Frontier nomads of Iran

Richard Tapper's fascinating book traces the political and social history of the Shahsevan, one of Iran's major nomadic peoples, living on the sensitive frontiers of Azarbaijan. The story, which is based on ethnographic fieldwork and extensive documentary research over more than three decades, is both tragic and dramatic. It recounts the mythical origins of the tribes in the seventeenth century, their unification as a tribal confederacy in the eighteenth century and their eventual decline under the Pahlavi Shahs when they were systematically stripped of both their economic and political influence. Although the confederacy has now ceased to exist, several thousand families of Shahsevan nomads still migrate near the frontier and thousands of other Iranians still acknowledge their identity as Shahsevan.

The book is intended as a contribution to three rather different debates. One concerns the riddle of Shahsevan origins, how and when the confederation was formed, while another considers how far changes in tribal social and political formations are a function of relations with states. The third discusses the relation between identity and history, and asks how different constructions of the identity of a particular people reflect or determine their view of the past. The author's synthetic approach to the history and anthropology of the region promises to make a major contribution to theoretical debates in both disciplines.

Cambridge Middle East Studies 7

Cambridge Middle East Studies has been established to publish
books on the nineteenth- and twentieth-century Middle East and
North Africa. The aim of the series is to provide new and original
interpretations of aspects of Middle Eastern societies and their
histories. To achieve disciplinary diversity, books will be solicited from
authors writing in a wide range of fields including history, sociology,
anthropology, political science and political economy. The emphasis
will be on producing books offering an original approach along
theoretical and empirical lines. The series is intended for students and
academics, but the more accessible and wide-ranging studies will also
appeal to the interested general reader.

Frontier nomads of Iran

A political and social history of the Shahsevan

Richard Tapper

School of Oriental and African Studies

CAMBRIDGE
UNIVERSITY PRESS

PUBLISHED BY THE PRESS SYNDICATE OF THE UNIVERSITY OF CAMBRIDGE
The Pitt Building, Trumpington Street, Cambridge CB2, 1RP, United Kingdom

CAMBRIDGE UNIVERSITY PRESS
The Edinburgh Building, Cambridge, CB2 2RU, United Kingdom
40 West 20th Street, New York, NY 10011–4211, USA
10 Stamford Road, Oakleigh, Melbourne 3166, Australia

First published 1997

Printed in the United Kingdom at the University Press, Cambridge

Typeset in 10/12pt Plantin

A catalogue record for this book is available from the British Library

Library of Congress Cataloguing in Publication data

Tapper, Richard.
    Frontier nomads of Iran: a political and social history of the
Shahsevan / Richard Tapper.
        p.   cm. – (Cambridge Middle East studies)
    Includes bibliographical references and index.
    ISBN 0 521 58336 5 (hardcover)
    1. Shahsevan (Iranian people)   2. Iran – History – Qajar dynasty,
1794–1925.   3. Iran – History– 20th century.   I. Title. II. Series.
DS269.S53T34   1997
955'.04–dc21   96–47890
                                                              CIP

ISBN 0 521 58336 5 hardback

Contents

Contents

Illustrations

Maps

Preface

The social order in Iran, like many other Middle Eastern countries, was marked until well into the twentieth century by a tension between the central government and powerful, semi-independent chiefs of nomadic tribes. At the same time, the rulers themselves were either of tribal origins or dependent on tribal support – the Pahlavis (1925–79) were the first for nearly a millennium to be neither. Under the Pahlavi Shahs the major tribal chiefs were systematically stripped of their economic and political influence, but tribal loyalties and forms of social organization survived in many parts of the country, and indeed have continued relevance in the Islamic Republic.

In recent decades, the tribes of Iran have attracted the attention of both anthropologists and historians. Several book-length ethnographies and histories of individual tribal groups have been published, as have some broader historical and theoretical analyses of the tribe–state relation.

The present work, the fruit of both extensive documentary research and intensive fieldwork, attempts a synthesis of anthropological and historical approaches. It tells the story of one of the great tribal confederacies, the Shahsevan of Azarbaijan. The confederacy had ceased to exist by the middle of the twentieth century, and the changes that have now occurred are probably irreversible, but many thousands of Iranians still claim or acknowledge their identity as Shahsevan, many of them continue a pastoral way of life, and the component tribal groups persist. Although few Iranians now mourn the passing of the great confederacies, their history is central to that of the country as a whole. The story of the Shahsevan is a dramatic one; there are acts of glory and honour, but there are also darker scenes, and in the end, as with the other confederacies of Iran, it is a tragedy.

The book addresses three main themes. The first is the riddle of Shahsevan origins. The best-known story is that the Shahsevan were a special composite tribe formed in about 1600 by Shah 'Abbas the Great as a militia loyal only to himself; although it was discredited as history many decades ago, it has acquired a mythical status and remains the standard version. There are, however, two other versions: one tells of the immigration of Shahsevan ancestors from Anatolia and presents the confederacy as divided between nobles (descended from the original immigrant leaders) and commoners; the third declares that the Shahsevan have always been 'thirty-two tribes', all of equal status. In Parts I and II (Chapters Two to Seven) I examine contemporary evidence from the sixteenth to the eighteenth centuries in an attempt to establish the historical origins of the contemporary Shahsevan tribes, and how and when the tribal confederacy was formed.

Secondly, the book is intended as a contribution to current debates on 'tribe–state relations' in the Middle East and elsewhere. In Parts III and IV (Chapters Eight to Thirteen) I examine nineteenth and twentieth-century sources on the Shahsevan and their relations with various states, which are detailed and circumstantial enough to permit the reconstruction, informed by fieldwork, of transformations in Shahsevan social and political organization, and to explain how the confederacy broke down.

Thirdly, the book is concerned with the relation between identity and history: how different constructions of the identity of a given people may reflect or determine different understandings of their past. Having, during the course of the book, examined and evaluated each version of Shahsevan origins in detail, in the concluding Chapter Fourteen I show how each of them not only represents the perspective of a different class of actors (rulers, chiefs, and ordinary nomads), but validates a different construction and interpretation of Shahsevan history and identity.

Although these three themes run through the book, and it is thus intended as a contribution to three rather different debates, I shall be glad if it is read for its methodological interest too, as the work of a professional anthropologist with some pretensions as a historian. In the Introduction (Chapter One) I discuss some of the problems of writing the history of people without their own written records, and survey the sources used. I have tried to keep within the limits of my own competences, in an effort to avoid the criticisms that I level at a number of widely read recent publications which I consider to contain serious flaws. At the same time, I am only too well aware of many of the remaining real and possible shortcomings of this study.

The book has taken a long time to complete. It began life as part of a doctoral thesis, for which the research was done in the 1960s. In the summers of 1963 and 1964, as an undergraduate student, I visited the Shahsevan, both nomad and settled, and collected ethnographic field materials including taped interviews with older tribespeople on historical matters. During the remainder of 1964 and much of 1965, as I prepared for more extended fieldwork, I began reading published sources on

Shahsevan history. In Tehran in the autumn of 1965, while awaiting permission for field research, I completed a preliminary historical paper (Tapper, 1966).

During fieldwork in 1965–6, although my major research focus was on contemporary economics, social organization and ritual behaviour among the nomads, I continued to record legends and personal memories among tribespeople of various classes. I also talked, and in some cases recorded interviews, with a number of outsiders who had had personal dealings with the Shahsevan, or were able to relay historical accounts they had themselves heard earlier.

On returning to London in late 1966 to write up my field material, I soon decided that further documentary research was necessary in order to try to establish, first, what could be said of Shahsevan historical origins, secondly, what was the nature of the tribal political organization which seemed in the 1960s to be in a state of fragmentation, and thirdly, how the Shahsevan came to have a system of individuated grazing rights which seemed unique among pastoral societies. This led me to extensive work in the archives at the India Office Library and the Public Record Office in London, and in Russian and Persian published and manuscript sources.

The thesis was completed in 1970; subsequent field research in Afghanistan (between 1970 and 1972) and Turkey (between 1979 and 1984) have limited my publication on the Shahsevan so far to an ethnographic monograph, some comparative anthropological papers and a number of historical papers (parts of the book are revisions of material published elsewhere (especially R. Tapper, 1974, 1983c, 1986, 1988b, 1991a, 1991b, 1994)). During 1986 I began the revision that was necessary to update the historical part of the thesis in order to make it into a book; in 1992, 1993 and 1995 I was able to make further visits to Iran, during which I collected new materials for the book.

In all this long gestation, I have revised and refined my own thinking about the subject, and have attempted to keep abreast of relevant publications that have appeared since my original research in the 1960s. Although I have come across significant further materials, published and unpublished, there are others which time or other limitations have prevented me from tackling, and which, as sources for Shahsevan history, await the attentions of another day – and perhaps another researcher.

Acknowledgments

I list here numerous individuals to whom, collectively, I owe an immense debt of gratitude for help and support during the long gestation of this book, at the inevitable risk of offending some I may have omitted, and in the sad knowledge that several of those listed are no longer alive. Initial stimulus and continuing encouragement at the early stages were provided by Peter Avery, Abdallah Bujra, Meyer Fortes, Edmund Leach, Peter Lienhardt, Lawrence Lockhart, Adrian Mayer, Vladimir Minorsky, Cornelius Op't Land, Jonathan Parry, Brian Spooner and Eric Sunderland. Christoph von Fürer-Haimendorf, Ann Lambton, David Morgan, Sandy Morton and Paul Stirling read various early drafts and offered valuable comments. My researches among the Shahsevan were facilitated in Iran, initially by Ehsan Naraghi, Nader Afshar-Naderi and Paul Vieille of the Institute of Social Studies and Research, and latterly by Ali Ghanbari and Seyed Hasan Nurbakhsh of the Organization for Nomadic Affairs. Nancy Lindisfarne-Tapper shared much of the fieldwork in 1965–6 and 1968, and I am deeply indebted to her for help and support during the initial historical research and the writing of the thesis. My thinking about Shahsevan history benefited much from discussions and correspondence with numerous fellow researchers and experts on Iran, particularly Peter Andrews, Hasan Arfa, Peter Avery, Marcel Bazin, Lois Beck, Dan Bradburd, David Brooks, Patrick Clawson, Stephanie Cronin, Jean-Pierre Digard, Eckart Ehlers, Willem Floor, Gene Garthwaite, William Irons, Nikki Keddie, Mehdi Mizban, Pierre Oberling, Mohammad-Hussain Papoli-Yazdi, Fereydoun Safizadeh, Philip Salzman, Günther Schweitzer, Parichehreh Shahsevand-Baghdadi, Brian Spooner, Georg Stöber, Jon Thompson, Martin Van Bruinessen and Sue Wright. Iraj Afshar, Jaber Anasseri, F. Ershad, Pierre Oberling, Hans Roemer and Mehdi Mizban kindly sent books or documents relating to Shahsevan history. Several people helped with translations of tapes or documents at earlier stages of my research: Leslie Collins, Michael Cook, Tourkhan Gandjei, Caroline Humphrey, Farokh Ebrahimi, Hasan Javadi, Shery Majd, Sandy Morton, Brian Spooner,

Christine Woodhead. Library staff at SOAS, the Public Record Office, the India Office Library, the British Library, the Organization for Nomadic Affairs in Tehran, and elsewhere were unfailingly helpful. Individual Shahsevan who provided information or other assistance are acknowledged at appropriate points in the text or notes. The book has been much improved by Catherine Lawrence's maps. In the final stages, Ziba Mir-Hosseini has given loving and expert assistance, encouragement and support. I am indebted to her, Hugh Beattie, Gene Garthwaite, Sandy Morton and Ruard Tapper for reading and commenting on all or part of the final manuscript.

A note on transliteration

I have been concerned mainly with ease of reading and some closeness to spoken Azarbaijani Turkish and Persian. The full range of English vowels is used to convey those in Persian words and names, though long and short 'a' are not differentiated except in the Glossary below.

For Shahsevan Turkish, I have not attempted an accurate or consistent representation in either proper names or vernacular terms. I use 'ı' for the Turkish back vowel (e.g. in 'Qızılbash'), pronounced as in spoken English 'the' before consonants, but the upper-case version remains undistinguished from that of 'i'. Umlauted 'ü' and 'ö' represent Turkish vowels similar to those so written in German; 'ä' represents the 'a' as in 'flat' (plain 'a' is rounder, as in 'dark'; not so far back as the Persian 'long a'. At the risk of occasional confusion, I have used 'sh' and 'ch' for sounds pronounced as in English; 'kh' for the 'ch' in Scottish 'loch'; 'gh' is like Parisian French 'r'; 'j' as in English 'jug'; the glottal plosive 'q', when final, is usually pronounced as 'kh' or 'gh'. Palatalizations of j > dz, ch > ts, k > ch, g > j, strong in Tabriz and Ardabil, are much weaker among the Shahsevan.

Diphthongs:
     ai as in 'high'
     ei as in 'hay' (except with *bey* and *elbey*)
     oi as in 'boy'
     ou as in 'owe'
     au as in 'how'

Glossary

alachıq – Shahsevan tent; round, felt-covered, with self-supporting wooden frame.

äläfchär – payment for grazing.

anjoman – Constitutional local cell; *änjini*, Shahsevan term for a raiding expedition, derived from *anjoman*.

aq-saqal (P. *rish-safid*) – grey-beard, elder of tribal section or camp.

'äshayer (pl. of Ar. *'ashira/'ashiret*) – nomad, tribesman.

äshrar (*lıq*) – (time of the) rebels, disorder.

bajanaq – relationship between a man and his wife's sister's husband.

bey (*baiğ*) – chief of taifa (P. *bīg, bīk*).

beyzadä – sons of chiefs; the 'noble' class.

binä – herding camp, often herding animals of absentee owner such a chief.

chob-bashı – grazing dues.

divāni/mamālek – state lands.

el (P. *il*; pl. *ilāt*) – tribe, tribal confederacy, people.

elbey (*elbeği*) – paramount chief, chief of *el*.

gholām – servants, slaves (cf. *qollar*).

göbäk – lineage, often equivalent to *tirä*.

hākem – governor of sub-province, district.

hāmpā – non-chiefly, commoner; companion, worker.

hokumat (T. *hökümät*) – government.

ilkhāni – paramount chief, e.g. of Bakhtiari, Qashqa'i, Qajar, Kurds; not Shahsevan.

jamahat (Istanbul T. *cemaat*, Ar. *jamā'at*) – community.

kalāntar – chief (not Shahsevan) equivalent to *bey*.

katkhodā – headman of village or tribal section (not Shahsevan).

khāleseh, khāsseh – Crown lands.

khān – lord, self-declared chief.

khankhan(*lıq*) – (time of) independent khans.

kümä – smaller Shahsevan tent, felt-covered, barrel-vaulted structure.

nasaqchi-bāshı – Qajar police chief (Chapter Eight).

nökär – servant, retainer.

oba/obeh – camp.

oimaq – tribe, section.

ojaq – hearth.

olka (ölgä) – tribal territory.

oulād (aulād) – lineage; lit. children, descendents (not Shahsevan).

qabila – tribe (not Shahsevan).

qanlı – feud (from *qan*, blood).

qıshlaq – winter pasture, winter camp.

qollar – 'slaves'.

qorchi (-bāshı) – royal guard, praetorian guard.

qoum/qaum – tribe, 'ethnic group', people, family.

qrān – unit of currency, one tenth of a toman; equivalent to present rial.

qurultai – general gathering and council.

rayät – commoner, farmer, subject.

rish-safid (P.) – white-beard, elder of camp or tribal section (not
      Shahsevan; cf. *aq-saqal*.

sarparast – supervisor, leader.

soltān – army rank.

soyurghāl – land grant, exemption.

tabaqeh – class.

taifa (tayfa/tayfeh/taifeh/tāyefeh) – tribe.

tira (tirä, P. *tireh,* Basseri *tira)* – tribal section.

tiyul (-dār) – (holder of) land grant, immunity from taxation

vaqf – endowment.

yailaq, yeilaq – summer quarters, summer pastures.

yurt, yort – camp-site, pastoral territory.

yüzbashı – captain of one hundred men.

zakāt – religious alms.

1 Introduction: writing tribal history

Anthropology, history and 'tribes'

In the mid-twentieth century, social scientists of all persuasions expected tribal and ethnic minorities within contemporary nation-states to succumb sooner or later to policies of modernization and national integration, and many were confident that class would replace ethnicity as the major dimension of social identity. Many anthropologists began to regard the study of their traditional subject-matter – tribal peoples – as an antiquarian irrelevance, turning instead to the newly fashionable sub-disciplines of urban anthropology and the anthropology of the state.

These expectations and trends have been confounded towards the end of the century by the persistence or creative revival of ethnic minority identities in virtually all countries of the world, and by increasing academic and popular perception of violent inter-community conflicts as ethnic in nature. Sociologists, political scientists, historians, geographers and others have shown renewed interest in the study of ethnic and tribal minorities of the 'Fourth World' – no longer the sole preserve of anthropologists. There has been a particular convergence between anthropologists and historians; the former 'do history', adding depth to their accounts of social and cultural change by scouring archives and chronicles, while the latter, not content with the often meagre 'facts' about tribal peoples to be established from such sources, enrich their interpretations with ethnographic, theoretical and comparative insights from anthropology.[1]

There are new focuses and interests. Both historians and anthropologists once concentrated on the actors and levels of society of which their sources treated – typically ruling families and dynasties, political institutions, warriors, bureaucrats, scholars – and were content with a largely narrative history, seeking to establish 'what really happened': facts and

---

[1] For a review of contributions to this field, see Krech (1991). Relevant debates have appeared in the pages of journals such as *Comparative Studies in Society and History* and *History and Anthropology*. See also Cohn (1987), Asad (1993).

1

events. They often allowed theory and interpretation to remain implicit in the categories used to translate the sources and to suggest causal relations. Now descriptive and analytical categories are more carefully examined; tribal and minority peoples and their histories are more firmly located within the context of the history of states and the world; and there is a growing concern to hear indigenous voices and to allow for the possibility that minorities as well as the state, ordinary people as well as their leaders, women as well as men will have their different pasts. Researchers now investigate these multiple pasts, who claims them, what motivates the claims, how they construct them and negotiate with their rivals.

Various minorities have participated in the economics and politics of states and empires long and actively enough to have left a considerable mark in the archives; some have produced their own chronicles, histories and anthropologies, often as part of their articulation of cultural identity and political aspirations. In other cases, relevant documentation is thin or lacking, and authentic indigenous voices are hard to discern. It is increasingly recognized, however, that particular cultural and political concerns are likely to motivate and colour not only indigenous accounts (whether oral or documentary), but those of apparently objective outsiders.

Recently too, serious attempts have been made to come to terms with the methodological – and ethical – problems involved in writing the history of other people, particularly where – as still is often the case with tribal peoples and minorities – the people themselves are silent, and the only sources relating to them have been written by outsiders. Often the only strategy available for a construction of the past is some form of extrapolation, the projection of understandings and analyses arising from one conjunction of time and space onto another.

Early European studies of the Middle East often attempted to extrapolate between 'the society of the patriarchs' and contemporary Bedouin in the Levant. Not only were Biblical texts used to construct what life among the Bedouins must be like, but observations of the contemporary Bedouin were applied to pad out the information on Biblical patriarchs that could be extracted from the texts. Most successful of such extrapolators perhaps was W. Robertson Smith; others were more or less fanciful and romantic.

This type of historical reconstruction – and indeed history generally – went out of fashion in British anthropology with the dominance of structural-functionalism in the 1930s–50s. Historical perspectives were reintroduced by Evans-Pritchard, Barnes and others, who were more interested in documenting at least recent historical changes. Two main trends in anthropological history developed: anthropologically informed histories; and histories of 'anthropological' subjects: tribes, rural society, the poor, the fourth world. Historians have for some decades applied anthropological insights, drawn from ethnographic analyses of the cultural systems of non-literate peoples, to help in reconstructing the pasts of Western societies, and to provide ethnographic readings of fragmentary historical texts. A prominent source here has been Evans-Pritchard's study of Zande witchcraft, and his analysis of the logic of magical thought, and the relation of witchcraft accusations to kinship and other social classifications.[2] More recently, historians have drawn on other concepts and insights from anthropological studies of kinship, tribalism, ethnicity and identity. At the same time, following the French *Annales* school, there has been a proliferation in studies of the social history of the 'people without history', in reconstructions of the social life of classes mentioned only indirectly in the sources.[3] This has often involved interpretations justified by reference to current social theories, as well as more imaginative historical writing which leans heavily on extrapolation from fieldwork-based ethnographies.

Extrapolation in history or anthropology is a form of comparative method which involves extracting insights and often elements from the analysis of one society, and applying these to another society where the same detailed information is not available. Anthropologists need not go so far as either Evans-Pritchard, who held social anthropology to be 'a special kind of historiography', or Radcliffe-Brown, who advocated comparison as the 'methodological equivalent of experiment'; but they must acknowledge that both anthropology and history are inherently comparative. Indeed, any study of culture at a distance – the business of both anthropology and history – involves both translation and comparison.

One problem in writing other people's history can be a failure to recognize the full implications of the cultural distances involved, which call for several translations. Ethnographic description and analysis involve, as is well recognized, translation from the language and categories of one contemporary people into those of another. Less recognized is the translation performed by historians studying the past of their own people – 'another country'.[4] When anthropologists reconstruct the past of a

---

[2] Evans-Pritchard (1937). Cf. Lewis (1968); and the work of Alan Macfarlane, Keith Thomas and others.

[3] The skilful reconstruction of a fourteenth-century French village by Le Roy Ladurie (1975) 'has been hailed as opening the possibility of a more ethnographic history and a more historical ethnography' (Rosaldo 1986: 77). See also Schneider and Rapp (1995), and the works of Eric Wolf which are the focus of that volume.

[4] See Ingold (1994); and cf. Asad (1986) on 'strong' and 'weak' languages.

people among whom they have done ethnographic fieldwork, a double filtering is now involved, a translation over cultural differences of both space and time. If historians, studying the past of another people, then make use of an ethnographer's account of the same people, they are now separated from their subjects by three filters, and must perform a triple translation. Already, such a history is a long way from an indigenous production.

A final degree of distancing is introduced when a historian or anthropologist attempts to reconstruct the society of one historical people by extrapolating from an ethnographic study of quite a different present-day people. Given the cultural distances involved, a convincing reconstruction through extrapolation must not only avoid ethnocentrism and anachronism but employ a theory of society that does not decontextualize, misrepresent, or distort the materials to which it is applied. Such exercises in comparison and interpretation are legitimate when approached with extreme caution, for example in presumptions about the nature of continuity and similarity between the two societies, in careful accounting for differences in their economic and political contexts as well as internal cultural differences between their values, understandings, motivations and experiences.

Now, in their study of the pasts of rural or tribal peoples, anthropologists have not always been careful or critical enough in their use of archival and other sources, and have sometimes failed for example to make adequate allowance for the impact of state policies or the forces of world economic and political systems. Historians who practise extrapolation, however, have not always done so with due consideration of the problems involved. How far is it legitimate to extrapolate from Central African witchcraft to mediaeval European witchcraft, or to popular religious practices in the Muslim world? Or from present-day Bedouin to early Israelites? Or from nomads in Iran today to mediaeval Turkish nomads?

I shall consider these problems further below by examining the ways in which certain historians have used one particular ethnographic study of nomads in Iran as the basis for reconstructing several very different nomadic societies of the past. First it is appropriate to note that not least of the problems involved is the question of the categories and terms of description and analysis to be employed, a problem which is – or should be – common to both ethnography and history.

Prominent among such terms have been 'tribe' and 'tribalism'. These refer to a category of human society whose study was once regarded as largely the prerogative of anthropology, yet anthropologists themselves have notoriously been unable to agree on how to define them. Small wonder then if historians too, and for that matter political scientists and others interested in 'tribalism', have differed widely in their understandings of the terms.

In writing a history of tribes in Iran, it would seem essential, not so much to lay down definitions (the experience of anthropologists has shown this to be a tedious and indeed futile enterprise), but rather to examine the assumptions behind different usages, and indeed the sources from which they derive. It will be helpful first to consider the main conceptions of 'tribe' current among anthropologists, the current academic and administrative usages of the term in studies of the Middle East and of Iran in particular, and the semantics of various indigenous terms that have been translated as 'tribe'.

'Tribe' in anthropology and the Middle East

Three fundamentally distinct conceptions of 'tribe' have had currency among anthropologists. Perhaps the closest to popular English-language usage is the loose equation of 'tribe' with 'primitive society', once applied to the pre-colonial populations of many parts of the world. In this classificatory usage, the population of a country or a continent was divided into 'tribes' in the sense of objectively apprehended cultural-linguistic groups. Political structure and ideology, and usually scale, were discounted, so that 'the tribes of Africa' ranged in size from a few hundred people to millions, and from a scattering of hunter-gatherer bands to complex stratified states. Post-colonial politicians, academics and governments objected to the connotations of 'tribe' and 'tribalism', and adopted more appropriate (but still unsatisfactory) terms such as 'ethnic group', 'people', or 'nation(ality)'.

More precisely formulated is the notion of 'tribe' as a particular type of society, usually in some kind of evolutionary scheme, in which tribes (with neolithic production techniques, and egalitarian and clan-based political organization) are intermediate between simple hunting bands and more complex chiefdoms and states.[5] A basic characteristic of such 'tribes' is the pervasiveness of kinship and descent as principles of social and political organization.

A third usage, common in British social anthropology, follows Evans-Pritchard's analysis of the Nuer people of the Sudan as a collection of tribes, that is political groups defined by territorial boundaries and by accepted mechanisms for the resolution of internal disputes.[6] Each such tribe divides into sub-sections at different structural levels down to that of

[5] See Sahlins (1968).   [6] Evans-Pritchard (1940).

the local community, and each tribe and section has a dominant descent group (clan or lineage). Descent groups in turn divide, from the level of the dominant clan in a given tribe, to that of the minimal lineage in the local community; but frequently the majority of members of the descent group reside elsewhere than in the territory of the section where it is dominant, and Evans-Pritchard carefully distinguished the genealogical framework of descent from the territorial-political structure of tribes and their sections.

Not content with any of these three usages, many ethnographers (myself included) have defined 'tribe' – or used the term without definition – to fit their analysis of a particular society, often attempting to translate a specific indigenous term. Indeed, anthropologists have followed their own varying epistemologies to emphasize widely differing criteria and thus have failed to agree on a general definition of what constitutes a 'tribe'. As with so many would-be general or universal concepts, it seems impossible to find an analytic terminology that both applies widely enough to be useful for comparison and classification and takes account of indigenous categories.

There has been much recent discussion of 'tribe' in relation to the Middle East.[7] The first of the anthropological concepts listed above – 'tribe' as a culturally and linguistically bounded 'primitive society' – is inappropriate for the major cultural-linguistic groupings such as Arabs, Berbers, Turks, Persians, Kurds, Pashtuns, Baluches, which can hardly be termed either 'tribes' or 'primitive societies', if only on grounds of scale, complexity and lack of unity.[8] But many writers on the Middle East, adopting either the second or the third anthropological conception of 'tribe', use the term for major subdivisions of some of these 'ethnic groups', 'peoples' or 'nationalities'. For some, a tribe is essentially an egalitarian descent group, the classical model of tribal society among Arabs and in the Middle East generally, conforming with Ibn Khaldun's conception as well as with Durkheim's notion of 'mechanical solidarity'. This criterion best fits Arab tribal society, where tribal genealogies are particularly extensive; a well-known example are the Rwala, a 'tribe' of some 250,000 souls, though some even larger non-Arab groups such as

---

[7] See, for example, Eickelman (1981/1989), Beck (1986), Bradburd (1987), Tapper (1991a), several contributions to Khoury and Kostiner (1991) and reviews by Gingrich (1992) and Crone (1993). Eickelman identifies four different notions of 'tribe' in the Middle East: anthropological analytical concepts, state administrative concepts, indigenous explicit ideologies, and indigenous practical notions (1981: 88–9). A few scholars, for example Marx (1977), consider 'tribes' to have an economic or ecological basis.

[8] Historically, however, city-dwellers in different parts of the Middle East have labelled rural and nomadic peoples as Turk, 'Arab, Berber, Kurd, Baluch, with connotations of 'primitives'. Cf. Tapper (1991b: 53–4) on urban images of tribespeople.

the Bakhtiari Lurs (500,000) of Iran or the Durrani Pashtuns (2 million) of Afghanistan have been called 'tribes' on the same grounds. Many proponents of this view would deny the term 'tribe' to any group without a descent ideology. Others, however, define a tribe as essentially a territorially distinct political group, and expect it to be led by a chief; they apply the term 'tribe' to almost equally large groups that lack unifying descent ideologies and are heterogeneous in origins and composition, such as the Qashqa'i, the Khamseh or the Shahsevan in Iran.

At this level of major cultural-political groups of 100,000 or more people, then, there is disagreement as to whether the term 'tribe' is applicable on the grounds of culture (a descent ideology) or political structure (chiefship and/or political-territorial unity). Other writers (such as myself), however, are unwilling to take either extreme position, and refer to these larger groups (whatever their apparent basis) as 'confederacies', locating 'tribes' at a lower level of political structure, that of first- or second-order components, numbering at most some thousands of individuals.[9] Such tribes commonly (but still by no means always) combine territorial and political unity under a chief with an ideology of common descent.

It is not often recognized, however, how far the ambiguity that thus remains in discourses about 'tribes' – over whether they are primarily political or cultural – not only divides academics but obscures current political debates at national level about the future role of tribes and tribalism.[10] Further ambiguity and misunderstanding arise from a notion of 'tribe' which is no part of standard anthropological conceptions but which is strongly entrenched in both academic and administrative discourses in many parts of the Middle East; that is, 'tribe' as the political and socio-cultural dimension of pastoral nomadism, such that the category of 'the tribes' is conventionally synonymous with 'the nomads'. This notion is held by numerous historians and other writers, who also assume tribes to be descent groups, often borrowing from anthropology the term 'segmentary lineage'.[11] Crone, for example, writing of early Islamic society, holds that it is likely that 'tribe in the specific sense of the word is an overwhelmingly or exclusively pastoral phenomenon (or so at least if we add the criterion of segmentary organization)'. The tribe, moreover, 'is that descent group within which control of pasture land is vested',

[9] E.g. Barth (1961) on the Khamseh, myself (1979a etc.) on the Shahsevan, Garthwaite (1983) on the Bakhtiari, Beck (1986) on the Qashqa'i, Loeffler (1978) on the Boir Ahmad.   [10] Cf. Tapper (1994).
[11] Where members claim descent from a common ancestor (the founder of the lineage, which often bears his – or her – name) and form a series of nesting subgroups (segments) descended from more recent ancestors.

which shares the obligation to pay blood-money for an injured member, and which has a chief and forms a community.[12]

But there is nothing in either pastoralism as a system of production or nomadism as a mobile way of living that necessarily leads to organization in tribes, whether defined politically in terms of territory and chiefship, or culturally in terms of common descent. Numerous observers have noted how the geography and ecology of most Middle Eastern countries favour pastoral nomadism. The terrain and climate made large areas uncultivable under pre-industrial conditions, and suitable only for seasonal grazing; and as only a small proportion of such pasture could be used by village-based livestock, vast ranges of steppe, semi-desert and mountain were left to be exploited by nomadic pastoralists. Such nomads until very recently numbered tens of millions, and almost all were organized politically into tribes under chiefs. Equally, tribes (defined in political terms) have commonly also had a pastoral economic base and led a nomadic way of life. But an insistence that tribes in the Middle East and Central Asia were necessarily pastoral nomads, organized in descent groups, ignores major tribal groups in Anatolia, Iran and Afghanistan, which often included both settled cultivators and pastoral nomads and were complex and heterogeneous in composition.[13] Thus, most of the Pashtuns of Afghanistan are (and have always been) farmers or traders, with little or no leaning to pastoralism or nomadism, and well-known groups in Iran such as the Qashqa'i, Bakhtiari, Kurds, Baluch, Turkmen and Shahsevan have been at least partly settled agriculturalists. Of course, by conventional anthropological definitions, many of these were not 'tribes' at all, but 'chiefdoms', or even 'proto-states'.

Any coincidence between nomads and tribes (whether descent-based, or led by chiefs) was not so much a causal relation as a function of relations of both with central states. Settled state administrations intent on registering and taxing the inhabitants of territories which they claimed to control have classically had ambivalent attitudes to both tribespeople, with their personal allegiance to each other or to chiefs, and nomads, with their shifting residence. Many earlier states, however, were themselves founded on military forces drawn from pastoral nomadic tribes, often organized in military units of tens, hundreds and thousands. Rulers have fostered pastoral nomadism in strategic parts of their territories, and have sometimes actually created tribes, tribal organization and tribal chiefs.

Officials – and many academics – have taken a highly positivist view of tribes, expecting them to be mappable, bounded groups, with little membership change, and wanting an exact terminology for classificatory

---

[12] Crone (1986: 55); Tapper (1991a). Crone (1993) seems to have changed her mind.
[13] Elsewhere (for instance in Yemen), 'tribes' are not nomadic at all.

and comparative purposes. From a government perspective, even the most autonomous rural populations should have identifiable patterns of organization, and leaders who may be treated as representatives; if they do not have these patterns or leaders, they may be encouraged to produce them. Some rural and nomadic populations have avoided government control and exploitation, and even the attention of historians, by failing to produce such leaders or recognizable forms of 'tribal' organization.[14] But government-created 'tribes', whose names may appear in the records as such, may exist only on paper. Further, tribal names found in official sources imply a uniformity of socio-political structure which, in so far as it exists, may be entirely due to administrative action, and may disguise fundamental disparities in culture and in forms of social organization.

A desire to establish a consistent and stable terminology for political groups has too often obscured the nature of indigenous concepts and terms, which are no more specific than are English terms such as 'family' or 'group' – or 'tribe'. Even in the most apparently consistent segmentary terminology, individual terms are ambiguous, not merely about level, but in their connotations of functions or facets of identity: economic, political, kinship, cultural. However, as with equivalents in English practice, the ambiguity of the terms and the flexibility of the system are of the essence in everyday negotiations of meaning and significance.[15]

Most of the terms that have been translated 'tribe' – for example qabila, il, 'ashira, taifa – contain such ambiguities, and attempts to give them – or 'tribe' – precision as to either level, function or essence, are liable to be misdirected. 'Tribe' as an analytical concept, I have argued elsewhere, is best viewed as – and best matches indigenous concepts for – a state of mind, a construction of reality, a model for action, a mode of social organization essentially opposed to that of the centralized state. A precise terminology may aid comparison, but is unlikely to explain behaviour or to provide an adequate translation of local categories and perceptions.[16]

---

[14] Irons (1974); Glatzer (1983); Bradburd (1990).

[15] See R. Tapper (1979a) and below on the ambiguity between *tira* (tribal section, political-administrative grouping under an elder), *göbäk* (patrilineage), and *jamahat* (community, congregation) among Shahsevan nomads; and see N. and R. Tapper (1982) on the ambiguities of *qoum* (family, nation, endogamous group), *wolus* (political community), *aulad* (patrilineage), and *tayfa* (local tribal section) among the Durrani in Afghanistan. See also van Bruinessen's discussion (1978: 52–3) of Leach's and Barth's difficulties with the terms *ashiret, tira* and *tayfa* among the Kurds of Iraq.

[16] These issues are discussed further in R. Tapper (1983b, 1988a, 1991a). Beck, writing of the Qashqa'i, defines tribe, subtribes and confederacies functionally (1986: 14–15, 174f.), and does not consider indigenous (Turki, Persian) terminology as analytically significant, noting just that the ambiguity and interchangeability in usage of *tireh, tayefeh, il* add to the confusion in tribal lists (1986: 178). In his important history of the Aq-Qoyunlu, Woods (1976) does not make analytical use of the notion of tribe, but concentrates on the structure of dominant tribal groups in fifteenth-century Anatolia and Iran: composite political confederacies of nomadic 'clans', with a dynastic paramount 'clan'.

That said and understood, I shall continue in this book to use 'tribe' as a convenient translation for the Shahsevan term *taifa*, as it is most often used, without expecting it necessarily to correspond with 'tribe' in any other cultural context. Below, indeed, I shall examine some of the ways in which the 'tribal organization' of the Shahsevan differs from that of others in Iran.

The tribes of Iran: classifications and comparisons

Sources for the history of tribes in Iran are mostly written from a distance by outsiders viewing the tribes with hostility or some other bias. They usually concern such matters as taxation, military levies, disturbances and measures taken to quell them, and more or less inaccurate lists of major tribal groups, numbers and leaders. They rarely deal specifically or in reliable detail with the basic social and economic organization of tribal communities; and they mention individual tribes only when prominent in supporting or opposing government, when involved in inter-tribal disorders, or when transported from one region to another.

For example, we still have only the vaguest notions of tribal economics in pre-modern times: what the relations of production were and how they have changed; who controlled land and how access was acquired; what proportion of producers controlled their own production; how many were tenants or dependants of wealthier tribesmen or city-based merchants; and whether control of production was exercised directly or through taxation or price-fixing. The sparse information in the sources must be supplemented and interpreted by tentative and possibly misleading extrapolations from recent ethnographic studies. Despite the recent shift of perspective from that of the state to that of minorities, the nature of the sources has continued to dictate a history of politics and dynasties, of the political interaction of the state with powerful chiefs and tribal confederacies. Tribal economic and social history remains nearly as obscure, and the tribespeople as faceless and voiceless, as before.[17]

In Iran, the 'tribes' (*ilat va 'ashayer*) were generally assumed to be pastoral nomads, and in addition were strongly associated with powerful leaders, who at points in the past rivalled – and on occasion overthrew and replaced – the rulers of the state. At the same time, Iran has perhaps a longer history than elsewhere of governments creating 'tribes' where none existed previously, and appointing 'chiefs' from among either local notables or complete outsiders, in order to administer rural populations

---

[17] This is regrettably true of almost all the pioneering historical work relevant to the tribes by Minorsky, Petrushevskiy, Lambton, Lockhart, Aubin, Dickson, Savory, Hambly, Oberling, Perry, Atkin, Gilbar, Abrahamian, Arjomand, Floor (see Bibliography).

and minorities, whether nomadic or settled. One of the best-known examples was the foundation of the Khamseh confederacy in Fars in 1861–2 under the chiefship of the Shiraz merchant family of Qavam al-Molk, in order to balance the power of the Qashqa'i. Another example is the supposed origin of the Shahsevan confederacy, discussed in this book.

The tribes of Iran maintained a diversity of cultures and forms of social and political organization. Recognizing the diversity, observers have classified them in a variety of ways, for different purposes. In official or historical documents, and some recent accounts taking the perspective of the state, tribal groups are often listed by 'ethnic' affiliation, that is, by language and/or supposed origins. The major categories, typically, are: (a) Iranians, held to be native to the country, such as Lors and Laks, Kurds, Baluches and Brahuis; (b) immigrant Turks; and (c) Arabs. One example from the eighteenth century listed named tribal groups under these headings, together with numbers of families, names of chiefs and assessments of revenue and military levies, but Lambton and Towfiq employed similar categories in their recent *Encyclopedia* articles.[18] Some scholars attribute political and sociological correlates to such an ethno-historical classification. Barfield, for example, has revived the idea that 'indigenous Middle East tribes' (among Arabs, Kurds and Pashtuns, and presumably the Lors and Baluches in Iran) – had egalitarian lineage structures and were resistant to domination, features which differentiated them from the powerful but more ephemeral centralized confederacies and dynastic states associated with the Turco-Mongol nomadic tradition originating in Central Asia.[19]

Other sources classify the tribes by province, listing the dominant named groups present in each, and estimates of their numbers. Examples include Lambton's key article again, and several local histories, as well as the 1987 *Socio-economic Census of the Nomadic Tribes* and associated official publications concerned with the practical issue of the provision of services for the nomads.[20]

A further mode of classification of the nomad tribes focuses on socio-political structures.[21] The best-known tribal groups, for obvious reasons, were the large confederacies, led by powerful chiefly dynasties. Earlier examples included the Aq-Qoyunlu and Qara-Qoyunlu in the fifteenth century, and various Qızılbash groups and others who founded dynasties or challenged the rulers in the sixteenth to eighteenth centuries. Examples from the nineteenth and twentieth centuries are the Bakhtiari

---

[18] Danesh-Pazhuh (1974) – see Chapter Four below; Lambton (1971); Towfiq (1987).
[19] Barfield (1991).   [20] Census (1987).
[21] Cf. Beck's classification of tribal groups by size and location in relation to frontiers (1991a: 199).

and Qashqa'i. None of these major groups were exclusively pastoral nomads, and their chiefs were not merely leaders of nomads, but had legitimate sources of personal wealth and power: not only livestock, but agricultural land and commonly city-based trading houses. In addition, chiefs received income through tax collection, and often subsidies from the Iranian state and sometimes others, including (for the Bakhtiari early this century) royalties from oil exploration. Some chiefs depended on recognition by rulers, others were strong enough to challenge them. They commanded well-armed irregular cavalry, drawn from their extensive entourage of kinsmen and personal followers as well as from the families of subordinate chiefs. These warriors did not participate actively in the pastoral or agricultural economy. They might be mobilized as levies by a strong government to fight its campaigns, but could, and sometimes did, bring the chiefs to power in government. Even where government had created these major confederacies and appointed their leaders as part of a 'tribal policy', controlling them continued to constitute a 'tribal problem' for the central state.

Less powerful and numerous were a range of locally centralized chiefdoms, including the Shahsevan and Qara-Daghi in Azarbaijan, different Kurdish groups in Western Iran and Khorasan, the Boir Ahmad, Mamasani and other Lors of the central Zagros, the Khamseh tribes of Fars, and different Baluch groups in the southeast. These groups were usually of concern to the state only at a regional level, but several on occasion could pose a major threat and ranked politically alongside the major confederacies.

Other tribal groups in Iran had no centralized political structure. They were diffusely organized and had no prominent leadership – like 'jellyfish', as Malcolm Yapp put it – and followed a strategy of 'divide that ye be not ruled', in Ernest Gellner's felicitous phrase.[22] The best-known example was the Yamut Türkmen of Gorgan, a powerful collection of tribes who resisted government control longer than many others by virtue of their diffuse organization, as well as having the advantage of being located on a frontier across which they could escape. Smaller and weaker groups, such as the Sangsari of the Alborz, or the Komachi and others in Kerman, managed to avoid the attention of central government and historians, and their existence and numbers were more or less unrecorded, at least until recently.[23]

Clearly, no unitary model of 'the tribes' or 'nomads of Iran' will be adequate, unless perhaps for very specific and drastic administrative or

---

[22] Yapp (1983) and Gellner (1983).
[23] Irons (1974); Bradburd (1990) – he has other arguments to explain Komachi lack of political centralization. Cf. Glatzer (1983).

political purposes. Many tidy-minded investigators, however, whether academics or government officials, have assumed that each tribe was necessarily ordered in a hierarchical or segmentary structure, with distinct terms referring to groups at separate levels, that could be translated, for example, as confederacy, tribe, clan, lineage or section. Representations of tribal structure in recent monographs and comparative studies (mainly in Persian) typically include the following elements:[24]

- A segmentary structure of nesting territorial/political units, with groups at each level distinguished by terminology (for example, *il*, divided into *taifeh*, each divided into *tireh*, and so on); the structure is usually depicted graphically as a radiating star or tree, or as concentric circles.
- A matching segmentary framework of nesting descent groups, with a genealogical charter of pedigrees of patrilineal descent from a common ancestor; again, a tree or a series of concentric circles are common models.
- A matching hierarchical structure of political leadership roles (*ilkhani*, *khan*, *kalantar*, *kadkhoda*, *rish-safid* and so forth), accompanied by pyramid-shaped diagrams.
- A matching pyramid model of class structure, for example: chiefly families, independent commoners, employees, dependants and servants.

The major Zagros confederacies (Bakhtiari, Qashqa'i, Khamseh), despite radical differences between them, have all at times been represented as the archetypes of this structure, while other tribal groups were held to be more or less imperfect approximations to them, with fewer levels of organization, less centralization, less powerful chiefs and so forth. However, the idea that there is – or was – either a uniform or an archetypal tribal structure of Iran, a fixed pattern of hierarchical political and social organization among nomads, is mistaken, and based on false assumptions.

Even if certain tribal groups had similar social and political structures on paper, this says little about the functions of groups at any level, the power and role of a particular leader, or the political behaviour of particular individuals. Indigenous terms for political and descent groups, according to which nomads and tribespeople identified themselves and acted, were not as systematically related or consistent as typical hierarchical models of tribal structure suggest. Terms tended to denote facets or functions, rather than levels in a hierarchy of groups. Ethnographers often

[24] A typical example is Amanollahi-Baharvand(1992); cf. Wright (1992).

report that individual nomads could not specify whether a given named group of people was, for example, a *taifeh* or a *tireh* or an *il*; however, this is not evidence of confusion or imprecision on the part of informants, but rather of the contextual nature of such terms. Many were used interchangeably or apparently inconsistently, partly because – like 'section', 'department', 'division', 'family', 'group', 'lineage', 'tribe', 'clan', 'community' in English – they were ambiguous, partly because different terms were appropriate descriptions of the same collection of people in different contexts of action. The same Shahsevan social group could be called a *tira* in the political context of tribal sections, a *göbäk* as a descent group, or a *jamahat* as a ritual and moral community. In different tribal cultures the same term might have different connotations – for example community, grazing-group, tribal section, followers of a leader, descent group. The Qashqa'i and the Shahsevan shared an identical formal structure, whereby the *il* divided into *taifeh*, which divided into *tireh*, which divided into *oba*; but groups so denoted differed widely in size and functions as between the two.[25]

Much the same was true of the terminology of leadership positions. Terms such as *khan*, *bey*, *katkhoda*, *aq-saqal/rish-safid*, which might be neatly listed in a hierarchical, quasi-military model of tribal political structure, in practical usage in different tribal contexts might rather differentiate between leaders who were self-promoted, government appointees, or popularly elected or approved, or might be applied to the same individual to stress different aspects of his leadership.

As for the assumption that nomads conceived their tribal identity in terms of a 'nesting' or branching set of patrilineal descent groups, this was true in only a very limited sense. The Bakhtiari, and one or two other groups, reportedly had a unifying tribal genealogy, but other major groups such as the Qashqa'i, Shahsevan and Khamseh, with histories and traditions of heterogeneous origins, made no pretence at such unity, and invoked frameworks of common descent only at low levels of organization. Commonly, indeed, pedigrees and descent claims were only invoked where they brought rights of access to an important resource such as pasture land. At the level of the local community, common descent was often no more important than other kinds of inter-personal ties as a basis for day-to-day relationships and loyalties. Local-level groupings tended to be of very mixed and changing composition, like the major confederacies themselves; most commonly, ties between women structured the composition of the smallest groupings of households.

---

[25] *Il*, the official term for all major tribal groups throughout Iran, in Türkmen language and culture means 'peace', 'obedience'.

Formal segmentary and hierarchical models of nomadic tribal society, as reproduced in academic and official analyses, appear to create rather than depict or discover structures. They are convenient as administrative blueprints, models for use by central government or by tribal chiefs, but they seldom represent tribal structure as experienced and reproduced by ordinary nomads, whose stories of the origins of different tribal sections and the connections between them often differed radically from the official, chiefly version.[26] They certainly do not explain the political behaviour of individual nomads: the networks of personal ties of loyalty and friendship, modes of negotiation and accommodation, the formation and maintenance of alliances and rivalries, and the emergence of leaders, including women (whether as wives or mothers of male leaders, or in their own right). These informal processes occurred at all levels of nomadic society. At the local level, they reflected day-to-day economic and social forces in nomadic society, beyond the usual concern and influence of government. At the level of tribes and confederacies, on the other hand, informal processes tended to be obscured if not suppressed by processes emanating from the state, following the official hierarchical political model.

Tribal political structures, as we have seen, had nothing much to do with either pastoralism or nomadism per se. Tribes in Iran formed and derived their character from their relation to particular rulers and states at particular times, and there has been much discussion of the complex factors and processes involved.[27]

Earlier scholars assumed pastoral nomads to be egalitarian, and asked why they united and produced chiefs and hierarchy, tribes and confederacies, finding the answers partly in internal factors such as population density and pressure on resources, but mainly in external factors such as the policies and strength of central government.[28] Others have challenged as a myth the notion of egalitarian pastoral nomads, claiming that even the smallest pastoral group contained conflicting classes and competing leaders; and that in order to disguise these inequalities successful leaders promoted unifying ideologies such as common descent or a call to religion, promising booty in military campaigns and granting rights to pasture and farmland in return for service. Moreover, tribes and confed-

---

[26] See Chapter Fourteen on the different versions of Shahsevan origins, and Wright (1992) on Doshmanziari and others.

[27] Different historical patterns of tribal relations to the state have been explored by Digard (1973; 1987), Garthwaite (1983), Beck (1991a), Kiavand (1989), Tapper (1983b; 1991a) and others. See also Crone's (1993) and Gingrich's (1992) reviews of Khoury and Kostiner (1991); and, specifically in relation to Iran, see Bradburd's (1987) review of Garthwaite (1983a), Tapper (1983a) and Beck (1986).

[28] See, for example, several contributions to Equipe (1979).

eracies were the creations of chiefs, often non-tribal opportunists seeking to defend their own interests, particularly in circumstances of the increasing demands for revenue brought by the imperial rivalries and spreading capitalism of the nineteenth century.[29] The chiefs (with their tribal warriors) differed little from the merchants (with their bazaar crowds) and the landlords (with their tenants) as dominant forces in the political economy of early modern Iran, with near equivalents in European feudal systems.

It would appear that the major tribes and confederacies in Iran were chiefdoms created or fostered by governments, rulers and chiefs themselves; they were political organizations with a complex economic base, in which pastoral nomads played an important part, both as valuable (but ecologically vulnerable) producers of surplus, and as a military resource. The chiefs, whether or not of pastoral nomad origins, liked to identify their tribes as nomadic, and often supplied a unifying (but mythical) ideology of common descent, while keeping their own class separate from the ordinary, working pastoralists, who commonly had no such unifying ideology themselves.

I have argued elsewhere that socio-dynamic and demographic forces led to the formation among nomads of two kinds of communities of determinate sizes and levels of organization, commonly coinciding with groups formed on other principles. The smaller one was an egalitarian local pastoral community of some fifteen to fifty families. In many cases, shared or joint grazing rights were one of the common interests of this basic pastoral community. It was usually led by a 'grey-beard', and members, linked by common patrilineal descent or other ties of kinship and affinity, moved and camped together or near by, made certain joint economic decisions, formed a congregation for certain religious ceremonies, and maintained social integrity through shared customs and knowledge. These smaller communities were most clearly identifiable in larger tribal groups, within which they were encapsulated by chiefly action and by forces emanating from the state.

The smaller communities, at least among the major tribal systems of western Iran, joined to form larger communities of one to several hundred families, groups of some continuity, independent of leadership, with a strong degree of cultural identity and notions of common origins, maintained by endogamy and other cultural practices. These larger communities, for which the English term 'clan' might be appropriate, commonly also constituted politically defined tribes or tribal sections, with jealously guarded territories and in many cases hereditary chiefs. But

---

[29] Bradburd (1990); and see Black (1972, 1986).

when the existence of these communities was thus obscured by coincidence with political and often state-sanctioned groups, they were more 'imagined' than experienced. Indeed, terms used by nomads themselves for the larger communities are hard to identify; perhaps the most common were *taifeh* and *tireh*, both terms often implying a group that was itself part or section of a yet larger grouping, such as an *il*: a tribal cluster, confederacy or chiefdom.[30]

Another regular feature of nomadic tribal organization in Iran (and elsewhere), not predicted by standard hierarchical models, was the formation of alliances and rivalries. The historical evidence indicates that pressure on resources commonly led not to unified leadership but to conflict and competition, and that alliances and rivalries tended to form regional chequer-board patterns; when strong rulers did emerge – or appeared from elsewhere – they had to take account of these patterns, and might even foster them to achieve their own ends.[31]

Interestingly, official definitions of tribes since the Islamic Revolution in Iran have played down the political dimension, omit all reference to chiefs, and focus instead on the social: tribes – or at least the major components, the *taifeh* – are now defined as kinship groups, virtually extended families:

An *il* is composed of several *taifeh* united on the basis of kinship, or social, political or other ties; usually located in a defined geographic area, known as the tribal territory (*qalamrou*). *Taifeh* of an *il* usually have distant kinship links with each other by blood (*nasabi*) or marriage (*sababi*); but some have no kinship links but form an *il* through social or political necessity (*zarurat*). The speech, customs and manners and way of life of the different *taifeh* of an *il* are by and large the same. The most well-defined and important pastoral nomad (*'ashayeri*) social level is the *taifeh*, a community (*jama'at*) usually united by near and distant kinship, linked through a number of generations, by blood or marriage, to a common origin (*mabna*); a pastoral nomad (*'ashayeri*) individual is usually identified primarily by his[/her] *taifeh* name.[32]

These official definitions in effect recognize changing political realities: the chiefs no longer exist. But they also fix current reality in a way that facilitates government control. This is also evident in the implication that there is, and always has been, a more or less uniform pattern of political and social structure among the nomadic tribes, which as we have seen is far from the case. Even the upper level of the structure (*il* divided into

---

[30] Tapper (1979b). In sparsely populated areas of the south and east, such as Kerman, where large-scale organization is rare, the larger community coincides with a *taifeh* such as Komachi, and is unstable in composition (Bradburd 1990). Cf. Anderson (1983).

[31] Tapper (1983b). Cf. Munson (1989: 395–6); Hart (1989).

[32] Census (1987, II-2, Ilsevan (Shahsevan): vi); also in ONA (1990; 1992). See Tapper (1994).

taifeh) is idealized. The model is not an exact representation of any one tribal group, but somehow an average of all of them, a model of uniformity, and it is a fiction for the purposes of administration, in the grand tradition of many centuries during which governments have defined, created and classified 'the tribes'.

Within the historical context of changing relations between central governments and the tribes, there remains agreement that the demographic, ecological and socio-economic processes governing the organization of pastoral nomadic camps were quite different from the politico-economic forces which produced tribes and tribal confederacies; an argument put forcefully by Fredrik Barth in his analysis of the Basseri nomads of southern Iran.

Historians and the tribes: the problem of extrapolation

Some historians, seeking to reconstruct mediaeval nomadic and tribal societies, have unwisely extrapolated from a limited range of recent ethnographies. Perhaps the most popular has been Barth's *Nomads of South Persia*, the earliest detailed ethnography of Iranian nomads.[33] This study of the Basseri, a tribe of some 3,000 nomad households belonging to the Khamseh confederacy in Fars, has now become a classic in social anthropology, and the Persian translation is widely read in Iran.

Based on fieldwork in 1958, the book offers an account of the Basseri tribe at two levels. First, it is a study of the ecological and economic processes generating the forms of social life among Basseri pastoral nomads. Basseri households, based on nuclear families and averaging 5.7 members, owned their own flocks. The average household flock was nearly 100 head of sheep, while the smallest flock on which a household could survive as nomads – given the productivity of the flocks, sales of lambs, skins and produce to the market, and expected levels of household consumption – was 60 head. When a father found a bride for his son, he soon provided him with a separate tent and his share of the flock as anticipatory inheritance, enabling the new couple to set up a separate household. Groups of roughly five households, not necessarily close paternal relatives, co-operated to herd joint flocks of about 400 animals. The basic nomadic community was the 'camp', ten to forty households which moved and camped together on migration between winter and summer quarters. The camp had a leader with limited personal authority over his followers.

Secondly, Barth shows how higher levels of organization than the camp

---

[33] Barth (1961). Earlier studies in Persian by Bavar (1945) and Bahmanbegi (1945) are interesting but not very specific on socio-economic detail.

depended on processes involving the Basseri chief (khan) and factors outside the tribe: the government, settled society, and other nomadic groups. The Basseri tribe (*il*), as administered by the chief, divided into sections (*tira*), which comprised one or more *oulad*. The *oulad* was a group usually of between 50 and 100 households whose male heads claimed common descent and thereby had grazing rights in specific pasturages in winter and summer quarters; to have access to grazing, a nomad must be able to claim membership of an *oulad*. Most *oulad* comprised two or more camps, but these were not defined patrilineal descent segments of the *oulad* and their membership was irregular and liable to change. The *tira* – the larger kind of nomadic community (as described above) – were weakly developed as groups, and the chief dealt directly and arbitrarily with *oulad* headmen (*katkhoda*) and often with camp leaders. To be effective as a leader and patron, the chief must have power and resources which set him, his family and his entourage apart from ordinary nomads, and on a level with regional and national elites. Barth's account of political structure and leadership is qualified to an extent by the fact that at the time of his study the chiefship had recently been abolished, and a new system integrating the Basseri into the state administrative structure via army officers had yet to take full effect.

Barth details the external economic relations and demographic processes affecting the nomads; and discusses the political relations between different tribal and ethno-linguistic groups in Fars province. As members of the Khamseh ('Five') confederacy, the Persian-speaking Basseri were linked with the Il-e 'Arab and the Turkish-speaking tribes Inanlu/Inallu, Nafar and Baharlu. They were collectively known as 'Arabs' and were traditional rivals of the Qashqa'i confederacy of 'Turks'. All of them had market and other relations with the settled peasantry who were mostly Persian speakers.

Barth made clear that Basseri economic, social, religious and political organization was highly dependent on specific historical, economic and political contexts. Ignoring this, however, many readers have extrapolated from the Basseri in both space and time, assuming them to typify Iranian pastoral nomads. Both Iranian and outside academics have frequently read Barth's account of Basseri (and Khamseh) tribal structure as confirming the elements of the unitary model of tribal structure in Iran outlined earlier, though a careful reading shows the Basseri to diverge at many points from that model. Anthropologists have constructed the Basseri into a 'type' of pastoral nomadic society,[34] while historians have

---

[34] Among many others, Sahlins (1966), but also Barth himself (1961: 49). The above paragraphs are an idiosyncratic 'reading' of Barth's study; others have read (misread, in my view) Barth's text as a study of segmentary lineage organization (Street 1990, 1992; Wright 1992, 1994); see Barth's response (1992) and Ganzer's comments (1994).

used the Basseri as a guiding 'text' for their reconstructions of pre-modern, especially mediaeval, nomadic and tribal societies in Iran, Turkey and elsewhere.[35]

For example, in an article on 'Turanian nomads', John Masson Smith laudably attempts to demolish some stereotypes of nomads as primitive vagrants. He refers to Barth's figures on Basseri herd sizes, claiming that Mongol pastoralism produced similar figures; and to Barth's analysis of Basseri 'capitalization' and 'profit', backed up by Daniel Bates' study of the Yürük nomads of Southeast Anatolia. But he quite ignores the fact that the production of most recent nomads in the region has been, and quite possibly was in mediaeval times, oriented towards market exchange, principally for wheat or some other agricultural product which was their staple food; moreover, he ignores the fact that nomad prosperity and flock size were determined, as Bates has clearly shown, by the ever-changing 'terms of trade' between wheat and pastoral produce. Masson Smith as a consequence constructs an idealized picture of nomad self-sufficiency, well-being and 'middle-class' prosperity. He makes further questionable generalizations from the hostility of the Basseri to settlement and their rates of settlement (among very rich and very poor only). Finally, from a misreading of Barth's account of the Basseri khan and a misunder-standing of Barth's analysis of the Basseri 'tribe', he accepts the necessity for nomad chiefs and extrapolates from the Basseri chief of the 1950s and his social and political characteristics onto mediaeval Saljuqs, Mongols and Safavids.[36] But his political model in no way accounts for Qashqa'i, Shahsevan, Durrani, Yürük, or many other recent instances of 'Turanian nomadism', and hence throws in doubt the extrapolation to cases from the past.

Masson Smith's treatment of the Basseri text is followed closely by Rudi Lindner. In his book *Nomads and Ottomans in Medieval Anatolia* he constructs a model of nomadic society under the Ottomans on the basis of extensive extrapolation from a selection of recent ethnographies, notably Barth on the Basseri, Bates on the Yürük, and Robert Pehrson on the Marri Baluch of Pakistan.[37] He claims with some justification that, in an examination of Ottoman cadaster records,

---

[35] Apart from works discussed below, see Manz (1989: 29–30), Abrahamian (1982: 18–20), Foran (1993: 52 – who acknowledges the problems of extrapolation) and others. Bournoutian uses a range of anthropological studies in his attempt to reconstruct nomadic societies in eastern Armenia under the early Qajars; the result is, unfortunately, confusion (1992: 51f.).

[36] Smith (1978); Bates (1973); he also refers to Irons' (1975) analysis of the Yamut Türkmen.

[37] Lindner (1983) and (1982); Barth (1961); Bates (1973); Pehrson (1966).

entries describing nomads, listing adult male tribesmen, locating their pastures, and summarizing their financial obligations, help us to perform some primitive, incomplete, but nonetheless suggestive fieldwork among medieval pastoralists . . . [and give] the opportunity to follow a group's fortunes over the generations.[38]

In the central chapter, his main objective is to make sense of Ottoman tax regulations relating to the nomads, for which purpose he states that he has to make certain assumptions, and to construct a model of the structure of a herd, for which historical accounts are inadequate.

It thus seems wise to follow the accounts of ethnographers who have given detailed accounts of the economics of herding practiced by their nomad hosts. Unfortunately, few modern anthropologists have studied herds as closely as they have studied the herders. The two best studies applicable to this study are by Barth and Bates.[39]

Much of this is skilfully done, and undoubtedly throws considerable light on the nature of mediaeval nomadic societies in Anatolia. Lindner is admirably cautious about some of his assumptions and careful in his interpretations of the ethnographic account – for example, the determinants of herd size, the issue of the 'terms of trade' between pastoral and agricultural produce and the politics of nomadic adaptations to village cycles, and the nature of nomadic migratory schedules.[40]

Unfortunately he makes a number of less appropriate extrapolations, and crucially misreads and misunderstands some complex analytical issues. For example, he quotes the Basseri early on as representing (like the Ottomans) 'the nomads of Inner Asian and Turkish history', whereas there is no historical reason to make this connexion. Later, he quotes a passage from Barth's description of the authority of the Basseri khan, without comment, as a representation of that of the Ottoman Sultan. Further, when constructing a model of nomadic herd structure under the early Ottomans, he uses Barth's material on the Basseri, and puts aside Bates' model of the Yürük because they 'are integrated into a market economy'; but so were the Basseri, whose livelihood depended on selling skins and other pastoral produce, while the economies of most present-day and probably many mediaeval pastoral societies were also oriented to market production of meat. Lindner's consequent assumptions about the sex and age distribution of herds, and rates of lambing and attrition, leading to conclusions about tax take-off and the burden on nomadic society under the Ottomans, are quite unjustified and must remain

---

[38] Lindner (1983: 75).
[39] Lindner (1983: 60); he missed detailed studies of pastoral herding in Iran by Afshar-Naderi (1968), Black (1972; 1976) and myself (1972, 1979a), and the comparative study by Dahl and Hjort (1976).   [40] Lindner (1983: 57, 59, 77).

suspect. He proceeds, like many others before him, to base some calculations on Barth's analysis of the minimum viable Basseri household flock, without realizing how far it is specific to certain economic, political and cultural conditions.[41]

As regards nomad political organization, though he underplays the role of kinship ideologies in recruiting and uniting tribal groups, Lindner correctly observes that in the Middle East all tribal political groups, whether large confederacies or even quite small tribes, are historically of mixed origins, sometimes recognized, sometimes forgotten. However, like Masson Smith, he distinguishes 'tribes' ('pragmatic, often temporary political groupings around a successful chief') from 'clans' (patrilineal descent groups, 'the most important structural segment of the tribe') in a way which demonstrates a misunderstanding, not only of general anthropological formulations of those terms, but also of Barth's analysis. He fails to appreciate that descent groups are directly associated with access to resources (grazing rights; holy descent or other claims to authority), that genealogies are 'constructed' and 'maintained' for this purpose, and that genealogies are in effect indigenous models of 'tribes'.[42]

In a later chapter, Lindner puzzles over references in the cadastral records to subtribal groups called *cemaat* (communities). Promisingly he begins, 'the traditional social organization of nomads is our key to answering this question, and Barth's study of the Basseri is a convenient source for this data'; he proceeds to discuss herding 'camps' as the most obvious nomadic communities, but not necessarily the most significant, and certainly not the most durable; instead he fastens on the 'clan', a subunit of the tribe.[43] However, he misses the significance of the *cemaat*. There is every indication that these are the basic nomadic communities of fifteen to fifty families, which in some societies, as outlined earlier, do coincide with herding 'camps' and/or subtribal administrative units, but are certainly not defined as such.

Lindner, in short, is led to suggest as necessary to nomadic society a number of economic, social and political characteristics that are in fact highly contingent; an error that he would have avoided if he had used a wider selection of available ethnographies of nomads, such as (for only Iran) the Bakhtiari, the Qashqa'i, the Shahsevan or the Türkmen, which on grounds of scale and culture at least are more directly comparable with nomads under the Ottomans than are either the Basseri, the Yürük or the Marri.

In his history of the Bakhtiari, Gene Garthwaite extrapolates at a

---

[41] Lindner (1983: 23, 52, 60f.). He does acknowledge some basis for variation in the last point, including alternative sources of income within the pastoral economy (p. 72 note 57).   [42] Lindner (1982; 1983: 93f.).   [43] Lindner (1983: 93).

number of points from the Basseri 'text'. He refers to Basseri flock sizes and the cash values of the animals and their produce, affirming that they 'corroborate' James Morier's early nineteenth-century observations of nomads in Iran, and implying that such figures were valid for the Bakhtiari too; he also implies that the Bakhtiari resembled the Basseri in the role of the nuclear family, pasture rights and descent structure, and quotes at length from Barth's analysis of Basseri anticipatory inheritance of animals as inhibiting the development of larger herds. He does question whether contemporary observations are relevant to earlier periods, but he fails to ask which groups were the basis of Morier's generalizations, or to note that there are innumerable significant social, economic and political differences among nomadic societies in Iran, and specifically between the contemporary Basseri and Bakhtiari, whether in terms of their own nomadic and pastoral organization, or in their natural, social and political environments.[44]

I would argue that these historians have been remarkably ahistorical in their use of the Basseri text. Besides, the Basseri example is inappropriate for such extrapolation onto other 'nomadic tribes', whether mediaeval or contemporary, for various reasons. First, Barth's observations derive mainly from his residence in the camp of the Basseri chief's personal entourage, the Darbar, which must throw doubt on their representativeness even of 'ordinary' Basseri nomadic society. Moreover, he was able to reside there for only the three months of the spring migration.[45]

Secondly, comparison with other contemporary nomadic societies, whether in Iran or elsewhere, shows the Basseri, in virtually all the features outlined in the summary above, to constitute just one pattern among many. This is not surprising, given the very specific ecological, economic, political and historical circumstances of the Basseri, most of which are ignored by those who extrapolate from the text, and are quite different from those of other tribal and nomadic societies, whether Ottoman, Bakhtiari or Shahsevan.[46]

Thirdly, Barth's own limited comparison with the neighbouring Qashqa'i Turks and Khamseh Arabs, and other sources on the social, economic and political organization of nomadic tribal groups elsewhere or at other times, suggests that the Basseri case is not merely specific but rather unusual. A rather different model is suggested by the remarkable similarities, for example, between confederate clans of the fifteenth-century Aq-

---

[44] Garthwaite (1983: 28, 32, 174, 80ff., 175, 29).   [45] See Tapper (1979a: 252).

[46] Irons (various articles) many years ago made the same point about the specificity of the Basseri by comparing various aspects of Basseri and Yamut Türkmen economy, politics and society. For a detailed comparison between Basseri, Türkmen and Shahsevan nomadic social organization, see Tapper (1979a: 240f.).

Qoyunlu, the sixteenth-century Qızılbash *oimaq*, nineteenth-century tribal confederacies such as the Boir Ahmad, or the Shahsevan described in this book.[47]

None the less, Barth's two-level analysis is valid and useful generally: the factors operating at each level are quite different. It seems likely, though relevant historical sources are only suggestive on this, that internal demographic and socio-economic factors and the ecological conditions of nomadic pastoralism have always shaped basic communities, and that larger political groupings, such as confederacies – and indeed tribes – are the product of external political, economic and cultural relations, notably with neighbouring groups and with central authorities.

The decades since Barth's pioneering study have seen the publication of numerous ethnographies of nomads and tribal groups which differ substantially from the Basseri. Undoubtedly, historians will be tempted to extrapolate from these works too, in their effort to reconstruct earlier nomadic and tribal societies; but their reconstructions will only be plausible if their readings of ethnography are more circumspect and comparative and more firmly contextualized than hitherto.

One such ethnography was my earlier study of the Shahsevan of Azarbaijan. The present book is my own reconstruction of their history, in which extrapolation from my fieldwork inevitably plays a major part. At the same time, it is an attempt to use history to deepen understanding of the political, economic and ecological contexts of my ethnography. As history, the book is a narrative of events and an analysis of processes, but it acknowledges that all historical – and ethnographic – descriptions and analyses are compilations of representations, resulting from negotiation between differently motivated claims to truth. In Chapter Fourteen, I examine the sources of the main different representations of Shahsevan history, and attempt to determine how they were motivated and negotiated. In the concluding parts of this Introduction, I outline Shahsevan history and recent social and political organization, constructed on this occasion so as to point up ways in which they differ from comparable – and better-known – tribal groups in Iran such as the Basseri, the Bakhtiari and the Qashqa'i; finally, I add a note on the sources used in the book.

The Shahsevan

Shahsevan is the name of a number of tribal groups located in various parts of northwestern Iran, notably in the region of Moghan and Ardabil

---

[47] Barth (1961: 123–33); Woods (1976); McChesney (1981); Loeffler (1978). But see Barfield (1991).

in eastern Azarbaijan and in the Kharaqan and Khamseh districts between Zanjan and Tehran. There is evidence that some if not all of the latter groups also came from Moghan.[48] Shi'a Muslims by faith, and speakers of Azarbaijani Turkish, the Shahsevan traditionally pursued a pastoral nomadic way of life, though by the present century this was in various combinations with settled agriculture.

The main discussion of this book concerns the history of the present Shahsevan tribes of Moghan, which once formed a unified confederacy, and continue to share language, religious beliefs and practices, technology and patterns of social organization.[49] Many features of their culture and way of life – notably their distinctive dwellings, the hemispherical, felt-covered *alachïq* – differentiate them from most other tribal groups in Iran, including the Shahsevan of Kharaqan and Khamseh. Some of these features are of Turkic origins and are found among other Turkic groups in Iran and elsewhere, and can often be traced to the cultures of the Ghuzz Turkic tribes of Central Asia which invaded Southwest Asia in the eleventh century AD. Although several component Shahsevan tribes are of non-Turkic origins, and preserve distinct cultural features that are evidence of this, Turkic identity and culture are overwhelmingly dominant among them.

Unlike the Bakhtiari and Qashqa'i confederacies of the Zagros, the Shahsevan live in an accessible and much-frequented frontier zone. Their winter quarters were in the fertile Moghan steppe, which was extensively irrigated in mediaeval times and was the site chosen by two conquerors, Nader Afshar (in 1736) and Agha Mohammad Qajar (in 1796), for their coronations as Shah of Iran. Shahsevan summer quarters, surrounded by rich farmlands on the slopes of Mt Savalan, lay between Ardabil, a historically important shrine city and trade centre, and Tabriz, until recently second city of Iran and the capital of several past rulers. Grain, fruit, wool and meat from the region have long been widely marketed. Raw silk produced in the neighbouring provinces of Gilan and Shirvan figured prominently in the international trade which crossed through or near Shahsevan territory, and control of which was a major motivation for conquest. Between the sixteenth century and the present, Iranian, Ottoman, Russian and Soviet forces claimed or occupied Shahsevan territory on several occasions each. In such a location, Shahsevan relations with central governments have taken a rather different course from those of the Qashqa'i and the Bakhtiari, and the tribal confederacy has not been a unified, centralized political structure since before 1800.

---

[48] On the Zanjan and Tehran Shahsevan, see Appendix One. The district of Khamseh should not be confused with the tribal confederation in Fars, bearing the same name (= 5).   [49] Discussed in detail in Tapper (1979a) and elsewhere.

The Shahsevan confederacy took shape during the upheavals of the early eighteenth century, when Nader Shah recovered Ardabil and Moghan from the Ottomans and Russians and appointed a khan over the Shahsevan pastoral nomads of the region. The khan's immediate descendants became established as chiefs of the Shahsevan and governors of Ardabil, though they soon split the confederacy into two, associated with the districts of Ardabil and Meshkin. The chiefs participated actively in the rivalries and alliances that characterized political relations in Azarbaijan until the Russo–Iranian wars of the early nineteenth century, ending in the Russian conquest of much of Shahsevan winter quarters in the Moghan steppe.

Shahsevan territory, straddling the sensitive Caucasian frontier, became an important arena for the Great Game of Asia. The old chiefs lost control of the tribes, and the tribal structure, with the emergence of a new elite of warrior chiefs, reformed on new principles; martial success and wealth now counted for more than noble descent or government sanction. No longer a unified confederacy, the Shahsevan were dominated by the actions, rivalries and alliances of the new chiefs, each leading a cluster of dependent tribes.

This system reached its heyday around the turn of the twentieth century, when the Shahsevan of Moghan numbered over 10,000 families and for nearly four decades were virtually independent of central government. Then, in the 1920s and 1930s, the Pahlavi regime pacified, disarmed and forcibly settled the Shahsevan. In the 1940s they resumed pastoral nomadism and revived a loose, decentralized, tribal confederacy, but by the 1960s the dismissal of the chiefs and the Shah's Land Reform programme deprived the confederacy of its economic and political foundations, and settlement and detribalization proceeded on a large scale. After the the Islamic Revolution of 1978–9, pastoral nomadism experienced a modest revival among the Shahsevan, as elsewhere in Iran, and the census of 1987 recorded nearly 6,000 families as pursuing this way of life, but in the mid-1990s it did not seem likely to survive much longer with the inexorable spread of various government-supported developments, notably agro-industrial schemes started in Moghan under the Shah.

In the twentieth century, the Moghan Shahsevan have been organized in a series of some forty *taifa*, units which I have termed 'tribes', which ranged in size from as few as fifty to several hundred households, and each of which had a chief, known as the *bey*. Most *taifa* comprised from two to over twenty *tira* (tribal sections), which were usually based on a *göbäk* ('navel', descent group), led by an *aq-saqal* ('grey-beard', elder), and formed a basic nomadic community (*jamahat*) – comparable to the

Basseri 'camp'.[50] As discussed in Chapter Fourteen, there is good evidence that the *taifa* (the larger communities), and possibly the *tira/göbäk/jamahat* (the smaller communities), have been the most important elements of Shahsevan nomadic and tribal organization since at least the mid-nineteenth century, and it seems reasonable to assume that they were so considerably earlier, possibly since their advent in the Moghan region.

This formal 'organization diagram' displays numerous similarities and differences when compared with those of other nomadic tribal groups in Iran, but reveals nothing of distinctive features of Shahsevan society, economics and politics which I have described in detail elsewhere, from the size and composition of households, patterns of pastoral production and marketing, and marriage and inheritance practices, to migration patterns and ethnic and economic aspects of tribal-settled relations. Perhaps the most important of the features that distinguished the Shahsevan from other nomadic tribal groups in Iran was their unusual system of grazing rights. Where other nomads operated some version of the expected system of communal access to grazing, in the twentieth century the Shahsevan developed a tenure system whereby individual pastoralists inherited, bought or rented known proportions of the grazing rights to specific pastures.[51] One theme that runs through this book is an attempt to trace the origins of this system; I remain convinced that access to grazing is both the most important and the most neglected aspect of pastoral nomadic social, economic and political organization.[52]

A note on sources

During the period of gestation of this book, historical studies of Iran have been reinvigorated, in two main respects. First, since the Islamic Revolution of 1978–9, particularly during the 1990s, there has been an explosion in the publication of documents from official and family archives in Iran. As regards the tribes, students of their history have not yet had the opportunity, or the skills, to take full advantage of these newly accessible documents; it has to be said, moreover, that the information in these documents concerning the tribes does not always repay the effort necessary to glean it.

Secondly, trends in social and economic history have begun to influ-

---

[50] For detailed discussion of the Shahsevan nomadic community, and comparisons with Barth's account of the Basseri, see Tapper (1979a).

[51] Described in detail in Tapper (1979a).

[52] Cf. my remarks in Tapper (1979c). An important recent volume (Casimir and Rao 1992) brings together a number of contributions which remedy this neglect.

ence a field hitherto dominated by older traditions of historical writing. Not surprisingly, this development has had an impact on studies of the tribes, since most of those who have attempted tribal history have had a social-science background.

Thus, there have been some recent attempts, mainly by scholars based in North America, to replace traditional 'orientalist' narrative and dynastic history by social and economic (i.e. 'theorized', often Marxist) history relating to the tribes. However, problems of competence and accuracy – perhaps inevitable, given the plethora of primary sources now available – have meant that authors of ambitious syntheses often ignore relevant available sources (historical or ethnographic), or misunderstand or misrepresent those they use. In the 1990s, it may be argued, the wealth of newly published materials, both primary and secondary, makes it considerably more difficult than it was for earlier generations of scholars to keep up with relevant literature in various languages, even with the benefit of electronic aids; but inaccuracy, omission and misrepresentation severely diminish the value of several otherwise interesting new studies.[53]

Published literature on the tribes of Iran now consists of a number of surveys and comparative studies, and several historical and ethnographic monographs.[54] Most ethnographic studies have some historical depth, however brief: but they are not based on much primary research, drawing rather on existing histories or easily available sources. A few make more serious efforts at history, and anthropologists have contributed some notable historical articles.[55]

Beck's monograph on the Qashqa'i stands out as an historically informed ethnography, particularly valuable on the fortunes of the ilkhani family in Pahlavi times and after. The bulk of the book deals with the mid to late twentieth century. Only sixty pages are devoted to earlier

---

[53] See my comments (Tapper 1991a) on the Helfgott/Reid debate; and in Chapter Two on Foran (1993).

[54] The most notable historical overview is Lambton's *Encyclopedia* article (1971). General surveys include Towfiq (1987), Spooner (1987), comparative essays by Varjavand (1965), Amanollahi-Baharvand (1992), myself (1983b, 1991b), Kiavand (1989), Shahbazi (1990), Beck (1991a, 1991b: 443–9). Other useful recent general studies include the compendium by Afshar-Sistani (1987), and two bibliographies published by the High Council of the Tribes: one lists foreign-language sources (Larijani 1990), the other Persian (ISSR 1987). Historical monographs include Oberling's studies of the Qashqa'i (1974) and other Turkic groups (1960, 1964a, 1964b), and Garthwaite's of the Bakhtiari (1983), both informed by anthropological insights.

[55] Historically interesting ethnographies include van Bruinessen (1978), Stöber (1978) and Bradburd (1990). Important articles include Digard (1973, 1979, 1987); Loeffler (1973, 1978); Singer (1982); Brooks (1983).

times: Beck talks of 'lack of historical information on practically all other
[than ilkhani] aspects of tribal organization and structure until the
twentieth century . . . Although the Qashqa'i tribal confederacy took
form in this period [1796–1906] little specific information is available
about Qashqa'i people . . . beyond their military role.'[56] She relies, naturally, on Oberling's earlier book (with some updating) and on the oral testimony of khans, referring to (but not quoting) 'family documents'; but
she treats as 'history' the khans' stories of events occurring two centuries
earlier, even though unsupported by documents.[57] Theoretically, she
focuses on centralization and hierarchy, the development of an elite
which separated the state and the ordinary nomads, and asks why and
how this happened among the Qashqa'i and not elsewhere. She relates
the Qashqa'i case to their location in particular, and more generally to
processes of state formation. The Qashqa'i polity developed with the
early Qajars (late eighteenth century), but Qashqa'i identity not until a
century later, with the impact of capitalism – in other words, the Qashqa'i
began to flourish at a time when Shahsevan unity had already broken
down.

Although records of the Shahsevan too are much richer for the past
100–150 years, earlier sources are apparently not so scarce as they are for
the Qashqa'i. For the period up to the early eighteenth century (Part I), I
have used the major secondary sources for general outlines,[58] but I have
scoured primary sources for mention of Shahsevan tribes and their activities: chronicles and published court documents, and foreign travellers'
accounts. For the next hundred years (Part II), such sources, supplemented increasingly by Russian and Azarbaijani archive-based historical
studies,[59] are much more productive of information on the Shahsevan,
though again I have also made use of general secondary sources.[60]

For the Qajar era (Chapters Eight to Twelve), materials on the
Shahsevan are apparently fuller than on other major groups like the
Qashqa'i.[61] In the second half of the nineteenth century, sources, particu-
larly in Russian, are detailed and circumstantial enough to permit the

---

[56] Beck (1986: 52, 60).   [57] Beck (1986: e.g. pp. 46–7).
[58] Notably Jackson and Lockhart (1986); and see notes in text.
[59] Notably: Butkov (1869); Abdullaev (1958, 1965); Dälili (1971, 1974, 1979);
Petrushevskiy (1949); see Ricks (1973), Perry (1979) on eighteenth-century sources.
[60] Esp. Avery *et al.* (1991), especially chapters by Avery, Hambly, Perry.
[61] They are not so extensive as those available for tribes on the North-West Frontier of
India. The extent of British contact and sympathy with, and understanding of, the
North-West Frontier tribes was very different from that of the Russians with the
Shahsevan and other tribal peoples on their frontiers; there is scope here for comparative
investigation.

reconstruction, informed by fieldwork, of transformations in social and political structures.[62] These materials are supplemented and often complemented by Persian chronicles and local histories[63] and British diplomatic and consular archives, especially those from the Tabriz consulate, from the early nineteenth century onwards;[64] meanwhile, huge numbers of Persian documents (Ministry communications, diaries, memoirs) relating to the Qajar era are becoming available, and general and critical studies are increasingly comprehensive.[65]

From around 1900 to 1925 (Chapter Twelve), archival and other materials are so varied and prolific that I have had to be summary and selective. I have also made use of interviews in the 1960s with Shahsevan men (and a few women) of various classes and non-Shahsevan individuals with knowledge of tribal affairs.[66]

Published and unpublished sources in European languages on the Shahsevan are few for the Pahlavi era (1925–79), though again Iranian documents and memoirs are rapidly becoming available.[67] I have again made use of my own field notes, and the reports of other individuals and organizations who have worked among the Shahsevan.[68]

It must be common for researchers – whether in anthropology or history – to find that the further they delve the less they seem to know; or rather, the more there seems to know. This has certainly been my experience, both in the field and in the libraries and archives. In the field, every honest ethnographer knows that she or he can never do enough fieldwork. In the case of archives and literary sources, just as the excavation of one seam passes the point of diminishing returns, so it seems another seam beckons. I cannot pretend that I have read every existing written source on the Shahsevan, however I believe I have covered more than any previ-

---

[62] Especially: Ogranovich (1870, 1876); Krebel (in Markov 1890, Radde 1886); Artamonov (1890); Tigranov (1909). See discussion in Chapter Fourteen.

[63] These include both older chronicles such as Bakikhanov (1926) on Qobbeh, Qara-Baghi (1959) on Qara-Bagh, as well as more recent memoirs and compilations: Baiburdi (1962) on Qara-Dagh/Arasbaran, Sa'edi (1965) on Khiou/Meshkin-Shahr, Safari (1971 etc.) on Ardabil, Rava'i (1984) on Khalkhal. I know of no published history of Sarab, although Naba'i announced that one by him was in press (1987: 182).

[64] Foreign Office files in the Public Record Office, and India Office files in the India Office Library, both in London.

[65] Iraj Afshar has been particularly prolific in publishing scholarly editions of such documents. For critical comments on sources on and studies of Qajar Iran, see Gurney (1990), Bakhash (1978: 405–14), Amanat (1983: 1ff.). Useful general studies include Yapp (1980), Lambton (1987, 1991), Hambly (1991a), Keddie and Amanat (1991) and collections like Pakdaman (1983). *Encyclopedia Iranica* is notably useful for its biographical entries.   [66] For sources on the time, see notes to Chapter Twelve.

[67] For background: Abrahamian (1982), Sabahi (1990), Avery et al. (1991).See *Iranian Studies* 1993 for articles on the early Pahlavi era, and on new collections of documents.

[68] See notes to Chapter Thirteen.

ous researcher, if only to learn both how little I know, and how little is known about Shahsevan history.[69]

Let me summarize some of the sources that I know I have missed.

I have not visited the archives in Istanbul, which contain unpublished materials concerning the Shahsevan from times when Ottoman forces occupied their territory between the 1580s and the 1720s. For example, during their occupation of much of Azarbaijan in the 1720s (see Chapter Five), the Ottomans undertook a population and land survey of the region, preserved in the Başvekalet Arşivi in Istanbul.[70]

Russian and Soviet authors have published or quoted from documents in similar (*mutatis mutandis*) archives in Baku and elsewhere in the former Soviet Union: Persian (and Georgian, Armenian) documents from pre-Russian times,[71] and Russian documents relating to invasions and occupations of Shahsevan territory such as in the 1720s and during the two Russo-Iranian wars. I have not consulted these, nor US State Department and French Foreign Ministry archives relating to nine-teenth- and twentieth-century Iran, which would also repay attention which I have not been able to give.

Above all, I have not consulted Iranian archives directly, and indeed I have found it impossible to keep abreast of the tide of published documents that have poured off the presses in the 1990s. The Ministry of Foreign Affairs has recently opened its archives, especially for the Qajar period; it has published lists of documents and several collections of them. Another major repository is the National Archives Organization (Sazman-e Asnad-e Melli) in Tehran, which has been publishing documents from the Interior Ministry and private archives in books and their journal *Ganjineh*. Although, as noted earlier, official documents rarely deal with the tribes, which until recently were – for various reasons – of more interest to outsiders, such of these publications that I have seen suggest that the archives would repay systematic study.

In short, there is a wide range of sources for Shahsevan history which await the attentions of another day, and probably another researcher.

This text has other limitations. Sources for the early modern history of Iran are richer than those for most other parts of the non-European world, but they consist almost entirely of materials (dynastic histories and chron-icles, diplomatic records and travel narratives) which focus on – or take

---

[69] I comment in the text on studies by Minorsky (e.g. 1934a), Rostopchin (1933), Balayan (1960), Sa'edi (1965), Schweizer (1970), Dälili (1974), Roemer (1989b), Hasani (1990), Shahsevand-Baghdadi (1991), Mizban (1992), Begdili (1993). Recent publica-tions devoted to the Shahsevan by photographers (Kasraian, Baharnaz) and carpet experts (such as Tanavoli 1985) add nothing to knowledge of Shahsevan history and society.   [70] Frye (1960: 625–6).   [71] See e.g. Puturidze (1961), Musävi (1977).

the perspective of – state and government, the centres of power, privilege and literacy. Ordinary people have been even less well served than their European counterparts. Contemporary nomads' constructions of their identity have been shaped by administrative – and scholarly – writings; the state, through official chronicles and documents, has constructed tribal peoples such as the Shahsevan as peripheral, defined their identities and written their histories, silencing them in the process. Even memoirs and local chronicles – invaluable in this case for at least recent periods – are written with a strong urban focus and a pronounced bias against the nomadic tribes of the hinterland and the geographical periphery.

Although this history of the Shahsevan is, to an extent, a history of Iran, seen from the unusual perspective of one such 'periphery' (in this case a crucial zone of international contact), the nature of the sources still means that it is largely a political history of chiefly dynasties, of leaders and their named groups of followers – tribes, confederacies – and their relations with the state. Rarely, and only latterly, do ordinary nomads, their households and camps – and women – emerge. Nomads produce little in the way of records:[72] they have no 'history' except as followers of named leaders, or when they become leaders themselves. When there are no chiefs to attract attention – as with the Shahsevan before the eighteenth century – there is little or no tribal history to write about.

Members of the Bakhtiari and Qashqa'i chiefly families and a few other tribal elites have produced memoirs and chronicles since late Qajar times. This has not been the case with the Shahsevan, whose main chiefly dynasty fell from power before the writing of such memoirs became fashionable. If there was a central historical voice of the Shahsevan, it has not been written down, though possible traces of it are found in legends recorded by Russian officials in the last century (Chapter Three); these, and legends recorded later, more likely reflect the competing voices of later rival chiefs of individual Shahsevan tribes. To my knowledge no Shahsevan has yet published a family or tribal history. In the past few years, individuals of Shahsevan descent or connections have produced books and theses which include valuable historical documents and memoirs of recent events, but on earlier periods they have little or nothing to add to published, externally derived sources.[73]

---

[72] But see Cribb (1991).
[73] E.g. Hasani (1990), Shahsevand-Baghdadi (1991), Mizban (1992), Begdili (1993). Since the 1950s students of Shahsevan background have written a number of dissertations at the University of Tabriz and elsewhere on agricultural and other topics concerning the Shahsevan. 'Ali Khan, former chief of the Geyikli, on reading Bahmanbegi's personalized account of the Qashqa'i (1989), was motivated to write a book-length history of the Shahsevan: in autumn 1995 he showed me the MS (which was being considered for publication in Tabriz), but he would not allow me to read it.

A book like this inevitably fails to capture and represent indigenous voices, at least for earlier periods. Only in the late nineteenth century do hints of Shahsevan voices begin to emerge, for example in the texts of telegrams (Chapter Twelve), and in stories I recorded in the field (see Appendix Three) from participants or their children – as it happens, few of them former chiefs. Otherwise, the voices that are heard in the written sources are those of outsiders, with their varied perspectives and biases, some of which are discussed in Chapter Fourteen.

Moreover, the sources were written by and almost exclusively about men, and there is little or nothing here about women. There are highly suggestive sixteenth-century accounts of tribes that were probable Shahsevan ancestors, where women, at least among the elite, are in powerful economic, social and political positions; and there are a few more recent interesting cases, such as the possible participation of Shahsevan in the women's revolt of 1896–7 in Ardabil, and 'Azamat Khanom, a woman who was chief of the Polatlu Shahsevan tribe in the 1920s (Chapter Twelve); but otherwise the sources are silent on Shahsevan women's history.[74]

In other words, the perspectives of the Shahsevan, chiefs or ordinary nomads, men or women, are under-represented in the sources. On occasion, I attempt to interpret events imaginatively through Shahsevan eyes, conscious of my presumption in doing so. I am conscious too that my trajectory – from living with 'real' Shahsevan into the historical texts and images – is the opposite to that of most Iranian counterparts writing about the tribes, who begin with often mythological images from (school) books and only progress later to the 'reality'. Am I creating a new mythology?

One of my hopes is that my comments and interpretations, when read by those who find them at fault, will provoke the production of hitherto unpublished documents that might resolve some of the riddles about earlier periods – or at least support some of the arguments I have dismissed as lacking evidence. The debate about Shahsevan origins and identity could prove lively.

---

[74] For an account of Shahsevan nomad women's socio-political organization in the 1960s, see N. Tapper (1978).

Part I

The Safavid state and the origins of the Shahsevan

[Shah 'Abbas I] had been early compelled to repress the ambition of the principal chiefs of the Kûzel-bash tribes, and had put several of them to death. He sought another defence against the effects of their turbulence, by forming a tribe of his own, which he styled *Shah Sevund*, or 'the king's friends'; and he invited men of all tribes to enrol themselves in a clan, which he considered as devoted to his family, and therefore distinguished by his peculiar favour and protection. Volunteers could not be wanting at such a call: and we have one instance of ten thousand men being registered by the name of Shah-Sevund in one day. This tribe, which became remarkable for its attachment to the Suffavean dynasty, still exists in Persia, though with diminished numbers. It could once boast of more than a hundred thousand families.

Sir John Malcolm, *History of Persia*[1]

The history of the Shahsevan since the early eighteenth century is fairly well documented, but their origins are obscure. They appear to be a collection of tribal groups brought together in a confederacy some time between the sixteenth and the eighteenth centuries.

By the twentieth century, they had acquired three rather different versions of their origins. The accepted, 'official' version of Shahsevan origins is that recounted by the historian Sir John Malcolm in the passage reproduced above, to the effect that Shah 'Abbas I (1587–1629) formed a special composite tribe of his own under the name of Shahsevan, in order to counteract the turbulence of the rebellious Qızılbash chiefs, who had helped his ancestor Shah Esma'il to found the Safavid dynasty a century earlier. In later readings of Malcolm's account, the Shahsevan were formed as a personal corps or militia, a royal guard.

Vladimir Minorsky, in his article 'Shah-sewan' for the first edition of the *Encyclopedia of Islam*, noted that 'the known facts somewhat complicate Malcolm's story', and that the references in contemporary Safavid chronicles did not amount to evidence that 'a single regularly constituted tribe was ever founded by Shah 'Abbas under the name of Shah-sewan'.[2]

Minorsky drew attention to the writings of a number of Russians who

---

[1] Malcolm (1815, I: 556).   [2] Minorsky (1934a).

recorded the traditions of the Shahsevan of Moghan with whom they were in contact towards the end of the nineteenth century. These traditions – which differ from but do not contradict Malcolm's story – vary in detail, but agree that Shahsevan ancestors immigrated from Anatolia; they present Shahsevan tribal structure as divided between chiefly nobles (descended from the original immigrant leaders) and commoners, and refer to an original royal grant of pastures and contemporary royal appointment of the chiefs, which appear to legitimate the latter's authority, as well as their control of the pastures, the most important resource for all the tribespeople.

This second version has given way in the present century to both the first, 'official' version, and a third, commonly articulated among the ordinary tribespeople and in modern writings on them, which declares that the Shahsevan are 'thirty-two tribes', all of equal status, and even denies that they were ever centralized under a paramount chief.

As we shall see, there is indeed no historical evidence to support Malcolm's story, which is based on a misreading of chronicle sources; but it has been adopted by most later historians, both Iranian and foreign, and has been assimilated into Iranian, and even, through modern education, into current Shahsevan mythology. Most influential in perpetuating the story have been Curzon, Fasa'i, Browne and Sykes; more recently (since Minorsky's article) Wilber, de Planhol, Bayani, Bosworth and Lapidus.[3] Among modern writers on the Safavids, only a few (Bausani, Petrushevskiy, Roemer, Morgan) acknowledge the doubts that have been expressed about Malcolm's story;[4] others such as Lambton, Smith, Reid and Louis Bazin, while referring to Minorsky's and sometimes my own previous investigations of the Shahsevan, nevertheless ignore the conclusions and reproduce the old myth as historical fact;[5] while Bellan, Petrushevskiy (in an earlier work), Falsafi, Lockhart, Röhrborn, Savory and Haneda refrain from comment on Shahsevan origins.[6]

[3] Curzon (1894, II: 270); Fasa'i (1895–6: 143); Browne (1928: 106, 119); Sykes (1930, II: 260); Wilber (1948: 68, and 1981: 62); de Planhol (1968: 249, 1993: 511); Bayani (1974: 68); Bosworth (1980: 174); Lapidus (1988: 289). Another influential version, close to (perhaps based on?) Malcolm's, is that of Shirvani (1898: 346–7). Porter (1821–2, I: 433), when describing the 'Ali Qapu in Esfahan, tells a romantically embellished version of Malcolm's story of the 'Shah Sewends'; but he did not connect it with the 'Shassivani' he encountered at Takht-e Soleiman (II: 561).

[4] Bausani (1962: 191); Petrushevskiy (1977: 183); Morgan (1988: 128); Roemer (various, and see below).

[5] Lambton (1971: 1102); Smith (1978: 74); Reid (1983: 30); Bazin (1988: 50). Similar inconsistencies are to be found in the historical summaries contained in several recent lavishly produced books on Shahsevan weaving, notably Azadi and Andrews (1985); Tanavoli (1985).

[6] Bellan (1932); Petrushevskiy (1949); Falsafi (1953); Lockhart (1958); Röhrborn (1966); Savory (1980a; 1987); Haneda (1987).

Minorsky's discussion of Shahsevan origins does not do justice to the available evidence. In Chapters Two to Four, I re-examine the evidence and adduce a number of important sources which have not yet been considered. There have been a few other attempts to solve the riddle of Shahsevan origins, in particular those of Rostopchin, Balayan, Dälili and Roemer.[7] I consider their contributions at relevant points, but it is appropriate to say here that, while Roemer's arguments are largely in accord with my own, the speculations of the others are not, being unsupported by contemporary sources.

Most discussions of the term 'Shahsevan' refer to its original meaning as extreme personal loyalty and religious devotion to Shahs of the Safavid dynasty, who reigned in Iran from 1501 to 1736. These Shahs owed their continuing legitimacy to their supposed direct descent from the Shi'ite Imams, through Sheikh Safi, eponymous founder of the Safavid Sufi order of Ardabil. In Chapter Two I briefly sketch the development of this order into a royal dynasty, in order to help elucidate the nature of its religious and political control over its followers; I then discuss the sources of the 'official' version of Shahsevan origins as a composite tribe formed as part of the military and tribal policies of the Safavid rulers.

Prevailing theories of the origins of the present-day Shahsevan tribes of Moghan tell of their ancestors' location there during Safavid times, but differ as to whether they were indigenous to the region or immigrants, and, if the latter, when they arrived. Chapter Three relates the traditions of the Shahsevan tribes, both those recorded and published during the late nineteenth century and more recent versions including those collected by myself, and also examines the possible bases for the twentieth-century 'popular' notion of the Shahsevan as thirty-two independent tribes. Chapter Four examines contemporary records from the Safavid period linking the name Shahsevan, and names of component groups, with the region of Moghan and Ardabil.

Neither the 'official' nor the traditional versions of Shahsevan origins can be fully documented. Tribal groups bearing the names of later Shahsevan tribes did inhabit the Moghan region in the sixteenth century, and some bearing the name Shahsevan itself are recorded there in the second half of the seventeenth century, but the evidence (as described in Part II) indicates that no tribal confederacy as such was formed until the following century, in the time of Nader Shah.

[7] Rostopchin (1933); Balayan (1960); Dälili (1974); Roemer (1989b).

2 'Shahsevani': Safavid tribal policy and practice

Background: Azarbaijan and the early Safavids[1]

The Safavid Shahs who ruled Iran between 1501 and 1722 descended from Sheikh Safi ad-Din of Ardabil (1252–1334). Sheikh Safi and his immediate successors were renowned as holy ascetic Sufis. Their own origins were obscure: probably of Kurdish or Iranian extraction, they later claimed descent from the Prophet. They acquired a widespread following at first among the local Iranian population, and later among the Turkic tribespeople who had been advancing from Central Asia into Azarbaijan and Anatolia from the eleventh century onwards.

Ghuzz/Oghuz Turkish tribes came into Khorasan under the Saljuqs in late Ghaznavid times (around 1000 AD) and soon expanded to the west and south, large numbers concentrating in Azarbaijan. The Saljuq conquest meant a victory for the Sunni religion and the eventual adoption of the Turki language by the indigenous Iranian population of Azarbaijan. In the late twelfth century, while the Turks moved forward into Asia Minor, Azarbaijan was ruled by the Atabey Eldigüz and his successors. In the 1220s the Mongols swept into northwestern Iran; from Hülegü Khan's advent in 1256, the Il-Khanids and their Jalayerid successors dominated Azarbaijan for 130 years, finding there the best pastures for their animals. Timur (Tamerlane) conquered Azarbaijan in 1386 and brought large numbers of Turks back from Asia Minor to Azarbaijan; others he sent further east, to Khorasan. Meanwhile, other descendants of the Ghuzz tribes in Armenia, Upper Mesopotamia and Anatolia formed the rival Turcoman[2] nomad confederacies of the Qara-Qoyunlu ('Black-sheep')

---

[1] On the early Safavids, see e.g. Ross (1896), Rumlu (1931, 1934, 1979), Sarwar (1939), Minorsky (1943), J. Aubin (various), Roemer (various), Glassen (1968), Efendiev (1981), Savory (various), Allouche (1983), Haneda (1987, 1989), Grönke (1993).

[2] Turcoman (Turkoman, Torkman, Türkmen) is the name generally used for the tribes descended from the Ghuzz Turks. The name was also that of one particular tribal group under the Safavids, for which I shall use the form Torkman, to avoid confusion. On the organization of mediaeval Turcoman tribal groups, see Woods (1976: 7f.), İnalcık (1994: 37–41).

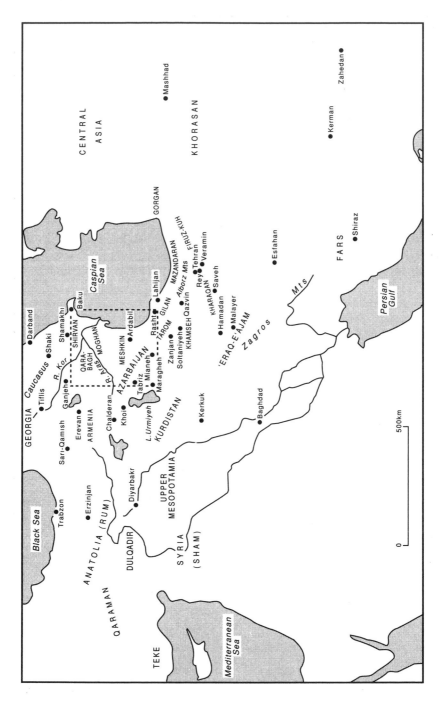

Map 1. Part of South-West Asia, to show places mentioned in Chapters 1–4 (enclosed area is enlarged as Map 2)

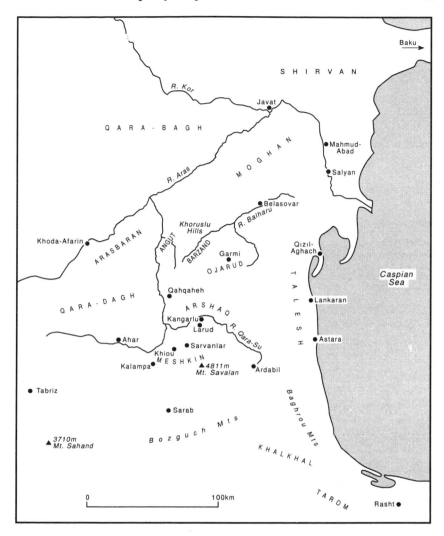

Map 2. Northeast Azarbaijan, to show places mentioned in
Chapters 1–4

and Aq-Qoyunlu ('White-sheep'). After Timur's death in 1407, the Qara-
Qoyunlu seized Azarbaijan from his son Miran Shah, while the Aq-
Qoyunlu were established in Diyarbakr to the west, in alliance with the
Timurids of Khorasan.

Sheikh Safi's order enjoyed the favour of the Mongols and possibly of
Timur, and grew in wealth and power during the fourteenth century. In

the mid-fifteenth century, however, the Safavids underwent a major change. No longer quietistic Sufis, they became one of several millenarian politico-religious movements to emerge, in the wake of the Mongols and Timurids, in the lands of the Qara-Qoyunlu and Aq-Qoyunlu confederacies. Safi's great-great-grandson Joneid appears to have espoused an extreme form of popular Mahdism, with elements of Shi'ism, but involving beliefs in reincarnation, and he is reported to have claimed quasi-divine attributes. He certainly began to foster military-political aims, directed largely against Caucasian Christians.

Early support for Joneid's political movement came from the Turcoman nomads of Anatolia, Syria and western Iran. He soon fell foul, not only of orthodox Sunnis such as his uncle Sheikh Ja'far, head of the order at Ardabil, but of Jahan Shah, the Qara-Qoyunlu ruler of Azarbaijan, who forced him to abandon Ardabil in about 1448. Joneid spent several years wandering in Anatolia and Syria, before being welcomed in 1458 at Diyarbakr by Uzun Hasan, the Aq-Qoyunlu ruler of eastern Anatolia, who married his sister to Joneid. He returned to Ardabil in 1459, but was again expelled by Jahan Shah Qara-Qoyunlu. After a further campaign against the Christians, he was killed in Shirvan in 1460, on his way back to Ardabil.

Joneid's son Heidar, born after his father's death, was brought up at his uncle Uzun Hasan's court, and married one of his daughters. Meanwhile, having in 1467 disposed of Jahan Shah and the Qara-Qoyunlu opposition, Uzun Hasan in 1469 defeated the Timurid forces of Abu Sa'id, Miran Shah's grandson, in battle in Moghan, and came into effective control of western Iran, setting up his capital in Tabriz. The next year, aged ten, Heidar Safavi moved to Ardabil to join his great-uncle Sheikh Ja'far, who seems to have neglected Heidar's religious training and allowed the development of his martial skills.

At all events, having remained quiet until Uzun Hasan's death in 1478, Heidar then indulged his inclination to military adventure, gathering around him Turcoman warriors who believed him semi-divine. Supposedly prompted by a vision, he had his followers wear a red cap with twelve scallops, in memory of the twelve Imams, from which they became known as the Qızılbash ('Red-heads'). He campaigned successfully against the Christians in 1483 and 1487, but aroused the anxiety of his brother-in-law Ya'qub Aq-Qoyunlu, son and successor of Uzun Hasan, who did not share his father's attraction to the Safavids. In 1488 Heidar too was killed in Shirvan, in a battle with the forces of Ya'qub and the Shirvanshah Farrokh Yasar.

Heidar's sons remained for some years in Aq-Qoyunlu custody before moving to Ardabil. The eldest, Soltan 'Ali, also died in battle (1494), whereupon his seven-year-old brother Esma'il fled to the Shi'i centre of Lahijan in Gilan. He left Lahijan in the winter of 1499–1500 with a small party of Sufi devotees, returning to Ardabil in the spring; but he had to leave again for Talesh and Moghan, whence he undertook an expedition via Qara-Bagh and the Caucasus to Anatolia during the summer, the numbers of his entourage constantly increasing. At Erzinjan he was joined by devoted Qızılbash tribespeople, with whose aid he defeated Farrokh Yasar in Shirvan in December, and the Aq-Qoyunlu leader Alvand the following summer (1501) at Sharur in the Aras valley. This allowed him to take Tabriz, though he did not defeat the Aq-Qoyunlu under Morad until two years later.[3]

When Esma'il became Shah at Tabriz in July 1501, he is reported to have proclaimed Twelver Shi'ism as the state religion. This would appear a deliberate political act, both to help legitimate the new Safavid state and to differentiate it from its Sunni rivals – the Aq-Qoyunlu, the Ottomans, and the Uzbeks. The Aq-Qoyunlu had already collapsed, and Esma'il took over their realm; the Uzbeks were to prove a problem in the east for many years, but the Ottomans in particular, as their power expanded, found a real threat in Esma'il's appeal to the tribes of central and eastern Anatolia.

The religious practices of Esma'il and the Qızılbash would appear to have been far from orthodox Shi'ism. Esma'il and his close advisers transformed Iran into a theocratic state based on the Safavid Sufi order, with extreme allegiance owed to him as grand master (*morshed-e kamel*). His associates were given Sufi titles such as *dede* (dervish-guide) and *khalifeh* (deputy) and the followers were known as *morid* (disciple). It is clear from his writings that Esma'il was accepted by many of his followers as the Mahdi, as an incarnation of Imam 'Ali. Some scholars interpret Qızılbash practices – which included eating the flesh of dead enemies and the ritual consumption of alcohol – as a development of the messianic shamanism of the Turcoman nomadic tribes.

The Qızılbash tribes

The Qızılbash military forces on whom Esma'il came to rely were mostly Turcoman nomads from Asia Minor, Syria and Armenia. Many of them came from groups that had already been components of either the Qara-

---

[3] On the Safavid rise to power, see e.g. Sohrweide (1965), Mazzaoui (1972), Petrushevskiy (1985), Arjomand (1984).

Qoyunlu or the Aq-Qoyunlu confederacies, sometimes both.[4] Accounts of the Sufis accompanying Esmaʻil from Lahijan to Ardabil in 1499–1500 name individuals from the Shamlu, Qaramanlu, Kheneslu, Qajar and Afshar Turcoman tribes, as well as local recruits from the districts of Qara-Dagh, Arshaq, Talesh and Moghan, seemingly villagers without tribal affiliation.[5] Meanwhile, the activities of Esmaʻil's ancestors had ensured that the movement had masses of followers over a much wider area. Qızılbash recruits at Erzinjan included Turcoman contingents from the Ostajlu, Shamlu, Rumlu, Tekelu, Dulqadır, Afshar, Qajar and Varsaq tribes, of which the first two were probably the most important at this stage. Other Qızılbash adepts were widespread in Anatolia and Syria, causing considerable trouble to the Ottomans until the massacre by Soltan Selim soon after his accession in 1512. Safavid Iran was a magnet for those suffering from plague and famine, as well as from Ottoman policies which were antagonistic not only to extremist Shiʻa but to nomads and tribes, and immigration continued throughout the sixteenth century.

These named Qızılbash 'tribes' probably had an open membership. They were not based on common descent, but were complex and heterogeneous collections of people of varied origins, like the original Turco–Mongol 'tribes'.[6] Some elements were not Turcoman, but of Iranian origin, particularly Kurdish. Membership probably comprised, in the first place, relatives and personal followers of a given chief, who was personally devoted to the Safavids; secondly, each tribe would have included fragments of other tribes, who had changed allegiance either voluntarily, or as a result of redistribution by the Shah, perhaps after immigration to Safavid lands; and finally, non-tribal settled peasants frequently entered the tribal ranks.

The presumption that the Qızılbash tribes were neither descent groups nor exclusively pastoral nomads has led some historians to deny them the label 'tribes', and the desire for a suitable standard 'technical' term has led some to pick *oimaq* (*aimaq/uymaq*), though it is not clear why; even less clear are the grounds on which one writer has built a whole argument around the notion of an '*uymaq* system'.[7] However, as Petrushevskiy noted,

---

[4] Efendiev (1975: 24–33), in Roemer (1985: 35).
[5] See Chapter Four; Khuzani (n.d. I: fol. 60a), quoted in Haneda (1987: 35).
[6] Morgan (1988: 52); della Valle (1972: 348f.); Petrushevskiy (1949: 94–5).
[7] See my comments (Tapper 1991a: 57–8) on the debate on the nature of Qızılbash organization in the pages of *Iranian Studies*, between Helfgott (1977, 1983), Reid (1978, 1979, 1984) and McChesney (1981). There is little or no evidence to support the notion

There is no precisely and strictly established terminology either in official documents or in narrative sources . . . to designate the nomadic tribe and its various sub-divisions – clan, family, etc. . . . . The same terms – *il, ta'ifah, aymaq, ashirah*, etc. – are used sometimes to designate an entire tribe, sometimes a subdivision (clan), and sometimes a family, and any distinction in the terminological significance of these synonymous expressions is not perceptible.[8]

If one can extrapolate back from present usage here, the terms indicated not specific groups but groups in specific contexts: for example, *il, olus* and *qoum* indicated a confederacy or an independent chiefdom, possibly a culturally distinct 'people'; *oimaq, taifeh* and *qabileh* connoted parts of a larger, but heterogeneous collection of groups; probably *tireh* had the same sense; only terms like *oulad* might indicate common descent as a factor of unity.

Elsewhere in the book I use the terminology suggested in Chapter One, which would recognize each major Qızılbash group as a 'confederacy', and the components of each group as 'tribes', but in this chapter, I shall keep to the conventional terminology, whereby the Qızılbash was a 'confederacy' of 'tribes', and the components of these were 'clans'.

Under the early Safavids, most of these named Turcoman tribes remained nomadic pastoralists, migrating between summer and winter quarters, though as the sixteenth century progressed many, particularly the leaders and the wealthier members, settled in the countryside and in towns. The pastoral nomads lived in tents apart from the surrounding population, whom they called *tat* or *tajik* with some scorn. They raised stock and pastoral produce for sale and to supply the military forces and the court; beyond this fact, little or nothing is known of the pastoral political economy of the Qızılbash tribes, though several historians have recently offered reconstructions, based largely, in the absence of contemporary sources, on extrapolation from what is known of other places or other times. Perhaps Fragner's is the most plausible account. However, his statement that 'the flocks and herds were regarded as the communal property of the tribe concerned' has not been true of Turkic nomads for a

---

that *uymaq/oimaq* was the standard term for major components of the Qızılbash. Della Valle (1972: 354) and one or two other Safavid contemporaries use it, but most sources use other terms (*il-va-olus, taifeh*, etc.) just as frequently; while they regularly use *oimaq* also for far smaller component groups, 'clans' or 'subtribes'. It is surprising that scholars such as Savory (1980b) and Aubin (1984: 6) have adopted the term '*uymaq*', even if only temporarily (see also Sümer 1967: 201). Reid (1983 etc.) is the main proponent of '*uymaq*' (apparently following Dickson); his book is, as Aubin remarks in a later article (1988), unusable, though unfortunately its thesis and terminology have been accepted by some distinguished general historians of the Middle East, notably Lapidus (1988: 940–1; 1991: 33f.).   [8] Petrushevskiy (1949: 94–5), quoted by McChesney (1981: 88).

long time, if ever, though it was possibly the case that the disposition of animals, like pasture-lands, was controlled by the chiefly classes.[9]

The Qızılbash chiefs – amirs – were appointed as provincial governors in different parts of the realm, and rewarded with land grants in the form of revenue assignments (*tiyul*) and territories (*ülkä/ölgä, yurt, ojaqlıq, java-maqam*) for their nomad followers. The grants were not necessarily permanent at this period, and the governors of some places were appointed from non-local tribes. Otherwise, this 'feudal' arrangement of giving loyal amirs land in return for service was probably necessary (and conformed with the practices of earlier dynasties) in order to ensure adequate military support, but it inevitably laid the grounds for future trouble, as amirs and their followers began to settle on the land.[10]

The tribes provided warriors for campaigns, usually only in summer; probably one horseman for every two to ten families, depending on the cause. Military organization probably followed the Turco–Mongol model of decimal units, each with a commander of appropriate rank: *yüzbashı* (head of one hundred), *onbashı* (of ten), *minbashı* (of a thousand); the commanders were usually chiefs (*amir*), ranked in ascending order of prominence as *bey, soltan, khan*. A further Turco–Mongol military feature, though not recorded until the latter part of the sixteenth century, was the division of the Qızılbash and the army into two wings, left and right. The Qızılbash are supposed to have numbered thirty-two tribes (though there is no consistent list of them), sixteen on each wing.[11] A special 'praetorian guard' (again on the Turco–Mongol pattern), the *qorchi* cavalry, comprising contingents from the different tribes, was directly loyal to and paid by the Shah. Both chiefs of tribes, and on a

---

[9] Fragner (1986: 496–7). The reconstruction of Qızılbash tribal society is based on the following: Minorsky (1943); Petrushevskiy (1949: 89f.); Dickson (1958: 6–10); Mélikoff (1975); Efendiev (1975, 1981); Sümer (1976); McChesney (1981); Anon. (1982); Allouche (1983); Fragner (1986: 496–7); Roemer (1985, 1986, 1989a, 1990: 29–30); Savory (1987); Aubin (1988: 29f.); Morton (1993a)/Membré (1993); Morton (1993b). Foran's recent (1993) ambitious historical sociology of Iran includes an interpretation of Qızılbash political and social structure which is largely based on Reid (1983). Foran's account is more plausible (he at least acknowledges the dangers of extrapolation), but it is marred by an inappropriate and unnecessary concern to characterize the 'social formation' of Safavid Iran with the aid of a static and deterministic model of 'modes of production', for which he has to make questionable assumptions about a pastoral nomadic 'mode of production' (1993: 25–8, etc.). As with other such 'Marxist' analyses, it is odd that Foran takes no account of Soviet versions of Iranian history.

[10] On *tiyul* and *soyurghal* under the Safavids, see e.g. Fragner (1986). According to Reid (1983), the most powerful chiefs, and often less important ones, came to control complex enterprises (the *uymaq*) which comprised not only pastoral nomads but peasant cultivators and artisans, co-ordinated, with the aid of a large bureaucracy, from a central household compound – echoing the Shah's palace in the capital – in the city where the chief was governor.

[11] See esp. Haneda (1987: chapter 2); Ulug Beg (1926: 45), della Valle (1972: 348f.).

smaller scale chiefs of clans and other tribal subdivisions (the grey-beards, *aq-saqal*), had similar retinues (*nökär/molazeman*) of tribesmen with no other loyalties, who performed military, administrative, house-hold and other services.

Chiefs had no links of kinship or common descent with most of their nomadic followers, as was indeed the case with Esma'il himself. In these times of transition and insecurity, both religious devotion and economic and political expediency would have counted for more than blood ties as a basis for both allegiance and conflict, at least at the level of the tribes. There was no clear rule of succession to chiefship: within each tribe, there was usually a dominant clan, a family of chiefs, but each succession entailed a struggle among competing candidates to demonstrate ability to lead; and possibly competition from another clan. There is evidence that, at least at the level of the chiefly classes, women held powerful positions: mothers and wives often controlled their sons' and husbands' purses, went out in public barely veiled, rode on horseback beside their men, par-ticipated in military campaigns, and in several cases controlled the leader-ship personally.[12]

Most Qızılbash tribes were, then, complex confederacies, heterogene-ous in origin and socially stratified. Dissent or incompetent leadership regularly led to some clans changing allegiance, to the chief of another tribe. Probably clans were similarly heterogeneous, stratified and fluid in membership.

Shahsevani: Safavid military and tribal policies

At first, Esma'il's state was run at least nominally by Turcoman Qızılbash amirs, but from early on major offices were entrusted to Iranian (non-Turcoman) administrators. In 1514, the Ottoman Soltan Selim's modern-ized army completely defeated Esma'il's forces at the battle of Chalderan. This disaster undermined Esma'il's claims to quasi-divinity and showed that reliance on Qızılbash tribal military levies was an inadequate founda-tion for a new state. The Qızılbash amirs, whose economic and political interests now diverged from their spiritual loyalty to the Shah, began to compete violently for office and dominant positions in the state. Ostajlu and Shamlu amirs were already squabbling on the eve of Chalderan. After Esma'il's death in 1524, Rumlu, Ostajlu, Tekelu and Shamlu amirs in turn dominated his successor, the young Shah Tahmasp, until in 1530–1 he crushed a Tekelu revolt. From 1533–4 he had the upper hand for forty

---

[12] See e.g. Morgan (1988: 129–30), Membré (1993: 31), Szuppe (1994, 1995), Gholsorkhi (1995); cf. Peirce (1993).

years. Meanwhile, as the Ottomans consolidated control of Eastern Anatolia, further waves of Qızılbash recruits entered Iran.

Shah Tahmasp tamed the Turcoman amirs by various policies. Like his father Esma'il, where possible he appointed Iranians to major administrative positions; and like Mongols and Ottomans before him, he sought to use slaves to balance and replace the unstable forces – the Turcoman Qızılbash, with their vulnerable pastoral nomadic economic base – on which he originally relied, taking Christian (Georgian, Circassian) prisoners in the Caucasus for this purpose. He increased the numbers of his *qorchi* personal guards, drawn from different Qızılbash tribes, and formed his own Safavid family into a new, neutral tribe, the Sheikhavand, to be set alongside the Qızılbash; one Sheikhavand cousin, Ma'sum Bey, he appointed over the Qızılbash as state *vakil*. He also divided each Qızılbash tribe internally and moved them around, in order to prevent any one amir from gaining excessive power or establishing a special claim to government of a specific area. Some chiefs he kept at court in administrative positions, others were given provincial governorships. All these policies had the effect of moving the level of conflict and competition from inter- to intra-tribal,[13] and laid the ground for more radical reforms under Shah 'Abbas.

Towards the end of his long reign, however, Tahmasp met more trouble from the Qızılbash, mainly directed against his newly acquired followers from the Caucasus. In 1574, two years before his death, there were two main factions struggling to influence the princes who were the main candidates to succeed him; the Ostajlu amirs, the Sheikhavand and Talesh and the Georgians favoured Heidar Mirza; the rest of the Qızılbash (Rumlu, Afshar, Torkman, Shamlu, Qajar, Dulqadır, Bayat, Varsaq) and the Circassians were for Esma'il Mirza. After Tahmasp's death, the latter faction managed to end Esma'il's twenty-year incarceration (in the castle of Qahqaheh near Moghan) and brought him to the capital as Shah Esma'il II.

According to Eskandar Beg Torkman, author of *Tarikh-e 'Alamara-ye 'Abbasi*, a major source for early Safavid history, the new Shah's faction had called themselves *shahisevan*, that is 'friends of the Shah'.[14] This is the first mention of the term, apart from two earlier references by Torkman to 'loyalists' in Baghdad: Seyyed Beg Kamuneh in 1507–8, and the followers of Mohammad Khan Tekelu in 1534. As an earlier source for these years does not use the term, it may be supposed that Torkman's usage here is anachronistic.[15]

---

[13] See esp. Haneda (1987, 1989).   [14] Torkman (1971: 119–20); Efendiev (1981: 130).
[15] Torkman (1971: 34, 68); Rumlu (1979). However, see also the enigmatic story by Yazdi (1987: 32) which seems to support Torkman's usage.

In 1577, after a bloody reign of eighteen months, Shah Esma'il II died in mysterious circumstances and was succeeded by his brother Soltan Mohammad Khodabandeh, a weak and ineffectual ruler who was faced with renewed Qizilbash rebellions. Torkman and Tekelu amirs took the Shah's side, while their rivals from Shamlu and Ostajlu supported the heir apparent Hamzeh Mirza. In order to deal with these internal dissensions and to be able to oppose invasions from the Uzbeks in the east and the Ottomans in the west, recourse was had, according to Torkman, to the principle of appealing to those who love the Shah (*sala-ye shahisevani, shahisevan kardan* or *farmudan*). For example in 1584, when Hamzeh Mirza dismissed and imprisoned Amir Khan Torkman, governor-general of Azarbaijan, the Torkman and Tekelu tribes revolted. Hamzeh Mirza, 'having appealed to those who love the Shah' (*shahisevan kardeh*), commanded that

all those of the Torkman tribe who were slaves and partisans of this family should rally to the palace . . . When the Torkman tribe heard the appeal (*sala*) of *shahisevani*, they . . . rallied in their masses to the Shah's palace gates and enlisted among the *shahisevanan*, so that even Amir Khan sent his sons and brothers lest they be excluded from the congregation (*zomreh*) of the *shahisevanan*.[16]

I know of no record earlier than the reign of Soltan Mohammad, in Torkman's account or elsewhere, of the principle of 'appealing to *shahisevani*'. There are, indeed, only three references by Torkman to such appeals to loyalty, all dating from the period 1578–88: the first in the case of a rebellion in Mazandaran, the second in 1584 as already narrated, and the last in the first year of Shah 'Abbas' reign as described below. These three instances would hardly seem to justify the frequency implied in Minorsky's 'Shah-sewen' article of 1926:

These ad hoc appeals played upon the religious sentiments of the adepts of the Safawi family (*dudman, odjakh*). The sovereigns of this dynasty not only traced their origins to the Shi'i imams, but even claimed to be incarnations of the latter . . . The formula called of [*sic*] Shah-sewan thus recalled to political recalcitrants their obligations to their superiors.[17]

However, Torkman frequently uses the word *shahisevani*, in the sense of 'loyalty to the Safavid dynasty', in expressions such as *sho'ar-e shahisevani zaher sakhtan, ezhar-e shahisevani kardan*, or just *shahisevan shodan*, when individuals or groups make declarations of loyalty and submission to the Shah. *Doulatkhvahi* ('support of the state') and *ekhlas* ('loyal devotion') appear to be almost synonyms of *shahisevani*. In addition, as in the above quotation, the plural *shahisevanan* ('friends of the Shah', 'Shah-lovers') is

[16] Torkman (1971: 299).
[17] Minorsky (1934a: 267; translation of French edition of 1926).

used collectively, or with a collective noun – the 'class' (*selk, tabaqeh*) or 'community' (*jama'at, jomleh, zomreh*) of the 'friends of the Shah' – to denote those among the Shah's supporters who remain faithful, particularly in confrontations with the Ottoman (Sunni) Turks and with rebels among the Shah's own people.[18]

Earlier writers are not clear when the term was first employed or what it signified. Bellan, and Minorsky in a work later than his 'Shah-sewan' article, equate Shahsevan with Qızılbash as referring in general to the tribes which supported the Safavid monarchs, though Torkman's usage does not bear out this equation. Falsafi asserts that *shahisevani*, loyalty to the Shah and devotion to him as head of the religious brotherhood, was a bond which united all the Qızılbash tribes from the time of Shah Esma'il I onwards, and Minorsky too, in 1955, dated *shahisevani* to Esma'il's reign; expanding on his earlier comments, he pointed out that to the Shi'i Sufis 'Shah' also signified "Ali', and that the Qızılbash Shahsevans were thus a 'religious party' devoted to the Shah as their supreme head. Finally, Lockhart, following Minorsky, writes of Esma'il I that 'When in times of crisis the Shah found himself in need of military aid, he would invoke the principle of *shahisevan*.'[19]

None of these authors, however, in putting forward such interpretations of the term, supports them with reference to contemporary sources. Roemer points to precedents for *shahisevani* in loyalty-appeals among Turkish rulers elsewhere (in the book of Dede Korkut, and in Egypt among Mamluks in the fourteenth century and Ottomans in the sixteenth), and argues on these and other grounds that the concept was current among the early Safavids, even if the literary sources do not mention the term.[20] But it remains unlikely that the term was used earlier than Soltan Mohammad Khodabandeh's reign – if then.

Whatever the case, such appeals under Soltan Mohammad had no

[18] Roemer (1989b) lists and analyses Torkman's uses of *shahisevani*, although he misses nearly half of the instances.

[19] Bellan (1932, esp. Introduction); Minorsky (1943: 30); Falsafi (1953, I: 169f.); Minorsky (1964: 252); Lockhart (1958: 20).

[20] Roemer (1989b). Of the other Safavid chronicles written in the period up to and including Shah 'Abbas I's reign, Afushteh'i Natanzi (1971, written in c. 1599), Yazdi (1987, written in c. 1613) and his son Kamal Khan (1677), as well as Pietro della Valle (1972; in Iran 1616–23), Arakel of Tabriz (1874, written in 1669) also use the term *shahisevan(i)* in describing some of the same events as Torkman, and in similar senses, but much less frequently. Khwandamir (1954, written c. 1524), Shirazi (1990, written c. 1571), Hasan Beg Rumlu (1979, written c. 1578), Qomi (1980, written c. 1594), Bedlesi (1868–75; written 1599) and *Tarikh-e Qızılbashan* (Anon. 1982, written c. 1600) do not use the term. A firman of 1607 gives the Georgian Malek Nazar authority over the Sonqorabad district in Qara-Bagh in return for his *ekhlas, doulatkhvahi* and *shahisevani* (Puturidze (1961: 6)). I have not yet had a chance to examine the following: Khuzani n.d.; Jonabadi n.d.

lasting effect. The Qızılbash amirs continued to disobey and to quarrel among themselves, while the Ottomans invaded Azarbaijan and Georgia and in 1585 captured Tabriz. Two years later, however, the Shah abdicated in favour of his sixteen-year-old son 'Abbas, a brilliant, shrewd and tireless leader who in the succeeding years managed not only to crush the Uzbeks and drive out the Ottomans, but also to tame the Qızılbash amirs who had for so long controlled political and military affairs in Iran.

In the first year of 'Abbas' reign (1587–8), some of the Qızılbash amirs rebelled against the authority of his chief minister Morshed-qoli Khan Ostajlu. The Shah having appealed to (*farmudeh*) the *shahisevan* – this is the third and last reported instance of the appeal – the Qızılbash assembled *en masse* in front of the palace. The rebels began negotiations for forgiveness and reconciliation, but their proposals were rejected by Shah 'Abbas, and a few days later they were rounded up and executed. As Minorsky notes, Torkman says nothing of the permanent effects of this appeal, adding only that the community (*jama'at*) of *shahisevan* who came at the Shah's call mounted guard until morning.[21] This time, however, the measure appears to have been successful, for 'Abbas had little further trouble from the Qızılbash. There are no further references to the appeal as such: the many later references to *shahisevan(-i/-an)* during 'Abbas's reign are to scattered groups and individuals, often from outside the Qızılbash, who declare their loyalty to the Shah at one time or another.[22]

Malcolm's version

Shah 'Abbas I deliberately cultivated his charismatic public image, but rather than rely entirely on the spiritual elements in his authority, he conducted a radical reorganization of his armed forces and administration. To counter the unruly Qızılbash, he promoted the *qollar* or *gholaman*, slave cavalry of Caucasian Christian origin, and the *tofangchian*, infantry musketeers drawn from various peoples, mainly Iranian peasantry. At the same time, he further expanded recruitment from the Qızılbash into the *qorchi* praetorian guards, and elevated their status. All these forces were both paid by and devoted to the Shah himself.[23] To pay for them, and

---

[21] Torkman (1971: 383–4); Minorsky (1934a: 267).

[22] Including a party of Georgian peasants in 1618, as reported by della Valle (1972: 170). See also note 20 above.

[23] On the military reforms, see particularly Haneda (1984). Also: Minorsky (1943: 16–19, 30–6); Lockhart (1959); Röhrborn (1966: 31–7, 44–53); Babaev (1973); Savory (1986: 363–6); Fragner (1986).

besides to break further the power of the amirs, he transferred large areas of land (for example in the Ardabil region) from the state domains (*divani/mamalek*) to the Crown (*khasseh*). In addition, he ruthlessly broke up, dispersed, resettled, and regrouped several Qızılbash tribes, and, where their amirs had formerly still provided the bulk of the administrative bureaucracy, he now appointed his personal devotees from among the *qollar* and the *qorchi* to the offices as they fell vacant, including the chiefships of some of the tribes. He also promoted the Sheikhavand tribe, and gave Ma'sum Bey Sheikhavand's grandson, 'Isa Khan, the key job of *qorchibashı*, commander of the *qorchi* guards.

With this reformed army and administration, 'Abbas acquired direct secular obedience to himself as ruler, and no longer depended on the religious devotion of the Qızılbash to the dynasty.[24] At the same time, he encouraged other significant changes in society, such as the settlement of nomadic elements, and the promotion of Shi'a orthodoxy which resulted in increased seclusion both of the women of the ruling classes and of their sons: a factor often blamed for the subsequent decline of Safavid fortunes.

According to some later historians, a major item in Shah 'Abbas' military reforms was the creation of a 'tribe' or militia called Shahsevan. The most well-known instance, and the source of most of the others, is the passage in Malcolm's *History of Persia* (1815) quoted earlier.

Fortunately we are able to identify Malcolm's sources. First of all, he had read the *Tarikh-e 'Alamara* and must have been familiar with Torkman's use of the term *shahisevani*, as we have surveyed it. Secondly, he gives a specific reference for the registration of 10,000 men as Shahsevan: Kamal Khan's *Zobdat at-Tawarikh*, a chronicle which he frequently uses for events under Shah 'Abbas I. Thirdly, his account of 'Abbas' 'forming a tribe of his own' sounds remarkably like Tahmasp's creation of the Sheikhavand tribe, mentioned above; it probably also derives from Krusinski's account of the 1720s, written nearly 100 years before his own, but still a century after the supposed event.

Kamal Khan twice uses the term *shahisevan*, both cases echoing Torkman's usage. The passage to which Malcolm refers runs as follows:

News came of the impending arrival of 10,000 Jalalis under the leadership of Mohammad Pasha, who had become *shahisevan*. It was accordingly arranged that Mirza Hatam Bey E'temad ad-Douleh should go to Tabriz and allot them winter quarters, and 12,000 *tuman*, 12,000 *kharvar* of grain, and 12,000 sheep were set

---

[24] Arjomand (1984: 111) considers the appeals to *shahisevani* to mark a process of secularization of the military, replacing earlier appeals to specifically Sufi loyalties (*sufigari*); this may be, but he gives no evidence to support the suggestion.

aside for them. After winter quarters had been allotted to this community (*jama'at*), the E'temad ad-Douleh came to Esfahan to the Shah's presence, with Mohammad Pasha and 300 of their notables.[25]

Torkman reports the same incidents, in much greater detail. Why did Malcolm single out this passage from Kamal Khan as indicating the formation of a 'tribe' of Shahsevan? There are many other such passages in Torkman – though none of them is any more convincing as evidence of the origin of a Shahsevan tribe. Moreover, in the next sentence Kamal Khan adds that 'in the year 1017 [1608–9] . . . they gave the Jalalis permission to depart, so that whoever so desired might go to his own country'.[26]

If, as Malcolm states, Shah 'Abbas created a 'tribe' called Shahsevan, one would surely expect to find some contemporary references, if not to a 'tribe' or 'clan' (*il, ta'efeh, oimaq*) of Shahsevan, at least to people bearing this tribal name. Torkman does refer (some examples have already been given) to the *shahisevan* 'class' (*tabaqeh*) or 'group/community' (*jama'at*), terms often used of groups otherwise referred to as 'tribes' or 'clans', but not once does he or any other chronicler refer to a 'tribe' or 'clan' of *shahisevanan*. I have found only one individual to whom Torkman gives the name *shahisevan*: Mohebb 'Ali Bey Shahisevan Shamlu. All other persons or groups who have 'become Shahsevan' he later refers to by their own former tribal name; if of Qızılbash origin, he continues to include them in the ranks of the Qızılbash. He uses *Shahisevan* as an epithet for both Qızılbash tribal names, as with Mohebb 'Ali Bey Shamlu, and groups of *qorchis*.[27] On this evidence, one must conclude that Shah 'Abbas did not create the Shahsevan as a tribe to oppose the Qızılbash.

The Polish Jesuit priest Tadeusz Krusinski was in Esfahan in the 1720s. In his memoirs, the term Shahsevan is applied not to a tribe, but to a reserve militia, not necessarily of tribal origins or organization:

Il y avoit une autre milice dans le Royaume, établie par Schah-Abas . . . Ceux qui la composoient *s'appelloient Schah-Seven, c'est à dire, affectionés au Roi.* C'etoient des personnes de la Noblesse à qui Schah-Abas avoit distribué des terres, à condition de servir avec un certain nombre de leurs Vassaux, quand ils seroient mandés . . . cette milice . . . alloit à trois cens mille hommes, et . . . dans un besoin subit et pressant fournissoit une ressource sûre.[28]

---

[25] Kamal Khan (1677: fol. 69a–b); see also Yazdi (1987: 347f.).

[26] Torkman (1971: 765f.); Kamal Khan (1677: fol. 69a–b); see Griswold (1983: 201, 206–7).   [27] Torkman (1971: 813, 1049); Vahid Qazvini (1951: 109).

[28] Krusinski (1728a: 160–1). This is Père J. A. du Cerceau's recension of Bechon's translation of Krusinski's memoirs. An anonymous English translation (Krusinski 1728b: 80–1) omits the words emphasized. De Clairac (1750, I: 317) paraphrases the passage; Hanway (1753, III: 136–7) translates de Clairac without acknowledgment.

Though he does not give a source for this, Krusinski's account of the distribution of fiefs fits the descriptions by Chardin and others of the military organization of the later Safavid state. But neither Torkman nor European writers earlier than Krusinski call this 'reserve militia' by the name of Shahsevan, and indeed the words emphasized above, which do not appear in all editions of the memoirs, may be an inept editorial gloss.

The passage probably refers, not to any militia called Shahsevan, but to those provincial Qızılbash tribespeople who had not been recruited into the expanded regular *qorchi* guards and who, after the reforms of Shah 'Abbas I, had a diminished role in the army. Haneda shows how seventeenth-century European travellers like Chardin, followed by recent historians Minorsky and Savory, have wrongly equated the Qızılbash with the *qorchi*. His explanation is that when, after 'Abbas' reforms, the Qızılbash lost military and political significance, their famous name became attached to the newly favoured (and Qızılbash-based) *qorchi*. This could also account for the apparent further confusion here, as well as in the passages from Minorsky and others referred to earlier, between Shahsevan and Qızılbash.[29]

There are, however, more contemporary references which might indicate that Shah 'Abbas I did indeed form another military corps – not a reserve militia – called Shahsevan, with special loyalty to the Shah, similar to the *qorchi*, the *qollar* and the *tofangchi*. For example, among the components of victorious armies in the Caucasus in 1604 and 1607, Jalal ad-Din Yazdi lists a *jama'at* of *shahsevan*, alongside those of *qorchi* and *gholam* (*qollar*). Haneda's translation of *jama'at* as 'corps' rather than simply 'group' or 'community' is barely justified by the context, in which a *jama'at* of Moqaddam (a Qızılbash tribe) and others from the provinces of Khorasan and Mazandaran and the district of Talesh also figure.[30] However, when the Ottoman traveller Evliya Chelebi was in Baku in 1647, he observed: 'This place being a frontier fortress opposed to Russia is garrisoned with excellent troops called Shahseven and Dizchoken (who love the Shah and bend their knees before him).'[31]

If such a Shahsevan corps did exist, it probably would have differed from the other new elements in 'Abbas' army: from the *qorchi*, by including non-Turcoman elements; from the *qollar* ex-Christian 'slaves', by freedom and spiritual allegiance to the Shah; and from the *tofangchi*, in being mounted and armed with spears and bows. In composition (mainly

---

[29] Haneda (1987: 146f.); Röhrborn (1979: 35); see Chardin (1811, V: 298–302). In the eighteenth century, and later, Qızılbash was a term applied by the Ottomans to all Iranians, and indeed by Kurds to non-Kurds in Iran.

[30] Yazdi (1987: 258–9, 323), quoted by Haneda (1987: 163–4).

[31] Evliya Chelebi (1850, II: 162). I know of no other references to Dizchoken (*diz-çökän*).

but not entirely Turcoman) the Shahsevan corps would have been closest to the Qızılbash themselves: a further possible reason for the confusion between them in more recent sources, from Krusinski onwards. Shahsevan, *qorchi*, and indeed Qızılbash, were not themselves regarded as tribal identities so much as titles, which could be inherited; as titles, they took temporary precedence over tribal identities; but the latter, it would seem, persisted in the long term.

However, the likelihood that the Shahsevan were a corps separate from the *qorchi* is lessened by references, from the latter part of the seventeenth century onwards, to troops which carried both names, as we shall see.[32] It is significant that contemporary analyses of the military forces of Shah 'Abbas and his successors, by Fryer (from 1677), della Valle (from 1618), Chardin (1655–77) and others, do not mention the Shahsevan as such.[33]

Whatever the reason, there was no further trouble from the Qızılbash in Shah 'Abbas' reign. Appeals to *shahisevani* are not recorded after 1588, though groups of various origins continue to be reported as 'becoming Shahsevan' in the 1630s under 'Abbas' successor Shah Safi.[34] Under the later Safavids, the Qızılbash tribes became increasingly marginalized, and their military contingents were rarely called on. Later historians tell how the dynasty, in its last years, had quite lost the ability to rouse the people to devotion. When they refer to a final appeal to enthusiasm for the Shi'a cause against the Sunni, they base themselves ultimately on Krusinski's account. In 1722, Shah Soltan Hosein was besieged by the (Sunni) Afghans in Esfahan; his son Tahmasp Mirza was declared successor and escaped to Qazvin, where he tried to raise an army for the relief of the capital. Krusinski relates Tahmasp's desultory efforts, such as his appeal to the militia of landed nobility established by 'Abbas I, which could have been of great help to him if it had not been quite neglected in recent reigns, particularly that of Soltan Hosein. Having not been called on for years to fulfil the obligations attached to their land grants, these nobles had come to look on these grants as private property, and through lack of use the military potential of this 'militia' was reduced to nothing. As a result, scarcely any of them recognized their duty to respond to the appeal, declaring that they were obliged to march only in a general expedition led by the Shah himself. A small number of peasants were duly

---

[32] See below, Chapter Four: a garrison at Darband, to the north of Baku, composed of *qorchi* of the Afshar and Shamlu Shahsevan in 1668 (Musävi 1977: document 15).

[33] Fryer (1915, III: 62–3); della Valle (1972: 348f.); Chardin (1811, V: 292–332).

[34] Mohammad Ma'sum (1978: 145, 151, 156, 157, 172). Minorsky (1943: 12) writes: 'appeals to the feelings of the *shahiseivani*, so common under Shah Tahmasp [on his own evidence, he means Soltan Mohammad Khodabandeh], are hardly ever heard of under the later Safavis'.

despatched, ill-paid and ill-equipped, but they returned home in disorder before covering half their journey.[35]

It is doubtful whether this account amounts to evidence for a 'final appeal' to *shahisevani*. Krusinski, moreover, gives no information as to the location of these people and their lands. Similar (the same?) appeals are recorded in a series of firmans issued by Tahmasp between June and December 1724, during his residence at Ardabil, in which he seeks emergency levies among local people to resist the Russian invaders; but neither the term *shahisevan(i)* nor the tribal name Shahsevan are mentioned.[36]

In summary, four separate features of Safavid policy appear to have given rise to Malcolm's mistaken account of the creation of the Shahsevan tribe.

(i) The strategy used by Soltan Mohammad Khodabandeh and Shah 'Abbas, as documented by Eskandar Beg Torkman and others, of appeals to *shahisevani* as a means of breaking the influence of rebellious Qızılbash amirs. More common than such appeals was the application of the term *shahisevan*, as a kind of category or title, to those who either surrendered to the Shah's forces or immigrated to his territory. Most groups that acquired this title do not seem to have retained it for long, but preserved their original names.

(ii) Shah 'Abbas' promotion of regular cavalry personally attached to and paid by the Shah, to counter the military strength of the irregular Qızılbash provincial tribal cavalry and their amirs. These included the established Turcoman *qorchi* guards, the new Caucasian *qollar*, and perhaps a further corps of mixed origins, known as Shahsevan, probably including the above immigrants.

(iii) The practice of breaking up, dispersing, regrouping and resettling the various tribal groups.

(iv) The practice of paying both regular troops and the provincial reserve militia with land assignments, with their attendant obligations of service.

Malcolm appears to have confused all four features of the policy, and may well also have confused the Shahsevan with Shah Tahmasp's creation of the Sheikhavand tribe. Krusinski (or his editor), referring primarily to (iv), attaches the name Shahsevan to the Qızılbash holders of land assignments; this is probably an error.

In fact, some of the groups that later came to be known as the

---

[35] Krusinski (1728b: 160–2). See note 28 above. Based on this (or on Hanway) are the statements by Malcolm (1815, I: 637), Sykes (1930, II: 318), *Gazetteer* (1914: 554).
[36] Fragner (1975a).

Shahsevan tribes probably acquired the name as a result of policies (i) and (ii). Though there is no evidence for the formation in Shah 'Abbas' time of a single composite tribe by the name of Shahsevan, as a result of his military and tribal policies certain distinct geographical areas now contained fragments of various tribes. As we shall see, in at least one case, that of Ardabil, these fragments eventually came to unite into a confederacy, under the only name they had in common: the title 'Shahsevan'.

In Chapter Four we shall review the evidence linking the name Shahsevan with Ardabil in Safavid times, to try to establish when the ancestors of present-day Shahsevan first reached the region. Meanwhile, in Chapter Three, a very different kind of evidence will be considered: that of the traditions of the Shahsevan tribes, recorded in the nineteenth and twentieth centuries, which emphasize the heterogeneous origins of the tribes but are not otherwise consistent with Malcolm's account.

3 Shahsevan traditions

The 'noble' tribes: nineteenth-century traditions

Three versions of the traditions of the Shahsevan tribes of Ardabil were published in the late nineteenth century. The first was written by Col. I. A. Ogranovich in 1870, soon after his appointment as Russian frontier commissar for the Shahsevan at Belasovar. The second, published by the German naturalist Gustav Radde, who travelled in Talesh and among the Shahsevan on the slopes of Savalan in 1880, derives from a manuscript sent to him by Ogranovich in 1884. The third was published in 1890 by Vl. Markov, Russian political agent, whose main source appears to be a report compiled in 1879 by E. Krebel, Russian consul-general in Tabriz at the time. Passages in Markov's account are identical with passages in Radde's, so we may assume that the manuscript which the latter was sent by Ogranovich was a copy of Krebel's report.[1] All of the authors had first-hand acquaintance with the Shahsevan tribespeople, but to judge from their accounts none of them were familiar with any Persian sources, and their knowledge of Iranian history was rudimentary.

At this time the tribes were extremely turbulent, being notorious for their raiding activities across the Russian frontier, but they were still nominally within the control of two hereditary paramount chiefs, the *elbeys*. All versions of the traditions agree that the nineteenth-century Shahsevan *elbeys*, and also a number of the component tribes of the Shahsevan, who collectively constituted a class of 'nobles' (*beyzadä*), were descendants of Yunsur Pasha, or possibly his brother Allah-qoli Pasha; the other tribes, the 'commoners', were descended variously from associates of Yunsur Pasha or from dependants of the noble tribes. Radde's and Markov's versions differ, as will be shown, as to the exact pedigrees of the chiefs, and as to which tribes were nobles and which commoners by origin. These discrepancies may well be explained by revisions or annotations in either copy of Krebel's report, by Ogranovich, by Radde or by Markov. They may also reflect differences in the tribal affiliations of the

---

[1] Ogranovich (1870); Radde (1886); Markov (1890). See Chapters Nine and Ten.

sources and their claims to nobility, but we cannot establish any such relationship without knowing the identity of the informants, which none of the accounts mentions.

The stories do agree in presenting Shahsevan tribal structure as a descent-based hierarchy, legitimating the authority of the chiefs, as well as their control of the pastures, the most important resources for all the tribespeople, with reference to an original royal grant and to contemporary royal appointment. All three versions agree that the origin of the Shahsevan was as follows: a certain Yunsur Pasha brought his nomadic tribes from Asia Minor to Iran and asked the Shah for permission to stay. According to Radde and Markov, the Shah (in their version, 'Abbas I) graciously acceded to Yunsur Pasha's request, gave the tribes the name of Shahsevan, and directed Yunsur Pasha to go and choose them a suitable area for winter and summer quarters. After much wandering around the country, Yunsur Pasha's choice fell on the Ardabil province, including the Savalan mountains and the Moghan plains, and that is where he settled, with his followers to the number of 3,300 tents.

The versions vary considerably as to the names of the tribes that came over with Yunsur Pasha, and those which are descended from him.

Ogranovich states that Yunsur Pasha lived at Khoi, 'near lake Urmiyeh', where he eventually died, leaving six sons – Qoja, Band 'Ali, Polat, Damirchi, Sarı Khan, Nouruz 'Ali – who split up, each having a tribal group or 'clan' named after him. Later offshoots separated from each 'clan', though remaining dependent on their original 'clan'. Ogranovich lists them all, together with the number of tents he counted. The original clans still total 3,300 tents: he seems to assume that they would not have increased since the time of the ancestors.[2]

> Qoja-Beyli (2 sections, 400 tents): with offshoots Moratlu (200), Udulu (100), Khalfali (400)
>
> Band-'Ali-Beyli (3 sections, 800): with 'Ali-Baba-Beyli (200), Bey-Baghlu (100), Khalafli (50)
>
> Polatlu (3 sections, 600): Sheikhli (250), Abu-Beyli (100), Qozatlu (400), Yortchi (400), Dursun-Khojalu (350), Takleh (2 sections, 600), Yekali (50)
>
> Damirchili (3 sections, 800): Inallu (400), Hajji-Khojalu (600), 'Arabli (100)
>
> Sarı-Khan-Beyli (400): Ajirli (700), Milli-Khalfali (250), Bala-Beyli (100), Beydili (600), Homunlu (50), Zargar (100)
>
> Nouruz-'Ali-Beyli (300): Geyikli (400), Pir-Evatlu (500)

---

[2] In the following lists of tribal names I give Anglicizations of formal versions of the modern names rather than of those given in the sources. In brackets I give emendations or comments. For more accurate transliterations of the tribal names as they are spoken, see Appendix Two.

The following groups, Ogranovich adds, also came out of Turkey and other places at various times and joined the Shahsevan:

Galesh (250 tents)
Sarvanlar (100)
Jeloudarlu (300)
Talesh-Mikeilli (600)
Qahraman-Beyli herding camps (*binälär*) (50)
Moghanlu-Heidar (300)
Reza-Beyli (50)
Jahan-Khanomlu (300)
Bey-Baghlu (separate from group of same name mentioned above) (50)
Gamushchi (50)
(Grand total: 12,350 tents)

Radde and Markov agree that on arrival some groups separated from Yunsur's tribe and went, with the Shah's permission, to Khorasan, where they still lived. After Yunsur's death the Shahsevan broke up into smaller groups, the heirs dividing not only the property of their father but also his authority over the nomads.

According to Radde, Yunsur Pasha had six sons, for whom he gives the same names as Ogranovich but in a different order. From them six tribes descend:

Sarı-Khan-Beyli
Band-'Ali-Beyli: from Band 'Ali Bey's three sons three further tribes descend: Mir-'Ali-Beyli (Mast-'Ali-Beyli), Kekili-Qasem-Beyli (Qara-Qasemli), 'Ali-Baba-Beyli ('Ali-Babalu)
Qoja-Beyli
Polat-Beyli (Polatlu)
Damir-Beyli (Damirchili)
Nouruz-'Ali-Beyli

One of the most influential Shahsevan chiefs who came with Yunsur Pasha to Iran, Radde continues, was Kurt (Qort?) Bey, who had three sons, after one of whom the Qozat-Beyli were named. From Kurt Bey's tribe, other tribes separated and migrated to Arak (sc. the region of 'Eraq-e 'Ajam in central Iran). Two other tribes came over from Turkey in Yunsur Pasha's time, the Inallu and the Beydili. Finally, the tribes Reza-Beyli, Sarvanlar, and Gamushchi came to Iran. The subgroups that left Kurt Bey, and divisions of the Inallu and Beydili, are given as follows:

Kurt Bey's group: Talesh-Mikeilli, Khalfali, Moghanlu, Udulu, Moradlu, Zargar, etc.
Inallu: Pir-Evatlu, Kalash, Kor-'Abbaslu, Geyikli, Yortchi, Dursun-Khojalu.

Beydili: Ajirli, Hajji-Khojalu, Yeddi-Oimaq, 'Arabli, Chakherlu,
Qobadlu.

In Markov's version, Yunsur Pasha had three grandsons, Sarı Khan
Bey, Beid 'Ali Bey and Qoja Bey, from whom came the following tribes:

Sarı-Khan-Beyli.

Beid-'Ali-Beyli, which divided further into four tribes, named
after Beid 'Ali Bey's sons: Mast-'Ali-Beyli, Qara-Qasemli, 'Ali-
Baba-Beyli, Nouruz-'Ali-Beyli.

Qoja-Beyli.

Qurt Bey, in this version, also had three sons, from whom came the following tribes: Polatlu, Damirchili, Qozatlu. Markov gives listings, identical to Radde's, of the clans of Inallu and Beydili and of the other three
tribes that came from Turkey at the same time as Yunsur Pasha, and also
of the six tribes which left Qurt Bey's tribe, though in his version they
went to live on the Araks (sc. here the river Aras).

Finally, Radde and Markov give different versions of the genealogies of
the Shahsevan *elbeys*: in Radde's account they are descended from Yunsur
Pasha's brother Allah-qoli Pasha (also mentioned by Ogranovich)
through his two sons Bedyr (Badr) Khan Pasha and Nazar 'Ali Khan. The
latter, and Bedyr Khan's son Kuchek Khan, divided the Shahsevan
between them and quarrelled for a long time, until Kuchek Khan's son
'Ata Khan drove Nazar 'Ali Khan and his followers out of Meshkin; they
settled in the Ardabil district, and from that time dates the present (sc.
1884) cleavage of the nomadic Shahsevan into the Meshkin and Ardabil
branches, each of which has its own chief.

In Markov's version, the *elbeys* are descended from Yunsur Pasha
himself, through his grandson Sarı Khan Bey. One of his descendants was
Badr Khan, whose sons Kuchek Khan and Nazar 'Ali Khan divided the
Shahsevan between them. 'Ata Khan, son of Kuchek Khan, drove Nazar
'Ali Khan's grandson (also called Nazar 'Ali Khan) out of Meshkin, and
so on as in Radde's account. The differences between these versions can
best be illustrated by Figures 1–3.

It is worth adding, as a footnote to these Russian versions of Shahsevan
origins, that British consular agent Keith Abbott, who in 1844 was the
first to list the Shahsevan tribes of Ardabil and Meshkin (Appendix Two),
in 1864 gave a very similar estimate to Ogranovich's of 1870 for
Shahsevan numbers (12,000 families) and hints at a similar story of
Shahsevan origins: 'Of the original race there are said to be only 3,500
families, the remainder being the descendants of strangers who have
joined themselves to the Tribe.'[3] Quite likely Abbott's information came
from the same source as that of Ogranovich, or a similar one.

---

[3] Abbott (1844: 27–8), and (1864) in Amanat (1983: 229).

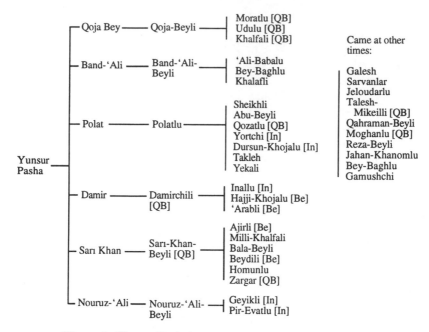

Figure 1. Yunsur Pasha's sons, their tribes, and the tribes that followed them, according to Ogranovich.

Later 'noble' traditions

The *elbeys* lost control of the Shahsevan by the end of the nineteenth century, and members of their family dispersed into various settlements in the region and elsewhere. Further versions of their traditions have been recorded from scions of the old dynasty. Probably from such a source is the following brief account quoted by the Soviet writer Balayan:

The Shahsevan tribes formed in two branches: one came to Moghan from Urmiyeh in the sixteenth century during Shah 'Abbas I's reign, and the other from ['Eraq-e 'Ajam]. The one from Urmiyeh was that of Band 'Ali Bey, and his sons Yunsur Khan, Sarı Khan and Kechi [Kuchek?] Khan.[4]

Balayan does not quote any further, and I do not know what is reported of the branch from 'Eraq.

Another Soviet writer on the Shahsevan, Dälili, apparently had access to an archive source of 1828, recording some Shahsevan traditions; but his use of this, and of Markov, is so loose and uncritical that the only

---

[4] Tairov and Pavlenko (1922: 1), quoted by Balayan (1960: 345). See also another source mentioned by Balayan: Shkinskiy and Averyanov (1900); I have not managed to trace either of these originals.

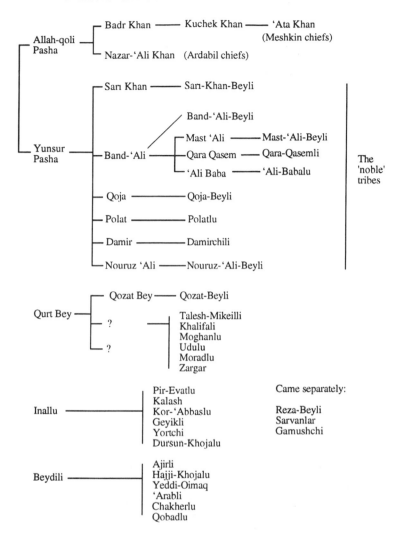

Figure 2. Original connections between the tribes, according to Radde.

definite point that can be taken from his account is the notion that the *elbeys* came from Urmiyeh and were of Afshar origins.[5]

The same point was made by Hosein Baiburdi, a retired Iranian army colonel from an old family of Arasbaran, a district bordering Shahsevan territory on the east, who wrote:

[5] Dälili (1974) and (1979: 22f.); see Chapters Five and Fourteen below.

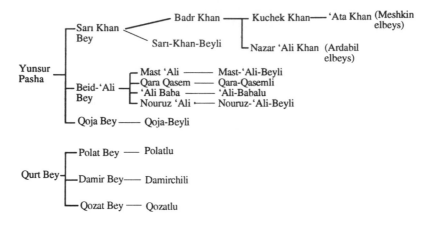

(The tribes following Qurt Bey, Inallu, Beydili, Reza-Beyli etc., as in Figure 2)

Figure 3. Original connections between the tribes, according to Markov.

The Shahsevans connected with the Arasbaran sphere are one part of the descendants of Kan'an Bey and Sarı Khan Bey Afshar. From the time of Nader Shah Afshar the leadership and paramount chiefship of all the Shahsevan was with the family of 'Ataollah Khan Sarı-Khan-Beyli, who was Afshar by origin . . . all Meshkin and Moghan were under his command, and the tribe of Qoja-Beyli is named after his brother Qoja Bey. In the same way, the tribes Jeloudarlu and Sarvanlu were his grooms and camel-herders, and the rest were servants, workers, chattels, and subjects.[6]

The origin of the *elbeys* in Urmiyeh, and the connection with the Afshar, were further supported by Aqa Bozorg Ebrahimi, another retired army officer, who had on a number of occasions been closely involved with Shahsevan affairs, and with whom I talked in December 1965. He recorded for me a detailed story, of which the following is a summary:

The Shahsevan *elbeys* and their cousins the *beyzadä* tribes Qoja-Beyli with 'Isa-Beyli, Mast-'Ali-Beyli, Reza-Beyli, Sarı-Khan-Beyli, Bala-Beyli, are descended from one Amir Aslan, who lived with his tribe in the district of Sarı-Qamış in eastern Anatolia in about 1500. They were Shi'i Muslims, and when Soltan Selim began his persecution of the Shi'is they decided to flee from Turkey and take refuge in Iranian territory. They fought their way across the frontier, reached Diyarbakr and delivered themselves into the protection of the Safavid governor, Soltan Mohammad Ostajlu, one of the Afshar chiefs. According to the Shah's instructions, the tribe was moved to the interior of Azarbaijan and granted winter

---

[6] Baiburdi (1962: 102).

pastures around Lake Urmiyeh and summer pastures on the Sahand mountains. Meanwhile Soltan Selim invaded Azarbaijan. At the battle of Chalderan [1514], in which Shah Esma'il's forces were out-armed, outnumbered and heavily defeated, Amir Aslan's men fought valiantly and barely three or four of them survived. Shah Esma'il appreciated their valour and loyalty and, when the tribe had once more grown numerous and there was no longer any room in the Urmiyeh region, they were sent to the Ardabil region and given the Moghan plains and the Khoruslu hills (which were then areas of lush grazing) as winter and summer pastures. Towards the end of the century, when Shah 'Abbas had trouble with the Qızılbash tribes, he called on Amir Aslan's people, on whom he knew he could rely, and formed them into a new tribe called Shahsevan, to counteract the Qızılbash. The most notable descendant of Amir Aslan was 'Ata Khan, after whom the *elbey* dynasty became known as 'Ata-Khanlu, and also as Sarvanlar, 'camel-drivers', presumably because they had hired out camels along the old Silk Road from Trabzon to Zahedan [*sic*], which was straddled by their original habitat of Sarı-Qamış.

I did not ask my informant's sources, but I suspect the story to be the product of his reading of Iranian history and of traditions he heard from his friend, the late Amir Aslan, chief of the 'Isalu, an offshoot of the Qoja-Beyli tribe. I talked with Amir Aslan's son in September 1966, when he gave me a genealogy going back to one Shah-qoli Bey, but an account similar to the above of the ancestor's arrival in Iran, participation in the battle of Chalderan, and so on.

Two stories so far have mentioned the Sarvanlar/Sarvanlu tribe. According to a manuscript of 1800 based on Mirza Mohammad Hosein Mostoufi al-Mamalek's *Tohfeh-e Shahi* (1716), Sarvanlu was one of four branches (*jama'at*) of the Afshar tribe (*ta'efeh*).[7] In Moghan in December 1965, Khan Aqa of the Sarvanlar tribe, who lived in a village of the same name not far from Meshkin-Shahr, told me that he was the paternal grandson of the last Meshkin *elbey*, 'Ali-qoli Khan, grandson of the famous 'Ata Khan, son of Mahmud Khan, son of Kuchek Khan, son of Boyuk Khan, son of Yunsur Pasha, son of Shah-qoli Pasha, who was a Sunni Muslim and an important man in Turkey. Under the early Safavids, he went on, Shah-qoli Pasha came with his people into Iran, was converted to Shi'ism, and was sent by the Shah to watch the marches in the region of Moghan and Meshkin. The tribes of 'Ata-Khanlu/Sarvanlar, Qoja-Beyli, Bala-Beyli, Sarı-Khan-Beyli and 'Isa-Beyli are cousins, descendants of Shah-qoli Pasha. The latter, he

---

[7] Danesh-Pazhuh (1974: 412). The other three branches were Shamlu, Qırqlu and (formerly) Bayat-Donboli. Kunke (1991) has published an edition of the *Tohfeh-e Shahi*, apparently aware of neither Danesh-Pazhuh's edition, nor many recent sources on the tribes. In her translation and interpretation she misreads and mis-attributes many tribal names: Sarvanlu, for example, she reads as Shirvanlu (as does Lambton, 1971: 1102).

concluded, died in Ardabil and was buried in the precincts of the Safavid shrine there. I visited the shrine shortly after and was directed by the gate-keeper to a gravestone plaque located under the outer gateway, bearing the inscription, 'The tomb of Abo'l-Qasem Bey son of Shah-qoli Bey'. The gatekeeper assured me that Shah-qoli Bey was the ancestor of the famous Qoja-Beyli tribe, but he knew no more about him or about the history of the Shahsevan. There were documents in the shrine library, he said, which might reveal more about Shah-qoli; but I did not have the necessary authorization to consult them.

None of the ancestral names mentioned in these traditions (Yunsur, Amir Aslan, Shah-qoli, Sarı Khan, Band 'Ali, Kan'an, Allah-qoli) can be definitely established in the contemporary sources on Safavid times. The name Yunsur Pasha I have found nowhere. No Amir Aslan is recorded as immigrant from Anatolia in the early sixteenth century, nor among the Safavid army at Chalderan, though an Amir Aslan Afshar was prominent somewhat later on, for example among Prince Esma'il's supporters in 1574, who according to Torkman called themselves *shahisevan*. Aqa Bozorg Ebrahimi referred to Amir Aslan's protector Soltan Mohammad Ostajlu as an Afshar chief; this is probably a mistake for Khan Mohammad Ostajlu, Shah Esma'il I's brother-in-law, who was Governor of Diyarbakr and a principal general at Chalderan, where he was killed. The Ostajlu were related to the Shamlu, but in any case we have reason to connect both the Afshar and the Shamlu with the Shahsevan. At that time, the major cleavage among the Qızılbash saw the Torkman and Tekelu opposed by the Ostajlu and Shamlu, with the Afshar usually allied with the latter. As for Sarı Khan, in the Safavid chronicles there are a few individuals of this name, while Shah-qoli Bey is among the commonest names for the Qızılbash chiefs; but there is no reason to connect any par-ticular ones of those mentioned in the sources with presumed Shahsevan ancestors.

It may be significant that names figuring in the traditions often have closely related religious meanings for extremist Shi'ites: Shah-qoli = 'slave of the Shah' or 'of 'Ali'; Allah-qoli = 'slave of God'; Band 'Ali = 'slave of 'Ali'. Indeed, the first presumed *elbey* ancestor to appear in con-temporary sources is named 'Ali-qoli Khan – as we shall see below, he may well be the Allah-qoli of the traditions.

All versions so far have probably originated with members of the old ruling *elbey* dynasty or its offshoots. The most consistent element in the stories appears to be the association of their ancestors with the Afshars and/or with the district of Urmiyeh, which in fact became the domain of the Imanlu branch of the Afshar after their arrival there at the end of the sixteenth century. The evidence from tradition, that the nineteenth-century Shahsevan *elbeys* were of Afshar origins, seems overwhelming.[8]

Traditions of the other tribes

Apart from the former 'noble' (*elbey* and *beyzadä*) tribes, many others of the Shahsevan tribes of Moghan and Ardabil today (see Appendix Two) believe that their ancestors came from 'Rum' (Anatolia) and/or 'Sham' (Syria), but nobody claims common descent or a unitary origin for all of them. Further, although the forty or so 'commoner' tribes are generally social units of some continuity, in few of them do all the component sections claim common descent or origin, and there is sometimes documentary evidence for their heterogeneity; while the 'noble' tribes themselves include subordinate sections of different origins.

Among the ordinary tribespeople (and indeed villagers in the region), by far the commonest response to a question about origins was that the Shahsevan had always been 'thirty-two tribes' (*otuz-iki taifa*), which were in theory of equal status, though they clearly differed in size and in the power and influence of the chief (*bey*) who headed each tribe. Most informants, asked to give a list of the Shahsevan tribes, would begin: 'Well, there are thirty-two tribes . . .' and proceed to list somewhat fewer. An expression that I recorded again and again was *otuz-iki Shahsevändä*, with the meaning 'throughout the Shahsevan'.

The origin of the dogma of 'thirty-two tribes' has proved elusive. None of the nineteenth-century sources on the Shahsevan mentions it, and all lists of tribes but the earliest (Abbott's) contain considerably more than thirty-two names.[9] In Radde's and Markov's accounts of Yunsur Pasha's arrival, and of the tribes that grew from his immediate descendants and associates and their dependants, it is possible to count thirty-two named tribes; but nowhere do they mention this figure themselves, and ambiguities in their accounts make totals of thirty-one or thirty-three equally feasible. Besides, their lists of contemporary tribes contain many more names.

The first specific mention of 'thirty-two' that I have found is in a British intelligence report of 1919, which states of the Shahsevan of Meshkin that

---

[8] It is further supported by the reconstruction of Shahsevan history in the eighteenth century, to be discussed in Chapters Five to Seven below. The Qurt Bey group mentioned in both Radde's and Markov's accounts may also be of Afshar origins; see Appendix One. On the Afshars, see especially Stöber (1978), Oberling (1985).

[9] Abbott (1844); Ogranovich (1870, 1876); Radde (1886); Markov (1890); Artamonov (1890); Tigranov (1909).

'there are 32 branches in this region', but then lists only eleven. At the same time, 'the Shahsavans of Ardabil are divided into 14 tribes', which are then listed.[10] Then in 1924 the Azarbaijani historian Zeinaloghlu relates, without citing a source, that the tribes that came with Yunsur Pasha originally divided into thirty-two *qabila*, though they later proliferated.[11] An influential Iranian geography from the 1930s states that there are thirty-two Shahsevan *taifa*, and gives a highly inaccurate list of thirty-two names; this version has been used in most general Iranian geographies, local histories, and other accounts of the tribes since then, in combination with Malcolm's story of the origin of the Shahsevan.[12] Some writers attach the number to all the Shahsevan tribes of Moghan, some only to those associated with Meshkin, or only to those of Ardabil.

It is tempting to connect this dogma with the Otuz-iki ('Thirty-two') tribe, who are first recorded in 1604 as 'having become Shahsevan' when submitting to Shah 'Abbas' forces on the recovery of the neighbouring region of Qara-Bagh from the Ottoman occupation forces. According to Minorsky, 'the opposite number of the Otuz-iki were the Yigirmi-dört, i.e. the Twenty-Four Kurdish tribes of Qarabagh'. The Yirmi-dört were associated with, or were part of, the Qajar tribe of Qara-Bagh, while the Otuz-iki persisted until very recently there in association with, or as part of, the Javanshir and Moqaddam tribes. But from 1604 until 1919 there is no recorded link of the name (or number) Otuz-iki with the Shahsevan of Ardabil and Moghan, none of the known subdivisions of each bears the same name, and it is unlikely that a branch of the former separated and developed into the latter.[13] It seems that the title Shahsevan stuck to the Otuz-iki no longer than it did to most of the numerous other tribal groups recorded as acquiring it at the same period.

The number thirty-two appears to have a proverbial value, like the number forty. Apart from the Otuz-iki and the Moghan Shahsevan, the Qızılbash confederacy itself is said in some sources to have comprised thirty-two tribes.[14] Perhaps it is the latter connexion that gave rise to the association of the same number with the Shahsevan; but we cannot know how old this association is – conceivably it has been current for centuries

---

[10] Anon. (1919).
[11] Zeinaloghlu (1924: 125). He inserts this number into a narrative otherwise entirely based on Markov (1890).   [12] Keihan (1933: 105). See e.g. Eqbal (1941: 26, 28).
[13] Minorsky (1943: 167); Torkman (1971: 857, 1085, 1089); Falsafi (1985, I: 215); Qara-Baghi (1959); Jävanshir (1961); Sümer (1976: 198–200); Petrushevskiy (1949: 135–6).
[14] See Chapter Two. The number thirty-two also has associations with both Sufi organizations and bazaar guilds. The largest Shahsevan *alachıq* tents had thirty-two struts; most have twenty-four, twenty-six or twenty-eight struts, never thirty (Andrews 1987). The number twenty-four has similar resonances: the original Ghuzz tribes numbered twenty-four.

among ordinary tribespeople, whose constructions of their identity have not been recorded before the present century.

While the 'thirty-two tribes' dogma is dominant, several non-noble tribes have distinct traditions. One other group of tribes, the Yeddi-Oimaq/Beydili complex, has traditions of common origin. In 1965, Savad Khan Jahangirzadeh, chief of the Beydili, and a villager in Moghan, told me that there was once a tribe Yeddi-Oimaq, composed (as its name indicates) of 'seven clans', which he listed as Beydili, Homunlu, Aivatlu, Hajji-Khojalu, Gabali, Inallu and 'Arabli. All of these are now Shahsevan tribes, though he knew nothing further of their origins. Several nineteenth-century sources mention the Beydili in the region of Moghan and Ardabil, together with but still distinct from the Shahsevan, while other groups of this name have long been found in various parts of Iran. Beydili was one of the original Ghuzz Turkoman tribes, and had arrived by the fourteenth century in Syria and Anatolia, where large sections of them have remained ever since. A branch came thence to Iran to join the Qızılbash as part of the Shamlu confederacy, and provided many important Safavid administrators, particularly under Shah 'Abbas I. Among numerous references to Beydili personages, Torkman tells that one of the Shamlu notables,

Gündoghmush Soltan Bekdilu, who lived in Ta'uq of Kerkuk, with his followers, having in [Shah 'Abbas'] first campaign to Baghdad [1623] become Shahsevan, presented himself to the Shah, received the rank of Soltan, and has various assignments (*tiyul*) in the lands of Azarbaijan.[15]

There is, however, no tradition or other evidence to connect this individual, or any of those mentioned in the seventeenth and eighteenth centuries, with the present Beydili tribe among the Shahsevan of Moghan.[16]

Apart from the Beydili, a number of other Qızılbash tribal names are found among the Shahsevan: Inallu, Ajirli, Takleh/Tekelu, and perhaps Delaqarda/Delaqadarlu, which may be identified with Dulqadır,[17] also perhaps Qaramanlu, if this is the same as Qahraman-Beyli.[18] Inallu,

---

[15] Torkman (1971: 1085).

[16] A sizeable compilation of documents relating to the Beydili has recently been published (G. H. Begdili 1988); the compiler's nephew has also published a monograph on the Shahsevan (M. R. Begdili 1993), which unfortunately adds nothing to already published accounts.   [17] See Roemer (1985: 230, n.17).

[18] See Appendix Two. Qahraman-Beyli were settled by the late nineteenth century. According to Oberling (1964a: 28), referring to a list of tribes held at Iranian Army headquarters in Meshkin-Shahr, Qahramanlu was both a village in Ojarud district, and a branch of the 'Delagherlu' tribe (presumably Delaqarda) living in that district. The recent census lists sections named Qahramanlu in both the Hajji-Khojalu and the Jeloudarlu tribes.

Dulqadır, Qaramanlu and three other groups whose names are among those listed in the nineteenth-century Shahsevan traditions – Chakherlu/Jagerlu, Yortchi and possibly Hajji-Khojalu – bear the names of components of the earlier Aq-Qoyunlu confederacy.[19] I was unable to consult present-day members of any of these except Ajirli, who appear however to have preserved no distinctive traditions other than possible membership of the Yeddi-Oimaq group.[20]

Sections of the Shamlu confederacy were named Inallu, Ajirli and Beydili. In Markov's and Radde's versions of the traditions, most of the non-chiefly Shahsevan tribes are descended from the Inallu (including Yortchi) and Beydili (including Ajirli, Hajji-Khojalu and Chakherlu). They do not mention Shamlu, but this is not surprising since this confederacy, like many Qızılbash groups, had disintegrated by the nineteenth century into its component parts; some of them at least became part of the Afshar and lived mainly in the Hamadan and Malayer regions to the south of Azarbaijan.

Several other tribes have preserved traditions of origin separate from the 'nobles'; and the names of others indicate different provenance for them too. Thus the Moghanlu tribe, traditionally large, rich and peaceable, and somewhat different in character from other Shahsevan groups, is said by some to have come to the region from an original homeland in Baku or Shirvan. According to Tairov and Pavlenko, however, 'The Moghanlu tribe came earlier than all the other tribes from ['Eraq-e 'Ajam] and took winter pastures in Moghan along the Aras, and received their name in this way.'[21] It is possible that the Moghanlu originated as the Moghani, indigenous settled farmers of Moghan, and acquired the Turkish name Moghanlu after becoming pastoral nomadic and adopting Turkic culture. In the sixteenth century, long before the name Shahsevan is first heard of in Moghan, there are references to individuals named Moghani; one was an ambassador, another a landowner in Meshkin and Moghan, though there is no indication whether either were nomads or tribal chiefs.[22] Then in 1623, travelling through the Moghan steppe south of the Kor, K. F. Kotov met nomads called Moghani living in felt tents.[23]

---

[19] See Woods (1976: 201 – Chakirlu/Jagirlu; 211 – Khoja-hajjilu; 212 – Yortchi).

[20] Ajirli may derive from the ancient Turkish tribe Aghaç-eri (Toğan 1943: 93, 102).

[21] Quoted in Balayan (1960: 369).

[22] After Chalderan, a diplomatic misson to the Ottomans at the end of 1514 included a Moulana Shokrollah Moghani, a divine who was later executed by Shah Tahmasp (Bacqué-Gramont 1987: 83). I am indebted to Mr A. H. Morton for the information that a *vaqfnameh* concerning properties in Meshkin and Moghan belonging to one Malek Mirza Bey ibn Seifal Bey Moghani is copied in the *Sarih al-Melk*, original dated 977/1570, Tehran National Library MS *fa'* 2734, pp.144–5. The original document, badly damaged, is in the *chini-khaneh* of the Ardabil shrine, no. 403 in Mr Morton's inventory.   [23] Kotov (1958: 36, 73).

In eighteenth- and early nineteenth-century sources, Moghanlu nomads are mentioned as neighbours of but still separate from the Shahsevan, and possibly of Kurdish origins; and the nineteenth-century noble traditions include them, along with Talesh-Mikeilli and others, in Qurt Bey's group.[24]

Like the Moghanlu, the Alarlu tribe has only just been accepted into the number of the Shahsevan. They preserve traditions of comparative autochthony in the Ojarud-Talesh district. Others of the present tribes (Khosroulu, Ja'farli) have plausible stories of comparatively recent advent to the region from Qara-Bagh. The names of others (Sheikhli, Seyetler, 'Arabli, Talesh-Mikeilli) suggest separate, non-Turkic origins, though they may well have been in the Shahsevan confederacy since its formation.

The traditions argue that, with a number of distinct exceptions, the present Shahsevan tribes originated in Anatolia and that they arrived in Iran in association with, if not as part of, certain Qızılbash groups. In particular, the noble tribes of the nineteenth century appear to descend from former members of the Afshar, while a number of commoner groups (Inallu, Ajirli, Beydili and others) may well have had Shamlu ancestors.[25] It is now in place to examine the contemporary sources concerning the nomadic and tribal population of the Ardabil region, and the first appearances there either of groups named Shahsevan, or of the various Qızılbash, Aq-Qoyunlu and other names mentioned above.

[24] In the early nineteenth century, there was a group of 1,000 Moghanlu 'Turkic nomads', in Armenia (Bournoutian 1992: 53–6).

[25] Clearly, given the continued existence in the Ardabil region of the groups named as followers of Qurt Bey, Markov's version, that they went to the Aras, is more likely than Radde's version that they went to Arak.

4   Moghan and Ardabil in Safavid times

The eastern Transcaucasus has always offered a highly favourable environment for both pastoral and agricultural activities. High mountains, with abundant summer pasturages, command the vast and fertile Shirvan, Qara-Bagh and Moghan plains of the lower Aras and Kor rivers, which provide correspondingly extensive winter grazing. The plains, a favourite wintering place of conquerors, also invite the construction of large-scale irrigation works, such as the canal restored by Timur in Moghan, which seems to have continued in operation throughout Safavid times. Shirvan was second only to Gilan to the south as producer of raw silk. The area is a natural crossroads, and trade and travel between Russia and Iran and between Anatolia and Central Asia passed through or close by. From Safavid times, travellers and merchants from Europe commonly journeyed overland through Russia and took ship on the Caspian at Astrakhan to land at Shirvan and halt awhile at the growing trading centre of Shamakhı, before crossing the Kor at Javat and passing via Moghan and Ardabil into central Iran, and beyond to India.

It is not surprising that the whole area was long the object of intense struggle between powerful rulers. The Safavids gained control at the beginning of the sixteenth century, but had difficulty keeping it from the Ottomans, the Russians and various Caucasian powers, and when the dynasty crumbled in the early eighteenth century, the area was divided briefly between the Ottomans and the Russians. It was the latter who eventually, after a further eighty years of Iranian hegemony, annexed most of the area for good.

Of the several excellent pastoral nomad habitats that centre on this area, the only one still left in Iranian territory is that part of Azarbaijan which stretches from the mountains of Savalan, Bozgush and Baghrou around Ardabil northwards to Moghan. While the other plains fell within the provinces of Qara-Bagh and Shirvan, the Moghan steppe south of the Aras and Kor, together with its irrigated lands, though usually under Shirvan, seems at times to have been included in the province of Azarbaijan. It is not clear, however, exactly how the Moghan-Ardabil region was divided administratively during the Safavid era. The following districts are often distinguished: Qara-Dagh (Qarajeh-Dagh), Sarab, Khalkhal, Ardabil, Talesh, Moghan, Ojarud, Barzand, Angut, Meshkin and Arshaq. Of these, Qara-Dagh (and its component districts), Ardabil and Talesh were governed separately, while the rest, on occasion independent districts, were usually administered by the governor of one or other of the three already mentioned (see Map 2).

Important trade routes passed through Ardabil, leading to the Caspian, to Mianeh and the south, to Tabriz and the west, and to Moghan, Shamakhı and the north. After the city of Ardabil, the major centres were Sarab, Ahar in Qara-Dagh, Lankaran and Astara in Talesh, and Salyan and Mahmud-Abad on the edge of Moghan. There was also a substantial settlement at Javat with its strategically important pontoon bridges over the Kor and Aras.[1]

From Safavid times until the development of the market-town of Khiou (Meshkin-Shahr) in the present century, a whole range of country in the centre of the region, stretching from the Savalan mountains to the Aras and Kor rivers, and covering the districts of Meshkin, Arshaq, Angut, Barzand, Ojarud and Moghan, did not contain a town of any size. The largest villages in this tract were Garmi, Barzand and Larud, each with a population probably not exceeding 2,000 souls, not large enough ever to have provided a governor's residence. However, this tract contained not only rich pastures but also fertile agricultural lands, and it also straddled two of the important trade routes: between Ardabil and Moghan and between Ardabil, Ahar and Tabriz. Control over these resources and their revenues would have been, in the Safavid period just as certainly as it was later, the object of competition both between chiefs of pastoral nomadic tribes and among provincial administrators and landowners.

The tribal and nomadic population of the region

The question of the origin, history and distinctiveness of the Shahsevan and other Turkic tribal groups of north and west Iran is not a genetic matter. A systematic physical-anthropological study would probably, in my view, confirm that these groups are genetically similar not only to each other and to the populations of modern Turkey, but also to the 'indigenous' (Kurdish and other) population of modern Iran. They are also probably distinct from the Türkmen and other groups of Central Asia, to

---

[1] These bridges were there in Mongol times (Rubruck 1900: 265); they were apparently destroyed during the course of the Ottoman occupation at the end of the sixteenth century, and rebuilt by Shah 'Abbas I in 1607 (Torkman 1971: 753).

whom they are, however, culturally related. This anomaly arises largely from two processes: Turkic culture has dominated much of Southwest Asia since its introduction there, while its bearers have intermarried with the indigenous non-Turkic populations.

Nor is this question a genealogical matter. Few named tribal groups in the area preserve even fictional genealogies of any depth, and groups of more than a few hundred people tracing common unilineal descent are rare. Throughout the millennium of their presence in Southwest Asia, apart from extensive intermarriage with local populations, Turkic tribal groups have been subjected by various rulers to systematic policies of breakdown, dispersal, regroupment and resettlement. All the major Turkic groups in the area are of quite heterogeneous composition. This is true particularly at the level of the tribal confederacies: Qızılbash, Qara-Daghi, Shahsevan, Qashqa'i, Khamseh (partly Turkic); but also at the level of their major constituent units.

The resultant problems for the investigator – historian or anthropologist – were summed up by Nikitine many years ago:

Les notions d'unité ethnique et d'organisme politique ne sont plus les mêmes dès qu'on pénètre sur le terrain d'ethnologie asiatique. A un certain moment on y constate en effet des molécules qui tantôt se réunissent sous une forme de vague confédération, tantôt, avec la même facilité, se désagrègent. Les noms mêmes n'offrent aucune constance ni certitude . . . Ce sera le nom du chef de la période de prospérité auquel pourra avec le temps se substituer un autre. Ajoutons à ceci des scissions et des regroupements constants à travers l'histoire et nous nous apercevrons de tout ce qu'il y a de délicat dans la tâche du chercheur.[2]

In tracing the ancestry of present-day Turkic tribes in Iran, the only possible initial procedure is to attempt to trace geographical movements of groups and individuals bearing specific tribal names. The assumption that justifies this procedure is that, even if there has been a regular process of changes of identity and of allegiance by individuals and groups, by and large the continuity of a tribal name and identity also involves a continuity of major cultural features and personnel. At the same time, if a named group is recorded as leaving a particular place, some of their number may be left behind, bearing the same name even though integrated, perhaps only temporarily, as a subordinate section of a group of another name.

In fact, at a certain structural level within the confederacy, represented in the Shahsevan case by the *taifa* ('tribe'), named communities of at most a few hundred families do exhibit considerable continuity, stability and cultural distinctiveness, due largely to territorial factors and to a strong tendency to endogamy, and it is on this basis that I attempt to elu-

---

[2] Nikitine (1929: 122–3).

cidate the origins of the tribes in the Shahsevan confederacy, by tracing the earlier movements of groups and individuals bearing their names.[3] The main sources for these, for the Safavid period, are chronicles and administrative documents, which refer to tribal chiefs and governors (often the same) of relevant provinces (Shirvan, Ardabil) and districts in between; as well as to land assignments: *soyurghal*, hereditary land grants with exemption from tax; *tiyul*, nominally temporary assignments of tax revenue from particular lands; *olka'/ölgä*, grazing rights on pastoral territories, granted to the tribal/nomad followers of particular chiefs. European travellers too, in their accounts, often mention the names of governors and describe sightings of nomads, sometimes with names or other details, and sometimes giving information on land tenure and society.

Tribal names present two problems. First, as we have seen, tribal groups were complex, heterogeneous and stratified, with considerable mobility, both compulsory and voluntary, of tribes and their leaders between confederacies and of tribal sections/clans between tribes. Secondly, it is not easy to be sure of the nature of any named group mentioned in the sources (tribe? clan? pastoral nomads? militia? a group of peasants?), given the highly fluid terminology, where groups at various levels are labelled *il/el*, *oimaq*, *taifeh*, *'ashireh*, *qoum*, *nasib* almost interchangeably, and sometimes with distinctly non-tribal terms such as *jama'at* (community) or *tabaqeh* (class).[4]

The tribal or pastoral nomadic groups inhabiting the Moghan-Ardabil region in early Safavid times were probably, by origin, a mixture of Kurdish, Turkic, Mongol and other elements. Kurds, and others speaking Iranian languages, were autochthonous, while Turks and Mongols were comparative newcomers. When Oghuz Turkish nomad groups from Central Asia began moving into Azarbaijan in the eleventh century, they apparently found the rangelands largely unoccupied, and more than likely many were attracted by the excellent pastures of Moghan and Ardabil. Their leaders the Saljuqs were themselves settled in orientation, and did little to disrupt the settled Iranian society whose administration they took over.

Very different was the effect of the Mongol onslaught in the thirteenth century. These invaders were militarily organized and despised agriculture and settlement; they destroyed irrigation and crops, and massacred villagers and townspeople. The Mongols, and the fresh wave of Central Asian Turks they brought with them, swept through Iran westwards;

---

[3] See Chapters Seven and Fourteen, and Tapper (1979b).
[4] See passages quoted from Nikitine (above) and Petrushevskiy (in Chapter Two).

many remained around Maragheh, Tabriz and Soltaniyeh, and in 1258 Hülegü located large numbers of Turks in Transcaucasia. The Mongol generals Jebe and Subutai had wintered in Moghan in 1220–1, and after them the Ilkhanid rulers (1256–1336) and Timur (Tamerlane; 1370–1405) liked to winter in the pastures of Qara-Bagh and Moghan. Timur himself travelled surrounded by nomadic families and flocks. Mongol elements were quickly assimilated, losing their own culture, religion and language and adopting those of the Turks, which had formed the majority element of the Mongol armies.[5] At the same time, in Moghan and Ardabil, as elsewhere, many settled, indigenous (non-Turkic) farmers probably had to take up nomadic pastoralism in order to survive. Cultivation certainly continued in the region, however; much of it on land owned by the Safavid order at Ardabil.[6]

Pastoral nomadism was further reasserted under the Qara-Qoyunlu and Aq-Qoyunlu nomad dynasties in the fifteenth century. They and the Safavids after them brought three new waves of Turcoman tribes to Azarbaijan, this time from the West.

Qızılbash governors and chiefs often bear the name of one of the original Oghuz tribes (Afshar, Beydili, Inallu), or of the place they presumably came from in the West (Shamlu from Syria; Rumlu, Dulqadır, Qaramanlu, Tekelu and Baiburdlu from regions of those names in Anatolia). Other Qızılbash groups found in the Ardabil vicinity bear the names of local districts (Qara-Daghi, Talesh, Moghani); though sometimes it is not clear whether or to what extent they constituted tribes (often their named leaders appear to be, or to be equivalent to, Qızılbash tribal chiefs), or whether they were local peasant communities.

It is reasonable to suppose that the ancestors of some at least of the nineteenth and twentieth-century Shahsevan of Moghan were already there by the beginning of the Safavid era in 1501, though others, as the legends tell us, may well have arrived some time later. The Italian travellers Barbaro and Contarini witnessed the life of pastoral nomads (unnamed) in the region in the 1470s under the Aq-Qoyunlu; the former describes the construction of a Turkish tent near Ardabil very similar to the present-day Shahsevan *alachıq*.[7]

Two names from the nineteenth-century lists are found in Moghan before 1500, as members of both the Qara-Qoyunlu and then the Aq-Qoyunlu confederacies. From the late fourteenth to the end of the fifteenth century, the chiefs of Chakerlu (Chakherlu/Jagirlu), a tribe of possible Kurdish origins, headed their own Amirate in Moghan, based at

[5] Minorsky (1943: 188); also Spuler (1960: 25).
[6] To judge from Grönke (1993: 340–1).   [7] Contarini (1873: 88).

Qızıl-Aghach (where the river Kor joins the Caspian, north of Talesh), with the backing of their nomadic followers; for a time they also held Ardabil for the Qara-Qoyunlu. In the 1490s Hasan Bey Chakerlu was a supporter of Rostam Aq-Qoyunlu; and it was Soltan 'Ali Bey Chakerlu, governor of Ardabil and Moghan for the Aq-Qoyunlu in 1499–1500, who advised Esma'il to leave Ardabil. The Chakerlu remained in Talesh and Moghan until 1612, when Shah 'Abbas moved them northwards to Salyan and nearby districts. In later years they are mentioned in connection with Shaki and Shirvan, and they do not reappear south of the Kor–Aras rivers until the early nineteenth century, when some came over to join the Hajji-'Alili tribe of Qara-Dagh.[8] However, although the Shahsevan traditions according to Krebel mention Chakherlu as originally associated with the Beydili (see Chapter Three), they are not otherwise listed among the nineteenth-century Moghan Shahsevan.

The Qaramanlu (Qahraman-Beyli?) had land in Qara-Bagh and perhaps Shirvan. They appear to have been associated with the Chakerlu, and by 1500 they too wintered at Qızıl-Aghach and probably summered near Ardabil.[9] Later in the century Qaramanlu chiefs were still prominent at Lankaran in Talesh, and in Ardabil and Shirvan.

From all accounts, Ardabil around 1500 was a city of importance. The Safavid shrine was located there, the wealth of the order was concentrated in the vicinity, and it was a major centre of craft and commerce. Though Esma'il chose the larger city of Tabriz as his capital, and his successors moved first to Qazvin and then to Esfahan, Ardabil retained its key position for the dynasty. Much village land in the surrounding districts (Moghan, Talesh, Khalkhal, Arshaq and Meshkin) belonged to the shrine, which probably also controlled the pastures, though they were grazed by flocks belonging to Turcoman nomads such as Qaramanlu and Chakerlu. With the start of Safavid rule, although the centre of power was elsewhere, the lands of Moghan and Ardabil must have been an important prize for competing tribal chiefs and their followers.

A variety of tribal names is associated with the region in the early sixteenth century, including several Qızılbash names with later Shahsevan connections: Shamlu (and their associate Ostajlu), Dulqadır, Tekelu/Takleh. Probably it was these groups whose membership was swollen by local village devotees of the Safavids, such as the villagers without previous tribal affiliations who were included in Esma'il's early

---

[8] Torkman (1978: 385, 398, 1312); Yazdi (1987: 429); Oberling (1964b: 72); Woods (1976: 135, 143–4, 180f., 201–2); Sümer (1976: 2, 17, 197); Anon. (1982: 23); Aubin (1984: 6; 1988: 8–11).

[9] Aubin (1984: 8; 1988: 9–11). On the Qaramanlu, see further Woods (1976: 210–1); Reid (1980).

party (1499–1500) and recruited into the Qızılbash, some of them into the *qorchi* guards:

> from among the Sufis of Moghanat, Avughli [Angut?], Tavalesh [pl. of Talesh], Qaracheh-Dagh [= Qara-Dagh], Arshaq, Ardabil and Gilanat, who under the Turcoman dynasties . . . had not entered the ranks of the Qızılbash tribes and the army but were occupied with purifying themselves and being faithful Sufis, the [people of] Tavalesh, Arshaq and Qaracheh-Dagh [now] enrolled in the ranks of the Qızılbash tribes. A *yüzbashı* [captain of 100] was appointed for them and a certain number of them registered in the ranks of the royal guard (*qorchi*), and land assignments and appropriate salaries were accorded them.[10]

Esma'il's closest associates in the first decade (the 'Sufis of Lahijan') included Qaramanlu and Shamlu chiefs, both married to his elder sisters, and other individuals from Talesh, Shamlu and possibly Dulqadır. The Shamlu, who, alongside people of Talesh and Qara-Dagh, had been local devotees of Sheikh Heidar in 1488, held lands in Ardabil, Khalkhal and Tarom. Also in Tarom and Khalkhal were Ostajlu: already in 1501 Qarpuz Soltan Ostajlu was governor of Ardabil, presumably a replacement for Soltan 'Ali Bey Chakerlu.[11]

From 1509, Qaramanlu, Shamlu, Talesh chiefs and other early associates were replaced at court by Ostajlu and Rumlu and sent to distant locations such as Khorasan and Esfahan; though the governor of Moghan in 1514, Aghzıvar Bey, was possibly a Shamlu. In 1526 the governor of Moghan (killed as a rebel) was Hamzeh Soltan Ostajlu. Badınjan Soltan Rumlu was governor of Ardabil from 1524 until he was killed in 1527/29.[12]

Tekelu first appear in the region in 1540. Having fled in 1531 to Baghdad after defeat by Shah Tahmasp, nine years later 'Ghazi Khan Tekelu deserted the Turks, and came to Court with 5,000 men, and was given as assignment (*tiyul*) the territories (*olka'*) of Salyan and Mahmud-Abad, among the districts of Shirvan.'[13] These were farming communities in Moghan along the lower Kor, probably including the steppe pastures, and perhaps also part of the lands irrigated by Timur's canal, known as *anhar-e Moghan*, though some of these were *vaqf* of the Ardabil shrine.[14]

---

[10] Khuzani (n.d., I: fol. 60a) as quoted in Haneda (1987: 35), with minor emendations.
[11] Petrushevskiy (1949); Efendiev (1981: 39f.); Aubin (1988: 85f.). On Ostajlu, see Bacqué-Grammont (1976).
[12] Dickson (1958: 13); Sümer (1976: 37, 43); Aubin (1984: 13); Bacqué-Grammont (1987: 183).
[13] Seddon (1934, I: 295–6); Kamal Khan (1677: 45a); Aubin (1988: 86f.). On Ghazi Khan Tekelu, see Membré (1993: 45, and Morton's comments: 69–70); he is also mentioned in connection with Salyan on the back of a land document of 1541 (Puturidze 1961: 2).
[14] Fragner (1975b: 187f.).

Shirvan continued to be nominally in the control of the Shirvanshah until 1538. Then it was given to the Safavid prince Alqas Mirza, who held the province until 1547, when he was replaced by another prince, Esma'il Mirza. Between 1550 and 1579 a succession of Qızılbash chiefs governed the province for the Safavids: 'Abdollah Khan Ostajlu until his death in 1566; Aras Khan Rumlu until 1576, Abu Torab Soltan Ostajlu in 1576–8 (under Shah Esma'il II), then Aras Khan again until his death soon after. All of these presumably had large numbers of their followers living a pastoral life in the vicinity. Anthony Jenkinson noted pastoral nomads in Moghan in 1562, but did not name them; they may have been Tekelu, or tribal followers of 'Abdollah Khan Ostajlu.[15]

To the south, Shah Tahmasp's half-brother Sam Mirza governed Ardabil and Tarom between about 1540 and 1561. At other times, until about 1592, they were governed by Ostajlu chiefs.[16] Meanwhile, members of the Sheikhavand and Zahedi families, both closely related to the Safavids, held considerable land in Ardabil and Moghan in *soyurghal*.[17]

Ostajlu were clearly dominant in the Ardabil–Shirvan area until Shah 'Abbas' reign. By 1580, their clans included Chakerlu and Qaramanlu.[18] After Morshed-qoli Khan Ostajlu's death in 1588–9, however, 'Abbas broke up the Ostajlu; some of their component tribes probably joined Shamlu, which became more important under 'Abbas; others (such as Qaramanlu and Chakerlu) remained independent – and some at least may eventually have joined the Shahsevan. Although the name Ostajlu does not survive in Azarbaijan, present villages in the Meshkin district bear the names of two other former components, Kangarlu and Kalampa.

B. P. Balayan, having referred to Ghazi Khan Tekelu's reported advent in Moghan in 1540, states that Tekelu tribesmen occupied Moghan for half a century after this, during which time they became more and more refractory. They rebelled with the Torkman in 1584, and their loyalty became so suspect that finally in 1596–7 Shah 'Abbas issued an order for their total destruction. In Balayan's view this meant their abandonment of Moghan and was the occasion for the steppe to be set aside for the newly created Shahsevan tribe.[19]

Now it may be that this was indeed the time when a new tribe was

---

[15] Jenkinson (1885–6, I: 128–9); see Dorn (1840).
[16] Morton in Membré (1993: 77–8); Torkman (1978: 339, 418, 613). In 1534, when the Ottomans penetrated Azarbaijan beyond Tabriz, a governor was appointed to a sanjak composed of Ardabil, Sarab and Meshkin (Sümer 1976: 62). In 1573–4, plague killed 30,000 at Ardabil (Torkman 1978: 196).
[17] See Petrushevskiy (1947; 1949: 162f.); Martin (1965).
[18] Petrushevskiy (1949: 205); Torkman (1978: 384).   [19] Balayan (1960: 338, 360).

formed, given the name Shahsevan, and allotted the pastures of Moghan and Ardabil, but Balayan presents no evidence for this, nor for the continued occupation of Moghan by Tekelu between 1540 and 1596. Actually most of the Tekelu lived in the Hamadan area towards the end of the century, and the massacre was carried out there. Some of Ghazi Khan's tribesmen may have remained in the Moghan region, however; two Tekelu chiefs had *olka'* in nearby Gilan in the 1570s; and Moseyeb Khan Tekelu accompanied Mohammad Khan Torkman from Talesh and Ardabil to court at the very beginning of Shah 'Abbas' reign (1587).[20] Other Tekelu may have dispersed to Moghan after the massacre. In 1638, as we shall see, Tekelu nomads were definitely in Moghan, presumed ancestors of those there today; while by the nineteenth century separate groups of Tekelu were to be found dispersed over Russian Azarbaijan.[21]

Ottomans occupied Shirvan from 1579 to 1607, and much of Azarbaijan from 1585 to 1603. By the treaty of 1591–2, Shah 'Abbas held the area to the east of Sarab and Khoda-Afarin, and south of the Aras. Qara-Bagh and Qara-Dagh were occupied, but Meshkin, Moghan and Talesh were left in Iranian control and administered from Ardabil.[22] In 1598 the Shah moved the capital from Qazvin to Esfahan, remote from the Ottomans. The Ardabil region was now a politically sensitive frontier, though probably also by 1600 in a state of considerable desolation. 'Abbas' usual border policy of creating a buffer zone, occupied by semi-independent tribes, would not have sufficed for Ardabil and the shrines, and the defenders of this region would have enjoyed the Shah's extreme confidence.

For the first part of Shah 'Abbas' reign, chiefs from the Dulqadır, Ostajlu, Ziad-oghlu Qajar and Qara-Daghlu nominally governed occupied Shirvan. When not campaigning for the restoration of their lands, they and their followers would seem to have resided in the Ardabil region.[23] What was left of Azarbaijan was governed from Ardabil: by Mahdi-qoli Khan Chaushlu Ostajlu until 1591–2, and then, until the campaign to recover Shirvan, by Zo'lfeqar Khan Qaramanlu, who built a palace in the city.[24] There is a reference to *shahisevanan* which might, if supported by other evidence, be taken to refer to a tribal group under that name. In 1590–1, Amir Hamzeh Khan of Talesh tried to prevent Alvand Soltan Qaramanlu, governor-elect of Lankaran, from taking up his post.

[20] Torkman (1971: 529); Haneda (1987: 123–4); Müller (1964: 30).
[21] Ismail-zade (1960: 125 and map 1).
[22] Röhrborn (1966: 7). See also Efendiev (1981: chapter 4).
[23] Torkman (1978: 359, 384, 389, 399); Petrushevskiy (1949: 122–3).
[24] Torkman (1978: 615, 828); Anon. (1982: 5, 38); Mohammad Ma'sum (1978: 221).

The latter prevailed and was installed, with the help of Safavids from Ardabil and the 'class (*tabaqeh*) of the Sheikhavand and *shahisevanan*'.[25] This isolated early reference to Shahsevan in the Moghan region remains ambiguous and can of itself hardly be taken to constitute proof of the existence of a tribe of that name.

There is no specific reference to named tribal or nomadic peoples in the region, though we hear that in 1603–4 the nomad tribes (*il va oimaqat*) of the districts of Ardabil, Arshaq and Talesh were ordered to help the Georgian Prince Constantine to recover the province of Shirvan, to which he had been appointed governor. This venture failed, and when Shirvan was regained in 1607, it was the same Zo'lfeqar Khan Qaramanlu who became governor. While in Moghan in the winter of 1611–12, the Shah order the Chakerlu under Akhi Soltan to be moved from Talesh and Moghan northwards to Salyan, Mahmud-Abad, 'Abdal-Abad and Fakhr-Abad (Ghazi Khan Tekelu's former *olka'*).[26]

Throughout 'Abbas' reign, there are frequent references to declarations of *shahisevani*, that is, loyalty to the Shah, submission on the part of immigrants and refugees from outside Iran, and surrender on the part of enemies. Arakel of Tabriz, a contemporary observer, mentions three such declarations, by Ottomans and Armenians at Erevan in 1604, and by Kakhetians in 1615.[27] References by Torkman are numerous, and many of them concern events not far from Moghan and Ardabil, but none of them concerns a Yunsur Pasha or any other supposed Shahsevan ancestors, nor can any be interpreted as evidence for the formation of a tribe or militia called Shahsevan. Some of these references are worth citing, however, partly as negative evidence, and partly to show the kinds of processes which would have been affecting the region at this time.

It was particularly at the time of Shah 'Abbas' recovery of Azarbaijan from the Ottomans (1603–4) that various groups joined him to declare their loyalty. In 1604 Amir Guneh Khan Qajar was sent to occupy Qara-Bagh; when he crossed the Aras at the Khoda-Afarin bridge, 'many of the Qajar, Otuz-iki Torkman and other tribes (*il va oimaqat*) of Qara-Bagh, having become *shahisevan*, assembled before him'.[28]

At this time too, the former Qızılbash groups Qazaqlar, Shams-ad-Dinlu and Hajjilar from Qara-Bagh, who had officially recognized Ottoman authority, now came to submit to Shah 'Abbas and to declare

[25] Torkman (1971: 441f.). Savory's translation (Torkman 1978: 615) – 'the Shaikhavand and Shahsevan tribes' – does not seem justified.

[26] Torkman (1971: 670, 733); Yazdi (1987: 429).

[27] Arakel (1874: 285–6, 328–9); cf. della Valle (1972: 170).

[28] Torkman (1971: 657). On the Otuz-iki, see Chapter Three.

themselves once more eager to adopt the 'flashing twelve-notched cap of the Twelvers',[29] in other words to re-enter the ranks of the Qızılbash.

Immigration of Turks from Anatolia had continued throughout the sixteenth century; now many more groups, both Shi'i and Sunni, left the expanding and oppressive Ottoman Empire to take refuge with the Safavids in Iran. In both Ottoman and Iranian domains, tribal confederacies were being deliberately broken up, regrouped, diluted and displaced. At the turn of the century, eastern Anatolia in particular was in a state of thorough turmoil due to the Jalali rebellion, whose initial anti-Ottoman activities increased after Soltan Morad's death in 1602–3, and intensified still further in the terrible famine that lasted from 1605 to 1609. In 1608 some 15,000 Jalalis, having been heavily chastised by Ottoman troops, fled to Iran and declared themselves *shahisevan*. They were warmly but cautiously received at Erevan and Tabriz, and their chiefs were brought to court at Esfahan, while they spent the winter in Iraq. The following spring they were granted lands in Kurdistan.[30]

Other groups left the Ottoman frontier provinces at the same time to become the Shah's subjects:

Meanwhile a body of clans (*oimaqat*) of mixed origins from Asia Minor, who had called themselves in Turki Sil-süpür, i.e. 'Sweep-clean', having become *shahisevan*, to the number of 2,000 households applied in expectation at the royal Court. They would pass through every district of Anatolia, and whatever they found they swept clean with the broom of disaster, in conformity with their name. Their elders [came to the Court and] *qıshlaq* and *yailaq* having been appointed for the above tribe (*ta'efeh*) in the province of Rey, Saveh, Khar and Firuz-Kuh, they were sent on to [Persian] 'Eraq.[31]

Later Torkman states that the above Sil-Süpür immigrants were led by one Khalil Soltan. On their reception in Iran, 'some of them were enrolled in the ranks of the great *qorchi*, the rest were appointed to the retinue (*molazemat*) of the same Khalil Soltan'. The latter, retaining his name Sil-Süpür, figures among Shah 'Abbas' generals, and later under Shah Safi.[32] Sümer writes that the Jerid Sil-Süpür came from the Dulqadırlı district of Anatolia, whence also came the Qızılbash groups Dulqadır(lu), Shamlu, and Imanlu Afshar.

A manuscript of Torkman used by Petrushevskiy differs from the published edition in the passage just quoted, adding that the Sil-Süpür were appointed land for settlement (*yurt va maqam*) in Veramin and military fiefs (*iqta*) in Saveh. Balayan is led by this, by his former assumptions

[29] Torkman (1971: 648–9).
[30] Torkman (1971: 771–82), Griswold (1983: 201) and see Chapter Two.
[31] Torkman (1971: 648).
[32] Torkman (1971: 781, 797, 1087); Mohammad Ma'sum (1978: 117).

concerning the population of Moghan, and by confusing the *qorchi* with the *qollar*, to the conclusion that Shahsevan tribal organization was already in existence by this date (1604), and that it was now overflowing from the Moghan–Ardabil region.[33] He also suggests, more reasonably perhaps, that some of the Jalali refugees found their way to the region, and that the famine of 1605–9 may have forced some of the settled population to adopt a nomadic existence.[34] But there is no evidence to link any of the above groups of immigrants with either Moghan or the present-day Shahsevan, and none yet of 'Shahsevan' as a definite tribal name.

There is little further information to indicate the nature of the tribal and nomadic population of the region in the early seventeenth century. After Shah 'Abbas recovered Azarbaijan, the governor-general once more resided at Tabriz, and Ardabil and the rest were districts within the province – except for interludes such as the Ottoman invasion of 1618, when Tabriz was sacked and Ardabil seriously threatened. By 1628 the governor of Ardabil and Sarab was from the Espehrlu tribe, but there must have been nomads from other groups in the vicinity: Kotov's observation of Moghani nomads in 1623 was mentioned earlier.[35]

In Shirvan, Zo'lfeqar Khan Qaramanlu was followed as governor-general by a number of *gholam*s, until in 1635, under 'Abbas' successor Shah Safi, the post went to 'Arab Khan Shamlu, a man of humble origins from the Sarab district. Other notables in Shirvan in the early seventeenth century came from the Alpa'ut and Kheneslu tribes. Shah 'Abbas regularly appointed governors of Qara-Dagh and Arasbaran, districts to the west of Moghan and Ardabil, from the Qara-Daghlu and Baiburdlu tribes, whose descendants remain there today.[36]

By the early seventeenth century, then, apart from groups with local names such as Moghani and Talesh, from the Aq-Qoyunlu and Qızılbash tribal names we have reason to connect with the Shahsevan the following have been mentioned in the region between Moghan and Shirvan in the north, Talesh in the east, Qara-Dagh in the west, and Ardabil, Khalkhal and Tarom in the south: Chakerlu, Qaramanlu, Tekelu, Shamlu, Ostajlu and Dulqadır. In almost all cases, the references are to particular chiefs;

---

[33] Sümer (1967: 152; 1976: 197); Petrushevskiy (1949: 33–5, 95–6); Balayan (1960: 347–8). See also Tapper (1972: 408–9).

[34] Balayan (1960: 341, 347, 352). Arakel (1874: 290), describing Shah 'Abbas' wholesale transfer of the Armenian population from Erivan to Esfahan, mentions that, having passed down the Aras valley, they spent the winter of 1604–5 in the districts of Meshkin, Ahar, Khalkhal and Tarom. Some of these Armenians remained in parts of Azarbaijan in communities that exist today.

[35] Torkman (1971: 1085). For Kotov, see Chapter Three. In 1623–4 a cholera epidemic in Ardabil and surrounding districts caused unprecedented fatalities (Torkman 1971: 1021).   [36] Torkman (1971: 1085f.); Petrushevskiy (1949: 131).

presumably they brought their nomadic followers to the region with them, and though they might have taken them away later, some of the nomads would have remained, possibly retaining their names. Meanwhile, Afshar, Beydili, Inallu, Ajirli, Yortchi, Hajji-Khojalu, Sarvanlar have yet to make their appearance.

Although the evidence is lacking, it remains quite likely that, of the many Turkish tribal groups that did at this time declare themselves *shahisevan*, whether on immigration to Iranian territory or as a result of some upheaval within it, one or more were allotted pasture-lands in Moghan and Ardabil, as the Shahsevan traditions tell us they were; possibly for service in a *shahisevan* cavalry corps.

Shahsevan nomads in Moghan

Not long after Shah 'Abbas' death (1629) we begin to hear more detailed travellers' reports concerning the nomadic tribes of that region. The Holstein ambassadors, whose journey to Iran was narrated by Adam Olearius, passed through Moghan in 1637. Between Shamakhı and Javat in the last days of March they met

a company of Sheep-herds and Cow-herds, who march'd with their Houses and all their Houshold-Stuff, their Wives and Children, all as it were shuffled together in Wagons, or pack'd up upon Horses, Cows, Asses, and other Creatures, not ordinarily us'd in carriage, after a very odd manner, and such as represented a very Fantastick kind of Trans-migration.

At Javat they crossed the Kor by the boat-bridge into Moghan and travelled on south to the Balharu, spending some nights in 'shepherd huts' on the way, until they arrived in Ardabil on 10 April, to stay there until June before proceeding south. Olearius notes that the Ardabil shrine not only owned many villages but collected the pasture-dues for Moghan and half those for Khalkhal and other districts to the south. The Shah received substantial amounts from pasture-dues (*abkhur-alafchar* or *ot-bash* in Turkish) and animal sales-tax (*choban-begi*) collected from Arabian and Turkish shepherds who are 'allow'd to feed their Cattel thereabouts [the Ardabil plain], and to Trade therewith in those Parts, after they have purchased the *Schach*'s Protection, or embrac'd the Religion of the *Persians*'.[37]

This account fits well with traditional versions of the origin of the Shahsevan as ex-Sunni immigrants, though none of the local tribes are yet named. However, the ambassadors returned in February 1638 via Astara,

---

[37] Olearius (1669: 168–77, 180, 230). See Emerson (1993) on texts of Olearius.

Lankaran and Qızıl-Aghach to Moghan. Again they stayed in nomad huts. Olearius then observed of the steppe that the Turks call it Mindünlük, i.e. 1,000 smoke-holes or tents;

It is inhabited by several peoples and families, whose Predecessors, having born Arms under the command of *Jesid* against Hossein, were banished into this Desert, and they are not permitted to live either in Cities or Villages. In Summer, they encamp at the foot of the Mountain, and in Winter, they lodge in Tents upon the Heath.

They subsist by their Cattel, but so poorly, that it is as much as they can do. Whence it comes, that they are called *Sumek Rajeti*, either for that, from *bone to bone*, that is, from Father to Son, they are subject to the King no otherwise than as the most miserable Slaves are, or that they have hardly left them wherewith to cover their bones. They are a kind of Savages, and their chief families are called *Chotze Tschaubani, Tekle, Elmenku, Hatzikasilu, Sulthan bacshelu, Carai, Ardenduschenlu, Chaletz*, &c. I speak in another particular Treatise of the origins of these families, and the manner of life of these people.[38]

Of the names, Tekle (Takleh/Tekelu) and Carai (Qara'i/Qaralar) are those of present-day Shahsevan groups. Chaletz (Khalaj) are also found in eastern Transcaucasia in the nineteenth century. Chotze Tschaubani (Khoja-Chubani) are also mentioned in 1649 as being responsible for the flocks belonging to the Ardabil shrine.[39] Sulthan bacshelu may be Soltanchelu, mentioned in a document issued by Shah Soltan Hosein in 1704 as a community living in Moghan.[40] Hatzikasilu (Hajji-Qazilu) may be Hajji-Khojalu, a Shahsevan tribe of today.[41] Elmenku and Ardenduschenlu are hard to decipher.

As for their 'Predecessors, having born Arms under the command of *Jesid* [sc. Yazid] against Hossein', this is presumably a periphrasis for 'having fought for the Sunni Ottomans against the Shi'i Safavids', which would clearly be true of what we know of the Tekelu, and the presence of a Tekelu remnant in Moghan could be regarded as the result of banishment. Yet, on their way across Moghan, the ambassadors passed the grave of 'Bairam Tekle Obasi', a famous robber of Shah 'Abbas' time, who gathered 12,000 men and did more damage to the Turkish invaders than the royal army could. Shah 'Abbas rewarded him with villages, lands and the title of Khan.[42] Now in early spring 1608 the Ottoman governor of Baghdad declared himself *shahisevan* and sent an envoy to Shah 'Abbas to invite him to take over the city; the envoy was one Bairam Khan Tekelu, who had been among the Tekelu chiefs who fled earlier from Iran to

---

[38] Olearius (1669: 295). *Sumek Rajeti* is presumably the Turkish *sümük rayäti*, i.e. subjects of the bone; I know of no other instance of this name.   [39] Zahedi (1924: 49).
[40] Musävi (1977: document 19).   [41] Suggested by Toğan (1943: 93).
[42] Olearius (1669: 295).

Baghdad. The Shah accepted the invitation, but before his Qızılbash army had time to reach Baghdad, an Ottoman army attacked the city, and the governor changed his mind. Meanwhile the Jalalis arrived in Iran, and further plans for Baghdad were postponed.[43] Bairam Khan Tekelu, who presumably remained in Iran, was perhaps sent to Moghan on this occasion, though the story told by Torkman hardly amounts to documentation for Olearius' account. In any case, Olearius' story of Bairam Tekelu is not consistent with the 'exile' story he relates earlier on the same page. We are left wondering, was it Olearius' Iranian escort, or the tribesmen themselves, who told him of the latter's origins; no doubt his 'particular Treatise' could tell us more.[44]

Given the exceptional qualities of the pasture-lands and the strategic importance of the Ardabil region, even at this time of famine and scorched-earth frontier zones, it is most unlikely that groups would have been sent there by Shah 'Abbas as exiles. The traditional version, that these pastures were granted as a reward for loyalty, or to trusted supporters, seems more credible. Too much store should not be set by Olearius' and later travellers' observations on the poverty-stricken appearance of the nomads in Moghan; but it must have taken many years for the area to recover from the devastations of the Ottoman–Iranian wars, and Olearius' visit was only a year or two after serious epidemics of both plague and cholera.[45]

The most notable conclusion that can be drawn from Olearius' account is negative: that, apart from Tekelu and perhaps Hajji-Khojalu, there is no evidence of any of the names for which we are looking: Shahsevan, Chakerlu, Afshar, Shamlu, Ostajlu, Qaramanlu, Sarvanlar, Beydili, Inallu, Ajirli, Dulqadır, Moghanlu.

A few years before Olearius' first visit, however, when Shah Safi's army returned from Georgia to Azarbaijan, Salim Khan Shams-ad-Dinlu had been sent to Georgia with 'a collection of princes and soldiers and tribesmen (*'ashayer*), particularly Sil-Süpür and Shahsevan of all classes (*tabaqeh*) of Shamlu and Afshar, who had their homelands (*yurt va maqam*) in the districts of Azarbaijan'.[46] These might have come from the Moghan–Ardabil region, leaving just the tribal remnants of which Olearius speaks; but there is no evidence that they did so, nor that they

[43] Torkman (1971: 764).
[44] Peter Andrews kindly passed me a copy of a letter written to him on 21.6.1994 by Dieter Lohmeier, specialist on Olearius, pointing out that the last sentence from the passage quoted is missing from the later, expanded edition of the work, that the author never published such a Treatise, and that he has not come across any notes which the author might have compiled towards it.
[45] Kamal Khan (1677: 78b); Mohammad Ma'sum (1978: 178).
[46] Torkman (1938: 134).

ever came back from Georgia, though this too is likely. In 1636, Shah Safi himself visited Ardabil. Mohammad Ma'sum reports this, and enthuses about the pastures on Mt Savalan, where the Shah spent a couple of days, but makes no mention of pastoral nomads thereabouts. At Ardabil, the Shah appointed Kalb 'Ali Bey Qajar guardian of the shrines and governor of the district.[47]

There is no evidence from the first half of the seventeenth century for the formation of a tribal group called Shahsevan in this region, while evidence for the arrival there of groups later connected with or part of the Shahsevan is still thin. It remains possible either that, contrary to the traditions, the Shahsevan ancestors had not yet left Anatolia, or that they (or some of them) had not yet reached the Moghan–Ardabil region.

Although a peace was arranged between Iran and Turkey in 1639, which lasted until 1721, migrations across the frontier evidently still occurred, for in July 1667 Jean-Baptiste Tavernier witnessed the reception of such a group of immigrants at Shah Soleiman's court at Esfahan:

> After them enter'd three hundred *Turks*, which were fled from the Borders of *Turkie* . . . All these were order'd to advance into the middle of the *Piazza*, where they made their obeysance to [the Shah] three times, and then humbly besought him that they might dwell in his Kingdom, with their Wives, their Children and their Cattel. The King order'd Money to be distributed among them, and that they should have Lands assign'd them to manure.[48]

We have no record of this group's name nor of the lands assigned to them. The narrative is strikingly reminiscent of the (presumably mythical) story of Yunsur Pasha's arrival at the court of Shah 'Abbas I; it also resembles Torkman's account, given above, of the reception of the Jalali chiefs some sixty years before – and also Michel Membré's description of the arrival of the 'Turcomans of 'Ali' at Tahmasp's court in 1539.[49]

From all accounts, in the late seventeenth century most ordinary Qızılbash tribes conducted a pastoral nomadic life relatively undisturbed, especially in outlying areas, sometimes led not by their own chiefs but by state-appointed *gholam*s. On the whole, Shah 'Abbas' successors did not continue his policy of resettling the tribes in new areas, and the above instance is hardly typical of later Safavid policy. Yet there are strong indications that by this time some groups named Shahsevan were already in Moghan.

In 1668 the garrison in Darband to the north was composed of *qorchi* of the Afshar and Shamlu Shahsevan: here again, Shahsevan is attached as a

---

[47] Mohammad Ma'sum (1978: 219f.). Kalb 'Ali Bey died in 1638/9. Nazar 'Ali Khan Söklan Dulqadır may have been his replacement (Torkman 1938: 215).
[48] Tavernier (1678, I: 162).
[49] Membré (1993: 18). Morton suggests that these might have been Tekelu.

label to other tribal names, not as a tribal name on its own.[50] But already in 1647, as we saw in Chapter Two, Evliya Chelebi saw troops stationed in Baku named Shahsevan *tout court*. A document from the Ardabil shrine, dated 1660–1, mentions a Shah 'Ali Bey Shahsevan, while a year later an 'Ali Bey Shahsevan figures in a marginal note to the inventory known as *Sarih al-Melk*. A further note, datable to no later than 1669–70, mentions villages in the steppes of Moghan as being in the possession of the '*jama 'at* of Takleh and Shahisevan'.[51]

Of travellers who passed through Moghan in the later seventeenth century, neither Jean Struys (in November 1671) nor Engelbert Kaempfer (in 1683) recorded the existence of pastoral nomads, though the former remarks on the local hut-dwellers: 'Ils sont extremement pauvres et apeine avoient-ils dequoi couvrir ce qu'il faut cacher. Avec cela ils étoient gais, et nous donnérent de ce qu'ils avoient pour trespeu de chose.'[52]

Père de la Maze, however, the Superior of the Shamakhı Jesuit mission, who crossed Moghan in October 1698, had more to say on the inhabitants. He and his companions did not like the desolation of the Moghan 'deserts', but were hospitably entertained by the local nomads. After describing the construction of their round, felt-covered tents, he notes that Moghan 'est habité par des Turcs, qui se donnent le nom de *Chaseven*: c'est à dire, ami du Roy, parce qu'ils ont passe de la domination du Grand Seigneur sous celle du Roy de Mougan'[53] – sc. from the Soltan to the Shah.

This information seems to confirm the 'traditional' rather than the 'official' theory; the Shahsevan of Moghan were immigrants to Iran from the Ottoman Empire. It is also, of course, quite consistent with Tavernier's account of immigrants just twenty-one years before.

Cornelis de Bruin passed through Moghan in September 1703 and again in April 1707, when he remarked on the large numbers of 'Tartar' nomads and their animals. The Russian mission under Artemii Volynskiy was in Moghan in December 1716; with them was John Bell of Antermony, who noted that 'The inhabitants are the KURDY, live in tents all the year. The soil is very dry and barren, notwithstanding the cattle are in good condition, and the mutton particularly good.'[54]

One might infer from these two references that the prosperity of the Moghan nomads had increased since the times when Olearius and Struys

---

[50] Musävi (1977: document 15).
[51] I am indebted to Mr A. H. Morton for bringing this document to my attention and for the dating; see Shirazi (1570), Morton (1974, 1975), Tapper (1974: 350, n. 86).
[52] Struys (1681: 276); see Floor (1993).   [53] De la Maze (1723: 409).
[54] De Bruin (1759, IV: 1–13; V: 206–9); Bell of Antermony (1764: 70).

observed them. In 1700, indeed, de Bruin says, a new canal from the Aras was constructed by order of the khan-governor, who lived in Moghan during the summer and wintered in Ardabil. This may have been 'Abbas-qoli Khan, governor (*hakem*) of Moghan and Lankaran in 1703.[55]

In his own journal, Volynskiy wrote that in 1717 the inhabitants of Moghan, nomadizing between the Kor and Aras rivers, revolted against their Khan, an Iranian noble imposed on them by the Shah, chose their own leader (*kalantar*) and fought the Iranian troops sent against them. The leader is not named, but an influential Moghani chief was active elsewhere at this time: Mansur Khan Moghani, Safavid governor-general of Mashhad, who was defeated by the Abdali/Dorrani Afghans and dismissed from his post in 1716; he returned to Azarbaijan, where he was involved in disturbances and executed in 1734, as will be described in the next chapter.[56]

Meanwhile, there is more information on the role of the Shahsevan in the area. A farman (decree) of Shah Soltan Hosein, dated July–August 1704, discusses the salaried appointment, in the district of Shaki and Shirvan, of one Emam-qoli Bey, son of Mohammad Bey (Baiburdlu), deputy of Soleiman Bey *yüzbashi* (captain) of the Shahsevan Ajirli *qorchi*. There is also a reference to Shah Verdi Bey, son of Mohammad Bey Inallu.[57]

Another farman of Shah Soltan Hosein, dating from 1709, concerns salary payments from the pasture-dues of Qara-Bagh and Ganjeh and other taxes. The recipients listed are almost all followers (*tabin*) of Afshar and Beydili chiefs, most of whom are also called Shahsevan: 'Abbas Bey Shahsevan Afshar, Zo'lfeqar Bey Shahsevan Afshar, Mostafa Shahsevan Afshar, 'Ali Bey Shahsevan Beydili, Emam-qoli Bey Afshar, Mirza 'Ali Bey Afshar, Ahmad Bey Beydili. We are not told where these chiefs lived, nor what difference (if any) was marked by the label Shahsevan.[58]

It seems reasonable to infer that communities of Afshar, as well as former Shamlu groups Inallu, Beydili and Ajirli, were now living in the Moghan region, some of them also bearing the name Shahsevan. Beydili are also among the thirty-six communities (*jama'at*), apparently from the Moghan area, listed in a *shajareh* of Shah Soltan Hosein dated December 1704, issued on the appointment of their spiritual guide (*khalifeh*). The first name on the list is Soltanchelu, which may be the same 'Sulthan

---

[55] De Bruin (1759, IV: 12); Schimkoreit (1982: 368).
[56] Zevakin (1929: 13), quoted by Abdurakhmanov (1964: 17); Mohammad Kazem (1960: fol. 16a).   [57] Baiburdi (1969). See also Schimkoreit (1982: 556).
[58] Musävi (1977: document 17). Emam-qoli Bey Afshar and Mirza 'Ali Bey Afshar were the names of *qorchi* leaders in the Darband garrison mentioned in a 1668 farman of Shah Safi (Musävi 1977: document 15).

bacshelu' of Moghan mentioned by Olearius. Another is Shekhlu (Sheikhlu), a common name but also that of a Shahsevan tribe settled near Ardabil in the nineteenth century; two other names (Borbor and Sabunji) we shall meet in association with the Shahsevan twenty years later; another, Bajervanlu, is the name of a section of the Moghanlu tribe today; but the rest, perhaps surprisingly, have no recognizable link with the Shahsevan or other names of Moghan tribes.[59]

The Shahsevan and/or Moghan are mentioned in three court documents of Shah Soltan Hosein's time, but their position is not clear. In his *Dastur al-Moluk*, Mirza Rafi'a states that the province of Tabriz together with Moghan and some other districts of Azarbaijan were entrusted to the *sepahsalar*, immediate military subordinate of the *qorchibashi*, who was chief of all the tribes (*ilat va oimaqat*) of Iran.[60] In the *Tazkerat al-Moluk* (c. 1726), Mirza Sami'a lists the Urmiyeh Afshar, the Shaqaqi, and the Inallu Shahsevan (possibly Inallu *and* Shahsevan) separately as dependencies of the Tabriz *beglerbegi*, though no other named Shahsevan group is mentioned.[61] In the *Tohfeh-e Shahi* (1716), Mirza Mohammad Hosein apparently classifies the tribes of the realm as Iranians, Turks, and others, and lists the Shahsevan as one of the six major Turkish tribes (*ta'efeh*), alongside Afshar, Qajar, Shaqaqi, Zanganeh and Qaraguzlu; they comprise two groups, one in Fars, the other in Azarbaijan and Gilan, and their chief is 'Ali Khan. The Afshar subdivisions are Shamlu, Qırqlu and Sarvanlu. It is not clear how much of this information is specific to the *Tohfeh* and how much was added in 1800.[62]

We have now heard evidence that by around 1700 a tribal group (or groups) called Shahsevan existed, part of it at least in Azarbaijan, and that most of the groups for which we were looking were indeed living in the Moghan region or just to the north in Shirvan, though not yet to the south in Ardabil, Meshkin or the Savalan mountains. Possibly the nomads of Moghan did not migrate so far south in the summer.

One substantial group of whom we shall hear much more in succeeding decades in association with the Shahsevan is the Shaqaqi, a large former

---

[59] Musävi (1977: document 19). The name Moghan is not mentioned in the document, but Musävi in his commentary asserts (it is not clear on what grounds) that these communities are from Arran (Qara-Bagh) and Moghan. The other names are: Azad Badali; Azad Cha'i; Akarlu; Amkul Khasi; Hajji Mansurlu; Hajji Pir Malek; Chuli Khani; Ulajlu va oulad; Visallu; Chullu; Sulfa; Kur Ahmadlu; Qarajeh Alpaut; Tarzboneh; 'Asheq Musalu; Jalayer; Qarachilu; Takash; Maslub; Sari Khaled; Chahar Dangeh and Hajji Kord; Paplu and Shekhlu (second time) and Qaderlu *et al.*; beneh (boneh?) 'Ezzaddinlu; Soltan Ahmadlu; Baba Kuran; Bahmani; Riyub Rumlu. Several of these names have echoes in present-day villages, or earlier tribal groups, without any necessarily Shahsevan connection.   [60] Danesh-Pazhuh (1968–9: 78, 80).   [61] Minorsky (1943: 100).
[62] Danesh-Pazhuh (1974: 414). See Chapter Three, note 7.

Qızılbash Shi'i tribe of Kurdish origins. They were probably the main occupants of Meshkin and Sarab (and perhaps Ardabil), where they were certainly dominant by the 1720s. If they were pastoral nomads, they would have found it difficult to stay in the high country there during the winter, but there is no mention of them yet in Moghan.[63]

Several Shahsevan leaders in the region have been named, many of them also carrying the names of Qızılbash tribes Afshar, Beydili and Ajirli. But there is nothing yet to indicate to what extent these various groups, and others whose names were mentioned, formed any sort of unified tribe or confederacy, nor what the relations between the leaders might have been.

Whatever unity there was, was quite disrupted by the events of 1725–30, when the Ottomans once again overcame Azarbaijan. Ardabil and Moghan once more became a frontier district, and the tribal population figures more prominently in the records.

[63] Cf. Minorsky (1934b).

Part II

The rise of the Shahsevan confederacy

> The Kurds and Shaysevans nomadizing on the Moghan steppe, who make a habit of coming in winter to the Salyan district with their flocks, became Russian subjects in 1728 and remained such until 1732, when Gilan was abandoned to Shah Tahmasp. The Kurds live on the River Aras on the Moghan steppe, after which they also are called Muganis. The Shaysevans have their residence mainly on the River Kura. Both peoples were at that time peaceful, supported themselves by stock-raising, and lived a nomadic life in tents.
>
> Butkov, *Materiali dlya Novoy Istorii Kavkaza.*[1]

The beginning of the eighteenth century found Iran in a condition of steadily worsening administrative and military decay under the weak and misguided Shah Soltan Hosein. The death throes of the Safavid dynasty began with the Afghan invasions in the south and east, culminating in 1722 in the siege and capture of Esfahan by Mahmud Ghilji, while the west and northwest soon fell carrion to the voracious Ottomans and Russians, both newly freed from military commitments elsewhere to expand in the direction of Iran.

The frontiers of Iran in Shah Soltan Hosein's time were almost as they had been left by Shah 'Abbas I: they included much of Georgia and Daghestan in the northwest, while Khorasan and large areas of present-day Afghanistan and Pakistan lay within Iran's eastern frontier. Some territory in the west had been lost to the Turks in the 1630s, but since the Treaty of Zohab in 1639 the frontier province of Azarbaijan had been so secure from invasion that it had for much of the time been counted as an internal province and ruled directly from the capital. Early in the eighteenth century, however, the situation changed drastically. For several crucial years Moghan and Ardabil were at the meeting point of three empires, and the Shahsevan and other tribal groups of the region were thrust into a political role as frontiersmen for which they must have been ill prepared.

The records for those years are the first that mention in any detail the activities of the Shahsevan and other tribal groups of the Moghan–Ardabil region, which allows us to construct somewhat more of a narra-

---

[1] Butkov (1869: 92), based on Gärber (1760: 137–8), Lerch (1776: 468).

tive than has been possible so far. Chapter Five examines these records, together with those relating to the subsequent period of Nader Shah Afshar, when it appears that a unified and centralized confederacy was first formed. The evidence suggests that Nader Shah appointed Badr Khan Sarı-Khan-Beyli of the Afshar tribe as chief of the Shahsevan of Moghan and Ardabil, and that the nineteenth-century paramount chiefs descended from him.

For several decades after Nader's death in 1747, members of Badr Khan's family governed the city and district of Ardabil, and the Shahsevan confederacy which they led played an increasingly important role in the turbulent years until the establishment of the Qajar dynasty at Tehran at the end of the eighteenth century. Chapter Six puts the history of the confederacy and its ruling family, so far as it is known, into the context of the competition for control of the region between the semi-independent neighbouring khans of Qara-Dagh, Qara-Bagh, Qobbeh, Sarab and Gilan, the Afshar, Afghan, Zand and Qajar tribal rulers of Iran, and agents and forces of the Russian Empire.

A narrative of the complexities of conquest, opposition and alliance among the khans does not make for easy reading, but is essential to the analysis in Chapter Seven, which summarizes the results of the enquiry in an attempt to interpret the evidence relating to the origins and early development of the Shahsevan tribal confederacy. The substantive evidence consists largely of references to the activities of a number of tribal chiefs. For this period, the social and economic life of the ordinary tribespeople is still largely a matter of inference from what is known of conditions elsewhere and in the region as a whole. Inevitably then, Chapters Five and Six constitute a narrative and dynastic history of the Shahsevan, with the recurring problem of fitting the various names of chiefs, as mentioned in the contemporary sources, with the names recorded in the various, often contradictory, later legends and genealogies.

5 Badr Khan Sarı-Khan-Beyli

Ardabil and Moghan under Russian and Ottoman occupation

In Chapter Two, I related Krusinski's account of the failure of the 'Shahsevan' to respond to Tahmasp Mirza's appeal from Qazvin in 1722, arguing that this was probably not an appeal such as those issued by Soltan Mohammad and Shah 'Abbas some 150 years earlier, but rather a general appeal to a provincial militia of former Qızılbash chiefs and their followers.

If the Shahsevan of Ardabil and Moghan were included in this appeal, and we may assume they were, it is not surprising if they were unwilling to leave their homeland. The previous year, in response to Shi'i maltreatment of the Sunnis in Shamakhı, just to the north of Moghan, Sunni Lazgi tribesmen from Daghestan had raided that city, and had sought and obtained protection from the Ottomans, who appointed a Governor there. During the raids, Russian property in Shamakhı had suffered, thus providing Peter the Great – nominally Shah Soltan Hosein's ally, and freed that year from his military involvements with Sweden – with a pretext for sending an expedition into Iranian territory. So, late in the summer of 1722, at the very time when Tahmasp's appeals from Qazvin would have been arriving, the tribes in Moghan and Ardabil must have been more than apprehensive for themselves and their own lands, menaced by both Ottoman supporters in Shamakhı and the great Russian army which was steadily making its way down the west coast of the Caspian.[1]

This year, in fact, Peter came no further than Darband before being

---

[1] Indeed Lockhart does not mention the Shahsevan in this context at all (1958: 160–1). For late-Safavid Iran, I have relied on Lockhart (1958) and sources used by him (but cf. Dickson 1962). For events in the Ardabil region in the 1720s, see particularly Chelebizadeh (1740) (used by Hammer 1965), Astarabadi (1962), Mohammad Kazem (1960/1990).

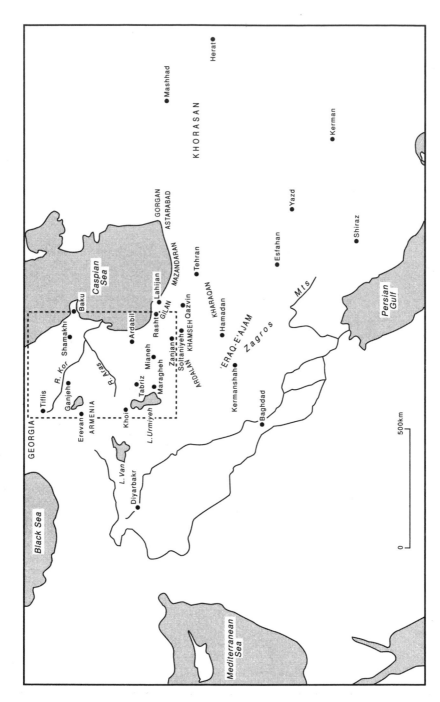

Map 3. Part of South-West Asia, to show places mentioned in Chapters 5–7 (enclosed area is enlarged as Map 4)

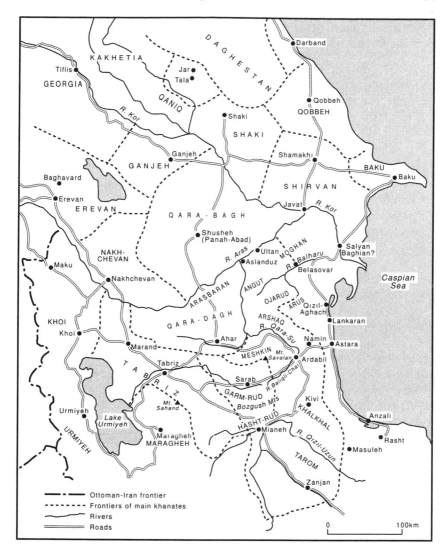

Map 4. North-West Iran, to show places mentioned in Chapters 5–7

forced to turn back in September by the lateness of the season and the destruction of a supply convoy. A separate expedition, however, landed near Rasht during the winter and occupied part of Gilan, and Baku was taken the following summer (1723).

In November 1722, with Soltan Hosein the prisoner of Mahmud Ghilji the Afghan in Esfahan, his son Tahmasp declared himself Shah. His envoy was now in St Petersburg negotiating a treaty with Peter, who promised help against the Afghans in return for the cities of Baku and Darband and the Caspian provinces of Gilan, Mazandaran and Astarabad. Although Tahmasp eventually refused to ratify this treaty, the Russians were soon in control of the southwestern shores of the Caspian.

While the Russians were treating with Tahmasp, the Ottomans were inclined to support their fellow-Sunnis, Mahmud and his Afghan tribesmen. They already had their Sunni Governor in Shamakhı, which Peter had threatened in 1722. However, neither the Turks nor the Russians wanted a clash; negotiations were conducted during 1723 and a treaty was concluded in July 1724 by which north and west Iran were partitioned between the two Powers. The Turco–Russian frontier was to bisect Shirvan and Moghan, leaving Shamakhı in the Turkish sphere and Salyan and the coast to Russia. From Javat in Moghan, the Turko–Iranian frontier was to run south towards the Safavid shrine-city of Ardabil, which was left to Tahmasp, and then straight on to Hamadan. Shahsevan territory in Moghan clearly straddled the proposed frontiers. The Russians were to retain control of the Caspian provinces they had already won, while the Ottomans had still to take possession of their allotted zone.

The Ottomans had launched the 1724 season with expeditions against Erevan and Tabriz. They besieged and captured the former stronghold with great loss, but the latter valiantly resisted siege by 'Abdallah Köprülü Pasha of Van, whose expedition was a costly failure, though Khoi, Marand and Nakhchevan were taken. The next year 'Abdallah Pasha was reinforced, and in August 1725, after a short but bloody siege, he entered Tabriz. Ganjeh fell a month later. The Ottomans had soon reached their agreed frontiers. By this time, however, Peter had died, and the Russians' conquering ardour had cooled, so the Ottomans pushed on to occupy Ardabil as well. In fact only a small sector of the proposed frontier, north of Shamakhı, was ever demarcated.[2]

Shah Tahmasp, who had first set up his capital in Tabriz, and then moved to Ardabil in July 1723 in the face of the Ottoman threat, now in late summer 1725 had to make a hurried retreat to Qazvin and Tehran. The Ottomans possessed Georgia, Armenia, and the greater part of Azarbaijan and Shirvan. Most of the region of Moghan and Ardabil was in the hands of the Ottomans, who appointed a governor, Safi-qoli Khan, to their sector of Moghan, and confirmed 'Abd ar-Razzaq Khan as governor of Qara-Dagh.[3] The latter district then included Meshkin, which was

---

[2] Lockhart (1958: 354f.).
[3] Chelebizadeh (1740: fol. 83b–85b). The Safavid (nominal) governor of Moghan in February 1726 was Ughurlu Khan (Fragner 1975a: 205).

the home at least of the Shaqaqi. The Russians had already entrusted their territories in Salyan and Moghan to the authority of 'Ali-qoli Khan Shahsevan, the big landowner in those parts, who was probably a dependant of the khan of Qobbeh to the north.[4]

Meanwhile the Ottomans had turned against Ashraf Ghilji, Mahmud's successor at Esfahan, declaring him an usurper, and hostilities were prepared in 1726. The campaign season began in spring, when the Shahsevan and Shaqaqi rose, not in support of Ashraf, but apparently in anger at the Ottoman occupation of the Safavid shrine city of Ardabil. Our source for these events, the Ottoman chronicler Chelebizadeh, refers to Shahsevan and Shaqaqi as distinct tribal groups, without naming any leaders; they appear, however, to have been under the command of 'Abd ar-Razzaq, whom the Ottomans had appointed as Governor of Qara-Dagh but who was now leading resistance to the occupation.

In May, 'Abdallah Köprülü's son 'Abd ar-Rahman Pasha left Ardabil with some 20,000 men against these rebels. According to Chelebizadeh, the tribes had left their usual quarters at Arash and fled to the Chai gorge, where the Ottoman forces confronted them, three days out from Ardabil. The tribesmen attacked, but were defeated and dispersed, fleeing down through the mists and forests of Qızıl-Aghach into Moghan, pursued by Ottoman troops who managed to capture their baggage before being forced by the waterless steppe to turn back to Ardabil.[5]

Chelebizadeh, writing from the Ottoman point of view, is the main source for this engagement, and his accounts of Ottoman 'victories' are similar in tone to Russian accounts of their Cossacks' campaigns against the Shahsevan tribesmen nearly two centuries later. It may be that the tribesmen were not defeated at all. When engaged against the Cossacks in the early twentieth century, the Shahsevan led their enemy into the Moghan steppe in summer (and if necessary into the mountains in winter), with two ends in view: to keep the troops away from the nomad families and flocks, which were in the mountains; and to force them to fight in climatic conditions in which the lightly armed tribesmen had a distinct advantage. Indeed, the other source for the same engagement suggests that the Shahsevan had already taken Ardabil and that the battle was fought outside the city.[6]

In any case, the geography of these events is not clear. Arash may be the Aras river, or it may be Arus, a hilly area in the west of Talesh, but most likely it is Arsha(q), the district northwest of Ardabil through which the nomads of today pass during May on the way from Moghan to the moun-

---

[4] See note 20 below.   [5] Chelebizadeh (1740: fol. 96a–b).
[6] de Clairac (1750, II: 322) – based on a specially written Summary of Events in Persia from October 1724 to April 1727, by M. Thomas. See Chapter Twelve below.

tains. Chai (= river) may be any of the gorges leading down from the Talesh hills, or it may be the Balıqlı Chai, the stream which passes Ardabil before feeding the Qara Su and thence the Aras. Qızıl-Aghach is presumably the coastal town in the north of Talesh on the southern borders of the Moghan steppe.

In September 1726, Chelebizadeh says, some Shahsevan from Ardabil joined an Armenian guerrilla rising, but were defeated by the Ottomans and pursued into the Moghan steppe, where they were reported to have suffered 2,000 killed and 600 captured. Nearly 5,000 families were plundered, their women and children taken prisoner, made up of the following: 700 from the Shahsevan tribe ('ashiret), 2,000 from the Takleh, 500 from Delaqarda, 300 from the Chandruz, 400 from the Yurbur, 600 from the Hajji-Eshaqlu, 200 from the Sabunji.[7] The first three names are immediately recognizable as those of twentieth-century tribal groups of Eastern Azarbaijan; Yurbur/Burbur and Sabunji were among the communities in Moghan listed in a document of 1709;[8] Chandruz and Hajji-Eshaqlu are not otherwise recorded.

These and other qualified Ottoman successes in the north were offset by disasters in the south against Ashraf Ghilji himself, and were not enough to justify the prodigious campaign expenses, nor to quell the rising Ottoman public opinion against a war with fellow-Sunnis. In 1728–9 peace was negotiated by both Ottomans and Russians with the Afghans at Esfahan.

The Shahsevan, however, continued to resist Ottoman occupation of their territory. In the summer of 1728 they joined a rising led by a dervish, Zeinal of Lahijan, who claimed to be Esma'il Mirza, a son of the late Shah Soltan Hosein (murdered in Esfahan in 1726). He and his followers had gained control of much of Gilan, defeating the governor, Mohammad Reza Khan 'Abdallu (Ostajlu?); the latter recovered, and (perhaps with Russian help) drove Esma'il/Zeinal westwards (possibly via Moghan) to Masuleh and Khalkhal. Here Esma'il regrouped his forces, recruiting local Shaqaqi and Shahsevan tribesmen, and defeated Mohammad-qoli Pasha, Ottoman governor of Khalkhal.[9]

At this point the sources diverge. Chelebizadeh states that Mohammad-qoli Pasha returned and in June fought a bloody battle with Esma'il at Kivi near Khalkhal, in which both the Shahsevan chief (unnamed) and the Shaqaqi chief (named as Shah-bandeh yüzbashı) were slain and a huge booty taken. Esma'il fled with the survivors to the

[7] Chelebizadeh (1740: fol. 123a; also 107a, 120b).
[8] Musävi (1977: document 19); see Chapter Four, note 59.
[9] Astarabadi (1962: 25); Mohammad Kazem (1960, I: fol. 35a–b); Chelebizadeh (1740: fol. 146b–148); Lockhart (1958: 302); Perry (1971: 61).

Masuleh mountains, then allied himself with 'Abd ar-Razzaq Khan, the rebel governor of Qara-Dagh. The latter had joined forces with the Shahsevan under another rebel governor, Safi-qoli Khan of Moghan. They defeated the troops sent against them by 'Ali Pasha, Governor of Tabriz, and in early August besieged Ardabil; after fifteen days they had to lift the siege and retreated to the pass of Mahmud (?), where their forces were increased to 20,000 by Shahsevan, Moghanlu, Qoloqjanlu and Teletekne (Tekelu/Takalu/Takleh?) tribesmen led by Esma'il. This army was however defeated with heavy loss by Rostam Bey, whose booty included Esma'il's drums and plumes and the war-trumpets of 'Abd ar-Razzaq.[10]

The Iranian chronicler, Mohammad Kazem, does not mention 'Abd ar-Razzaq, but states that Osman Pasha came out from Ardabil to face Esma'il's army; on being deserted by 2,000–3,000 Qızılbash from the garrison, the Ottomans fled to Tabriz. Esma'il entered Ardabil and paid respects at the shrine of his presumed ancestor Sheikh Safi. His army having increased to 10,000–12,000, he headed for Moghan to confront his old enemy Mohammad Reza Khan, governor of Gilan; on his arrival in Moghan, the Ottomans there fled to Ganjeh without a fight, and he won over some of the Shahsevan chiefs, planning now to take Shirvan, Azarbaijan and Gilan. He moved back to Masuleh, but here one night some of the Shahsevan in his following killed him and took his head to the Russians, who had instigated the deed.[11]

A second Iranian source, Mohammad Mahdi Astarabadi, says that Esma'il was defeated at Ardabil by the Russians; he then recruited some Shahsevan support and went to Moghan, but having been defeated there by 'Ali-qoli Khan Shahsevan (the Russian-appointed governor), he returned to Masuleh where he met his end as stated by Mohammad Kazem.[12]

Whatever the course of this rising, the pretender and his sizable local support clearly caused the Ottomans considerable trouble that year (1728).[13] Such resistance efforts (especially 'Abd ar-Razzaq's claim to be

---

[10] Chelebizadeh (1740: fol. 147–8). I read Qoloqjan(lu) for Hammer's (1965, VII: 353) 'Killibedjan'; I cannot identify the latter, while the former is a tribe of Kurdish origins (and still Sunni) at present inhabiting Khalkhal, said to be an offshoot of the larger Shatranlu, itself a branch of Shaqaqi; see Eichwald (1834, I, pt 2: 562–3), Oberling (1964a: 53f.), and Fortescue (1922: 322).   [11] Mohammad Kazem (1960, I: fol. 35b).

[12] Astarabadi (1962: 25). A later source, Kuhmarreh'i (Golestaneh 1965: 483–4) combines elements of Astarabadi's and Mohammad Kazem's accounts, but acknowledges only the former. Rabino (1917: 465) summarizes the relevant passage of Astarabadi's *Dorreh-ye Naderi*, which seems very similar to that in his *Tarikh-e Naderi*. See also Perry (1971: 61); Lockhart (1958: 301–2).

[13] Abdurakhmanov states that the greater part of Azarbaijan south of the Aras was involved in the revolt (1964: 52).

Esma'il's general) led the Ottomans to reinforce the Tabriz garrison. Shortly after, in October, the Ottoman general, Kord Ebrahim, Governor of Diyarbakr, attacked the Shaqaqi tribe, drove them to their headquarters at Meshkin, destroyed a thousand of their tents, and took their women and children captive to Tabriz.[14]

Another general, Cholaq Sorkhai Khan, chief of the Lazgi tribes of Ghazi Qumuq and now governor of the Ottoman portion of Shirvan, led an army of 20,000 to deal with the Shahsevan. In January 1729, he joined forces with the governors of Ardalan and Diyarbakr at Angut, south of Moghan. In the face of this formidable army, the Shahsevan, who were encamped with their families and possessions at the Balharu river, had arranged with Russian agents to conduct them to Salyan; they were taken at night to the Kor river and ferried across opposite the settlement of Baghian by means of forty to fifty boats. Presumably one 'Russian agent' was 'Ali-qoli Khan, who lived at Baghian/Bakhian.[15] The Ottoman forces, according to Chelebizadeh, caught up with some of the Shahsevan as they were crossing, cut the stragglers to pieces and plundered their baggage.

Meanwhile, 3,000 families of Inallu and Afshar had apparently abandoned the Shahsevan and fled northwest along the Kor towards the bridges at Javat on the confluence with the Aras, where they were surrounded and submitted to the Ottomans. 'Abd ar-Razzaq, rebel governor of Qara-Dagh, and the Inallu chiefs Mirza 'Ali Bey and Hosein Bey, with fifteen elders, approached the victors with shrouds round their necks and were pardoned.[16] At Sorkhai Khan's recommendation, Mirza 'Ali Bey was appointed deputy of Inallu and Afshar.[17]

The Shahsevan joined the Moghani as Russian subjects, and remained so for the next three years, with 'Ali-qoli Khan as their chief. The protection given them at Salyan angered Sorkhai Khan at Shamakhı, and the Ottomans complained to the Russians. The latter countered that Sorkhai Khan had been raiding widely in the Russian zone, including Moghan and Salyan.[18]

According to Major Gärber, one of the Russian commissioners appointed to the frontier delimitation with Turkey, in 1728 (before their defeat) Shahsevan and Moghani nomads would come in winter to rent grazing in the Salyan district, whose excellent pastures were due to the

---

[14] Chelebizadeh (1740: fol. 151–3); the same reservations apply to this report as before.
[15] Lerch (1769: 19). According to a footnote (by Brosset) in Butkov (1869, I: 92), the Shahsevan chief who arranged for their transition to Russia was Adar Khan, though nothing more is heard of this name.
[16] Chelebizadeh (1740: fol. 153–4); I read Inallu for the text's Anballu.
[17] Refik (1930: 183).   [18] Hammer (1965, VI: 369); Lockhart (1958: 356–7).

annual summer flooding in the Kor delta. Their horses were the finest in Iran. In summer, he says, they lived south of the Kor, the Shahsevan upstream from Salyan, the Moghani in the steppe along the Aras.

If this report is correct – though in the light of later practice it is hard to imagine nomads summering in the fierce heat of the steppe – it would explain why there has so far been no clear mention of Shahsevan nomads in the mountains around Ardabil and Meshkin, summer pasture-lands which may well have been in the hands of the Shaqaqi. But the Shaqaqi appear to have migrated north to Moghan in winter, and it is possible that the Shahsevan and others from Moghan joined them in the south for the summer – Gärber also mentioned 'Arab nomads as renting winter pastures like the other groups near the lower reaches of the Kor, in Russian territory, but moving to summer quarters in Ottoman territory.[19]

Gärber described all these nomads as peaceful people. However, leaving aside the disturbances already described, some at least of the Moghani may have had sympathies with the Ottomans rather than the Russians, for it was when they had given refuge to the exiled Soltan of Salyan, Hasan Bey, who had killed a Russian officer in 1724, that the Russians entrusted their territories in Salyan and Moghan to 'Ali-qoli Khan Shahsevan.[20] Abdurakhmanov quotes a Russian archival source to the effect that the Ottomans, apart from sponsoring Sorkhai Khan's incursions from Shamakhı, in 1731 sent another agent, Mansur Khan, who organized his bands in Moghan to raid the property of 'Ali-qoli Khan.[21] This is presumably the Mansur Khan Moghani who was earlier Governor-General of Mashhad (until 1717); he is almost certainly the same who was later executed by Nader Shah, as mentioned below.

Nader Shah in Ardabil and Moghan

At the end of 1729, the brilliant general Tahmasp-qoli Khan of the Qırqlu branch of the Afshar, later called Nader Shah, disposed of the Afghans and restored Safavid rule at Esfahan in the person of Shah Tahmasp.[22] In the following year he managed to recover from the Ottomans all western Iran and most of Azarbaijan, including (in August 1730) Ardabil, which he took with Russian help. Later in the year he was distracted by an Afghan uprising in Khorasan; in his absence from Azarbaijan in 1731, Shah Tahmasp rashly attacked the Ottomans there, and lost most of the

[19] Gärber (1760: 137–8, 146–7); Lockhart (1958: 246, 351–5).
[20] Gärber (1760: 139); Lerch (1769: 19); Butkov (1869, I: 91); Abdullaev (1965: 186f.).
[21] Abdurakhmanov (1964: 56).
[22] For Iran under Nader Shah I have relied on Lockhart (1938) and works used by him, while consulting more recent work for specific events.

newly recovered territory – Ganjeh, Tiflis, Erevan, Nakhchevan, Shirvan and Daghestan – the Ottoman frontier with Iran being fixed at the Aras. However, Nader returned and retrieved the lost ground; by the end of 1733 Turkey gave up all claim to the territory that had been seized, and the frontier of the Treaty of Zohab (1639) was resumed. By the Treaty of Rasht in 1732, Russia ceded the Caspian provinces south of the Kor, including Moghan. 'Ali-qoli Khan Shahsevan continued to hold the Salyan district for the Russians, but the Shahsevan were among the peoples who now returned to Iranian control.

In August 1734 Nader marched through Ardabil to Moghan and Shirvan to attack Sorkhai Khan the Lazgi chief and former Ottoman governor, who fled to the mountains but was pursued and defeated. Nader besieged Ganjeh in November; the Russians assisted him, then, by the Treaty of Ganjeh (March 1735), restored Baku and Darband to Iran and withdrew their occupying army, which had suffered terrible losses in the south Caspian climate.

In Salyan, 'Ali-qoli Khan had served the Russians well; he was now recommended to the mercy of Nader, who took him into his retinue, having, as Lerch puts it, clipped his wings. According to one source, Nader drove him to Herat (and probably had him killed there), and replaced him at Salyan by one Mohammad Khan, removing the district from the domain of the khanate of Qobbeh.[23]

After a further campaign in western Transcaucasia against the Ottomans, culminating in the victory of Baghavard (June 1735), Nader received the surrender of Ganjeh, Tiflis and Erevan by October. He then spent the end of the year ravaging Lazgi country.

In January 1736 a huge camp was set up in Moghan near the Javat bridge, where Nader held his famous *qurultai* assembly of the chiefs, mullahs and nobles of the newly reconquered Iranian Empire.[24] He had

---

[23] Lerch (1769: 19–20); Dälili (1974: 29), referring to Äliyev (n.d.: 274); Abdullaev (1965: 187f.).

[24] The journalist Amir Taheri, after visiting Moghan in 1970, reported that Shahsevan he met near Aslanduz pointed to a mound (known as 'Nader's Hill') as the place where the tribal chiefs who supported Nader came on his request and each poured a handful of earth on the spot where he had addressed the assembly. 'The tribal chiefs came forward each pouring his share of earth on that spot. The procession lasted from dawn to dusk. And as the sun was setting a huge mound had grown. Nader then climbed the mound and crowned himself the Shahanshah of Iran. For many decades after that momentous day Nader's Hill was a place of national pilgrimage. The Shah-savans considered it a symbol not only of their own unity but also of the unity of the whole nation' (Taheri 1970). I know of no contemporary source to corroborate this story, which I did not hear myself while in Moghan in 1965–6 (though I spent very little time at Aslanduz). It is apocryphal – contemporary sources unite in locating the site of the *qurultai* over 100 km away at Javat. Other features of Moghan's topography are mistakenly attributed to Nader, and besides, the hill in question has more recent associations, as the site of the last stand

decided that the time had come to assume the title of Shah, but he wanted there to be a show of legitimacy, and pretending to wish nothing but retirement for himself he told the assembled notables to choose themselves a Shah.[25] Mohammad Kazem describes the guile with which Nader ensured both that there were no Safavid supporters left and that he himself should be publicly acclaimed the most suitable ruler. In one case, Nader

commanded a rope to be thrown round Badr Khan's neck and said, 'I am going to put you to the sword; leaving me, nominate whomever [else] you favour to be Shah.' Even though they had put the rope round his neck, Badr Khan stuck to his former words [sc. that Nader was the best man to be Shah]; [Nader] said that the people of Iran were quite shameless, removed the rope from Badr Khan's neck and set him free.[26]

It seems likely, as will be discussed below, that this Badr Khan was of Afshar origins, the son of 'Ali-qoli Khan Shahsevan, and was later appointed chief of the Shahsevan tribes of Moghan and Ardabil.

Lockhart accepts an estimate of 20,000 delegates assembled in Moghan. Although none of the sources mentions nomads camped in Moghan that winter, John Cook, who passed through eleven years later, was told that 'upwards of a hundred thousand tents were in these happy plains when Kouli Khan [Nader] mounted the throne of Persia'. Catholicos Abraham, though he nowhere mentions the pastoralists themselves, tells of the abundance of pasture for the sheep and other animals in Moghan in December and January, by which time the lambs were already born and growing up[27] – this is still today the lambing season among the Shahsevan in Moghan, by contrast with the Zagros and Kurdistan, where lambing takes place towards spring.

Various considerations may account for the lack of explicit reference to Moghan nomads in 1736. First, the Shahsevan, as mentioned earlier, used to winter near Salyan on the Kor, some way to the southeast of the

---

of the Iranian forces at the disastrous battle of Aslanduz in 1812 (see Chapter Eight). Monteith (1833: 30) camped at the foot of the mound, which he was told had been erected by Timur (see Plate 6).

[25] Astarabadi (1962: 266f.), Mohammad Kazem (1960, II: fol. 1f.), Asef (1969: 203–4) and Abraham de Crète (1876: 282–310) give eye-witness descriptions of events that winter. Cf. Morgan (1988: 55) on the precedent of Chengiz Khan's assumption of leadership. Ahmad Shah Abdali of Afghanistan adopted the same pretence in 1747.

[26] Mohammad Kazem (1960, II: fol. 10a); in his recent edition (1990: 456), Riahi has changed all three instances of Badr Khan in this story (very clear in the MS) to Baba Khan (Chaushlu), presumably on the grounds that previous remarks referred to the latter, a senior and much better known figure than Badr Khan. Such emendation is not warranted.

[27] Cook (1770, II: 402–3); Abraham de Crète (1876: 292), who also reported that at the *qurultai* Pir Ahmad Khan of Herat was named khan of Moghan (pp. 289–90).

qurultai site near Javat, and if they were there in 1736 they would probably have endeavoured to keep their homes and flocks well out of the way of the assembly and its huge demands for provisions. Secondly, the Moghani had probably moved north and taken refuge with the Lazgis in Daghestan (see below). Thirdly, some of the former tribes of the area, particularly the Shaqaqi, Inallu Shahsevan, and Afshar groups, having come under Ottoman control in 1728–9, had apparently been removed from Azarbaijan by Nader in 1730. According to Mohammad Kazem,

> At this time, when the Shah's forces arrived in [Iranian] 'Eraq and Azarbaijan, he sent off about 12,000 households of the Afshar tribe (*jama'at*) and forty to fifty thousand households of the tribes of Torkman, Bakhtiari, Kurds, Lors and various other tribes of camel- and cattle-rearers to Khorasan, so that they should dwell in the dependencies of Mashhad, Jam, Abivard and Soltan Meidan.[28]

This account may be based on the very similar one by Astarabadi, who gives much the same names and numbers. Kuhmarreh'i, however, states that in about 1734–5 Nader moved 60,000 households of Qashqa'i, Shahsevan and Afshar of Azarbaijan and settled them in the cities of Khorasan.[29]

These passages may refer to two different migrations, but more likely Kuhmarreh'i's is a misdated version of the others. Although there is evidence for a removal of Qashqa'i to Khorasan in about 1739, and their return to Fars in the 1750s,[30] 'Qashqa'i' here, in a passage referring to areas far to the north of their territory, is probably a mistake for 'Shaqaqi', another tribal group which is known to have been sent east by Nader and to have returned thence some time after his death (see below). The Shahsevan referred to are most likely the Inallu and Afshar, who like the Shaqaqi had submitted to the Ottomans; the rest of the Shahsevan, still Russian subjects in 1730, did not come under Nader's control until 1732, and there is no definite record of other groups named Shahsevan in either 'Eraq-e 'Ajam or Azarbaijan at this time.[31] Besides, the present Inallu of Kharaqan and Khamseh trace their departure from Moghan to Nader's time; and so do most of the Afshar groups of that region, who later became known as Shahsevan, so it seems reasonable to assume they all took part in this mass exodus.[32] Although in the twentieth century small

---

[28] Mohammad Kazem (1960, I: fol. 116a).

[29] Astarabadi (1962: 134–5); Golestaneh (1965: 377).

[30] Oberling (1974: 36–7); Mohammad Kazem (1960, III: fol. 57a, 66b).

[31] Among the groups exiled from Azarbaijan were Javanshir, Otuz-iki and Kebirli from Qara-Bagh (Abdullaev 1965: 90).

[32] See Appendix One. According to Astarabadi (1962: 134–5), 2,000 of the transported Afshar families were from Nader's own clan of the Qırqlu, but most of them must have been from the tribal centre near Urmiyeh. Nikitine's Afshar chronicle states that of the Urmiyeh Afshars, 2,000 horsemen were enrolled in Nader's bodyguard, 12,000 families were transported to Khorasan, 6,000 inhabitants (?) were delegated to defend the fron-

groups of Inallu still nomadized in Moghan and to the west of Qara-
Dagh, and some more were settled southwest of Ardabil, neither Inallu
nor Afshar are reported in any numbers in the Moghan–Ardabil region
after Nader's time.[33]

It is unclear what did happen to the Shahsevan once they left Russian
control in 1732. The fate of 'Ali-qoli Khan has already been mentioned.
In 1734 Nader sent Mansur Khan Moghani, after his involvement in a
Lazgi rebellion, from Tabriz to Shiraz with thirty-nine other rebel
Azarbaijani chiefs for execution. He had apparently fallen out with the
Lazgis, and fled to Nader to ask pardon; but Nader refused, simply
adding him to the other condemned rebels so that their numbers should
make up a round forty. Other Moghani chiefs were more fortunate; the
rebel Najaf-qoli Soltan Moghani was forgiven and appointed Soltan of
Darband. Behbud Khan Moghani and a Shahsevan chief, 'Abbas 'Ali
Bey, were among Nader's victorious commanders at the battle of
Baghavard in 1735. At the time of Nader's death in 1747, his son 'Ali-qoli
Khan included among his rebel forces in Khorasan an 'Alam Khan Tork
Moghani, who shortly after (as a reward for his support?) was made
governor of Yazd.[34]

When Nadir's army had marched back from Daghestan with great
suffering in early 1743, they camped for twenty days in Moghan to allow
men and animals to recuperate. The Moghanis may have earlier retreated
north (with Najaf-qoli Soltan?), for later in 1743 troops from Moghanlu
('a tribe inhabiting the Qaniq district [of Daghestan]'), who were garri-
soning Qobbeh, joined a Lazgi revolt led by Sam Mirza, another Safavid
pretender, and Mohammad, son of Cholaq Sorkhai Khan. Sam had
appeared earlier in Ardabil, claiming to be Shah Soltan Hosein's son, but
had been captured by Nader's nephew Ebrahim, who cut his nose off. His
new revolt was more successful at first, spreading to Shirvan before being
crushed at the end of the year. Many Moghanlis were killed, the rest
blinded and sent home to Moghan – or to Khorasan.[35]

This last statement originates in a report by Cook who, when he passed

tiers of Azarbaijan, and 3,000 moved to Sa'in-Qal'eh district. The Urmiyeh Afshars
retained no pleasant memories of Nader, and the chronicle throws doubt on his Afshar
origins (Nikitine 1929: 88).

[33] Oberling (1964a: 26–7). Nader appointed an Emam-qoli Khan Afshar as governor of
Ardabil in 1735, replacing the former incumbent, Mohammad-qoli Sa'dlu, who now
went to govern Shirvan (Mohammad Kazem 1960, I: fol. 311; Bakikhanov 1926: 113;
Abraham de Crète 1876: 289). It is not clear whether Emam-qoli was a local man or a
clansman of Nader's; possibly he was the same Emam-qoli Khan who forty years later
was governor of Urmiyeh (Nikitine 1929: 78f.).

[34] Mohammad Kazem (1960, I: fol. 277b, 280b, 301a); Na'ini (1974: 3, 287f.).

[35] Butkov (1869, I: 217); Lockhart (1938: 231, 238–9); Bakikhanov (1926: 123); Hanway
(1753, I: 388). In the early nineteenth century there were 1,000 Moghanlu in Armenia
(Bournoutian 1992: 53f.).

through Moghan in 1747, saw near Javat a pyramid constructed from the skulls of Sam and Mohammad's supporters. Enthusing, like other writers of the period, over the rich Moghan pastures, where the royal horses were said to be raised, he noted that they were however virtually deserted, as were the nearby villages. He was told that 'These plains were formerly inhabited by roving people living in tents . . . Indeed we passed by, in our way to Gilan, two or three of the last going to settle, by order of the tyrant, in the province of Chorassan.'[36]

It seems that Nader emptied the Moghan steppes of local inhabitants, settled or nomadic, Shahsevan or other. Later sources appear to confirm that his policy of tribal resettlement had also affected the Shahsevan. Apart from Kuhmarreh'i's possibly mistaken reference to Nader's removal of Shahsevan and others to Khorasan in 1734–5, referred to earlier, there are reports of Shahsevan employed in campaigns there in 1747, and Ahmad Shah Durrani's chronicler Ahmad al-Hoseini mentions 3,000–4,000 households of Shahsevan and Bakhtiari tribespeople, sent by Nader to Herat, returning to their original homes after his death.[37] In the early nineteenth century, James Morier learnt that 'Nadir dispersed [the Shahsevan] throughout different parts of Persia', and Zein al-'Abedin Shirvani wrote in 1831 that 'Now among [the Shahsevan] there are different tribes; their residence is in Moghan, Azarbaijan, 'Eraq and Fars, while sections live in Khorasan, Kabul, and Kashmir.'[38] Finally, one of the four assassins of Nader Shah in Khorasan in June 1747 was Musa Bey, chief (*sarkardeh* – commander?) of the Shahsevan.[39]

These passages need, however, refer only to the dispersal of the Inallu and Afshar and other groups originally from Moghan who did not return there but were known as Shahsevan. Musa Bey, for instance, appears to have been from the Erili Afshar of Tarom, and was brother of Amir Guneh Khan the later chief of that tribe.[40] The traditions of the present Shahsevan tribes of Moghan and Ardabil, summarized in Chapter Three, give a different picture of events during this period. For example, in 1870 Ogranovich recorded no recollection among these tribes of a period spent in Khorasan by their ancestors little more than a century before; but both Radde's and Markov's accounts note that on Yunsur Pasha's arrival in Iran some groups left his tribe and went to Khorasan, where they are to this day; this would be consistent with Kuhmarreh'i's, al-Hoseini's,

---

[36] Cook (1770, II: 402–3, 406–7); Lerch (1776: 413f.).
[37] Mohammad Kazem (1960, III: fol. 240a–b, 245b); al-Hoseini (1974: fol. 20b).
[38] Morier (1837: 237); Shirvani (1898: 346–7). In 1830, Masson too found Shahsevan in Kabul, as well as Javanshir and many other Azarbaijani tribes said to have been left by Nader Shah (1842, II: 297).   [39] Mohammad Kazem (1960, III: fol. 249b).
[40] Astarabadi (1962: 426); Lockhart (1938: 262); Perry (1979: 37).

Morier's and Shirvani's accounts. As for the emptiness of the pastures, this is of course consistent with the exile of large numbers of the former inhabitants, but also with the lean times the remnant Shahsevan must have been suffering, like other inhabitants of the country under Nader Shah.

The traditions relate that the confederacy achieved unity under Nader Shah, who appointed a paramount chief. According to Markov and Radde, this chief was 'Bedr Khan Pasha . . . who accompanied Nader Shah on numerous campaigns and distinguished himself by his bravery'.[41] This may well be the Badr Khan whose predicament at the Moghan *qurultai* in 1736 we enjoyed earlier. Mohammad Kazem gave him no tribal name at the *qurultai*, but refers later to Badr Khan Shahsevan as an officer under Baba Khan Chaushlu in the army of Nader's eldest son Reza-qoli Mirza, campaigning in Turkestan in 1737. The traditions state that the Shahsevan *elbeys* were of Afshar origins; although Nader Shah and his successors, like former rulers, governed the tribes largely through their own leaders, Nader was also inclined to appoint Afshar fellow-tribesmen to office and leadership. So perhaps, too, Badr Khan Shahsevan is also Badr Khan Afshar, beglerbegi of Herat, who (in Astarabadi's account) was entrusted with the defence of Balkh.[42]

Markov states that Badr Khan was descended from Sarı Khan, son of Yunsur Pasha, the original leader of the Shahsevan when they came from Anatolia; Radde, that Badr Khan was son of Yunsur Pasha's brother Allah-qoli Khan. A combination of these is likely: Badr Khan's descendants are known as Sarı-Khan-Beyli, while Allah-qoli may be 'Ali-qoli Khan Shahsevan, whom we have already met as landowner in Moghan and friend of the Russians, and who could have been Badr Khan's father.

This at least is the conclusion reached by the Azarbaijani historian Hüseyin Dälili, who states that 'Ali-qoli was of the Sarı-Khan-Beyli Afshar: Nader, having exiled him to Khorasan, but wishing to keep the support of the Shahsevan, showed kindness to his young son Badr Khan, made him one of his officers and put him in command of a company of royal guards, in which capacity he shared Nader's campaigns and won fame and influence. Though highly plausible, there is unfortunately no evidence to support this embroidery on the known sources: Dälili misses Mohammad Kazem and Astarabadi and cites only Markov, whose remarks on Badr Khan are confined to the statement mentioned above,

---

[41] Markov (1890: 6); Radde (1886: 421).
[42] Mohammad Kazem (1960, II: fol. 105b, 106b, 113a); Astarabadi (1962: 314). Tigranov (1909: 106) states that the Shahsevan served Nader's military enterprises in the Caucasus; instances of this would be the Moghani chiefs, and 'Abbas 'Ali Bey Shahsevan, mentioned earlier.

and Jahangir Zeinaloghlu, whose account is in fact a straight translation of Markov.[43]

More recent traditions, as we saw in Chapter Three, indicate that Yunsur Pasha, Sarı Khan and Badr Khan came from Urmiyeh and were, like Nader Shah, of Afshar extraction.[44] This again is consistent with several reports that Yunsur Pasha was Sunni on arrival in northeast Azarbaijan. Nader himself professed a form of Sunnism at Moghan and at various points during his reign.[45] It is possible, though less likely, that Badr Khan and his forebears were from one of the Shamlu groups (Ajirli, Beydili, Inallu) which came to northeast Azarbaijan under the Safavids; some sources state that Shamlu was one of two Afshar clans.[46]

Badr Khan's fate after Nader's death in 1747 is not known. In the traditions, his son and successor as chief of the Shahsevan was Nazar 'Ali Khan, whom we shall meet in the next chapter as governor of Ardabil; perhaps he was the Nazar 'Ali Bey Azarbaijani and (presumably the same individual) the Nazar 'Ali Bey Afshar mentioned as a junior commander in campaigns in the east in Nader's last years.[47]

With the apparent absence of the Shaqaqi from the vast summer grazing grounds of Ardabil and Meshkin, these would appear to have fallen into the hands of the Shahsevan nomads, while their chiefs established themselves for the first time in Ardabil. Nazar 'Ali Khan and his successors appear to have ruled as khans of Ardabil for most of the next fifty years, a confused but eventful period during which they and their tribespeople clearly established occupation of the region's pastures, but had to struggle against a variety of competing powers – as described in the following chapter.

---

[43] Dälili (1974: 29); Zeinaloghlu (1924: 124).   [44] See also Dälili (1974: 26).

[45] Lockhart (1938: 100, 278f.). According to Ogranovich (1870: 79), the Qoja-Beyli tribe of the Shahsevan – descendants of Yunsur Pasha – were still said to be Sunni in 1870.

[46] Morier (1837: 233); Houturn-Schindler (1898: 49); Nikitine (1929: 73); Lambton (1971: 1102).   [47] Mohammad Kazem (1960, III: fol. 106, 114b).

6 Nazar 'Ali Khan Shahsevan of Ardabil

The Khanates of Azarbaijan after Nader Shah

Nader Shah's empire disintegrated under the conflicts of his successors: for two years his surviving close relatives strove against each other for control, before succumbing to the efforts of leaders of various other tribes. Azarbaijan was for some years occupied by one of Nader's Afghan generals, Azad Khan Ghilji, who contended with 'Ali Mardan Bakhtiari at Esfahan, Karim Khan Zand at Shiraz, and Mohammad Hasan Khan Qajar in Gorgan.[1]

While Karim Khan Zand won over the Bakhtiari tribes and defeated the Afghans in southern Iran, Mohammad Hasan Khan, chief of the Qoyunlu branch of the Qajars, gained control of Gorgan, beat off the Afghans in the northeast, and in 1756 headed for Azarbaijan against Azad Khan. The Qajar now had with him the Safavid scion Esma'il III, and with good reason hoped for support from the chiefs of eastern Azarbaijan, such as Panah Khan Javanshir of Qara-Bagh, Kazem Khan of Qara-Dagh, Hosein 'Ali Khan of Qobbeh, and the Shahsevan tribes. But he was made to feel less than welcome in Azarbaijan. As he passed through Talesh on the way to Moghan in early 1757, he was attacked by Qara Khan of Lankaran and suffered heavy losses. In Moghan he waited more than a month but, of the expected allies, only Kazem of Qara-Dagh appeared.

In spring and summer he proceeded to capture Tabriz and Urmiyeh from the Afshars and Afghans, drove Azad out to seek refuge in Baghdad, and then in autumn joined forces with Kazem of Qara-Dagh to besiege the latter's neighbour, the powerful Panah Khan of Qara-Bagh, in his new stronghold of Shusheh; but they made no headway and, with Zands and Afshars threatening his homeland in Gorgan, the Qajar abandoned the

---

[1] For Azarbaijan after Nader Shah, see especially Perry (1979), Golestaneh (1965), Nami (1938), Butkov (1869). A number of monographs have collected information on social, economic and political conditions in the different Azarbaijani and Transcaucasian khanates in the second half of the eighteenth century. On Azarbaijan north of the Aras, see Abdullaev (1958, 1965). For the Sarab, Qara-Dagh and Ardabil khanates, see Dälili (1979: esp. 40–63).

siege. Apparently some Shahsevan had joined his forces, for we hear that when he made his way back through Moghan towards Tabriz, cavalry from Qara-Bagh and Shaki so harassed his troops that the Shahsevan and other Azarbaijanis among them deserted and went home. Mohammad Hasan Khan withdrew and prepared a campaign against Karim Khan Zand for 1758, leaving his former Azarbaijani supporters to the mercy of the vengeful Panah Khan.[2]

In 1758 Mohammad Hasan Khan penetrated as far south as Shiraz, but Karim Khan, though unable to meet his forces in battle, managed to win many of them over, especially the Afghans, without an engagement. The Qajar chief, who had been Karim Khan's most dangerous rival, was defeated and killed in Mazandaran in early 1759.

Azarbaijan was now in the hands of Fath 'Ali Khan Afshar of Urmiyeh, who had dominated the province since 1749 with considerable local support, though part of the time in service to Azad Khan and sub-sequently allied briefly to Mohammad Hasan Qajar. In spring 1760, Karim Khan headed for Azarbaijan to reconnoitre the position. Fath 'Ali Khan held out at Tabriz with his allies from the Donboli Kurds of Khoi. The Shahsevan and Shaqaqi of the Sarab and Hasht-Rud region, who had earlier submitted to Karim Khan, now switched to support Fath 'Ali Khan, but Karim Khan sent a strong force to subdue and punish them before returning to Tehran. Meanwhile, in the summer, Azad Khan returned from the west: at Maragheh, faced by Fath 'Ali Khan's tribal army, he was defeated for the last time, and fled to Georgia. In 1761, neither Fath 'Ali Khan Afshar nor Karim Khan Zand was ready for a confrontation with the other. In spring and summer, Fath 'Ali Khan's forces held Ardabil and Mianeh; and probably it was at this time that he defeated Panah Khan at Shusheh, taking his second son Ebrahim Khalil Bey hostage.[3]

In spring 1762, Karim Khan advanced again on Azarbaijan. At Mianeh, 'Ali Khan, chief of the Shaqaqi, and other local leaders of the Shahsevan and Shaqaqi, submitted once more, bringing fighting men and horses, cows and sheep as presents for the army.[4] Fath 'Ali Khan's forces were with difficulty defeated near by, Tabriz fell, and the Afshar chief fled to his stronghold at Urmiyeh, which was besieged and eventually surren-dered in February 1763. Karim Khan spent the following months appointing or confirming governors in Azarbaijan, and the province remained largely peaceful and loyal for the rest of his reign. By September he was in Ardabil, planning to cross the Aras against the northern

[2] Perry (1979: 67–9); Butkov (1869, I: 243–5, 418–25); Jävanshir (1961: 22); Abdullaev (1965: 232).   [3] Perry (1979: 86); Butkov (1869, I: 246); Bakikhanov (1926: 130–1).
[4] Ghaffari (1887: 81).

khanates, when news came of his half-brother Zaki Khan's revolt in the south.[5] In October, with a huge retinue, including chiefs and their families as hostages, and troops from all the local tribes, Karim Khan left Ardabil and passed south through Khalkhal, Khamseh and Soltaniyeh to defeat Zaki Khan.[6] He was now master of Iran, apart from Khorasan which remained in the hands of Shahrokh Afshar.

Qara-Dagh and Kazem Khan

One Azarbaijan district whose population seems not to have experienced exile under Nader Shah was Qara-Dagh. The local chief, Kazem Khan, opposed the Ottomans during their occupation of Azarbaijan in the 1720s. Later, having fought at Baghavard in 1735 as one of Nader's officers, he was appointed governor of Qara-Dagh, though he later aroused Nader's jealousy and was blinded.[7] Despite this disability, after Nader's death he collected the local tribes and sought to extend his influence by strategic alliances.

In 1748, during the rivalries of the Afshars, Amir Aslan Afshar, sardar of Azarbaijan, was defeated at Maragheh by his cousin, Ebrahim, who had just taken power from his own brother, Nader's successor 'Adel Shah ('Ali-qoli Khan). Amir Aslan sought refuge with Kazem Khan in Qara-Dagh, but the latter handed him over to Ebrahim, who had him executed and proclaimed himself Shah at Tabriz.

Two years later Kazem Khan was among the supporters of Mahdi Khan Afshar, governor of Tabriz, when he was defeated by Azad Khan Ghilji. For some time, it seems, Kazem Khan resisted Azad, making alliances with his neighbour Panah Khan of Qara-Bagh and others in 1752, but eventually he had to submit, sending hostages and withdrawing into the Qara-Dagh mountains. In 1757, however, he was the only local chief to come to Moghan to join Mohammad Hasan Qajar, whom he later helped in the siege of Panah Khan in Shusheh, then in 1760 he took his warriors to join Fath 'Ali Khan Afshar in the final defeat of Azad Khan. In 1763 Kazem Khan was among the last to submit to Karim Khan Zand, and was taken in the party of hostages to Shiraz. His subsequent fate is not recorded, but by the 1780s he had been succeeded by his son Mostafa-qoli (?) Khan, who continued the family loyalty to the Qajars.

It is not clear which Qara-Daghi tribe Kazem Khan belonged to; oddly, neither Baiburdi or Oberling mentions him in their historical accounts. Under Shah 'Abbas I the Qara-Daghlu amirs had a special position as

---

[5] Ghaffari (1887: 117f.).   [6] Perry (1979: 86f., 104f.).
[7] Chelebizadeh (1740: fol. 149); Mohammad Kazem (1960, I: fol. 301a); Golestaneh (1965: 188–9).

spiritual advisers to the Qızılbash; perhaps there is a continuity with their later loyalty to the Afshar and Qajar dynasts, who (unlike Afghans and Zands) had Qızılbash antecedents.[8]

Qara-Bagh and Panah Khan

Neighbour and rival of Kazem Khan was Panah Khan of Qara-Bagh; he was from the Sarıjalı branch of Javanshir, who with their associate (or clan?) the Otuz-iki (= thirty-two) had for long been rivals of the Yirmi-Dört (= twenty-four) and Ziad-oghlu Qajars of Ganjeh, whose chiefs had been official rulers of Qara-Bagh since Safavid times.[9]

Nader Shah had sent large numbers of Otuz-iki, Javanshir and Kebirli tribespeople of Qara-Bagh to Khorasan, but he kept Panah Khan with him at court as hostage. When his brother Behbud 'Ali Bey was executed (about 1744), Panah Khan fled in fear of his life, hiding with the Lazgis (a common refuge of resistance to Nader) and evading capture until Nader's death, when he returned to Qara-Bagh and declared himself Khan.

Most of the exiled nomads now returned;[10] but, still feeling weak, Panah Khan sought alliance with Amir Aslan Afshar. Together they subdued the neighbouring khanates, and Panah Khan was confirmed in control of Qara-Bagh by Nader's successor 'Adel Shah. Within a year, however, both his Afshar patrons were dead, and in 1750 he was among the Azarbaijani chiefs defeated by Azad Khan.

Two years later he joined his neighbours of Georgia, Ganjeh, Nakhchevan and Qara-Dagh in resistance to the powerful Khan of Shaki. Around this time he fortified the settlement of Shusheh as his capital, naming it Panah-Abad. Here he withstood Mohammad Hasan Qajar's siege in 1757, and shortly after captured Ardabil, appointing a clansman Dargah-qoli Bey as governor. A few years later, Panah Khan's capital was besieged again, this time by Fath 'Ali Khan Afshar. He bought the latter off by handing over his second son Ebrahim Khalil, who was taken as hostage to Urmiyeh.

In 1762, while at war with Kazem Khan of Qara-Dagh, Panah Khan submitted to Karim Khan Zand, who was about to besiege Urmiyeh. After the fall of that city, Karim Khan took Panah Khan himself among the hostages to Shiraz, where he soon died.[11] His son Ebrahim Khalil was sent back to Qara-Bagh as governor. For a while he was busy consolidating his domestic power and was overshadowed by some of his neighbours,

---

[8] Baiburdi (1962); Oberling (1964b).   [9] See Chapter Three.
[10] Some Javanshir stayed in Kabul, see Masson (1842, II: 297), Jävanshir (1961: 48).
[11] Jävanshir (1961: 20–3); Qara-Baghi (1959: 19–24); Bakikhanov (1926: 128–31); Butkov (1869, I: 246; III: 89f.); Dälili (1971); Huart (1927).

but he emerged after Karim Khan's death as a major rival to the Khan of Qobbeh and an implacable enemy of the Qajars.

Qobbeh and Fath 'Ali Khan

Meanwhile, for much of the Zand era, the major power of eastern Transcaucasia, balancing the Georgian kingdoms of Kartli-Kakhetia in the west, was the khan of Qobbeh (including Daghestan and Darband). Fath 'Ali Khan of the Qaitaq succeeded his father Hosein 'Ali Khan in 1758, and came to dominate the region during and after Karim Khan's rule in Iran. He paid Karim Khan not even nominal allegiance; a marriage alliance of his sister to Karim Khan's eldest son Abo'l-Fath Khan, promised in 1763, was never implemented. He spent much of his time dealing with commercial and consular agents of Russia, who had established posts in Darband.[12]

In the later 1750s Hosein 'Ali Khan had recovered his former control of the khanates of Salyan[13] and Darband, and Fath 'Ali Khan expanded further southwards during the following decade. By 1768 he also controlled Shirvan, Baku and the small khanate of Javat and Moghan; at Javat he appointed Hasan Khan, and in 1770 he was said to collect taxes from the Shahsevan. In 1771–2 he seized Shamakhı, but in 1773 an alliance led by the ousted khan, sponsored by Erekle of Georgia and supported by neighbours from the Shaki and Ganjeh khanates, rose against Fath 'Ali Khan. The following year they besieged him within his own stronghold, until in 1775 a Russian expedition came to his aid. He then set about regaining his power; he suffered a further temporary setback in 1778 when Moghan was invaded by Hedayat Khan of Gilan, but in 1784 he himself briefly occupied Ardabil and surrounding districts. He maintained his regional hegemony until his death in 1789.[14]

Ardabil, Moghan and the Shahsevan

Nothing is heard of Badr Khan after Nader's reign. According to the 1828 archival source referred to by Dälili, Badr Khan was succeeded as Khan of Ardabil, at an unknown date, by his son Nazar 'Ali Khan, who ruled a united Shahsevan tribe of Ardabil, Khalkhal and Moghan, with trusted kin and followers delegated as beys to head the Meshkin, Namin and Moghan districts under him.[15] As suggested in the previous chapter,

---

[12] And also in Gilan; see summary in Perry (1979: 250f.).
[13] On the khanate of Salyan, see Abdullaev (1965: 186–8), Gmélin (1779, I: 382–3).
[14] See Bakikhanov (1926: 129–39); Abdullaev (1958) and (1965); Perry (1979: 209–14).
[15] Dälili (1974: 29), referring to Zapiska (1828).

Nazar 'Ali Khan may be the officer Nazar 'Ali Bey Afshar/Azarbaijani
fighting in the east shortly before Nader's death, but he is not mentioned
in the Ardabil–Moghan context until the end of Karim Khan's reign;
various other individuals are named earlier as chiefs of, or in association
with, the Shahsevan of Moghan. Thus in 1749 one Ahmad Khan
Shahsevan and his brother were involved in a vendetta with the Shamakhı
khans. Meanwhile, 'Alam Khan Tork Moghani, who had joined the rising
against Nader Shah in Khorasan in 1747, after Nader's death went to
Yazd as Governor, taking 200 'Moghan Turks' with him; but he was
turned out by the populace after only a few months.[16]

In 1757 (as mentioned earlier) some Shahsevan joined and then
deserted Mohammad Hasan Qajar's forces on his passage through
Moghan, though no chiefs are named. When, later in the year, Panah
Khan of Qara-Bagh made Dargah-qoli Bey Javanshir governor in Ardabil,
it is not recorded whom he replaced or how long he stayed. Shortly after,
Fath 'Ali Khan is reported as taking some Shahsevan nomads from
Moghan to Qobbeh, though it is unclear if this is the same group that one
Tavabi Mohammad Khan took to Qobbeh from Ardabil.[17]

Between 1760 and 1762 we hear of Shahsevan and Shaqaqi tribesmen
around Sarab vacillating in allegiance to Karim Khan. There is no record
of who was appointed governor/khan of Ardabil when Karim Khan left in
October 1763. Unnamed Shahsevan chief(s) went as hostage to Shiraz,[18]
though quite probably they, like the others, were in due course appointed
as governors and sent back. Nazar 'Ali Khan (Sarı-Khan-Beyli) was governor of Ardabil at some point under Karim Khan.[19]

In 1768, however, elders of Ardabil and Tabriz wrote to ask Fath 'Ali
Khan of Qobbeh for protection against the extortions of their respective
(but unnamed) khans.[20] In the same year, Fath 'Ali Khan gained control
of Moghan and appointed as khan at Javat his supporter Tala Hasan, chief
of the Shahsevan nomads in Moghan, who were said in 1770 to pay taxes
to Qobbeh. At this time, the district of Moghan, coterminous with the
khanate of Javat, covered roughly the major, northeastern portion of the
steppe; present Iranian Moghan to the southwest was the district of
Ojarud, under Ardabil.[21]

---

[16] Bakikhanov (1926: 128); Na'ini (1974: 287f.).
[17] Butkov (1869, I: 249); Abdullaev (1958: 17, 193; 1965: 238).
[18] Nami (1938: 114).   [19] Asef (1969: 352).
[20] Abdullaev (1958: 60, 158–60; 1965: 244). The khan of Tabriz was Najaf-qoli Donboli.
[21] Butkov (1869, I: 253–4); Abdullaev (1958: 52, 160; 1965: 231). Tala Hasan Khan's iden-
       tity remains a mystery: he does not figure on any of the Shahsevan genealogies; possibly
       he was from the Talesh khan family. On the economic importance of Moghan see
       Abdullaev (1958: 58; 1965: 124f., 229f.). On social and economic conditions in the
       Ardabil khanate at the time, see Dälili (1979: 54–63) – his account is necessarily a some-

In the anti-Qobbeh revolt of 1773, raids in Salyan, Shamakhı and Moghan made life very difficult for Shahsevan and other local nomads and settlers, and Tala Hasan Khan was taken captive; Moghanlu were among the raiders, but Moghan nomads were also said to be prominent in Fath 'Ali Khan's support.[22] In early 1778, Hedayat Khan of Gilan, authorized by Karim Khan Zand and supported by the exiled khan of Shamakhı, took the field against Fath 'Ali Khan; he invaded Talesh, plundered Salyan, seized Javat and took Hasan Khan prisoner before withdrawing to Gilan.[23] After both these captivities, Hasan Khan was presumably restored to his seat, as he is recorded as khan until his death in 1789.

Sarab and the Shaqaqi

The Shaqaqi were a tribal group of Kurdish origins, but by now Shi'i and Turkicized.[24] Counted at one time among the Qızılbash, they were led by a dynasty of chiefs, called 'Ali Khan and Sadeq Khan in alternate generations. In the 1720s, when we heard of their risings, together with the Shahsevan, against the Ottoman occupation forces, they were one of the largest groups in the Ardabil region, with headquarters in Meshkin.

Shaqaqi were probably among the exiles moved to Khorasan by Nader Shah after his arrival in Azarbaijan in 1730, returning some time after his death. In the late 1750s 6,000 families of Shaqaqi, reported to be newly returned from Khorasan, went via Gilan to join Azad Khan at Esfahan, but were offended by him and proceeded to Fars to join the Zands, for whom their warriors fought in several campaigns, notably around Kermanshah and Hamadan. Either some Shaqaqi did not go to Khorasan, however, or they did not all return at once, for in 1750 'Ali Khan Shaqaqi had been among the Azarbaijani chiefs at Tabriz defeated by Azad Khan.[25]

At any event, by the time Karim Khan gained control of western Iran, the Shaqaqi had returned to Azarbaijan, not to Meshkin and Ardabil but to their present territory of Sarab (Garm-Rud) and Mianeh (Hasht-Rud) to the south. The Shahsevan must now have consolidated their hold on

---

what speculative reconstruction, and not always consistent; for example, Khalkhal is marked on his map, but not in the text, as a district of the Ardabil khanate; whether this was so, or whether Khalkhal was an independent (but little reported) khanate remains unclear; possibly the district was under the control of the Shahsevan or the Shaqaqi, or of the Shatranlu who are known to have lived there later (Fortescue 1922: 322; Oberling 1964a: 53f.).

[22] Abdullaev (1958: 167), (1965: 265, 521, 538).   [23] Abdullaev (1965: 232, 565f.).
[24] For the Shaqaqi see Minorsky (1934b: 290), Oberling (1964a: 80), Tavahodi (1987–8).
[25] Nami (1938: 33–4); Golestaneh (1965: 130–4, 301–3).

Ardabil, Meshkin and Moghan, being no longer willing to share that region with them; elderly Shahsevan told me in 1966 that when their ancestors arrived in Moghan the plains were dominated by the Shaqaqi, and that when the Shahsevan came, the Shaqaqi went (*Shahsävän gäldilär, Shäqaqi getdilär*). Perhaps it was conflict over territory that led to both groups' being reported as troublesome and slow to submit to Karim Khan. On the other hand, the Shaqaqi may also have been in conflict with their neighbours to the east and south, the Afshar and Doveiran of Khamseh and Tarom.[26]

In summer 1760, 'Ali Khan Shaqaqi joined Fath 'Ali Khan Afshar's army for the final defeat of Azad Khan Ghilji. When Karim Khan returned to Azarbaijan in spring 1762, 'Ali Khan, who was now apparently leader of both Shaqaqi and Shahsevan beyond Mianeh, submitted and supplied animals and troops to the Zands.[27]

With the pacification of Azarbaijan and the surrender of the last Afshar chiefs, Karim Khan appointed Najaf-qoli Khan Donboli as governor-general of Tabriz and dependencies; among his instructions were 'to treat with compassion the Shaqaqi tribes and other tribes in the province, and to settle them in their original dwelling places and to cause them to engage in agriculture and service to the government'.[28] These remarks probably applied not only to the newly returned Shaqaqi but also to the Shahsevan who had taken over their original dwelling places in Meshkin and Moghan. But there is no evidence either that the Shaqaqi moved from their new territory, or that they continued to dispute the old one with the Shahsevan. They remained quiet for the rest of Karim Khan's reign, except for their support of an abortive revolt by Zo'lfeqar Khan Afshar of Zanjan in 1772.[29]

The rise of the Qajars

After nearly twenty years of comparative peace, prosperity and security, the death of Karim Khan Zand in 1779 precipitated a new period of disorder in Iran. In the south, the Zand chiefs struggled for supremacy, while Agha Mohammad Khan, eunuch son of Mohammad Hasan Qajar, soon gained control of most of the north. Azarbaijan remained for some years divided among various semi-autonomous local chiefs. The most powerful

---

[26] See Appendix One. For an account of social, economic and political conditions in the Sarab khanate at this time, see Dälili (1979: 40–2).
[27] Golestaneh (1965: 455); Nami (1938: 98); Perry (1979: 86); Ghaffari (1887: 80–1).
[28] Lambton (1953: 133), quoting Nader Mirza (1905: 174).
[29] Perry (1979: 123); Ghaffari (1887: 172).

of these, Ebrahim Khalil Javanshir of Qara-Bagh, son of Panah Khan, was the Qajar's most bitter enemy, supported by Mir Mostafa Khan of Talesh, son of Qara Khan, replicating their fathers' alignments of a quarter of a century earlier. Ebrahim Khalil also won the allegiance of many other neighbouring khans, at least those of Shirvan, Shaki, Ganjeh, Nakhchevan and Ardabil – 'by force or by marriage', as Qara-Baghi puts it.[30] Two of his daughters married sons of Nazar 'Ali Khan Shahsevan and 'Ali Khan Shaqaqi.

Gilan and Hedayatollah Khan

One khan who submitted early to Agha Mohammad Qajar, but continued to seek independence and indeed to expand his power, was Hedayat(ollah) of Gilan. After being in and out of control of Rasht for several years, he had been confirmed as governor by Karim Khan in 1763, and in 1767–8 his sister was successfully (unlike the daughter of Fath 'Ali Khan of Qobbeh) married to Karim Khan's son Abo'l-Fath Khan. He more or less stayed out of trouble as governor of Gilan, though, fearing Qajar resurgence in Mazandaran, he attempted intrigue with the Russians (in 1773) and with Fath 'Ali Khan of Qobbeh after his raid on the latter's domains in 1778.

After Karim Khan's death, Hedayat Khan seized his neighbour Nazar 'Ali Khan Shahsevan of Ardabil and imprisoned him in Anzali, but the people of Gilan rose against him and threw him out, freeing Nazar 'Ali Khan. Hedayat Khan fled to Zanjan, where he was arrested by the governor, Zo'lfeqar Khan Afshar. Hedayat Khan's friend 'Ali Morad Khan Zand came north to rescue him, and restored him to Rasht, with the help of Zo'lfeqar Khan's rival, 'Ali Khan Shahsevan of Zanjan. Nazar 'Ali Khan Shahsevan of Ardabil, whose son Nasir Khan was married to a daughter of Ebrahim Khalil Khan of Qara-Bagh, received troops sent by his affine and returned to Rasht to drive Hedayat Khan out to Mazandaran. There in June 1780 Hedayat again sought Russian help, though it was 'Ali Morad Khan Zand who once more restored him to power in August.

The next summer (1781), Agha Mohammad Khan Qajar moved into Gilan; this time Hedayat Khan fled to the Qobbeh khanate to ask assistance of his old enemy Fath 'Ali Khan. In early 1782, a concerted anti-Qajar force from Qara-Bagh, Shaki, Shamakhı, Javat, Talesh and the

---

[30] *khvah ba zur khvah ba khvish* (Qara-Baghi 1959: 25); Qara-Baghi claims Ebrahim Khan also subdued Tabriz, Khoi, Maragheh, and Erevan, but this is unlikely. On Ebrahim Khan, see Atkin (1979).

Shahsevan of Ardabil recovered Gilan for Hedayat Khan, but a few years later Agha Mohammad Khan returned to help Hedayat Khan's enemies in Rasht put an end to him.[31]

In spring 1784 Fath 'Ali Khan of Qobbeh carried out his long-planned invasion of the khanates to the south. Bringing with him yet another Safavid pretender, 'Abbas Mirza, supposed grandson of Shah Soltan Hosein, he moved into Talesh, and then in August he occupied Ardabil and Meshkin – without opposition, according to a Russian source.[32] He turned out Nazar 'Ali Khan Shahsevan and appointed Tala Hasan Khan of Javat (or Qara Khan of Talesh?) as governor of Ardabil, and Khoda-verdi Bey over Meshkin, but left the region himself a few months later, after receiving heavy hints from Russia. Meanwhile Nazar 'Ali Khan collected support from his patron Ebrahim Khalil Khan of Qara-Bagh, together with Ahmad Khan of Khoi, and when Fath 'Ali Khan withdrew in early 1785 they ejected the puppet chiefs he had left behind.[33]

For the next few years, it seems, Nazar 'Ali Khan Shahsevan stayed in power at Ardabil, probably maintaining his allegiance to Ebrahim Khalil Khan north of the Aras, and his alliance with his neighbours 'Ali Khan Shaqaqi and his son Sadeq Khan, who for some years held sway in southern Azarbaijan. (Sadeq Khan and Nazar Ali Khan's son Nasir Khan were *bajanaq*, both married to daughters of Ebrahim Khalil Khan.)

Agha Mohammad Qajar in Transcaucasia

During the local struggles after Karim Khan's death, while Ebrahim Khalil Khan of Qara-Bagh was competing beyond the Aras with Fath 'Ali Khan of Qobbeh, much of Azarbaijan came under the control of the Shaqaqi. 'Ali Khan was succeeded on his death in 1786 by his eldest son Sadeq Khan, who the following year, with Shahsevan support, captured Tabriz and killed the governor, Khoda-dad Khan Donboli, son of Karim Khan Zand's governor Najaf-qoli Khan. Sadeq Khan's followers also raided widely in Gilan.[34]

When Agha Mohammad Khan Qajar set out for Azarbaijan in early

---

[31] On Hedayat Khan, see Nami (1938: 229–30); Butkov (1869, II: 79f., 92, 99, 302–4); Bakikhanov (1926: 135); Rabino (1917: 473–5); Nikitine (1929: 79f.); Abdullaev (1958: 102); Atkin (1980: 34–5). The course of events in 1779 is not clear: Nami dates what must be the same episode to 1775; Brosset's chronology (in Butkov 1869, III), based on contemporary Russian reports, gives a very complex picture. Hedayat Khan seems to have been in and out of power in Rasht every few months from 1779 to his death.

[32] Abdullaev (1958: 123).

[33] Butkov (1869, II: 141); Abdullaev (1958: 51; 1965: 123–4, 185); Perry (1979: 213). Bakikhanov (1926: 138) gives the date of the invasion as 1788, which must be wrong.

[34] Busse (1974: 16); Butkov (1869, I: 307); Nami (1938: 332); Nader Mirza (1905: 176).

1791, twenty-five years after his father Mohammad Hasan Khan, Sadeq Khan Shaqaqi opposed him but had to abandon Tabriz in order to defend his headquarters at Sarab. The Qajar defeated him, destroyed Sarab and laid waste the surrounding countryside. Sadeq Khan escaped across the Aras to his father-in-law Ebrahim Khalil in Qara-Bagh.

Agha Mohammad proceeded to Ardabil, sending a detachment to Talesh to subdue Mir Mostafa Khan. When the detachment returned, with booty but no submission, the Qajar army marched on Ahar, whence Mostafa-qoli Khan of Qara-Dagh had been sending welcoming messages; and to Tabriz, where Agha Mohammad received the homage of all the Azarbaijani khans south of the Aras, other than Talesh, and reinstated the Donboli khans. Many chiefs came in as hostages, including Sadeq Khan Shaqaqi and one of his ten brothers, as well as the brothers of Nur 'Ali (possibly Nasir) of Ardabil and the (unnamed) chief of the Shahsevan and their wives.[35]

Having already effectively united the Qoyunlu and Davalu factions of the Qajars behind him by remarkable diplomacy, Agha Mohammad Khan completed his subjection of northern Iran by using the well-tried policies of taking hostages and setting one faction of a rebel tribe against the other. It was not until 1794, however, that he finally defeated Karim Khan's great-nephew Lotf 'Ali Khan and extinguished the Zand dynasty with his customary extreme cruelty, despoiling their strongholds of Shiraz and Kerman. Now in control of the Iranian plateau, he was able to turn to the urgent problem of relations with neighbouring powers.

In Iran's former Caucasian provinces, there was the problem of Georgia in the west, and strife among the khans in the south and east. Although Russian aggression had ceased with Peter the Great, under Catherine II Russian commercial and imperial influences had steadily continued to penetrate, especially in Christian areas. Georgia, once Peter's vassal-state, emerged as independent under King Erekle, who in 1783 signed a treaty with Catherine which guaranteed Russian protection. Now, in 1794, the khans of Erevan, Qara-Bagh, Qobbeh, Shirvan and Talesh all refused homage to Agha Mohammad. Fath 'Ali Khan of Qobbeh had been succeeded by his sons, Ahmad Khan in 1789 and Sheikh 'Ali Khan in 1791; they apparently made up their father's dispute with Ebrahim Khalil of Qara-Bagh; at any rate, the khanates of Qobbeh and Qara-Bagh now became allies. This situation on the northwest frontier Agha Mohammad judged more serious than the Türkmen threat and Dorrani Afghan expansion in the east, while the Ottomans in the west had their own Russian preoccupation.[36]

---

[35] Butkov (1869, II: 319–20).   [36] Hambly (1963: 168).

Eager to reassert Iran's former hegemony over Georgia, early in 1795 Agha Mohammad Khan gathered his forces in Tehran, his new capital, and headed for the northwest. At Ardabil, an army of some 60,000 divided into three corps: the first advanced through Moghan to subdue the khans of Shirvan and Qobbeh; the second, under 'Ali-qoli Khan Shahsevan, marched on Erevan;[37] the third, under Agha Mohammad himself, was to reduce the fort of Shusheh in Qara-Bagh, held by his old enemy Ebrahim Khalil Khan, who was now at the height of his domination over much of Transcaucasia.[38]

With no effective artillery, Agha Mohammad had to abandon the sieges of Erevan and Shusheh. Leaving garrisons to blockade them, he proceeded to join the first column which, having passed unopposed through Moghan, had received the submission of Qobbeh; at Ganjeh, Javat Khan too came over. The combined forces marched on Erekle in September, defeated the small but valiant Georgian army, and took the capital Tiflis. They ransacked the city and massacred all the inhabitants or took them into slavery. At this news, Erevan surrendered, but Ebrahim Khalil Khan held out in Shusheh.

Agha Mohammad Khan withdrew from Tiflis to Shaki and Shirvan, putting Mostafa Khan of the latter to flight and sacking his capital Shamakhı. He ravaged the Qara-Bagh and Shirvan countryside as he had Georgia; desperate famine prevailed, and much of the population fled. Having virtually restored the Safavid domains, Agha Mohammad then camped for the winter in the plains of Moghan where, in March 1796, following the example of Nader Afshar sixty years before, he was crowned. The new Shah put on the sacred sword of the Safavids from the Ardabil shrine, and then proceeded to Khorasan, where he spent the campaigning season of 1796. Sadeq Khan Shaqaqi acted as one of his most trusted commanders, especially in the capture of Mashhad.

Meanwhile, Catherine was hoping to expand Russian commercial interests in the south, to challenge the other Europeans, and to defeat Agha Mohammad Khan. In rather belated fulfilment of her treaty obligations to Erekle, she sent a Russian army of 30,000 men under Valerian Zubov, who quickly won over eastern Transcaucasia as far as Salyan and Talesh.[39] At the end of 1796, some sixty-five years after their departure, the Russians in their turn camped for the winter in the Moghan plains.

---

[37] I cannot trace an 'Ali-qoli Khan of the right age among the chiefs of the Moghan Shahsevan; he was perhaps from the Shahsevan of Khamseh or Qazvin. He may be the same 'Ali-qoli Khan Shahsevan who was an active commander in the early years of the first Russian war (1804–12 – see Chapter Eight); but the latter, much more likely than his namesake here, may have been the great-grandson of Nazar 'Ali Khan Shahsevan as recorded on Radde's genealogy (1886: 444).

[38] According to Qara-Baghi (1959: 26–9).   [39] See Atkin (1980: chapter 3).

In November, however, Catherine died, and her son Paul reversed her aggressive policy. Zubov was recalled and the Russian threat disappeared, even before being confronted by Agha Mohammad Shah, who was preparing a new Caucasian campaign for the spring. Intent on revenge none the less, in June 1797 he set out again for Qara-Bagh and Georgia via Ardabil. Hearing of his approach, Ebrahim Khalil Khan abandoned Shusheh and fled to Daghestan. Agha Mohammad hurried forward, crossed the Aras with only his light cavalry, including Sadeq Khan and his Shaqaqis, and entered Shusheh. There, on 16 June, he was assassinated.

The Shaqaqi debacle

The assassins handed the crown jewels and royal insignia to Sadeq Khan, who was later suspected of having backed them. The camp at Shusheh broke up, Sadeq Khan immediately hurried back over the Aras, collected his Shaqaqis and harried the main body of the Qajar army as it dispersed towards Tehran. Ebrahim Khalil Khan's nephew took over Shusheh and sent Agha Mohammad Shah's head to his uncle, who soon recovered the allegiance of all the Transcaucasian khans, including the Shahsevan chiefs Nasir Khan and 'Ata Khan.

Meanwhile Sadeq Khan had gained control of most of the rest of Azarbaijan, clearly planning to establish yet another tribal dynasty on the throne of Iran. He appointed two of his brothers as governors of Tabriz and Qara-Dagh and, with an army of 15,000 tribesmen, marched on Qazvin, where members of his family were being held.

The Qajar princes and their army had returned to Tehran, while the heir apparent, Agha Mohammad's nephew Baba Khan, governor of Shiraz, hastened to the capital and became Fath 'Ali Shah, then quickly headed an army against Sadeq Khan, who had so far failed in his assault on Qazvin. Outside this city the Shaqaqis were defeated by the less numerous Qajar forces. Sadeq Khan managed to escape to Mianeh and Sarab, but his brothers were defeated in Azarbaijan by Ja'far-qoli Khan Donboli of Khoi for the Qajars, and he himself was persuaded to submit to the Shah at Zanjan. On the delivery of the crown jewels and insignia, he was pardoned and appointed governor of Garm-Rud and Sarab.

Ebrahim Khalil Khan sent Agha Mohammad Shah's body to Tehran, and in return Fath 'Ali Shah appointed him governor of Qara-Bagh and proposed marriage with his daughter Agha Beyim. Agha Baji, as she came to be called, was brought to court, accompanied by her brother Abo'l-Fath Khan, and became Fath 'Ali Shah's twelfth wife; highly respected at court, for some reason she remained a virgin.[40]

---

[40] Qara-Baghi (1959: 35); Ahmad Mirza (1976: 14).

Fath 'Ali Shah also married, as his thirteenth wife, the daughter of Sadeq Khan Shaqaqi.[41] This persuasive but deceitful individual turned coat once more, however; the following year (1798), when Ja'far-qoli Khan Donboli arrived in Azarbaijan as the Shah's newly appointed governor of Tabriz and Khoi, Sadeq Khan attacked him. The Shaqaqi forces were again defeated, their centre Sarab once more laid waste. Sadeq Khan fled through Moghan to take refuge with Mostafa Khan of Shirvan; shortly after, he won over both Ja'far-qoli Donboli and Mohammad-qoli Khan Afshar, another powerful chief; after convening in Sarab they took over the whole of Azarbaijan. It was not long, however, before Sadeq Khan betrayed the other two and put them to flight, to return once more to royal favour.

Not surprisingly the Qajars had had enough of Sadeq Khan's continual intrigues and tergiversations, and in 1800 he was arrested and emprisoned in Tehran at the Golestan palace, in a room of which Fath 'Ali Shah had him walled up.[42] His brother Sarı Khan was appointed chief of Shaqaqi and governor of Sarab, and another, Mohammad 'Ali Soltan, was named commander of the Shaqaqi cavalry, which from then on provided important contingents to the Qajar armies.

The successors of Nazar 'Ali Khan Shahsevan

The sources relating to the 1790s mention several names of Shahsevan leaders and possible successors of Nazar 'Ali Khan, but there are inconsistencies and problems of identification. According to Butkov, the khan of Ardabil (though not it seems of the Shahsevan) in 1791 was Nur 'Ali, who (along with other Azarbaijani khans) sent his brother and wife as hostages to Agha Mohammad Khan; in 1795, Nur 'Ali was in charge of the forces being prepared at Ardabil for Agha Mohammad's expedition across the Aras.[43] In August 1795, however, Nasr (sc. Nasir?) 'Ali Khan Shahsevan was reported as fleeing the camp at Ardabil to join his father-in-law Ebrahim Khalil Khan in Qara-Bagh.[44] In early 1797, when Ebrahim Khalil abandoned Shusheh to the advancing Agha Mohammad Shah and fled to Qobbeh, he was still accompanied by his son-in-law Nasir Khan, as well as 'Ata Khan and other Shahsevan chiefs.[45] Nasir Khan, governor of Ardabil and the Shahsevan, is also paired with

---

[41] Sepehr (1958, I: 330).
[42] Baiburdi (1962: 296), who writes that Sadeq Khan shared this fate with one Fath 'Ali Bey Shahsevan; the latter is not mentioned in any other sources.
[43] Butkov (1869, II: 319–20, 331).
[44] Contemporary document referred to by Brosset in his chronology (Butkov 1869, III: 289).   [45] Qara-Baghi (1959: 29).

Shokrollah among the Shahsevan chiefs who a few years earlier (after the death of Fath 'Ali Khan of Qobbeh in 1789) appealed to Ebrahim Khalil to declare himself Shah.[46]

According to Dälili's 1828 archival source, Nazar 'Ali Khan died in 1792 and was succeeded by Nasir Khan, who like his father kept the Shahsevan tribe and the Ardabil khanate united until the Qajars ousted him from Ardabil during the Russian war – the date, not given by Dälili, was 1808.[47] Only when Nasir died (date again not given) did the tribe and the district divide. Nasir's brother Farajollah Khan stayed in Ardabil with part of the Shahsevan; Nazar 'Ali's grandson 'Ata Khan (also called Kuchek Khan) took control of the Meshkin district; Khoda-verdi Khan went to settle in the Talesh mountains; and Shükür 'Ali Khan took the camping grounds in Moghan. 'Ata Khan, and also it seems Khoda-verdi and Shükür 'Ali, were in effect dependants of Farajollah Khan.[48]

'Ata Khan and Shükür 'Ali (Shokrollah) we have already met, and shall be meeting again, while Khoda-verdi may be the same who was appointed Bey over Meshkin by Fath 'Ali Khan of Qobbeh in 1784–5, as mentioned above; as for his going to the Talesh hills, he is unlikely to have been in control there, for after Qara Khan of Talesh died in 1786 he was succeeded by his son Mir Mostafa Khan, who ruled until 1814.

Dälili's account of Nazar 'Ali Khan's immediate successors is the most detailed available, besides being based on a near-contemporary source. Unfortunately, we have found Dälili's use of sources at other times to be fanciful and less than reliable, so this account cannot necessarily be fully credited. However, I am inclined to accept it in preference to the rather different ones recorded some decades later by Radde and Markov.

According to Radde, Badr Khan and Nazar 'Ali Khan were brothers; the latter, and Badr Khan's son Kuchek Khan, divided the Shahsevan between them and quarrelled for a long time, until Kuchek Khan's son 'Ata Khan drove Nazar 'Ali Khan and his grandson and their followers out of Meshkin; they settled in the Ardabil district, and from that time dates the cleavage of the nomadic Shahsevan into the Meshkin and Ardabil divisions, each with its own chief. Nazar 'Ali Khan's sons are named as Mohammad Khan and Balaja Khan; there is no mention of a Nasir Khan, but Nur 'Ali Khan was Kuchek Khan's eldest son, followed by Shükür Khan, Shah 'Ali Bey and 'Ata Khan.

In Markov's account, Badr Khan's sons Kuchek Khan and Nazar 'Ali

---

[46] Qara-Baghi (1959: 130). For Nasir Khan's marriage to a daughter of Ebrahim Khalil Khan, see also Ahmad Mirza (1976: 53), who also implies that yet another daughter married 'Ata Khan, though Qara-Baghi does not support this.
[47] See Chapter Eight below.   [48] Dälili (1974: 29–30; 1979: 23, 28).

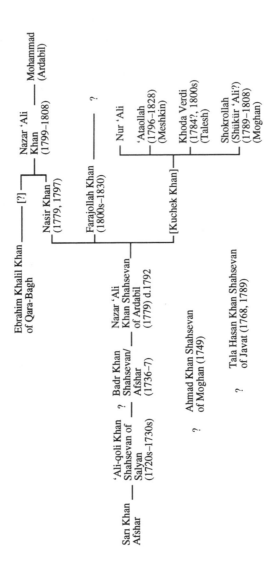

Figure 4. Lineage of Nazar 'Ali Khan, according to Däiili. (In brackets, dates mentioned in other sources.)

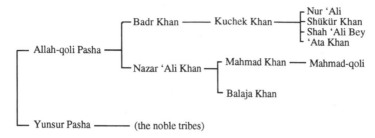

Figure 5. Lineage of Nazar 'Ali Khan, according to Radde

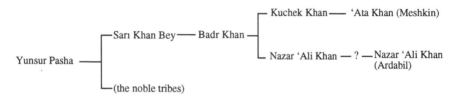

Figure 6. Lineage of Nazar 'Ali Khan, according to Markov

Khan divided the Shahsevan between them; Kuchek Khan's son 'Ata Khan drove Nazar 'Ali Khan's grandson, also called Nazar 'Ali Khan, out of Meshkin, and so on; neither Nur 'Ali nor Nasir is mentioned.[49]

The existence of a second Nazar 'Ali Khan is certain: by 1799 he was governor of Ardabil,[50] and in contemporary accounts of the early 1800s, Nazar 'Ali Khan and Farajollah Khan of Ardabil, and 'Ata ('Ataollah) Khan and Shükür (Shokrollah) Khan of Meshkin, do figure prominently, as we shall see in Chapter Eight. In the sources there is a possible (orthographic?) confusion between the names Nur ('Ali), Nasir/Nasr, and Nazar ('Ali), all apparently (*pace* Radde) chiefs of the Ardabil division. Unless Nur 'Ali and Nasir are one and the same, the references from the 1790s given above might indicate that the former was a reliable Qajar supporter, unlike the latter with his father-in-law Ebrahim Khalil Khan.

Later events show Nazar 'Ali Khan and Farajollah Khan of Ardabil to have co-operated with the Qajars even after their deposition from the governorship in 1808, while the khans of Meshkin opposed them. Indeed,

---

[49] Radde (1886: 420f., 444); Markov (1890: 6).
[50] Farman from 'Abbas Mirza ordering Nazar 'Ali Khan governor of Ardabil to see the *vaqf* revenues reached the shrine, Dhu'l-Hijja 1214; Ms. in Chelleh Khaneh of the shrine, no. 415 in A. H. Morton's inventory. I am indebted to Mr Morton for this reference.

'Ata Khan, a legendary figure among the Meshkin tribes, is said to have been blinded by Agha Mohammad Qajar, though it is not related on what occasion. In 1965–6 I heard a number of anecdotes concerning him and his retinue, often reminiscent of stories told elsewhere of Mollah Nasruddin; some represent him as more of a patriot than events show him to have been.[51] As we shall see, he and his brother Shükür played a dubious role in the first Russo–Iranian war of 1804–12, and openly welcomed the Russians in the following war of 1826–8, which raged across their territory.

[51] For example, Baiburdi (1962: 102–3).

7   The Shahsevan tribal confederacy

Organization of the early Shahsevan

In the foregoing chapters, we have sought and examined evidence for the first appearance in their present habitat of the ancestors of the Shahsevan tribes of Moghan, and the first formation there of a recognizable tribal confederacy. The prey has been elusive, and the narrative has been at times dry, dense and complex. The materials have inevitably been of a dynastic and political nature, to do with administration, campaigns and rebellions. With the establishment of the confederacy in the region, finally, in the second half of the eighteenth century, we may attempt, in the absence as yet of any definite information, to imagine the social and economic circumstances of the Shahsevan peoples at the time. First we should summarize the political history we have traced.

Among the tribal names of groups and individuals reported in the Moghan-Ardabil region by the first quarter of the eighteenth century were the following:

• Tekelu/Takleh, Dulqadır/Delaqarda, Afshar, Shamlu (including Inallu, Ajirli, Beydili) are reported in or near Moghan. All these are names of former Qızılbash Turkoman confederacies, with known or suspected descendants among nineteenth-century Shahsevan. The original confederacies were all large and complex, with sections in many parts of Iran by this time. The sections in Moghan may have arrived with Esma'il Safavi as early as 1500, but they may not have come until long after 1600. Two other Qızılbash groups, Ostajlu and Qaramanlu, were prominent in the area betwen 1500 and 1600, but by 1700 they are no longer recorded there. The Ostajlu were broken up, some components joining the Shamlu, possibly to become Shahsevan ancestors; the small nineteenth-century tribe Qahraman-Beyli, and perhaps the Qahramanlu sections of two contemporary Shahsevan tribes, may be relics of the former Qaramanlu.

• The Chakherlu/Jagerlu who inhabited the region before 1500 were later associated with the Qaramanlu as part of the Ostajlu; having moved north of the Aras–Kor, they were never among the Shahsevan of Moghan, but some of them returned after 1800 to join the tribes of Qara-Dagh.

• Groups of reputed Kurdish origins include the Shaqaqi and Qoloqjanlu, based in Meshkin, and the Moghani/lu, which could be a composite group of descendants of the pre-Turkoman inhabitants of Moghan, possibly partly of settled origins.

• Other names recorded and later found among the Shahsevan tribes of Moghan include Qara'i/Qaralar; Sheikhli; and Hajji-Qazili, who may be the present Hajji-Khojalu.

• Names recorded more than once in Moghan up to the early eighteenth century, but not afterwards, include Khoja-Chubani and Soltanchelu.

• There were ''Arabs', possible ancestors of the present 'Arabli tribe among the Shahsevan.

• Several names mentioned by Olearius (in 1638) and Chelebizadeh (for the 1720s), and particularly in the 1704 *shajareh*, are hard to identify.

Part at least of this population was now known as Shahsevan. Chiefs of the former Afshar and Shamlu (Ajirli, Beydili, Inallu) groups usually bear the name in addition to their tribal name, but two others (Shah 'Ali Bey and 'Ali Bey) were referred to in the 1660s with no other tribal name than Shahsevan (as indeed were some other individuals active elsewhere the country). By the 1720s the nomads of Moghan were under the authority of a landowner 'Ali-qoli Khan Shahsevan; later evidence points to his being of Afshar origins. However, it is not clear to what extent the Shahsevan – or indeed the other named groups – formed a 'tribe' or a 'confederacy' of tribes at this stage.

What can we say of the way these nomads were organized during this time? First, those who bore or claimed the name Shahsevan in the early eighteenth century probably were, or were attached to, descendants of those who had made a declaration of *shahisevani* in the time of Shah 'Abbas or earlier, or so we must assume, in the absence of evidence of such declarations under later monarchs. We should look further at the meaning of this term, which seems to have involved a series of linked symbolic values. Primarily and explicitly, the word *shahisevani* meant 'loyalty to the Safavid Shahs'; this implied, secondly, fidelity to the Safavid Sufi order and the Shi'i faith, especially to 'Ali ('the Shah') and the Imams, of whom the monarchs were representatives if not incarnations; this produced, thirdly, keen hatred and opposition towards the Sunni Ottomans, archenemies of Shi'i Safavid Iran (replacing the Safavid order's initial targets of *jehad*, the Caucasian Christians). Just as a declaration of *shahisevani* by a tribal chieftain implied that he regarded it as a religious and moral duty to follow his sovereign the Shah, without hope of reward, so also the authority of this chieftain over his own followers would depend largely on the same quality of moral duty, reinforced by stronger charismatic principles when he (or the Shah) also proved particularly pious or successful militarily. Doubtless adherence to such moral principles also depended to a great extent on how far the Shah, or the chief, ensured the continuing flow of material benefits to his respective followers.

Tribal groups of the region, Shahsevan or other, appear to have provided military contingents, such as the Shahsevan garrison mentioned by Evliya Chelebi in Baku in 1647, or the Shahsevan *qorchi* (apparently from Azarbaijan) campaigning in Khorasan in the same year, or the Afshar and Shamlu Shahsevan *qorchi* stationed in Darband in 1668, or the Shahsevan Ajirli *qorchi* at Shaki and Shirvan in 1704.[1]

The *qorchi* military organization into centuries, with corresponding leadership by *onbashı* (captain of ten) and *yüzbashı* (of hundred) officers (such as Soleiman Bey Ajirli Shahsevan in 1704), may have been more generalized: Gärber reports of the 'Arab nomads in Moghan in 1728 that they were organized in units of one hundred families headed by elected chiefs called *yüzbashı*.[2] Perhaps these were the *taifa* and their chiefs, the *Bey*s of more recent years. But we do not hear of any larger units of tribal organization, and only occasional mentions of a khan such as Mansur Moghani, and 'Ali-qoli Shahsevan.

By the early eighteenth century, both the military organization of the nomads and the unifying symbolic power of the concept of *shahisevani* are likely to have lost their effectiveness. Not once, during the hundred years between the presumed occupation of the region by these tribes (early seventeenth century?) and the beginning of the Russian and Ottoman threat, was any of the three *shahisevani* principles seriously called into question. The Safavid dynasty seemed safely in control, Shi'ism was the unchallenged state religion, and the Ottomans, after the Treaty of Zohab, were held in the west, far beyond the ken of the nomads of Moghan and Ardabil. Indeed, despite the references to military organization, service and leadership, there was no call in the whole period for the tribes to unite for military purposes. Minorsky, pursuing his conception of the Shahsevan (sc. Qızılbash) as a religious party of extremist Sufis, remarks: 'About the end of the seventeenth century the former Shahi-sevans served only decorative ends and were relegated to their *tauhid-khana* where they practised their *dhikr*.'[3] Conceivably the nomads near Ardabil were influenced by the anti-Sunni and anti-Sufi revival of Shi'a orthodoxy which took place in Iran at the end of the seventeenth century.[4]

---

[1] Chapter Four; Vahid Qazvini (1951: 109).   [2] Gärber (1760: 146–7).
[3] Minorsky (1964: 258, note 32).   [4] Lockhart (1958: 70f.); cf. Arjomand (1984).

Shah 'Abbas made sure to reward his *shahisevan* followers, like all his military forces, materially. Chiefs might be given grants of *tiyul* (temporary right to collect revenue for specific lands) or, in the case of pastoral nomads, summer and winter pastures as their *olka/ölgä* (territory). The evidence concerning such grants of land in Moghan and Ardabil in Shah 'Abbas' time is thin. As mentioned earlier, much land in these districts was held by Safavid relatives of the Sheikhavand and Zahedi families, or was endowment (*vaqf*) of the shrine.[5] In 1637–8, Olearius noted that the shrine collected rent from local Turkish and 'Arab nomads for the use of the rich grazing lands of the vicinity, including those of Moghan and half those of Khalkhal, Garm-Rud and Hasht-Rud, while the farmlands were probably still largely in the control of powerful local families.[6]

Shah 'Abbas I and his successors increasingly transferred land from state (*divani*) to Crown (*khasseh*) administration, in order both to weaken the Qızılbash leaders (who had held *tiyul* grants and governorships in state lands) and to increase royal revenues. This happened to Gilan and Astara in Shah 'Abbas' time, and in 1656–7 to Ardabil. In 1647 Nazar 'Ali Khan Söklan Dulqadır was governor of Ardabil, but in 1657 he was dismissed by Shah 'Abbas II for 'unworthy conduct, the complaints of the peasants, embezzlement of the Ardabil *vaqf* revenues'; he was imprisoned and his property sequestered; his *tiyuls* were transferred to Mortaza-qoli Khan Bijarlu (Beydili? Ajirli?) Shamlu, former *qorchibashı*; and the district was removed from the state domains (*divani*) and placed under direct control of the Crown administration (as *khasseh*).[7] There is no indication of what lands were then included in the Ardabil district (did they include Moghan and any districts north of the Kor and Aras?), when they had become *divani*, or how long they remained in the *khasseh*. After 'Abbas II, the process was often reversed, 'as the threat of war once more necessitated the appointment of (Qizilbash) governors and these were naturally expected to raise troops.'[8]

One effect of the transfer of land out of Qızılbash control into the Crown domain was that tribal troops were increasingly paid individually (rather than through their amirs), as with the salaries for the several Afshar and Shamlu Shahsevan '*qorchi*' mentioned in the early eighteenth-century documents cited in Chapter Four, who appear to be low-ranking officers at most.

Around 1700, Moghan and Tabriz and some other districts of Azarbaijan were entrusted to the *sepahsalar*, the most important military official after the *qorchibashı*, who was *inter alia* the chief (*rish-safid*) of all

---

[5] Fragner (1975b: document 2).   [6] Olearius (1669: 177, 180).
[7] Vahid Qazvini (1951: 109, 216).   [8] Fragner (1986: 523).

the tribes of Iran. According to the *Tazkerat al-Moluk*, written about 1726, the governor-general of Azarbaijan controlled Meshkin and the irrigated parts (*anhar*) of Moghan, but Ardabil appears neither among the *divani* districts in his control, nor among the *khasseh* domains.[9] In 1726, of course, Ottomans occupied most of Azarbaijan, including Meshkin and much of Ardabil and Moghan, appointing their own governors.

By the end of the eighteenth century, after many interruptions, pasture dues for Moghan were collected by the landed khans of Talesh; possibly this had been the case since Safavid times. The pastures of Moghan, whatever the traditions of the noble tribes of the Shahsevan claim, may well have been owned, not by nomads, but by settled landowners, or the Crown.

I have come across no further information on the land tenure and administration of the region during the seventeenth century. Towards the end of Safavid rule, districts like Ardabil, Meshkin, Qara-Dagh, Qara-Bagh, Shirvan, Talesh, Sarab and Garm-Rud were probably administered from urban bases by governors who, if they had roots in tribal and nomadic society, were now alienated from them and 'citified', in conformity with Ibn Khaldun's theory of the circulation of tribal elites. In such a situation, as with city–nomad relations everywhere, district officials had a strong interest in preventing the emergence of unity among the local tribal groups, and would indeed foster any divisions and oppositions among them.

Before the eighteenth century, there is an almost complete lack of contemporary information on the economic organization of the nomads or of the districts in which they ranged. Chardin mentions that the Turkoman nomads reared sheep for sale, implying an economy similar to that of the Shahsevan today, but differing from that of some of the nomads of southern Iran, who sell skins and milk products rather than livestock for slaughter.[10] In any case the nomads were, it is fair to assume, economically dependent on access to markets, for sale of their stock or pastoral produce, and for purchase of various essential items, especially grain and foodstuffs which they did not produce themselves. In addition, then as in both earlier and more recent times, nomad chiefs would have sought to supplement the insecure natural foundations of their pastoral economy by gaining control not only of agricultural production but also of trade routes passing near or through their lands, and, when conditions permitted, of the market centres of the region.

For nomads in Moghan the nearest market centre would have been the

[9] Röhrborn (1966: ch.3); Danesh-Pazhuh (1968–9, II: 80); Minorsky (1943: 101).
[10] Chardin (1811, V: 300), Barth (1961); cf. Bradburd (1990).

town of Salyan; a little further away were the city of Shamakhı and the town of Lankaran. To the south were Ardabil and Sarab, both surrounded by mountain rangelands, as was the town of Ahar, which was then, as it has been ever since, within the sphere of the tribes of Qara-Dagh. The best agricultural lands were attached to Ardabil and the neighbouring district of Meshkin, which as we have seen had no urban centre but lay between Ahar and Ardabil.

In those times, as later, state authorities would have needed large and determined forces to find and subdue rebellious nomads, as we saw with the Ottomans in the 1720s. Despite the comparative accessibility of their habitat, in the southern uplands the nomads would have been able to escape control by taking refuge in the mountains, while nomads in Moghan could equally have found refuge in the steppe. They would have been most vulnerable on their spring and autumn migrations.

Scattered references to the tribal population of Moghan and Ardabil in late Safavid times suggest a picture of a rather insignificant group of tribal fragments occupying a remote, but not frontier, territory; a highly favourable pastoral habitat where, in times of peace and non-interference such as were enjoyed for a century before 1725, human and animal populations would have grown steadily, both naturally and by immigration, to a point of substantial overcrowding, suffering only occasional setbacks due to climatic disasters or epidemics. At the same time, the transfer of the Ardabil district to the *khasseh* Crown domain, to judge from the effects of such moves elsewhere at the time, would have led to increased oppression, the Shah's officials being even less interested in the welfare of the rural populace than the former provincial governors had been.[11]

So, by the early eighteenth century, I suggest, the tribes of Moghan and Ardabil were overcrowded, disunited, and oppressed. As evidence, one might cite observations by travellers such as Struys (in 1671) and de Bruin (in 1703 and 1707) on the prevalence of fearsome robbers in Moghan, the mass flight of peasants from the *vaqf* villages of the Ardabil shrine which was the subject of a 1714 document issued by Shah Soltan Hosein, and the rebellion of the people of Moghan in 1717 against the khan imposed on them by the government.[12] At another period, a strong monarch such as 'Abbas I or Nader Shah would have dealt with this situation by removing troublesome elements and resettling them elsewhere, but Iran was not then ruled by such a monarch and no such measures

[11] See Chardin (1811, V: 250–4). Roemer (1986: 295) argues that in *khasseh* lands, though officials were under fewer constraints in exploiting the peasants, the latter often complained effectively to the Shah.
[12] Struys (1681: 276–8); de Bruin (1759, IV: 13–14; V: 206–9); Fragner (1975b: document 5); Abdurakhmanov (1964: 17).

were taken. Rather, local officials probably attempted to exploit the disorder.

These factors – absence of an external threat; consequent disappearance of the need for military unity; overcrowding of pastures; and increased administrative oppression – would have transformed the social, economic and political organization of the tribes. The meagre relevant evidence suggests something along the lines of processes known to have occurred in similar conditions two centuries later.[13]

If we can extrapolate back from more recent studies, basic nomadic communities were probably of two kinds: first, the egalitarian pastoral camp (*oba, jamahat*) of twenty to thirty families (150–200 individuals) in daily contact, with a core of members of a patrilineage (*göbäk*), named after the eponymous ancestor of the lineage, and led by an elder (*aqsaqal*); secondly, the permanent union of several such camp communities into a larger named community of a few hundred families – the tribe (*taifa*) under a hereditary chief (*bey*). Almost all marriages were within the tribe, which maintained notions of common origins (perhaps as a named patriclan – *boy, ojaq*) and had its jealously guarded pastures, controlled by the chief.[14]

In conditions of insecurity and disorder, and so as to deal with a predatory government, several tribes would gather around a chief who had demonstrated his ability to offer protection and security. Such a gathering of a thousand or more families constituted an *el*, probably bearing the name of the tribe of the chief, who might acquire the title of *khan*, but it was not sufficiently large or institutionalized to warrant terming it a 'confederacy'; a better term, I suggest, is 'tribal cluster'. The khan (and on a smaller scale, the chief of a tribe) would have a retinue of servants and armed henchmen, the latter including both levies from the dependent tribes and refugees and outlaws from elsewhere; he might be a landowner, with his main residence in a village or even in town; he would certainly own farmlands in the vicinity of the pastures and would attempt to control any trade routes passing through or near by.

While tribes were remarkably stable and long-lasting groups, a tribal cluster's composition, unity and continuity would depend on the success of the khan in ensuring both security and access to resources for dependent tribes in the cluster. Neighbouring khans would be in constant competition for followers and for control of pastures, farmland and trade routes, and would make temporary alliances with more distant chiefs in order to prosecute feuds against intervening mutual enemies. Khans

---

[13] See Chapters Nine to Twelve below.
[14] See Tapper (1979a) and (1979b), and Chapter Fourteen below.

would also compete for the favours of government officials, but a weak administration, fearful of the emergence of a strong, unified tribal confederacy, would, as I have suggested, encourage local rivalries and alliances.

The half-dozen or more named groups that we encounter in the early eighteenth-century sources (especially Inallu, Beydili, Ajirli, Afshar, Takleh, Moghanlu, Shaqaqi) were probably not 'tribes' (*taifa*) as I have just defined them, so much as 'tribal clusters' (*el*). We know nothing of their size or composition – it would be unwise to accept figures mentioned by sources such as Chelebizadeh – but to judge from their number and the carrying capacity of the local pastures in later years, they probably each contained 1,000–2,000 families. That some of these groups or their chiefs (Afshar, Beydili, Ajirli, Inallu at least) also bore the name Shahsevan, and that 'the Shahsevan' are sometimes referred to separately, may indicate a union or 'coalition' of these groups, at a greater level than the 'cluster'. The basis of this coalition, other than local territorial and political patterns, could have been some claim to common origins as *shahisevan* a century earlier.

The Shaqaqi seem to have been a more substantial group than the rest, and possibly constituted a coalition or even a confederacy of their own, as they certainly did later in the century. The Moghani may have been another coalition: they too were a group of some substance, with numerous chiefs mentioned as active in the early eighteenth century.

Despite the insecure times, some nomads may have settled, especially in Moghan. Here, apart from the ancient canal system restored by Timur in 1401, which may or may not still have been operating, in 1700 the local khan ordered the construction of a new canal from the Aras; and by the 1720s the irrigated lands (*anhar*) of Moghan must have been of some extent, to judge from the revenue assessment recorded in the *Tazkerat al-Moluk*.[15] Canals irrigated a considerable area by the lower Aras and Kor (the Moghan, Shirvan and Qara-Bagh steppes) at least until 1733, but Nader Shah probably destroyed them shortly after; so says Monteith, who observed the remains of some of these canals in spring 1829. One can see traces of them today in Iranian Moghan, alongside the ruins of mediaeval cities (such as Ultan/Altun/Vartan) that must have thrived on them, all somewhat dwarfing late twentieth-century irrigation schemes. Ironically, local people know Nader Shah as their builder, not their destroyer.[16]

Possibly the Moghani were not even nomads at all, but farmers settled

[15] Minorsky (1943: 165); de Bruin (1759, IV: 12).
[16] Lerch (1769: 18–20); Monteith (1833: 30) describes Altun/Ultan, and also Timur's canal (now known as Nader's Canal) from near Aslanduz at the mouth of the Qara-Su; Abbott (in Amanat 1983: 228) also mentions Altun. See also Minorsky (1936) and (1938).

in the irrigated lands, who took to pastoral nomadism only in the troubled times of the 1720s, then had no other choice after Nader destroyed the canals. Perhaps only then (if they were indeed Kurds by origin) did they adopt the Turkic language and a Turkic name (Moghanlu as opposed to Moghani) alongside their Shahsevan fellows.

Formation of the Shahsevan confederacy

Whatever the processes that may have produced the Shahsevan coalition, its unity and the relevance of the values implied in the name were soon put to the test. Suddenly the Safavid monarchy was tottering; Sunni Ottoman power penetrated dangerously close to the Moghan–Ardabil region, while Russian expansion towards the southern Caspian shores renewed the Christian factor in the equation.[17] How would local tribes – or their chiefs, at least – react?

For those who bore the name Shahsevan, the issue would seem to have been clear: the main threat and arch-enemy was (as before) Sunnism and the Ottoman Empire. The Shi'i Safavid monarchy had allied itself with the Christian Russians, so Shahsevan chiefs too had a clear duty to side with them, and an interest in defending their pastures and farmlands in Moghan and Ardabil against the Ottomans. Other groups, whether nomads or settled farmers, though interested in protecting their lands, would not be quite so committed to either side. Meanwhile, the problems of the Safavid Shah Tahmasp II, routed from the south by Sunni Afghan invaders, could not have inspired further assistance from the tribes of Moghan and Ardabil, who were already desperately engaged with the enemy on their own territory. Krusinski's testimony on the decay of the 'reserve militia' by 1722 could well have applied to the nomad tribes of this region.

In fact, Shahsevan, Shaqaqi and Moghani seem to have resisted the Ottomans strongly; they attempted to keep them out of the Safavid shrine city of Ardabil, and joined an uprising led by a locally based Safavid pretender. They joined Armenian Christian guerrillas, and eventually, when no alternative was left to them, the Shahsevan and Moghani abandoned pasturelands in western Moghan and moved east to take refuge with the Russians at Salyan, while the Shaqaqi, having had their homes in Meshkin destroyed by the Ottomans, were forced to surrender, as were, soon after, the Inallu Shahsevan and Afshar.

Shortly after this cataclysm, Nader Afshar recovered Ardabil and

---

[17] This was the first organized Christian military threat for a century; Christian Cossack raiders and Russian traders had been known for some time in Shirvan and on the Caspian.

Moghan, nominally for the Safavids, and probably removed Inallu, Afshar and Shaqaqi groups to the frontiers of Khorasan. He thus revived Shah 'Abbas' tribal policy, for various reasons. First, it must be remembered that in Iran, like other Middle Eastern states until modern times, rulers at any level were interested in territory only if they could control a population who might exploit it and provide a source of revenue and manpower; this was a major rationale of both the 'forced migration' and the 'scorched earth' policies of Shah 'Abbas and Nader Shah.

Perhaps the most important reason for Nader's policy of forcible movement of populations to Khorasan was to concentrate 'tribespeople of good fighting qualities' there to garrison his metropolitan province.[18] Further, the migrants were to provide supplies for the regular armies that were maintained or campaigning there. But the policy would also have served to put an end to disorders due to overcrowding and overgrazing in the original lands of the tribes in question – Perry holds that 'Nadir's prime motive was to fragment recalcitrant tribes, particularly in Azarbaijan and the central Zagros, by sending large numbers of them where he could keep them under surveillance'.[19]

The particular choice of the Shaqaqi, Inallu and Afshar for exile may thus have been a punishment for abandoning the Safavid cause in 1729. It could, however, have been related to Nader's policy of 'building up a non-Persian (and non-Shi'a) army upon which he could wholly depend under any circumstances',[20] particularly in the event of a final trial of strength with Tahmasp or any other Safavid elements. The Shaqaqi were Kurdish, and possibly still Sunni, while the Inallu and Afshar were Turks like himself and had demonstrated, by their submission to the Ottomans, a willingness at least to compromise with Sunnism.

Inallu and Afshar, however, had already borne the name Shahsevan; and even though, by surrendering to the Ottomans, they had abandoned the values the name represented, they became known by it later when they had settled in the present lands between Zanjan and Tehran. Perhaps their spell of exile in Khorasan encouraged them to manipulate the symbolism in this name among new neighbours who may have known little of their actions in 1729. The Shaqaqi, on the other hand, who had also submitted to the Ottomans but did return to Azarbaijan, never did bear the name Shahsevan, and would have had no credible excuse for pretending to it.

Both tribal clusters and larger coalitions were probably groups of mixed and shifting composition, though some continuity in the leader-

---

[18] Lockhart (1938: 54).   [19] Perry (1975: 209); cf. Morgan (1988: 87).
[20] Lockhart (1938: 54).

ship must be reflected in the continuity of group names. If we chart the presumed relations of common origins between the named groups, we find one main set (Inallu, Beydili, Ajirli) related as Shahsevan and former Shamlu; a second set (Afshar, Takleh, Delaqarda) as other Qızılbash; and a third (Shaqaqi, Moghani) as presumed Kurds. It may be significant, and indicative of the way the coalitions had formed, that one group from each set (Inallu, Afshar, Shaqaqi) is recorded as surrendering to the Ottomans and was exiled; the others remained and were eventually united in the Shahsevan confederacy. Such a coalition pattern, which probably also had a territorial dimension, conforms to the 'anti-segmentary', chessboard model common elsewhere;[21] it may also reflect the success of government policies of 'divide and rule'.

Those groups which were left − Shahsevan (Beydili, Ajirli), Takleh, Delaqarda, Moghani and perhaps others − who really had acted consistently with the values of *shahisevani*, now faced a dilemma, for Nader, though from a tribe once as strong as themselves in support of the Safavids, was endeavouring to modify their Shi'a religion, and had moreover imprisoned the Safavid Shah Tahmasp II. The evidence, or perhaps the lack of it, indicates that the Shahsevan tribes at first avoided Nader, then, like the departed Inallu, Afshar and Shaqaqi, decided to compromise in order to maintain their pastures. Only the Moghani continued to resist, fled northwards, and apparently suffered severely as a result.

Like other strong rulers, and in conformity with his policy elsewhere, Nader now it seems united the tribal groups in Moghan and Ardabil as the Shahsevan confederacy (*el*); as chief over them he appointed Badr Khan Sarı-Khan-Beyli Afshar, possibly the son of landowner 'Ali-qoli Khan, who was earlier recorded under the name Shahsevan. Whatever his origins or connections with the tribespeople, Badr Khan was presumably given the post as a reward for military services. There is no indication that he was made governor of Ardabil.

To judge from present tribal names that appear in eighteenth-century sources, the early Shahsevan confederacy included fragments of various former Qızılbash groups: Ajirli and Beydili (from Shamlu), Takleh/Tekelu, and whatever Afshar elements (Sarvanlar?) were associated with the Sarı-Khan-Beyli leadership and eventually formed the 'noble' tribes, as described in Chapter Nine. The new confederacy was, we may surmise, joined sooner or later by Qaralar, Sheikhli, Hajji-Khojalu/Hajji-Qazili, Qahraman-Beyli/Qaramanlu and remnants of the Moghani/lu, though sources as late as the nineteenth century still on occasion refer to Moghanlu − and also Beydili, Takleh and perhaps Ajirli −

---

[21] Cf. Chapter One, and below.

alongside but apparently distinct from the Shahsevan of the region,[22] while other groups with the same names continued to nomadize independently in Shirvan or elsewhere to the north in the nineteenth century. Delaqarda/Delaqadar, who fought alongside Shahsevan and Takleh against the Ottomans in 1726, and who probably originate from the Qızılbash Dulqadır, were mentioned to me in the 1960s as among the settled Shahsevan of Ardabil, having once wintered in Ojarud in southeastern Moghan. Their affiliation to the Shahsevan was very late; possibly they never fully assimilated. In the early twentieth century Fortescue mentioned a small tribe of this name in Tarom to the south of Khalkhal.[23]

Significantly, perhaps, several of these named groups were among the largest in the earliest census of individual Shahsevan tribes, over a century later (1870). Apart from the 'noble' tribes, the largest of the 'commoner' tribes were the following: Ajirli (700 families), Beydili, Takleh and Hajji-Khojalu (600 each). The last of these was probably originally associated with the Beydili, Ajirli and Inallu in the Shamlu confederacy.[24]

In other words, to conclude, it was probably not Shah 'Abbas but Nader Shah who first organized the Shahsevan 'tribe'. As Oberling remarks, 'Persian tribesmen tend to ascribe all past tribal movements to Shah 'Abbas or Nadir Shah, the only two names of former rulers with which they are familiar',[25] but such ignorance is unlikely on the part of tribal chiefs of the nineteenth century, from whom the traditions published by Radde and Markov must have been recorded. The error in the 'official history' of the Shahsevan, for which Malcolm must be blamed, remains that of the historians.

Consolidation and fission of the confederacy

In the second half of the eighteenth century, members of Badr Khan's family, the Sarı-Khan-Beyli, controlled the city of Ardabil and presumably the nomad population of the region, though at some stage the family, the tribes and the territory divided into two. Both divisions, through their chiefs, became involved in the complex network of alliance, opposition and intrigue that occupied the khanates and tribes of Azarbaijan and Transcaucasia during the fifty years between the death of Nader Shah and the establishment of the Qajars.

Nader's reign had left much of Iran, particularly Azarbaijan and the northwest, drastically depopulated. Many groups fled beyond the frontiers or into mountain fastnesses to escape transportion, slaughter

---

[22] See, for example, Dupré (1819, II: 461); Eichwald (1834, I pt 2: 589); Donboli (1972: 22).   [23] Fortescue (1922: 322); see also Oberling (1964a: 28).
[24] Ogranovich (1870); see Appendix Two and Chapter Three.   [25] Oberling (1960: 74n.).

and the ravages and requisitions of his campaigns. Given the devastation of the area, and the rapid changes of control which the people of the territory experienced – to a degree probably not found in any other part of Iran during the period – the usual characterization of the eighteenth century as a 'time of troubles' would seem more appropriate than Ricks' view of it as one of 'little disruption of the social strata of towns and villages'.[26]

For ten years after Nader's death we hear nothing of the nomad tribes of Moghan and Ardabil. Various exiles began to return to Azarbaijan, though it was not until Karim Khan came to power that serious attempts were made to restore the country's population, and the region must have remained for some time comparatively empty and its resources under-exploited. In the absence of information, we must assume that, as else-where, the chiefs in the Ardabil district would have been largely preoccupied with consolidating their positions and attracting followers to their respective territories.

Khans of neighbouring districts were concerned with their own affairs and with other frontiers. Most likely to have affected the Shahsevan at first was blind Kazem Khan of Qara-Dagh, who ventured into the wider sphere of conflicts among the Afshars and Azad Khan Ghilji, and may well have been a dominating influence among his local neighbours. In Qara-Bagh, however, Panah Khan Javanshir was establishing his own position, building his new stronghold at Shusheh, and dealing with rivals to the north and west. The Shirvan khanate was unsettled for many years before eventually succumbing to the expanding power of Qobbeh in the north. Qobbeh's first move south was not until 1757, when the khan managed to regain Salyan and placed a garrison there. Qara Khan of Talesh may already have controlled Moghan, receiving rent from the nomads, but otherwise never displayed any ambitions to expand west-wards into the Ardabil region, unlike his neighbour Hedayat Khan of Gilan. To the south, the upland valleys of Khalkhal, Sarab and Mianeh may have remained empty of nomads until the return of the Shaqaqi in the late 1750s.

External pressures on the nomad tribes of Moghan and Ardabil were thus once again light. At the same time, the absence of pressure on their own resources must have allowed them a decade of expansion and prosperity, and Badr Khan's family would have been able to consolidate their leadership of the new confederacy.

Only in 1757 did things begin to change. In that year, Mohammad Hasan Khan Qajar swept through the region, then Panah Khan of Qara-

[26] Ricks (1973: 116).

Bagh invaded and placed a governor in Ardabil, while to the north Salyan fell to the khan of Qobbeh. A few years later Karim Khan Zand conquered Azarbaijan.

To deal with the tribes, Karim Khan did not continue Nader's policy of transportation, but rather made the khans responsible for their followers, by appointing them as chiefs or district governors, and by taking hostages from their families. Some time after Karim Khan left Ardabil in 1763, he appointed Nazar 'Ali Khan Shahsevan governor of the town and (presumably) chief of the local tribes – it is even conceivable, in the absence of a contemporary source for Badr Khan's appointment, that it was neither Shah 'Abbas nor Nader Shah but Karim Khan Zand who 'created' the Shahsevan confederacy by giving the governorship of Ardabil to Nazar 'Ali Khan, though the date for this remains unknown.[27]

Karim Khan's sovereignty over much of Transcaucasia was nominal. During his reign the area experienced conditions of 'neglect, anarchy and economic stagnation'[28] but political calm, compared with the years before and after. There was an expectation that taxes would be collected and order maintained, but local chiefs were in effect autonomous; this was probably the case in those districts from which Karim Khan took hostages (Qara-Bagh, Erevan, Ganjeh, Nakhchevan and the Azarbaijani khanates south of the Aras), and certainly in those from which he did not, especially the Georgian kingdoms and the Qobbeh khanate and its dependencies.[29]

The political organization of Ardabil and the Shahsevan tribes no doubt conformed with the pattern for the Caucasian khanates as sketched by Atkin. The khan had broad military and judicial powers, possibly subject to consultation with a council of elders and mullahs, and liable to popular revolt and emigration if traditional norms were violated. He collected revenue from cultivators, pastoralists and other exploiters of his territory, as well as commercial and other taxes. Khans had their own retinues of courtiers, servants and guards, and all these people were probably exempt from taxes, as were any tribesmen who fought for the chiefs.[30] The headquarters of the khanate was a substantial palace in the city, with offices for different branches of the administration, and barracks for the guards. Authority was delegated to beys, who might be members of the khan's family, and to a hierarchy of public officials. As the khans emulated the court administration and style of life of a state ruler, so subordinate beys, on a far more modest scale, would imitate those of

---

[27] Cf. Perry (1979: 224f.) for other such appointments of tribal leaders by Karim Khan.
[28] Perry (1979: 250).
[29] Perry (1979: 212f.); Lambton (1977: 126); Atkin (1980: 10–21).
[30] Cf. Atkin (1980: 12f.).

the khan. The economy and society of the ordinary pastoral nomads were probably not radically different from what was recorded a century later by Russian observers, as will be described in Chapter Nine.

At some time in the second half of the eighteenth century, the new Shahsevan confederacy divided into two. Dälili is at pains to insist that, according to his 1828 source, the Shahsevan did not divide until the nineteenth century and that the senior division was that of Ardabil. Markov's and Radde's accounts, dating from half a century later, state that the confederacy divided in the generation after Badr Khan, and that the Meshkin khan drove out the khan and people of Ardabil. Part of the discrepancy may be explained simply by supposing Dälili's source to be information recorded from Ardabil informants, and the others from Meshkin ones.

To evaluate which version is more likely, we should recall that Ardabil, even in this period of economic stagnation and political disorder, was a city of continuing commercial and religious importance, control of which would have been both a source and an indication of power; while there was at this time no town or trade centre of any size in the Meshkin district at all. Until the twentieth century the Meshkin Shahsevan were the only group of tribes in the area without an urban centre: the Shaqaqi controlled Sarab and Mianeh; the Qara-Daghis had a centre at Ahar; the Javanshir of Qara-Bagh were based at Shusheh, the tribes of Shirvan at Shamakhı and Salyan, and those of Talesh at Lankaran.

Here we have, in effect, a classic illustration of Ibn Khaldun's centre–periphery model. The Ardabil khans acquired their urban base, and by the time they lost control of it in 1808 they had already become used to 'civilized' ways and alienated from their nomadic roots. Many of their followers settled in or around the city. Not long after the Treaty of Torkman–Chai (1828) the khans lost control of their nomad followers too. Meanwhile the Meshkin group remained relatively a 'backwoods' nomadic people, with a 'desert culture', tribal solidarity and organization. After the Ardabil khans fell from power, the Meshkin chiefs came to dominate the nomad tribes.[31]

Dälili's account of the seniority of the Ardabil khans seems more credible, probably originating from them when they were still dominant; fifty years later they had given place to the Meshkin khans from whom Markov's and Radde's reports were presumably drawn. The original division of the confederacy is more likely to have been a matter of the secession or expulsion of the Meshkin group from Ardabil. However, this division must have occurred – or at least begun – before the end of the

[31] See Tapper (1983b: 62f.).

eighteenth century, since chiefs of the two divisions are already named by the 1790s.

Meanwhile, with the renewed political activity after Karim Khan's death, distinct patterns of opposition and alliance emerged among the khanates of the area. In the early eighteenth century, I have suggested, the weak late-Safavid administration sought to prevent the formation of local tribal coalitions and confederacies, so that the major political units were those I have termed tribes and tribal clusters, under petty khans at most. The stronger rulers Nader Shah and Karim Khan, on the other hand, appointed local khans and formed or fostered their confederacies, so that these much larger and more powerful groups were the main units of local opposition and alliance by the end of the century. As before, there was a distinct tendency for each unit to be opposed to its neighbours and allied with more distant ones, resulting in an overall chequer-board pattern.

The pattern was not, however, rigid or unchanging. Apart from changes of allegiance by component tribal groups in each khanate or confederacy, which must have occurred but of which we have no information, several of the khans had their own domestic opposition – close relatives, ousted rivals or dissatisfied subjects – who attempted intrigue with neighbouring khans. For example, Mehr 'Ali Bey, younger brother of Ebrahim Khalil Khan of Qara-Bagh, took refuge in Shirvan and sought the help of Fath 'Ali Khan of Qobbeh. We also heard earlier of elders of Tabriz and Ardabil seeking support from Fath 'Ali Khan against their khans. Other local groups sought Karim Khan's support against Fath 'Ali Khan. Perhaps some such intrigue was involved in the separation of the Meshkin from the Ardabil Shahsevan.

Further, at different times Fath 'Ali Khan of Qobbeh, Ebrahim Khalil Khan of Qara-Bagh, and 'Ali Khan Shaqaqi and his son Sadeq Khan, sought a wider hegemony and led alliances of khans; the Shahsevan chiefs do not appear to have had such ambitions themselves. The only ideology that might have united all or most of these khanates was Islam, and Shi'ism in particular. This undoubtedly was an important and necessary support to the legitimacy of any established ruler, especially those who claimed to be ruling for the Safavids (as did Karim Khan) or in succession to them (as did the Qajars),[32] but in practice religious claims were not decisive in unifying the khanates, either behind any aspirant to the Iranian throne[33] or even against the Russians. Rather, at this period both ambitious local khans and outside powers provoked divided responses,

[32] Perry (1971) and (1979: 214f.); Lambton (1977: 119).
[33] Cf. Ebrahim Khalil Khan's reputed refusal of the offer of all the khans of Azarbaijan (Qara-Baghi 1959: 130); and Fath 'Ali Khan's Safavid pretender in 1784.

and alignments reflected less ideological commitments than local boundary enmities between neighbours.

At the end of the eighteenth century, the most successful conqueror (Agha Mohammad Khan Qajar) made a firm alliance with one bloc of allies, and used them to defeat the other. Thus, he received support from the khans of Khoi, Qara-Dagh, Shirvan, the Shahsevan of Ardabil, and the Shahsevan/Afshar of Zanjan and Tarom; and was opposed by their neighbours and rivals, the khans of Qara-Bagh and Talesh, the Shahsevan of Meshkin, the Shaqaqi of Sarab and Mianeh and the Turkicized Kurds of Khalkhal.[34]

Local alliances were often marked by marriage links between the khans. Marriage alliances were also used by some powerful outsiders: Karim Khan married his son to sisters of Hedayat Khan of Gilan and Najaf-qoli Khan Donboli, and was promised the daughter of Fath 'Ali Khan of Qobbeh – but he relied more on the hostage system. Agha Mohammad Qajar also took hostages, but he and his nephew Fath 'Ali Shah made a very wide range of marriage alliances, including among their affines the khans of Qara-Bagh, the Ardabil Shahsevan and the Shaqaqi. As Lambton writes,

Marriage alliances were used [by the Qajars] . . . as a means to consolidate the royal power, to cement alliances, and to terminate, or prevent, blood feuds. Qajar women were given in marriage to local tribal leaders, important members of the bureaucracy, and leading religious dignitaries, and women taken from these and others into the royal household.[35]

Badr Khan and his successors remain shadowy figures, mentioned incidentally and inaccurately in contemporary records. There are no accounts of them by travellers or chroniclers, and we are ignorant of their lives and those of the people they controlled. Where did the khans live – did they occupy the Qaramanlu palace in Ardabil? What was their relationship with the Safavid shrine? How educated were they? Did they maintain a library? What were their relations with their tribal followers, and with the townspeople of Ardabil? Presumably they maintained a 'court' there, like those of their more powerful allies of Qobbeh and Gilan, but inevitably on a smaller scale.[36] But unless and until some further documentation is unearthed, this must all remain speculation.

---

[34] See Hambly (1991a: 137). A persistence of this pattern of rivalries can be seen over a century later, at the end of the Qajar period, as will be described in Chapter Twelve.

[35] Lambton (1961: 127). The Qajar rulers were notoriously prolific: Fath 'Ali Shah had a vast number of wives and over a hundred children, see Sepehr (1958, I: 313f.). For royal marriages with tribal chiefly families, see Garthwaite (1983).

[36] See Perry (1979: 207–9) for references to the splendid court of Hedayatollah Khan of Gilan; and Abdullaev (1958) for Qobbeh.

Various earlier authors have speculated on the development of the Shahsevan tribal confederacy in the period from its supposed origins under Shah 'Abbas I until it first became the object of study in the nineteenth century. Their ideas do not take into account and are inconsistent with the eighteenth-century materials discussed here, and should be located within the nineteenth and twentieth century contexts in which they were produced. They will be discussed in Chapter Fourteen.

We must now proceed with the narrative and enter the nineteenth century. As international and imperial conflicts are fought out on their home territory, the Shahsevan of Moghan become once more crucially involved. This time the source materials are far more revealing about the economic, social and political organization of the tribes.

1. Women at a ground-loom on the slopes of Mt Savalan, July 1963

2. Camp of the chief of Geyikli tribe on the lower slopes of Savalan, before migrating north to Moghan, September 1963

3. A family on migration in Moghan, May 1966

4. Flocks and camel-train on migration in the Salavat hills, May 1966

5. The Safavid shrine in Ardabil, November 1995

6. 'Nader's mound' at Aslanduz, Moghan, November 1995

7. Chiefs of Qoja-Beyli, 'Isalu, Geyikli and Hajji-Khojalu tribes, with Amir Lashkar 'Abdollah Khan Tahmaspi and other officers, presumably in spring 1923:

Standing at the back, left to right: Ildir Bey Qoja-Beyli, Emam-'Ali Khan Qoja-Beyli, Amir Khan Qoja-Beyli (Amir-Tomar), Moharram Bey Qoja-Beyli, Esma'il Bey Qoja-Beyli, Nouruz Khan Qoja-Beyli, Ayaz Bey Qoja-Beyli, Minbashi Bey Hajji-Khojalu, 'Aleshan Khan Geyikli, Javat Khan Hajji-Khojalu, Hatam Khan Geyikli, Bahram Khan Qoja-Beyli, Hajj Faraj Geyikli, Amir Aslan 'Isalu and his brothers Musa Bey and 'Isa Bey, unknown.

Squatting are nökar of some chiefs, left to right: Amini, Ja'far-qoli Khan, unknown, Gorshad Khosroulu, Aqa-Kishi Pir-Evatlu, Amini (nökar of Bahram Khan), Mahmadeh (nökar of Nouruz Khan).

Standing in front: Abol-Qasem Khan Sartip (Brigadier), 'Abdullah Khan Amir Lashkar (General), Sarhang (Colonel) Mohammad 'Ali Khan.

8. Chief men of Geyikli and dependent tribes (Kalash, Hüsün-Hajılı, Küravazli) and their wives in the pastures, after the dress reforms, probably in the early 1930s:

Front row: men on the left inclde Esma'il Khan Hajji-Imanlu (in white coat), Agha Bey Khan-Hoseinlu. First woman on left is Sarfenaz (of Kalash; wife of Esma'il Khan). Men on the right are 'Aleshan Khan and Hatam Khan, chiefs of Geyikli; to their left are Gila Khanom (wife of 'Aleshan) and Kabi Khanom (in white; wife of Hatam Khan, and mother of 'Ali Khan). Other women unidentified.

Back row, from the left: 'Aleshan Hüsün-Hajılı, Gholam-Reza Khalilli, Hajji 'Ali Hüsün-Hajılı, Karbala'i Gha'eb Ramazanlu, 'Abdollah Kalash. Then unknowns until Badr Khan Kalash, Agha Jan Küravazli, Rostam Beg Kalash (Küravazli?), Pasha Beg Hüsün-Hajılı, Hajji Agha Mirza'i.

9. Memorial to the martyrs of 21 Azar 1324 (December 1945), in the grounds of the shrine at Meshkin-Shahr, September 1993. The names of the martyrs on the memorial are: District-governor 'Abbas-qoli Arbab-zadeh; Captain Asadollah Adib-Amini; Captain Qasem Ardabili; First Lieutenant Qeiz-'Ali Sho'eifi; First Lieutenant Saduqi; Warrant Officer 'Ali Hushyar.

Part III

The Shahsevan tribes in the Great Game

'Shahsevan' is a Turkish word, which means 'lover of the Shah'; the
measure of their Shah-love in the past was that, whenever the central
state was strong enough, they were obedient servants of the state and the
Shah, otherwise they brought ceaseless unrest by their plundering . . .'

Baba Safari, *Ardabil dar Gozargah-e Tarikh*, p. 160.

Russia's Caucasian frontier with Iran was in many ways as crucial an
arena of the nineteenth-century Great Game as British India's frontier
with Afghanistan. Both were of considerable strategic importance, and
were crossed by major Asian trade routes. The main differences were in
the nature of the terrain and the population. While the mountain ranges
of the North-West Frontier of India were of marginal agricultural value,
rugged, remote and defensible, Transcaucasia included some of the most
fertile agricultural lands of the area and for this reason, as well as its
comparative accessibility, could not provide so remote and defensible a
refuge where tribal populations could flaunt their political autonomy in
the face of the competing states and empires.

The two Russo–Iranian wars of the early nineteenth century raged
across Shahsevan territory and resulted in the conquest of the best part of
their winter quarters in Moghan by Russia. Chapter Eight narrates the
main events leading to this turning point in Shahsevan history, laying
stress on the role which the tribes and chiefs of Moghan are known to
have played during the campaigns, and on the movements of tribes southwards at the end.

The mid-nineteenth century is the first period for which there is any
detailed information on Shahsevan tribal society. Chapter Nine examines
what is known of Shahsevan culture, economy and political organization
at the time, in the context of changing economic and social conditions in
the region, settlement among the nomads, and the diminishing role of the
khans. The main sources are the reports of Russian officials. As a result of
the Russian conquest of Moghan, most of the Ardabil tribes settled, like
their khans. The Meshkin khans too established settled bases and in their
turn lost overall control of the nomadic tribes, which began to realign
behind new leaders who were better able and more willing to take advantage of prevailing conditions. From this period dates the complex system

of grazing rights that distinguishes Shahsevan social organization in the twentieth century; while the escalating economic and political pressures on the tribespeople saw descent and delegated authority give way, as sources of economic power and political legitimacy, to more material factors of wealth and manpower.

For some decades Russia permitted the Shahsevan nomads limited access to their former pasturelands; but they failed to observe the limitations. During the latter part of the century both Iran and Russia used Shahsevan disorder to political advantage, and it was an important factor in Great Power rivalry in Iran. In this context, European commentators, especially British and Russian agents, did not hesitate to express opinions on the activities of the nomads, judging them by the standards of the modern European state: observance of territorial frontiers, security for the conduct of trade, obedience and orderly payment of taxes to central government.

The Russians wished to develop their newly acquired territories in Moghan, and for this and other more strategic reasons found Shahsevan disorder a convenient excuse for bringing moral and political pressure to bear on the Iranian government, insisting that they restrain or settle the 'lawless' nomads. Iranian government policy towards the tribes varied from virtual abdication of authority to predatory expeditions and an attempt in 1860 at wholesale settlement. This typically twentieth-century measure provoked one British consular official to an illuminating and surprisingly modern assessment of the role of the nomad tribes within the state. Chapter Ten relates these troubles on the frontier up to the inevitable final closure of Russian Moghan to the nomads in 1884.

8   The Russian wars and the loss of Moghan

The Russian conquest of eastern Transcaucasia

Fath 'Ali Shah Qajar was occupied until 1803 in dealing with internal opposition, but he maintained his uncle's policy of regarding Georgia and the other Caucasian districts as part of Iran, while fearful of Russian aims there. Tsar Paul annexed Georgia in 1801; when he was assassinated soon after, his successor Alexander I reverted to Catherine's policy of expansion in the Caucasus. In the next two years, unsuccessful attempts were made to negotiate the submission of the khanates of Erevan, Ganjeh and Nakhchevan, all of which had substantial Christian populations.

The Russian advent in the Iranian vassal territories of eastern Transcaucasia met with a mixed reception. Atkin gives an authoritative account of the mutual misunderstandings and prejudices that characterized relations between Russians and both the Iranian authorities and the local rulers and their subjects, in the years leading to the outbreak of war. She points out at length how the khans had 'for generations . . . profited from the weaknesses of neighboring empires by asserting their own autonomy. They continued to pursue their traditional objective, then including Russia and Iran in their maneuverings.'[1]

In some parts, for example the cities of Baku, Shaki, Qobbeh and Darband, the troops were apparently welcomed by the populace, who took the opportunity to throw off the oppressive yoke of the khans. Qara-Bagh was in a desparate economic state after the ravages of the 1790s; Ebrahim Khalil Khan maintained allegiance to Fath 'Ali Shah for some years after his submission and gift of a daughter in 1797, but he was in no position to resist the Russians, and declared for them by 1805. Like him, Mir Mostafa Khan of Talesh was a longstanding opponent of the Qajar

---

[1] Atkin (1980: 66, and passim). For the early Qajar period in Transcaucasia, from Agha Mohammad Khan to the end of the Russian wars, see also Donboli (1972), Brydges (1833), Bakikhanov (1926), Qara-Baghi (1959), Jahangir Mirza (1948), Sepehr (1958), Dupré (1819), Eichwald (1834), Watson (1866), Monteith (1856), Baddeley (1908), Jävanshir (1961), Nafisi (1956), Hambly (1963, 1991a).

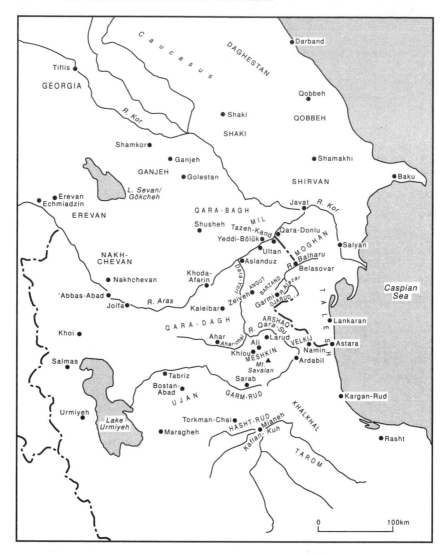

Map 5. North-West Iran, to show places mentioned in
Chapters 8–10

monarchy, and supported the Russian invasion. Their Muslim subjects,
whom they began to oppress even more than before, would have preferred a return to Iranian countrol, and had well-justified fears of Russian
intentions. A third khan, Mostafa of Shirvan, was on permanent bad
terms with his neighbour and namesake of Talesh, and was besides
involved in a blood-feud with Ebrahim Khalil of Qara-Bagh, so he was

supposedly an ally of the Qajars; but he intrigued with the Russians whenever it proved advisable to do so, in an attempt to maintain his autonomy.[2]

The nomadic tribes of the eastern Transcaucasian khanates, being relatively mobile and autonomous by virtue of their way of life, had perhaps suffered less oppression than the peasant and urban population, and were less worried about exchanging one overlord for another. If properly treated, the tribal element was a valuable source of regular cavalry for any ruler who could gain their allegiance, as well as of pastoral produce and other wealth which could be levied as tax. Once the Russian presence was recognized as permanent, the Iranian government concentrated its military efforts in the region on inducing these nomad tribes to migrate to Iranian territory and to remain subjects of the Shah.

After the rigours of the dynastic struggles of the eighteenth century, the Shahsevan had no particular ideological commitment to support the Qajar dynasty in Iran. Only seventy years before, their grandfathers had already accepted and benefited from Russian authority, a resumption of which they had no reason to dread. However, the Meshkin and Ardabil divisions were in somewhat different situations. The Ardabil group – its chiefly family at any rate – would be prepared to support the Qajars as long as they were allowed to maintain their control of the city. The Meshkin chiefs had no such investment in an urban centre, while their opposition to their Ardabil cousins, and presumably also factors like the treatment which their chief 'Ata Khan is said to have suffered at the hands of Agha Mohammad Qajar, would make them more likely to welcome the Russian return.

The occupation of the Iranian territories of the eastern Caucasus took the Russians from 1804 to 1812. For much of this time Russia was involved in the European war, and so the forces available to the commanders in the Caucasus were greatly inferior in numbers to the Iranian armies that opposed them, and the commanders themselves were often unreliable. The Iranians scored some notable military successes. The Russian troops were, however, better organized, even after the Iranians had benefited from some drilling in the European manner. A brilliant general like Kotlarevski, taking advantage of incompetent enemy leadership, had no difficulty in driving the Iranians south of the river Aras. The war ended with the battle of Aslanduz (1812), fought on the western edge of the Moghan steppe. The peace which followed recognized as Russian territory the greater and better part of the steppe, leaving the Shahsevan nomads, in theory, a choice of becoming Russian citizens or retreating south into Iran.

---

[2] Qara-Baghi (1959: 34–5); Dorn (1840: 423).

The first Russo–Iranian war

In January 1804 General Paul Tsitsianov[3] stormed the citadel of Ganjeh and renamed it Elizavetpol, making the khanate a district of Georgia, and then headed for Erevan. Fath 'Ali Shah ordered his third son, 'Abbas Mirza, the fifteen-year-old heir apparent and governor of Azarbaijan,[4] to proceed to Erevan and hold the city against the Russian invaders, and to organize Azarbaijan for defence. In June he confronted Tsitsianov's 5,000 Russians outside Erevan with an army of 20,000, including Shaqaqi and Shahsevan cavalry, the latter commanded by 'Ali-qoli Khan Shahsevan.[5] At the ensuing battle of Echmiadzin (the Armenian capital), the Iranians were eventually worsted, and the Russians besieged Erevan; but they were so harassed by the Iranian light cavalry, among whom 'Ali-qoli Khan's Shahsevan were prominent, that they were compelled to abandon the siege in September. A letter of 'Abbas Mirza relating to early successes in this campaign mentions 'Ataollah Khan Shahsevan, a leading chief (*'omdat al-khavanin al-a'zam*), alongside Mostafa Khan the governor-general of Azarbaijan, but it is not clear whether either was involved in the siege.[6]

The Iranian forces were, as was customary with them, disbanded for the winter with instructions to reassemble in the spring for a new campaign. The following year (1805), in spite of her involvement in the European conflict, Russia also managed to prosecute a full-scale war in Transcaucasia, though Tsitsianov's forces were again inferior in numbers to the Iranians'. 'Abbas Mirza's spring campaign began with an advance on Qara-Bagh to subdue Ebrahim Khalil Khan, who in May abandoned his marriage alliance with the Qajars and once more threw in his lot with the Russians. In engagements near the Khoda Afarin bridge, the Qara-Baghis and Russians were defeated and driven back to Shusheh, which the Iranians besieged. (On his way to attend the siege, Fath 'Ali Shah passed through Ardabil, presumably to be entertained by the governor, Nazar 'Ali Khan Shahsevan.) That year, however, Tsitsianov managed to retain Qara-Bagh and Ganjeh, and Russian forces landed on the Caspian coast of Iran at Anzali and Sari, though an attack on Baku was repelled.

Mostafa Khan of Shirvan at first asked for Iranian aid against Tsitsianov's advance from Ganjeh. General Pir-qoli Khan Qajar was sent,

---

[3] On his character and attitudes, see Atkin (1980: 70f.). He was known to the Iranians as Ishipokhtur (an approximation of his rank, Inspector), which in Turkish means 'his work is shit'.

[4] From Fath 'Ali Shah's time onwards this office was normally held by the heir apparent.

[5] Probably from the Khamseh Shahsevan, though just possibly son of Nazar 'Ali Khan Shahsevan of Ardabil (see Chapter Six).

[6] *Raqam* of June–July 1804 to Feghan 'Ali Khan Qajar: Anon. (1992: 92).

but on arrival in Moghan found that Mostafa Khan had begun intriguing with the Russians. Another expedition was sent during the winter to the aid of Baku, 'Abbas Mirza himself marching to Ardabil with the intention of proceeding to Moghan. However, Tsitsianov was entrapped by Hosein-qoli Khan of Baku, and assassinated (February 1806). Meanwhile, at 'Abbas Mirza's approach, Mir Mostafa Khan of Talesh had fled to join the Russians, but the heir apparent's minister, Mirza Bozorg, won him over and persuaded him to blockade the Russian force in Sari, off the Talesh coast; and Mostafa Khan of Shirvan also made promises of loyalty once more, despite his 1805 treaty of submission to the Russians.

At this point (June 1806), seeing the Russian reverses and the lenient treatment received by Mostafa of Talesh, and no doubt worried about his daughter Agha Baji, and his son Abo'l-Fath Khan (who was still in the Iranian camp), Ebrahim Khalil Khan of Qara-Bagh asked Fath 'Ali Shah's pardon, which was granted. He then requested help of 'Abbas Mirza, who had spent the winter at Ardabil, where Napoleon's agent P. A. Jaubert visited him in May 1806.[7] Abo'l-Fath Khan was sent ahead with Farajollah Khan Shahsevan to help the Qara-Baghis to oust the Russians, and 'Abbas Mirza himself followed. However, Ebrahim Khalil Khan was betrayed by his grandson to the Russian garrison at Shusheh, who, before the Iranian detachment arrived, fell on the Khan and killed him and members of his family, replacing him with another of his sons, Mahdi-qoli Khan.[8]

At the same time, Salim Khan of Shaki, brother-in-law to Ebrahim Khalil Khan, sought Iranian help to keep the Russians out, so 'Abbas Mirza, himself now approaching Shusheh, sent Farajollah Khan Shahsevan to his aid. In addition, according to Brydges' translation of Donboli:

As most of the tribes of Karabagh, after the massacre of Ibrahim Khalil Khan, had entreated permission to remove from that place and settle themselves in [Qara-Dagh], therefore Farraj Allah [Shahsevan] was ordered to conduct their movements.[9]

Farajollah Khan Shahsevan and Abo'l-Fath Khan Javanshir were resisted by one of the tribes, the Jabra'illi, who called in Russian support. The Iranian chiefs were defeated, but 'Abbas Mirza advanced into Qara-Bagh himself, and the Russians withdrew to Ganjeh, leaving a garrison in Shusheh.

---

[7] Jaubert (1821: 169f.).   [8] See Atkin (1979).
[9] Brydges (1833: 268). Brydges was apparently unfamiliar with the Shahsevan: throughout his translation he transliterates their name as 'Shahun'.

According to the published text of Donboli, this last mission was conducted not by Farajollah Khan but by 'Ataollah Khan Shahsevan, while Sepehr, also referring to Donboli, mentions both Farajollah and 'Ataollah.[10] The latter we have already met as chief of the Meshkin Shahsevan, while Farajollah Khan was father's (possibly grandfather's) brother as well as deputy (*na'eb*) of Nazar 'Ali Khan, chief of the Ardabil Shahsevan and governor of Ardabil. This Farajollah Khan must not be confused with another Farajollah Khan, who played a prominent role in events described below as 'head of military police' (*nasaqchi-bashi*), Khan of Khamseh and chief of the tribes of that region, of whom Morier was told that 'they had been the principal heroes in the war with the Russians'.[11]

The confusion of names given in different texts of Donboli is perhaps significant. The text from which Brydges made his translation was much earlier, and incomplete; 'Ata(ollah) Khan's name may have been added to the roll of Qajar generals in later texts, at a time when the Meshkin Shahsevan were in the ascendant, in an attempt to re-establish the respectability of the Meshkin khan family after 'Ata Khan's disloyalty in 1827, to be recounted below. The exclusion of Farajollah Khan, similarly, may follow from his disgrace in 1829–30.

Meanwhile the Russian army under Tsitsianov's successor, Ivan Gudovich, was campaigning in the northeast. A popular rising in Darband against Sheikh 'Ali Khan threw open the gates of that city to the Russians. 'Abbas Mirza had planned to besiege Ganjeh, but at this latest news he determined to proceed to Shirvan and Darband. The intriguer Mostafa Khan of Shirvan was hesitating in his loyalties, so after the Iranians had plundered Shirvan, Najaf-qoli Khan of Garus and Farajollah Khan Shahsevan (so Brydges, though the later texts again give 'Ataollah Khan) were sent to his stronghold at Fit-Dagh, but they were unable to persuade him to join them. At this point, disturbances on the Turkish frontier, among other considerations, forced 'Abbas Mirza to abandon his plans and to retreat from eastern Transcaucasia to Tabriz, leaving Pir-qoli Khan Qajar in Moghan,

with a detachment of the vengeance-breathing army; and with instructions to halt there, if he thought it advisable; or otherwise to remove the people of Shirwan, Rudbar, and Mughan, and proceed to Taulish.[12]

The Russians went on to 'liberate' Baku, Shirvan and Salyan and to occupy Moghan. Salim Khan of Shaki, the last of Iran's allies in the region to hold out, was in his turn deserted by his subjects and fled to

[10] Donboli (1972: 171); Sepehr (1958, I: 87).
[11] Morier (1812: 261–2). This Farajollah Khan of Khamseh is perhaps also the same Farajollah mentioned in Nikitine's Afshar chronicle as Khan of Khalkhal some twenty-five years earlier (1929: 29).   [12] Brydges (1833: 287).

Ardabil, whence he was conducted to Tabriz by Farajollah Khan Shahsevan. 'Abbas Mirza gave him and his followers permission to reside in Ardabil until matters should be favourably settled. The Russians handed his khanate to Ja'far-qoli Donboli, former khan of Khoi.

Pir-qoli Khan, in spite of Russian-inspired attacks by Mostafa Khan of Shirvan and his cronies, duly conducted the tribes of Shirvan, Rudbar and Moghan (presumably including the Shahsevan) south into Talesh and himself returned to Ahar in Qara-Dagh. The Russian commander in Javat threatened Mostafa Khan of Talesh, but he proved for the moment more loyal to Iran than his namesake of Shirvan, refused to send the immigrants back, and informed 'Abbas Mirza, who once more sent Pir-qoli Khan to Moghan to help him.

A truce was arranged with the Russian commander-in-chief as the winter set in, and the following year (1807) was spent preparing a fresh army. General Gardanne and his French officers trained bodies of Iranian troops in the European manner, including a Shaqaqi infantry battalion; and were also employed unsuccessfully in negotiating a peace agreement.

Late in 1808 Gudovich advanced on Erevan, and engaged 'Abbas Mirza and the Iranian armies in western Transcaucasia. Qara-Dagh, Ardabil and Meshkin had been left unguarded, so Amir Khan Qajar, uncle of 'Abbas Mirza, was sent to look after the security of those districts.

By this time the hegemony of the Shahsevan chiefs at Ardabil had apparently come to an end. With Gardanne's help, 'Abbas Mirza had constructed a European-style fortress in the town, and had appointed Najaf-qoli Khan of Garus to command it. This was the signal for the Ardabil chiefs to abandon the Qajars, and they fled to join their neighbour Mostafa Khan of Talesh, who was now intriguing with the Russians, and with whose daughter Nazar 'Ali Khan Shahsevan was 'involved in a love affair':

Nuzur Aly Khan, and Farraj Allah Khan, the governor and Na'ib of Ardebil, having entertained unfavourable sentiments concerning Najuf Kuly Khan Garus, who had been appointed to put the fort of that place in order, had fled from thence with their tribe, and having arrested Husain Kuly Khan of [Baku], who had been the cause of putting to death the Russian General [Tsitsianov], had proceeded to Lankaran, the residence of Mustafa Khan Taulish. This latter also, on account of his relationship and alliance with the fugitives, became quite alarmed for his own safety; and they all joined in endeavouring to introduce the Russians into that country.[13]

When Fath 'Ali Shah heard this news, he ordered Amir Khan, commanding the troops in the region, to bring the rebels to order, by force if neces-

---

[13] Brydges (1833: 346).

sary. Late in the year (1808) he reported to 'Abbas Mirza that he had succeeded in winning over Mostafa Khan of Talesh. The latter now repented
of his treachery and had reassured the Shahsevan fugitives, and requested
that 'the dust of their crimes may be washed off by the pure stream of
[Abbas Mirza]'s beneficence'. This request was granted and Nazar 'Ali
Khan was reinstated (as governor?).

In the spring of 1809 the Shahsevan chief came to Court to pay homage
and to atone for his misdeeds. When he arrived, he asked that Farajollah
Khan the *nasaqchi-bashi*, who had just been ordered to advance against
the Russians in Qara-Bagh, should on the contrary be instructed to
proceed to Ardabil, where Nazar 'Ali Khan would bring the Shahsevan
cavalry, fully equipped, to join forces with him and 'render some important service'; he promised, moreover, to deliver the other daughter of
Mostafa Khan of Talesh as bride for 'Abbas Mirza's brother. These plans
were approved, and the two khans were sent to Ardabil. Upon arrival,
Nazar 'Ali Khan Shahsevan was sent on to Lankaran to open negotiations
for his inamorata's sister, daughter of Mostafa Khan. Farajollah Khan the
nasaqchi-bashi waited several days in Ardabil,

anxiously expecting Nuzur Aly Khan to bring the [Shahsevan] cavalry, according
to promise, to his camp; but as the dust of that cavalry arose not in the quarter in
which it was looked for, and as the stipulated nuptials were not effected, it was
evident that Nuzur Aly Khan's proceedings were only based on pretences and
delays.[14]

Mostafa Khan of Talesh was meanwhile preparing to repel any further
Iranian expeditions, and to welcome the Russians. He forced the people
of Talesh to emigrate (northwards?), while he conveyed his valuables to
the sea-girt fortress of Jamishwan, his own capital of Lankaran being
indefensible. He sent his son Mir Hasan Khan to surprise the Iranian
commanders stationed in the neighbouring district of Ojarud; these were
routed, and among the prisoners taken was Mohammad Khan Beydili
(Shahsevan?). In Ardabil, Farajollah Khan the *nasaqchi-bashi* was
instructed to take action, and he sent a detachment into Talesh. Nazar
'Ali Khan Shahsevan and his kinsman Farajollah Khan were arrested,
imprisoned and then sent to Court. Mostafa Khan withdrew from
Lankaran to the Jamishwan fortress. Eventually reinforcements of
Russians and of 'Tartars' sent by Mostafa Khan of Shirvan drove the
Iranians back and out of Talesh.[15]

---

[14] Brydges (1833: 389).
[15] Baddeley (1908: 78), though Donboli (1972: 226–8) writes that Mostafa Khan of Talish
was brought to submission by 'Abbas Mirza's Minister, Mirza Bozorg (see also Brydges
1833: 400f.).

In the west 'Abbas Mirza had caused great losses to Gudovich's forces, which failed in their attack on Erevan in 1808. Alexander Tormasov replaced Gudovich as commander-in-chief, but there were no more major operations against Iran until 1812.

In spring 1809 the French officers, who had been training Iranian infantry and giving other military assistance, were expelled. The Shah was exasperated that they had failed to provide a promised peace agreement with their allies the Russians. He now received a series of British missions, including those led by Malcolm and Brydges (then known as Harford Jones), which in their turn brought (among other things) military training and assistance.

In 1809 the Iranians advanced through Georgia, while a reconnaissance expedition of Beydili Shahsevan horsemen under Abo'l-Fath Khan Javanshir was sent to report on the Russian position in Baku; they ambushed a party of Russians and cut them to pieces. 'Abbas Mirza reached Nakhchevan, where he received peace overtures. The embassy was sent on to the Shah at Tabriz, and a ceasefire was agreed on. As winter approached, 'Abbas Mirza confronted the main Russian forces at Ganjeh, and narrowly avoided defeat.

During the winter of 1809–10, an incident occurred in Moghan:

A body of [Russian] troops from Shirwan made a sudden incursion, irresistible as the visionary form of his mistress makes at midnight on the sleeping lover's heart, into Mughan, and drove off from the tribes of Karachehdagh nearly 20,000 head of sheep.[16]

The tribes did not retaliate; a complaint was lodged, but Tormasov denied responsibility.

In spring 1810 the Russians forced the Iranians back over the Aras river and occupied Qara-Bagh. The Iranian army spent the season sending raiding expeditions into Qara-Bagh and making new military preparations. These involved the construction of a European-style fortress at 'Abbas-Abad on the Aras, and the drilling of troops, including Shaqaqi infantry, under British officers. Various plans were formed for taking advantage of the crisis of leadership which was affecting the Russian forces. Several mojtaheds declared jehad against Russia for its oppression of Muslims in Iranian territory. The deposed Salim Khan of Shaki and Hosein-qoli Khan of Baku were in the royal camp at Ujan, and it seemed likely that Sheikh 'Ali Khan of Qobbeh and Mostafa Khan of Shirvan would co-operate in ousting the Russians.

Pir-qoli Khan Qajar was once more deputed to put affairs in Moghan

---

[16] Brydges (1833: 409–10).

and Qara-Dagh in order. He proceeded thence to Qara-Bagh where, unable to persuade Mahdi-qoli Khan and the Russians to meet him in the field, he occupied himself with reducing the recalcitrant Jabra'illi tribe and seizing their property. He also forced the Yusefanlu and Chalabianlu tribes, which had emigrated from Qara-Dagh north into Qara-Bagh, to return south of the Aras.

The Iranians spent the next campaigning season (1811) similarly, the main objective being to induce the tribes of Qara-Bagh to migrate south to Iran. Large numbers of nomads were brought across the Aras, while major confrontations between Russian and Iranian forces were avoided.

Early in 1812, now with about 13,000 European-trained troops at his disposal, 'Abbas Mirza decided on a more serious invasion of Qara-Bagh. He succeeded in overcoming a newly established Russian outpost, and 'brought away 2,000 families of Ilyats [nomadic tribespeople], thus nearly depopulating this region of Kara Baug'.[17] In August, the Iranian army left Ahar for Meshkin. An elite, British-trained column under Amir Khan was sent to drive the Russians out of Talesh, whereupon Mostafa Khan again retired to his fortress of Jamishwan, but his subjects willingly submitted to the Iranians, and the small Russian garrison had to withdraw. In spite of the advice of his British officers, Amir Khan refused to attack Mostafa Khan's stronghold.

These various successes bolstered Iranian hopes for the 1812 season, though the new Russian commander in Qara-Bagh, General Kotlarevski, was already beginning reprisals. Then Napoleon's invasion of Russia made the British and Russians allies, and in October most of the British officers in the Iranian army were withdrawn.

At this point the main Iranian forces were moving into the Moghan region, while the very much smaller Russian army was encamped across the Aras from Aslanduz. The Russians made overtures of peace, and in this connexion the British envoy Gore-Ouseley left the Court at Tabriz and travelled via Ahar to the Russian camp, before returning to Ardabil and Tehran.[18] The negotiations were unsuccessful, the Iranians being unwilling to make concessions. Indeed, when they encamped at Aslanduz they felt themselves to be so secure from attack by Kotlarevski that they omitted to post pickets along the river.

On 30 October 1812 the Russians were conducted unobserved across the Aras by Morad Khan Delaqarda, and they took the Iranian camp at Aslanduz by surprise. Although they were held off that day, a further surprise the following night ended in the complete rout of the Iranian army.

[17] Monteith (1856: 56).   [18] See Morier's account of this journey (1818: 233f.).

Kotlarevski was unable, however, to follow up his victory, and 'Abbas Mirza retreated to Meshkin.[19]

The next move for the Russians was to drive the Iranian garrison from Lankaran in Talesh and to reinstate their ally Mostafa Khan. An Iranian force was sent from Ardabil to intercept them, but it got stuck in the snow in Arshaq. In December Kotlarevski advanced across the snow-covered Moghan steppe, where he was met by a 'fine body of Kurdish cavalry'.[20] The Russians formed squares and beat them off, inflicting heavy losses. They proceeded unopposed to attack the Iranian force in Lankaran, but suffered great casualties before they took the town. Kotlarevski himself was shot in the head and permanently disabled.

Meanwhile the Russians were welcomed by the 'Qara-Baghi' tribes in Moghan under 'Ata Khan and Ja'far-qoli Khan: these were presumably 'Ata Khan of the Meshkin Shahsevan and his eldest son, named Ja'far-qoli Khan by Radde.[21]

The disasters of Aslanduz and Lankaran were in effect the end of the war. For some months of 1813 border skirmishes continued; the Iranians drilled fresh troops, and by summer had regained their former strength, seeing hopeful signs in Russian involvement in Europe, while knowing they could rely on a continuing British war subsidy. But Britain was no longer interested in the continuation of the war, and forced Iran to make a disappointing peace.

In October 1813 the Treaty of Golestan confirmed parts of Talesh and Moghan as Russian possessions, to the great chagrin of Iran. The Russians, however, were equally disappointed that their frontier was not extended to the Aras in western Transcaucasia, where the khanates of Erevan and Nakhchevan remained subject to Iran.[22] The wording of the regulations concerning the frontiers was vague, and in the ensuing years both sides seized on the ambiguities to justify infringements, particularly in the region of the Moghan–Talesh hills, and around Lake Gökcheh/Sevan in Georgia.

The second Russo–Iranian war

The Iranians had managed, as we have seen, to convey a great number of nomads across the Aras inside their now diminished frontiers, but they

---

[19] For accounts of the battle see Monteith (1856: 88f.), Donboli (1972: 149f.), Campbell (1931: 229–30), Nafisi (1965, II: 30f.), Atkin (1980: 138–9 – where further references are given).

[20] Monteith (1856: 96); were these Shahsevan? *Gazetteer* (1914), under 'Mughan', quotes Monteith's narrative but dates it wrongly to the winter of 1828–9.

[21] Donboli (1972: 153b); Radde (1886: 444).   [22] See Atkin (1980: 139–44).

lost vast areas of valuable grazing lands, notably in the Moghan region. Many contemporary travellers comment, usually from secondhand information, on the Moghan plains. For example, Ker Porter wrote in 1822:

During the winter and spring months, this immense tract, which is computed at sixty farsangs [350 km] in length, and twenty [120 km] in breadth, becomes abundant in fertility and the richest pasturage, feeding thousands of flocks belonging to the Eelauts [nomads] from the mountains of Azerbijan. It being in the power of the Russian government to shut out these subjects of Persia, from their customary annual fattening on a land now passed to other masters, the recovery of this district cannot but be in the heart of the Shah. From the peculiar luxuriance of the pastures, it has always been a favourite place of encampment with conquering armies, as well as with peaceable tribes.[23]

The extent of Moghan is overstated here; but when Kinneir reports: 'The Persians say, that the grass is sufficiently high to cover a man and his horse, and hide an army from view, when encamped',[24] my own experience of conditions there in spring 1966 suggests this is only a slight exaggeration.

The Shahsevan remained Iranian subjects, but as Porter implies they were for the moment allowed to continue winter grazing in Moghan, on two conditions: that they continue payment of the pasture-dues (*chobbashı*) to the khan of Talesh, under whose jurisdiction the pastures remained; and that nomadic Russian subjects from Talesh should be permitted to enter Iran in the region of Ojarud during the summer months, as they had done before.

Mostafa Khan of Talesh had been reinstated after Kotlarevski's last expedition, but he died in 1814, to be succeeded, with Russian approval, by his son Mir Hasan Khan. Three other khanates in eastern Transcaucasia – Shaki, Shirvan and Qara-Bagh – were also restored to their former rulers as Russian puppets, for a period following the Treaty of Golestan.

In the years that followed, two tendencies built up into the outbreak in 1826 of the second Russo–Iranian war. First, the advent in 1816–17 of Alexis Ermolov as Commander-in-Chief of the Caucasus led to the Russian take-over of direct local authority, and their pressure on the ambiguous areas of the Iranian frontier. Secondly, the protests of the Iranian religious classes, infuriated by the loss of the Caucasian districts, encouraged a resurgence of military power under 'Abbas Mirza, and his determination to recover them.

The people of Azarbaijan had suffered particularly from exactions to

[23] Porter (1821–2, II: 512–13).   [24] Kinneir (1813: 153).

finance the first war, and with the cholera of the 1820s conditions continued to be desperate. In the northeast of the province, the Shahsevan nomads, straddling a critical frontier and totally dependent on Russian benevolence for permission to use their traditional winter quarters, could not be relied on to support the Iranian armies. As early as 1821 it was reported that some families of Shahsevan fled to Talesh, pursued across the frontier by Iranian troops, who were rounded up, their commanding officer being taken prisoner and sent to Georgia.[25] The Meshkin group at least was to welcome the Russians when they once more encroached upon Iranian territory. At Ardabil, however, the Qajar princes who had governed from 1810 onwards succeeded in securing regular military levies from the local, already semi-settled Shahsevan tribespeople.

In the years after his appointment, Ermolov took over the khanates of eastern Transcaucasia one by one and deposed their khans: Shaki in 1819, Shirvan in 1820, and Qara-Bagh in 1822. Only Mir Hasan Khan of Talesh was allowed autonomy, Ermolov understanding him and his family to be implacably hostile to Iran. In fact Mir Hasan threw the Russians out in the year that hostilities reopened, and a strong Iranian force came to help him. He retained control of the khanate, in the name of the Shah, until he was forced to abandon it in 1828 by the Treaty of Torkman–Chai.

Mostafa Khan of Shirvan and Mahdi-qoli Khan of Qara-Bagh fled to Iran, where they were installed near the frontier. They soon began intriguing with supporters in their former capitals, and instigated border infringements by the Shahsevan in Moghan, in retaliation for which Russian troops occupied parts of some Iranian districts such as Ojarud.

These disputes originate in the licentious conduct of the wandering tribes who every winter resort to Moghan and the banks of the Arras, for the sake of pasturage. Thefts are mutually committed, which brings on retaliation; hostile clans arrange themselves on different sides, and scarcely a year passes without some scene of rapine and bloodshed.[26]

This tale, like the tone in which it is reported, becomes increasingly familiar as the century proceeds. No doubt the 'hostile clans' belonged to the Meshkin and Ardabil sections of the Shahsevan.

Meanwhile some efforts were being made towards demarcation of the frontier in western Transcaucasia; but the commission could not agree on any part of the line that they discussed, and the attempts were abandoned in December 1823. The Russians began encroachments in the Gökcheh region, which they eventually occupied in 1825.

'Abbas Mirza chose the summer of 1826 to open a full-scale campaign

---

[25] *Papers Relative to the War* (no. 12 of 10.2.1821): 8.   [26] *Ibid.*, no. 14 of 10.5.1823.

for the recovery of the former Iranian territories in the Caucasus. In addition, once again 'one of the principal objects of the war carried on by the Persians against Russia was to induce the Iliyats of Karabagh, Sheki, &c. to return to their allegiance to the Shah'.[27] He launched a surprise attack on Georgia and Qara-Bagh, and met with immediate success, Ermolov being caught quite unprepared. Qara-Bagh rose against the Russians, and Shusheh was invested. Soon Iranian troops reoccupied Ganjeh, Shirvan, Shaki and Talesh, and menaced Tiflis. Mostafa Khan was reinstated in Shirvan.

In September, however, in a major engagement at Shamkor, Prince Madatov's courage won the day for the Russians. The Iranian commander, Mohammad Mirza (later Mohammad Shah), was taken prisoner but rescued by a Shahsevan chief.[28] In a further battle at Ganjeh on 26 September, Cavalry-General Paskevich defeated 'Abbas Mirza. The Iranian troops, after their few months of glory, were forced back over the Aras at Khoda-Afarin, bringing with them many families of tribespeople as before. Mostafa Khan of Shirvan once more escaped south of the Aras with a few followers, but Mir Hasan Khan continued to occupy Moghan and Talesh in the Shah's name. For some weeks 'Abbas Mirza delayed in camp on the Iranian bank of the Aras, and conducted raids into Qara-Bagh. In mid-October he rejoined his father at the royal camp at Ahar, then moved to Tabriz for the winter. The last major Iranian military effort in eastern Transcaucasia had failed.

Meanwhile General Paskevich took a small expedition over the Aras into the Iranian district of Qara-Dagh, partly to prevent any further military activities, particularly raiding, on the part of the Iranians, and partly to forage for provisions for his army. He found that 'Abbas Mirza had already moved south to Ahar, so before returning north he rounded up some of the numerous groups of nomads whom the Iranians had brought over, and sent them back to their homes in Qara-Bagh.[29]

Early in 1827 a second Russian expedition entered Iranian territory in Moghan and penetrated as far as Meshkin, with similar intentions to the first: to collect provisions, which were very scarce in Qara-Bagh and Shirvan that winter, and to induce the Qara-Baghi nomads to return north of the Aras.[30] This expedition, led by Prince Madatov, an Armenian of Qara-Baghi origins, crossed the Aras at Aslanduz and ascended the Dara-Yort canyon by forced marches, coming across wintering camps of Shahsevan, 'Adschalinen' (Ajirli? Hajjili?) and other nomads, from whom they took 15,000 sheep and large numbers of camels and horses. Some

[27] Morier (1837: 241).   [28] Watson (1866: 214).
[29] Eichwald (1834, II, 2: 587–8).   [30] Monteith (1856: 132).

500 families of Qara-Baghi nomads were sent back. Eichwald gives the following account of the further progress of the expedition against the Shahsevan:

Lieut. General Prince Madatov then spread a report that he was intending to invade Talesh; but he proceeded slowly, so that the nomads which were staying on the Talesh side under Iranian authority [i.e. the Ardabil section of the Shahsevan] could seek refuge in the Meshkin district, where he could far more advantageously attack them. His plan worked. In the still of the night of 1st [13th] January, he marched into the Meshkin district, was told of the nomads' whereabouts, and at once sent out a detachment of light cavalry and Armenian infantry, to put them to flight. The enemy, in disorder, made only a brief, token resistance; they [the nomads?] lost 18 men killed and a number wounded, and 2,000 camels, 10,000 head of cattle and 60,000 sheep were driven off from the Shahsevans. Meanwhile Madatov pitched his camp at Lari, a small town of the district. The district chief, 'Ata Khan and his brother Shukur Khan, came before him and asked for protection, which Madatov willingly granted.[31]

Madatov's own account of this expedition is very similar to Eichwald's, but adds that at Lari, apart from these Meshkin chiefs, he also received a deputation from the Shaqaqi chiefs. It is not clear what any of these chiefs were doing in the high country of Meshkin and Lari in January, unless it was to divert the invaders from the nomad families and flocks which were presumably in the Moghan plains to the north. Madatov intended to proceed to Ahar and threaten Tabriz, but his force was too small, and in any case another detachment, which had been sent into Qara-Dagh to meet him at Kaleibar, was repulsed by Iranian forces. So he returned north to Moghan, taking back with him many of the Shirvan and Qara-Bagh nomads whom the Iranians had brought south, and crossed the Aras at Yeddi-Bölük after some two weeks on Iranian soil.[32]

'Abbas Mirza's son Jahangir Mirza, who was responsible for an Iranian force at Ardabil, gives a very different account of Madatov's expedition, its purposes and outcome. He writes that Madatov advanced on Ardabil, which was temporarily without a commander; Jahangir Mirza came to the rescue via Sarab, frightened Madatov off in the direction of Moghan, and sent Shahsevan and Shaqaqi troops after him, who caught him up and captured horses, guns and prisoners before driving him back over to Qara-Bagh.[33]

According to Monteith, apart from 'having harassed the Persians by obliging them to assemble at a very inconvenient season of the year', Madatov was more successful in wasting the country and depriving the emigrants of their livestock than in persuading them to return to Qara-

[31] Eichwald (1834, II, 2: 589–90).   [32] Madatov (1837: 123–7).
[33] Jahangir Mirza (1948: 65–8).

Bagh. In addition, Madatov is said today to have robbed the Safavid shrine in Khiou (present Meshkin-Shahr) of its golden dome.[34]

In spring 1827, Ermolov was replaced as Commander-in-Chief by Paskevich, who advanced on Erevan. That city, as well as Nakhchevan and the new fort of 'Abbas-Abad, soon fell, though 'Abbas Mirza's last supreme effort, at Abaran near Echmiadzin in September, was an Iranian victory, at great cost. Paskevich swept the Iranian forces across the Aras, and by October had captured Tabriz. 'Abbas Mirza submitted and entered negotiations with the Russians in November.

Jahangir Mirza relates how he himself led an Iranian force, composed of Shahsevan and other local tribesmen, from Ardabil to Talesh and Moghan, and how he succeeded, in conjunction with Mir Hasan Khan, in recapturing Salyan from the Russians.[35] At the same time, Prince Vadibolski crossed the Aras at Aslanduz and headed towards Ardabil for two days. Then, hearing of the fall of Tabriz, he supposed his mission ended and returned to Qara-Bagh. Paskevich, however, wanted the Tabriz–Ahar–Ardabil road opened as a route for the eventual withdrawal of the Russian army, as the Jolfa road was liable to become snowed up in winter, so he ordered Vadibolski back across the Aras. With about 5,000 men Vadibolski forded the Aras once more at Aslanduz in early December, by which time the roads were already in ruin through heavy rainfall and then snow. They were welcomed in Moghan by the people of the Meshkin district. 'The local governor 'Ata Khan was one of the first people to surrender to the Russians, and for that reason Paskevich gave him the governorship of Meshkin; and all the nomadic tribes of the region followed him.'[36] Vadibolski set about opening the road between Ahar and Ardabil, but found this extremely difficult, as he was short on provisions. The weather conditions were terrible, the men sickened and the animals died.

General Paskevich was himself having trouble provisioning his army in Tabriz. Though the Shahsevan of Ardabil remained faithful to the Qajar princes in this town, the tribes of Khalkhal and Tarom and the Shaqaqis of Sarab and Garm-Rud, who had until then resisted Russian influence, now came forward and hired transport animals to the Russian army, and even offered their military support. Paskevich provisionally appointed the Shaqaqi chief, son of Sadeq Khan, as governor of Ardabil.

'Abbas Mirza and Paskevich agreed a treaty at Tabriz, but Fath 'Ali Shah rejected it on hearing that it stipulated that he pay an indemnity of 20 million roubles. As a result of this, and of news of the battle of

---

[34] Monteith (1856: 132); Eichwald (1834, II, 2: 590).   [35] Jahangir Mirza (1948: 73–7).
[36] Nafisi (1965, II: 146, 155), who appears to be using Russian sources.

Navarino, the Russians broke off negotiations and, although it was mid-winter, prepared to march on Tehran. Paskevich appears to have intended marching via Ahar and Ardabil, but, as Vadibolski's column was still stuck there in the snow, he determined to march via Mianeh and Kaflan-Kuh. His Lieutenant Pankratiev was to take a division to Maragheh and join the khan of the Moqaddam tribe, while Count Sukhtelen was to proceed via Sarab to Ardabil, where his division was to unite with Shahsevan and Shaqaqi recruits. Khoi, Salmas, Urmiyeh and the rest of Azarbaijan had surrendered when Tabriz fell, so that the Russians, on Monteith's estimate, could now command 20,000 of Iran's best troops, including 10,000–12,000 cavalry, against their own countrymen. According to Jahangir Mirza, 2,000–3,000 Meshkin Shahsevan horsemen gathered to threaten Ardabil.[37]

Sukhtelen marched to take possession of Ardabil. He occupied the town in early February, but 'Abbas Mirza's two sons, Mohammad Mirza (later Shah) and Jahangir Mirza, who were in command of the town, were unwilling to abandon the castle, even though 'Abbas Mirza, in arrangement with Paskevich, had written formally ordering them to surrender. According to Jahangir Mirza, his father secretly ordered the princes to defend the castle: only after a few rounds of artillery had been fired into it did they surrender.[38]

At that time, Nafisi points out, Ardabil did not have the commercial importance it had once possessed and which it was later to recover, but the Russians were keen to control it, as it lay astride an important military route. The Iranians, on the other hand, had been even more anxious to hold the city, as pilgrims came from all over the Shi'a world to visit the Safavid tombs. Sukhtelen packed up the most valuable portion of the shrine library, which was later transported to St Petersburg 'on loan'. The volumes were never returned, but the Tsar contributed 800 toman towards repair of the shrine. The money appears to have been embezzled.[39]

The Shah had soon been alarmed at these further movements, and at Russian threats to annex Azarbaijan. Helped by a British contribution, 'Abbas Mirza delivered the first instalments of the required indemnity, and a treaty was signed at Torkman–Chai on 18 February 1828, fixing the northern frontier of Iranian Azarbaijan almost exactly as it remains today. The Shah recovered Tabriz and Ardabil, but renounced any claims to territory north of the Aras, and confirmed the loss of Talesh and Moghan.

[37] Monteith (1856: 148–50); Jahangir Mirza (1948: 104–8); Nafisi (1965, II: 163–8).
[38] Jahangir Mirza (1948: 107–8).   [39] Nafisi (1965, II: 166–8); Abbott (1844: 32–3).

The aftermath of the wars

During the wars, Iranian troops had brought a large number of nomads south of the Aras, as described above. Some returned to become Russian subjects, but many remained, including ancestors of large Qara-Daghi groups of today: Chalabianlu, Yusefanlu/Mohammad-Khanlu, and sections of the Hajji-'Alili.[40] Others, such as the ancestors of the present Ja'farli tribe, and probably the Khosroulu and parts of several other tribes, joined the Shahsevan.

Most tribes indigenous to Iranian Azarbaijan had co-operated with the Russians during Paskevich's occupation of the province. Article 15 of the Treaty of Torkman–Chai granted them an amnesty and allowed them one year in which to migrate, if they chose, into Russian territory and settle there as Russian subjects.

There was indeed considerable movement in a northerly direction: Seidlitz lists twenty-one villages in the Talesh, Salyan, Shirvan and Baku districts that were completely or partly settled by Shahsevan tribespeople at this time, while certain nomads based in Talesh (and perhaps also the other districts), formerly loosely attached to the Shahsevan confederacy, now chose to take up Russian nationality, though some of them continued to come to Iranian territory during the summer months.[41] Eichwald mentions other nomads who left Iranian territory at this time, particularly Kurdish tribes from northwestern Azarbaijan. Fraser, writing of the Iranian authorities' oppression of their subjects in 1833–4, notes that

Frequent migrations of the Nomade population take place from the Persian territories into those of Russia; while many of the fixed inhabitants rather long for the hour which shall bestow upon them the fancied protection of the Russian sway.[42]

Atkin, however, feels that there was much greater movement southwards; as a result of the two wars, 'the total number of Muslims who emigrated [to Iran] exceeded by far the number who returned . . . most parts of the eastern Caucasus had far fewer inhabitants at the end of the Russian take-over than at the start'.[43] This, and the fact that a substantial population of peasants and nomads – including the Shahsevan – still remained in Iranian Azarbaijan, despite Article 15 of the Treaty, and despite official oppression, is probably chiefly explained by the aversion which Muslims felt to the prospect of subjection to Christian overlords.

Meanwhile Mahdi-qoli of Qara-Bagh and Mostafa of Shirvan returned

---

[40] Baiburdi (1962); Oberling (1964b). See also Mohammad Mirza's order concerning the Chalabianlu, dated early 1830, in Anon. (1992: 167–8).

[41] Seidlitz (1879: 498); cf. Ismail-zade (1960), and see further below.

[42] Fraser (1838, II: 404).   [43] Atkin (1980: 149–50).

to their khanates as Russian subjects and were both restored to partial control over their former lands and given military rank. Towards the end of the nineteenth century, however, Hasan Khan, a descendant of Mostafa Khan of Shirvan, founded a number of settlements such as Tazeh-Kand on the banks of the Aras in the extreme north of Iranian Moghan: these villages and their inhabitants are known today as Hasan-Khanlu.

Mir Hasan Khan (son of Mir Mostafa Khan) of Talesh, who had thrown out the Russians in 1826, was now obliged by the terms of the Treaty to evacuate Lankaran. He acquiesced at first and came to Astara and Ardabil, but on several occasions in the following years he escaped to cause trouble in his old territory and was recaptured, until finally, when both Russian and Iranian forces had been sent against him, he fled to Mazandaran and Tehran, where he succumbed to dropsy. His son Mir Kazem Khan, to whom 'Abbas Mirza had given one of his daughters in marriage, was appointed to the new khanate of Namin, based on the village of that name near Ardabil. He was given jurisdiction (subject to the governor of Ardabil) over the 'Three Districts' of Ojarud, Velkij and Astara, all of which bordered his father's old khanate of Talesh, and he was allowed to appoint the governors of these districts and also that of the district of Arshaq, so that he and his successors had some control over the affairs of the Shahsevan nomads, most of whom had to pass through these districts on their semi-annual migrations.

Mir Kazem Khan was succeeded by his son Mir Soltan Ahmad Khan, and the latter by his son Mir Lotf 'Ali Khan in 1876. Meanwhile another branch of the family was apparently of some official standing in Russian territory: in 1880 Radde found Mir Taqi Bey, grandson of Mir Mostafa Khan, recognized as Khan of Russian Talesh. The neighbouring Iranian khanate of Kargan-Rud, which had been taken over by Mostafa Khan, after Torkman–Chai voluntarily seceded from the Astara district and from subjection to the Talesh khan family, and was included in the Iranian province of Gilan. There had been, and continued to be, a relationship of feud between the Talesh and Kargan-Rud khan families.[44]

In Moghan, the Russo–Iranian frontier delineated by the Treaty of Torkman–Chai has not been significantly altered since, but the Shahsevan nomads were for nearly sixty years able to cross the frontier to their traditional winter quarters, as they had been after the Treaty of Golestan in 1813. In 1828 the Iranian government asked the Caucasian administration to permit the Shahsevan nomads to continue their migrations to Moghan as before, offering to pay the annual sum of 2,000

[44] Rabino (1917); Nikitine (1922).

roubles (£350 at exchange rates of the time), equivalent to the 700 tomans formerly paid as pasture-dues to the khans of Talesh. In 1831 a preliminary contract concerning this was drawn up at Tiflis between Count Paskevich and 'Abbas Mirza's envoy Mirza Saleh. The contract specified conditions by which the nomads' migrations should proceed and the dues should be paid. The third article laid down that the Shahsevan tribes should use only that part of the steppe which had formerly belonged to the Talesh khanate, specifically excluding the Shirvan part of the steppe; this latter, comprising much of the territory on the southern banks of the Aras and Kor rivers, was reserved for the use of Russian nomads and village-based flocks. A copy of the contract was sent to Tehran for ratification, pending which the Shahsevan were allowed to use the Moghan pasturage free of charge. According to Markov, it was not until 1847 that the Iranian government paid the first instalment of the pasture dues.[45]

Meanwhile Russian colonization of the steppe proceeded apace. After 1828, 'the situation was radically altered and the tsarist government energetically set about consolidating their territorial gains, the more so since this coincided with the intensified settlement of nomadic Russian subjects'.[46]

From the beginning, however, the new colonists complained that their agricultural efforts were hindered by Shahsevan nomads, who destroyed crops, stole animals and plundered villages. In the course of time, the division of Moghan into the Shirvan and Talesh sectors lapsed, and the whole territory south of the Kor and Aras was abandoned to the Shahsevan in the winter. Moreover, some of the Iranian nomads had been used to crossing the Kor and Aras and wintering on the Mil (Qara-Bagh) and Shirvan steppes to the north, and many of them continued to do so, but they now fell foul of the local nomads for whom these pastures had been set aside by the Russian authorities, and both there and on the southern banks of the rivers there was continual bloodshed.[47]

---

[45] Markov (1890: 23).   [46] Rostopchin (1933: 98).
[47] On nomads in Russian territory at this time, see Ismail-zade (1960) and Kobychev (1962).

9   The Shahsevan nomads in the mid-nineteenth century

Economic conditions in the region

There has been a lively debate on the nature of the Iranian economy in the nineteenth century, focusing on the importance of such factors as population increase, urbanization, famine and drought, changes in production, and patterns of trade.[1] In 1953, Lambton wrote that 'the picture of the land revenue system and administration of the early Qajars is one of decay, maladministration, oppression and insecurity', but the more recent consensus is expressed by Hambly: 'Fath 'Ali Shah's reign ultimately afforded sufficient order and effective government to make possible some economic recovery ... Fath 'Ali Shah's Iran was more tranquil and prosperous than it had been at any time since Safavid rule had ceased to be effective.'[2]

Azarbaijan continued to be, politically at least, the most important province of Iran. It was the chief recruiting ground for the Qajar armies, if not also the chief supplier of agricultural produce, and Tabriz, with around 200,000 inhabitants, was the largest and most important city of the country and usually the seat of the heir apparent, as well as the main emporium of the rapidly expanding trade with Russia and the West. Russia was naturally the paramount foreign influence in the political and economic affairs of the province, though the British often managed to exert some pressure through their consular officials in Tabriz.

Tabriz flourished particularly under 'Abbas Mirza, but it was overtaken by Tehran in size and importance by the end of the century, and it would seem that for Azarbaijan the nineteenth century was a period of decline, when the resources of the province were steadily drained away by a succession of officials of all ranks who came simply to make their fortunes. Their salaries were commonly paid by tax assignments (*tiyul*), whether on Crown Land (*khaleseh*, formerly *khasseh*) or on privately owned land, and much Crown Land was sold to the officials and others

---

[1] E.g. Bakhash (1978), Amanat (1983), and contributions to Issawi (1971), Pakdaman (1983), Avery *et al.* (1991).   [2] Lambton (1953: 150); Hambly (1991a: 144).

such as wealthy merchants and thus became private. The landowning classes increasingly included government officials, merchants and tribal chiefs, who squeezed the cultivating peasants for what they could contribute. The tribal chiefs, at least among the Shahsevan, also leased out their pastures at steeply rising rentals. The burden of taxation and other dues was passed on, in the case of the nomads, by the chiefs and tax-collectors, who as a rule demanded cash payments from the ordinary nomads. Members of the chiefly families had no employment other than occasional military service, and raiding expeditions were a characteristic preoccupation. Social relations generally were marked by an increasing polarization between landowning (non-productive) chiefs and hard-pressed pastoralists, between predatory officials and their victims, between nomads and villagers.

Until the end of the nineteenth century, the sub-province of Ardabil was divided into the following districts (*mahal*): Ardabil itself, Meshkin, Arshaq, Ojarud, Astara and Velkij. As mentioned earlier, the sub-governors (*na'eb al-hokumeh*) of the last four districts were appointed by the khan of Namin, from the former Talesh khan dynasty. The plains of Iranian Moghan appear to have been under the direct administration of the governor (*hakem*) of Ardabil through the Shahsevan chiefs; the district of Angut, west of Ojarud but east of the Qara-Su river, was administered by a khan resident in the village of Zeiveh and subject to the governor of Qara-Dagh at Ahar. The sub-provinces of Ardabil, Sarab and Qara-Dagh, which for most of the eighteenth century had been ruled by semi-autonomous local chiefs, were for much of the nineteenth century administered by members of the Qajar royal family, 'often the most rapacious of mankind', who subjected their charges to continual and grinding oppression.[3] This oppression fell most heavily on the people of the towns and the nearby villages, which became noticeably depopulated.

A number of European travellers passed through the region in the years following the Russian annexation of Moghan. William Monteith, visiting on behalf of 'Abbas Mirza, spent the winter of 1828–9 at Ardabil, then in early March travelled north along the Talesh frontier to Moghan, noting that

The greater part of this road from Ardabile had been over a very rich country, but totally abandoned as pasture to the great tribe of Shah Sewund, who would allow none but themselves to cultivate the rich lands of Guerney, Alzer and Burgund [Garmi, Alazar, Barzand – i.e. the district of Ojarud].

Apparently the spring rains had not yet come, as he found in Iranian Moghan, northwest of the Balharu river, that 'The Illiauts had aban-

---

[3] Abbott (1844: 11).

doned the central part of the plain, and were only to be met with in the bed of the river Aras. I fortunately had provided myself with forage, for we found no grass fit for horses.'[4] He reached the Aras at the frontier post Yeddi-Bölük, then rode up-river, past the ruins of Altun/Ultan and Timur's canal, to Aslanduz.

In mid-winter 1837 d'Arcy Todd travelled from Tabriz to Tehran via Ahar, Meshkin, Ardabil and Talesh: he comments on the richness of the cultivation in both Ahar and Meshkin. The largest villages in the latter district were Ahmad-Beyli, Barzil (residence of Rostam Khan, chief of Meshkin) and Ali. Ahar he estimated to contain about 700 households, and to be in a dilapidated condition. Ardabil too, having suffered from plague in two recent years, was very much depopulated and in ruins. From Ardabil he headed north on Monteith's route as far as Garmi, which was 'the chief place of the district of Ujarud, a large and populous village on the bank of a ravine; the inhabitants chiefly pastoral, possessing large flocks of sheep and droves of cattle'. Much of the local pasturage belonged to 'the Persian tribe of Peranbili' (Perambel, Russian subjects based in Talesh); he also remarked the tribes of Mirankuh (Moranlu?) and Dilloghardalu (Delaqarda) in the region. He did not pass into Moghan and made no mention of the Shahsevan by name.[5]

Seven years later, in his report on a journey in November 1843 from Tabriz to the Caspian via Ahar, Meshkin and Ardabil, Keith Abbott gave a lengthy account of the land tenure and revenue situation in these parts of northern Iran. His general impressions of northeast Azarbaijan confirmed those of Todd. Ahar he found in a wretched condition, suffering the oppressions of a succession of Qajar princes, each of whom 'hastens to collect as much wealth as possible before his removal'. Considerable numbers of the inhabitants had fled the extortions, and of the 1,500 families left only 600 paid the taxes, amounting, with the commercial dues, to 1,000 tomans.

The Meshkin district, on the other hand, appeared populous, quite prosperous and much cultivated, with a deep, rich soil except on the mountainsides. The district was famous for the rice cultivated in the valleys of the Qara-Su and the Ahar-Chai rivers, and there were fruit groves in abundance. The town of Lari was said to contain 500 houses and was taxed at the rate of 700 tomans plus one fifth of the crop, of which half went to the government. Wheat yields were said to be ten- to twenty-fold on unirrigated and twenty- to thirty-fold on irrigated lands.

The Ardabil district, though containing several villages and a well-watered plain, was neither well cultivated nor populous, with only some

---

[4] Monteith (1833: 29).   [5] d'Arcy Todd (1838: 30–34).

1,000 families. The soil was not very productive and the climate was too extreme for many crops. Ardabil itself was in a wretched condition, much impoverished after the recent plague and cholera, and the 3,000 families paid tax at a reduced rate of 8,000 tomans, increased by dues from the customs house. Ardabil had some importance commercially in the transit-trade between the Caspian (Russian and Iranian ports) and the interior of Iran.

Villages, Abbott found, fell into three types, according to their owner-ship. First there were villages owned by the Crown, of which few existed in northern Iran, though there were some in the Ardabil district: here the government was the sole collector of revenue, taking a share of the produce that varied according to the quality of the land, the kind of crop grown, and whether or not the land was irrigated. Often the government share amounted to one fifth, the peasant providing the labour and bearing the expenses; when the government provided seed, oxen and ploughs, it took a half-share of the crop. Cattle, sheep, goats, mares and donkeys (but not horses or oxen) were taxed, as were fruit trees, and a poll tax was levied on villagers but not on townsmen.

The second type of village was private property, founded, bought or inherited by individual owners. Here the government took a share of the produce and a cash tax on cattle, etc., while the landowner took a further share. When the peasant provided labour and bore other costs, the land-owner might get three in ten, from which the government got four sev-enths, so that the government share amounted to 17 per cent and the landowner's to 13 per cent of the produce. The government also took other dues, such as 5 qrans (half a toman) for every *kharvar* (600 kg) of grain it received, as 'straw-money'. Sometimes the government share amounted to only 10 per cent. Whoever founded a new village or opened cultivation on waste, unappropriated land, became the landowner, but the inhabitants of this or other private land were not serfs, in that they were free to move, which they often did in response to oppression – 'a salutary restraint where otherwise [the landowner] might have too much power to injure or oppress them'.

A third class consists of Villages the Government revenues of which are given in Teule [*tiyul*] or assignment to any person in payment of Salary or for other claims he may possess on the Government. This system is very common in the North of Persia and it saves the Government the expense of collecting the Revenue. It sometimes happens that the Proprietor of a Village farms the Government Revenues himself – this arrangement does not afford him any pecuniary advan-tage but it relieves him and his Villagers from the trouble and annoyance which the interference of Government Agents sent to collect the Taxes would occasion.[6]

---

[6] Abbott (1844: 21–5); see Amanat (1983).

Abbott says nothing, however, of the tenure of grazing rights in pasture-lands, nor does he indicate who, apart from some of the Shahsevan nomads, were the landowners or *tiyuldars* in this region. Abbott's companion Holmes reported that Lari and some other nearby villages belonged to a Manuchehr Khan of Tabriz,[7] and by the end of the century officials and merchants from Ardabil and Tabriz were the most prominent landowners.

A number of documents dating from the 1830s have recently been published, however, recording grants of *tiyul* in Meshkin to Hosein 'Ali Khan Javanshir, a descendant of Ebrahim Khalil Khan: these included the villages of Pari-Khan, Qurt-Tepe and Saru-Khanlu. In the case of the latter, Hosein 'Ali Khan appears to have been given the *tiyul* over the head of Ja'far-qoli Bey, son of the village founder Saru Khan Shahsevan (perhaps the son of former Meshkin Shahsevan khan, 'Ata Khan Sarı-Khan-Beyli).[8] Most of the documents in this collection concern the career – and the *tiyuls* in Qara-Dagh – of Kazem Khan Javanshir, presumably another exiled member of Ebrahim Khalil Khan's family; he was appointed governor of the neighbouring district of Khalkhal and Shatranlu in 1838–9. Another Javanshir, 'Abbas-qoli Khan, son of Ebrahim Khalil Khan's eldest son Abo'l-Fath Khan, was governor of Ardabil, Meshkin and Qara-Dagh in 1849–50.[9] Lambton's observation that 'the greater part of the Shahsevan country in Azarbaijan, which was crown land, was granted towards the middle of the century in tuyul to the family of Abu'l-Fath Khan, a Qarabaghi chief of some consequence', is puzzling since Rawlinson, in the passage to which Lambton refers, is discussing the rich farmlands between Lake Urmiyeh and Maragheh, whose inhabitants may include settled Shahsevan (not mentioned by Rawlinson), but which is far from the main Shahsevan country of Ardabil and Moghan.[10] It may be, however, that Abo'l-Fath Khan also had lands in Meshkin.

Abbott and Holmes passed many groups of Shahsevan nomads on their way north to winter quarters in Moghan. There were reckoned to be 6,000–7,000 families in the Meshkin region and about 5,000 in Ardabil; the former were wealthier as well as more numerous, and paid 4,000 toman in taxes, as opposed to 1,500 toman paid by the Ardabil division. The latter, however,

possess several villages in the Ardebeel district inhabited chiefly by the common Peasantry of the Country mixed with people of the Tribe and for which the

---

[7] Holmes (1845: 27).   [8] Anon. (1992: 295, 303, 309–11, 314–18).
[9] Bamdad (1968, II: 227–8), with pictures of both 'Abbas-qoli Khan and his father.
[10] Lambton (1991: 491); Rawlinson (1841: 5). Cf. Lambton (1953: 139, 155) on *tiyul*-holding at this period.

Government demand on the Tribe is 1,000 Tomans yearly ... It is to be understood that the above sums are claimed of the Heads of the Tribe and they are known to extort a great deal more from their followers ... The Tribe, as a Body, is rich in cattle and flocks but many of them are very poor ... and commonly given to petty theft and robbery but they are not accused of marauding and pillaging on a large scale.[11]

Not many years would pass before Abbott had cause to revise this charitable judgment; indeed the Shahsevan were already involved in raids and skirmishes with the Russian population of Moghan, but clearly reports of this had not yet filtered through to the British agents.

Pastoral economy and society

The basic husbandry practised by Shahsevan pastoralists was much as in the present century, and could sustain much the same rate of production, but higher costs and heavy impositions probably meant much lower standards of consumption. James Morier, who was acquainted with the Shahsevan earlier in the century, writes of Iranian nomads in general at that time:

An Iliyat of middling fortune possesses about a hundred sheep, three or four camels, three or four mares, ten asses, &c., which may yield him a revenue of forty to fifty tumans. A man who possesses a thousand sheep, thirty camels, twenty mares, &c., is reckoned a rich man. Each sheep may be valued at two piastres [qrans?], a camel at ten, a mare at eight, an ass at three. Such a property would yield a revenue of four hundred tumans. This is to be derived from the wool and milk of the sheep, the wool and hire of the camels, the colts from the mares and asses ... The encampments of the Iliyats are generally of about twenty to thirty tents together, which they pitch mostly without any great attention to regularity ... The tents are close to each other, but the different encampments may be a mile or two asunder, according to the convenience of grass and water ... excepting their clothes, copper utensils, pack-saddles and ornamental luxuries, they supply all their own necessities ... Their mode of calculating property is by sheep ... A shepherd has the care of three hundred sheep, and is paid in kind, both in wool and lambs.[12]

The same rate of income is reported for Russian eastern Transcaucasia in the 1840s: 100 sheep give an annual income of 100 to 150 roubles, i.e. 35 to 50 tomans.[13] Morier's account is highly generalized but, with minor modifications, it still applied to the Shahsevan in the mid-twentieth century.

Two Russian officials who dealt with Shahsevan nomads in the mid-nineteenth century collected much information on their social organiza-

---

[11] Abbott (1844: 19, 28–9).   [12] Morier (1837: 239–41).   [13] Ismail-zade (1960: 111).

tion (I discussed their accounts of Shahsevan traditions in Chapter Three). Colonel I. A. Ogranovich, first appointed Frontier Commissar for the Shahsevan at Belasovar in 1869, wrote various articles about them. A Report for the Caucasian administration by E. Krebel, Russian consul-general at Tabriz from 1877, was (I have suggested) used extensively by the German naturalist Gustav Radde and the Russian official Vl. Markov, both of whom visited the Shahsevan themselves in the 1880s and collected further information. These accounts are worth quoting at some length, even if, as will be noted, they make no attempt to assess the direct or indirect effect of the Russian presence in Moghan on Shahsevan behaviour and institutions.

Ogranovich reckoned in 1870 that the Shahsevan of Moghan numbered over 12,000 households in 47 'communities' (*obshchestvo*), i.e. *taifa*, tribes: 9,000 (32 tribes) in the Meshkin and 3,200 (15 tribes) in the Ardabil division. The tribespeople owned over 6,000 herds of wethers, each herd consisting of about 300 head, and about 30,000 head of camels and the same number of horses. This indicates, not only that animals were tended in herds of a similar size to today, and that the nomads raised one- to two-year wethers for sale, but that the average household owned about 150 head, which matches good years in the mid-twentieth century.

That year, however, was the second of a famine which ravaged this region like others in Iran, and, besides, the two following winters were terrible; by 1875 Ogranovich revised his estimate of the nomad population down to about 6,000 households. Krebel in 1878 counted about the same number, but in 1884 Ogranovich reckoned the Shahsevan once more totalled around 10,000 households, and the stock numbers had reached their 1870 levels.[14]

On this evidence, the total number of Shahsevan households migrating to Moghan in the period 1828 to 1884 probably fluctuated between 6,000 and 12,000. Estimates of numbers of Shahsevan actually crossing the frontier to Russian Moghan vary even more widely than those for the total. According to Russian statistics mentioned by Avdeyev, there were no more than 3,500 Shahsevan households wintering in Russian Moghan in the late 1860s, while Ogranovich's first report of 1870 indicates almost three times that figure. Krebel found under 3,500 households there in 1878, yet in 1884 Ogranovich reckoned there were nearly 5,500 wintering in Russia. Abbott's estimates of 1860 tend to agree with Ogranovich's in most respects. However, given the considerations mentioned later by Artamonov and Tigranov, bearing on the difficulty of collecting accurate

[14] Ogranovich (1870: 71–2; 1876: 201f.); Markov (1890: 7–13); Radde (1886: 442); on the famine, see Gilbar (1976: 134, 143f.), Okazaki (1986).

statistics of the nomadic population, it is likely that all these figures erred by as much as 50 per cent either way.[15]

The following details of domestic and economic activities give some idea of the extent to which the nomads depended on access to markets within Russian territory:

The way of life of the Shahsevan is almost exclusively nomadic . . . Members of some tribes do a certain amount of agriculture, in which case they do not go on migration but live continuously in villages in Meshkin, Ardabil and other places near Moghan. The main occupation of the Shahsevan is stock-rearing. They rear (i) sheep, from which they get milk and wool, the milk and its products being eaten and the surplus sold and the wool also being partly sold and partly used for various things; (ii) cattle, which are mainly used for heavy transport; (iii) camels and (iv) horses, both in small numbers, extremely unprepossessing but hardy animals. The Shahsevan do not occupy themselves with trade, handicrafts or generally with any sort of commerce. Only the women make crude cloth from sheep and camel wool, and also carpets of poor quality, and the felt for their tents.[16]

Having disposed and arranged their pastures for the winter in Moghan, the Shahsevan would then set out with camels and pack animals back to their villages in Iran, where they would collect bread, flour, wheat, rice and barley and bring these to their pastures for their own consumption. A quarter of the Shahsevan remained in the villages of the Ardabil province and were occupied with grain cultivation both on their own account and for the remaining members of the community's nomads. Such journeys to their homeland were essential for the Shahsevan, since they were unable to take up and transport a six-months' supply of wheat for themselves and barley for their horses at one go. But apart from this transportation, they were often forced to purchase wheat from our people, especially in years when there was a poor harvest in Iran. The imported grain was milled in our mills by the Aras, in Talesh and in two mills in Belasovar. During the winter grazing the Shahsevan would visit our bazaars at Qara-Donlu, Javat, Abdulyan, Salyan, Masalin, and Asulin, to sell their produce: thick felt, *palas*, *mafrash*, *jejim* [all flat-woven goods], hides, skins, wool, butter, cheese, cattle, horses, rams, wethers, goats and camels – these transactions proceeded without their paying any tax to the [Russian] treasury.[17]

They buy the following produce: flour, rice, salt, onions, garlic, dried fruit, *doshab* (grape-juice) . . . They do not smoke tobacco and very few use a *qalyan* (water-pipe). Of domestic fowl, they keep only roosters, which serve as clocks for the times of prayer, milking, driving the flock to pasture. Each man keeps several

---

[15] Artamonov (1890: 445f.); Tigranov (1909: 126f.); Avdeyev (1927: 11); for Abbott, see Chapter Three above, and Amanat (1983: 229): Ardabil 6,200 families, Meshkin 5,400. Details of the various tribal lists and population estimates are given in Appendix Two. Rostopchin (1933), declaring an increase from 6 tribes (3,500 tents) in 1815 to 48 tribes (12,500 tents) in 1872, appears to be interpreting Ogranovich's report too literally.

[16] Radde (1886: 424); Markov (1890: 19). The last item is possibly wrong: felt in the twentieth century is made exclusively by men.   [17] Markov (1890: 24).

dogs. At the time of migration all the property is loaded onto camels and oxen. Twice a year they shear the sheep: at the beginning of April for felt, at the end of August for sale.[18]

Out of the household produce they sell the following:

Sheep's wool at 2–5 *qran* a *batman*.
Camel's wool at 2 *qran* a *batman*.
Felts, measuring about 1.5 by 1 metre, at 5 *qran*.
Horses at 45 to 400 *qran*.
Camels: *nar* (for transport) at 400 *qran*.[19]
       bughur (two-humped) at 250 *qran*.
Bulls at 25–100 *qran*.
Cows at 15–65 *qran*.
Wethers at 7–13 *qran*.
Ewes at 7 *qran*.
Lambs at 3 *qran*.
Donkeys at 35–50 *qran*.
Carpets from 10–50 *qran*.
Mats at 7–15 *qran*.

They buy weapons in Ardabil, Qara-Bagh and Salyan; powder from the Jahan-Khanomlu tribe, more than half of whom are occupied in manufacturing it; lead for shot is bought from Tabriz and Ardabil. Salt is purchased in Sarab at a quarter *qran* per *batman*; copper pans are bought in the village of Lahij and in Ardabil.[20]

A comparison of these prices with those current a century later permits a striking if not perhaps surprising observation. The relative values of the different animals and their products, and the 'terms of trade' with grain, are virtually the same, prices in the mid-1960s being a little more than one hundred times greater in each case, in terms of Iranian money values. In addition to the commodities mentioned by Ogranovich, the price of wheat-flour at the time was about half a *qran* a *batman* (average 5 toman = 50 *qran* in 1965–6); rice then was just over 1 *qran* a *batman* (in 1965–6 it varied, depending on quality, from 90–180 *qran*). Only the price of mutton has risen much more than a hundred times over the century.[21]

The general framework of the nomadic economy, in terms of pastoral

---

[18] Ogranovich (1870: 81). The details on shearing may be mistaken; nowadays the spring clips are sold, the summer clips are used for felt-making (Tapper 1979a: 57).

[19] The *nar* is a highly prized bull, hybrid between the two-humped Bactrian camel and the one-humped dromedary; it can usually carry up to half a ton, and is the only one of the variety of Shahsevan camels that can carry a complete tent; see Tapper (1985).

[20] Ogranovich (1870: 81–2). I have converted some of Ogranovich's figures from Russian into Iranian measures. A *qran* is and was a tenth of one toman: nowadays it is officially known as the *rial*. At that time the *qran* was worth about a shilling, and the toman was worth three Russian silver roubles (10s.). The *batman* in use in most of Shahsevan territory was and is equivalent to about 6 kg, 14 lb, or 0.4 Russian *pud*.

[21] Figures for 1860 abstracted from FO 248/192 (Abbott to Alison no. 38 of 29.11.1860); cf. Gilbar (1978, 1983). For 1965–6, see Tapper (1979a).

production and marketing, has not changed substantially, but consumption of items like sugar, tea, oil and charcoal, was then at a much lower level than now, the balance of income being exacted in taxation and other dues. Ogranovich continues:

The Shahsevan spend summer and winter in round felt tents . . . and a whole family lives in each tent; if the sons are married they hang up a partition of dark blue cotton. The father is the head of the family; if he separates his son off during his lifetime then he gives him a separate tent and part of the property to live on. After the father's death, the property is divided in the following fashion: the eldest son receives the best horse and bull, the father's weapons, sabre and knife; then the rest of the property is divided equally among the sons. The eldest brother takes the father's place and is considered the head of the family. To the widow they give two half-imperials [?] which she keeps for her funeral; if she lives with her sons, then they must provide her full dowry (*kabin-ishtahi* [?]) and then she lives separately. If she remarries after the mourning period, which is about a year, then her sons give her clothes and a bed. Daughters receive nothing at property divisions . . . men look after the herds . . . while women are obliged to look after everything in the house.[22]

Ogranovich and Krebel give details of Shahsevan religious rituals, in which they judge the nomads to be generally lax and ignorant of the correct Shi'i practice and dogma. Wedding and funeral customs appear to have been essentially the same as today: for example, the custom of serving sugar to wedding guests, who then contribute presents of animals or money, is mentioned specifically.

Weddings usually take place in the summer in the *yailaq*, They take girls from various societies, even from among the daughters of the Lankaran and Javat settlers, to whom they also give their daughters. A man of 16 and a girl of 15 are considered adult; they are engaged from childhood. Polygamy is allowed but few people have two wives.[23]

In Krebel's judgment, the Shahsevan have no conception of 'honour' and set little store by promises or oaths, and 'from this directly stems their lack of understanding of property rights and their recognition only of the skill and daring involved in robbery, and not of the crime'. The Shahsevan are, however, exceptionally hospitable, and eagerly entertain and protect all guests, whether friends or enemies. 'The women are very moral, which may be due less to a sense of morality than to fear of the dire penalties for misbehaviour.' Different tribes are renowned for different qualities: some are more honest, or cleaner, or more pious, or more warlike than others.

Krebel adds the following on Shahsevan lawlessness, which he blames on the vices of the oppressive, inefficient and avaricious Iranian administration:

[22] Ogranovich (1870: 80–2).   [23] Ogranovich (1870: 82–3); cf. Tapper (1979a: 45–6).

However, it may also be said that the main occupations of the Shahsevan are robbery and violence, which result from the blood feuds which are so common among them. When, as frequently happens during the raids of one tribe on the herds of another, a man from one tribe is killed by a man of the other, then the whole tribe of the victim enters a feuding relationship (*qanlı*) with the killer's tribe. This enmity cannot be settled except by bloodshed: the victim's fellow-tribesmen consider it their duty to try and kill any member of the killer's tribe, wherever they may meet them, and therefore any customary meetings between the two tribes cease, and they avoid each other so far as possible. No kind of legal criminal investigation and punishment of the murderer will satisfy or pacify the injured party, and the only means of restoring peace between them is by the long-sanctified custom of blood vengeance. Conciliation is effected as follows: the elders and most respected persons of the killer's tribe, or respected men of some other tribe, act as mediators and go to the injured tribe to make overtures of peace; meanwhile they offer presents; then the killer himself apologizes and offers blood-money, and they usually conclude the matter by arranging a marriage between the two sides, the injured side taking a bride from the offender.[24]

The statement above, that the 'enmity cannot be settled except by bloodshed', is rather contradicted by the later details of conciliation, unless Krebel means 'after vengeance has been taken'. In Radde's version, on the argument that the expenses in a Shahsevan marriage are mostly borne by the groom's side, it is stated that the the girl is provided by the injured party for the offenders, and the usual prestations are exchanged, so that the former are materially better off; but this is not consistent with what I was told, which confirms Krebel's version.

The economic and cultural features so far described have changed little since the time to which they refer; it may perhaps be assumed that they have obtained at least since the eighteenth century. In one major respect, however, the nineteenth century, with the Russian acquisition of the better part of Moghan and the eventual closure of the frontier to the nomads, brought a radical upheaval in economic conditions for the Shahsevan, which in turn transformed their tribal political organization, as we shall see.

The Shahsevan chiefs

The Shahsevan khans reached the height of their power at the end of the eighteenth century; they then sharply declined as a result of both internal divisions in the chiefly dynasty, as sketched in Chapter Seven, and the Russian conquest of their territory (Chapter Eight). This decline continued with the resumption of firmer central government in Iran.

---

[24] Ogranovich (1870: 84); Radde (1886: 423–4); Markov (1890: 21).

As Lambton says,

To establish control over the tribal areas was . . . one of the hardest problems which faced the Qajars. In general at this period they attempted, as had rulers before them, to rule the tribes through the tribal chiefs, but the control they established was seldom more than precarious. Thus, an Il Khan and Ilbeg were appointed over the larger tribes; they collected government taxes and were generally responsible for tribal affairs. These officers were usually, but not necessarily, tribal chiefs, and the tendency was for the office to be hereditary.[25]

According to Krebel, Shahsevan *elbeys* were officially constituted in 1839 following Russian complaints about disorder among the tribes. 'Before that, the Shahsevan tribes were governed by their own leaders and by officials who were sent to them from time to time by the government.' Apart from the *elbeys* – one for each of the two *el* (the Ardabil and Meshkin divisions) – each tribe (*taifa*) had its chief (the *bey*), and all these officials were appointed by and were responsible to the governor of Ardabil.[26]

After his dismissal, rebellion and subsequent arrest, Nazar 'Ali Khan was taken to court in 1809 and does not figure in the records again. Lambton notes that 'frequently relatives of the tribal leaders, or even the leaders themselves, would be kept at court as hostages for the good behaviour of the tribe', while 'the tribal leaders also often found it expedient to have their representatives in the capital or the main provincial centre to transact their business and to watch over their interests'.[27] In the case of the Ardabil chiefs, even if they were close to the centres of power, they lost their overall dominance of the Shahsevan, and it seems they suffered a major eclipse. Probably many of the tribes joined the Meshkin confederacy under 'Ata Khan and Shükür Khan, though Ardabil tribes supplied troops for the Qajar princes governing Ardabil right up to the end of the second Russian war.

One of Nazar 'Ali Khan's daughters was married to one of Fath 'Ali Shah's numerous sons, who was born in 1813 and cannot have been married much earlier than 1825–30. Ahmad Mirza relates in some detail the wedding arrangements (he does not mention the date) for Shah Beyim Agha, daughter of Nazar 'Ali Khan Shahsevan Sarı-Khan-Beyli, who was brought from Ardabil as wife of Hajji Soltan Mohammad Mirza Seif ad-Douleh. Among other extravagances, this was the first Qajar wedding when the bride was brought to court on an elephant. The reason for the splendour of this wedding was that the bride's maternal aunt was

---

[25] Lambton (1953: 158–9).   [26] Radde (1886: 424): Markov (1890: 17).
[27] Lambton (1961: 130).

Agha Baji, the Shah's highly respected wife and daughter of the late
Ebrahim Khalil Khan of Qara-Bagh, while the groom's mother was the
Shah's favourite wife, Taj ad-Douleh, who was on very good terms with
Agha Baji. Agha Baji apparently wrote announcements to all the queens
of foreign countries, who duly sent wedding presents, the most fabulous
of which was a jewel-encrusted smelling-bottle from the Queen of
England.[28]

Further evidence for the comparative sophistication of the Ardabil
branch of the dynasty is the report by 'Abbas Mirza's son Jahangir Mirza,
governor of Ardabil and Meshkin, that in winter 1828–9, when his father
was preparing a trip to St Petersburg, he was ordered to accompany him
as far as Tiflis, bringing a party of fifty young Shahsevan nobles from
Ardabil, mounted on the finest horses and decorated with rich trappings.
The mission was in fact cancelled on the news of the murder of the
Russian envoy Griboedov in Tehran.[29]

It is difficult to establish who succeeded Nazar 'Ali Khan. His former
deputy (and uncle?) Farajollah Khan appears to have returned to Ardabil,
for in about 1829 he murdered a Shahsevan chief and was imprisoned
there by Jahangir Mirza. He escaped, possibly with Jahangir Mirza's con-
nivance, but the latter was forced by his father to recapture him and bring
him to court.[30] (Soon after, Jahangir Mirza was replaced as governor by
his elder brother Mohammad Mirza. When 'Abbas Mirza died in 1833,
Mohammad Mirza became heir apparent and governor-general of
Azarbaijan, and he succeeded his grandfather Fath 'Ali Shah on the
latter's death the following year. Meanwhile Jahangir Mirza and various
other royal princes were incarcerated in 'Abbas Mirza's castle at Ardabil,
which had become the state prison of Iran.)

Abbott noted in 1843 that the Ardabil chief was Mohammad Khan;
according to Radde's genealogical chart, 'Mamed Chan Il-Begi' was son
of Nazar 'Ali Khan. In 1853, Tahmasp-qoli Khan (on Radde's chart,
brother's son of Mohammad/Mahmad Khan, but not *elbey*) was dismissed as *elbey* as a result of complaints by the tribesmen, and replaced by
Rostam Khan. Radde shows Rostam Khan *elbey* as grandson of Mahmad

---

[28] There is some ambiguity about the identity of the couple: Ahmad Mirza also names a
Gelin Khanom, daughter of Nazar 'Ali Khan Shahsevan Sarı-Khan-Beyli, as wife of
Soltan Mohammad Mirza Seif ad-Douleh; perhaps these were two separate women;
perhaps one of them was married to Seif ad-Douleh Mirza, another son of Fath 'Ali Shah
(Ahmad Mirza 1976: 16–17, 53, 186). Fasa'i (Busse 1974: 139) reports that a perfume-
bottle (the same one?) studded with jewels worth 20,000 toman was presented to Banu,
daughter of Ebrahim Khan Javanshir, in November 1811 by envoy Gore-Ouseley's wife
on behalf of the Queen of England.
[29] Jahangir Mirza (1948: 124).   [30] Jahangir Mirza (1948: 130–1).

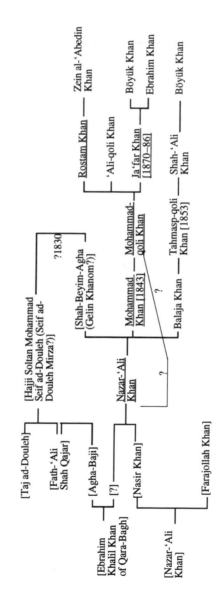

Figure 7. Genealogy of Ardabil *elbeys*

Khan *elbey* and elder brother of Ja'far Khan *elbey*, who had succeeded him by 1870 and continued as *elbey* until the late 1880s.[31] So far so good: however, Radde names Mahmad Khan's son (and father of Rostam and Ja'far) as Mahmad-qoli Khan *elbey*, while Ogranovich names Ja'far Khan as son of Nazar 'Ali Khan. Even allowing for the likelihood of there having been two (or more?) Nazar 'Ali Khans, and the possibility that by 'son' may be meant 'descendant', it is hard to sort out this discrepancy.

The Meshkin chiefs, who probably took over dominance of the Shahsevan tribes after the fall of Nazar 'Ali Khan of Ardabil, played a notably pro-Russian role in the second war, as we saw in the previous chapter. 'Ata Khan and Shokrollah/Shükür Khan not only offered support to Madatov and Vadibolski, but they threatened Mohammad Mirza Qajar in Ardabil when he was preparing to defend the town against Sukhtelen.

A firman of Mohammad Mirza dated April–May 1828 (after the Treaty of Torkman–Chai), still addresses 'Ata Khan politely as governor of Meshkin.[32] But neither he nor his brother is mentioned after this, and they most likely took refuge in Russian territory; their sons, however, remained. Ogranovich and Radde indicate that 'Ata Khan's son Farzi Khan succeeded him as Meshkin chief, though in 1837 d'Arcy Todd found Rostam Khan (shown on Radde's chart as son of Shükür Khan) as Meshkin chief, while in 1843 Abbott recorded the incumbent as 'Cosseim' Khan – presumably Farzi Khan's younger brother Qasem Khan (Radde). Farzi Khan was, however, chief by 1849, when he was dismissed soon after Naser ad-Din Shah's accession. His immediate successor is not recorded, but in 1853 Qasem Khan was reappointed *elbey* and his son Böyük Khan (so also in Radde's chart) was given command of the Meshkin Shahsevan sowars. According to Krebel (in Radde and Markov), Farzi Khan was *elbey* from 1850 to 1880 with a few interruptions: Radde says that he was twice replaced briefly by his son Mahmadqoli Khan. In 1880, when Mahmad-qoli was dead, Farzi Khan, reportedly an old and debauched menace, was finally set aside and put in custody in Tabriz. He was succeeded as *elbey* by his son 'Ali-qoli Khan, who retained the title at least until 1903.[33]

The *elbeys* had almost unlimited power over the tribespeople. They were responsible for collecting taxes and military levies, for policing the tribes, and for holding court in serious cases. They adjudicated and sentenced according to religious law (*shari'at*), local custom (*'adat*) and expediency (*maslahat*), but at their own discretion they could sentence offenders to fines, corporal punishment, imprisonment, confiscation of

---

[31] Maraghe'i (1877–80, II: 123); Garusi (1910: 94–6); Ogranovich (1870: 70).
[32] Karimzadeh-Tabrizi (1971: 186).
[33] Maraghe'i (1877–80, II: 123); Radde (1886: 434); Tigranov (1909: 112–13).

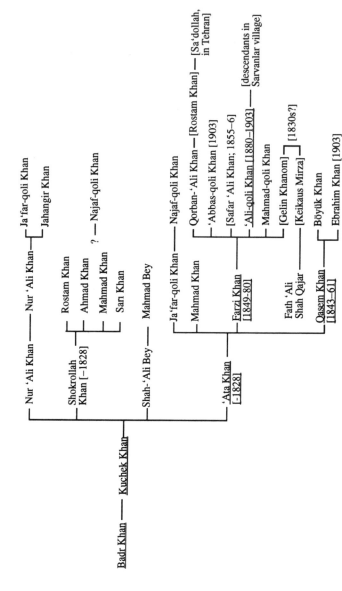

Figure 8. Genealogy of Meshkin *elbeys*

property and even death. They profited substantially when judging cases of theft, and appeal against their judgments was impossible. According to Ogranovich, *elbeys* had the right to take to wife any girl from among their subjects (*rayāt*). *Beys* of individual tribes had lesser duties and kept order within their own tribes, assisted by elected elders (*aq-saqal*) of camp communities (*oba*).[34]

As Lambton notes,

The main body of the shah's military forces . . . was formed by tribal levies. They were required to attend court annually at the feast of the New Year; if their services were not required that year they would be given leave to return to their homes. The provincial governors were also able in time of need to levy contingents from the tribes and villages in their governments.[35]

The Moghan Shahsevan were expected to provide 500 fully equipped horsemen for military service. However, with their record in the Russian wars, the Shahsevan tribes that remained in Iranian Azarbaijan could hardly have a high place in the regard of the Qajar government. Moreover, to judge from Russian reports a few decades later, in mid-century more than two-thirds of the Shahsevan wintered customarily in Russian Moghan, so, having to spend half the year in Russian territory and being thus dependent on the goodwill of both governments, they were unlikely to inspire trust in their patriotism, and it would be surprising if extensive use were made of their military capacity.

The Shahsevan of Moghan did contribute levies to the Qajar campaigns at that time in Khorasan and Afghanistan, although troops from the Shaqaqi and from the Inallu, Baghdadi and Afshar Shahsevan tribes of Kharaqan and Khamseh figured more prominently.[36] In 1271/1854–5, Hasan 'Ali Khan Afshar became colonel of the Ardabil and Meshkin regiment; in 1278/1861–2 he was promoted to general-adjutant. Minorsky quotes a Russian history of the Türkmen to the effect that in 1856–7 an Inanlu general and an Afshar general participated in the expedition against the Türkmen of Astarabad, but both came from Moghan; perhaps the latter was Hasan 'Ali Khan, and his regiments including Shahsevan warriors.[37]

[34] Ogranovich (1870: 80); Radde (1886: 424–5); Markov (1890: 17–18).

[35] Lambton (1961: 131); see also Hambly (1991a: 159–60).

[36] See Appendix One, and compare the references to Shahsevan regiments and leaders from the respective Shahsevan groups in 'army lists' of the time, e.g. Maraghe'i (1877–80: various; and 1889: Appendix, pp. 6–26). In Andreski's terms (1954), there was a low 'Military Participation Ratio' among the Moghan Shahsevan.

[37] Bamdad (1968, V: 72); Minorsky (1951–2: 3); C. M. MacGregor, who passed through Khorasan in 1875, observed that 'amongst the troops at Mushudd, was a body of cavalry, drawn from the Shah Sewunds, a large tribe, I believe, of Toork descent, who came from the districts of Mishkeen and Ardebeel, in the province of Azurbaijan' (1879, I: 297), quoted by Gurney (1983: 173).

The nomad taxes were assessed on the 'horse-standard' (*at-mah*): 1 horse (valued at 3 tomans) = 2 camels = 5 cows = 100 wethers. Tax ratings per nomad tent ranged from 10 to 100 tomans – though Ogranovich does not make clear what was being assessed; it does not seem to be the capital value of the animals, nor the expected value of their annual produce. In 1843 5,500 tomans were officially collected from the nomads (4,000 tomans from the Meshkin and 1,500 tomans from the Ardabil division; the numerous settled Shahsevan of the Ardabil division paid separate taxes) and delivered to government. Forty years later, the figures were more than doubled. The Russian officials seemed shocked when they reported that the cash annually collected from the nomads totalled two to three times the official amount that reached the Treasury. The governors, the *elbeys*, the *beys* and the tax-collectors (*mohassel*) all took their legitimate percentages, while the *elbeys* extorted a whole range of customary and irregular 'dues', such as tribute in pack-camels, tent-felts, butter, sheep, and cash for 'household expenses' and for 'presents' to government officials. The *elbeys* continued to collect the pasture due (*chop-bashi*) for Moghan, at the rate of one toman per household, long after the Russians had ceased receiving it. The mullahs received various dues: one *qran* annually (presumably as *zakat* alms) from each household and one toman for each funeral or wedding.[38] All these payments, except where specified, had to be made in cash, which to this extent must have stimulated pastoral production and marketing activities.

Shahsevan tribal organization

The various Shahsevan tribes (*taifa*) formed a hierarchy: members of the *elbey* dynasties, and those half-dozen or so tribes which could claim common descent with them from Badr Khan's ancestor Yunsur Pasha, were classed as 'nobles' (*beyzadä*); the rest were 'commoners' (*rayät* or *hampa*).

Each noble tribe consisted of two 'classes'. Members of the ruling lineage formed the nucleus of the tribe, which bore their ancestor's name, and they dominated not only by delegated authority and by control of pasture, but also through their superior descent. With their retinue of 'servants' (*nökär*), they constituted the *beyzadä*, who 'do no work, pay no taxes, own everything and in many tribes amount to half or more of the population'. The rest of the noble tribe were *hampa* (Radde) or *hämra* (Markov), both terms meaning 'companion', though according to my own information the former, which also means 'peasant', was the term

---

[38] Ogranovich (1870: 72–3).

used; they were 'workers' and peasants, who had no control over pasture or farmland, but tended the flocks, paid the taxes and cultivated the farmlands owned by the *beyzadä*.[39] In other tribal groups in Iran, this retinue goes by the name *'amaleh* ('workers'); although I have not come across this name in relation to the retinues of Shahsevan chiefs, it seems appropriate, as well as convenient, to follow Russian usage in translating *hampa* as 'workers'.

In addition, every commoner tribe was subordinated to one of the noble chiefs, and its own chief or members of his family joined the latter's retinue. To judge from earliest records mentioning individual tribes, the nobles' dominance over the commoner tribes at this time depended partly on their descent claims and partly on the *elbey*'s delegation of authority to them, though they probably also had some control over the pastures of the commoner tribes.

There is little information on the nature of political and territorial organization within these noble tribes, or the tribal 'clusters' which they led, but it was probably echoed in that of the dominant tribes later in the century, to be described below. Certain important differences of organization distinguished noble tribes from commoners. Neither workers, nor members of commoner tribes, however strong, could take leadership of a noble tribe; their allegiance was to the chiefly lineage, but not to individual chiefs. There was no formal rule of chiefly succession other than patrilineal descent from a former chief, and retinues and commoners would follow whichever candidate offered greater economic and political advantage. Noble lineages could and did experience fission; when this occurred, the workers and the commoner tribes divided accordingly, each new noble tribe continuing to be dominated by a noble lineage.

The following noble tribes all formed by fission, probably originally from the Sarı-Khan-Beyli tribe: Bala-Beyli, Band-'Ali-Beyli, Nouruz-'Ali-Beyli, Qoja-Beyli, Damirchili and Polatlu. The sources are not consistent on identifying all these tribes as 'nobles', but this list seems most likely. In 1843, all but Polatlu belonged to the Meshkin division, but some of them may once have been under the Ardabil *elbeys* before the latter declined; other noble tribes of Ardabil may already have settled. Later fission divided Band-'Ali-Beyli into the separate tribes Mast-'Ali-Beyli, 'Ali-Babalu and Qara-Qasemli; 'Isa-Beyli ('Isalu) separated from Qoja-Beyli; Khamesli, Asefli and Jurughlu from Polatlu; Qurtlar from Damirchili; and Mast-'Ali-Beyli divided, one half emigrating to Russia.

Chiefly lineages in commoner tribes had no such claims to legitimacy.

[39] Radde (1886: 424f.); Markov (1890: 17).

Few commoner tribes bore an ancestral name or even had an ideology of shared descent, through which access to joint pasture-lands might be regulated. All lineages could identify equally with the tribal name, and were equally eligible to lead. The chiefly lineage's authority thus depended largely on the support of the nobles and the *elbey*, and it could not afford to be weakened by fission, which might allow another lineage to take over the whole tribe. I have no record of fission in commoner tribes, but there are cases where leadership of such tribes was taken over by a new chiefly lineage; this happened in Geyikli in the middle of the nineteenth century, and in Talesh-Mikeilli around the turn of the century.[40]

By 1850, many commoner chiefs had acquired independent economic power over their followers. We have no information on the nature of pasture ownership and tenure before the Russian acquisition of Moghan (other than ownership of at least part by the Talesh khans, to whom some form of rent was paid), but it is clear that this event, and its immediate consequences in restricting Shahsevan pastures, brought violent changes in patterns of economic and political organization. Although Krebel and Ogranovich say little on these changes (discussed in Chapter Eleven), they do give details of the main features of pasture tenure in Moghan in the mid-nineteenth century.

Briefly, the evidence indicates that all the available pastures fell into the hands of the tribal chiefs, who leased them at escalating rentals to their followers, and thus gained an unprecedented degree of power over them. In 1850 or soon after, the chiefs

quickly divided Moghan into *qıshlaqs* and marked off the boundaries. When this division was completed, the chiefs began to lease the *qıshlaqs* both to their own followers and also to others . . . Moreover, the chiefs have gained such control over the *qıshlaqs* that they are distributed before the annual migration of the Shahsevan to Moghan; each person is authorized to go to a certain *qıshlaq*: they have secured their seizure with written orders granting the right to graze. If someone dares to take a *qıshlaq* arbitrarily and use it, they then extort double and sometimes treble the sum due, as a fine, like an arbitrary quit-rent . . . As a result of this awkward situation the poorest of the Shahsevan, on coming to Moghan, first sought free *qıshlaqs* from Russian subjects, renting them from nomads and villagers, especially from Russian settlers, with whom they drew up written contracts, remaining on these *qıshlaqs* until the end of March. Many such poor people even join our nomads, contract marriage alliances with them, and some serve most willingly as shepherds for our chiefs and wealthy nomads, performing even further duties and services only for the sake of feeding their sheep and cattle.[41]

[40] See Chapters Thirteen and Fourteen below.
[41] Ogranovich (1872, nos. 130 and 144) as quoted by Rostopchin (1933: 101); see also Radde (1886: 429–30); Markov (1890: 26).

Elsewhere, Ogranovich listed 736 *qıshlaqs*. The Shahsevan, he claimed, would lease out all their *qıshlaqs*, then cross the boundary set by the Russian authorities and seize the land of Russian subjects on the river banks, which they would then lease out also. In years of bad harvests, they would lease their grazing lands at high rentals to Russian subjects from Javat and Lankaran, or they would lease both their own *qıshlaqs* and the lands they had seized to Iranian nomads brought in from Sarab, Sa'uj-Bolagh, Urmiyeh, Khoi and Hamadan. The animals (camels, horses, sheep) brought to Moghan in the latter half of the century numbered over two million head. Naturally, as the pastures became more crowded, so rents rose: 'initially the *qıshlaqs* rented at between 15 and 40 roubles, but at the end of 1860 they had risen to 40 toman (about 120 roubles)'.[42]

The old hierarchy of tribal groups and classes and chiefly authority was already breaking down and a new structure was emerging, partly as a result of internal contradictions and partly as a response to the drastic changes in the economic and political environment beginning with the Russian advent in Moghan. As the pasturage became more and more restricted, so the division widened between owners of pasture and tenants. The *elbeys* lost the monopoly of authority. The Ardabil branch of the chiefly dynasty was already assimilated to the administration and to urban life and had lost touch with the tribes, while the Meshkin *elbeys* either could not or would not control the most recalcitrant brigands and were unacceptable to the Russians. The noble tribes meanwhile were weakened through rivalries within their chiefly lineages, and, though they continued to control their own workers, many of them were now diminished in numbers and had lost control of their 'cluster' of commoner tribes. In each division, however, one noble tribe continued to dominate the rest: Polatlu in Ardabil, Qoja-Beyli in Meshkin. The half-dozen or so larger and wealthier commoner tribes now declared their independence of the nobles and collected their own clusters of weaker tribes. The weaker commoner (and noble) chiefs, if only to secure their control of their own workers, sought the support of a dominant chief. By the time the frontier was closed to the Shahsevan in 1884, the original stratification of the tribes into nobles and commoners had broken down, and a new one was emerging, based no longer on descent claims and delegated authority, but rather on numerical strength, material resources and territorial and political alliances.

These changes are described in greater detail in Chapter Eleven, after the events leading to the frontier closure have been narrated.

---

[42] Ogranovich (1872, nos. 130 and 144) as quoted by Rostopchin (1933: 101), and (1870: 74–5).

10 Nomads and commissars in Moghan

The troubles begin

After the end of the wars, the Russians colonized and settled their new Transcaucasian territories, and dealt with local uprisings. They were not interested in the annexation of Iranian Azarbaijan. They put pressure on the Iranians to settle their frontier tribes, but both sides had much to gain from keeping groups like the Shahsevan nomadic. Iran relied on the nomads' pastoral produce and on their role as frontier guards, while the Russians not only gained considerably themselves from the Shahsevan contribution to the economy of the Moghan settlers, but also were able to put to good political use their tally of the latter's complaints of Shahsevan raiding. The officials and diplomats concerned were well aware of these factors in the situation. Though the Russians pressed for settlement of the nomads, they knew the Iranians would not be keen, and anyway the British agents advised the Iranians against such a policy. So the Iranian officials took half-measures, succeeding only in lining their pockets and further antagonizing the nomads.

According to Radde and Markov, it was in response to Russian complaints concerning Shahsevan raids and disturbances that the Iranian authorities in 1839 created the offices of *elbey* for the two sections of the Moghan Shahsevan tribes. The only other Iranian move concerning the Shahsevan that I know to have been carried out before 1849 was the visit of Mohammad Shah's brother Bahman Mirza, governor-general of Azarbaijan, to Ardabil, Meshkin and possibly Moghan, in November 1843, when he 'arranged the frontier'.[1]

In 1849, to try to keep the Shahsevan nomads away from the settled colonists and the Russian nomads in Moghan, Baron Wrangel, military governor at Shamakhı, took steps to give precise definition to the tract which the Iranian nomads were to be allowed to use. This timing was probably not fortuitous but calculated to take advantage of the comparative weakness of the Iranian government under the young Naser ad-Din

---

[1] FO 248/107 (Bonham to Sheil, various).

Shah, who had succeeded his father Mohammad Shah on the latter's
death in September the previous year; it also coincided, however, with
some repressive measures by the Iranian authorities against the
Shahsevan, to be described below.

Ogranovich sets out the boundaries decided on. A strip not less than
5–7 versts wide (a verst is a little over 1 km), between the nomadic tract
and the banks of the rivers Aras, Kor, Akosha and Balharu, was reserved
for the use of the settlers there and their own cattle. The zone of Russian
Moghan allotted to the Shahsevan flocks to graze amounted to over 2,000
square versts (about 250,000 hectares). In addition, the Shahsevan were
shown places on the rivers at which their flocks might drink, and tracks
along which they should lead them there. These last provisions were
absolutely necessary because, although Moghan had been widely irrigated centuries before, there was now no surface water at all within the
central part of the steppe, other than a number of salt lakes. The provisions were not enough, however, to satisfy the Shahsevan, who had been
accustomed to camping by the rivers and to using pastures within easy
reach of the banks, and did not regard the waterless central part of the
steppe as usable grazing.[2]

Russian policy and Wrangel's measures gave rise to misunderstandings
from the start. In late 1849, Consul-General Richard Stevens at Tabriz
wrote to Colonel Farrant, the British envoy in Tehran, that the Russians
were refusing to permit the Shahsevan to winter in Moghan; and in
January 1850, Stevens reported to Farrant's successor, Lieutenant-
Colonel Sheil, that

The Shahsevens on preparing to take up their winter quarters on the [Russian]
side of Moghan were informed that the Russian Government would no longer
permit it. The cold weather setting in earlier than usual, and before the question
could be settled, the tribes suffered a great deal, and lost a large portion of their
flocks. The prohibition was subsequently withdrawn, when they occupied their
customary ground.

This message was transmitted to London, and the Foreign Office
instructed Lord Bloomfield in St Petersburg to call Russian Chancellor
Count Nesselrode's attention to the matter. The latter explained to
Bloomfield that

it was perfectly true that the permission enjoyed by these Tribes to cross the
Russian frontier had been suspended, and that this measure had become necessary in consequence of their ill conduct and marauding propensities, but that after
some Communications the prohibition had been withdrawn and the old privilege
restored to them.

[2] Ogranovich (1870: 73); Radde (1886: 429); Markov (1890: 25).

Markov too, enumerating Russian grounds for complaint against the Shahsevan, writes that the cause of the above incidents was the nomads' occupation of areas not allotted to them, and the subsequent disputes.[3]

In autumn 1850, Sheil wrote to London that the Russians again intended to forbid the Shahsevan to enter Moghan, and the Foreign Office once more briefed Bloomfield. This time the Russian government denied that they had communicated any such instructions: the Viceroy of the Caucasus must have taken these steps on his own authority.[4] In the outcome, the Russian measures had little permanent effect. According to Ogranovich, the Shahsevan chiefs seized the Moghan pastures, divided them and rented them out, as related in Chapter Nine.

Meanwhile, the Iranian authorities were taking their own forceful measures. For a year or so after Mohammad Shah's death in September 1848, lawlessness reigned in the Ardabil region as elsewhere in Azarbaijan. His young successor, Naser ad-Din Shah, sent 'Abbas-qoli Khan Javanshir (grandson of Ebrahim Khalil Khan of Qara-Bagh) to govern the districts of Ardabil, Meshkin and Qara-Dagh. He had particular instructions to free the frontiers from robbers and highwaymen, and to capture and imprison Eskandar Khan and the brothers Shah Palang and Shah Mar, all of the Meshkin Shahsevan, and Hajji Mohammad 'Ali of the Ardabil Shahsevan. He left the capital in summer 1849, and on his way met Hamzeh Mirza Heshmat ad-Douleh, who was going to Tabriz to take up his appointment as governor-general of Azarbaijan. In Zanjan they were warned that the Hajji-Khojalu and Damirchili tribes (both from the Meshkin division of the Shahsevan) had been fighting, and that several people had been killed, so, as they approached the Ardabil region, they sent letters to various Shahsevan and Qara-Daghi chiefs, bidding them collect forces and bring the Hajji-Khojalu to submission. This move was apparently successful. The governors then proceeded together to Tabriz, whence they sent word to the nobles of Qara-Dagh to arrest certain Shahsevan chiefs and send them in custody to Tabriz, appointing 500 cavalry for the purpose. Hamzeh Mirza deposed the Meshkin *elbey* Farzi Khan, who then began widespread raiding activities.[5]

Towards the end of the year (1849) 'Abbas-qoli Khan himself left Tabriz for Qara-Dagh and Meshkin, where he took several Shahsevan chiefs prisoner. In January 1850, Stevens reported to Sheil that 'Abbas-qoli's 'severe but necessary punishments' had 'produced a salutary effect'

---

[3] FO 248/142 (Stevens to Sheil no. 3 of 13.1.1850); FO 97/345 (FO to Bloomfield no. 25 of 29.1.1850); FO 65/376 (Bloomfield to Palmerston no. 77 of 8.3.1850); Markov (1890: 27).   [4] FO 65/380 (Bloomfield to Palmerston no. 324 of 22.10.1850).
[5] Sepehr (1958, III: 76, 111f.).

in those districts, which were now in a 'tolerably quiet state'.[6] The Shahsevan had no doubt been shocked into submission by an unprecedented threefold attack, for (as we have seen) the Russians had just prevented them from crossing the frontier, and they were now besides experiencing an unusually severe winter.

In spring 1851, after the second winter in which the Russians had tried to stop the Shahsevan from wintering in Moghan, Naser ad-Din Shah's great minister, Mirza Taqi Khan Amir Kabir, was reported to be contemplating removing the Shahsevan south to the region of 'Eraq-e 'Ajam, between Hamadan and Zanjan. In the summer, Hamzeh Mirza was sent to Ardabil and Meshkin, to adopt 'measures for preventing the Shahseven tribes from wintering on the Russian side of Moghan'. Stevens reported in September that

The Prince Governor of Azerbijan [Hamzeh Mirza] during his recent visit to Mishkin invited the principal chiefs of the Shahsevend Tribes to wait upon him, assuring them that his object was to consult with them on certain measures connected with the welfare of the Tribes, and that they would be permitted to return to their homes. As soon as they had all collected in the Prince's camp, they were seized, and put into heavy irons, and sent to the common gaol of Tabriz. I am not aware that these persons have given any cause of complaint against them, and am at a loss therefore to account for such a gross breach of faith on the part of the Prince Governor.[7]

The following chiefs were mentioned: Farzi Khan, Eskandar Khan, Salim Khan, Roushan Khan, Qasem Khan of Shaki, Shah Palang, Shah Mar, and Mollah Mo'men. It is not at all clear which tribes were involved. Farzi Khan is presumably the deposed Meshkin *elbey*. Eskandar Khan, Shah Palang and Shah Mar were mentioned above; in Sepehr's chronicle, Eskandar Khan is named son of Shükür Khan, though Radde does not mention him on his genealogical chart of the Meshkin *elbeys*. Qasem Khan may be a relative of Salim Khan of Shaki, given permission by 'Abbas Mirza in 1808 to reside in Ardabil. Sepehr relates the story of Mollah Mo'men. Salim, Shah Mar and his brother Shah Palang were apparently notorious robbers; of Roushan Khan nothing further is told.[8]

When the Amir Kabir was dismissed in November 1851, a number of the Shahsevan prisoners were among those to be recommended to the

---

[6] FO 248/142 (Stevens to Sheil no. 3 of 13.1.1850). Later in the year 'Abbas-qoli Khan was replaced, in Ardabil by Mohammad Reza Khan Qajar, and in Qara-Dagh by Qasem Khan Qajar (Sepehr 1958, III: 130).

[7] FO 248/145 (Stevens to Sheil no. 51 of 12.6.1851, and no. 80 of 4.9.1851); FO 60/166 (Sheil to F.O. no. 19 of 26.6.1851, and no. 35 of 24.9.1851).

[8] Sepehr (1958, III: 111).

Shah's pardon. Hamzeh Mirza felt that all the Shahsevan chiefs should be kept in custody in order to preserve security on the frontier, while Stevens, the British consul-general, considered that only Salim Khan and the brothers Shah Palang and Shah Mar need be detained.[9] There is no mention of what actually happened to the prisoners, though Farzi Khan at least was eventually released and reinstated as *elbey* of the Meshkin tribes.

In 1852, according to Markov, the Azarbaijani administration nominated Colonel Heidar 'Ali Khan as commissar for the Shahsevan, to be attached to the Russians and to introduce order on the frontier. The Iranian authorities gave their new commissar no instructions about satisfying Russian claims against the Shahsevan, and neither the power nor the authority to deal with them, 'and therefore this measure brought us no advantage at all'.[10]

Meanwhile the Iranians continued to pay 2,000 roubles as the pasture-due for Moghan. Soon the Russians became involved in war with Turkey, and endeavoured, through their envoy in Tehran, to win Iranian support. In 1853 the Amir Kabir's successor as prime minister, Mirza Aqa Khan Nuri, who was anxious to rid Iran of foreign political influence, took advantage of the Russian predicament to refuse payment of the Moghan dues, claiming on behalf of the Shahsevan that the grass had been burned by Russian subjects before the nomads' arrival, while the Russians alleged that the Shahsevan themselves had fired the pastures. A subsequent inquiry, according to Markov, supported the Russian allegations. Mirza Aqa Khan then swung back to a pro-Russian position and in 1856 the Iranian government paid over the outstanding dues – though after that year the payments ceased permanently.[11]

Mirza Aqa Khan had been intriguing against the British, and in December 1855 British envoy Charles Murray withdrew his mission from Iran. The following October the British representative in Tehran, Consul Stevens (who had had to leave Tabriz himself in 1854 as a result of Iranian complaints of his 'interference' in government affairs, notably in the question of the widespread use of torture), wrote home:

The Russian authorities in Georgia have recently been complaining very loudly against the insecure state of the frontier, from the organization of large bands of brigands from the Shahseven tribes of Persia. The Governor of Lankeran goes so far as to declare that disorders have reached such a degree that he cannot collect the taxes of his district. The Consul-General in Tabreez [Keith Abbott] reports to the Legation that the Kaimakam [minister to the governor-general of Azarbaijan] had taken no notice of as many as forty official letters addressed to him in the

---

[9] FO 248/145 (Stevens to Sheil no. 195 of 10.12.1851).
[10] Markov (1890: 27).   [11] Markov (1890: 24).

course of a month, all more or less connected with the above-mentioned affairs. Formerly such a state of things would have produced serious threats, if not coercive measures, on the part of Russia. Now, however, the Chargé d'Affaires has simply brought them to the attention of the Persian Prime Minister, who has promised to inquire into the complaints.[12]

In 1856, in defiance of Treaty undertakings to the British in India, Iran sent a military expedition to capture Herat, whereupon Britain invaded Iranian territory in the Gulf area. After the Treaty of Paris, ratified in spring 1857, Murray returned to Tehran. Naser ad-Din Shah dismissed Mirza Aqa Khan Nuri and took over direct control of government and foreign affairs. Relations with the British were now favoured, principally since they appeared more able to supply the financial aid of which Iran was increasingly in need, while relations with Russia entered a decidedly cooler phase.

An attempt at settlement

On the Azarbaijan frontier the Russians now began to demand satisfaction of the claims which they had to date merely stored up. For example, the Russian consul-general in Tabriz insisted to the governor of Azarbaijan, Mirza Feizollah Khan Vazir Nezam (brother of Mirza Aqa Khan Nuri), that Mir Soltan Ahmad Khan of Namin (grandson of Mir Hasan Khan of Talesh) should meet Russian demands for compensation for frontier infringements. Markov writes that Mirza Feizollah Khan was both bribed by Soltan Ahmad Khan, and secretly instructed by his brother the prime minister, to leave the khan of Namin in peace.

As for Shahsevan affairs in Moghan, at the end of 1857 the Caucasian administration sent a special official, Colonel Bartholomey, to restore order on the frontier, in the presence of a delegate from the Iranian government, Hajji Mohammad Khan. Markov wrote of this measure that Hajji Mohammad Khan, like his predecessors, had no local influence, inadequate powers and inadequate salary, so that he was compelled to provide for his own maintenance out of 'percentages' from the disputes which he adjudicated.[13]

A somewhat different picture is painted by contemporary British diplomatic reports. Thus in February 1858 Consul-General Keith Abbott wrote to Murray from Tabriz that the Joint Frontier Commission had met in 1857, had been suspended for a while, and was about to reconvene. Apparently in this connexion, a quantity of artillery was being surrepti-

---

[12] IOL L/P&S/20 (A.7, 2: Affairs of Persia, Jan.–Dec. 1856, p. 237).
[13] Markov (1890: 27–9).

tiously despatched from Tabriz to Ardabil. A week later, however, Abbott wrote:

> The Persian Commissioner and secretaries had indeed been waiting for some time past at Ardebeel and a Russian officer had been appointed as Commissioner from the Govr. Genl. of Georgia but had not reached Mogan. The Persian Consul at Tiflis has just reported that the Govr. General had, after all, relinquished his intention of sending a Commission and would refer the cases in dispute to the Consulate here – He added that the Russian authorities appeared to be very indifferent to the subject.[14]

The Iranian prime minister wrote to the envoy in St Petersburg on 16 June 1858, giving the Iranian version of these incidents, and also indicating fears of the increasing coolness of the Russian attitude. The governor-general of Georgia and the Russian legation in Tehran were complaining, he wrote, of Shahsevan disturbances within Russian territory; they also complained that the Iranian authorities were refusing to allow the culprits responsible to go to Russian Moghan for the winter, and demanded the extradition of certain named persons.

> The Persian Ministers . . . deputed Hadgee Mahommed Khan to proceed to the frontier, and arrange this matter in a suitable manner, and they also addressed instructions daily to the authorities in Tabreez to render every assistance in their power in order to settle this matter. A writer was consequently sent from Tabreez, and it was arranged that an agent on the part of the Russians should be present, and the whole matter arranged in accordance with his opinion. A Russian agent was accordingly named, but it is to be regretted that he did not fulfil his duty. He even refused to identify the fugitives alluded to, and demanded peremptorily and violently that according to his list these fugitives should be delivered up, and would not allow the Shahseven Tribe to visit their winter quarters at Mughan (in Persia) [?]. He also said that Kassim Khan the Chief of the Tribe [probably Qasem Khan, younger brother of the dismissed Farzi Khan] must be dismissed as well as Sultan Ahmed Khan [of Namin]. The Persian Ministers have given this matter every attention, but it has been of no use in carrying out the views of the Russian authorities, and they are again beginning to act with harshness.

The letter proceeds to emphasize to the minister in St Petersburg that Russian as opposed to British goodwill is to be sought.[15]

Soon after this, however, relations between the Iranian and British governments improved, inevitably incurring Russian jealousy and the adoption of a harder line, particularly concerning satisfaction of their complaints about the Shahsevan. In January 1860, William J. Dickson,

---

[14] FO 248/177 (Abbott to Murray no. 11 of 23.2.1858, and no. 13 of 3.3.1858). Keith Abbott was appointed consul-general in July 1857. See Amanat (1983).

[15] Translation secretly sent to London: FO 60/232 (Murray to Malmesbury no. 17 of 3.7.1858).

British vice-consul in Tabriz, discussed the situation with the governor-general of Azarbaijan, Sardar 'Aziz Khan, who stated that

So long as Persia showed herself indifferent to the friendship of England, Russia did not press her real or imaginary claims, but contented herself with notifying her grievances, as they occurred, to the Persian Government and then registering them in a book kept by their agents for that purpose, – by which means a long list has been formed.

A further Iranian commissioner, Ja'far-qoli Khan, had been sent to Moghan the previous autumn to investigate, but a Russian counterpart had not yet appeared. Dickson strongly advised Sardar 'Aziz that the Iranian authorities should spare no effort to settle the various claims and show themselves eager to remove misunderstandings, though the Sardar feared the Russians' main aim was to embarrass the Iranian government by pressing claims the following summer, when the tribes were out of Moghan and no possible settlements could be reached.[16]

In March 1860, Sardar 'Aziz himself took a body of infantry and artillery to Ardabil, in order to be in closer contact with Ja'far-qoli Khan, the commissioner; Dickson believed they were doing everything in their power to satisfy the just Russian demands. Meanwhile it was reported that General (sic) Bartholomey was to be sent to the frontier. No Russian officer had yet appeared by the time the Shahsevan nomads left Moghan in May, but the Georgian authorities did despatch one Aqa Bey to meet Ja'far-qoli Khan in the summer, and in July a mixed commission, having settled some important claims, was concluded.

This was reported by Consul-General Abbott, who had returned from leave in June; but he soon had any illusions about the Sardar's good intentions dispelled. The governor-general remained at Ardabil until July, being occupied in providing for the settlement of large numbers of the Shahsevan nomads in that district and in Meshkin, to keep them from causing trouble on the frontier. He planned to prevent them from wintering in either part of Moghan, arrested several Shahsevan chiefs on charges of theft and murder, and disposed of them with the utmost cruelty; in addition, he accumulated a great deal of the nomads' wealth in extortions and confiscations. At the same time, though there had also been inroads by plunderers from the Russian side of the frontier, and no attention had been paid to consequent counter-claims, the Iranians did not seem to mind.

Meanwhile, along with other authorities in the province, Sardar 'Aziz

---

[16] FO 248/192 (Dickson to Rawlinson no. 3 of 22.1.1860). On Sardar 'Aziz, see Calmard (1989) and Eqbal (1947).

had been indulging in such speculations that food prices had risen in mid-1860 to five or more times their 1857 levels, and much of the population was starving. Abbott remonstrated with the Sardar, particularly about the last, with the result that by the end of the year the former close British–Iranian relations in Tabriz were completely reversed, and Abbott was virtually ostracized.[17]

The Shahsevan nomads cannot have retained much, for the winter of 1859 had been one of the severest known, 'when there was snow in Moghan for over a month and the river Kor was frozen and all their property lost: they named it "killer-year" (qıran-yıl)'.[18] The events of 1860, marking a significant moment in Shahsevan history, are not mentioned in Markov's or the other Russian accounts of frontier incidents, perhaps because the Sardar's measures to settle the nomads were undertaken at Russian instigation. However, Abbott's reports to Tehran, this year and in 1861, are illuminating and deserve to be quoted at length. In June 1860 he commented that the Sardar's settlement policy,

supposing it to be successfully carried out, is questionable, for although the Tribe may possibly be induced through fear to relinquish their nomadic habits and in time to turn their attention to agriculture, so great and sudden a change in their circumstances would occasion much distress among them – their usefulness as a pastoral tribe would cease and their old haunts in Persian Moghan becoming deserted would probably fall into the hands of that division of the community which belongs to Russia – an event which would hardly fail to become a source of disquiet to the Persian Government.

Abbott did not believe any such change would last long; the nomads would return as soon as possible to their former way of life.[19]

When the Sardar returned to Tabriz in July, he boasted to Abbott of having settled 15,000 families of nomads. Abbott was thoroughly sceptical both of the numbers and of the permanence of the supposed 'establishment in villages'. 'Indeed', he wrote, the nomads

appear to have demanded certain conditions of the Persian Government in return for their acquiescence in the scheme and it is not yet known whether these will be agreed to at Tehran. The Shah had however consented to a remission of one year's taxation amounting to Ten or Twelve Thousand Tomans as some compensation for the loss and inconvenience to which they would undoubtedly be put by the contemplated change in their condition. It is proposed by the Serdar to restrict the whole of the Tribe from resorting to winter quarters in Moghan the greater part of which is held by Russia – and here I believe consists the main difficulty to the execution of the scheme of settling this people in villages. The Tribe is rich in

---

[17] FO 248/192 (Abbott to Alison no. 13 and no. 14 of 23.7.1860, and no. 38 of 29.11.1860).
[18] Ogranovich (1876: 201).   [19] FO 248/192 (Abbott to Pelly no. 1 of 13.6.1860).

flocks, camels and cattle, to abandon which would be ruinous to them, and to maintain them, they require to resort to the rich pasture lands of Moghan in winter.

The Sardar also intended to establish guardposts in Moghan, 'to maintain that frontier and the country immediately South of it when abandoned by the Tribes'. According to Abbott's own information – he wrote the 1844 report quoted at length in Chapter Nine – the Shahsevan nomads residing south of the Aras numbered no more than 12,000 families, of which some 5,000 already had village bases in the Ardabil and Meshkin districts. It was the remaining 7,000 nomadic tent-dwellers, mainly of the Meshkin division, who were affected by the settlement plan.[20]

This is confirmed by a recently published document, dated 1277 (between July 1860 and June 1861; no month is specified), which is a request to the Shah, apparently from Sardar 'Aziz (though his name does not appear), on behalf of Farzi Khan Sartip *elbey*, to grant certain places as permanent residences for the Meshkin Shahsevan, who had been settled the year before (i.e. 1276/spring 1860). The job was given to Hosein 'Ali Khan Javanshir (whose land assignments in Meshkin were mentioned in Chapter Nine) and Qasem Khan, governor (*hakem*) of the Meshkin Shahsevan (and Farzi Khan's younger brother, see Chapter Nine). The document lists the names of the Meshkin tribes and the places where they are to settle, but the reproduction is poor and several names are hard to decipher.[21]

In November, following his fall from the Sardar's favour, Abbott elaborated on a number of the points already mentioned, particularly on the value to the province's economy of the nomads' contribution, which would be lost if they were settled. The Sardar's severity at Ardabil, he wrote, and his measures to settle the Shahsevan,

have rendered this Tribe more discontented and greater enemies of the Government than ever, so that for some time to come it will probably prove a scourge rather than an advantage to the province . . . there is no doubt the Tribe has been the cause of pretty constant annoyance to the Russian frontier Authorities and their petty depredations have been the subject of unceasing complaint – but the remedy for all this will scarcely be found, I think, in the measures taken to make them a stationary people, at least for some years to come, and for the present matters are rendered worse than before by the Tribe pillaging far and

[20] FO 248/192 (Abbott to Alison no. 12 of 17.6.1860).
[21] Shahsevand-Baghdadi (1991: 198–201). Notes on the copy state that the original, which I have not been able to consult, belongs to a Mr Firuzi Zargar and is to be found in the library of Hajji Hosein Javadi of Talesh-Mikeilli; and that it bears the seal of Mozaffar ad-Din Mirza.

near in revenge for the treatment they have experienced. A regiment and two guns have been posted in the vicinity of Mooghan to cut off their access to those plains and some trifling resistance has been offered by the Tribe which no doubt finds itself in great measure ruined by the change it is being compelled to make in it's habits and mode of life.

I think it impolitic in the Persian Government to seek to render it's great nomad Tribes a stationary people. Persia is differently circumstanced to most other countries and the nature of it's climate, it's natural features and the general habits of the people require that it should possess a population which can adapt itself to variations of mountain and plain and draw from that condition of life resources which are in a great measure denied the fixed inhabitants. It is on these great pastoral communities that the population of the cities and plains nearly depend for their supplies of animal food – for the flocks – for the butter, cheese and other preparations from Milk which are so largely consumed in Persia and for many coarse but useful articles of woolen and other manufacture for which the produce of the fields and cities is exchanged. The Tribes are a further advantage to the country in consequence of their wealth in camels which afford a cheap means of conveyance for merchandize to the most distant parts; but these advantages are in great measure lost to the country when the tribes are compelled to renounce their nomadic condition to become cultivators of the soil – and the State in authorizing these changes lessens it's resources in a military point of view – for whereas the Young men of the nomad Tribe are to a great extent available for military service, the duties and labour of the community being chiefly performed by the females, the labour of cultivating the soil must fall principally on the males – and no doubt also the hardiest races in Persia and the most valuable for military duties are the men of the wandering Tribes.[22]

These observations on the nature of nomadic pastoralism in Iran are remarkably modern in tone, and would have held good until quite recently as an assessment of the value of the nomad tribes and of the arguments against a policy of enforced settlement. At the same time, Abbott was clearly ignorant of the extent to which Shahsevan nomads increasingly sold their produce and bought their supplies during their winter stay in Russian Moghan, as detailed in the account by Ogranovich quoted in the previous chapter. During the second half of the century, to judge from later reports to be discussed in Chapter Eleven, demand for Shahsevan produce grew among the Moghan settlers.

In the same report, Abbott noted that the good harvest had at last brought prices down, but complained of the system by which the province was governed: nominally by a royal prince, but effectively by his minister (in this case Sardar 'Aziz), a system which was responsible for most of the oppression in the province. He also mentioned that the governor of Ardabil, Mohammad Reza Khan, having nearly provoked a rising by his oppression, had to seek another appointment, and was replaced by a

[22] FO 248/192 (Abbott to Alison no. 38 of 29.11.1860).

young prince, Akbar Mirza, 'whose antecedents as Governor of Oroumieh [Urmiyeh] and general character for profligacy afford no hope of any good resulting from his present appointment'; while the governor of Qara-Dagh, Khosrou Khan, 'is favourably spoken of, but he is appointed to a district which for a succession of years has been exposed to oppression and the ruinous effects of over-exaction and spoliation'.[23]

Some weeks later Abbott was able to report on the Sardar's financial situation. He had a salary of 3,000 tomans with allowances of 3,500 tomans, while, in addition to a private income, he had in the previous nine months received at least 40,000 toman in 'presents' (*pishkash*) from subordinate officials in the province. This figure included the following contributions:

Khosrou Khan, governor of Qara-Dagh	500 toman
Akbar Mirza, governor of Ardabil	500 toman
elbey of the Shahsevan	6,000 toman

The latter is not named; his is almost the highest single contribution in the province.[24]

In early March 1861 Sardar 'Aziz Khan was in Tehran, where he was interviewed concerning the state of Azarbaijan by the British envoy, Charles Alison. The Sardar claimed that, thanks to his attention, the frontier was at present tranquil.

A fruitful source of dispute between Persia and Russia had arisen from the depredations of the nomadic tribes who, during the winter months, frequented the plain of Moghan. Persian tribes committed depredations on Russian territory, and Russian Tribes on Persian. The only remedy was to oblige them to renounce their nomadic habits. This was no easy matter, considering that one of the Persian Tribes – the Shahseven – counted upwards of 12,000 families, and would strenuously resist any attempt to deprive them of a privilege which they and their ancestors had enjoyed for centuries. To have transferred them to another province would have been to deprive an important frontier of a strong barrier. The Serdar, therefore, proceeded in person to Ardebil, and finding its neighbourhood a suitable locality, summoned the tribe and by a due mixture of fair proposals and threats induced about 9,000 families to build houses and settle. The remainder, he expects, will soon follow their example. By this means the chance of a War with Russia has, he hopes, been averted; the annual payment to that Power of 5,000 Tomans to permit the tribe to pasture their flocks on the other side of the Arras, will be saved, and should the necessity ever unfortunately arise, the tribe will henceforth for the protection of their own homes, be compelled the more efficiently to defend the frontier. The settlers have already contributed 500 horse to the Persian Army, and the Serdar hopes the number will next year be increased to 1,000. The Russian Authorities, he added, have expressed their intention to

[23] *Ibid.*   [24] FO 248/199 (Abbott to Alison no. 3 of 6.1.1861).

take similar measures with regard to their own frontier tribes, in which case a source of continual ill-feeling and irritation between the two countries will be radically removed.[25]

Alison sent a memorandum on the interview to Abbott in Tabriz for comment. He did so at length, reiterating most of his former points. He agreed that the Moghan frontier was now tranquil, though the province in general was in an appalling state of insecurity. The Shahsevan had at first acquiesced in their settlement, 'under fear and with a bad grace', but the scheme was as yet far from a success. A large part of the tribe had broken through the inadequate force stationed in Moghan, which appeared to have confined its activities to 'plundering of all its wealth one respectable division of the tribe on it proving refractory'. Abbott's objections to the policy still held:

There is still every cause to apprehend the downfall and ruin of that great and flourishing pastoral community, for should they be forced to abandon their nomad habits it will be at a sacrifice of much which at present constitutes a source to them of wealth and prosperity – and should they continue refractory the Government may make this a pretext for plundering them as it is reputed has already happened to one division. Any such change in the condition of the Tribe as was contemplated by the Serdar will be attended likewise with injurious effects to the country generally – the prices of meat and of other articles of animal food which this people usually furnish, produce of their flocks and herds, will be greatly increased – indeed there is already every appearance of this having already happened through the unsettled state of the Tribes, in the present high prices of Animal Food in Azerbaijan.

Abbott was further sceptical about the Sardar's estimation of the seriousness of Shahsevan raids on the frontier: there was no real danger of war there. The Russian Shahsevan tribes were equally responsible for raiding activities, but their Iranian cousins 'being the most numerous were better able to protect their own property and they retaliated severely on those who molested them'. The figure of 5,000 toman for the pasture dues was exaggerated: only 750 tomans used to be paid.[26] Abbott believed that the nomads did not cross the Aras but kept themselves to the south of the river in the Moghan plain. On the increase of the long-established levy of 500 horsemen, Abbott commented, 'the Tribes generally are ready enough to furnish horsemen to the State when their services are remunerated', and the Shahsevan could afford to contribute 1,000 men – but not if they were settled. He had no information on Russian intentions

---

[25] FO 248/201 (Wm J. Dickson's Memorandum of 12.3.1861, enclosed in Alison to Abbott no. 2 of 13.3.1861).

[26] Russian sources confirm this, giving the figure of 2,000 roubles (= 750 toman), though the payments ceased after 1857, as mentioned above.

to settle their own tribes (though Russian sources indicate that this settlement was in fact proceeding).

In conclusion, Abbott noted that the removal of the Shahsevan from
the frontier would undoubtedly improve the situation there, but the
trouble would only move to a new locality,

and the Persian districts would be exposed more than before to the depredations
of a people who whether stationary or erratic is not likely to abandon all at once
it's ingrained and inherent propensity for appropriating the property of it's neighbours. The Shakakee Tribe may be taken as an example that a once pastoral
people does not relinquish the habit of plunder and pilfering on abandoning in
some degree it's former unsettled mode of life.[27]

These last comments do not agree with Abbott's assessment of the
Shahsevan eighteen years earlier, as not given to 'marauding and pillaging
on a large scale', but this correlation of pastoralism with kleptomania is
perhaps the only jarring note in an otherwise perceptive analysis of the
Shahsevan situation at the time. He refrains in fact from explicitly suggesting alternative and more effective measures for dealing with the
problem, implying only that given better government in Azarbaijan and
less extortion on the part of officials the Shahsevan might be persuaded to
restrict their lawless activities; in all of which the Russian commentators
would have agreed with him.[28]

Improvement in government was not yet to occur, however, for Sardar
'Aziz retained control of the province for some years. In 1862, following
the disastrous campaign against the Marv Türkmen in 1861, a review of
the survivors and new recruits to the Iranian army was held in Ujan, the
plain between Sarab and Bostan-Abad, favourite summer quarters of the
Qajar court and mustering ground for their armies. Sardar 'Aziz took a
body of troops from the Ujan camp to Ardabil in September, 'ostensibly
to settle some frontier business, but really, in all probability to lay the
country under contribution for his own private advantage, his former
journey in that district about 2 years ago having proved very successful in
this respect'.[29]

Abbott's assessment of the effectiveness of Sardar 'Aziz's policy
appears to have been accurate. In 1864 he reported of the Shahsevan:

Those of Ardebil inhabit villages during part of the year and encamp about
Savalan for the remaining months. Those of Mishkeen were until lately nomadic
all the year through but three years ago the Persian Government resolved on com-
pelling them to take to fixed abodes instead of resorting to Moghan in conse-

[27] FO 248/199 (Abbott to Alison no. 14 of 17.4.1861).
[28] E.g. Radde (1886: 423–4), Markov (1890: 21).
[29] FO 248/207 (Abbott to Alison no. 41 of 9.9.1862).

quence of the irregularities they were continually committing on the Russian frontier. Though they were at first obliged to yield obedience they have since then however generally thrown off the restraint and returned to their old habits which their wealth in cattle and sheep seems to render necessary. The Tribe is held in bad repute from its plundering propensities and occasions much embarrassment and trouble to the Persian and Russian Frontier Authorities.[30]

Shahsevan disorders increased, until even the appointment to the Ardabil governorship in 1867 of Mohammad Rahim Mirza, Zia ad-Douleh, a man with a reputation for justice and energy, could do little to alleviate the situation.

The Russians increase the pressure

The reports of the British consul-general at Tabriz are the main source for the preceding events, yet after Abbott (who was transferred to Odessa in July 1868) British representatives were apparently not aware of the Shahsevan again until 1883. Russian sources by contrast, having remained silent on the 1860–1 attempt at settlement, describe the next phase of the story in some detail.

Presumably under the influence of the new policy prescribed by the Gorchakov memorandum of 1864 for the frontiers of Central Asia, the Russians determined to set in train a solution of affairs on their Moghan frontier too. In 1869 for the first time they appointed a permanent frontier commissar, Colonel Ogranovich, the source of much information on the Shahsevan tribes in the nineteenth century.

Iran had had commissars since Ja'far-qoli Khan's first appointment in 1859, but so far they had dealt with temporary officials from the Baku government, and with local chiefs and their assistants. Now both commissars were supposed to be present at Belasovar from October to April, throughout the Shahsevan residence in Moghan. Ogranovich complained that his counterparts did not arrive until February, leaving only one month in which disputes could be settled; there was nothing to check Shahsevan lawlessness earlier in the season, when complaints could have been dealt with and satisfaction rendered on the spot. Actually, if the Iranian commissars were late, it would have been understandable in view of their previous experience of the unpunctuality of Russian officials. Markov also writes of the venality of the Iranian officials, who would accept any suit so long as it was accompanied by material inducement, but the only example he quotes was from a different locality and involved different persons.

[30] FO 60/286 (Abbott of 19.4.1864), published in Amanat (1983: 229).

The rules according to which crimes and disputes were dealt with were, first of all, those of local customary law (*adat*): presentation of the case by both sides with witnesses; if this did not solve the case, mediators were called; if they could not agree, the matter was referred to a court of mullahs, who decided it according to the Shari'a, by means of oaths and 'public expediency' (*maslahat*). These procedures were complicated for Ogranovich by certain 'unofficial' Iranian and Shahsevan practices: for example, plaintiffs tended to demand twice or three times what they expected by way of compensation, so as to be able to afford the fees of 'informants' or 'detectives' (*müshtülükchi*). There was also a form of self-help, whereby the victim of theft could seize property from the suspected thief – or anyone else – as a guarantee (*gerou*) not to be returned until his own property had been restored. If the thief happened to be a chief or one of his henchmen (*nökär*), the 'detectives' were easily bribed to drop their investigations, and if the victim himself appeared he might well be beaten until he swore he had secured reparation. Finally, the Iranians recognized no distinction between criminal and civil law: if caught, thieves were not punished but had only to restore the stolen property; the same was true of homicide, for which the Russian law demanded the death penalty, while Iranian law allowed reconciliation and compensation.

Ogranovich was clearly much frustrated by a lack of precision in his instructions as to how to deal with this situation. Similar frustrations appear in Iranian reports of the time: in February 1870, General Hasan 'Ali Khan, now special emissary to Moghan, wrote to Foreign Minister Mirza Sa'id Khan that Zia ad-Douleh, governor of Ardabil and Meshkin, was hamstrung by lack of power to coerce the Shahsevan; he begged for royal orders to command Farzi Khan *elbey* to leave Meshkin and appear at Belasovar, and to take responsibility for the Shahsevan, who all fear him like dogs. 'How should I know where so-and-so is to be found, which tribe (*taifa*) he comes from?' Hasan 'Ali Khan complained. 'The Shahsevan consider Farzi Khan their *ojaq* (ancestral hearth) and won't swear an oath falsely on him.'[31]

Many disputes were solved, however, and law and order improved. New settlements were formed in Moghan, even on the Iranian side; for example, the Talesh-Mikeilli tribe founded a village of 100–200 households at this time on the Iranian side of Belasovar, and the Zargar tribe

---

[31] Hasan 'Ali Khan to Mirza Sa'id Khan, Zi-qa'da 1286 (Safa'i 1974: 167–9; see also Report from Special Emissary Javad, Rabi ol-Aval 1286/June–July 1869, *ibid*: 149–50). Safa'i confuses General Hasan 'Ali Khan, later to become Governor of Ardabil and Meshkin and chief (*ra'is*) of the Shahsevan tribes, with Hasan 'Ali Khan Garusi, later to become famous as the Amir Nezam (see below, and Bamdad 1968, V: 72). Safa'i also footnotes Governor Zia ad-Douleh as Anushirvan Mirza, not Mohammad Rahim Mirza.

another not far away along the Balharu-Chai.[32] Possibly these villages
were settled after the unprecedented drought of summer 1870, which was
followed by a terrible famine throughout Iran, and in 1871–2 by cholera
and harsh winters. According to Ogranovich the Shahsevan nomad
population was literally halved:

Almost half their property was lost, their cattle, camels, horses, rams and ewes,
particularly the latter, two-thirds of which died . . . one third of the Shahsevan
households became destitute, many died of hunger and cholera, and part of them
scattered into the different villages of Lankaran, Javat, Shamakhı and Shusheh
districts, in order to find food, and they settled there. At present [1875], on the
basis of carefully checked information, I estimate the Shahsevan nomads to
number 6,000 families.[33]

Passing through Ardabil in October 1872, von Thielmann came across
a few Shahsevan nomads, finding them 'very ragged'. In December the
newspaper *Kavkaz* reported that 'wealthy nomads who had several thousand sheep can now scarce count a few hundred, while their cattle have
positively all perished'. The same article proposed full settlement of
Moghan, even industrialization of the central, waterless steppe: a network
of canals, possibly opening up the ancient canal system, would, through
cultivation of rice, cotton, madder, mulberries (for silk), and so on, bring
enormous profits to the entrepreneur.[34]

Reports of border incidents in Moghan in the 1870s mainly concern
the Qoja-Beyli of Meshkin, now emerging as the most powerful and
lawless of the Shahsevan nomad tribes,[35] while the Shatranlu of Khalkhal
were raiding caravans to the south. The winter of 1879–80 was again one
of terrible famine in Azarbaijan, and bread was extremely scarce and dear
in the spring. The districts of Ardabil and Ahar were among the worst hit,
yet reports from the Shahsevan indicate that they were surviving these
disasters well enough, largely through the success of their raiding activities. Radde, visiting several Shahsevan camps on his climb from Ardabil
to the heights of Savalan in July 1880, found them to be flourishing: 'The
prosperity of the Shahsevan . . . must be considerable, since, as I was told,
they know well how to pay off the administration, apart from the many
robberies and murders which have brought them notoriety far and
wide.'[36]

In late summer 1883, the heir apparent Mozaffar ad-Din Mirza visited
Sarab and Ardabil to collect huge sums of money as 'presents' from the
Shahsevan chiefs, and thoroughly alienated the tribes, but the troops and

[32] Markov (1890: 33f.), Radde (1886: 435–6).   [33] Ogranovich (1876: 201).
[34] Von Thielmann (1875, II: 29); *Kavkaz* as quoted by Rostopchin (1933: 104–5).
[35] See Appendix Two; Iranian reports mentioned above (note 31); Markov (1890: 29–30).
[36] FO 450/8 (various); Radde (1886: 173).

artillery he brought with him indicated the inadvisability of resistance, and he succeeded in taking three of the most notorious chiefs (not named) back with him as hostages to Tabriz. In William Abbott's absence on leave, French consul Bernay reported to the British minister in Tehran that the prince seemed as surprised as his subordinates that the Ardabil affair had been resolved so smoothly and that his expedition had escaped serious opposition and returned safely to Tabriz.[37]

That autumn, the Russians put into effect measures which led to a final resolution of the Shahsevan problem, for which they had been planning for some years. Internal troubles and failures of policy in St Petersburg, in addition to recent British successes in Afghanistan, had moved the Tsar to more aggressive policies on his eastern frontiers, particularly in Central Asia.[38] In 1876 the Caucasian government had entrusted E. Krebel with the Shahsevan question, and he was instructed, on becoming consul-general in Tabriz the following year, to go to Moghan, report on the state of affairs, and advise on Russian policy.[39]

Krebel left for Qara-Dagh and Moghan in October 1878. One reason for his visit to Qara-Dagh was that the Chalabianlu tribe there had been raiding in the Qara-Bagh and Moghan steppes, as well as causing trouble to the Armenian communities of the district, who were under Russian protection. Abbott at Tabriz reported Krebel's departure, considering the mission to be concerned not only with the mutual depredations of Iranian and Russian nomads, but also with the Iranian complaint that the Shahsevan went to Moghan not simply for pasturage but to avoid paying their taxes. He did not hear of the result of the expedition.[40]

In his report of 28 February 1879, Krebel declared that in the Shahsevan affair there were two policies open to the Russian authorities: either they must bring the nomads under their complete control while they were in Moghan, and all interference by Iranian officials or the Shahsevan *elbeys* must cease; or they must prevent the Shahsevan from coming to Moghan.[41] At this stage the Caucasian government would not favour the second solution, as it would lead to loss of the nomads' herds and consequent disorder and intensified raiding:

---

[37] FO 248/400 (Bernay to Thomson, enclosed in Thomson to Granville of 2.10.1883). Keith Abbott's next successor but one was his cousin William Abbott, who had been acting consul 1863–5, consul in Rasht 1865–75, and took over at Tabriz in 1877 (Amanat 1983: xxviii).   [38] See Kazemzadeh (1968: 57f.).   [39] Markov (1890: 37).
[40] FO 450/8 (Abbott to Thomson no. 55 of 21.10.1878).
[41] Krebel's report as it concerned the Shahsevan was I believe the basis of Markov's account (1890: 37f.). According to Ogranovich, the *elbeys* had been officially removed from control of the Shahsevan in 1874 and the tribes put under the direct authority of the Ardabil governor (1876: 204); if this was so, then the *elbeys* regained control soon after, to continue causing a nuisance to the Russians.

instead of a unified group of nomads, there would appear on our frontiers numerous mutually aggressive bandits, against whom it would be even more difficult for Russia to protect her frontier population; and the Iranian government would be in no position to facilitate the execution of such a measure in the near future.[42]

There were of course other reasons why the Russians wanted to keep the frontier open: for example, their settlers in Moghan were economically dependent on Shahsevan pastoral produce, as became clear later. They also no doubt hoped, as American envoy S. G. W. Benjamin suspected, that the Shahsevan could eventually be recruited as valuable irregular cavalry.[43]

So the first policy was adopted. The Caucasian authorities drew up a list of 13 regulations to cover the administration of the Shahsevan, which was approved by the Tsar on 21 December 1882. Markov gives the full list: the main provisions were that the Shahsevan should be subject to the Belasovar commissar during their stay in Russian territory; the commissar would deal with the *beys* of individual tribes and not with the *elbeys*, who must not interfere in the nomads' affairs while in Russia; the commissar might grant or refuse admission to specific tribes at his own discretion; those admitted were to be shown their allotted grazing grounds and handed documents defining their boundaries; the commissar, responsible to Baku and assisted by the tribal chiefs and by two police officers and a special detachment of one hundred Cossacks (apart from the regular frontier garrisons), would hear and judge minor complaints and disputes, and would investigate more serious cases which became subject to martial law; persistent Shahsevan offenders must be deported to Iran. The frontier authorities had wanted to be able to sentence Shahsevan offenders to exile within Russia, but this was not possible under current international agreements.

Russian Moghan was divided into two districts, each with a special garrison of thirty Cossacks, one attached to Javat, the other to Lankaran. Trouble was anticipated, since no more than 6,000 families of the Shahsevan were expected to cross the border, while up to another 7,000, in 17 tribes, would remain in Iran under the authority of the *elbeys* and Iranian officials, just the other side of a thin cordon of Cossacks. At the same time, the Russians took steps to prevent their own nomads from entering Iranian territory during the summer – the two groups concerned, Perembel and Darvishli-Panahvand, comprising something over 500 families, were already partially settled and converted to bovine pastoralism, so adequate summer grazing was easily found for them in Russian territory.

---

[42] Markov (1890: 38).   [43] Benjamin (1887: 479–80).

During 1883 the Iranian authorities were informed of these measures. Their request that they be permitted to send an official to co-operate with the Russian commissar was refused, as it would have been contrary to the main purpose of the regulations. A further request for an Iranian vice-consul in Moghan was also turned down, as there was already a vice-consul in Baku who was free to visit Moghan as an observer. Having given the Iranian authorities time to warn the nomads of their new position, and also hoping that 'this new measure might persuade the Iranian government to try to end the migration of the Iranian Shahsevan onto our territory, to which end it might set aside winter quarters for the Shahsevan within Iran', the Caucasian command put their new policy into effect in autumn 1883.

As the nomads crossed the frontier, the commissar officially informed them of the new system. The chiefs claimed they had not been warned; that the governor of Ardabil, Akbar Mirza, had in fact told them to continue to obey their *elbeys* in everything; he had, moreover, authorized two of the most lawless tribes – Polatlu and Jurughlu – to cross the frontier, and had also permitted Qoja-Beyli to return to their settlement of Barzand in spite of Russian prohibitions. The commissar met with no co-operation from the chiefs, and the rate of crime, raiding and robbery began to rise to its previous levels. According to Markov, the commissar received claims from Russian subjects against the Shahsevan, for the 1883–4 season, amounting to some 35,500 roubles.

The new system had failed. The Caucasian administration decided the time had come for a 'final solution': the Shahsevan must be banned from Moghan, whatever the consequences.[44]

The closure of the frontier

The Russians had always regarded this ban as inevitable if not desirable, but hoped they would be able, by diplomatic means, to get the Iranians to initiate it. Russian nomads had now been banned from Iran, so the Iranians could no longer insist on the Shahsevan right of reciprocity.

In March 1884 the heir apparent was ordered, in response to the new system in Moghan,

to proceed to the spot and make arrangements for the localization of such portion of these tribes as can settle down to a sedentary life. With regard to those whose circumstances render it impossible for them to do so, some place within the Persian borders is to be fixed for their annual migration.[45]

---

[44] Markov (1890: 41–9).   [45] FO 60/460 (Thomson to FO no. 57 of 5.4.1884).

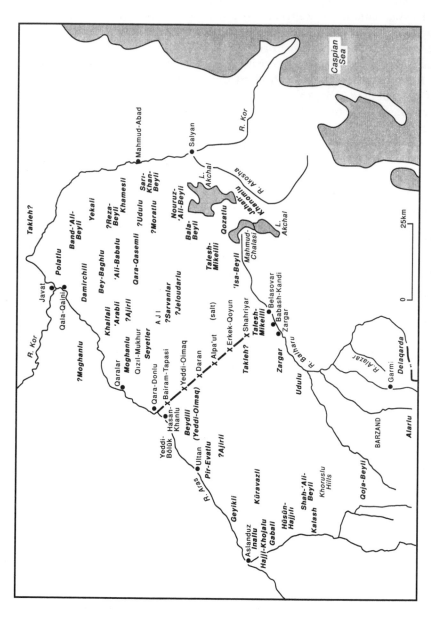

Map 6. Moghan, showing approximate location of tribes 1870–85 (Chapters 10 and 11); mainly after Ogranovich (1870), Avdeyev (1927) (names of tribes are shown in bold italics)

Presumably less than eager to face the Shahsevan again after his narrow escape of the previous year, the heir apparent asked his father for 100,000 tomans as expenses for the journey to Moghan. The Shah refused, so the prince did not go. Instead, Mohammad Sadeq Khan Qajar, Amin Nezam, was appointed to the mission, and left Tabriz in May for Meshkin and Moghan to carry it out. Reporting it, Consul Bernay expressed doubt that the Shahsevan would submit to settlement within Iranian territory, as they had been too often deceived and oppressed by agents of the Shah.[46]

According to Markov, in autumn 1884 the Russian envoy Melnikov began talks with the Iranian government, who commissioned the governor of Ardabil to examine the question of settling the Shahsevan within Iran. Finally in early November the Iranian foreign minister sent Melnikov the note for which he had been waiting, stating that the Iranian government could not accept the regulations which the Tsar had approved in 1882.

Despite the fact that the prohibition of the nomad tribes from migration to their customary wintering places presents great difficulties and occasions these nomads a considerable loss, nevertheless the Iranian government has forbidden them to return to that part of Moghan which is Russian territory and to remain in winter quarters there. It has been decreed that on no account are the Shahsevan to migrate to Moghan, nor to remain there in winter quarters. The necessary instructions have already been sent to the Azarbaijan authorities and to the governor of Ardabil and Meshkin, concerning the measures to be taken to prevent the Shahsevan from returning to Moghan and the implementation of the present order. The Azarbaijan authorities have already, specially and seriously, taken the necessary steps to carry out the Imperial Decree, but as it may happen that several of the Shahsevan secretly escape to Moghan, which would clearly be against the orders of their government, and as the Russian government is obliged by treaty to return such fugitives, your excellency will not neglect to instruct the Russian frontier authorities in good time not to allow those tribes to remain in Russian territory. On their side the Iranian authorities will show the utmost diligence in preventing the Qoja-Beyli, the Jurughlu and other Shahsevan tribes from crossing to Moghan, and in carrying out the stated decrees.[47]

Meanwhile Bernay reported that the Shahsevan were preparing to cross the frontier as usual, in spite of Iranian attempts to stop them. It seemed that if the nomads crossed, the Russians might not let them return the following spring. The Shah, in fear of losing his subjects, had just instructed the heir apparent to stop the migration at all costs. The prince was on the point of leaving Tabriz for Moghan via Ahar, since he had no alternative but to present himself personally so as to prevent the crossing of the Polatlu tribe, the nearest to the frontier, whose moves would be followed

[46] FO 248/413 (Bernay to Thomson of 6.5, 17.6 and 31.8.1884).
[47] Quoted in Markov (1890: 49–50).

by all the others. He would not hesitate to use force if necessary, and might take the risky step of putting the nomad chiefs to death. Sending Bernay's report on to London, Ronald Thomson commented that he had been informed by the authorities in Tehran that the heir apparent's purpose had been achieved, 'and that winter quarters on the Persian side of the border have been assigned to the tribe in question'.[48]

Abbott returned to his post in Tabriz in December and sent Thomson a long report on what, according to his information, had actually happened when the heir apparent visited Moghan. He set out a history of the present situation, the frontier raids that had led Russia to her latest measures to control the Shahsevan. At the Russians' suggestion, the heir apparent was considering settlement of the nomads, even though the attempt several years before (1860) to introduce such a policy had led to failure. The prince had travelled via Ahar and Ardabil to the Aras at Aslanduz and then along the river to Hasan-Khanlu near the frontier.[49] Abbott's information led him to doubt whether any definite progress in settling the Shahsevan would be made so late in the season, but the heir apparent was said to have effected a satisfactory solution to the present difficulties. Abbott summed up the situation as follows:

The Azerbaijan Government have a somewhat difficult task to perform in the present instance: – the adoption of such measures as will, on the one hand, be acceptable to Russia and, on the other, tend to secure the loyalty and affection of the Shah's tribal subjects.[50]

Markov writes that Ogranovich met the Iranian heir apparent in Hasan-Khanlu and informed him 'of the real state of affairs and of the oppressions which the Shahsevan suffered from their self-interested ruler'. The prince told the governor of Ardabil, Mohammad Sadeq Khan, Amin Nezam, that he hoped such excesses would cease. He stayed on the frontier until early March, 'and while there he settled almost all the Shahsevan tribes on the lands put aside for them'. The Shahsevan remained peaceful throughout the winter and made no attempt to cross the frontier.[51]

Abbott in Tabriz did not mention the Shahsevan during 1885, the year when he wrote: 'Azerbaijan – bound hand and foot by Russia, her trade crippled, her army in rags, without a single carriageable road, corruption permeating every pore';[52] and the year when Hasan 'Ali Khan Garusi, Amir Nezam, became the heir apparent's minister (*pishkar*), took over the

---

[48] FO 60/461 (Bernay in Thomson to FO no. 173 of 27.11.1884).
[49] Hasan-Khanlu was a small collection of settlements along the Aras founded by descendants of Mostafa Khan of Shirvan, as mentioned in Chapter Eight.
[50] FO 450/8 (Abbott to Thomson no. 6 of 28.12.1884); also in FO 248/413 and FO 60/464.   [51] Markov (1890: 50–1). For details of his settlement, see Chapter Eleven.
[52] FO 248/425 (Abbott to Thomson no. 25 of 21.9.1885).

governorship of the province with a firm hand and began to clear up the mess.

The Shahsevan were desperate, however, on their return to winter quarters at the end of 1885. Unfortunately the sole source for the events in Moghan that winter is Markov, a Tsarist official whose main purpose was clearly to justify Russian actions and presumably to cover up any errors or injustices. I have extracted the more circumstantial details from Markov's account, but they may still need to be treated with reserve.

On 7 December (25 November by the Russian calendar in Markov's narrative), over 700 families broke through the insufficient Iranian and Russian guards strung out along the frontier, which was marked by the road from the Aras at Qara-Donlu to the Balharu at Belasovar. They were quickly followed by thousands more, some of whom declared it their wish to escape harassment by the Iranian authorities and to take Russian citizenship or death rather than return. The Russian authorities could not allow this, not least since the Shahsevan were hardly desirable as immigrants, but also since Iranian permission would properly be required. They took hasty measures, sending 500 Cossacks as reinforcements from Salyan, and had their envoy in Tehran request the Iranian government to prevent the incursions and remove the Shahsevan from the frontier.

Meanwhile the governor of Baku, accompanied by the commissar, went round the Shahsevan pastures trying to persuade the nomads to return to Iran. When they refused, they were granted two days' grace before they were driven out by force. On 22 December, the 500 Cossacks arrived and set off in the direction of areas where nomads were said to be encamped. The first day they came across scattered camps, including one hundred households of Sarı-Khan-Beyli, who packed up their tents and possessions on the arrival of the troops and headed back towards the frontier, promising they would not stop until they had crossed back into Iran; and they sent word to the elders of two other tribes, Nouruz-'Ali-Beyli and Jahan-Khanomlu, to move on by the following day. Then reports arrived that a mass of nomads was encamped in the centre of the steppe, known as Aji, so an agent was sent to find out more and to tell the camps to return to Iran. On the second day the Jahan-Khanomlu camps were found to be on the move as instructed; the troops quickly cleared their pastures and proceeded towards Belasovar, which they reached two days later without coming across any further nomads. Their agent had now returned with the news that up to 1,500 families of nomads were indeed encamped at Aji; he was accompanied by several chiefs, who asked for a few more days' grace, since their animals were exhausted from the snow and lack of fodder. They were allowed four more days, until the 28th, in which to leave Moghan by the Daran guardpost, which the nomads themselves selected as being the nearest to the quarters set aside for them by the Iranian authorities.

On 27 December the Moghanlu, a large but peaceful tribe numbering between 500 and 1,000 tents, broke through the cordon at Daran into Russian Moghan. Shots were exchanged and many of the nomads were killed (the Cossack guards suffering one killed and one wounded), but the rest escaped into the centre of the steppe leaving many of their animals and possessions in the hands of the Cossacks. The Russian commander took 200 men in pursuit, caught the Moghanlu after 35 km and surrounded them. The nomads, even though exhausted, turned back and crossed the frontier again by evening, having lost more of their animals, including all their newborn lambs. They claimed they had come over because of oppressions suffered at the hands of the Polatlu and Qoja-Beyli tribes, and because they had heard that they would be allowed to stay until spring. At the Yeddi-Oimaq post, several wretched groups of women and children and 6,000 of their sheep were taken; the former were allowed to return to their camps but the animals were taken eventually to Belasovar.

On the 30th it was learnt that the Aji camps had not yet moved, and now wanted a further week's grace. The commander sent a detachment to clear them out at once. On 1 January 1886, the detachment first came across camps of the Ajirli and 'Ali-Babalu tribes, and by the evening of the 2nd all the camps were rounded up and led eventually across the frontier between the Erkek-Qoyun and Yeddi-Oimaq posts. Large numbers of nomads were known to have hidden among the Russian camps and villages in the Javat and Lankaran districts, so energetic measures were immediately put in train to find them and return them with all their property to the Iranian authorities. Markov claims that within five days all Iranian subjects had been found and sent back, and that by 8 January (27 December, old calendar) Russian Moghan was clear of the Shahsevan nomads.[53]

For the rest of the winter, which was one of heavy snowfalls, the Shahsevan remained within Iran. On Russian recommendation the governor of Ardabil, Mostafa-qoli Khan, Mir Panj, had been sent to the frontier at the beginning of 1886 to take all possible measures in co-operation with the Russian authorities to restore order and to remove the most lawless groups far from the frontier. In a letter to the Shah, the Amir Nezam complained that the Mir Panj merely plundered two of the worst tribes, Polatlu and Qoja-Beyli, though in another letter he was more

[53] Markov (1890: 51–7).

complimentary and noted the arrest of Ja'far Khan, *elbey* of the Ardabil Shahsevan.[54]

In autumn 1886, the Amir Nezam, seen by all sides as a Russophile, and now 'alive to the importance of Persia scrupulously fulfilling her part of the agreement with Russia concerning the Shahsevans', decided to send the Mir Panj again to Moghan, with 1,000 special infantry, 500 cavalry and some artillery, to prevent any further border infringements.[55]

The Mir Panj died during the winter and was replaced as governor of Ardabil by another Russian nominee, Asadollah Khan Vakil al-Molk, who was persuaded to resign his post as Iranian minister in St Petersburg. He found further drastic measures against the Shahsevan to be necessary, and began by arresting and blowing from the cannon's mouth the Qoja-Beyli chief 'Ali Baba Khan, and another chief Javat Khan (Polatlu?); and he also imprisoned at Ardabil ten or twelve other Shahsevan notables, all of whom were said to have raided extensively in both Russia and Iran.

In July 1887 Abbott reported gloomily:

It is quite impossible on frontiers situated and circumstanced as are those of Ardebil and the Moghan to put a permanent stop to brigandage and other excesses – Russia and Persia both suffer from these causes; but the result must eventually be that the weaker of the two coterminous states will go to the wall, when Russia will annex the Shahsevend districts including Ardebil and convert these tribes into valuable irregular cavalry, utilizing them as she has the Turkoman tribes.

Order was for the moment maintained to the satisfaction of the Russian authorities, who attributed the prevention of conflicts to the Vakil al-Molk's energy and tact; but the Shahsevan question was seething, 'though dormant not dead, and at Russia's signal may crop up at any moment'.[56]

There remained the question of the confiscated property, which had now been sold. According to Markov, the governor of Baku and the frontier commissar brought the matter to the attention of the Caucasian government, who asked the Russian ministry of finance for money compensation to pay the nomads, but this was refused on the grounds that the property was contraband and had been legally sold, and that the Shahsevan would learn a salutary lesson from their loss. The Amir Nezam wrote to the Shah in 1886:

---

[54] Garusi (1910: 182, 94–6); the reference to Ja'far Khan is somewhat cryptic – he could have been in custody for some time.
[55] FO 248/438 (Abbott to Nicolson, 29.8.1886).
[56] FO 248/449 (Abbott to Nicolson, confidential memo. of 5.7.1887, no. 6 of 16.7.1887 and no. 8 of 27.7.1887). The imprisoned chiefs may have been those seen by the French archaeologist Jacques de Morgan (1912: 179).

Most of the Shahsevan tribes which had gone to Moghan have now returned, through either Russian measures or the diligence of our own officials. Only four of the tribes have remained and have not yet returned, but the Mir Panj has assured me by letter and telegram that he will have them returned also. As I have already reported, however, the Russian officials have behaved most immoderately towards those tribes which crossed over, and have not only confiscated their goods and baggage but have also seized over 20,000 of their sheep and caused them great loss. Although I have . . . telegraphed to the Mir Panj strictly enjoining him to request Russian border officials to restore the property and flocks of the Shahsevan and have also written a full account and sent it to Mo'in al-Vezareh [Iranian consul] at Tiflis, there has been no sign from the Caucasian government that the Shahsevan property and flocks are to be restored. There should be a further statement from the ministry on this matter, which is of the utmost importance, as a large section of the Shahsevan has been ruined.[57]

The Iranian government pressed their request for compensation, saying the nomads might be forced to take up brigandage if they were left without their pastoral resources. Finally the Tsar was personally informed of the matter, and in May 1886 agreed to allow compensatory payment to the Shahsevan. Although there is no record of this having been made, Markov writes that with it 'there ended the direct relations of Russia with the Iranian nomads. From 1885 to the present [1889] the Shahsevan have continued to conduct themselves peaceably and have made no more attempts to cross our frontier.'[58] These complacent remarks were premature, to say the least.

[57] Garusi (1910: 182).   [58] Markov (1890: 57).

Part IV

The end of the tribal confederacy

Life was good for the rebel tribes in the *äshrarlıq* times; you wouldn't believe the destruction they caused. They would go and raid in other countries and bring back the plunder. They would not go at the command of the chiefs, no one knew or cared about what anyone else said or did; the chiefs should have come together and decided to stop the anarchy, but in fact they were the cause of it. A different sound came out of every young man's mouth; that was *äshrarlıq*.

> Hajji Vali Khan of Khalifali, interview in summer camp, August 1964.

Fifty years ago was the time of rebellion (*äshrarlıq*), there was no government (*hökümät*), no Shah, it was the time of the khans (*khankhan*). Whoever was powerful (*güjlü*) himself would pillage, plunder, steal and rob – that was *khankhan*. If a man had much influence (*partı*) and many horsemen, then he would get ahead. This continued until 1340 [1921–2], when Reza Shah became Shah of Iran and restored the government, then they collected the Shahsevan guns and the *khankhans* disappeared, the villages prospered, food was plentiful . . .

> Amanollah Gobadi, interview in Pir-Evatlu village, August 1963.

For some years after the closure of the Moghan frontier, no major political disturbances brought the Shahsevan tribes to the attention of the central government, or to that of the representatives of the two imperial powers who had earlier been interested in their situation. At this time, however, the region of Moghan and Ardabil and the Shahsevan tribes confined there were undergoing a drastic social and economic upheaval, which was to erupt into political activity in the early years of the twentieth century, and whose causes were to be found not simply in the closure but also in the increased oppression perpetrated by the officials of the Qajar administration.

Chapter Eleven describes this upheaval and its immediate causes, relying particularly on the detailed and depressing picture given by Russian officials, who did not, of course, appreciate or admit the degree to which Russian imperialism and nineteenth-century rivalry with Britain were largely responsible for both the frontier situation and the abuses of the Iranian administration. Markov, our earlier source for events on the frontier, concerned only to justify Russian actions and their benefits to the inhabitants of Russian Moghan, does not consider the effects on the Iranian side. Artamonov, however, who visited the region to make a military–geographical study in November 1889, a year after Markov, was shocked at the poverty and oppression of the peasantry and the obvious distress and disorder suffered by the nomads as a result of the closure; his observations were mainly of the Shahsevan of Meshkin. Fourteen years later, Col. Tigranov of the Russian General Staff carried out an investigation of the region and published an informative and perceptive account of the economic and social conditions of the Ardabil province and of the nomad and settled Shahsevan tribes, particularly those of the Ardabil division.

The detailed reports of Artamonov and Tigranov, although clearly to an extent influenced by political bias, are corroborated by other sources. These include accounts recorded among elderly Shahsevan in the 1960s, which describe changes in Shahsevan social and political organization and the raiding which increasingly became part of the way of life of the chiefly retinues, as related later in the chapter.

The first quarter of the twentieth century saw a radical transformation of the political and social structure of Iran, where the period was as eventful as in much of the rest of the world. The Constitutional Revolution of 1906–9, occupation of parts of the country by Russian, British and Turkish forces, and the *coup d'état* of 1921, brought the end of the Qajar dynasty and its replacement by the Pahlavis. Russian and British influence predominated, denying any political or economic independence to Iran, but they were in turn checked by the Bolshevik revolution, by British economies overseas after the First World War, and by the rise of Reza Khan, who, in spite of the northern proximity of the new Soviet Union and the growing importance to Britain of her oil interests in the south, managed to create and unify a politically and economically independent Iranian state.

Chapter Twelve details the involvement of the Shahsevan tribes in various important events in this critical period. In spring 1908, border incidents involving Shahsevan tribesmen and Russian frontier guards provided the Russians with a pretext for military intervention in Azarbaijan on a scale which hastened the fall of the Constitutionalist government in Tehran. During the winter of 1908–9, some Shahsevan joined the Royalist forces besieging Tabriz. In late 1909, while the new Nationalist government struggled to establish control of the country, most of the Shahsevan chiefs joined a Union of tribes of eastern Azarbaijan, which proclaimed opposition to the Constitution and the intention of marching on Tehran and restoring the deposed Mohammad 'Ali Shah. They plundered Ardabil, receiving wide coverage in the

European press. Despite defeat soon after by Nationalist forces from Tehran, Shahsevan warriors engaged in sustained guerrilla resistance against the occupying Russian forces, and were wooed in turn by the other powers. Until the restoration of central government authority under Reza Khan, the major chiefs usually controlled the region, pursuing their local ambitions and rivalries, focused again on the city of Ardabil, and united only to oppose Bolshevik incursions in 1920 and 1921. During the winter and spring of 1922–3 the Shahsevan were among the first of the major tribal groups to be pacified and disarmed by Reza Khan's army.

Chapter Thirteen takes the story up to the time of my field research in the mid-1960s, and describes the final dissolution of the Shahsevan tribal confederation. At first the tribes were integrated within the new nation-state as equal units under recognized and loyal chiefs; they then suffered economic and social destitution as a result of the enforced settlement of the 1930s. After a brief revival in the 1940s, in the decades after the Second World War they experienced renewed discrimination under Mohammad Reza Pahlavi. A series of measures ended the chiefs' domination, broke down the tribal organization, and increasingly drew the pastoralists into national and wider economic and political structures. The pastures were nationalized under the Land Reform of the early 1960s. The desirability of settling the nomads remained an axiom of government policy but the mistakes of the 1930s were not to be repeated. The promotion of irrigated agriculture and industry in Moghan seemed likely to provide settled bases for most if not all of the nomads. The chapter concludes with a postscript outlining developments up to 1995.

11   Pastures new: the effects of the frontier closure

Azarbaijan at the end of the nineteenth century

Generally, at this time, Iran enjoyed increased security, particularly in the tribal areas and on the frontiers. Economic production increased and in most parts the peasants' lot improved.[1]

Azarbaijan and Shahsevan country seem to have been an exception to this trend. Contemporary reports agree that the peasantry of Azarbaijan suffered under an increasingly decadent and corrupt administration, paralysed by the influence of Russia, which practically controlled the nominations and activities of the most important officials. Lesser officials, from local district governors to tax collectors, acquired their appointments from their immediate superiors, and as there was some competition for offices these were usually auctioned. Agricultural settlements in the southern part of the Shahsevan region, that is the districts of Meshkin, Arshaq, Velkij and Ardabil, were the private property either of wealthy townsmen (officials, merchants and clergy from Ardabil and Tabriz), or of the chiefs of the tribes settled there, particularly in parts of Ardabil district distant from the town. These landowners (*molkdar*) collected a share of the village produce. In addition the government usually farmed the taxes of villages or whole areas as *tiyul* assignments to individuals, either as pensions for official or other services, or for a cash payment. Often the landowner also held the *tiyul*, while in the few villages left as Crown land (*khaleseh*) the *tiyul*-holder (*tiyuldar*) collected both the taxes and the government share of the crop. In other cases the landowner and the *tiyuldar* were in competition. The landowner, having a more permanent interest in the land, was more likely than the *tiyuldar* to be concerned for the peasants' welfare, and where he was stronger the landowner could protect his peasants from the interference and oppression of *tiyuldars* or other government officials, or he might acquire the *tiyul* himself. In either case, however, a strong landowner could, if he were so

[1] Gilbar (1978: 360f.); Lambton (1991: 481); Pakdaman (1983).

inclined, commit unchecked extortions. The most unfortunate villages were those owned by weak landowners who could not resist the *tiyuldar*'s exactions. Such villages, like those belonging to the Crown, were increasingly sold as private property to the *tiyuldars* themselves, which normally improved the peasants' conditions.[2] Even enlightened landowners and *tiyuldars*, who were few enough, themselves had to pay so much for their appointments and in 'presents' to their superiors that the peasants suffered an intolerable burden of exactions, and in many cases abandoned their villages.

For some years public order and security were maintained by the iron hand of the Amir Nezam, at least enough to satisfy the critical eye of the British consul-general at Tabriz, who was obliged to assess the effects of Russian influence on Azarbaijan and on the Shah's authority there. In 1890, Col. C. E. Stewart wrote from Tabriz

Since the time some five years ago that the Amir-i-Nizam took over the Government of this province, life and property have become safe, and riots, both in the city of Tabriz, and the provinces generally, have been put down and now very rarely occur, while before his time they were frequent.[3]

The Shahsevan question was dormant, he reported, and order was being maintained on the Moghan frontier, though in the neighbouring district of Qara-Dagh there was considerable turmoil due to raiding activities, both sides of the frontier, by the Chalabianlu tribe. The Russian authorities were putting considerable pressure on the Iranians to deal with such tribes and with Russian nomads who took refuge in the mountains of Qara-Dagh.

The following year, however, the Amir Nezam overstepped his mark. With his support, and incited by the religious classes and the Russian consul-general, the Tabriz populace demonstrated violently against Naser ad-Din Shah's granting (in 1890) of a tobacco monopoly to a British company. The monopoly was eventually cancelled; Amir Nezam was dismissed, and over the next five years public order broke down, the province suffering in addition from both starvation and cholera (a dreadful epidemic in 1892).[4] The weak heir apparent Mozaffar ad-Din had never exercised any control over the Amir Nezam, and now allowed the latter's successors to misgovern the province.

Mozaffar ad-Din became Shah in 1896, and for the next eleven years Azarbaijan endured the rule of his son Mohammad 'Ali Mirza, as bigoted

---

[2] Tigranov (1909: 82f.); cf. Lambton (1953: 155); Tagieva (1969: passim).
[3] FO 60/511 (Stewart to Wolff, report of 25.4.1890, forwarded in Wolff no. 163 of 4.5.1890).
[4] On the condition of Iran in the 1890s, see Sir Mortimer Durand's Memorandum of December 1895, in FO 60/581.

and corrupt as his father had been weak. The administrative machinery broke down; agitation by xenophobic reformist elements in the mercantile and religious classes increased following their victory over the tobacco concession, and now Russia, though she had contributed to that victory, became the sole target of opposition. Mohammad 'Ali identified himself with everything Russian, and his subservience to Russian influence was a major factor in his eventual downfall as Shah. He relied, though with little effect, on tribal leaders like Rahim Khan Chalabianlu of Qara-Dagh to control his disordered province; in practice, he encouraged the frontier tribes in banditry, while Russian troops hovered on the frontier, eager to be invited to restore order.

Russian commercial penetration of the Azarbaijan markets was able to expand apace. The main traffic from Russia came via Astrakhan and the Caspian to Astara and thence by road to Tabriz; Ardabil grew ever busier as entrepôt of this trade. At the same time, large numbers of Iranians from the Ardabil region migrated to Baku to work in the oilfields or the docks for several months of the year; some of them stayed and remitted their earnings to Iran.[5] In the 1960s I met elderly Shahsevan men who said they had worked around the turn of the century in the new cotton plantations in Russian Moghan and Qara-Bagh.

Among the Shahsevan tribes, the *elbey* dynasty had finally lost all control. After Ja'far Khan's arrest in 1886, nothing further is heard of an Ardabil *elbey*, but 'Ali-qoli Khan, third son of Farzi Khan, was nominally Meshkin *elbey* at least until 1903. Farzi Khan's first two sons, Qorban 'Ali Khan (d. 1886) and Safar 'Ali Khan, were of some standing at Naser ad-Din Shah's court, and Safar 'Ali Khan may be the general of that name who distinguished himself in various campaigns in the east in the 1850s.[6] According to Ahmad Mirza, Gelin Khanom, a daughter of Farzi Khan, was married to Fath 'Ali Shah's son Keikaus Mirza.[7] Tigranov names the district governors of Meshkin and Ojarud in 1903 as Ebrahim Khan and 'Abbas-qoli Khan, respectively; these may be sons of the brothers Qasem Khan and Farzi Khan.[8] As for the rest of Badr Khan's descendants, some were dispersed in the cities (Ardabil, Tabriz, Tehran), others had joined nomad Shahsevan tribes (such as Sarvanlar and Jeloudarlu) or had become impoverished villagers. The real power among the nomads had long been elsewhere: with the Qoja-Beyli tribe.

---

[5] Arfa (1964: 41). Swietochowski says the oil boom was over by 1900 (1985: 37).
[6] Maraghe'i (1877–80, I: App., 13); Baiburdi (1962: 103).
[7] Ahmad Mirza (1976: 53) names Gelin Khanom as daughter of Farzi Bey Shahsevan Sarı-Khan-Beyli. Sepehr, however, gives Keikaus Mirza's father-in-law as Fazl 'Ali (Farzi?) Bey Javanshir (1958, I: 321). Another of many royal brides named Gelin Khanom was daughter of Nazar 'Ali Khan, as mentioned earlier.
[8] Tigranov (1909: 95, 100); Radde (1886: 444).

After the 1870s, Nurollah Bey Qoja-Beyli and his successors collected taxes from the nomads of the Meshkin division, and also from those Ardabil tribes that continued migrating to Moghan. This was symbolically important: to pay taxes to someone, whether a tribal chief or a government official, amounted to accepting their authority – though the collector also of course profited considerably by exacting amounts in excess of the assessment.

Around the time of the frontier closure, Morad 'Ali Bey, chief of Moghanlu, the largest, wealthiest and most law-abiding of the tribes, was appointed 'overseer' (*sarparast*) of all the nomadic Shahsevan, responsible to government for communicating its directives to the other chiefs; but he could not exert his authority over the Qoja-Beyli chiefs, who continued to dominate the nomads.[9] More serious rivals to the Qoja-Beyli were the Hajji-Khojalu under Ahmad Khan Bey and later Hazrat-qoli Bey, whose traditional winter pastures near Aslanduz were the best in Iranian Moghan, and with whom Qoja-Beyli had been in conflict ever since they had themselves been banned from Russian Moghan.

I was told that towards the end of the century Hazrat-qoli, apparently encouraged by the Amir Nezam, confronted Qoja-Beyli and ended their hegemony; with none of the chiefs recognized as having authority over the rest, Mozaffar ad-Din Shah then appointed an aide of the governor of Ardabil as *elbey* to supervise the tribes. According to Safari, this was the Ardabil notable, Mo'taman al-Ro'aya, who was killed early in the Constitutional Revolution, after which his uncle Vakil al-Ro'aya held the position for many years.[10]

The government policy of no longer recognizing any Shahsevan as overall chief created the condition known as *khankhanlıq*, the time of the khans; the significance of the term is that, as opposed to the titles *bey* and *elbey*, which are usually government appointments, *khan* implies at least a degree of irresponsible power. A synonym more commonly used by the Shahsevan in recalling those days is *äshrarlıq*, anarchy, the time of the rebels or outlaws (*äshrar*). The policy was in effect one of divide and rule.

Pastures and production

The immediate effect of the closure of the frontier was an economic crisis for the Shahsevan. Restricted to Iranian Moghan, the livestock were short of adequate pasture and water resources, many succumbed to disease and

[9] Artamonov (1890: 448–9).
[10] Safari (1971: 249); he states that these two notables were descended from the old khans of Moghan who had lost Moghan to the Russians, i.e. the khans of Talesh/Namin, not the Sarı-Khan-Beyli dynasty.

starvation, and production was drastically reduced. Further, the pastoralists needed access both to new sources of grain and other commodities and to new markets for their produce, facilities for which they had increasingly come to rely on Russian Moghan. Many Shahsevan had to find alternative means of subsistence.

Before the closure, the nomads had had access to 300,000 hectares of Russian Moghan, including both the legitimate tract laid out by Wrangel in 1849 and areas along the banks of the Kor, Aras and Akosha which had since been abandoned to them. Only some 150,000 to 200,000 hectares of Iranian Moghan, those parts lying within reach of the various watercourses, had been then in use as winter grazing. Artamonov reckoned that reasonable pastures were to be found only in the north, towards the Aras and the Russian frontier, and in the west along the lower reaches of the Qara-Su, 'whose valley is accounted the pearl of all the pasturages on the Iranian side of the frontier'.[11] The southern third of Iranian Moghan, he thought, was rendered quite useless as grazing by its clayey and rocky soils and lack of water, though it might, with adequate irrigation, be turned to cereal cultivation. After the closure, however, the nomads had to open up these lands in order to feed their vast herds, estimated at 1.5 to 2 million head of sheep and goats and around 100,000 head of larger livestock.

In the 1960s the Shahsevan nomads referred to the division of the pastures in Iranian Moghan after the frontier closure as the basis for the current distribution. Interestingly, as I heard the story from them and from various officials who had been concerned with them in earlier decades, the person responsible for distributing the pastures was the Amir Nezam, that is Hasan 'Ali Khan Garusi, the governor-general of Azarbaijan: when I asked about the origins of rights to a particular pasture, the regular response was to refer to *Ämrenezam-säpki* (Amir Nezam's registration – *sapt*).

In fact, the original distribution was effected in 1884–5, before Amir Nezam's appointment as governor-general, by an official with a very similar title, that is Mohammad Sadeq Khan Qajar, Amin Nezam, governor of Ardabil. According to Krebel, the Amin Nezam had been nominated in 1872, for an unspecified period, as *ilkhani* or commandant of all the Shahsevan, but there is no record of his activities then.[12] However, we heard in the last chapter how in spring 1884 he was ordered to Moghan to assign lands to the Shahsevan in the Iranian sector; joined there in December by the heir apparent Mozaffar ad-Din, he duly settled the nomads during the winter on the lands put aside for them.

[11] Artamonov (1890: 450).   [12] Markov (1890: 26).

I could find no extant contemporary record of the distribution, and none of the tribesmen I asked had personal knowledge of any document relating to it. A document has recently come to light, however, in the archives of the Interior Ministry, recording a list, compiled in December 1922 by Amir Lashkar Tahmaspi (see Chapter Twelve), of

> the names of tribes (*taifeh*) of nomad Shahsevan of Ardabil and Meshkin, and the *qıshlaqs* which, after the abolition of the *qıshlaqs* of Russian Moghan by order of that government in 1304 HQ, the late Amin Nezam in the presence of the Shahsevan headmen in Moghan [illegible]; since after the revolution they paid no attention, the Qoja-Beyli and others destroyed the issue and names of tribes and *qıshlaqs*, and there was no document available, I, by the command of the High Army Council ... put together the following information.[13]

He lists forty-three tribes, together with the names and locations of their *qıshlaqs* in Arshaq and Moghan. He adds a further list of thirty-eight names of tribes (most but not all duplicating names in the first list) and pastures, representing changes and adjustments effected later by Mostafa-qoli Khan Amir Tuman Hamadani. This is probably the official mentioned in other sources as Mostafa-qoli Khan Mir Panj, who was apparently charged – by Hasan 'Ali Khan, Amir Nezam – with restoring order among the Shahsevan in their new pastures the year after the closure, i.e. in 1304 HQ (1886–7), the date given in the document; Amin Nezam's initial distribution had occurred two years earlier. It would seem that both Amin Nezam and Amir Nezam had a hand in the distribution, while in time the credit easily passed to the latter, by far the more famous of the two.

The distribution involved allotment of land for both pasturage and settlement. I was unable to discover the precise legal status of these lands at the time. Administratively, southwestern Moghan was in the Angut district, part of Qara-Dagh sub-province, but the rest of Moghan was in Ojarud district which, like Arshaq, was part of the Namin khanate in the sub-province of Ardabil. Much cultivated land in Ojarud once belonged to the Namin khans but had by now been sold to local chiefs – for example in the 1960s the chiefs of the Alarlu tribe farmed extensive lands near Garmi, bought (as they told me) from the khan of Namin in the nineteenth century.

The pastures were probably reckoned Crown lands (*khaleseh*), a status possibly dating from the seventeenth century, and the right to cultivate them had to be acquired from the Crown. At the end of the nineteenth century, large quantities of Crown lands from all parts of the country were sold to private individuals, to bring funds to the chronically needy

---

[13] Document dated Rabi i 1341 (Oct.–Nov. 1922), reproduced in Mizban (1992: 13–22).

Qajar treasury.[14] There are a number of firmans in existence, recording the transfer of parts of Moghan to Shahsevan chiefs at the time, specifically for the purpose of cultivation. In 1965 I saw and copied one such document, in the possession of the chief of the Jeloudarlu tribe but originally issued in 1309/1892 to 'Ali-qoli Khan *elbey* and some associates; they were assigned certain fields or hamlets (*mazra'eh*), mainly in Moghan but partly in Meshkin, as private property for cultivation and settlement, on condition that they paid the taxes assessed. In fact few of the lands mentioned were turned to the plough for another fifty years at least.

The rest of Moghan remained as pasturage, nominally Crown lands, but divided among the different tribes and their sections. I was told in the 1960s that Moghan had been divided into 364 *qıshlaqs*, which covered not only the steppe but much of the present districts of Angut, Barzand and Ojarud, as well as part of Garmaduz district, lying across the Dara-Yort from Aslanduz in Qara-Dagh, where the Hajji-Khojalu tribe of the Shahsevan had some pastures. Amir-Lashkar's list of the first pasture distribution (1884–5) names 274 *qıshlaqs*, many of them in Arshaq; the second list (1886–7) names 264 *qıshlaqs*, all in Moghan. Both lists, however, note several tribes only as continuing to occupy their former pastures, neither naming nor enumerating them – the total could well have matched the figure of 364 that I was given. Holdings ranged from the thirty-four or more *qıshlaqs* allocated to the Moghanlu tribe to the one or two given to some of the smallest tribes.

It would seem that the distribution was originally renewed annually. According to Artamonov, who was in Moghan in November 1889,

Usually at the beginning of November the nomads, having descended from the mountains, migrate in a broad front in loose formation into the Moghan steppe, staying a while on the boundaries of their winter pastures until the arrival of the governor of Ardabil, who is always accompanied by a considerable military detachment. Only after he has assigned parts of the steppe to the nomad communities [sc. tribes] does the governor give them permission to occupy their pastures. At that time he collects the taxes, sorts out misunderstandings between the communities and institutes a summary court without appeal, often accompanied by executions. The governor remains, with his military detachment, to supervise the Shahsevans in their winter pastures, usually close to our frontier near the village of Belasovar, where our frontier commissar also stays, whose duty is to sort out misunderstandings and incidents arising on the frontier between subjects of both states.

Artamonov writes that the Shahsevan, nomad and settled, were assessed for some 15,000 toman in taxes, but the governor actually exacted some

[14] Tigranov (1909: 3, 84); Lambton (1953: 147, 152).

35,000 toman. Each tribe was assessed at a certain sum corresponding to its population, each household being rated at 2 toman. Naturally the chiefs underestimated their census returns.[15] Overcrowding led to competition for the best pastures, and the governor presumably exploited this situation profitably, adding to his already considerable income from his legitimate percentage on the nomad taxes and from other 'presents'. It remains unknown when the distribution became permanent, but the wealthier and more powerful tribes were eventually able to acquire more and better pastures, while the poorer and weaker ones had to make do with inadequate, barren and rocky pastures far from sources of water.

Conditions in the western and eastern parts of Moghan differed. Several groups in Ojarud and the east, including some of the Ardabil nomads, continued for years to cross the frontier and winter in Russian territory, on payment of some kind of duty. Abbott reported in July 1887:

If what I hear be correct, the Russian frontier officials are unable to prevent or rather wink at the Shahsevends proceeding periodically to the Moghan – within the Russian border – to pasture their flocks, because the villagers in the Moghan have represented to the Russian commissary that they depend for their living upon the annual visits of these nomads.[16]

In the west, on the other hand, the new distribution curtailed the once-extensive pastures of several tribes (notably Hajji-Khojalu), in order to make room for newcomers, notably sections of the Qoja-Beyli, who had been moved from the vicinity of the frontier in Ojarud westwards to Angut and the Dara-Yort valley. There was regular fighting over the pastures here between them and Hajji-Khojalu, and between Hajji-Khojalu and their neighbours to the west, the Chalabianlu tribe of Qara-Dagh. Mahmud Khan Bey, brother of the Hajji-Khojalu chief Ahmad Khan Bey, told Artamonov in 1889:

Now they have divided the *qıshlaqs* between the tribes . . . We have few pastures, but thank God our cattle have nonetheless increased; so we have struggled and fought for every inch of land. We have never had such disorder as in the last four years. Almost all the tribes have fought each other. It is particularly difficult for us in bad years and at the end of winter, when all the tribes congregate in those places where grazing is to be found, and try to fight each other off. We, for example, have fine winter quarters, I don't think you would find better than the

---

[15] Artamonov (1890: 450–1); this system prevailed, I was told, until Reza Shah's time, but soon after 1900 taxes ceased to be collected regularly, and arrears had to be paid up after the disarmament in 1923. A new law of 1889–90 provided for the camels, sheep and goats of every village and tribe to be counted annually at the beginning of spring and taxes to be levied at 3 *qrans* per camel and 1 *qran* per sheep and goat (Lambton 1953: 168), but there is no evidence that this law was ever implemented in the Ardabil region.

[16] FO 248/449 (Abbott to Nicolson no. 8 of 27.7.1887); see also Tigranov (1909: 123, 128).

Dara-Yort valley in all Moghan; but unfortunately there is little room for us and
we are bitter enemies of the Chalabianlu tribe, and already at least 50 people on
each side are demanding blood . . . now we cannot graze [our animals] unless we
carry rifles. But our feud began over the pastures. Their sheep crossed onto our
pasture and we seized them. Soon after, some Chalabianlu approached our
animals at night; luckily our watchmen were awake, picked up their guns and a
battle ensued; our men killed two of theirs. Several days later we suffered
somehow one night – three of our men were killed. After that, it seems, we lost
count.[17]

Averyanov, who passed through ten years later, also records that

All autumn and winter there is firing in the Qara-Su valley between the Shahsevan
and the horsemen of Rahim Khan [Chalabianlu], whose villages . . . adjoin the
Shahsevan pastures; the tribes are hostile to each other and are constantly having
disputes and misunderstandings over the pastures.[18]

The locations and sizes of the tribes enumerated in the 1880s lists
match the rather sparser details given for 1903 by Tigranov, who estimated a total of 5,595 nomad households pasturing in Iranian Moghan in
1903 – that is, about fifteen households per *qıshlaq*. Little can be established of the way the pastures were allotted within a tribe, other than what
can be deduced from tradition and from the distribution in 1966 – when
they were still occupied by an average of about fifteen nomad families.
Though no one I spoke to knew of any relevant document, the chief may
originally have had title to the *qıshlaqs* allotted to his tribe. On these or
other grounds, he may have controlled the allotment of pastures within
each tribe, and been able to demand payments from his followers.[19]
Certainly, in the larger and richer tribes, the flocks and herding camps of
the chief and his relatives occupied several *qıshlaqs*, but among the ordinary nomads one *qıshlaq* was allocated to each camp-community of
twenty to thirty households, who managed it as an undivided estate.
Those *qıshlaqs* on which I collected information, mainly in the northern
and western parts of Moghan, averaged some 1,000 hectares in extent,
and were of very variable shape.

[17] Artamonov (1890: 452). In the 1960s, as clearly also in 1889, rights in a pasture were
observed only until all of the first growth (*kham*) had been grazed once by the owners'
flocks; after that, the second growth (*örän*) was open to all comers; this normally coincided with spring rains and plentiful grazing, but in a dry year violent disputes – such as
mentioned here – were common. It was also still the custom to seize, and often to beat, a
neighbour's animals that strayed onto one's pasture (cf. Tapper 1979a: 51–2).
[18] Averyanov (1900: 66), quoted in Rostopchin (1933: 108).
[19] Tagieva, referring to Georgian Central Historical Archives, puts the tribes into three categories: the majority, where all the lands used belonged to the chiefs; a few, where part of
the lands belonged to members of the chiefly family; and those nomad tribes where the
pastures were communally owned (1964: 92); but it seems (it is not clear) that she is
mainly discussing farmlands.

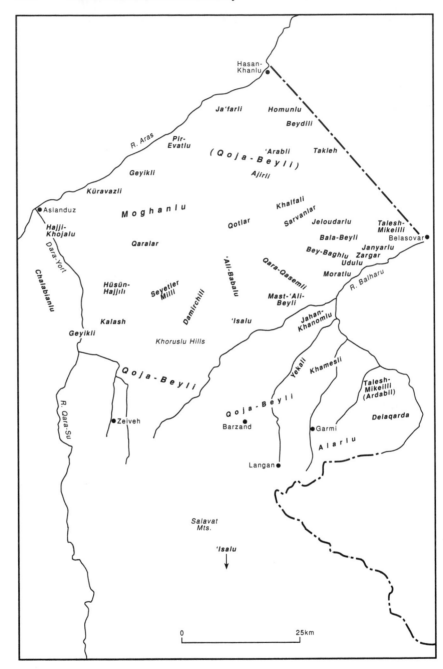

Map 7. Iranian Moghan, showing approximate location of tribes around 1900 (Chapter 11) (names of tribes are shown in bold italics)

In the twenty years or so after the distribution, there were occasional wholesale movements when powerful groups occupied the pastures of weaker ones, and other infringements of the original borders. For example, Nouruz Khan Qoja-Beyli moved his followers north from Ojarud and Khoruslu and occupied pastures among the subordinate Pir-Evatlu, 'Arabli, Ja'farli and Ajirli tribes. Much of the Ajirli, together with the Beydili and others, withdrew from the north of Moghan and took refuge with Alarlu in Ojarud. Later, the Geyikli tribe began to encroach on Qoja-Beyli lands in the Dara-Yort/Qara-Su valley. However, most of these moves were later reversed, and a comparison of Maps 7 and 8 shows that remarkably little redistribution of *qıshlaqs* has taken place between tribes, and so far as I could judge the same is true of the allotment of *qıshlaqs* within each tribe.

Artamonov was told that, before the closure of the frontier, every Shahsevan nomad houseold had owned at least three or four horses, two or three camels and forty to fifty head of sheep and goats (a modest flock at any time), while now the shortage of pasture meant there was scarcely one horse and one camel per tent.[20]

Indeed it seems that larger stock suffered far heavier reductions in numbers than did sheep and goats, which were better able to use the sparse grazing of southern Moghan and the Khoruslu hills than Artamonov imagined. A major deficiency at first was in water sources, and wells had to be sunk in many places. The evidence indicates that, although the Shahsevan flocks had to graze at a higher density than they had been used to in the lusher pastures of Russian Moghan, they did not fall permanently below about 1.5 million head for many years after the closure. The 700–800 pastures into which the chiefs had divided their legitimate tract of Russian Moghan around 1850 averaged around 350 hectares, and such pastures were considered adequate grazing for 1,000 sheep,[21] in other words a density of about 3 per hectare. In Iranian Moghan and surrounding districts Amin Nezam made available somewhat over 400,000 hectares for distribution as winter grazing, much of it previously underused. Now it supported 1.5 million sheep and goats (and numbers of larger livestock) at four to five per hectare, a little above the density practised today.[22]

The flocks deteriorated in condition sooner than in numbers, and in bad years their resistance to disease, cold and drought was impaired. Thus in 1888–9, when the rainfall was very poor, large numbers of animals did perish, leaving their owners destitute. As he passed through Moghan the following autumn, Artamonov saw spiritless animals and met angry tribesmen, bewildered by the disasters which had befallen

[20] Artamonov (1890: 200).   [21] Radde (1886: 429).   [22] Tapper (1979a: 48).

them and reproaching his government for its action in excluding them from their old lands.[23] Even in better years the flocks were far less productive than before, and this was where the pastoral economy suffered the most.

Markets

The nomads had been accustomed to marketing much of their produce in Russia as well as in Iran. Not only was there a substantial and growing demand in eastern Caucasia, where, for political and economic reasons and in advance of a change of taste, the Russian pastoralists had been converted from ovine to bovine stock-keeping, but also the most productive time in the Shahsevan pastoral cycle was the spring, so that before they left Moghan for the south the nomads disposed of their milk products, spring wool clips, woven goods produced during the winter and (most important of all) their fatstock. Those who camped in Russian territory visited the bazaars along the Kor and Aras banks, while those who remained in Iranian Moghan came to Belasovar or even crossed the Aras to Qara-Bagh to market their goods. Probably also Russian dealers visited the camps, though I have no information on this.

Now the inferiority of the winter pastures in Iranian Moghan greatly reduced the quantity of Shahsevan produce for sale in spring, and the closure of the frontier prevented them from selling direct to Russian consumers. If Abbott was right in his suspicions (see above) that Shahsevan nomads were still being allowed to enter Russian Moghan in 1887, it can only have occurred on a small scale at this time. The Russians for their part soon began to 'open up' the steppe for cultivation. Markov, writing in 1889, summarizes his government's justification for finally excluding the Iranian nomads from Moghan, and discusses the immense development potential of the steppe, pointing out the existence of the huge ancient canal networks which could easily be reopened, and the ruins of large and prosperous cities which had once thrived on them. He concludes:

the fact that the Shahsevan were forbidden to pasture in Moghan augurs well for this extensive part of the Baku province; with the improvement of communications up to the outskirts of Moghan itself, it will be cultivated all over and covered by tilled fields and cotton plantations . . . the cultivation of lands in Moghan will not require special complicated engineering works or huge investment of capital . . . Thus, at the present time, when the Iranian nomads have been removed once and for all from our territory, Russia has the prospect of reaping the benefit of its territorial gain by the treaty of Torkman–Chai with Iran, and with this aim she

[23] Artamonov (1890: 200, 451f.).

must turn special attention to the canals scattered throughout Moghan and with the aid of irrigation turn this almost waterless plain into one of the richest granaries of the Transcaucasian region.[24]

A later writer noted how 'the face of the steppe began to change under the cultivation and filled with settlers'.[25] After the closure of the frontier Shahsevan raids on Russian settlers increased, but the nomads did not try to use Russian Moghan again for pasturage until the Bolshevik revolution.

By contrast with Moghan, the situation in the Shahsevan mountain pastures was if anything ameliorated by the reduction of stock numbers kept by the nomads.[26] There the flocks could recover from the rigours of winter, and in any event summer now became the more productive time of year, especially for stock sales. The nomads now intensified their use of the local market towns in the vicinity of the summer pastures: Ardabil, Ahar and Sarab. Meanwhile Russian demands for Shahsevan produce continued, and much of the stock sold in the Iranian towns in summer was then taken on the hoof from Ardabil north to Belasovar and Russian Moghan.[27]

Russian markets had been not only outlets for Shahsevan produce but also sources of various commodities which they needed, particularly agricultural produce and manufactured goods such as firearms and ammunition. After the closure, the nomads, mainly from the Meshkin tribes, had to find alternative supplies of such commodities. As for grain, few of them owned any farmland themselves along the migration routes or near their pastures, and they were unlikely to be able to buy village lands in Meshkin and Arshaq, as these were already in the hands of large landowners who were unwilling to dispose of such a potentially profitable resource. They could buy the produce of these villages from the cultivators or the landowners, but the instability of the economic structure of Azarbaijan, where supplies and prices of grain were liable to enormous fluctuations due to speculation by merchants and landowners, made this option less than attractive to them. Encouraged by the attitude of the administration, many nomads chose two alternative sources of grain: opening up new lands to cultivation, and banditry – raiding the villages or extorting produce from them as 'protection money'.

---

[24] Markov (1890: 58–62); Monteith too wrote of Tamerlane's canal in Iranian Moghan: 'At a very small expense, it could again be opened, and the desert of Mojan [*sic*] converted into one of the most fertile districts of Persia' (1833: 30).   [25] Avdeyev (1927: 15).

[26] Amir Leshkar's letter accompanying his list of the tribes and their winter pastures (see note 13 above) implies that Amin Nezam also listed the summer pastures, and so I was told (of Amir Nezam) in the 1960s; but no copy of the latter list has yet come to light (Mizban 1992: 24).   [27] Aubin (1908: 107); *Routes in Persia* (II: 609).

Settlement

Both Artamonov and Tigranov remark on the aversion of the Meshkin nomads to taking up agriculture themselves. Artamonov wrote:

After the Russian frontier was closed to them the Shahsevan, in their own words, 'fell into the cauldron'; there is not enough room for all to pasture, but they are not interested in a sedentary and agricultural way of life; they despise the idea of settling somewhere within the boundaries of their pastures, since if there should be a small piece of land suitable for cultivation it would require very hard work and heavy expenditure to supply artificial irrigation. The Shahsevan definitely do not want to leave this region, and the Iranian government's feeble attempts to this end, made at [Russian] insistence, have led nowhere.[28]

Tigranov had another explanation for the nomads' attitude:

In the eyes of the true Shahsevan, agriculture is not a respectable occupation, and the settled folk evoke his contempt. The reality of his environment encourages this view, for the settled population seems to him like 'sheep, allowing themselves to be shorn without demur'. Out of this population there come to him people destitute and broken in spirit to seek protection, for which they are even prepared to accept the status of his slaves.[29]

Being disinclined to take up cultivation themselves, and presumably unable to persuade their nomad followers to do so, the wealthier Shahsevan invited destitute and landless peasants from the southern parts of the Ardabil province and elsewhere in Azarbaijan, and settled them in Moghan and along the migratory routes in Arshaq. They supplied the immigrants with land and dwellings – 'huts, half-buried in the ground and very skilfully braided with reeds'[30] – grouped them into small hamlets of ten to twenty households, loaned them seed, tools and draught-animals and set them to cultivating wheat, barley and rice (by the rivers), and to tending cattle and growing fruit. They provided them, finally, with some protection from the administration, and in return received about two-thirds of the produce.

Rudimentary settlements as they were, these hamlets also paid government taxes, and as a result their economic conditions were intolerable, even by Iranian standards, and development was out of the question. It was particularly difficult for them in autumn and spring on the governor's journey between Ardabil and Belasovar.[31]

The authorities officially favoured settlements sponsored by the nomads, but by their oppression in effect they also hindered their development.

---

[28] Artamonov (1890: 455).   [29] Tigranov (1909: 134).
[30] Artamonov (1890: 201); just such dwellings (*tam*) were standard equipment in winter camps in the north of the region in the 1960s.   [31] Tigranov (1909: 121).

Only those situated off the governor's line of march, for example in western Salavat, or lucky enough to be protected by a powerful land-owner, as in Meshkin, lived in tolerable conditions and even grew in size by attracting impoverished nomads to settle there.[32]

Artamonov considered that 'the most terrible scourge for the farmer is the damage done by the nomads' livestock, which sometimes compel the inhabitants to give up their land and find more peaceful if less favourable lands'; at migration time, violent brawls between nomads and settlers were commonplace.[33]

Two major factors affected the way each individual tribe adjusted to the economic crisis: the location of its winter quarters both before and after the closure, and the degree to which it already had access to alternative resources such as farmland. Already there were large differences in these respects between the tribes of the Ardabil and Meshkin divisions. Few of the latter had villages or agricultural lands, though many had had pastures on the Iranian side of the frontier. The Ardabil tribes, on the other hand, were already more committed to settled bases, and their nomadic sections were entirely former migrants to Russian Moghan, so, although a few of them were allotted new pastures within Iran, most of them chose simply to settle in the villages which they already had in the vicinity of Ardabil. The closure thus accelerated settlement processes that had been in train among the Ardabil tribes for a long time.

Some of the weaker Ardabil tribes, which had no villages of their own, had already disappeared before the closure, parts joining the stronger nomad tribes, parts settling in villages belonging to other tribes. Tigranov gives as examples the defunct tribes Farajollah-Khanlu, Mirza-Rahimli, Fathollah-Khanlu and Pasha-Khanlu. Other small tribes that already had village bases, or suitable places where they could now found them, were able to settle en bloc, and the villages now bore the name of the tribe: Tigranov mentions the Abu-Beyli and the Udulu as examples.

In the case of rather larger tribes which had numerous villages, such as the Dursun-Khojalu, Sheikhli and Qozatlu, their settlements all bore the tribal name and perhaps also the name of the village founder, and then after the closure the tribe settled in them without losing its name and identity. The locality of the villages acquired the tribal name too. But the name long outlasted other cultural features of the former nomadic society, and the settlers soon assumed the character of farmers, forgetting their nomad origins, often deliberately. The tribal identity of Reza-Beyli and Baibagli, however, whose villages were scattered over a wide area and did not form a compact group, was preserved after settlement only

[32] *Ibid.*   [33] Artamonov (1890: 442).

because their names remained as such in the governor's tax register (though a small group of Reza-Beyli continued as nomads until very recently).[34]

In each of the tribes discussed so far, there were formerly (according to Tigranov) about equal numbers of chiefly entourage and cultivating peasants (*rayät*). After full settlement, with the fragmentation of the village land through inheritance, most of the chiefly family became impoverished: some joined the entourages of more powerful chiefs, others were assimilated to the peasantry or forced to emigrate, and in the meantime powerful external elements – mullahs, merchants, officials – steadily bought up the tribal farmlands and acquired control of the settled nomads.

The strong tribes of Polatlu and Yortchi formed a separate category. Their chiefs had always owned large areas of land and controlled thousands of peasants and thus remained economically secure for some time. Their villages, moreover, were situated in compact territories, convenient for protection against bandits, officials and prospective purchasers. Conditions in these villages, however, were as bad as in those of weaker landowners where the *tiyuldars'* rapacity was unchecked, for the chiefs considered themselves *tiyuldars* rather than landowners, and were correspondingly inconsiderate of their peasants' welfare. They not only collected the government land taxes, but continued to levy the former nomad assessment from the settlers, paying the governor for the right to do so.

Tigranov describes the plight of the Yortchi tribe: in 1901 the notorious bandit chief of this tribe, Khosrou Khan, who had for some years bought the right to collect the former nomad assessment of 1,140 toman, was arrested and taken to Tabriz. His successor, hoping to take on his tax-farming rights, offered the governor of Ardabil, Emam-qoli Mirza, 5,000 toman. To raise this sum he had to borrow from a merchant at 80 per cent per annum, and in order to leave himself some profit this chief tried to extract about 11,000 toman from the tribe, nearly ten times the original assessment. The tribe could not provide such an amount and the chief had to resort to extensive banditry. Tigranov writes that, since other chiefs were in a similar position, the 'brigandized' condition of the Ardabil province was hardly surprising.[35]

The Ardabil chiefs, in other words, became assimilated to the predatory administration and further and further alienated from their former tribal followers. The only hope for the oppressed peasantry was the

[34] See Appendix Two.   [35] Tigranov (1909: 139–40); see also Safari (1971: 175f.).

purchase of the villages by a strong landowner, which was happening on the northern borders of the Yortchi and Polatlu territories.[36]

Meanwhile a few of the Ardabil tribes remained pastoralists, migrating in winter to their alloted pastures in the eastern and southeastern parts of Iranian Moghan. They included the Jahan-Khanomlu, Khamesli, and sections of the Ardabil Talesh-Mikeilli, Takleh, Qozatlu, Yekali and Reza-Beyli, amounting by 1900 to fewer than 1,000 households altogether. During their migrations and their residence in Moghan these groups became, to all intents and purposes, subject to one or other of the leading Meshkin chiefs, who now controlled the whole region north of Arshaq.

Among the Meshkin tribes, rather than nomad settlement, the opposite process of peasant nomadization appears to have been occurring. As we have seen, villages in Moghan and Arshaq had been settled not by nomad tribespeople but by destitute peasants brought in from elsewhere. By the time of the Constitutional Revolution (1905–11), when *tiyuls* were abolished, land ownership in the region was totally insecure. Few landowners were able to protect their peasants, or to collect their own shares of the produce without paying for 'protection'. Facing a combined attack from administrative extortion and tribal raiding, many peasants in Meshkin and districts to the north left their lands to join the nomad chiefs' retinues, while others even formed small new commoner tribes of pastoralists, for example Larili (from the small town of Lari), Khioulu (from Khiou), Seyetler-/Sadat-Zarinji (from a village of settled Seyeds) and Terit (from Aslanduz).

Changes in Shahsevan tribal organization

By 1900, with the decline of the *elbeys* and the emergence of *khankhanlıq*, there were changes in the organization of the different Shahsevan tribes. Government policy virtually sanctioned a state of uncontrolled feud between various powerful chiefs, giving free rein to the tribes' mutual depredations, the symptoms of desperate overcrowding in Moghan. It also kept the tribes from co-ordinated rebellion and ensured that a share of the spoils they collected should pass, in the form of fines, bribes and taxes, to the officials themselves. The latter abandoned any attempt at security or justice, such as were maintained earlier under the *elbeys*.

In the noble tribes, the ruling lineages continued to control the

---

[36] The preceding analysis of the situation of the settled Ardabil tribes is based on that of Tigranov (1909: 135–9).

'workers', but many of them (largely as a result of fission) grew very weak in numbers and lost their following of commoner tribes. None the less, one noble tribe in each division continued to dominate the rest: the chiefs of Polatlu in Ardabil, and of Qoja-Beyli and its offshoot 'Isalu in Meshkin, maintained a degree of traditional authority and continued to wield symbols of nobility and to rule their followers through a hierarchy of subordinate chiefs and elders. Meanwhile a new elite was emerging, based no longer on traditional descent claims but rather on numerical strength, material resources and territorial and political alliances. The chiefs of four of the larger and wealthier commoner tribes, Hajji-Khojalu and Geyikli in Meshkin, Yortchi in Ardabil, and Alarlu in Ojarud, now declared their independence of the nobles, collected their own followings of weaker tribes, and attempted to establish the same kind of dynastic rule and hierarchical structure of their following as had characterized the former noble tribes.

A common feature of the dominant tribes, the main basis of the chiefs' power, was that before the closure they all had either extensive village bases, or pastures in Iranian Moghan, or both. The almost wholly settled Polatlu and Yortchi have been discussed. Hajji-Khojalu and Geyikli, neighbours in both winter and summer quarters, had fine pastures in western Moghan, comparatively inaccessible both to the Russians and to the Iranian authorities. In the centre of the region, the Qoja-Beyli and 'Isalu chiefs were between them able to control both the access of other tribes to Moghan and the passing of trade caravans between Ahar, Ardabil and Belasovar. Alarlu, mainly settled with prosperous farmlands near Garmi, dominated Ojarud and the frontier between there and Ardabil.

The weaker commoner chiefs sought the support of a dominant tribe, if only to secure their control of their own tribes. Only Moghanlu, it seems, as the largest tribe of all, at once acquired a measure of independence and did not seek to dominate others. Each dominant tribe now had its chiefly lineage and its commoners, and so did each subordinate tribe. The hierarchical structure of each 'tribal cluster' now developed as follows:

The *beyzadä* – this term referred no longer only to those of noble descent, but to the chiefly lineages of all dominant tribes – comprised the chief (*khan*) of the dominant tribe and his entourage: his agnates and their households, who between them owned or controlled access to much of the available pasture and farmland; a suite of attendants (personal servants, secretaries, tutors, etc.), who might be of the chiefly lineage or refugees of rank from elsewhere; and also the chiefs of subordinate tribes in the cluster and a few selected members of their (much smaller) entourages.

The *beyzadä* provided military levies for the government when called on. Whereas twenty-five years earlier, as mentioned in Chapter Ten, the Shahsevan levy amounted to 500 horsemen, by 1886, perhaps in recognition of the hardships consequent on the frontier closure, the levy was reduced to 450: the Shahsevan of Ardabil and Meshkin were expected to contribute a troop of 400 cavalry, while the Qoja-Beyli were separately rated at 50 horsemen.[37] In 1902, 440 men were called up for service in the Persian Cossack brigade, with contingents from the tribes as follows:

Ardabil tribes		Meshkin tribes	
Khamesli (Polatlu)	80	'Isa-Beyli (Qoja-Beyli)	50
Yortchi	50	Hajji-Khojalu	50
Dursun-Khojalu	25	Talesh-Mikeilli	40
Takleh	25	Geyikli	30
		Hüsün-Hajjılı	15
		Damirchili	15
Alarlu of Langan	50	Ajirli	10

(Polatlu and Qoja-Beyli themselves apparently escaped the levy by resisting the governor of Ardabil's recruiting expedition of that year; the absence of a levy from Moghanlu is puzzling.) Each year, those who had served the previous year were replaced, and then had to serve again the following year, so in fact some 880 horsemen of the Shahsevan were regularly involved.[38]

Each chief (*bey*) had a retinue of armed and mounted henchmen or servants (*nökär*), including those provided by elders of commoner sections of the tribe, who would be detailed for various domestic military duties such as defence of the chief's property and camp, offensive raids, coercion of dissident followers. The retinue also included the chief's menial servants and herdsmen, most of them outlaws or refugee peasants or nomads without property or effective kin support of their own.

The commoners, formerly known as *hampa* ('companions'), now came to be known as *rayät* ('subjects'); these non-chiefly tribespeople probably amounted to the great majority of the Shahsevan nomad population, and continued during this period to occupy themselves with pastoral activities, migrating with their flocks between Moghan and the mountains to the south. The pastoralists lived in communities (*jamahat*) of twenty to thirty households whose heads usually formed a lineage (*göbäk*) – descendants of a common ancestor, camping together and usually managing as a joint estate the winter pasture (*qıshlaq*) allotted to them in the 1880s, as well as their traditional summer pastures. The chief recognized these

---

[37] FO 251/57 (Herbert to Nicolson, Army Report of 7.6.1886).
[38] Tigranov (1909: 109, 121, 144f.). Note that Alarlu is still not counted as a Shahsevan tribe; they acquired this identity very shortly afterwards.

communities as sections (*tirä*) of the tribe, and made the elder (*aq-saqal*) responsible for maintaining a small retinue of armed horsemen to protect the camp and the animals and also to be sent to join the chief's retinue. In order to do so, the elder had to make certain demands on his followers, as well as keeping a larger flock himself.

Life was hard for the ordinary pastoralists, and they had difficulty securing an adequate supply of necessities. The pastoral commoners still had to market what was left of their produce, after handing much of it to the chief as 'tribute' or 'protection money', and in addition had to supplement their income by sending their young men (*iyid* or *qızılbash*, as they were sometimes known), armed and mounted, to join the chief's retinue. To the extent that they could obtain necessary supplies without paying for them, they compensated for the reduced productivity of their flocks and avoided settlement. My informants indicated that a fairly general pattern at this time, at least among the chiefly entourages, was exchange: the herdsmen continued to tend their flocks and to supply produce to their employers for agricultural and manufactured goods, acquired by some means or other. Old commoners admitted that food had been scarce at this period, when so much farmland had been abandoned because of banditry.

Pastoralist commoners relied on the protection of one or other of the powerful chiefs. It would have been quite impossible for a small tribe or nomadic community to carry on a pastoral existence without joining the cluster of tribes following the dominant chief of the neighbourhood. Powerful chiefs sometimes turned both followers and weaker enemies out of the choicer pastures they had been allotted in Moghan, taking them over for the use of their own vast herds of camels, horses and sheep.

A tribal cluster was not effectively centralized. The supreme power in each cluster was too firmly rooted to be seriously challenged by commoners, but each dominant tribe was divided by dynastic factions, among which violence commonly broke out, particularly on the death of the chief. There was no rule of succession, but the chiefship almost always passed between close agnates. There was an inherent fissive tendency within each chiefly family, due to the same kinship principles that affect the organization of the pastoral household and camp: on the one hand, father and son, full-brothers and usually paternal uncle and nephew, co-operate without question, the juniors accepting the senior's authority unless the latter specifically abdicates it; on the other hand, paternal half-brothers and first cousins are inevitably rivals.[39]

A cluster chief could thus rely on, and share his power with, sons and

---

[39] See Tapper (1979a: 104, 126f.).

brothers, but had to be careful to conciliate his half-brothers and first cousins, especially those who inherited substantial shares of former chiefs' resources and owned and lived in lands remote from his own, and were thus a greater threat as rivals than more distant cousins could be. He could not hope to crush these rivals, nor to deprive them of their property; they too maintained retinues of armed henchmen, herdsmen and servants, locally recruited and owing their immediate loyalty to the leader who promised to protect their vulnerable pastoral resources. Rather, he persuaded them to keep outlying subordinate chiefs in order; chiefs of smaller and weaker tribes were then, as now, little more than the most prominent of the elders of their tribe. So long as the cluster chief supplied his agnates with sufficient spoils and armed reinforcements when necessary, he could rely on their support.

Rivals, whether close agnates, dangerous subordinate chiefs or wealthy commoner elders, could be compelled to make the pilgrimage to Mecca, which had two political effects advantageous to a dominant chief: it dissipated some of the rival's wealth, and usually indicated his retirement from political activity. Indeed, lists of names of subordinate chiefs, and the genealogies of elders, are full of Hajjis. Chiefly genealogies too contain numerous cousins and uncles of ruling chiefs who renounced claims to power by making the pilgrimage, while I know of only two cluster chiefs who went to Mecca while still in office: Hajji Faraj of Geyikli and Hajji Hazrat-qoli of Hajji-Khojalu, both of whom, as it happened, had powerful brother's sons ('Aleshan Khan and Javat Khan, respectively) to whom they handed over much of their political responsibility.

Dynastic rivalries within the chiefly lineage often threatened to split the dominant tribe, though the lineage, as a corporate descent group, could usually unite itself, its own tribe and its subordinates to meet an outside threat. Such rivalries had presumably caused the distribution of Shahsevan tribes among Badr Khan's descendants, first into the Ardabil and Meshkin divisions and then between the various noble tribes, as outlined in Chapter Nine. By 1900, of the former nobles among the dominant tribes, 'Isalu had already separated from Qoja-Beyli, while Khamesli was in the process of breaking from Polatlu; later Qoja-Beyli began to divide between Bahram Khan and Sardar Bey, and 'Isalu between Agha Bey's son Amir Aslan and his half-brother 'Isa Bey. Later family rivalries also began to divide the 'commoner' dominant tribes: Hajji-Khojalu between Hazrat-qoli's sons and his nephew Javat Khan, Geyikli between Faraj's son Hatam Khan and nephew 'Aleshan Khan; Alarlu between the cousins Najaf-qoli Khan and Gholam. That none of these threatened fissions was completed by 1923 indicates perhaps that each 'commoner' chiefly dynasty as a whole realized the threat to its control of the cluster and still did not feel so secure in its authority as the former 'noble' dynasties.

Given the dynastic rivalries within each of the seven dominant tribes (Polatlu, Yortchi, Qoja-Beyli, 'Isalu, Hajji-Khojalu, Geyikli, Alarlu), it is often more important to know the names of the chiefs involved in events at this period than the names of their tribes. On one or two notable occasions, most of the cluster chiefs were allied for a particular common purpose, but usually, as we shall see in Chapter Twelve, each was on terms of hostility if not blood-feud with his neighbours, and formed alliances among the other chiefs in the region and in neighbouring regions: those of the Chalabianlu and Hajji-'Alili of Qara-Dagh, the Shatranlu of Khalkhal, the Galesh of Talesh, the Dalikanlu of Sarab, and the Shaqaqi of Mianeh.

Banditry

The chiefs of the dominant tribes divided the pastures and village lands of the region between them and sent their armed henchmen to raid widely in neighbouring regions of Russia and Iran. Banditry, and the 'protection' of agriculture, pastoralism and commerce, became increasingly the means by which the Shahsevan chiefs acquired both their necessary supplies and their dominance over the population of the region.

Banditry was a source of revenue to the administration, and also of course a source of income in kind for the chiefly entourages. As the demands of the Iranian administration increased, the burden was passed on to the smaller and weaker communities, both nomad and settled, while the wealthy and powerful took advantage of the situation. Mutual raiding of tribe on tribe was used as a means of tax-gathering,[40] shares of booty from other sources found their way into the officials' pockets, and captured bandits bought their pardon and release. Artamonov was told by a Meshkin chief in 1889:

We have no order at all; a wealthy man can buy his way out of the most terrible crime, and among us only a lazy man does not try to oppress and rob the poor. When you stopped allowing us into your territory, the Vakil al-Molk and the Mo'taman took us in hand. We had not seen such robbery for a long time. Everyone had his price; if I wished to rob your home and to kill you, and did so, then I could ride to the Mo'taman and give him half of the loot; and thereafter I could deal openly and honourably with him.

Asadollah Khan Vakil al-Molk was governor of Ardabil in 1887–9; during his three years in office, according to Artamonov, he acquired thirty vil-

---

[40] See passage from Maslovskiy (1914: 7) quoted by Rostopchin (1933: 103–4); also Markov (1890: 30–2).

lages in the sub-province. Mo'taman al-Ro'aya was mentioned earlier as the governor's assistant with special responsibilities for the Shahsevan tribes.[41]

Armed henchmen of the chiefs terrorized the settled population, particularly in long-established villages of Meshkin, Arshaq and Ardabil districts. Villages were fortified, but many were abandoned and the destitute farmers fled, either to the refuge of larger and better protected settlements such as Lari or Khiou, or to the towns, or northwards to become tenants of the nomad chiefs. The poorer nomads too were destitute and forced to settle or take service with the chiefs, who grew ever wealthier and more powerful.

Tigranov analyses the developments as follows:

at the same time the immigrant element, forming the settled villages of the tribes, provides them not only with the grain they need but also with a view of a culturally superior way of life. Only the growth of income from the increasing number of villages belonging to the tribe, and the systematic depletion of the resources [necessary] for nomadic life, owing to the growth of the settled population, brings into the life of the tribe an irresistible urge to settle and take up agriculture. The core of settlers, peasants destitute of property and spirit, is joined by similar 'weak' people from the tribes, until finally there remain strong in spirit only the chiefs, their small entourage of [subordinate] chiefs, and their families. This entourage lives in plenty, deriving its means of subsistence from the villages, and consequently the need for migration lessens, and the nomadic element disappears. When the migrations cease, the school for the military education of the tribe also vanishes; there is a falling off in the regular confrontations with other tribes, over the winter pastures, on the migration route and in the summer pastures, and the mass loses its familiarity with the military situation which had guaranteed the tribe's survival, while for those who remain strong in spirit – the chiefs, who are quite alien to the agricultural economy – the only avenue for the release of their unemployed energies is banditry.[42]

Actually the economic situation of the nomads was not wholly dominated by banditry. A number of tribes like Moghanlu and Damirchili, and commoners within other tribes, confined their activities to pastoralism. But even in powerful tribes the pastoralist commoners were insecure, for it was they who suffered in inter-tribal reciprocal raiding.

In the 1960s, survivors of those times retained vivid memories of the anarchy fostered by the *äshrars* (lawless rebels) and the *khankhans* (independent chiefs) which contrasted with the peace and security they had enjoyed since 1923; I recorded countless statements such as those quoted at the head of Part IV. These memories naturally overstress the absence of

[41] Artamonov (1890: 452); Safari (1971: 193, 249); FO 248/449 (Abbott to Nicolson nos. 6 of 16.7.1887 and 8 of 27.7.1887); FO 248/722 (Wood no. 9 of 22.11.1900).
[42] Tigranov (1909: 134–5).

order, regularity and consistency in the social organization of the time, on which they are none the less the main source of information. In the absence of law (*qanun*), order (*edareh*), government (*hokumat*), state (*doulat*) or even Shah, the old men said, there was just irresponsible power (*güj*), based on the control of mounted riflemen. If a man could muster a party of horsemen and carry out successful raids, his following would grow and he might become khan; meanwhile the weak and defenceless suffered – 'the armless and legless disappeared (*älsiz ayakhsız aradan getdi*)'. As an old villager from the Ja'farli tribe put it, when talking to a young Iranian agricultural engineer who was assisting me at the time:

As you now acquire rank with your pen, just so in those times, whoever was smart would acquire rank. For example, one day I might raid a camp, or leave five men dead. They would then call me an *äshrar*, and fifty horsemen, say, would follow me. Just as you now order people around with your pen, and people call you Engineer and reckon you an important man – it was just the same system then. The smart man who took his gun and brought in most by his nightly raids – they would call him smart, they would call him chief, he was reckoned important, and fifty horsemen might follow him. That was how the great tribes became powerful *äshrars*: tribes like Geyikli, Pir-Evatlu, Ja'farli, Khosroulu;[43] another one, over there, was Alarlu, and another was 'Isalu, and over there Hajji-Khojalu. All the rest of them – Moghanlu, Damirchili and so on – were included within the others. These were the powerful *äshrar* tribes; the *äshrars* were chiefs, people who, if there were a hair in your eye, could snatch it away (*gözdä tük oleidi onu vurup apara-jaghdılar*).

Participation in a successful raiding party was the prime ambition of the young commoners: 'the same loud noise came out of every young man's mouth.' Raiding parties were called *änjini*.[44] They were of two types: the reciprocal raid against caravans, camps or villages protected by other tribes in the region, from whom retaliation might be expected; and the unilateral raid, usually a long-range expedition outside the region, into Iranian or Russian territory, where direct retaliation was unlikely and the spoils might be greater.[45]

The chiefs did not encourage reciprocal raiding by their followers unless there was a blood-feud in progress or some other immediate political purpose to be achieved. Prospective raiders naturally chose their enemies' weakest camps or villages as victims, and so long as they did not

---

[43] The last three were in fact small tribes, powerful by association with and subordination to Qoja-Beyli.

[44] A corruption of *anjoman*, the term for the revolutionary and regional committees of the Constitutionalists.

[45] My use of the terms 'reciprocal' and 'unilateral' raiding here is not quite the same as that of Sweet (1965: 1140), who is dealing with the very different context of Bedouin camel raiding in North Arabia. (See also Rosenfeld 1965, Asad 1973, on Bedouin raiding.)

provoke the retaliation of a powerful protector they were not impeded in their activity by their own chiefs. Honour in the Bedouin sense was not a factor in raiding:[46] it was not shameful but normal for the strong to rob the weak, though killing was avoided as far as possible, and women, children and old men were not harmed. The spoils sought were commonly horses, camels, sheep and cattle, but sometimes tents, clothes and household property might be brought off. As the same Ja'farli man said,

> No, we did not listen to the chief; everyone was chief in his own camp . . . If there was a smart fellow in such and such a camp, he would collect horsemen, ten or fifteen of them, and go off on a raid . . . when they brought the loot back, then he would get a larger share of it, whatever it was, sheep, horses, etc. The others would throw lots for their shares . . . If anyone was killed, they would add to his share; if someone borrowed a horse, the horse was allotted a share, that is if I had no horse and went and borrowed one from someone, then whatever I brought in with that horse, for example ten sheep, then five were for the owner of the horse and five for me. The horse's owner got a half share.

Unilateral raids required more organization. Sometimes chiefs would send raiding parties to attack villages and caravans in regions of Iran as far away as Zanjan, Hamadan and Tabriz. But the most prestigious expeditions were those sent into Russian territory, to steal animals and grain from camps and villages, but more often, in the years immediately after the closure, to attack Cossack guard-posts and carry off their firearms, with which the nomads were plentifully supplied by 1900. (Many Iranians and others suspected that the Russians were actually supplying the Shahsevan with arms, to help them embarrass the Iranian authorities, and indeed the evidence supports this, at least in the years around the turn of the century.) From caravans, raiders would take cash, valuables and merchandise of various kinds (e.g. cloth); but the favourite booty was horses, as they could be quickly and easily brought back, though stories are also told of summer raids into Qara-Bagh to bring thousands of sheep at a time back across the Aras. Stories I heard of Shahsevan raids into Russia agree substantially with the following account from 1904:

> Shahsevan raids into Transcaucasian territory have recently become an almost daily occurrence, for the following reasons: since the nomads may no longer take their flocks to [Russian] Moghan, their pastoral economy has been restricted and very many families have been ruined . . . since 1884 the animals have been short of grazing and fodder and have to be sold at ridiculous prices. The numbers of horses have decreased so far that many families no longer have a single one of these prized animals. Nowadays the owner of a horse often lends it to a bandit who lacks one, in return for a half share of any booty taken. On these conditions, the one stakes his life, the other his horse.

[46] Cf. Abou-Zeid (1965: 246).

Raiding parties into Russian territory are usually organized efficiently and with the encouragement of the chiefs. After each successful raid, the booty is brought to the chief, who takes the lion's share before dividing the rest, in the presence of the elders, between the members of the raiding party. Each party includes members of several descent groups.

The general plan of a raid is communicated to the chief, who picks a number of horsemen from each group and orders them to gather at a certain hour near the frontier. These horsemen do not leave their camps together, but in ones and twos and nearly always at night, so as not to call attention to themselves. When the leader has assembled his party, they are guided across the frontier by guides from the border settlements. Then the party divides into several small bands; the leader remains with a few horsemen on the frontier, the others move off into Russian territory, disposing themselves like chessmen at prearranged points, where they lie in ambush to cover the line of retreat of the leading band. This band, having achieved its aim and rounded up a herd of horses or cattle, or having robbed a caravan or a village, etc., immediately returns by the prearranged route; if it is pursued, the other bands which have lain in ambush let their comrades through and then open fire on the flanks and rear of the pursuers, so that the robbers usually manage to return without loss. The Shahsevan successes are due not only to such tactics but also to the excellent training of their horses.[47]

Tigranov pointed out that the clause in the Treaty of Torkman–Chai that guaranteed Russian support for the Qajar succession meant that former rival tribes could no longer entertain dynastic ambitions and now directed their energies to banditry. In Azarbaijan, the proximity of Russia and the tightening of her frontier controls towards the end of the nineteenth century pressured tribal groups such as the Shahsevan to abandon even this kind of activity and gradually to become sedentary farmers, thus losing their mobility and military effectiveness. The Azarbaijan administration, however, deliberately hindered this settlement. According to Tigranov, the heir apparent Mohammad 'Ali Mirza did not feel too sure of Russian favour and had alienated the settled population by his oppression, so he turned to cultivating the more powerful nomad tribes and their chiefs as potential military support. The Iranian army had deteriorated ever since irregular tribal levies had been replaced by regular troops early in the century, and was now virtually extinct as a fighting force. The nomad tribes remained the only effective militia, and even they were reliable only when defending their own territory. The old policy, of maintaining a frontier strip of endemic tribal 'disorder', was revived as some kind of defence against possible incursions, whether from Kurds and Turks in the west, or from Russians in the north of the province. The administration not only oppressed the settled population and hindered

---

[47] The original account, in Sh-f M-z-f (1908), is quoted by Rostopchin (1933: 112–3), and given in emended paraphrase by von Hahn (1910: 67). This translation is a slightly abbreviated and edited version of the original.

the nomads from settling, but they even as an instrument of policy encouraged the banditry which was the nomads' only alternative for survival. The prevalence of banditry grew more marked than elsewhere in the case of the Shahsevan, where it was aggravated by the Moghan frontier closure and the subsequent restriction of the pastoral economy, and by the attitudes of the Russians and the Iranian administration, both of which, for different reasons, stood to gain from Shahsevan raids.[48]

One of the most notorious bandit leaders of Azarbaijan, Rahim Khan Chalabianlu, acquired Mohammad 'Ali Mirza's full protection. Actually, Mohammad 'Ali's relations with the Russians were so favourable that he need have had no fear for his succession from that quarter, and indeed the Russians and chiefs like Rahim Khan became his staunchest supporters during and after his brief and troubled reign, as we shall see.

[48] Tigranov (1909: 106f.).

12 The Shahsevan, the Constitution, the Great War – and after

Azarbaijan and the tribes up to the Constitutional Revolution

After the setback to British prestige of the scandal of the Tobacco Monopoly in 1890–2, Russia steadily increased her domination of the north, where she won important economic concessions while the Iranian government grew heavily indebted to her financially. The British were concerned with the defence of India and with maintaining their power in the Persian Gulf, which became more vital after oil was discovered in commercial quantities in 1908. Russia wanted access to a warm-water port and further outlets for her expanding trade, and felt these could be achieved only by virtual subjugation of much of Iran. Defeat by the Japanese in 1905 and the Tsar's granting of the Duma did little to halt Russian forward policy in Iran. Without consulting Iran, Russia and Britain in 1907 clarified their respective positions in a Convention which carved the country into 'spheres of influence': the largest sphere, in the north and northwest, went to Russia, the southeast to Britain, while the southwest and a corridor to the northeast were to be neutral.

As described in Chapter Eleven, during the years of Mohammad 'Ali Mirza's rule as heir apparent (1896–1907) the province of Azarbaijan was in continual disorder and distress, with Russian influence paramount. The Ardabil region was in turmoil. There were repeated grain shortages, due not only to bad harvests and the insecurity of cultivation but also to hoarding and speculation by landowners. These included the religious leaders who, divided into Ne'mati and Heidari factions as in other Iranian cities,[1] pursued their own active and often violent rivalries while inciting the city populace against foreigners and against the governors, several of whom were forced to take refuge. Meanwhile, Shahsevan bands raided throughout the region and on occasion in the city itself. On a number of occasions Mohammad 'Ali Mirza sent Rahim Khan Chalabianlu to help quell disturbances in the city or to subdue the tribes. One notable inci-

---

[1] See Mirjafari (1979a).

dent was in 1896–7 when a party of women, led by one Begum Pasha, but incited by the Ne'mati leader, mojtahed Mirza 'Ali Akbar, came out on the streets, forced the bazaar to close and (with stones carried in chadors tied round their waists) attacked the castle, where the governor Nazem as-Saltaneh (a close kinsman of Mohammad 'Ali Mirza) was being guarded by Polatlu tribesmen under their chief Jurugh Bey. The Polatlu fired on the men who had come to watch, the crowd dispersed.[2] Mirza 'Ali Akbar fled, not returning for several months. Nazem as-Saltaneh was dismissed the following year, and in 1899 was appointed Governor-general of Azarbaijan, to replace the Amir Nezam Garusi, who had had a further, short and less than successful term in that office.

At Ardabil, the new governor 'Ali Khan Vali sought the help of Rahim Khan Chalabianlu to quell disturbances led by Mirza 'Ali Akbar, who was supported by Khosrou Khan of the Yortchi, the main rivals of the Polatlu. In March 1899 Rahim Khan captured Mirza 'Ali Akbar and sent him to Tabriz, but a year later Khosrou Khan took 'Ali Khan Vali prisoner and forced his dismissal too.[3] 'Ali Khan was replaced as governor by Samad Khan Shoja' ad-Douleh, who on arrival in the district in November 1900 took immediate severe measures: he had the 'brigand' chiefs Jurugh Bey Polatlu and Farrokh Bey Khamesli blown from the cannon's mouth, despite the intervention of the 'Mohtaman of Ardabil' (presumably Mo'taman al-Ro'aya, whom we met in Chapter Eleven). As British Consul-General Wood observed, 'the 'Shahsavans' have been deeply impressed by this determined action of Samat Khan, and are quiet'.[4]

In 1901 two major expeditions against the Shahsevan had some short-lived success: in February, Samad Khan, helped by Rahim Khan Chalabianlu, arrested the following chiefs: Hazrat-qoli of Hajji-Khojalu, Mohammad-qoli Khan of Alarlu, Sardar Bey of Qoja-Beyli, and Qara Bey Delaqarda; but these came to some arrangement with their captors, possibly through Russian intercession, and were released. For whatever reason, in spite of this success, Samad Khan was dismissed. His replacement as governor, Emam-qoli Mirza, refused to leave Tabriz without an adequate force, and, since many of the landowners suffering from Shahsevan depredations were prominent Tabrizi citizens, he was duly

---

[2] Safari (1971: 172f.); FO 248/654 (Wood to Hardinge no. 25 of 12.8.1897). Although public protests by women have a much longer history in Iran, these women were clearly inspired by those who played a prominent role in the Tobacco Protest a few years before. On the political situation in Ardabil at the time, see Safari (1971: 160–202).

[3] Safari (1971: 174–5); FO 248/698 (esp. Wood to Hardinge, 27.3.1899) and /722 (Wood to Hardinge no. 5 of 23.4.1900).

[4] FO 248/722 (Wood to Hardinge no. 9 of 22.11.1900); Safari (1971: 176–9). Samad Khan was a landowner from Maragheh; on him and his role in the period, see Mojtahedi (1948: 95f.) and Good (1977).

supplied with several thousand troops. With the aid of the governor of Qara-Dagh, by late summer he had subdued all the tribes, though he had to fight several battles with Sardar Bey Qoja-Beyli. Khosrou Khan Yortchi was tricked into submission, and sent to Tabriz, where Mohammad 'Ali Mirza freed him in return for a very substantial 'gift'; though shortly after he was again taken prisoner and executed.[5]

Despite these government successes, Shahsevan banditry continued unchecked in the following years, Qoja-Beyli and Alarlu raiding on the frontier north of Ardabil, Polatlu in the region of the city itself. Throughout these years, the Russian Caucasian administration and their representatives at Tabriz apparently continued to encourage the Shahsevan, supplying them with arms, allowing them to take refuge over the frontier when pursued, and intervening on their behalf when they were captured. Meanwhile they built up their Cossack garrisons at frontier points like Astara and Khoda-Afarin, offering their services to the Iranian government, which was able to refuse them only by sending expeditions such as that of Emam-qoli Mirza in 1901. In addition, the Russians took their own reprisals against those of the tribes (notably Qoja-Beyli and Alarlu) who raided too flagrantly over the frontier. Their policy was clear: to foster disorder within Iranian territory and to make their own military assistance and eventual occupation indispensable, though they did not achieve this for some years.[6]

Russian military expeditions visited Shahsevan districts for intelligence purposes.[7] Russian merchants and goods dominated the trade of Azarbaijan, and, after Tabriz, Ardabil was the most important commercial centre of the province. Russian subjects were buying numerous villages in the province, notably in Ardabil, Ahar and Sarab districts, using Iranian proxies in order to overcome legal restrictions. New roads and railways across the province were planned, though a proposed railway south from Aslanduz was rejected as it would run through bandit-infested country.[8]

Events in Russia in 1905 encouraged the now widespread Iranian movement for reform, and the mollahs and merchants of Tehran, protesting against the Shah's autocracy and the sale of the country to foreigners, headed the revolution which forced Mozaffar ad-Din Shah in 1906 to grant a Constitution providing for a Representative Assembly. He signed

---

[5] On the events of 1901, see Tigranov (1909: 139–144); FO 248/745 (Wood to Hardinge no. 3 of 7.2.1901); *FO Prints, Persia and Arabia* V to VII (1901: various Monthly Summaries); Aubin (1908: 105).

[6] See Safari (1971: 181–200); and Amir-Khizi in Taherzadeh-Behzad (1955: 472f.).

[7] E.g. Averyanov and Shkinskiy in 1899, Tigranov in 1903, Sh-f M-z-f in 1904.

[8] See Sumbatzade *et al.* (1985: 72); *FO Prints, Persia and Arabia* XV, no. 199 (November 1903), p. 204.

the Constitution on 1 January 1907, but died a few days later. Though his successor, Mohammad 'Ali, swore several times to uphold the Constitution, he had no intention of doing so. Supported by Russian advisors, he began intrigues and repressive measures which culminated in June 1908 in the bombardment and forcible closure of the Assembly, the arrest of the Constitutionalist leaders, and the outlawing of the *anjomans*, local committees which were the core of the Constitutionalist movement.

The populace of Ardabil, led by the Ne'mati mojtahed Mirza 'Ali Akbar, eagerly welcomed the turn of events in late 1906, and the granting of the Constitution. They pressed for the removal of the reactionary governor Sa'ed al-Molk, and on instructions from Tabriz set up a local *anjoman*. The Heidari, however, set up a rival *anjoman*, and hostilities between the factions intensified until the introduction of bands of Shahsevan warriors, Qoja-Beyli by the Ne'mati and Polatlu by the Heidari, brought violence and death to the streets. Naqi Khan Rashid al-Molk, a presumed supporter of the Constitution but later known as a Russophile, was sent from Tabriz to be governor. He suppressed the rival *anjomans* and initiated a new one with equal numbers from each faction, but he was unable or unwilling to pacify the Shahsevan.[9]

The attitudes of the tribes towards the Constitutional Revolution in its first year are unclear. When Böyük Khan Chalabianlu, at the instigation of his father Rahim Khan (who was in Tehran), attempted to end the Tabriz *anjoman* in May 1907, Hajji-Khojalu tribesmen halted his march on Tabriz by pillaging his villages in Qara-Dagh in his absence; but their action was probably more due to their longstanding enmity with the Chalabianlu than to the support for the Constitution that they were later to show.[10]

Pokhitonov, Russian consul-general at Tabriz, magnified every such instance of disorder in his appeals for the introduction of Russian troops to 'keep the peace'. The Constitutionalists sent Rahim Khan's rival, Karim Khan, to be chief of Chalabianlu, but although he quietened Qara-Dagh he failed in his avowed object of capturing Böyük Khan.

In the summer of 1907, a Russian vice-consul was appointed for the first time in Ardabil. The following winter, the townspeople began to agitate for the dismissal of Rashid al-Molk, and in early 1908, when Shahsevan warriors (probably Polatlu or Yortchi) raided Ardabil in force, the governor was forced to flee. Then in April a border incident in the

---

[9] Safari (1971: 187–200). On Rashid al-Molk and his role in Iranian history, see Mojtahedi (1948: 198–200).

[10] See *FO Prints, Affairs of Persia* XI (Spring-Rice to Grey no. 128 of 15.6.1907); Browne (1910: 141–2); Farzad (1945: 91–2); Taherzadeh-Behzad (1955: 472f.); Hedayat (1965: 170).

north of the region brought the Shahsevan into the very centre of events leading to the fall of the Constitutionalist government in Tehran.

The Belasovar affair

Some years previously, Shahsevan nomads migrating to and from the eastern part of Moghan had been given permission to use a track crossing Russian territory in the vicinity of Deman. Mohammad-qoli Khan of Alarlu constructed a small settlement beside the track. The Russian authorities, alleging that he based raiding expeditions on this settlement, which they thus interpreted as a fort, demanded that he dismantle it. As he paid no attention, a Cossack detachment was detailed to patrol the frontier between Deman and Belasovar.

On 11 April 1908 an officer of this detachment (Capt. Dvoyeglazov) crossed onto Iranian territory near Belasovar in pursuit of a runaway horse. On encountering a party of Qoja-Beyli tribesmen, he was shot dead and several of his escort were wounded. In immediate retaliation the Cossack garrison at Belasovar crossed to the Iranian side of the frontier, destroyed the customs post and killed some forty inhabitants. A week or so later, reinforcements arrived from Baku, and a force of several hundred men assembled and divided into two parties. The first, having entered Iran near Belasovar and destroyed one or two Iranian villages, set off in pursuit of the Qoja-Beyli, but after suffering heavily in an engagement with the tribesmen the party had to withdraw. The second party, under General Snarskiy, destroyed Mohammad-qoli Khan's settlement near Deman, then crossed the frontier and razed other Iranian villages to the ground before withdrawing. On 16 May Snarskiy – who was later to become notorious for his excesses during the occupation of Tabriz – gave the Iranian authorities an ultimatum to the effect that if certain demands were not fulfilled he would enter Iran again and see to their satisfaction himself. The demands included the handing over of Dvoyeglazov's killers, the return of stolen property, guarantees against further raiding by the tribesmen, and the payment of 80,000 roubles, a sum which the Iranians were most unlikely to be able to find.

Now the Qoja-Beyli had only too often in recent years raided Russian border posts for arms and Russian villages for other loot, but on this occasion not only had the original Cossack party been trespassing but the officer had fired first and was in other ways to blame for his own fate: some years before, he had killed two sons of a Qoja-Beyli chief, and though subsequently offered a transfer so as to avoid vengeance, he had refused. Moreover, the retaliations were brutal and unjustified. The Russian envoy in Tehran, somewhat embarrassed by these excesses, admitted the officer's trespass to his British colleague, but the Caucasian administration disguised what had really happened, refused to allow a joint commission of inquiry, blew the incident up to major proportions and publicized Snarskiy's expedition as a legitimate measure taken in exasperation against bandits of whose continual atrocities against Russian frontier guards this had been merely the latest and worst example.

The Iranian government took serious steps to satisfy some of the demands. Though the tribesmen concerned managed to escape to the mountains, the Qoja-Beyli and Alarlu chiefs were brought to Ardabil in custody at the end of May and most of the required indemnity was paid. Meanwhile the Tehran government was incensed by the Cossacks' and Snarskiy's excesses, and not deceived by their version of the incident. With the 1907 Convention, the British envoy Marling, though well informed on what had really happened and who was to blame, refrained from protests and simply advised the Iranian government to accede to Russian demands. The Shah intervened personally to ask for leniency, but many Iranians suspected him of having incited the Shahsevan so as to give the Russians an excuse for introducing troops to crush the Constitutionalists. At the end of May the cabinet resigned over the affair. The Russians saw that they had gone too far in alienating Iranian public opinion and early in June relented. Snarskiy's troops withdrew from the border and the unpaid indemnity was added to Iran's long-term debt, to be used to pressure the government in later years. Soon after, the Shah bombarded the Assembly and restored his autocratic rule.[11]

Rahim Khan Chalabianlu had gone to Tehran in Mohammad 'Ali's entourage, but in June 1907 the Shah had been forced to imprison him in the uproar following his son's attempt on the Tabriz *anjoman*. In April 1908 he was freed by the Tehran Assembly and sent to Tabriz with the mission of bringing the Shahsevan to order, and in May, assuring the Tabriz *anjoman* of his allegiance to the Nationalist-Constitutionalist cause, he persuaded them to give him arms and money towards his mission. These contributions he promptly used to raise Royalist forces to attack the Nationalists in Tabriz, which he entered and began plundering in July.

A most prominent part in the Assembly had been played by the repre-

---

[11] On the Belasovar incident, see FO 248/792 (Wratislav to Hardinge, no. 18 of 22.10.1903); *FO Prints, Persia and Arabia* XV (Oct.–Dec. 1903: Grant Duff to Lansdowne no. 296 of 30.12); *FO Prints, Affairs of Persia* XIV (Apr.–June 1908: Marling to Grey nos. 95 of 23.4, 115 of 20.5, 135 of 22.5, 138 of 29.5, telegraphic nos. 128 of 30.5, 129 of 3.6); *S.D.D.* I (139–88); Khakhanov (1908); von Hahn (1910); Sh-f M-z-f (1908); Safari (1971: 203); Hedayat (1965: 170–2); Kazemzadeh (1968: 517–19).

sentatives from Azarbaijan, the province which had suffered Mohammad 'Ali's oppressions for ten years as heir apparent, and the Shah's coup now served only to encourage the Tabrizis to rise in revolution against him, declaring his rule illegitimate. During the summer of 1908 the Tabriz *anjoman* made further efforts to forestall Royalist opposition from the tribes. One Mollah Emam-verdi of Meshkin, a Constitutionalist, was summoned to the *anjoman*, as the governor of Ardabil had complained of his activities. After the Shah's coup in Tehran, Mollah Emam-verdi was sent back to Meshkin to recruit Nationalist support and to dissuade the Shahsevan from attacking Tabriz, but he was apprehended by the governor of Ardabil and hanged; he is remembered locally as a martyr.[12]

During the following winter and spring, supported by revolutionaries from the Caucasus and inspired by the Young Turks, the Tabrizi Nationalists heroically withstood the besieging Royalist forces. In May 1909 Russian troops, called in to bring food supplies and protect foreign residents, lifted the siege and rescued the city from extreme deprivation and famine. However, the occupation forces soon alienated the Tabrizis and curbed the activities of the Nationalists, to whom they and the Russian consul-general were completely opposed. Meanwhile, Nationalists from Rasht and Esfahan, inspired by the example of Tabriz, marched on Tehran, and in July formally deposed Mohammad 'Ali Shah.

The Royalist forces besieging Tabriz until May 1909 were composed mainly of tribesmen from northern Azarbaijan, but apart from some 500 horsemen from Yortchi and Polatlu the Shahsevan refrained from joining Rahim Khan and his Qara-Daghis. Throughout the main period of the siege, the nomads were in Moghan, far from the scene, while there were indications in the spring that many of the settled Ardabil Shahsevan favoured the besieged Nationalists.[13]

The Tribal Union and the sack of Ardabil

Abandoning the siege of Tabriz on the arrival of Russian troops in May 1909, Rahim Khan withdrew to Qara-Dagh. That summer, northern Azarbaijan was quite insecure, with raiding by Rahim Khan's followers in Qara-Dagh and by the Shahsevan in Ardabil and vicinity and on the Tabriz–Tehran road. In June Constitutionalists regained control of Ardabil, driving out the tribesmen and forcing the leading reactionaries to take refuge in the Russian vice-consulate, whose guard was reinforced

---

[12] Amir-Khizi (1960: 40, 145); Sa'edi (1965: 88f.).
[13] On the siege of Tabriz see *FO Prints, Affairs of Persia* XV–XVIII; *S.D.D.* I and II; Browne (1910); Moore (1914); Wratislaw (1924). There are several Iranian accounts by contemporaries, e.g. Amir-Khizi (1960).

by one hundred Cossacks. After the Shah's deposition in July, Nationalists from Tabriz arrived at Ardabil, formed a new *anjoman* and took over the city, while the Tehran government appointed Mohammad-qoli Alarlu as deputy governor. The *anjoman* proceeded to dispose of their opposition and Mohammad-qoli Khan to loot the town. More Ardabilis, including the former governor, Rashid al-Molk, joined the refugees in the Russian vice-consulate. The Russians planned a punitive expedition against the Shahsevan for September, with the excuse that Snarskiy's demands of the previous year had not yet been met.

The Ardabilis sent to Tabriz in August for someone to relieve them from the tyrannies of the new *anjoman*. The governor of Tabriz, Mahdi-qoli Hedayat Mokhber as-Saltaneh, eager at the same time to put an end to Rahim Khan's banditry, decided on a joint operation from Ardabil and Ahar. He eventually managed to send Sattar Khan, the hero of the defence of Tabriz the previous spring, who had now become a drunkard and a nuisance. Accompanied by several hundred Nationalists, Sattar Khan set out for Ardabil in early September. At Sarab he was greeted by Mohammad-qoli Khan Alarlu, an old friend, and Nasrollah Khan Yortchi (brother of Khosrou Khan), Hosein-'Ali Polatlu and other Shahsevan chiefs. According to Amir-Khizi, who accompanied Sattar Khan on this trip, Mohammad-qoli Alarlu tried to persuade the Nationalist hero to lead the Shahsevan to Tehran and become Shah. On their arrival at Ardabil, Sattar's party had some success in restoring order. Rashid al-Molk was persuaded to leave the Russian vice-consulate and returned to Tabriz. Soon almost all the Shahsevan chiefs came to offer their submission to Sattar Khan, who was forming a camp outside Ardabil and preparing an expedition against Rahim Khan; but by the end of September he had alienated them by his abusive behaviour, his intrigue and his drunkenness. Led by Amir 'Ashayer of Shatranlu, one by one the chiefs abandoned Sattar and went to join Rahim Khan. Last of all, even the latter's bitter rivals Zargham Hajji-'Alili and the son of Hazrat-qoli Hajji-Khojalu (who had been entrusted by the Tabriz *anjoman* with opposition to Rahim Khan and the Qoja-Beyli) deserted Sattar and joined the new Tribal Union. Sattar Khan also antagonized the Ardabilis by his requisitions, and many of them went to join the Shahsevan.

In late August, Russian detachments had left Tabriz for Ahar; ostensibly they were to demand the return of goods looted by Rahim Khan's tribesmen during the siege of Tabriz, but they killed 'Ali Khan, one of his Qara-Daghi rivals, and appear to have encouraged Rahim Khan to raise the tribes of northern and eastern Azarbaijan in favour of the now deposed Mohammad 'Ali Shah. Telegrams were sent at the end of September to the Russian consulate at Tabriz for transmission to the ex-

Shah and to the Nationalist leaders in Tehran, signed by Rahim Khan and the chiefs of Qara-Dagh and of Qoja-Beyli and some other Shahsevan tribes, affirming opposition to the Constitution and their intention of first looting Ardabil and then marching on Tehran to restore Mohammad 'Ali.[14] The telegrams arrived too late, for the Shah had left Iran on 1 October.

A week or so later the Russian consul-general Miller sent his doctor to treat Rahim Khan for a paralytic stroke, and (as he told his British colleague) to counsel moderation. The doctor was believed however to have instigated Rahim Khan to further efforts to unite the tribes, for two days after his departure Rahim Khan marched on Ardabil. Whether or not he really had Russian support, he certainly gave out that he had, both to his allies and to his opponents.[15]

Towards the end of October the tribesmen surrounded Ardabil and were looting on the outskirts. After a token resistance, the defenders ran short of ammunition. On 1 or 2 November Sattar Khan escaped and fled to Sarab and Tabriz. There is controversy in the Persian sources over the actual date of Sattar Khan's departure, and whether he 'fled' or was 'persuaded reluctantly' to abandon the city. The question of the date is cleared up by the fact that Smart, British consul in Tabriz, was able to report Sattar Khan's escape from Ardabil on 2 November.[16] It was presumably Smart from whom Browne received the report on Sattar Khan which included the following remarks:

With regard to Sattar Khan, I hope you will be moderate in your praises of him in your Constitutional History. I went to Tabriz a fervent admirer of Sattar, and I came away with another lost illusion. Sattar is an illiterate, ignorant Qaradaghi horse-dealer, who has no more idea of what a Constitution means than Rahim Khan ... His conduct at Ardabil was despicable, and was mainly responsible for the rebellion of the Shah-sevens, whose chiefs had come into Ardabil to tender their submission. Sattar, in a drunken fit, insulted them in the coarsest language. Furious by this treatment by a man whom they looked on as a plebeian, they left the town and joined Rahim Khan. Sattar then ignobly abandoned the unfortunate town to its fate and fled to Tabriz.[17]

Two or three days later, the defence collapsed and the tribesmen entered and sacked the town. The Constitutionalists took refuge in the Russian

---

[14] Few of the names of the fifteen signatories are identifiable. The texts of the telegrams are in Kasravi (1938, III: 119–20) and many other places; English translations in FO 248/974 (Smart to Barclay no. 35 of 14.11.1909).

[15] On the question of the Russian instigation of the Tribal Union, see FO 248/1004 (Smart to Barclay, report no. 3 of 4.1.1910); *FO Prints, Affairs of Persia* XXI (Barclay to Grey no. 8 of 27.1.1910); Amir-Khizi (1960: 428f.); Kasravi (1938, III: 112–13, 118–19, 126f.); Hedayat (1965: 218); Safari (1971: 230f.); Browne (1910: 347).

[16] FO 248/974 (Smart to Barclay, telegraphic no. 206 of 2.11.1909).

[17] Browne (1910: 441–2).

vice-consulate, which resisted Rahim Khan's demands for their delivery. On 3 November Rahim Khan and most of the important Shahsevan, Qara-Daghi and Khalkhali chiefs signed the following Treaty of Alliance:

In the name of God the Compassionate and Merciful. On 19 Shawwal 1327 [we] the slaves of the Court, chiefs of the tribes of the Five Provinces [Qara-Dagh, Ardabil, Sarab, Khalkhal, Astara], have made an agreement and union for the restoration of security and monarchy in Iran and the repulse of the evil of the mischief-makers and the removal and suppression of those disobedient to the true religion and the propagation of the Ja'fari [i.e. Ithna-'Ashari Shi'a] faith (to which a thousand congratulations and praise); we have first of all taken measures in this province of Ardabil for total reform in the future and performance of this work, and have sworn on the holy word of God among ourselves, and are laying down conditions whereby we shall strive in total struggle from the beginning to the end of our project with our lives and property, to the last drop of blood and last grain of substance; we have appointed the honourable Sardar Nosrat [Rahim Khan] as our leader and hold it necessary for us to execute his commands. Whoever goes back from this Treaty and turns his hand to plundering, we shall expel him from the chiefly assembly; he has no tribal rights, no true religion, may this sacred word of God put an end to his house; we shall have to pillage his property all together and at once, and kill and execute him himself.[18]

The names of the thirty-four signatories, together with their known or suggested tribal identity in parentheses, are listed in Figure 9. Many are hard to identify, but they include most of the major Shahsevan chiefs; conspicuously absent are Hazrat-qoli Hajji-Khojalu and Amir Arshad Hajji-'Alili, Rahim Khan's two main rivals among the Shahsevan and in Qara-Dagh respectively. The names so far unidentified may include the aliases or titles of the following chiefs: Sardar Bey, Bahram Khan and Nouruz Khan of Qoja-Beyli; Qara Bey Delaqarda; Reza-qoli Bey Polatlu; Qılıj Khamesli; Faraj Geyikli; 'Emran Hajji-Khojalu.

The siege and sack of Ardabil caused great consternation not only in Tehran but in the European capitals, whose newspapers for some weeks carried leading articles speculating on the intentions of Rahim Khan and the Shahsevan tribes and on whether the Russians had instigated the anti-Constitutionalist Tribal Union, and, if so, whether they would continue to support its projected move on Tehran. Meanwhile both Iranian and Russian troops had been despatched belatedly to the relief of Ardabil. By the end of October a motley force of 3,000 Azarbaijani Nationalists, under Sattar Khan's associate Baqer Khan and Samad Khan Shoja' ad-Douleh, had assembled at Sarab, where they delayed. Tehran meanwhile despatched 1,500 men, a special effort which quite exhausted the new government's already minimal resources.

---

[18] The text, written in the margins of a Koran, was published by the then governor of Tabriz in his memoirs (Hedayat 1965: 218–19) and also in Amir-Khizi (1960: 429) and elsewhere.

Sardar Nosrat [Rahim Khan CHALABIANLU]
Amir 'Ashayer [Esma'il Khan SHATRANLU]
Salar As'ad [?]
Salar as-Soltan [YORTCHI; perhaps Aqa Khan DALIKANLU]
Salar Nosrat [?Shokrollah Khan SHATRANLU; ?perhaps a son of Rahim Khan]
Lotfollah Khan Sartip [DURSUN-KHOJALU/YORTCHI]
Eqtedar Nezam [?]
As'ad as-Saltaneh Hazar Khan [Amir Toman, QOJA-BEYLI]
Fateh al-Mamalek [Habibollah Khan Shoja' Lashkar CHALABIANLU, son of
    Rahim Khan]
Salar 'Ashayer [Zargham HAJJI-'ALILI; possibly Karim Rashid ad-Douleh
    CHALABIANLU]
Seif as-Soltan [?]
Sarem as-Soltan [Mir Sa'id Khan of NAMIN?]
Salar Firuz [Esfandiar Khan SHATRANLU, elder brother of Amir 'Ashayer]
Rashid al-Mamalek [Habibollah Khan SHATRANLU, younger brother of Amir
    'Ashayer]
Salar Divan [Hosein-'Ali Khan POLATLU, brother-in-law of Amir 'Ashayer]
Mosta'an al-Molk [?]
Badal Khan [ZARGAR]
Hosein-qoli [-'Ali?] Khan [GALESH of Talesh]
'Ebadollah ['Abdollah?] Khan [YORTCHI; possibly AJIRLI? or GEYIKLI]
Abo'l-Fath Bey [PASHA-KHANLU]
Qodrat Khan [?]
Masha'llah Khan [REZA-BEYLI; perhaps YORTCHI]
Ezzatollah Khan [ALARLU?; perhaps son of Rahim Khan CHALABIANLU]
Badr Khan [?]
Mohammad-qoli Khan [ALARLU]
Mohammad Khan [MAST-'ALI-BEYLI? PIR-EVATLU?]
Javad Khan [HAJJI-KHOJALU]
Ensha'llah Khan [?]
Nosratollah [Nasrollah] Khan [YORTCHI; perhaps a son of Rahim Khan]
Aqa Bey [DALIKANLU; perhaps 'ISALU]
Fathollah Khan [perhaps 'ISALU]
Mohammad Nasir Khan [perhaps SHATRANLU]
Hashem Khan [QOJA-BEYLI; perhaps YORTCHI]

Figure 9. Signatories to the Treaty of Alliance signed on 19 Shawal
1327 (3 November 1909) between the chiefs of the tribes of
Shahsevan, Qara-Dagh and Khalkhal

Russian detachments began to arrive from Astara on 7 November and
the tribesmen retired to a camp outside the town. If the Russians had
instigated Rahim Khan's Tribal Union in order to provide the pretext for
further armed intervention, as seems likely, this aim had now been
achieved, and indeed messages had been sent to Rahim Khan strongly
warning him against excesses in Ardabil. At Sarab on the 9th he met the

governor-elect (Rashid al-Molk once more) to whom he declared his loyalty to Russia and his intention of marching on Tehran. By the 14th, however, the formidable Tribal Union of Qara-Daghi, Shahsevan and Khalkhali tribes was already disintegrating. The immediate aim of plunder had been achieved, and the longer-term prospect of wintering in Tehran had become remote, so the Shahsevan nomads at least were eager to return to their usual winter quarters in Moghan, whither they departed a few days later. It is probable also that the tribes were disillusioned about the Russian support which Rahim Khan had claimed to enjoy, for over 3,000 Russian troops under Col. Averyanov, warmly welcomed by the populace, now occupied Ardabil. Rashid al-Molk was once more installed as governor.[19]

Yeprem Khan's defeat of the Shahsevan

In mid-December a detachment of 600 men from Tehran, comprising Bakhtiari tribesmen, Nationalist volunteers, Iranian Cossacks and artillery, under chief of police Yeprem Khan and the Bakhtiari chief Sardar Bahador, arrived in the region and joined the Tabrizi force at Sarab. The Russians decided to leave disciplinary measures to this combined force and withdrew up to half of their Ardabil garrison.

In a series of engagements in late December and early January, government forces defeated and pursued Rahim Khan's two eldest sons over snowbound country northwest of Sarab. While the Tabrizis stayed around Sarab, the Tehran detachment captured Ahar, occupied it as their base, and during January defended it against repeated attacks from Rahim Khan's warriors, who suffered considerably from the fire of the two Maxim machine-guns, weapons they had not experienced before. Meanwhile no help was forthcoming from the Shahsevan. The Meshkin tribes were in winter quarters in Moghan, the Ardabil and Khalkhal tribes were in their villages and some of them (such as the Yortchi) were negotiating with Rashid al-Molk at Ardabil.

On 1 February the Tehran detachment sallied northwards from Ahar. Rahim Khan was routed, fled with his retinue across the Aras and was given refuge in Russia. Most of his Qara-Daghi rivals and confederates tendered their submission to the government. Accompanied by the Qara-

[19] On the fall and relief of Ardabil, see Safari (1971: 230–306); Amir-Khizi (1960: 410–39); Kasravi (1938, III: 111–32); Hedayat (1965: 196f., 226); FO Prints, *Affairs of Persia* XIX and XX (various items); *S.D.D.* III (passim); *The Times* (articles almost daily from 3 to 18 November 1909); FO 248/974 and /1004 (telegrams and despatches from Smart and Shipley at Tabriz); Browne (1910: 441f.).

Daghi chiefs Amir Arshad Hajji-'Alili and his brother Zargham, the government troops withdrew to Tabriz and a victorious welcome.[20]

During February and March the Russians increased their pressure for further moves in the spring to subdue and disarm the Shahsevan, and for the fulfilment of Snarskiy's demands of two years before. They threatened to send a punitive expedition themselves. At Tabriz there was considerable turmoil, fomented by Sattar Khan, who bitterly resented having been sent to the Ardabil 'death-trap'. British and Russian representatives insisted on his removal to Tehran, which was effected in mid-March.

Meanwhile the Yortchi and Polatlu Shahsevan of Ardabil, together with the Shatranlu of Khalkhal, were restless and, according to the Russians, making the roads south and west of Ardabil quite unsafe. Rashid al-Molk appealed to the tribes to submit and to restore the plunder they had taken in November, but the tribes were alarmed by rumours of planned reprisals and declared themselves unwilling to submit except to someone they could trust. The government forces at Tabriz prepared for a spring expedition against them, planning to reach the Ardabil and Khalkhal tribes before those of Meshkin had arrived from Moghan and could come to aid them.

On 12 April the Tehran detachment under Yeprem Khan and Sardar Bahador left Tabriz for Ardabil. After passing through Sarab they fought an action on the 19th against the warriors of Nasrollah Khan Yortchi, Hosein-'Ali Khan Polatlu and Amir 'Ashayer Shatranlu, in which Reza-qoli Khan, one of the Polatlu chiefs, was killed. The tribesmen fled, Nasrollah Khan and Amir 'Ashayer to Khalkhal, Hosein-'Ali Khan to his home near by. The next day Nasrollah Khan's main rival, Lotfollah Khan Yortchi/Dursun-Khojalu, came over to Rashid al-Molk, and together with other local forces they joined the Tehran detachment at Nir. Soon after, Aqa Khan of the neighbouring Dalikanlu tribe of Sarab came over. On the 22nd, Nasrollah Khan's home at Aq-Chai was destroyed. Rashid al-Molk offered terms to Hosein-'Ali Khan Polatlu but was refused, so the army moved into Khalkhal and delivered an ultimatum to Hosein-'Ali and to Amir 'Ashayer and Nasrollah Khan, demanding that they surrender or lose both life and property. On the 23rd Amir 'Ashayer duly surrendered, followed by Nasrollah Khan and Hosein-'Ali. The victorious army proceeded to Ardabil, where the captured chiefs of the Polatlu, Yortchi, Dursun-Khojalu (except Lotfollah Khan), Dalikanlu and Shatranlu

---

[20] On the campaigns against the Qara-Daghis, see *S.D.D.* IV (4–27); FO 248/1004 (various); *FO Prints, Affairs of Persia* XXI (various); Amir-Khizi (1960: 443–8); Kasravi (1938, III: 138–41); Hedayat (1965: 199).

tribes were imprisoned in the castle. The revolt of the Ardabil tribes was over.[21]

The tribes of Meshkin were now just beginning to leave Moghan on their annual spring migration south to the mountains. None of the chiefs, of whom the seventy-year old Sardar Bey Qoja-Beyli was the most prominent and intractable, had paid any heed at first to Rashid al-Molk's appeal for submission, so on 2 May the government army, with some local levies, left Ardabil on the Meshkin road. As they marched west and then north towards Moghan, a number of Sardar Bey's opponents (Aqa Bey and 'Alesh Bey 'Isalu, Hazrat-qoli Hajji-Khojalu, Mohammad-qoli and Hamid Bey Alarlu) came to the government camp, submitted and offered their services. Not once did the tribes unite to offer resistance.

Finally an engagement was fought on 8 May, north of Langan, against the Qoja-Beyli, who suffered heavy losses from the machine-guns. Many of Sardar Bey's close kinsmen were killed, including his son Hazar Khan, and some 200 warriors were taken prisoner. The following day saw the surrender of Sardar Bey's cousin and rival Bahram Khan. Of the important chiefs now at liberty there remained only Sardar Bey himself and his son (later chief) Nouruz Khan, and Javat Khan Hajji-Khojalu, Hazrat-qoli's nephew. The government force proceeded on the 16th to Meshkin, where by the 23rd all the remaining chiefs had submitted or been captured. Hazrat-qoli and one or two others were set free, the others were sent in chains to Ardabil, but not before they had disgorged a vast amount of money, the taxes which the tribes had not paid for three years. At the end of the month the army returned to Ardabil and a triumphal welcome. With a total of ninety-three chiefs now imprisoned there, Yeprem and Sardar Bahador could congratulate themselves on complete success.

On 10 June the government army departed for Tehran, taking with them fifty-nine of the most important chiefs but leaving the others in the Ardabil castle. They entered the capital to a further magnificent reception towards the end of June. Much of the looted property of the Ardabilis had been recovered and was restored to its owners, but Yeprem and the Bakhtiari were said to have brought great loads of cash and booty to Tehran. The Shahsevan chiefs declared that they had been tricked into submission, that pledges made to them had not been honoured, and that they intended to hold an inquiry into the conduct of the expedition. Actually, Yeprem was later criticized for not having disarmed the tribes,

---

[21] On the campaign against them, see *S.D.D.* IV (139–55, 215f.); Amir-Khizi (1960: 481–3); Kasravi (1938, III: 149–51); Hedayat (1965: 200); Safari (1971: 300–2); Rava'i (1984).

though this might well have proved impossible, and the Iranian government probably still hoped to rely on the Shahsevan as some kind of frontier guard.[22]

Shahsevan versus Cossacks: the 1912 campaign

Elsewhere in the country, the Nationalist government was having problems restoring order, for although the Russians and British gave it official support they would not allow it to raise enough money to finance the necessary forces. In the Ardabil region, however, with the tribal chiefs in captivity, comparative tranquillity was maintained throughout summer 1910. Rashid al-Molk planned to disarm the Qoja-Beyli and their allies, and in September assembled outside Ardabil a ragged force of 1,000 men, comprising local levies and cavalry from Yortchi, Polatlu and Reza-Beyli.

On the 25th the Qoja-Beyli fell on his camp and broke it up; part of his force joined the assailants, some were taken prisoner, and a few, including Rashid al-Molk himself, abandoned the artillery and supplies and fled back to the city. The Russian vice-consul claimed that, but for the Cossack garrison, Ardabil would once more have been sacked and the captive chiefs released from the castle.[23] The Shahsevan took control of Meshkin, Ardabil and Sarab districts, while the Shatranlu and Galesh overran Khalkhal and Astara.

Meanwhile Hazrat-qoli Hajji-Khojalu, having been set free in spring, took over Ahar in the name of the Nationalist government. In September Rahim Khan Chalabianlu's sons Habibollah Khan and Böyük Khan returned from Russia. The former submitted to Hazrat-qoli, but the latter began widespread looting and on 23 October attacked Ahar, though he was driven off by Hazrat-qoli's tribesmen. By the end of October Hazrat-qoli had won over the Chalabianlu, and as a result of this pact the other Shahsevan tribes caused no more trouble before they went to Moghan in November, after which order was restored in the Ardabil vicinity. In December Rahim Khan himself returned to Iran, staying awhile in Moghan, but as he found the Shahsevan there unwilling or unable to join him in a further rising he let himself be taken to Tabriz in January 1911, a virtual prisoner.

At Ardabil Rashid al-Molk rallied his forces. He thought he could rely on the Hajji-Khojalu at Ahar and Meshkin and on the Yortchi and Polatlu

---

[22] On the subjugation of the Meshkin tribes, see Amir-Khizi (1960: 483f.); Kasravi (1938, III: 151f.); Safari (1971: 303); S.D.D. IV (161–204, 216f., 232).

[23] See S.D.D. V (106, 108, 135–9); FO Prints, Affairs of Persia XXIV (Grey to Barclay of 3.10.1910); Kazemzadeh (1968: 578).

at Ardabil, while he hoped to gain Shatranlu support by releasing from the castle Abish Khan (Habibollah Khan Rashid al-Mamalek), brother of Amir 'Ashayer (who was in Tehran). Early that winter several Shahsevan chiefs – notably Abish Khan Shatranlu, Sardar Bey (and other Qoja-Beyli chiefs), Lotfollah Khan Dursun-Khojalu/Yortchi, Hazrat-Qoli, Ahmad Khan and Javat Khan Hajji-Khojalu, Hamid Bey Alarlu, Firuz Khan Polatlu (son of Hosein 'Ali Khan), and others from Geyikli, Khamesli, Damirchili, Talesh-Mikeilli, Ajirli, Beydili and Zargar who were not prisoners in Tehran, joined the nominal *elbey* Ghafar Khan Salar-Movaqqar in sending a telegram to the Majles, assuring them that the misdeeds of their foolish young warriors were past, that they were loyal servants of Rashid al-Molk, and would carry out the commands of the Majles and the ulama, to defend their country against occupying foreign forces.[24]

During the winter all was relatively quiet in Moghan, but Rashid al-Molk, at his Russian mentors' insistence, prepared a further expedition against the Qoja-Beyli. This tribe now revolted against an alliance being formed between the Qara-Daghi tribes, the Hajji-Khojalu, and the Polatlu of Ardabil. Disorder at Ardabil increased. Nationalist elements demonstrated against Russian troops, and Abish Khan and others intrigued for the return from Tehran of the remaining captured chiefs, who were themselves seeking the dismissal of Rashid al-Molk from Ardabil. When Hosein-'Ali Khan Galesh and Mohammad-qoli Khan Alarlu reappeared in the neighbourhood and their bands caused trouble in the Astara district, further Russian troops were moved into Iran to take reprisals.

Late in April 1911 Rashid al-Molk set off on his new expedition to disarm the tribes. Though he began with some success against bands of 'Isalu and others, by the end of the month he found himself in a critical situation in Meshkin; aid promised by Hajji-Khojalu and Shatranlu failed to appear, probably through resentment at his Russian backing. The governor of Qara-Dagh was sent to his rescue, but at the end of May the Qoja-Beyli heavily defeated both forces in Meshkin, capturing the governor of Qara-Dagh. The Qoja-Beyli again threatened Ardabil, but could not take it because of the Russian garrison of some 1,000 men. Rashid al-Molk escaped to Ahar and made his way to Tabriz, where the Nationalists arrested him and were about to hang him for conspiring with the Shahsevan to restore Mohammad 'Ali, when he was rescued by a

---

[24] Telegram published in *Iran-e Now*, No. 38, Monday, 2 Zi-h-jja, 1328 = 5 Dec. 1910, as reproduced in Torkman (1991: 186). Several of the signatories were among those who had been captured in the spring, and must have already found their way back to Ardabil.

force of Cossacks sent by the Russian consul-general, for whom he had performed many services.

That summer the effects of a harsh drought and a poor harvest were aggravated by Qara-Daghi and Shahsevan bands which pillaged all over the Ardabil and Sarab region and right up to the gates of Tabriz. The Russian garrison at Ardabil was increased to nearly 2,000 men and employed in convoying caravans over the brigand-infested roads between Tabriz, Mianeh, Ardabil and Astara.

Early in July it was learnt that Mohammad 'Ali's favourite Mojallal as-Saltaneh had passed through Ardabil and was now residing with the Yortchi tribe, engaged in recruiting Shahsevan support for the ex-Shah's return. The Russians began to encourage the tribesmen: at the end of July a public proclamation was issued in Ardabil, apparently at the bidding of Mojallal and the Russian vice-consul Belyaev, to the effect that Mohammad 'Ali was in or near Tehran with a large army and vast resources, and had proclaimed an amnesty and overthrown the Constitution. The Nationalists went into hiding, nobody suspecting that the story was a fabrication. In August Mojallal entered the city unopposed, but soon enough the truth emerged, and his support, which does not seem to have been widespread among the Shahsevan, melted away in September when it was heard that the ex-Shah's army had been decisively beaten near Tehran by Yeprem Khan.

Measures taken by the Nationalist government to restore order in the Ardabil region had been somewhat unfortunate. At the end of July Samad Khan Shoja' ad-Douleh was sent (yet again) to punish the Shahsevan. He gathered a force of several thousand at Sarab, but in August began to recruit the Shahsevan into his army, with which he then threatened Tabriz, proclaiming himself governor-general of Azarbaijan in the name of the ex-Shah. He demanded the release of the Shahsevan chiefs from Tehran, and on 15 September invested Tabriz, though he did not press his advantage in view of the setbacks to the ex-Shah's cause in the rest of the country. Meanwhile the Tehran government had appointed the old reactionary 'Ein ad-Douleh as governor-general of Azarbaijan. His plan for dealing with the Shahsevan was to release the captive chiefs in Tehran and demand that they pacify their followers. Believing their assurances that they would do so and would capture Mojallal and ensure his own safe arrival at Tabriz, he took them with him on the road to Azarbaijan. Among them were Amir 'Ashayer Shatranlu, Bahram Qoja-Beyli, and Salar Dalikanlu.

Böyük Khan Chalabianlu brought his warriors into Samad Khan's camp, but the Nationalists in Tabriz promptly executed his father Rahim

Khan, to prevent his encouraging his followers. Amir Arshad Hajji-'Alili, who had at first also come to Samad Khan, now returned to Qara-Dagh and declared for the Nationalists. Böyük Khan, sent after him in October, suffered a heavy defeat and was captured, leaving Amir Arshad lord of Qara-Dagh. Among the Shahsevan, Samad Khan's only success was with some Ardabil tribes. Abish Khan Shatranlu managed to unite many Meshkin tribes against the Royalists and their Russian sponsors, and having rejected Samad Khan's overtures went to Mianeh to await the arrival of the now freed chiefs.

From October onwards the British pressed the Russians to withdraw troops from Iran, but the latter stated that 'measures of extreme vigour' would soon have to be taken to meet the situation in the northern provinces. Indeed, at the end of September a large Russian detachment arrived at Ardabil under General Fidarov, whose mission was to prepare a campaign for the following spring to punish and disarm the recalcitrant Shahsevan tribes. The tribes concerned – principally the Qoja-Beyli and others of the Meshkin division, for most of the Ardabil division were subject to the Russians at Ardabil – were now in Moghan and were joined by their chiefs some time during the winter.[25]

Russian troops now occupied northern Iran. The Tehran Assembly was dispersed in December, and Russian consuls and army commanders, or Iranians amenable to them, took control of affairs. On 1 January 1912 Samad Khan entered Tabriz with Russian support as governor, and the Nationalists now suffered worse atrocities of killing, torture and pillage than they had just experienced from the Russian occupying forces. With a general rising expected in the spring, Samad Khan's henchmen, such as Rashid al-Molk, agitated in support of Mohammad 'Ali; but he himself refrained from doing so, since his Russian sponsors had now abandoned the ex-Shah's cause in an effort to establish understanding with Britain (which would not accept the restoration) in view of events in Europe. The Russians acceded to British requests not to extend official recognition to Samad Khan as governor, but the British agreed that he was the only Iranian who could control the province, and the departure of the governor eventually appointed from Tehran was delayed.

Meanwhile, his hopes ended, Mohammad 'Ali left Iranian soil for the last time in March 1912. There were further movements in his favour that year but they were prevented from coming to fruition. Foreign influence in Iran was at its zenith. The country was nominally ruled by a regent for the

---

[25] On the events of 1911, see FO 248/1033 and /1038; *FO Prints, Affairs of Persia* XXV–XXVIII; *S.D.D.* VI and VII; Kasravi (1938, III: 208–32, 252–7).

young Soltan Ahmad Shah, with a cabinet composed largely of Bakhtiari khans, while Nationalists who had not fled to Europe kept out of sight.

As expected, the Azarbaijani chiefs, who had returned in the winter eager for revenge, commenced activity on a wide scale in spring 1912. In April the first encounter took place between Fidarov's troops and tribal warriors, in Khalkhal. Both sides suffered heavy losses. Fidarov delayed his movement against the tribes; he probably felt his force insufficient and was waiting both for provocation by the tribesmen – so that he could call for reinforcements – and for an Iranian force to be sent and to be shown to be inadequate.

Early in June a party of Cossacks left Ardabil for summer quarters near by, and the Qoja-Beyli duly attacked them, thinking them a punitive expedition. Fidarov then sent a real punitive force against them, and there was some fighting in Meshkin and further heavy losses on both sides. Strong reinforcements were brought to the region from Tabriz, Qara-Bagh and Astara. At Russian request, an Iranian force of 1,000 men was sent, once more under their ever-willing servant Rashid al-Molk, but having suffered the expected defeat the remnants did not reach Ardabil until mid-July, where they took up a strictly honorary role under Fidarov. According to one report, the Shahsevan who defeated Rashid al-Molk sent Samad Khan in Tabriz the following message: 'Do not send any more Mussulman soldiers against us. We do not care to kill our Mussulman brethren, but send all the Russians you can. We will settle our account with those yellow dogs!'[26]

Fidarov now had some 5,000 troops – Cossacks, infantry and artillery – and began a campaign which lasted several months. The Iranian authorities expressed their concern that he intended to annihilate the tribes, while the Russian newspapers played down the political nature of his expedition: the Shahsevan were not patriots defending their country against the invader, but lawless brigands who had proved a scourge both to the Russians and to their own countrymen, and were to be prevented from further banditry and to be forced to restore all the stolen goods.

The Shahsevan meanwhile were organizing themselves, having learnt the lesson of defeat from the Nationalist forces two years earlier. Chiefs of the two most powerful tribes, Hajji-Khojalu and Qoja-Beyli, made up their differences and collected their warriors. They detailed some of the client tribes to declare themselves neutral and take all the flocks and families aside to a place of safety, leaving the warriors free to deal with the Russians, to whom they swore never to submit. They were no longer

[26] Mirza Firooz Khan (1912), quoted by Cottam (1964: 57).

interested in the Royalist cause, which had become discredited, and even those who still favoured it were annoyed with Samad Khan for not openly declaring for Mohammad 'Ali on occupying Tabriz. Indeed, the chiefs returned from Tehran seem to have had encouragement and finance from influential persons there, to keep Samad Khan busy in Azarbaijan and prevent him marching on the capital in the ex-Shah's name.

Throughout July and August the Shahsevan and the Russians fought. The course of the campaign, and even its outcome, are hard to determine. The Russians declared their eventual complete success, but observers in Tabriz saw large numbers of casualties brought in, while the Shahsevan themselves maintained that their warriors killed thousands of Russians and that few tribesmen submitted.

The commander of the Russian detachment in Ardabil before the First World War (Fidarov?) commented on Shahsevan fighting tactics:

Well acquainted with the terrain, excellently deployed, making use of every rock, every hollow, mobile, light, accustomed to long movements over mountainous places, with their mountain-bred horses, the Shahsevans, when attacking, or repulsing an attack, never mass, but break up, make diversions on the front. They always try to outflank the enemy, flowing quickly round him, rarely taking a blow at close quarters, retreating at the point of greatest pressure, immediately reappearing on the flank and in the rear, trying to stretch the enemy line, using their constant numerical superiority, so as to gain the opportunity to break the enemy up and destroy him. Throughout an action or skirmish, they keep the enemy under well-co-ordinated observation, always having several observers on every high point around the enemy . . . Their tenacity in battle depends on the degree of danger to their flocks, families and property if these have not succeeded in getting away, or in their numerical superiority over the enemy. The greater the distance between the Shahsevan bands engaged in battle and their retreating camps, the weaker their resistance; on the other hand, their stubbornness increases as the distance decreases.[27]

I heard very similar accounts in the 1960s of how Shahsevan guerrilla tactics and superior knowledge and use of their terrain often brought them success when fighting the Russian troops. They never massed for an attack but kept their enemy under constant observation from scouts posted on the hilltops, and concentrated on sniping and skirmishing, trying to break organized troops into small bands that could be disposed of piecemeal. If they were attacked in force, they would immediately scatter, giving the impression of a rout, which the Russians would claim as a victory, only to find themselves harried by the same warriors soon after. One serious military drawback, which sometimes led to disaster for the

---

[27] Quoted by Rostopchin (1933: 113).

Shahsevan warriors, was the strictly observed duty to rescue the bodies of slain kinsmen.

The warriors' persistence and bravery depended very much on the danger presented by the enemy to their homes and property. For this reason, and also so as to wear down the troops with unfamiliar conditions, they would try to draw the Russians into the heat of Moghan in high summer, and to the snow of the mountains in winter. They soon learned how to deal with a machine-gun onslaught: they would draw the fire by waving hats on rifles, keeping watch until they saw the gun needed reloading, a lengthy process during which they had ample time to charge. In this way they captured a large number of Russian machine-guns and mountain guns.

Fidarov deployed his forces in four main columns, operating against Hajji-Khojalu, Qoja-Beyli, Alarlu, and the Khalkhalis, respectively. Javat Khan Hajji-Khojalu, with his Geyikli allies, led the Russians first into the torrid wastes of Moghan in mid-July, and then back in August to Qosha-Dagh; there, joined by a strong party of Qoja-Beyli, he held the forest of Qashqa-Mesha against Fidarov's greatly superior force, which (it is said) he eventually defeated and drove back to Moghan and across the frontier.

Meanwhile over a thousand warriors from Qoja-Beyli and associated tribes broke through a cordon with which the Russians had tried to trap them in the northeast of the region, and headed south to Mianeh, threatening the small Russian garrison in Qazvin. They asked government permission to migrate to Kurdistan or Turkey, to find winter quarters far from the Russians. They were eventually headed back north by an Iranian force sent by Samad Khan.

At Deman, the column sent against the Alarlu suffered heavily and lost a number of guns to the tribesmen. In September, however, the Russians achieved at least partial success, for they captured Mohammad-qoli Alarlu and executed him, and then captured Amir 'Ashayer Shatranlu, though he kept his life. They then cut off the nomads' retreat to Moghan. All the tribes that had submitted or been defeated, including those detailed by Hajji-Khojalu and Qoja-Beyli to look after their property, were collected at the Samian bridge over the Qara-Su near Ardabil, and the Russians proceeded, supervised by an Iranian official, to divide their property into two, confiscating one half of everything – animals, arms, tents or clothing.

This event is remembered by the Shahsevan as *bölgi-yılı*, the year of division, and as the end of their struggle against the Tsarist Russians. The warriors of Qoja-Beyli, Geyikli and Hajji-Khojalu are said to have remained unsubdued, but they retained none of their property except their horses, their rifles and their women, which they would have died sooner than give up. In October Fidarov's army withdrew with its booty.[28]

The Shahsevan during the Great War

From the end of 1912 until 1917 Shahsevan bands continued to raid throughout the region,[29] but they caused no major trouble to the Russian forces, which, apart from a brief evacuation in the winter of 1914–15, remained garrisoned at Ardabil. In Tehran, affairs were run by a Bakhtiari-dominated cabinet, under British and Russian influence. Anti-Bakhtiari feeling grew around the country; in winter 1912–13 a concerted campaign of telegrams to the Russian and British embassies, asking for a government headed by Sa'd ad-Douleh and for the dismissal of the Bakhtiaris, included one from the Shahsevan chiefs of Ardabil – who quoted a 'well-known tribal saying' to the effect that wood cannot make rope, Kurds cannot make saints, and tribes (ilat) cannot make ministers. The signatories, listed in Figure 10, include rather more recognizable and verifiable names than the 1909 Treaty.[30]

The young Shah was crowned in July 1914, the Assembly was

---

[28] On the 1912 campaign, see FO 248/1055 and /1059; *FO Prints, Affairs of Persia* XXX–XXXII; Mirza Firooz Khan (1912); Rostopchin (1933: 114f.); Baiburdi (1962: 105); Sa'edi (1965: 84–6, and 1968: passim); Safari (1971: 327–31); I have also used accounts of Fidarov's campaign recorded from Shahsevan participants and from Aqa Bozorg Ebrahimi, an Iranian army officer who knew Fidarov's artillery commander. The literary value of Sa'edi's account of Fidarov's campaign in the novel *Tup* (The Cannon) quite outweighs its many historical solecisms. The only contemporary source dating *bölgi-ili* at 1912 is *Gazetteer* (1914: 554). Rostopchin says that Fidarov's 1912 campaign was inconclusive, but that in a further one of 1916, 'the operation was successfully conducted, and the Shahsevan were cut off from their winter pastures. However, a tremendous bribe accepted by General Fidarov caused him to order the Shahsevans to pass on, so that the results of this expedition were favourable to the Shahsevan' (1933: 114f.). I know of no other record of such a campaign in 1916, though indeed some of my informants suggested that *bölgi-ili* was about then. Sa'edi states that it was in 1896 (1275 AHS), long before the Constitutional Revolution, but this (like much of his chronology) is definitely wrong; Tanavoli (1985: 23) compounds the error by reading Sa'edi's dating as 1858 (1275 AHQ), and Opie follows him (1992: 253).

[29] Cf. Cyren (1913: 306–7); Arfa (1964: 54). On the period 1915–23, see FO 248/1117, 1188, 1215, 1216, 1224, 1225 (especially the anonymous report in no. 291 of 17.1.1919), 1226, 1278, 1323 (esp. Bristow's report, no. 102 of 31.12.1921); IOL Persian Affairs 1920–3; IOL L/P&S/10, 4500/1920; IOL L/P&S/10, 56, Intelligence Summaries 1921–3; Tagieva (1956: 99–100, 108–13); 'Iranskiy' (1924: 107); Sa'edi (1965: 92–5); Safari (1971); Rava'i (1984); Afshar (1995: 194–8). I have again used tape-recorded interviews with Shahsevan informants, and with Aqa Bozorg, the army officer personally delegated by Jahanbani to collect Shahsevan firearms.

[30] Afshar (1995: 168–70).

Salar Divan, kadkhoda of FULADLU taifeh [Hosein 'Ali Khan]
Asad as-Saltaneh Amir Toman QOJA-BEYLI
Rashid as-Saltaneh, ra'is of YORTCHI taifeh
Ahmad Khan, ra'is of HAJJI-KHOJALU taifeh
Aqa Bey, ra'is of 'ISA-BEYLI taifeh
'Aleshan Bey QOJA-BEYLI, ra'is of NASROLLAH-BEYLI tireh
Fulad Khan Bey QOJA-BEYLI, ra'is of SHAH-BAR-BEYLI tireh
Sa'adat Khan QOJA-BEYLI JURUQLU,
Bahram Khan Saham-al-Molk QOJA-BEYLI
Hazrat-qoli Bey HAJJI-KHOJALU
Lotfollah Khan, ra'is of TALESH-MIKEILLI taifeh
Hatam Khan, ra'is of GEYIKLI taifeh
Bala Khan HAJJI-KHOJALU
Rahim, ra'is of SEYYEDLU taifeh
Qilij Khan, ra'is of KHAMESLI taifeh
'Alesh Bey, Shukur Bey, kadkhoda of Anvar
Yadollah Khan min taifeh ALARI
Mahmad 'Ali [-qoli] Beylu, Ruh taifeh ALARI [??]
Ahmad Khan Bey, ra'is of DURSUN KHOJALU taifeh
Zargham Homayun, ra'is of TEKELI taifeh
Shaji' al-Mamalek, ra'is of REZA-BEYLI taifeh
Dadash Khan TAKLEH
'Ali-qoli Khan, ra'is of 'ATA-KHANLU taifeh [presumably the former elbey of
     Meshkin]
Asadollah Bey, ra'is of JANYARLU taifeh
Javad Khan, ra'is of KUR-'ABBASLU taifeh and HOSEIN-HAJJILI
Mahmad Bey, ra'is of MAST-'ALI-BEYLI taifeh
Qal'eh Mirza [Gholam Reza] Bey, ra'is of PIR-EIVATLU taifeh
Heidar Bey, kadkhoda of 'ALI-BABALU
Qahraman Khan, ra'is of DELAGHARDALU taifeh
Qahraman Khan, ra'is of MOGHANLU taifeh
Musa Khan, ra'is of KHALAFLI [Khalifali] taifeh
Musa Bey, ra'is of QOZATLU taifeh, vakil of Ojarud
'Abd al-Hosein Bey QOJA-BEYLI
Rostam B y KALASH
Bala, ra'is of Tait [TRIT] taifeh
Heidar-qoli Bey HAJJI-KHOJALU
Mokhtar Bey QOSHA-BEYLI
Ruhollah Bey ALARI

Figure 10. Signatories to the Telegram from Ardabil to the Russian
and British Embassies, 14 Jadi 1331 (January 1913)

reopened the following January, Bakhtiari domination was relaxed, and
anti-foreign Democrats and Nationalists gained some influence. For the
next few years, while the government at Tehran was usually directed by
men acceptable to the Allies, tribal khans controlled most of the rest of
the country, and popular rebellions and secessionist movements proliferated.

Although the Iranian government declared neutrality at the outbreak of the War, this was ignored from the start by both Russia and Britain, now allies, and by Turkey, which soon joined the Central Powers. Turkish forces occupied Azarbaijan briefly in the winter but were defeated by Russians who advanced to Qazvin. In 1915 Russia abandoned to Britain the neutral zone defined by the 1907 Convention, in return for British assent to the occupation of Constantinople. Democrats and Nationalists, hoping to oust both British and Russians, had turned to Germany for support, but these efforts ended in a further dissolution of the Assembly in November 1915. A National-Democrat provisional government, supported by Germany, held sway briefly in Kermanshah, until driven out by Russian troops. In 1916 Sir Percy Sykes and his South Persia Rifles brought the south and east under some control, despite infiltration by German agents.

With the 1917 revolutions in Russia and the disintegration of Tsarist forces in Iran, the British, left alone to face the Turks in the west and northwest of the country, established a corridor from the Gulf to Baku via Qazvin and the Caspian. Northern and eastern Azarbaijan fell into the hands of Amir Arshad Hajji-'Alili of Qara-Dagh, Amir 'Ashayer Shatranlu of Khalkhal, and the leading Shahsevan chiefs of Ardabil and Meshkin. For several years these chiefs and their rivals competed for control of the region, and indeed a succession of bad harvests and harsh winters intensified the competition. After 1916, Bahram Khan Qoja-Beyli led some of the nomads back into Russian Moghan, reoccupied the banks of the Kor and prevented the settlers from irrigating their crops. Long-range raiding expeditions were commonest in the period 1917–22, after the Tsarist forces had left the area; on both sides of the frontier there was poverty and terrible famine, and in the eastern Caucasus they were probably substantially aggravated by Shahsevan depredations.

From 1917, Mirza Kuchek Khan's Jangalis controlled the neighbouring province of Gilan, while in 1918 Turkish forces occupied Tabriz and much of Azarbaijan and held the heir apparent in their power. Both Jangalis and Turks attempted, with some success, to recruit support from the Shahsevan and neighbouring tribes. Kuchek Khan appointed Amir 'Ashayer Shatranlu governor of the city of Rasht, though he returned home to Khalkhal when the Turks approached from Tabriz; he and his brother were taken prisoner, but they managed to escape. Meanwhile the Turks persuaded Javat Khan Hajji-Khojalu and possibly his allies of Geyikli and 'Isalu to act on orders when signed by the heir apparent. At the same time, Iranian Cossacks and British agents operating from Zanjan and Mianeh won support from the Ardabil Shahsevan tribes, from Salar Mozaffar of the Shaqaqi and eventually from Amir 'Ashayer Shatranlu.[31]

In September 1918, Turks and Azarbaijanis took over Russian Azarbaijan and declared an independent republic. After the Turks retreated at the end of that year, the first Azarbaijani parliament opened, with support from British forces at Baku. Iranian Cossacks, with British support, defeated Kuchek Khan in spring 1919. That year, tribesmen raided unchecked in Qara-Dagh, Meshkin, Ardabil and on the Tabriz–Mianeh road. The Iranian authorities at Tabriz, unable to afford an expedition against them, asked the British at Qazvin to send an aeroplane to fly over them and the Kurdish rebel Simko (Esma'il Khan Shakak) – 'both would be quiet immediately – it would have undoubtedly very good effect'. The plane was sent – probably the first the Shahsevan had seen – and apparently had the desired result.[32]

The British left Baku in August 1919; the Red Army entered and set up a Soviet in spring 1920, while many of the largely bourgeois Musavatists, who had dominated the parliament, fled to Iran. After the war, as non-belligerents, the Iranian delegation were not admitted to the Versailles Conference. Curzon was busy concocting an anachronistic Anglo–Persian treaty of protection, which might have been of benefit to Iran but would have recognized Britain's right to interfere in her internal affairs. After many months of sordid negotiations and passionate opposition from the Iranians, the treaty foundered when the British were unwilling to supply forces to counter a Bolshevik invasion of Gilan and Mazandaran in support of Kuchek Khan in 1920.

At Ardabil, Hosein-'Ali Khan of Polatlu was somewhat overshadowed by his remarkable wife, 'Azamat Khanom, widow of his older brother Jurugh Bey (killed in 1900 by Shoja' ad-Douleh) and sister of Amir 'Ashayer Shatranlu. In alliance with Najaf-qoli Alarlu, she intrigued briefly with the Bolshevik troops who gathered in large numbers at Astara and Ardabil in late May 1920, but they backed down in the face of opposition from the other Alarlu chiefs Ruhollah and Gholam, as well as the ulama of Ardabil: mojtahed Mirza 'Ali Akbar at Ardabil declared an anti-Bolshevik jehad. Ruhollah and Gholam Alarlu, Nouruz, Ayaz and Rahim Qoja-Beyli, Hatam Geyikli and Javat Hajji-Khojalu all made successful attacks on Bolshevik columns on both sides of the frontier. That summer, Amir 'Ashayer of Khalkhal formed an anti-socialist union of his Shatranlu with Salar Mozaffar Shaqaqi from Mianeh, the Khamesli, Bahram Khan

---

[31] Safari (1971: 370); Rava'i (1984: 77, 108); FO 248/1216 and 1188 (various); Dunsterville (1920: 126, 130, 189).

[32] FO 248/1225 (Bristow no. 496 of 28.9.1919) and 1226 (no. 554 of 12.11.19).

Qoja-Beyli, Najaf-qoli Alarlu, Mashallah Reza-Beyli, Nasrollah Yortchi and the khans of Talesh and Namin.

From April to September 1920 the Democrat Sheikh Mohammad Khiabani controlled Tabriz and much of Azarbaijan, proclaiming the separate state of Azadestan. Backed by Bolsheviks, he also received some support from Javat Khan Hajji-Khojalu and his ally Böyük Khan Chalabianlu, but was opposed by Amir Arshad Hajji-'Alili, who defeated a force sent by Khiabani to Javat's aid. According to Tagieva, the following Shahsevan chiefs were won over by a British agent to oppose Khiabani: Nasrollah Yortchi, Amir Aslan 'Isalu, Hatam Geyikli and Javat Hajji-Khojalu; British reports confirm the involvement of only the first of these chiefs.[33] Khiabani's state was suppressed by Iranian Cossacks in September.

In autumn 1920, with the excuse that Shahsevan bands were continually encroaching over their frontier and attacking their forces, the Soviet authorities prepared an invasion of Iranian Azarbaijan. One column crossed at Astara in January 1921, only to be heavily defeated. Another column invaded Moghan in the spring and was wiped out by warriors from Pir-Evatlu, 'Arabli and Ja'farli, client tribes of Nouruz Khan, son of Sardar Bey Qoja-Beyli, who were supported by Musavatist refugees from the Caucasus.[34]

Inter-tribal relations in the time of the khans

We have seen how, after the frontier closure, a few powerful Shahsevan tribes – or rather their chiefly families – emerged at the head of 'clusters' of weaker and smaller tribes. When the administration recognized the *elbeys*' fall from power and allowed *khankhanlıq*, it sought to create and maintain a balance of power between the clusters, checking their competition for resources and hegemony only when one seemed likely to overpower or unite the others, thus posing a threat to the administration itself.

Although it was possible, as old men liked to recall in the 1960s, for any individual to make a name for himself as a successful bandit, to gather a following and become a minor 'chief', this could only be done with the approval of the dominant chief of the cluster. The cluster chiefs entered the *khankhanlıq* period with control of vast pastoral and agricultural wealth. They soon increased their armed retinues, and acquired further

---

[33] Tagieva (1956: 108), quoting a Soviet archive source.
[34] See Tapper (1966), and Appendix Three.

resources which became essential to their effective leadership: in particular, control of information and communication from important centres of government. Each cluster chief had spies and representatives in Ardabil, Tabriz and Tehran, and contacts through whom powerful government officials could be influenced. The cluster chief himself exercised absolute authority over his retinue and the commoners of his tribe, and so long as he satisfied his rivals with adequate spoils, and his other followers with effective leadership and protection, he was permitted or even expected to exercise absolute authority over them too. He held court to judge such cases of theft or insubordination as were brought before him, and sentenced offenders to physical punishment or property confiscation, carried out by his henchmen.

With the breakdown of government authority, the major tribes seized effective control of the region. The chiefs of the four main nomad tribes of Meshkin came to an agreement. They divided the villages of Meshkin and Arshaq (and their inhabitants) into four 'spheres of influence', so that, from west to east: Hajji-Khojalu controlled the vicinity of Ahar and much of western Meshkin, Geyikli controlled the rest of western Meshkin, Qoja-Beyli most of eastern Meshkin, and 'Isalu the rest of eastern Meshkin and much of the country up to Ardabil. Qoja-Beyli and Alarlu chiefs meanwhile controlled Angut, Barzand and Ojarud, while further south the settlements of Ardabil and Khalkhal were in the hands of Alarlu, Polatlu, Yortchi and Shatranlu chiefs. Each assumed the 'protection' of his own territory, and caravans passing through it, against the raids of the others.

The chiefs then set about securing the available centres of commercial or strategic importance, market towns or large villages lying near or across the main highways, as defensible headquarters. The villages of Barzand and Langan commanded the Belasovar–Ardabil trade route, and the eastern migration trail of the Moghan nomads; Zeiveh in Angut straddled the western migration trail; Khiou and Lari/Lahrud, important new market centres (swollen by refugees from outlying villages), commanded the Ahar–Ardabil road; Nir lay astride the vital Tabriz–Sarab–Ardabil highway. By 1900 many of these were already occupied: Nurollah Bey Qoja-Beyli had fortified Barzand, but somewhat prematurely, for the government soon razed his fort; his son Bahram Khan and cousin Sardar Bey took over Zeiveh and Barzand respectively. In the last years of *khankhanlïq*, after Sardar Bey's demise, Bahram Khan seized Khiou, which had so far remained independent, but soon lost it, and Zeiveh, to Hajji Faraj of Geyikli and his nephew 'Aleshan. Amir Aslan of 'Isalu and his paternal half-brother 'Isa Bey fought each other for control of Lari and the neighbouring villages. Langan was controlled by Alarlu, Nir by Yortchi.

Struggles developed for control of the larger towns. The two main prizes, Ardabil and Ahar (Sarab remained dominated by Shaqaqi and neighbouring tribes), were beyond the control of a single tribal cluster, and coalitions formed in competition for them. Ardabil, the headquarters of Nazar-'Ali Khan Sarı-Khan-Beyli a century earlier, did not remain for long in the possession of any of the tribes in *khankhanlıq*; between 1909 and 1917 the Russian occupation troops kept them out, while at other times local govenors, notables, and the occasional Iranian military expedition had to strike alliances with different Shahsevan chiefs. In the later years, 'Azamat Khanom of Polatlu, in revolt against the Iranian government, sought control of the city. She allied Polatlu with the Shatranlu of Khalkhal, led by her brother Amir 'Ashayer, and Najaf-qoli Khan Alarlu, but this coalition was successfully opposed by the rival coalition of chiefs from the Yortchi, Khamesli and Qoja-Beyli, together with the Dalikanlu from Sarab. At Ahar, after Rahim Khan Chalabianlu's fall from power, Hazrat-qoli of Hajji-Khojalu seized the town, but he was not able to keep it for long from a Qara-Daghi coalition under Amir Arshad Hajji-'Alili; the latter, however, lost Ahar on occasion to Hazrat-qoli's nephew Javat Khan and his allies of Geyikli and Chalabianlu.

The old distinction between Meshkin and Ardabil Shahsevan was no longer of political relevance, nor indeed was that between Shahsevan, Qara-Daghi and Khalkhali. Rather, there were four tribal coalitions active in the region: Hajji-'Alili and their Qara-Daghi allies disputed Ahar with Hajji-Khojalu + Geyikli + Chalabianlu; Polatlu + Alarlu + Shatranlu disputed Ardabil with Yortchi + Khamesli + Qoja-Beyli. Meanwhile Bahram Khan Qoja-Beyli intermittently pursued his longstanding enmity with the neighbouring Hajji-Khojalu, Geyikli, 'Isalu and Alarlu, though these never all allied against their common enemy.

It was rare for the tribes to combine for a single purpose. For a few weeks in 1909 Rahim Khan united most of them to oppose the Constitution and take Ardabil, but the Russians soon retook the city and a relatively small force under Yeprem Khan defeated the union piecemeal. Having learnt their lesson, the tribes mounted a co-ordinated and nearly successful resistance to the Russian forces in 1912. External factors sometimes caused a major shift of allegiances, as when Chalabianlu, having lost control of Qara-Dagh in 1910, allied themselves with their traditional enemies the Hajji-Khojalu so as to oppose the new Qara-Daghi power of Hajji-'Alili.

Rivalries within chiefly dynasties, and consequent shifts of power,

meant that, while in 1910 Sardar Bey's Qoja-Beyli relentlessly opposed
the Constitution and the Nationalists, to whom Hazrat-qoli's Hajji-
Khojalu, Mahmad-qoli's Alarlu and Hosein-'Ali's Polatlu were prepared
to give their support, ten years later Javat Hajji-Khojalu fought the rest in
the name of the Nationalist government. Shortly before the disarmament,
the four coalitions aligned into two blocs: the Alarlu/Polatlu/Shatranlu
coalition was aligned with that of the Hajji-Khojalu/Geyikli and sometimes 'Isalu, in common opposition to the bloc comprising the Qoja-
Beyli/Yortchi/Khamesli alliance which (until Amir Arshad's death) had
common cause with Hajji-'Alili; but the allies in each bloc did not send
each other material support. Chiefly families would contract marriages
with each other, that is with allies in the same bloc, but affinal ties were no
guarantee of permanence in an alliance.

In these times, homicide within a tribe, or between tribes of a cluster,
led to vengeance killing and then reconciliation, arranged by the cluster
chief. Between tribes of different clusters, the results of a homicide
depended on the political aims of the clusters concerned: the chiefs might
arrange reconciliation and compensation, or they might use the killing as
an excuse for reopening hostilities, if these were not already in progress.
Hostilities would begin with a series of reciprocal raids, in which sooner
or later somebody would be killed, as a Ja'farli elder told me:

For example, the nomads would place old men on guard at their sheepfolds . . .
you might put me there, say; then you would go away and leave me, and someone
might come to rob the sheepfold and they might shoot me. The next day it would
be known that so-and-so's man has been shot, your man in this case, and you and
they would become enemies over the blood. Or one nomad might raid a village
and kill a man, and that man's boss (*sahib*) would go and attack the nomad's camp
and steal his sheep: for example you had killed one of my men . . . If sheep had
been taken, the chief, or the elder, would say, they've stolen my sheep, why are you
sitting there, sons-of-dogs, have you gone feeble? So twenty or thirty or a hundred
horsemen would assemble and then suddenly attack. They might catch up with
them and recover the sheep, but a battle would probably ensue and they would
shoot at each other, and if I was stronger I would kill five or six of your men, or it
might be the other way.

It was difficult to negotiate peace. The powerful chiefs, who respected each
other – Nouruz Bey [Qoja-Beyli], Najaf-qoli Khan [Arallu], Javat Khan [Hajji-
Khojalu], 'Aleshan Khan [Geyikli] – they might get together, or write messages to
each other, saying, come on, let us make peace between these tribes. Then the
chiefs would come to make peace and greet each other, and compensation would
be arranged for the spilled blood. They would give a hundred sheep, or one or two
camels, or a stallion, or if that were not enough they might give a girl, and say,
here, we give you this girl for the blood. She would be married to the dead man's
son or brother. God bless it, they would say, here is your blood-money (*qanpulu*).
That was the Shahsevan way.

When a small tribe of a cluster was at blood-feud (*qanlı*) with a tribe from another cluster, it could usually rely on assistance from other tribes in its own cluster, particularly the dominant tribe. Thus, the two small tribes Ja'farli and Pir-Evatlu were both at blood-feud with the powerful Geyikli tribe, but together and with the assistance of Qoja-Beyli they managed to survive. The following account of the blood-feud was given by the same Ja'farli elder; he afterwards admitted that Pirevatlu assistance had been important to his tribe's success:

Ja'farli had a battle (*dava*) with Geyikli, as a result of our blood-feud. They killed the brother of our chief Samad Khan . . . we entered hostilities with them. Our men collected a party and went off raiding towards Sarab. . . on their way they saw seven men over there, on Örkäläk, a rocky hill in 'Aleshan [Geyikli]'s lands, who suddenly ran away, so our party attacked them, surrounded them and cut them off; they took refuge behind a large rock, but our men had surrounded them, shot six of them dead and took the seventh prisoner. We brought him back and handed him to Nouruz Bey [Qoja-Beyli], who would not allow us to kill him. The man was terrified, but he was allowed to go home and to die there. After that they killed more of our tribe, and the hostilities, the blood-feud intensified. We were a small tribe, fewer than 200 households, but they had 500 or more – we could not hope to defeat them. However, our Ja'farli tribe were very brave men, some of them better than a hundred others.

Well, finally we fought a battle. We had camped by Qeinerjeh, on the slopes above Khiou, and then at night [Geyikli] came and dug themselves into trenches, thinking that in the morning when Qoja-Beyli had passed by on a raiding expedition, they could massacre us. That was their intention; however there were spies who took messages for us to Nouruz Bey at Qotor-Su, saying that Geyikli had come and made trenches against Ja'farli and that when Qoja-Beyli had passed in the morning, Geyikli would attack us in revenge for the men killed. Well, dawn broke and we saw how Geyikli lay in their trenches. At that time they had fine new 3- and 10-shot rifles, none of those old Berdans; they were firing them in the air, to show off their range, and the bullets landed in our camp. So poor Samad Khan said, let us attack them at once. Off we went and took their trenches, and chased them from trench to trench, until we routed them to Ay-Dagh, a large mountain in summer quarters on the west of Savalan. We defeated them and turned them out of their trenches and occupied them ourselves. Then a huge party of Qoja-Beyli horsemen turned up, it looked like a thousand of them, Nouruz Bey's men, and they saw what had happened. Well, we remained at blood-feud with Geyikli up to the arrival of 'Abdollah Khan Amir Lashkar Tahmaspi [see below].

The dominant tribes conducted intermittent warfare, marked by incidents such as the following, related by a Khalfali elder:

Qoja-Beyli wanted to fight Hajji-Khojalu; they had a battle at Malı-Qıshlaq near Zeiveh. Köntö, eldest son of Bahram Khan, went there and built himself a stronghold across the migration trail of Geyikli and Hajji-Khojalu. He blocked the road and said, 'I will not allow any migration to pass by here,' and when they came he opened fire on them. Now Hajji Hazrat-qoli of Hajji-Khojalu had given his daugh-ter in marriage to Baghish Bey, son of Shükür Bey Qoja-Beyli, who lived in Salim-Aghach nearby. Shükür Bey persuaded the two parties to negotiate peace; he persuaded Hazrat-qoli, who sent three men to negotiate with Köntö. But in the negotiations they shot Köntö; and after that the Qoja-Beyli killed Bala Khan Bey, brother of Javat Hajji-Khojalu. Two important men were now killed, one on each side. The fighting went on for years, each side raiding and killing the other, but after Köntö's death the road was opened again and people came and went along it.

Hostilities between the chief and his rivals sometimes developed into particularly bitter open warfare, though sooner or later peace was arranged. One notorious rivalry was described briefly by the same Khalfali elder:

Another feud was between Amir Aslan Bey and 'Isa Bey [both of 'Isalu]. They were brothers, with the same father but different mothers; they were always fighting, for four or five years, attacking each other's homes, plundering and so on. Each killed a full-brother of the other. They fought about land, villages in Meshkin such as Onar, Arzan, Lari, Fakhrevar – each wanted to be boss (sahıb), that's why the brothers quarrelled.

The main Shahsevan chiefs were certainly politically informed and aware, through advisers in their suites and contacts in the cities, of the course and implications of the events that were shaking Iran. Their actions were motivated not merely by short-term gain, but at least in part by consideration of the long-term relevance of national issues to their local interests. Probably they never assembled more than a few thousand horsemen for a campaign. Usually bands of a few hundred at most con-fronted the Russian Cossacks or other hostile forces. Contemporary Russian and British agents considered them a formidable fighting body, as great a potential military threat to government as any other tribal group in the country: they could muster 10,000–12,000 horsemen in their own defence – but not more than half that number for a campaign outside their home territory. It is this – the comparative vulnerability and access-ibility of Shahsevan pastures and property, both to Russian and to Iranian government forces – rather than any comparative lack of leadership or political commitment, that explains why the Shahsevan never made any concerted effort, in whatever cause, to emulate the achievements of the Bakhtiari in Tehran.

The rise of Reza Khan: the end of the Shahsevan revolt

In 1921, Iran was in a state of complete disunity. Foreign influences were for the moment in abeyance: the Turks had been defeated in the war, the British were discredited and were being forced by economies at home to withdraw their troops, while the Bolsheviks too were ousted from Gilan. In this situation Reza Khan, an officer in the Iranian Cossacks, began his rise to power, marked by his coup in February 1921, together with the intellectual Seyed Zia ad-Din Tabataba'i.

In 1921 the tribes of the Ardabil region continued to struggle for dominance. 'Azamat Khanom's Polatlu warriors attacked and looted the city on a number of occasions, but the religious leaders of the city, aided by Qoja-Beyli, managed to keep some order. Towards autumn the Polatlu were again allied with the Alarlu and in open rebellion against the government, whose side was taken by their rivals Qoja-Beyli and Yortchi. Many engagements were fought between these opponents, though usually with indecisive results.

In November Amir Arshad of Qara-Dagh, whose warriors had been relied on by the newly restored government at Tabriz since the downfall of Khiabani, was persuaded to take them and 600 Yortchi cavalry against the Kurdish rebel Simko, but his army was defeated and he himself was shot, supposedly by one of his own men whom he was trying to prevent from running away from the enemy. His brother and son were arrested next spring, and Qara-Dagh was soon restored to government control.[35]

During the autumn and winter of 1921–2, Reza Khan, now War Minister, reformed the army and set in motion his plans for pacifying and disarming the rebellious tribes, which he considered essential to the reassertion of central government control in the provinces. Rebellions in various northern regions, including that of Kuchek Khan in Gilan, were successfully suppressed, and efforts in 1922 concentrated on Azarbaijan, starting with Simko in Kurdistan.

In the Ardabil region disturbances continued in 1922. Polatlu again, probably with Bolshevik support, raided the town in February and June; other tribes attacked the Bolsheviks. With Simko defeated during the summer, Reza Khan gave orders for moves against the Shahsevan: they were to be disarmed – their weapons were needed for the new National Army – and their taxes, unpaid for many years, were to be collected. In September, General Jahanbani, commander-in-chief of the Tabriz Division, prepared a force of 800 men, which he sent to begin this task.

In November and December this army successfully conducted operations against the Hajji-Khojalu, Polatlu and Alarlu, in which Hazrat-qoli's son was killed and Najaf-qoli of Alarlu was taken prisoner. The latter's execution at Tabriz in December caused the Alarlu to break out into revolt once more. In February 1923 the new commander-in-chief, Amir

---

[35] On Amir Arshad and Ahar, see Mojtahedi (1948: 184–5); Arfa (1964: 121–2, 439–40); Taherzadeh-Behzad (1955: 505–7); Bahrami (1965: 588–92); Baiburdi (1962: 105–7).

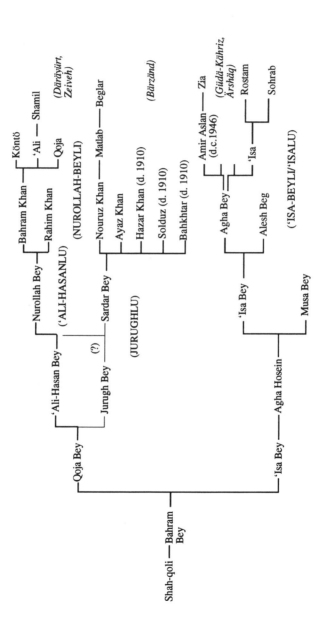

Figure 11. Skeleton genealogy of chiefs of the Qoja-Beyli tribe

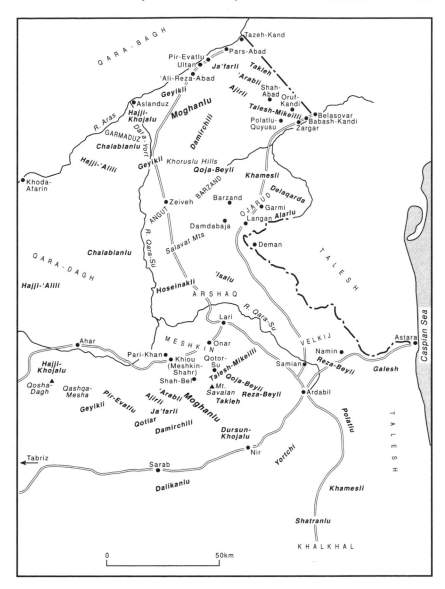

Map 8. Eastern Azarbaijan, to show places mentioned in Chapters 12 and 13 (names of tribes are shown in bold italics)

Lashkar 'Abdollah Khan Tahmaspi (the Shahsevan always mention his full name and title), brought reinforcements to Ardabil.[36] An efficient force of some 1,800 men, cavalry, infantry and artillery, was now in the field, and most of the chiefs, including Javat of Hajji-Khojalu, 'Aleshan of Geyikli, Bahram and Nouruz of Qoja-Beyli, and Nasrollah of Yortchi, sensing at last an Iranian leader whom they could respect and to whom they could surrender with honour, did so without fighting. Of the Shahsevan, only the Alarlu and Polatlu held out, the former in resentment at the execution of Najaf-qoli Khan, the latter either instigated by the Bolsheviks or fearing reprisals for their former intrigues with them. These rebels fled to Khalkhal, but they were all defeated there on Nouruz (21 March). Amir 'Ashayer, his brother Abish Khan, his sister 'Azamat Khanom, and her husband Hosein-'Ali, were among those captured, and in April 'Abdollah Khan had the men executed and 'Azamat Khanom's hair shorn off.[37]

During the spring, the Shahsevan handed over up to 30,000 rifles and a large number of mountain- and machine-guns. A sword of honour, inscribed with the names of the Shahsevan tribes, was prepared for presentation to Reza Khan. On 19 July it was exhibited in Tabriz, 'Abdollah Khan delivering a stirring speech in praise of Reza Khan and the patriotism of the Shahsevan. Some 200 Shahsevan horsemen then escorted the sword to Tehran.[38]

[36] He had already compiled the lists of tribes and their winter pastures referred to in the previous chapter.

[37] On Azamat Khanom, see Safari (1971: 450), Rava'i (1984: various). Her punishment is mentioned only by a British source: IOL L/P&S/10 (566/1921: Intelligence Summary 17 of 28.4.1923). For detailed accounts of the campaigns by townspeople who witnessed some of them, see Safari (1971: 437–48), Rava'i (1984: 149–68).

[38] Melzig (1938: 56), Sheean (1927: 72).

13   Settlement and detribalization

Reza Shah and the tribes

Reza Khan assumed the premiership in 1923 and became Reza Shah Pahlavi in early 1926, bringing the Qajar dynasty to an end. His aversion to the tribes in Iran is notorious, and he is widely thought to have broken the back of the tribal system. In his programme for unifying Iran and creating a modern, independent, secular, Persian-speaking country, he saw in the nomad tribes symbols of much that he was trying to replace: alien cultures and languages, allegiance to hereditary chiefs, a 'primitive' way of life, and a mobility that made them inaccessible to administration and the rule of law. He was also concerned by the extent to which the tribes had been subject to manipulation by foreign powers. Judging the organization and leadership of the tribes a continuing political danger, and their nomadism as anachronistic in a modern state, he eventually determined on the revolutionary step of destroying the tribal system altogether.[1]

Reza Shah's tribal policy had two main aspects, and was implemented in two distinct phases: a campaign of pacification and disarmament, carried out mostly before he became Shah, and a programme of nomad settlement enforced during his last decade. The pacification campaign, often quoted as a successful example of his strong-arm approach, is well documented, but there is little detailed record of the enforced settlement, which by contrast has received considerable – largely justified – notoriety as a brutal and catastrophic failure. Many aspects of the implementation of these policies and their impact on the tribes are little known and need investigation: the highly varied nature of the country's tribal groups, and of the threat they posed to state security; how individual groups responded to Reza Shah's policies; the extent to which pacification actually destroyed tribal political structures; and the impact of settlement on tribal economy and society.[2]

---

[1] Cf. Oberling (1964b: 89f.); Cottam (1964: 59–62); Brooks (1983: 340–342); Abrahamian (1982: 141–3); Hambly (1991b: 226–9).

[2] See e.g. Garrod (1946: 298–9); de Planhol (1968: 250–1); Oberling (1974: 149f.); Beck (1986: 129f.); Tapper (n.d.); see also articles in *Iranian Studies* 26 (3–4), 1993.

Before 1921, central government controlled only Tehran and the vicinity. Most of the country was under the sway of tribal, socialist or reactionary leaders, who paid no taxes to Tehran and ran their own well-equipped private armies. The nomadic and semi-nomadic tribes, amounting to a quarter if not a third of the total population, were virtually all independent of government authority. Most tribal groups were led by powerful chiefs, but some, such as the Yamut Türkmen, had no constituted leaders at all.[3]

During the five years of his rise to the throne, Reza Khan formed an efficient army and restored the unity essential to his programme of national regeneration. As Minister of War, one of his first steps towards restoring order to the country was to deal severely with the petty regional dynasts and the rebellious tribes, most of which he pacified, disarmed and brought under direct government control. It should be noted that he badly needed to collect their arms and unpaid taxes, not only to equip the army, but for the political symbolism which was universally accorded to taxes: the act of payment indicated recognition of authority. This campaign, although it was not completed by 1926, was none the less remarkably effective, and much welcomed by the large majority of the population, tribal and non-tribal.

The first years of peace among the Shahsevan

The new army achieved pacification and disarmament of the Shahsevan of Moghan and Ardabil in 1922–3 more quickly and more thoroughly than any other major tribal group. It brought banditry and armed inter-tribal hostilities to an abrupt end, and established an unprecedented degree of order and government control over the region. An army officer was appointed *elbey* or *ra'is-e 'ashayer* ('chief of the tribes'), responsible for political security. He maintained order with the backing of strong garrisons of troops, supplemented after 1924 by the gendarmerie (*amniyeh*) as a rural police force, which later took over frontier security.[4] Nevertheless, effective administration of the tribes still depended on co-operation with traditional leaders, and it was official policy to conciliate the chiefs so far as possible. Some of them had been killed in battle or executed during 'Abdollah Khan Tahmaspi's campaign. Others who proved recalcitrant were removed from the tribes; but most, tired of several decades of *äshrarlıq* and impressed with the strength of the new

---

[3] For the situation in various parts of the country in 1921, see Arfa (1964: 439–46).

[4] Cf. Monaco (1928: 157). Rostopchin (1933: 15) states that under a 1925 law the Shahsevan were one of five tribal groups with a Majles representative; I never heard any informant refer to this.

army, were willing to co-operate and give their allegiance to the Pahlavi regime.[5]

With their arms gone, the tribespeople were now in great fear of the army, whose firepower and resources rapidly increased, and whose successes against tribal rebels in the south were common talk. Sheep-lifting became almost unknown. The gendarmes too feared the army, and were sure to make arrests among the tribesmen to demonstrate their vigilance whenever an army officer was to visit the region. Most inter-tribal blood-feuds and hostilities were patched up, compensation arranged and marriages contracted between protagonists. Only a few enmities persisted, particularly within the chiefly families; sometimes these grew more bitter than before, now that raiding and warfare had been firmly suppressed.

There were a few uprisings among the Shahsevan at first, mostly provoked by the tactlessness and brutality of army officers. Thus in about 1926 Gholam of Alarlu and Bahram Khan of Qoja-Beyli broke into revolt. The former was soon disposed of, but Bahram captured Khiou and drove out the garrison, before being himself routed by government troops, reinforced by Geyikli tribesmen. He fled to Soviet Azarbaijan, where he is said to have died in exile, though his family later returned. In Moghan too there were occasional incidents, though these appear to have resulted from events on the Soviet side. For example, famine in the Caucasus between 1931–3 sent large numbers of refugees south, many settling in Shahsevan territory; they raided across the border, causing a brief Soviet occupation of Belasovar in 1932.[6] I also heard stories of continued raids into Soviet territory by Qoja-Beyli and others, and of small bands of outlaws who terrorized villages and camps in the mountains but were eventually hunted down by the army or the gendarmes with the aid of Shahsevan levies. Irregular Shahsevan cavalry were also levied once or twice in the 1920s for use against such rebels as the Kurdish chief Simko.

I have found no contemporary records concerning the condition of the tribes, and informants were themselves reluctant to speak on the subject except in generalities, so it has proved difficult to establish how far disarmament and the new order affected Shahsevan tribal political and economic organization. Although the immediate basis of their power – the ability to muster and deploy armed horsemen – was circumscribed, chiefs who co-operated with the new regime retained control of the other

---

[5] A recently published document records the army's appointment in 1928 of Savad Khan, son of Hazrat-qoli, as deputy of old Jahangir Bey, chief of the Beydili tribe (Begdili 1988: 501). In 1965 I talked with Savat Khan Jahangirzadeh in his village in Moghan.

[6] FO 416/90 and /91, various.

resources on which their power was founded. Thus they continued to receive large incomes from agricultural land, flocks and pastures, and to exercise control over tenants, herdsmen and servants who also derived their livelihood from these resources. Even the families of chiefs who had been punished by the government, such as Amir 'Ashayer Shatranlu, 'Azamat Polatlu, and Bahram Qoja-Beyli, eventually, after considerable efforts in Tehran, received back at least some of their former lands.[7]

The conditions in which the former tribal clusters and alliances had developed no longer prevailed, however, and dominant chiefs were no longer able to coerce or evict their subordinate tribes. Many of these, particularly larger tribes such as Moghanlu, Damirchili and Talesh-Mikeilli which had been subject to the Qoja-Beyli chiefs, now declared independence. The chief of each separate tribe now dealt directly with the *elbey* and other officials, especially in the symbolic matter of tax collection. For example, the small Khalfali tribe now broke free from Moghanlu, to which they had been attached, as one elder recalled:

We used to be mixed up with the Moghanlu; our ancestors were together. After Amir Lashkar came and collected our weapons, then everyone went to his own tribe. We had some twenty-four to twenty-five years' taxes unpaid [an exaggeration] and we now had to pay them all, and then Moghanlu said, Khalfali tribe is part of us, let us pay Khalfali's pasture taxes, and then we shall be in control of them. But we said, we would give up our women's and children's skirts, but not our lands. So we collected our own taxes and we became separated from Moghanlu. Hajji Mollah Hasan [one of the elders] said that if we wanted to move freely in our own lands, we must collect and pay our own taxes. So we got together and elected one of our cousins, Mashhad Musa Khan, to be our elder (*aq-saqal*).

The term *aq-saqal* (elder) tends to be used for any elected leader, including the chief of a tribe, who is called *bey* (chief) only if he is appointed or approved by government or other higher authority. In 1931, the titles Khan and Bey were officially abolished, though people continued to use them. 'Everyone went to his own tribe' refers both to independence from dominant chiefs and the restoration to individual tribes of lands allotted to them in the 1880s from which they had been ousted during *āshrarlıq*. However, apart from the return of a few small groups to the Moghan pastures from which Qoja-Beyli chiefs had ousted them, there appears to have been little change in the distribution of summer and winter pastures. As for the 'pasture tax', I was told that throughout Reza Shah's reign, and indeed until 1963, all those who sent flocks to graze on the

---

[7] Rava'i (1984: 175–7); Safari (1971: 450); FO 248/1416, Report of Colonel Galloway of 25.7.1942, and /1417, Macann to Millspaugh of 30.7.1943 and Macann to Nizam-ud-Din Imami of 17.8.1943.

Crown Lands of Moghan continued to pay a pasture due at a specific rate per animal; to the nomads this was a tax, while the government considered it to be rent.[8]

Despite the new independence, few other tribes as small as Khalfali felt secure enough to deal alone with army and other officials. Most sought the protection and patronage of chiefs such as Hatam Khan and 'Aleshan Khan Geyikli, Amir Aslan Bey 'Isalu, Javat Khan Hajji-Khojalu, Hosein Aqa Khan Alarlu, Nouruz Khan Qoja-Beyli, and Fazlollah Bey Talesh-Mikeilli. These chiefs were all from the Meshkin tribes. None of the Ardabil nomad groups had a powerful chief; in Moghan in winter they would ask protection of one of the Meshkin chiefs, in summer they might show allegiance to Nasrollah Khan of Yortchi, the most powerful settled chief in the Ardabil district.

In practice, the followings of the Geyikli, 'Isalu, Hajji-Khojalu and Alarlu chiefs differed little from the clusters they had formerly headed, though some small tribes which had belonged to the Qoja-Beyli cluster now joined the followings of one of the others, or of the new power, Fazlollah Bey of Talesh-Mikeilli. Each of these chiefs now mediated political relations between agents of the state and a large number of protégés, from his own tribe and others, and in return for his services was able to demand certain unofficial payments.

The new security enabled farmers to bring long-abandoned lands back into cultivation, and many former peasants who had taken refuge in the towns or in the tribal chiefs' retinues now returned to their villages. Others of the chiefs' henchmen took up pastoralism. The nomads, indeed, often recalled the ten years or so after Reza Shah's rise to power as a golden age, compared with the chaos that went before and the enforced settlement which was to come. In 1963, one old tribesman, recently settled, summarized the period as follows:

Reza Shah came and was made Shah of Iran and established the government, and they collected the rifles of the Shahsevan and the *khankhans* disappeared. The villages became cultivated, there was plenty of food, and people went safely to summer quarters and came back to winter quarters and looked after their

---

[8] This information on the Shahsevan does not quite accord with what is reported of Iran generally in more contemporary sources. According to Monaco (1928: 49) a new system of taxing livestock was introduced throughout the country in January 1926. Each type of animal was assessed at a certain number of *rials* annual tax, but those below a certain age were exempt, and the owner was allowed a certain number free of tax. Ten per cent of the revenue from this tax was to be devoted to combating animal diseases. In 1934 this system was replaced by a new law, according to which animals and their produce were taxed on entry to towns where they were to be sold (Lambton 1953: 184). A similar alternation of methods occurred in the 1960s, see note 45 below.

animals. The weak and powerless were no longer oppressed, things were put in order, and if there had been any criminals they were arrested and put in jail or executed; they did away with thieves; people relaxed and began to live comfortably.

For the farming population, however, life was less than comfortable. In Reza Shah's reign, Azarbaijan declined in political importance, and Tabriz lost its pre-eminence as a commercial centre.[9] The rural areas, such as the Shahsevan region, were little affected at first by the industrial, commercial, social and legal reforms and innovations of the new order. In spite of the end of tribal raids, the peasants, who farmed lands among the most fertile and productive in the country, continued to suffer as they had always done from the exactions of landowners and government officials. Reza Shah's plans for industrialization and modernization included little provision for the agriculture on which the economy of the country continued to depend. As Wilber wrote, 'agriculture and irrigation were neglected, so that the farming population received little direct benefit from the new industry and suffered a decline in its standard of living'.[10]

Both peasants and nomads became subject to the new conscription laws, which meant the dispersal of individual national servicemen to far-flung and culturally alien parts of the country where they could not expect help from fellow-tribesmen. In 1928, distinctive tribal clothing for men was banned, and they were forced to adopt 'western' forms of dress: jacket, trousers and the 'Pahlavi' peaked cap – replaced in 1935 by the felt brimmed hat. Shahsevan women, on the other hand, were comparatively unaffected by the new regulations, having never worn the veils that were banned in 1935; they continued as before to wear different types of head-scarf and to make up their colourful dresses from bought stuffs.

Reza Shah's sartorial reforms, bitterly opposed at first, were surprisingly permanent in effect. Oberling points out that, as the nomads had always relied on the bazaars for supplies of ready-made clothes, when the government instructed the merchants to supply only the new types of garment, the customers necessarily had to adopt them.[11]

Compulsory settlement

By the early 1930s the first stage of Reza Shah's tribal policy was virtually complete. He had removed the political danger he felt to be inherent in tribal leadership and autonomy, by imprisoning, executing, exiling or otherwise incapacitating many of the more powerful chiefs, abolishing

---

[9] Cottam (1964: 124–5).   [10] Wilber (1948: 100).
[11] Oberling (1964b: 92–3). Cf. Chehabi (1993).

their titles and offices and confiscating their landed properties or exchanging them for others in remote parts of the country. Direct government control was extended to the lower levels of the tribal political structure.

Now he determined to put an end to nomadism. The nomad families were to cease migrating, build houses, start cultivating their pastures, and submit to the same rural system of administration as other villagers. The policy of compulsory settlement was implemented during the 1930s.[12] The result was a disastrous reduction in the animal produce available in the towns and cities. Very soon, when the effects on the national economy were becoming apparent, the policy was modified. Settled nomads were allowed to entrust their flocks to herdsmen with special permits to continue migrating to seasonal pastures where necessary. This revised policy was consistent with the semi-nomadic, village-based pastoralism customary in various parts of the country, and also with the Cain-and-Abel kind of dual economy already practised by many tribal groups such as some of the Shahsevan, where settled sections sent their flocks to pasture with nomadic sections, providing the latter with agricultural produce from the tribal villages in return.

As with other tribal groups, there are no detailed contemporary records of the economic and social changes entailed among the Shahsevan by the settlement policy. The following account once more derives from the memories of survivors (all from Meshkin tribes) interviewed in 1963–6.

The new policy was implemented among the Shahsevan in 1933–4. The official aim was to settle the nomads on lands that had hitherto been used only as pasturage, and indeed some steps were taken to facilitate the opening of new cultivation in the winter pastures in the north of the region. In the districts of Khoruslu, Angut, Barzand and Ojarud there were already a number of villages, but these districts had been largely devoted to pasturage. Many nomads, particularly of the Qoja-Beyli and tribes formerly subject to them, settled here, acquiring title to the new farmlands from the government:

By the law of 7th Day 1311 (December 1932), the Ministry of Finance was empowered to transfer without exchange from the pastures and crown lands in the province of Azarbayjan, in the area where the Shahsivan reside, whatever amount it considered necessary as private property to the *khans* and individuals of those tribes.[13]

---

[12] According to various reports in FO 416/91, /92, /93, /94 and /95, settlement was begun in 1931–2 (see also Rostopchin 1933: 115, for the Shahsevan of Saveh), but drought and bad winters caused the Shah to postpone implementation in much of the country until 1933–4; in some parts, it would appear that settlement was only patchy, as late as 1937. See also Tapper (n.d.); and Magee (1948) on the Qashqa'i.   [13] Lambton (1953: 241).

In the plains of Moghan there were as yet only a few villages, scattered along the banks of the Dara-Yort, Aras and Balharu rivers. Further settlement did not seem so feasible in the absence of water supplies, but the nomads were encouraged to attempt it none the less. Nomads from Talesh-Mikeilli and other tribes commenced dry-farming in the vicinity of the old villages of Belasovar and Babash-Kandi, and founded the new settlements Oruf-Kandi, Polatlu-Quyusu and others.

In the winter of 1935–6 the Iranian press reported 'the inspection by experts of the Mughan Steppe . . . and the drawing up by them of schemes for its irrigation, in order to provide land for the settlement of the Shahsevan tribes'.[14] The French experts apparently advised the reopening of the ancient canal systems and the construction of a dam at the mouth of the Dara-Yort river as it meets the Aras. Further, 'A scheme is on foot for the formation, under Government auspices, of a company with 5 million rials (£55,550) capital for the purpose of irrigating and developing the Moghan lands in Azarbaijan.'[15]

The Shah himself toured Azarbaijan in September and October 1936, visiting Ardabil, Khiou and Ahar, though I know of no record of his encounter with any Shahsevan. The occasion gave rise to a Memorandum by the British consul-general in Tabriz, R. W. Urquhart, in which, after a long discourse on the Kurds, he wrote:

Shahsevans. The problem of the Shahsevans is simpler than that of the Kurds, since the only foreign Power which might take their part is Russia, and Russia used them so roughly in 1912 that they have little reason to turn to her. The question is almost a purely internal one.

The tribe has been described on occasion as the most powerful in Persia. Properly speaking, of course, it is a loose federation of many small tribes, who have frequently found themselves united into a strong force by common enmity towards the Central Government. Highway robbery and holding to ransom were everyday trades. That has been completely stopped, and while it is difficult to obtain information, the fact that security is perfect on the roads running through their territory and that no incidents are reported suggests that they have been completely subjugated by the Central Government.

As regards assimilation, this is being attempted as with the others. I have recorded in my diaries the attempt, suspended for the moment, but by no means abandoned, to induce the nomad tribes to settle in houses instead of in moving tents, and to have themselves registered and their flocks numbered. It appears that

---

[14] FO 416/93 (Intelligence Summary no. 25 for period ending 14 December), which went on to add, 'It is possible that this reconnaissance is not unconnected with oil, the existence of which in that area is known, and which, in 1932, formed the subject of Russo–Iranian negotiations.' See also ODDM (1966), Hawaian Agronomics (1971).

[15] *Ettela'at* of 6.1.1936, reported in enclosure in No. 41E from Knatchbull-Hugessen to Eden, 24.1.1936 (FO 416/94).

a good deal of land is available for settlement, while the proposed irrigation of the Moghan steppe on the Iranian side of the border is intended to provide more.[16]

The proposals could not be implemented at the time, but attempts had already been made to dig out the old canal near Ultan, for the benefit of the Pir-Evatlu tribe which had settled there. The narrow but highly fertile Aras river banks were now crowded with settlers from Moghanlu, Ajirli, Beydili, Ja'farli, Bala-Beyli, most of whom had winter pastures in the vicinity. In the Dara-Yort valley, groups of Qoja-Beyli, Hajji-Khojalu, Moghanlu and others settled. In these various settlements in the northern parts of the region, villages usually contained the whole of a tribal section or nomad community, or even in a few cases the whole of a small tribe.

Many of the nomads, however, chose to settle in the south, in Meshkin and Arshaq districts. Sometimes they found unoccupied lands suitable for farming, but usually they added themselves to the population of villages already inhabited by either peasants (known as Tat) or recently settled nomads. Most of the villages in these districts were wholly or partly owned by tribal chiefs and elders, who now settled in them, accompanied by large numbers of kin and dependants. There was rarely much extra land or water available for exploitation, and the original peasants continued perforce to do the work of cultivation, the new settlers remaining idle and living off their or their elders' shares of the crop.

Though one of the aims of Reza Shah's tribal policy had been to protect farmers from nomad depredations, in many cases they were now even more oppressed than before by both landowners and officials. More and more village land fell into the hands of wealthy ex-nomads, while there was a flow of both poorer nomads and oppressed Tats into the towns of the region. In particular, the market town of Khiou – officially renamed Meshkin-Shahr in 1938 – was growing in size and gaining importance as a district market and military centre.

As a Talesh-Mikeilli elder recalled:

The order was given for everyone to build houses; there were to be no more *alachıq*. Everyone gathered in their villages, hid their tent poles, and each man began to build a house on his own land. Then they gave permits to the herdsmen as 'supervisors' (*sarparast*) of the sheep, for example each owner appointed a herdsman to supervise his flock and this herdsman took them off to pasture . . . and of course he could not manage the sheep, and they suffered greatly. It was like that for five or six years, the owner not being allowed to accompany his sheep.

[16] FO 416/94 (Memorandum on Political Affairs in Azerbaijan; enclosure no. 2 in No. 467 from Butler to Eden, 12.10.1936, p. 82). I have not yet found Urquhart's diaries.

Supervisors were permitted to use only the smaller *kümä* type of tent. Yet those few allowed to migrate were not enough to tend the flocks efficiently, and they no longer had firearms to defend them against wild animals – or the thieves who had begun to reappear.

Some nomads disobeyed the first orders to abandon the *alachïq*: when they were caught, the gendarmes confiscated their tents, piled the felts and poles together and burned them. Some families, I gathered, succeeded throughout the period in migrating as before in their *alachïq*, by evading the gendamerie checkpoints along the route; others constructed enlarged *kümä* and crowded them with two or more households, all pretending to be 'supervisors'. But these evasions were exceptional, and the regulations were usually enforced with severity and sometimes brutality.

Sometimes households were split, only one or two members being permitted to go with the flocks as supervisors. Such separations caused great distress, as this old man from 'Arabli recalled:

One or two of a family used to come to *yailaq* with the sheep and a *kümä*. One brother would stay, the other would go. It was very sad and painful for brothers to be apart, and we used to weep so much that you would have thought we had just fought a battle and most of the people had been killed . . . Do you see this young man? I used to live with his father, and once, when he was a boy, I had to take him from our village in Arshaq up to *yailaq*. In those days the only shoes we had were these sandals. I hid the boy's sandals in my bag, so that when he came along with me he was barefoot and didn't imagine we were going to *yailaq*; but after a short distance he caught sight of his sandals and asked about them. I pretended it must have been a mistake, someone had put them in there or something; but he knew at once that we were going to *yailaq* and he started crying and ran away.

In the 1960s Shahsevan households with village bases were still averse to splitting in this fashion, though it was very common for two closely related households – brothers or other close agnates – to conduct a cooperative dual economy, the one remaining in the village and farming jointly owned land, the other taking the flocks to pasture.

The policy of settlement, known locally (as elsewhere in Iran) as *takhtaqapu* (wooden-door), struck at the roots of Shahsevan tribal identity, not just in the ban on migration but particularly in the outlawing of the felt-covered *alachïq* tent, which was increasingly the symbol by which the Shahsevan distinguished themselves both from house-dwelling villagers and from all other tribal groups in Iran (except the Qara-Daghis). In the 1960s, when few survivors of Reza Shah's time bothered to mention his other reforms such as the ban on their traditional clothing, all spoke with horror of the 'wooden-door' policy.

The Shahsevan probably suffered less than other tribal groups – though more than the neighbouring Qara-Daghi nomads, many more of whom were already accustomed to spending half the year in settled communities.[17] Some new settlements, particularly in the more fertile and better-watered parts of Arshaq and Khoruslu, persisted and flourish today. Nevertheless, most of their inhabitants, and indeed the great majority of the newly settled Shahsevan, returned to a migratory way of life in 1940–1.[18] The pastoral nomads had not been converted into settled cultivators; the tribesmen had learned no new attitudes, unless an increased contempt and hatred for the peasant life they had now experienced for themselves. The hidden *alachïq* were brought out; where they had been destroyed, new ones were built or replaced temporarily by *kümäs*; the pastures were reoccupied, the tribes reformed and the chiefs resumed control. A Soviet Army document of 1941 estimated 1,870 Shahsevan nomad families in the Ardabil district, and 5,026 in Meshkin.[19]

The settlement policy was politically less than successful, and a social and economic disaster. Lambton comments:

The policy was put into operation without adequate preparation. No detailed survey of the possibilities of settlement or the effect the destruction of the tribal element would have upon the economy of the country was made. Many of the tribal leaders were exiled and the annual migration of the tribes from winter to summer pastures was largely prevented. Suitable areas in which to settle the tribes were not always chosen, adequate provisions for health and education were not made, and sufficient facilities by way of agricultural training and the provision of agricultual implements were not given to the tribesmen to enable them to change over from a pastoral to an agricultural life.[20]

There was little increase in agricultural and a considerable drop in pastoral production. The health of the former nomads suffered in the unfamiliar sedentary life, and few medical or educational facilities were available to them. There were other deficiencies in the system, as a former officer in Reza Shah's army explained to me in 1966:

His Majesty Reza Shah intended migrations in Iran to be completely suspended, the tribes to be settled and to start stock-raising in a scientific manner. Naturally this was to be only a beginning . . . However the plan was not implemented as intended. Sheep need the attention of all the family, to care for them and milk them, to make the butter and other dairy produce. Unfortunately the ideas behind the programme were ill-informed; they imagined that taking the sheep to summer quarters was an easy matter, one herdsman went to summer quarters, put the sheep to graze in the pastures, and then returned. But it was Reza Shah's command and no one dared dispute it. Steps were taken to carry out the

---

[17] Oberling (1964b: 90–1).   [18] See Koetz (1983: 171).
[19] Wehrmacht (1941: 211); also 1,190 families in Khalkhal/Garus, and 2,700 in Qara-Dagh.   [20] Lambton (1953: 285).

beginning of the programme, but later Reza Shah himself realized that it was a mistake, relaxed his efforts and no longer took the matter seriously.

Lambton summarizes the effects of the enforced settlement as follows: 'The tribal policy of Reza Shah, ill conceived and badly executed, resulted in heavy losses in livestock, the impoverishment of the tribes, and a diminution of their numbers.'[21]

The question remains, however, whether any aspect of Reza Shah's policy actually achieved fundamental changes in the social structure of the tribes. The tribes of Iran were very heterogeneous, culturally and socially, and the impact of Reza Shah's reforms on them varied considerably. The Shahsevan were not typical: thanks to their frontier location and the comparative accessibility of their territory to government forces, they were sooner and more easily pacified than other tribal groups; and they suffered less during the compulsory settlement, probably because of the temperateness of the climate and the fertility of the local farmlands.

Quite possibly, however, pastoral nomad society in Iran generally emerged relatively unscathed, despite the death-toll of people and livestock. It has been argued that Reza Shah's military campaigns against the tribes removed a political superstructure that was in no way necessary to the existence of the ordinary nomads, while the period of settlement was too short to have left anything but the memory of a bad dream.[22] Certainly, the continued viability and resilience of pastoral nomadism in Iran in the late twentieth century would seem to bear this argument out. However, the picture of tribal life in Reza Shah's time remains hazy, and much remains to be achieved by further research.

After Reza Shah: Soviet occupation and the Democrats, 1941–6

On the excuse that Iran was harbouring German agents, British and Soviet troops invaded the country in August 1941. The Shahsevan nomads were in the mountains when Soviet aeroplanes flew overhead dropping propaganda leaflets, which few could read but whose import made the tribesmen wish desperately that they were armed with weapons other than slings and sticks. A few of them, it appears, did have firearms and were sent to join the Iranian army at the frontier,[23] but (as elsewhere in the country) the resistance was only a gesture in the face of a far superior force, which proceeded via Ardabil and Tabriz to Tehran. In September Reza Shah abdicated in favour of his son Mohammad Reza.

---

[21] Lambton (1953: 286).   [22] See, for example, Brooks (1983).
[23] Yekrangian (1957: 324f.); contrast the opinion of Mostoufi (1947, III, pt 2: 298f.).

For five years northern Iran was politically and economically isolated from the rest of the country, which suffered from the loss of the agricultural and pastoral surplus usually received from Azarbaijan but now diverted to the Soviet Union. Early on, Soviet agents apparently caused some minor incidents involving the Shahsevan in Ardabil and Sarab,[24] but otherwise their forces interfered little in tribal affairs during the first three and a half years of the occupation. Policing of the Ardabil region was still nominally carried out by units of the Iranian gendarmerie; an Iranian army brigade remained stationed at Ardabil, and a company at Meshkin-Shahr, the captain of the latter being responsible for political relations with nomad Shahsevan chiefs.

Meanwhile in Tehran, during 1942–3, 'Persian Government set up a Tribal Commission to enquire into claims for the restitution of dispossessed tribal lands. Commission sits regularly and entertains applications from all classes of tribesmen including those whose lands were seized by the ex-Shah as part of his Amlak.'[25] Most cases were in the British sector in the south of Iran, but one was in the name of the heirs of Bahram Qoja-Beyli, asking for restoration of lands in Moghan.

In spring 1945, as the war drew to a close, the Soviets went ahead with plans for achieving unification of Soviet and Iranian Azarbaijan. The Tudeh (Communist) Party of Azarbaijan, led by the Soviet-trained Ja'far Pishavari, a veteran of the Gilan Soviet Republic of 1920, roused popular support for a programme of provincial autonomy, though Pishavari denied the aim of secession from Iran. The more powerful Shahsevan chiefs, who were landowners and solidly anti-Soviet, became subjected to severe pressures from Soviet agents and officials, who hoped to neutralize their opposition and perhaps gain the support of the tribal masses. Early in May, Soviet officials sought, on various pretexts, to lay hands on Hatam Geyikli and Amir Aslan 'Isalu. Hatam Khan evaded capture, but his son Bala Khan was arrested, together with Amir Aslan, Nosrat Bey Ajirli, Fazlollah Bey Talesh-Mikeilli, and Böyük Bey Moghanlu. All but Amir Aslan were released after a few weeks, being warned that if they would not support the Tudeh Party they must at least refrain from interfering in its activities.[26]

General Hasan Arfa, Chief of Staff of the Iranian army at Tehran at the

---

[24] FO 248/1410 (various). Cf. also the Report (in *Zakhayer-e Enqelab* 5, 1988–9, pp. 247–8) of the Shahsevan capture and disarmament of a gendarmerie troop near Meshkin-Shahr in December 1941.

[25] FO 248/1416 (TG 27, Holman to all consuls, 4.7.1942); see also 248/1417 (various).

[26] Pesyan (1949: 82–4), using various Iranian military reports and communications of the time; FO 248/1463 (various). See also Appendix Three. Pishavari was born in Khalkhal in the 1890s; when he was aged 10–12, as a result of Shahsevan raid on his village, his family moved to Russian Azarbayjan (Bayat 1991: 119, 160).

time, writes that in summer 1945 there was little response to Tudeh activities in eastern Azarbaijan:

Even in those regions of the Soviet-occupied zone which were not under direct control of the occupational forces, the Soviet-supported Tudeh groups were attacked and driven away, people boycotting the pro-Soviet propaganda films shown by the Russians in the villages of the zone. This was particularly the case in the regions around Ardabil, Khalkhal, Arasbaran and Ujarud, near the Soviet frontier, where the patriotic and warlike Shahsevan tribes dwelt.

In order to subdue the Shahsevan, the Soviet authorities would have needed protracted operations in a difficult mountainous region, and according to Arfa they asked the Iranian authorities to see to the disarmament of the tribes and the restoration of order. Arfa agreed with the desirability of such measures, but complained that Soviet military occupation made it impossible; the request was dropped.[27]

Early in September, the Tudeh Party was absorbed in the newly declared Democrat Party of Azarbaijan. Soon after, the Soviet agent Mohammad Jalili (originally of the Sarı-Khan-Beyli tribe), summoned several Shahsevan chiefs, including Hatam Geyikli, Fazlollah Talesh-Mikeilli and Rostam 'Isalu (brother of Amir Aslan) to the Soviet consulate at Ardabil, on the pretext that they were to be paid for some sheep sold to Russia. The Soviet consul told them, however, that they must prepare for a journey to Baku to meet Jafar Baqerov, prime minister of Soviet Azarbaijan, from whom they would receive instructions concerning the establishment of Azarbaijan autonomy within Iran.[28]

Pesyan implies that the chiefs never went to Baku, but I was told by several reliable informants that several Shahsevan chiefs did go. They are said to have been first confined alone in cells for some days, then subjected to a mixture of threats and blandishments. Pointing out to them the racial, cultural and linguistic similarities uniting Soviet and Iranian Azarbaijanis, Baqerov offered them arms if they would rise in support of the Democrats. The chiefs responded that there was a religious difference (referring to Soviet atheism?), but more important, there was a wide cultural gap between them: they had seen women serving among the occupation forces, and such a custom was totally unacceptable to the Shahsevan. Most of the chiefs refused to co-operate, but all (I was told) returned to Iran.[29]

During October 1945, Soviet troop reinforcements entered Azarbaijan to back the forthcoming coup, and proceeded to intervene in civil affairs. On 16 and 17 November Democrat forces drove the Iranian army units

[27] Arfa (1964: 340).   [28] Pesyan (1949: 53–5).

[29] Kurdish Nationalist chiefs were brought to Baku at the same time, with very different results; see Eagleton (1963: 43f.).

from Tabriz and Mianeh, and Pishavari seized power. A relief force sent from Tehran was prevented by Soviet troops from passing Qazvin.

Meanwhile the Shahsevan nomads were in Moghan. At the beginning of November the Soviet consul-general at Tabriz had visited Hatam Khan's house in Meshkin-Shahr (Khiou) and delivered further threats to his host, to be passed on to Amir Aslan (who had now been released) and the other chiefs, that they must refrain from opposing the Democrats.[30]

At Ardabil there was an armed rising of Democrat supporters; the police and gendarmerie surrendered, but in spite of desertions the army garrison held out for some days. Nasrollah Khan of Yortchi offered resistance, killing a number of Democrats and seizing their Soviet-supplied weapons, but he was captured and brought to Ardabil with other chiefs. One army officer, Ruhollah Amir-Fatih, chief of Alarlu, was brutally killed as an example to the Shahsevan. Nosrat Bey Ajirli and Matlab Qoja-Beyli apparently decided to co-operate, and contrived the arrest of the Iranian army's agent for the Shahsevan, Captain Adib-Amini.[31]

By early December the Shahsevan, few of whom were armed, ceased active resistance. With Sarab and Ardabil in their hands, the Democrat forces proceeded against the Iranian units in Meshkin-Shahr. They overcame the gendarmerie, though with heavy loss, and put to death the commander and others. The army barracks surrendered and the officers were killed, as was the captive Adib-Amini soon after; Pesyan specifies, as did my informants, that the Democrats cut off Adib-Amini's finger in order to get his gold ring. There is also a much-told story, whose truth Pesyan denies, of the escape of the gendarmerie commander Ardabili in women's clothes, his subsequent betrayal, capture and murder. Whenever and however he was killed, the Shahsevan avenged his and Adib-Amini's deaths a year later.[32]

For just over a year, the Pishavari regime controlled Azarbaijan, continuing to declare their wish for autonomy, not secession from Iran. At first they attracted considerable support from the farming peasantry and the urban workers, and carried out some social and economic reforms, such as a distribution of land. In some areas, landowners were dispossessed, but the Democrat government now demanded payment of the same dues from the peasants.[33] Most of the Shahsevan tribespeople remained passively hostile, though the Democrats appointed Nosrat Bey Ajirli as

---

[30] Pesyan (1949: 59–61). I was told several stories of the honourable way in which these insults were received by Hatam Bey and the others; see Appendix Three.

[31] Pesyan (1949: 71–6, 101); Safari (1992: 88–90).

[32] Pesyan (1949: 86–8); Safari (1992: 90–2). See Appendix Three. There is a monument to Ardabili, Adib-Amini and other martyrs of the resistance in the precinct of the shrine in Meshkin-Shahr (see Plate 9).   [33] Lambton (1969: 37).

ra'is-e 'ashayer, chief of the Shahsevan. Hatam Khan and most of the other chiefs loyal to the Tehran government managed to avoid further involvement. Arfa claims that there was little he could do from Tehran during the Soviet occupation, except to reinforce the Shahsevan morally.[34]

As a result of diplomatic manoeuvres in Tehran, Moscow and the United Nations, Soviet occupation forces withdrew in May 1946, leaving the Democrat regime on its own.[35] Many of the promised reforms had to be abandoned, and popular support cooled, while Tehran prepared to recover the lost province, supplying the Shahsevan tribes and other loyalists with arms. Iranian troops left for Azarbaijan in December under General Razmara, and quickly reoccupied the province. Already those Democrats who had not escaped to Soviet Azarbaijan were caught and massacred by the populace, the Shahsevan being prominent among the avengers, and when the Iranian troops arrived it was apparently to almost hysterical scenes of welcome.[36] Nosrat Bey, the Democrat-appointed chief of the Shahsevan, was put in prison, where he died a year or two later. Cottam maintains that there was little popular desire in Azarbaijan for separation from Iran; this was probably the case, nevertheless the brief experience of the Democrat regime left a healthy legacy of political and social awareness in the rural as well as the urban population.[37]

Developments from 1946 to 1966[38]

After the War, the Iranian government pursued a modified version of Reza Shah's policies towards the nomad tribes: pastoralism was to continue, but on new terms, with a long-term development policy of planned settlement of nomads, mainly through neglect. Tribal leaders were removed, pastures were nationalized, commercial stock-breeders were allowed to invade – and overgraze – tribal rangelands, while traditional pastoralism was neglected and massive irrigation projects and agro-

---

[34] Arfa (1964: 342).
[35] See Pesyan (1949); Rossow (1956); Cottam (1964: 124–9, 196–9); Avery (1965: 378–401); Fawcett (1992).
[36] Arfa (1964: 368, 378, 380); *Journal de Tehran* of 26.12.1946, quoted in FO 248/1463.
[37] Cottam (1964: 124f.); cf. Philips Price (1946: 195); Lambton (1969: 37, 127); Tapper (1979a: 31).
[38] Apart from my own fieldnotes from research between 1963 (including unpublished notes by Jonathan Parry) and 1966 among Ajirli, Geyikli, Moghanlu, Arabli, Talesh-Mikeilli and some smaller tribes, and settled areas, I have made use of reports by Op't Land, Bessaignet and Rakhshkhorshid, who visited Moghan briefly at various points in 1961 and 1962; various postgraduate theses from the 1950s and early 1960s, mainly in Tabriz University; Sa'edi's book (1965), based on a visit to the region the previous summer; and Schweitzer's articles, based on brief visits to Moghanlu and Geyikli in 1969.

industrial schemes were launched in tribal territories. The government wilfully ignored the contribution pastoral nomads had made to the national economy, notably in exploiting otherwise inaccessible range-lands and supplying meat for the increasingly voracious domestic market.[39]

For the Shahsevan nomads, the most far-reaching changes began in Moghan. In the later 1940s, northeastern Azarbaijan suffered poor harvests and harsh winters. The winter of 1948–9 in particular was catastrophic for the Shahsevan; over 80 per cent of the livestock in Moghan was reported to have perished, including almost all the transport animals, leaving their owners starving and unable to move. Hundred of nomads died; those who had returned to their tents at the end of Reza Shah's reign now had to leave them once more, some making their way to the towns in search of a livelihood, others simply settling in the village bases they had recently founded in Moghan and elsewhere in the north of the region.[40]

Partly in response to this disaster, in 1949 the government transferred some of the Crown Lands of Moghan to the new Plan Organization (PO), for a development and nomad settlement project under the first Seven-Year Plan. Backed by various commercial companies and assured of assistance from the FAO and other bodies, the Azarbaijan Ploughland Company (*Sherkat-e Shiar-e Azarbaijan*) was formed and began mechanized dry-farming in eastern Moghan near what became the settlement of Shah-Abad, on Talesh-Mikeilli, Takleh, Sarvanlar and Jeloudarlu winter pastures.

Rainfall in eastern Moghan proved less than anticipated, and first results were unsatisfactory, so in 1951 PO directed the Company to commence irrigation by the Aras. With a base at 'Ali-Reza-Abad, by 1953 the Company had completed a canal system irrigating some 4,000 hectares, in winter pastures of the Geyikli and Pir-Evatlu tribes. Construction work then started on a larger network, to irrigate a further 28,000 hectares of the winter pastures of the Ajirli, Ja'farli, Petili, Beydili, Guwashlu, Homunlu, 'Arabli, Aivatlu and Takleh tribes; a new centre for the project was established and named Pars-Abad. In 1958 the Shiar Company handed the irrigation project for completion to the independent Organisation du Développement du Dachte Moughan (ODDM), but continued dry-farming activities based on depots at Shah-Abad and Belasovar.

The main canal suffered heavy damage from floods in spring 1962; the following year a chronic shortage of funds, lack of personnel, and deterio-

---

[39] A point made by Stauffer (1965), and much earlier by Abbott (see Chapter Nine).

[40] See FO 248/1492 (various reports, particularly Dr R. H. Burns and V. B. Maitland to Charles F. Bookwalter, 5.5.1949, G.122/19a/49); Douglas (1952: 45).

rating relations between ODDM and PO brought development in Moghan to a standstill. In 1964, the government once more took the scheme over as a project of the Azarbaijan Water and Power Authority. Two years later the engineering works were complete. Unfortunately the water now available was sufficient to irrigate only 18,400 of the projected 32,400 hectares, the deficiency being due to excessive silting and a rapid lowering of the level of the Aras. Meanwhile, agreement was reached with the USSR to build two dams on the Aras, one at Aslanduz and one higher up at Khoda-Afarin, with water to be shared between the two countries.

The irrigated lands were first divided into 12-hectare plots. Application for plots (for sale by instalments) was not restricted to the 1,000-odd nomad families evicted by the project from their winter pastures. Initial response to the project from Shahsevan nomads was slow, and suspicion prevailed. Later, however, particularly after the hard winter of 1963–4, and at the time of Land Reform, the trickle of applications increased to a flood. Even when plots were reduced to six (and later three) hectares, the lists were soon filled, and many applications were rejected pending completion of the later project.

By 1966, 12,500 hectares were distributed to 1,452 farmers in 12- and 6-hectare plots – the remaining land being taken up by buildings, gardens, plantations, roads and irrigation works. A further 2,500 Shahsevan worked as agricultural labourers or were otherwise employed within the project. Not all the farmers or other workers were household heads, nor were all of them of Shahsevan nomad origin, but probably around 3,000 families of Shahsevan ex-nomads were settled in the Moghan irrigation project area.[41]

Soon, work was started on the new Soviet–Iranian project, the Aslanduz diversion dam. This was planned to irrigate the remaining 14,000 hectares of the original project (largely frontier lands between Tazeh-Kand and Belasovar, ceded by the Soviet Union in 1957[42]), as well as another 58,000 hectares of Iranian Moghan; to provide the basis for a major agro-industrial complex; to supply power and other facilities for the whole region; and to allow the settlement of the remaining Shahsevan nomads.

These development schemes meanwhile improved conditions for the nomads still wintering in Moghan and migrating to Savalan summer pastures; in 1966 I estimated these at 5,000–6,000 households (about 40,000 individuals).[43] Along the main canal there were several watering

---

[41] See ODDM (1966), Hawaiian Agronomics (1971), Schweizer (1970, 1974). For an account of settlement processes among the Shahsevan, and of conditions in the ODDM villages, based mainly on research in summer 1963, see Tapper (1972: 821–47); see also Bessaignet (1961), Rakhshkhorshid (1962), Op't Land (1961, 1962).

[42] Cf. Jahanbani (1957).   [43] Tapper (1979a: 269–70).

places where nomads' animals could be brought to drink. The Health Centre in Pars-Abad was open to the nomads for free treatment and cheap medicines. Communications with Meshkin-Shahr, Ardabil and outside the region improved and increased, while the bazaars at Pars-Abad and Belasovar, and shops in many other villages in Moghan, enabled the nomads to make regular purchases of commodities throughout the winter, when they used to be cut off for long periods. With the expansion of government services after the disastrous winter of 1949, the nomads and their flocks survived rather better in two further bad winters, 1955–6 and 1963–4. The Livestock Department station, based near Shah-Abad, for some years successfully reared an experimental flock of sheep, crosses between the Moghani and a Rambouillet strain, taking them every summer to pasture with the Khalfali tribe near Shah-Bel on the slopes of Savalan; they also provided expert veterinary advice and treatment, though these were not much called on, except by neighbouring nomads and in times of disaster.[44]

Government controls on the nomads meanwhile steadily increased. From 1947 to 1963, agents of the Ministry of Finance (then in 1962–3 the Forestry Department, Jangalbani) collected pasture dues for Moghan from the Shahsevan on the spring migration. The collecting agents, with a large escort of soldiers or gendarmes, set up posts on the passes through which the migrating flocks had to pass: Langan, Damdabaja, Salavat. The elder of each nomad community usually went round the previous day to collect payments, making loans where necessary, and delivered the sums due in cash at the collecting post as they passed. The agents relied heavily on the nomads' own estimates of their stock holdings, and it seems that only a small fraction of the payments reached the government. The taxpayer was given a receipt, stating the name of the pasture used, the numbers of animals and the amount of tax paid. After 1963, all pasture dues were abolished and a tax was collected at the slaughterhouses, thus slightly lowering the price the pastoralists received when selling their animals.[45]

In 1963, as part of the Land Reform programme, the government declared the forests (jangal) of Iran to be national property. State-owned

---

[44] For other infrastructural and economic changes in the region affecting the Shahsevan nomads between 1946 and 1966, see Tapper (1979a: 31–3).

[45] The pasture dues and tax rates were as follows (in rials):

	up to 1960	1961–3	from 1964
	(on spring migration)		(in the slaughterhouses)
sheep	5	20	12
goats	4	22	12
cattle	10	45	25
donkeys	5	50	—
horses	30	50	—
camels	50	60	30

range lands such as Moghan and Savalan were regarded as 'forest', and government planned to register ownership and occupation of the pastures (as recorded on the tax receipts) and to ensure their efficient use, probably by a system of grazing permits.[46] The job was given to the Forestry Department, whose officials visited the Shahsevan camps in the mountain pastures that summer and demanded a further payment of grazing dues, giving out further receipts for the pastures occupied there. But the Department did not seem to have the personnel or the experience to undertake the task of registration efficiently or equitably, and they had not completed the job by 1966. Accurate maps were lacking, no one seemed to have a record of any previous registration such as that of the 1880s, and many wealthy chiefs and their families had bribed the officials to register in their own names pastures traditionally owned and used by their followers. Meanwhile, everyone seemed to be awaiting the outcome of Land Reform in the villages. In the event, the Land Reform, and the related nationalization of the range lands, marked the final stage in under-mining of the position of the chiefs.

The twilight of the chiefs

After demonstrating their loyalty to Tehran during the Democrat episode of 1946, the Shahsevan tribes were commended and some of the chiefs received medals. This probably occurred during the Shah's official visit to Ardabil in spring 1947, when large numbers of tribesmen played a major part in the ceremonial reception.[47] Parties of chiefs had visited Tehran earlier that year, and did so again in 1948 when a Tribal Congress was held to discuss political and military questions.[48] One result was the despatch of teachers to set up tented schools among the nomads; few of these lasted more than a year or so among the Shahsevan, the teachers finding the conditions intolerable, but two or three were still being run by educated tribesmen in 1966.[49]

In September 1950, in a further demonstration of their integration into the state, tribal chiefs from all round the country came to Tehran to attend the reinterment ceremonies for Reza Shah. From the Shahsevan came Amir Aslan 'Isalu, Hatam Geyikli, Farzollah Talesh-Mikeilli, Hosein-Aqa Vatandust Alarlu, Mir 'Abd al-Hosein Mansuri Khalfali, Karim Zand Qoja-Beyli, Mir Karim Farzaneh Sadat-Zarenji, Amir

---

[46] For further details, see Tapper (1979a: 273–5).
[47] Described in some detail by Safari (1992: 126–8).
[48] FO 248/1472 (Consul-general in Tabriz to Le Rougetel in Tehran, TG 19 of 29.1.1947); Arfa (1964: 380); Digard (1979: 45).
[49] Cf. Barker (1981) on tented schools among the Qashqa'i tribes.

Khaz'al Yortchi, Farman Shoja'i Reza-Beyli and Büyük Amir-Fatih Alarlu.[50]

For some years, while tension continued on the frontier, the tribesmen retained their arms – the chiefs were each given a stock of rifles, to be used only when authorized by the *elbey*, an army colonel responsible for the collection of taxes and for mobilizing the tribes in case of war. Two junior officers were appointed to each tribe as 'supervisors' (*sarparast*); based on Meshkin-Shahr, they paid regular visits to the tribes, to help the solution of inter-tribal disputes. The chiefs continued to mediate all political or administrative contacts, and remained responsible for order within their tribes and for the collection of taxes.

A chief might adjudicate in cases involving theft, pasture trespass or personal assault between different sections, but section elders usually decided disputes within the tribe, avoiding the chief's involvement, which tended to be expensive. When a plaintiff (or his elder) brought a case before the chief, he had to provide a substantial 'present' (*rüshvät*) in cash or kind, besides witnesses prepared to support him and to swear on the Koran. The chief summoned the accused, and if he could not produce a satisfactory defence (or present), he was liable to a fine or beating or both, carried out by the chief's henchmen. In the case of theft, the chief would also undertake investigations if necessary, and the thief would have to produce double the value of the stolen goods, half to be taken by the chief and his detectives. Mullahs might be consulted in inheritance and property disputes; homicide, and matters of family or community honour, could be decided by revenge killings, followed by reconciliation and compensation arranged by the chief, but inter-tribal disputes of this nature were more likely to attract the intervention of the 'supervisors' or the gendarmerie.

Apart from payments of 'expenses' incurred when travelling on behalf of their followers, and 'presents' received when cases were brought to them, at New Year the chiefs traditionally received a lamb or wether from every extended family within the tribe and often from other followers. In many tribes, the chief's permission was sought for every marriage, and he would expect a handsome present (customarily a stallion) before a wedding could be held. He would be on visiting terms with most section elders and sometimes other commoners, and he or a member of his family would attend their feasts and contribute to the expenses.[51] As there was no longer any commission attached to the collection of taxes, chiefs left this duty to the elders. Nor did they receive a salary for other official

---

[50] Listed in FO 248/1506 (Chancery to Consulates, 28.9.1950, P.88/10/50).
[51] Cf. Tapper (1979a: esp. 150–2) on *kheirüshärr* networks.

jobs performed on behalf of the authorities. Nevertheless, the rewards of chiefship were such that, when a chief died, there continued to be some rivalry over the succession, and the authorities, the chiefly family and the commoners sometimes proposed different candidates. The new chief was almost always a close agnate of his predecessor, while the authorities sought to appoint one acceptable to at least the majority of his followers.

Beyond the rewards of office, the chiefs based their power on ownership of farmland, pasture and flocks. As recounted earlier, they seized control of the villages of the region in the early years of the century. Though many of the previous landowners or their relatives recovered their property after the disarmament, and officials and others bought land in the region legally, nomad chiefs and elders retained control of many villages and often secured legal ownership of more. Some chiefs had shares totalling ten or more villages, while many elders had at least one or two 'sixths' (aqcha, dang). The annual income for an absentee landowner was reckoned to average up to 5,000 toman (£250) per sixth. Some nomad landowners built houses in villages where they held a majority share, but after the enforced settlement no Shahsevan landowner (to my knowledge) voluntarily resided in a village other than a settlement of his own tribespeople. Tat (i.e. non-Shahsevan) tenants were left to the supervision of a bailiff, or sometimes a member of the landowner's family, the landowner himself visiting irregularly if at all. The Tat population, often suffering extortion and oppression, remained alien to the chiefs and the nomads. Their resentment was enlivened by their experience of socialist ideas during the Democrat interlude – at least one Shahsevan landowner was killed by village tenants in the following decades.

A second source of power for the Shahsevan chiefs was grazing rights, a marketable commodity among the Shahsevan since at least the mid-nineteenth century. Chiefs and members of their families always controlled more pastures than they needed for their own flocks, partly allotted to them in the 1880s, partly bought by recognized transactions, partly seized. We saw earlier how the most powerful chiefs secured the best Moghan pastures for themselves in the years before disarmament, evicting weaker groups and demanding payments from others. Afterwards, the previous distribution was largely restored, and most nomads enjoyed some security of tenure, paying dues only to government. But when groups of nomads settled, it was usually their chiefs who were able to afford to buy up – or seize – their grazing rights. Chiefs would make their surplus available for rent, sometimes to landless members of their own tribe, sometimes to outsiders or commercial stock-raisers.[52]

---

[52] For further details see Tapper (1979a: Appendix IV).

The third base to the chiefs' power was their wealth in livestock. In spite of vulnerability to climatic disaster, flocks were a more productive and less troublesome resource than land, and less subject to government restrictions. After the War, government improved veterinary services, communications and facilities for marketing stock, wool and dairy produce. Many nomads took advantage of these developments, and the more powerful chiefs all owned flocks of considerable size, often several thousand head, which they entrusted to camps (*binä*) of hired herdsmen, supervised by junior relatives. As the herding camps followed the most pleasant climate, even those chiefs whose economy was largely based on farming liked to spend many months of the year with their main herding camp, which they regarded as home.

In 1956 the government gave greater powers to the army officers responsible for the tribes; the chiefs continued to co-operate, though now in a definitely subordinate role.[53] Then in 1960 the chiefly titles Bey and Khan were (again) formally abolished, as was the position of *elbey*, and the nomads were transferred from the control of the army to that of the gendarmerie, who were to deal directly with the nomads or their community elders, as they did with villagers and their headmen. The army continued to garrison the frontier until 1963–4, when the gendarmerie took over that duty too. After that, the tribes had few dealings with the army; the garrison at Belasovar was responsible for conscription, for which it dealt with the nomad elders. Government policy in the 1960s seemed to be to integrate the Shahsevan fully into the national administration. But the need for mediation in dealings between authorities and nomads, particularly those of a judicial or political nature, continued to be felt by both sides. Individual nomads were usually quite helpless and ignorant when faced by the mysteries and demands of the bureaucracy, while officials continued to be unable to contact the nomads conveniently without the aid of known Shahsevan leaders – though they knew the location of the main tribes and chiefs, they still did not always know the lands of sections and elders.

For most purposes the key role was played by the elders; many of them, however, felt the duties and expenses demanded of them, especially those involving contacts with officials, to be beyond their own abilities and resources, and they would try to enlist the assistance of more influential elders and sometimes their former chief as patron and mediator. Several chiefs retained control of much of the resources on which their power had been based, and remained men of influence in the region. Not surpris-

---

[53] All the chiefs had official appointments, such as that recently published relating to Savad Jahangirzadeh's chiefship of the Beydili, confirmed in 1957 by Col. Niknam, *sarparast* of the tribes of Shahsevan and Arasbaran (Begdili 1988: 513).

ingly both authorities and nomads continued to call on their mediatory services, though the extent to which chiefs responded to this call depended largely on the extent to which their own economic interests were now involved.

Rights in village farmlands and surplus pastures had continued to be a profitable and secure investment for wealthy nomads until the Land Reform of the 1960s, when absentee landowners were compelled to sell holdings above a total of one village, and to adjust their relations with the cultivating peasants in the holdings they retained. Implementation of the reforms was uneven, but generally in this region the power of the land-owners was effectively broken.[54] At the same time, the range-lands were nationalized, and despite various subterfuges attempted by many wealth-ier nomads, grazing rights seemed unlikely to be a source of income for much longer.[55]

In the mid-1960s, several leading Shahsevan chiefs were running busi-ness empires based on a combination of these resources, and were said to have annual incomes of hundreds of thousands of tomans, placing them among the wealthiest men in the region. With such incomes they could easily maintain the high level of consumption and expenditure expected of them as tribal leaders. At the same time, they still had direct control over the livelihood and activities of large numbers of people apart from their own families: employees, household servants and herdsmen. These all depended on their employer-chief, not simply for access to resources, but also for political patronage. All chiefs were prepared to perform small acts of patronage for their followers, such as writing to officials or other chiefs, and mediating in any disputes that were brought to them. Though they no longer had formal sanctions and could not demand 'presents' for these services, payment was usually provided in some form by their clients. But not all chiefs were now willing to spend time and money to travel and make personal visits on behalf of tribal followers. None of the chiefs now received New Year visits and presents from their followers on the same scale as they were reputed to have done formerly; nor did their followers ask permission for marriages, except when there was some immediate political purpose to be achieved by doing so. The more power-ful chiefly families were said to be similarly remiss at performing their former social obligations to their followers.

Wealthy chiefs whose resources consisted mainly of pasture and farm-land located near the camps and settlements of their followers, continued to play an active and prominent role in their political affairs. They did so

---

[54] On Land Reform in this region, see Tapper (1979a: 28–34); Lambton (1969: 100–1).
[55] On the nationalization of the range-lands here, see Tapper (1979a: 273–5).

largely for self-interest: to maintain conditions of security in the vicinity of their own resources. A few other wealthy chiefs deliberately opted out of local political affairs, having interests remote from their tribal lands, so that former followers found it hard to involve them in their affairs. Less wealthy chiefs, living near or among their followers, having lost their official position, often continued to be regarded as principal elders of the tribes; in several cases they asked minor patronage services of a nearby prominent chief to whom their tribe was formerly subordinated as part of a tribal cluster.

A chief no longer had the authority to decide disputes within his tribe. Criminal and civil cases of all kinds were supposedly matters for elders and gendarmerie, and no concern of the chief. The actual procedure of dispute settlement within a tribe varied with the position of the chief. If he was prominent, few non-criminal disputes would ever reach the gendarmerie. It often also depended on the relation between the parties concerned whether a dispute was allowed to reach the gendarmes' notice. Commonly, matters involving parties who were previously on good terms could be decided to mutual satisfaction without proceeding further than a meeting between the elders concerned. A mediator might be called in, perhaps a Hajji from an uninvolved section, or the chief, or a member of his family. In other cases, where a complaint of theft or trespass, for example, was a symptom of hostile relations between those involved, the plaintiff might go straight to the gendarmes and cause considerable difficulty and expense for his opponents; these would have recourse to their chief or other patron, who might be prepared to complete a dossier for the gendarmes, putting the case as seen by both sides. In more serious disputes, or where local gendarmes were clearly biassed, influential chiefs wrote letters over the heads of local officials.

In disputes involving members of two tribes, the chiefs might communicate by visit or letter, and all could then be settled between them. In criminal cases, the chiefs prepared a dossier and handed it over to the gendarmes with the offenders. In such cases, the plaintiff did not go straight to the gendarmes, since he knew his opponent would anyway call in his own chief or patron, and that the gendarmes too would work through the latter. The same kinds of processes occurred in disputes involving nomads and villagers. When the gendarmes did receive a complaint, they were expected to investigate the affair by interrogation, but unless the chief of the tribe was very far away his permission was asked first, if only as a matter of courtesy, and he probably helped in the investigation and compilation of dossiers. If an arrest was made, the prisoners were taken to jail in Meshkin-Shahr to await a hearing. Normally the prisoner's elder, and sometimes chief, took steps to provide legal assistance and other support.

Material and political incentives for chiefs to act as mediators and representatives nowhere approached their former scale. They were able and willing to act vigorously only in cases where their own interests were more or less directly involved, or where they had a chance of demonstrating and reinforcing their influential contacts in the region or province.[56]

Ordinary nomads told me that, when chiefs were responsible for order, theft and petty crime had been rare, as offenders were easily detected and caught and sanctions were both heavy and arbitrary. Now, in affairs where high authority was involved, the State was in firm control: activities such as banditry and raiding were quite out of the question and cases of homicide were speedily dealt with. Otherwise, tribesmen generally felt that, though they had benefited from the removal of the more autocratic and oppressive chiefs, law and order had deteriorated, largely through the incompetence and corruption of the local gendarmerie; dealing with them was just as expensive as was dealing with the chiefs, and usually less effective. They felt particularly exposed to the wayward demands for taxes on their animals and to increasing threats to their pastures by government or government-supported companies and individuals.

On paper, by 1966 the tribal system had ceased to exist along with the abolition of the chiefs. Among themselves, up to twenty active and influential former chiefs and their close kinsmen formed a loose elite, linked extensively but not exclusively by marriage and other social ties. They employed many servants and workers to tend their flocks, farm their land, and keep their households; they maintained houses in Ardabil, Meshkin-Shahr or Ahar. They owned motor vehicles; their sons and sometimes daughters were educated through twelve grades of school and some went on to University, sometimes abroad. They or their sons travelled regularly to Tabriz and Tehran; some sons of chiefs active in the region became Army officers or took other prestigious jobs, but most returned after their education to take up a pre-arranged role in the family business, as supervisor of flocks or farmland, or as secretary or personal assistant. These chiefs associated on equal terms with the regional elite (landowners, businessmen, senior officials), who were invited to the extravagant entertainments and feasting which the chiefs provided at the weddings and circumcisions of their children. Such chiefly feasts to some extent kept alive notions of tribal identity, yet the audience at whom the

---

[56] At several points in my fieldwork between 1963 and 1966 I followed and sometimes took part in the activities of chiefs, notably those of Ajirli and Geyikli. I observed the progress and eventual resolution of a number of major disputes in which those chiefs took leading roles, and which involved members of their own and other tribes and officials of the local, regional and sometimes the provincial levels of the gendarmerie and administration.

display was aimed was no longer the tribespeople, rather the elite guests to whose respect the chiefs aspired.

Meetings of Shahsevan elders (*aq-saqal*) were sometimes called to discuss important regional or national issues, or to represent the Shahsevan on ceremonial occasions; the elders concerned included the elite former chiefs, as well as the wealthier and more influential leaders of tribal sections or section clusters. But among the wealthiest of the chiefs were three or four men, widely recognized as the 'elders of the chiefs' (*beylärin aq-saqallari*): Hajji Hatam Geyikli, Fazlollah Pasha'i Talesh-Mikeilli (d. 1965), Qotaz Shahin Ajirli, and sometimes Sa'id Khan Hajji-Khojalu and Hosein Aqa Vatandust Arallu. These chiefs maintained close contacts with influential officials and others in Tabriz and Tehran, and acted as representatives and spokesmen for the Shahsevan on ceremonial occasions, such as Royal visits. Each had a following of client tribes for whom he was prepared to perform acts of patronage. There were several other chiefs, often of quite small tribes, who were nearly their equals in resources and influence, while some large tribes, such as Moghanlu and Qoja-Beyli, were without effective leadership.

Postscript: 1966–95

The last decade of Pahlavi rule brought a rapid decline in Shahsevan pastoral nomadism, hit by hostile government policies and an unfavourable market for pastoral produce. In 1971, government entrusted the agro-industrial development of Moghan to the Hawaiian Agronomics Company and the Agronomics Company of Iran. Shortly after, the Aslanduz dam and the new canal system were completed, and a total of 90,000 hectares of the plain were now under irrigation. On 42,000 hectares (including the older project lands), the farmer-owners were now formed into nine Agricultural Companies, with nearly 4,000 shareholders. The remaining irrigated area (48,400 hectares) was transferred to the new Moghan Agro-Industrial Company (*Sherkat-e Kesht va San'at-e Moghan* – KSM), evicting a further 1800 Shahsevan nomad families, mainly from the large tribes Geyikli, Ajirli and Moghanlu, from their winter pastures.

The best winter pastures had now disappeared under the canals. Many of the remaining nomads were in conflict with KSM and other groups and individuals who were scrambling for advantage in the booming development in Moghan. They also faced problems elsewhere in their habitat. Issued with grazing permits for Moghan and Savalan, they lost security of tenure and the right to cultivate their pastures, while the expansion of village agriculture along the migration routes deprived them of grazing and campsites. Increasing numbers of nomads met this threat by abandoning their camels and hiring trucks, trailers and pickups to transport their homes and animals. Disputes grew bitter with village farmers who were demanding exclusive use of water from springs in the higher pastures, and cultivating the lower mountain pastures.

Studies such as that done by Hawaiian Agronomics for the Livestock Organization had shown such highland cultivation to be uneconomic, demonstrated the continuing pastoral potential of the whole region, and recommended that livestock raising and fodder production be integrated with irrigated agriculture. Moghan and Savalan each offered 300,000 hectares of usable pasture, with a seasonal capacity of 1.5 million sheep units.[57] Unfortunately, government was not interested in the development of pastoralism. By the mid-1970s, following the oil boom, they undermined the Iranian livestock economy by subsidizing imports of meat and dairy products. This was partly offset by the fact that grain prices were also subsidized, but large numbers of former pastoral nomads were impoverished and settled, and many joined the mass migration to the cities. There was an official Organization for Mobile Pastoralists (*Sazman-e Damdaran-e Motaharrek*), but its brief is evident from the fact that it was part of the Ministry of Housing and Urban Development; in Azarbaijan, it had neither resources nor personnel, and I could discover nothing that it had achieved for the nomads, who were largely bypassed by developments elsewhere in rural infrastructure and services. In Moghan, in the years leading the Islamic Revolution of 1978–9, alleged corruption and collusion between former chiefs, gendarmes, Livestock and Forestry Department officials and directors of KSM brought a polarization of wealth and power which reflected the situation elsewhere in the country.[58]

Tribes were considered to have ceased to exist as a political element in Iranian society, while the pastoral nomads were marginalized to the extent that they could be regarded as colourful, folkloric relics from the past, a tourist attraction. The Pahlavi regime's defeat of the nomads and other minorities was celebrated in the Festival of Popular Traditions held in October 1977 in Esfahan, in which nomadic cultures were taken out of their social and especially political contexts and displayed in public as museum pieces – a 'culture bazaar', as one Iranian anthropologist has described it.[59] Shahsevan culture was not prominent on this occasion, which was dominated by the local Bakhtiari and other Zagros tribal groups, and no Shahsevan troupe took part in the public displays of

[57] Hawaiian Agronomics (1971).   [58] See e.g. Taimaz (1979: 35f.).
[59] Shahshahani (1986: 75–6). Cf. Beck (1982).

'tribal dancing' which caused such an uproar at the time. On the whole, the Shahsevan would have escaped the 'marketing' to which groups such as the Qashqa'i were subjected in the 1970s, but for the fact that the international Oriental Carpet trade had recently recognized that a whole category of what had previously been regarded as 'Kurdish' or 'Caucasian' tribal weavings were in fact the product of Shahsevan nomads.[60]

The Islamic Revolution of 1978–9 was largely an urban phenomenon, and Shahsevan nomads themselves played little part.[61] Settled tribespeople did participate in events in towns such as Meshkin-Shahr. Revolutionary elements killed three of the former chiefs in the fighting; others fled the region and some the country. There were clashes in Moghan where many Shahsevan, both nomad and settled, occupied KSM farmlands, demanding restoration of their former pastures, or a greater say in the organization of KSM. In spring 1979, a delegation of 400 Shahsevan elders from 30 different tribes went to Qom to pay their respects to Ayatollahs Khomeini and Shari'at-Madari, with a list of requests: abolition of the Forestry Department, purging of the gendarmes, the nomads to be given the right to cultivate their lands, improved facilities for both pastoralists and farmers, including health, education, credit and roads; the response from Shari'at-Madari was confined to condemnation of the seizure of KSM property.[62] However, some KSM land was officially returned to Shahsevan nomads and villagers, while more of it remained under their occupation; meanwhile, the nine Agricultural Companies were disbanded and their lands reverted to individual plots in control of the original farmer-owners. The Shahsevan were officially renamed 'Elsevan', literally 'those who love the people (or tribe)'.[63] The nomads themselves never accepted the new name, however, and by 1992 it was no longer widely used officially.

I visited Shahsevan territory in summer 1993 after an interval of twenty years, and then in November 1995. Many changes were evident. Ardabil was a city of a quarter of a million, and the capital of a newly created province of the same name. In Moghan, KSM was forging ahead, backed by the Ministry of Agriculture, who in 1986 transferred a further 18,000 hectares of Moghanlu and Ajirli winter pastures, apparently acquired by the Ministry twenty years before, to the new Pars Agro-Industrial Company (*Sherkat-e Kesht-o-San'at-e Pars* – KSP). Four factories were in

---

[60] See especially Housego (1978). More recent works devoted to Shahsevan textiles include Tanavoli (1985), Azadi and Andrews (1985).   [61] As elsewhere in Iran: cf. Beck (1980).

[62] Taimaz (1979: 36–7); Beck (1986: 320); Safizadeh (1984: 18).

[63] This conformed with post-revolutionary rejection of all mention of 'Shah' in names of places or groups; though it is not clear to me why one of the usual religious substitutes was not chosen, such as 'Imam' or 'Islam'.

operation in Moghan, producing sunflower oil, processing sugar-beet, pasteurizing milk and ginning cotton. Pars-Abad, now the centre of a new sub-province, had become the second largest town in the province, with a population of over 30,000, and there were two 'new towns' (*shahrak*) in the project area, constructed on the model of an American subdivision. Work on the Khoda-Afarin dam, and its massive further irrigation network, had stalled as the Soviet Union crumbled and war broke out between the Republics of Azerbaijan and Armenia.

The Islamic Republic has seen a revival in the fortunes of the nomadic tribes. Ayatollah Khomeini declared them to be one of two sectors of the population (the other being the Mullahs) particularly oppressed by the previous regime. He termed them Treasures of the Revolution (*Zakhayer-e Enqelab*), and the fourth Armed Force; officially they are considered to have had a vital historical role in protecting the independence and territorial integrity of the country. Special efforts have been made to foster their social, economic and cultural life and to make sure that they have the same facilities as the rest of the population. This has been largely the responsibility of the Organization for Nomadic Affairs (ONA – *Sazman-e Omur-e 'Ashayer*), since 1983 part of the new Ministry of Jehad/Rural Reconstruction (*Jehad-e Sazandegi*, MOJ). At the provincial level, where it is staffed partly by members of the tribes, ONA provides infrastructural services and organizes local and regional representation of the nomads. Other services for nomads, such as health, education, security and the control of pasture-lands, are organized through other Ministries, though the basic groundwork is done by ONA.

The continuation of nomadic pastoralism still has its advocates in some quarters. By 1993, however, settlement was again firmly on the government agenda, and many nomads themselves were said to be keen on settlement in some form; it was promoted as strongly as ever by traditionalists in Plan Organization, Ministry of Agriculture and MOJ.[64] These important changes in official attitudes were accompanied by economic, social and demographic changes at the national level that have affected nomads such as the Shahsevan.

The government had decided firmly that the future of Moghan is cultivation and industry, and that Shahsevan nomads must 'settle'. The local ONA, acting as the pastoralists' guardian (*motavalli*) in a losing battle with the Ministry of Agriculture, KSM and KSP over Moghan lands and the future of the Shahsevan, had made great progress in their own plans for 'settlement': the remaining winter pasture-lands were

---

[64] See Tapper (1994). ONA also conducts research, which it publishes in books and reports, and in the interesting quarterly journal *Zakhayer-e Enqelab*, started in 1987.

divided into nine pastoral habitats (*zist-bum*), each with a central base (*istgah*) in which were located power and water supply, bath-house, communications centre, health clinic, school and other facilities. MOJ had driven tracks from the centre to each winter campsite in the habitat, and ONA planned to allow the nomads to stay in their campsites or, if they wanted, to come and settle at the centre. These bases came into full operation in 1995.

Roads were also a prominent feature of ONA activity elsewhere in Shahsevan territory: jeepable tracks now reach the most inaccessible parts of the Savalan mountains. In regions of the country inhabited by more independent-minded tribes, this penetration clearly facilitates government control, but the Shahsevan nomads see it positively, as allowing them to perform the whole migration by motor-transport; the camels are now almost all gone. ONA also sells cheaper and more durable canvas tents, and runs stores and veterinary stations near both winter and summer quarters; they have also encouraged enterprises aimed at improving the marketing of pastoral produce. Improvements to the system of grazing permits are also planned, to give the nomads more security of tenure and more responsibility for conservation.

In the 1990s Shahsevan pastoral nomadism persisted in radically changed and changing conditions. Many of the old problems continued, such as encroachment by farmers on their summer pastures, and government-subsidized imports of meat and cheese,[65] but by 1995 pastoralism had became very profitable. Prices received for pastoral produce had increased faster than costs. In 1987, the Shahsevan sold sheep for about 7,000 toman a head; in 1995 they could get 30,000 toman. Milk fetched 75 toman a kilogram in 1994, 110 toman in 1995. Partly as a result, and despite substantial spontaneous settlement and urban migration following both the huge population increase in Iran and the general pressures on the Shahsevan territories, numbers of both nomads and their animals have increased. In the 1987 census of nomads, the Shahsevan numbered 5,897 families, more than they did a quarter of a century earlier;[66] and by 1995 there were 7,800 Shahsevan families registered with the ONA – though many of these were at least semi-settled.

Most of the former chiefs, consistently opposed by government (including ONA) as exploiters of the nomads under the Pahlavis, were

---

[65] I heard these complaints in 1993, as did Janebolahi (1991–2) on a tour of the summer pastures in early summer 1989; cf. Shahsevand-Baghdadi (1991).

[66] Cf. my estimate of 5,000–6,000 families for 1966, and those of Taj-Gardun (1959) of 4,800 families and Sadeq (1961) of 5,500 for the later 1950s; cf. Tigranov's estimate (1909) of 5,925 nomad families for 1903. In comparing these remarkably similar figures, some allowance must be made for different criteria for inclusion.

gone – though in the late 1980s, when capitalism became respectable again, some members of chiefly families quietly resumed their former economic activities in farming and livestock enterprises. Leadership among the nomads in the 1990s was negotiated between community elders and ONA officials. Significantly, as noted in Chapter One, official definitions of nomad tribes now omitted any reference to chiefs, and focused on pastoral production, seasonal migrations, and sentiments of kinship.[67] Among the Shahsevan, significantly, despite all the economic and political changes, the tribe (*taifa*) and the tribal section (*tira*) continued to be the main pastoral nomadic communities recognized by both the tribespeople themselves and the government, as will be shown in the final chapter.

[67] Tapper (1994). Accounts in English of nomadic life under the Islamic Republic are still few; cf. Beck (1992). In Persian several, including accounts of various visits to the Shahsevan, have appeared in *Zakhayer-e Enqaleb*; and see Shahsevand-Baghdadi (1991).

14   Conclusion: Shahsevan identity and history

On ethnicity and identity

In the opening chapter I showed how anthropologists have failed to agree on a substantive definition of 'tribe', arguing that as an analytical concept it is best used – and best matches indigenous concepts – for a 'state of mind', a mode of social organization essentially opposed to that of a centralized state. Some of the problems anthropologists have had with the concept of 'tribe' are echoed in debates over concepts of 'ethnicity' and 'identity'. I do not intend to review those debates here, but only to make clear my own perspective, which is the same as that employed in the discussion of 'tribe'.[1]

One dominant approach to 'ethnic groups' in history and anthropology has conceived them to be, or to approximate, bio-genetically self-perpetuating populations, whose members share elements of a common culture, identify themselves and are identified by others as a separate category. This 'primordialist' approach, fundamentally positivist and objectivist, is a refinement of an older anthropological tradition in which 'cultures' were treated as co-terminous with 'tribes', 'societies', 'peoples'. Even if adherents of this approach do not all take the genetic assumptions too literally, they still present populations as divided into formally bounded, clear-cut, ethnic groups, with every person belonging to one: a conception that facilitates tidy maps, neat lists of the traits associated with each group, a rigorous classification of types, and cross-cultural comparison.

The flaws in such a conception have become increasingly clear, not least its disregard for the identity claims of the populations concerned and for other cleavages such as those of class that might divide those populations. Worse, the search for accurate statistics and maps of 'ethnic groups' reflects an academic (and political) desire for order, with the danger that order thus created will be taken as real and authoritative, that a group so identified and located will become fixed, and that members

[1] Tapper (1988a, 1988b); cf. other chapters in Digard (1988). There is a huge and expanding literature, which more often pairs 'ethnicity' with 'nationalism'.

315

will be expected to conform and subjected to categorical policies of control – as shown in extreme form by many twentieth-century tragedies.

There has been for some time, however, a shift in conceptions and approaches, from a concern with ethnic groups as objectively apprehended divisions of a population, to a more subjective, cultural approach to ethnicity as one of a number of possible discourses on identity. Statistics and maps can only ever be very rough guides; this reflects not so much 'inaccuracies', as the reality of differing definitions of the identity being counted or mapped. There are no 'true' figures or boundaries. Earlier representations of the Middle East depicted a 'mosaic' distribution of peoples and cultures. Another model, particularly favoured in discussions of the post-war Middle East, was that of the 'melting pot'. Both have proved quite misleading. 'Ethnic' and other identities and distinctions are neither fixed as implied in the notion of the mosaic, nor declining as implied by the idea of the melting-pot. Rather, those who claim them or attribute them to others are constantly reproducing, renegotiating and redefining them in order to cope with new circumstances, opportunities and challenges.

The essence of ethnic labels and of conceptions of ethnicity is that they cannot be pinned down 'scientifically' by maps and lists of traits and attributes, but that they are ambiguous and shifting materials for the construction and manipulation of identity, by the people concerned, by their 'Others', by administrators, and by historians and anthropologists. Ethnic, tribal and other identities (religion, language, kinship, gender, occupation, region, class, nationality . . .) are essentially negotiable, changing, multiple and flexible. The ascription of an 'ethnic' identity to a group or individual varies with the speaker, the audience and the context. Ethnic groups do not 'exist' objectively, but rather all groups and associations display, to a greater or lesser extent, features commonly associated with 'ethnicity': a tendency to endogamy, and self-definition with reference to common values and traditions.

In other words, the initial question asked in a historical or anthropological discussion of any given population – who are they? – is far from unproblematic. We cannot simply accept a previous classification originating in some archive or administrative handbook. We have to allow that the people concerned, as well as those who have observed or written about them, may produce a wide range of answers; that different answers may come from different classes, genders and other categories of the population.

Such a perspective does not identify or distinguish between 'tribe' and 'ethnic group'; further, it acknowledges any use of the epithets 'ethnic' or 'tribal' as a political statement which defines the speaker and their relation to their audience as much as it defines the group or individuals so labelled. Similarly, it identifies the categories 'tribalism' and 'ethnicity' as ideological concepts and disqualifies them from analytical usage. The same disqualification applies to the use of any particular name for a population.

This perspective is necessary when attempting to understand the complexities of historical representations and identities of a population such as the Shahsevan. The Shahsevan are not a 'tribe', nor are they an 'ethnic group' in any conventional sense: they are of heterogeneous origins and have no ideology of common descent, they are not politically unified or distinct, and they share religion and language with neighbouring non-Shahsevan. What constitutes Shahsevan identity – apart from the name – appears to have changed over time, and to vary according to a number of factors.

In my earlier monograph I discussed in detail what it meant to belong to a basic nomadic community among the Shahsevan. The present book has been concerned with the history of larger communities, often more 'imagined' than experienced:[2] tribes (*taifa*), tribal clusters, the Shahsevan confederacy as a whole, and their respective chiefs. This concluding chapter discusses the elements of identity involved in membership of the larger collectivities, first by relating the different versions of Shahsevan origins to different constructions of their identity and the political history of the confederacy, secondly by investigating the reasons for the remarkable continuity displayed by the different *taifa*, and finally by exploring some of the implications of this study for debates over the relationship between tribal societies and wider, state-level political processes.

The Shahsevan confederacy: contested origins, political change

As we saw in Part I, by the twentieth century the Shahsevan tribes had acquired three different versions of the origins of the confederacy in the Moghan and Ardabil region: Malcolm's story of the foundation of a special tribe by the Safavid Shah 'Abbas; the traditions relating Yunsur Pasha's immigration from Anatolia and the unification of the tribes under his kinsman Badr Khan, henchman of Nader Shah Afshar; and the current dogma of thirty-two independent tribes with no central authority.

These different versions of Shahsevan origins are reflected in differing constructions of their identity, by themselves and by observers of their political behaviour. Moreover, various authors, mainly Russian and most

[2] Anderson (1983).

with some personal acquaintance with the Shahsevan, have offered widely differing reconstructions of Shahsevan history. Earlier chapters have examined the documentation used in their accounts; here I consider the assumptions behind them and how far they illuminate or are illuminated by the historical sources on the one hand and Shahsevan culture and self-identifications on the other.

From royalists to bandits

Those who 'know' the Shahsevan only from knowing the meaning of their name and the 'official' myth of their origins are led to associate them with a royalist ideology and to judge their behaviour and identity in later periods accordingly. But they rarely consider how far the original loyalty was solely to Shah 'Abbas, or whether it was extended to the Safavi dynasty or more generally to the Iranian state or to Shi'ism; and they do not ask how the Shahsevan might have been expected to behave towards other tribal dynasties (Afshars, Zands, Qajars) or the Russians, factors not present in Shah 'Abbas' time. Nor do they relate the supposed politico-religious ideology of the Shahsevan to their social and economic circumstances as pastoral nomads.

Historians who accept the official version of Shahsevan's origins, as a tribe formed by Shah 'Abbas with special loyalty to himself, inevitably see his period as the Shahsevan heyday. They point to various actions recorded of the Shahsevan since as indicating a sad degeneration, a betrayal of their name. As it happens, the three sets of incidents most commonly referred to, which occurred in the early decades of the eighteenth, nineteenth and twentieth centuries, all involved Shahsevan relations with the Russians. In all cases, a verdict of degeneration and disloyalty, apart from ignoring possible causes, is an unjustified distortion and oversimplification.

The first event, recounted in Chapter Two, was Tahmasp Mirza's unsuccessful appeal (according to Krusinski) in 1722 to the reserve militia, for help against the Afghan invaders. In the English translation of Krusinski's memoirs, the militia is called 'Shahsevan'; this was reproduced soon after by de Clairac and Hanway, and was one probable source of Malcolm's notion of the Shahsevan as a 'special tribe'. Without citing a source, Malcolm also refers to the Shahsevan as failing Tahmasp Mirza. Sykes too, no doubt relying on Malcolm, writes in his equally widely read *History* that 'even the Shah Savan tribe was false to its oath'.[3]

This may well be a calumny. For one thing, as argued in Chapter Five,

---

[3]   Malcolm (1815: 637); Sykes (1930, II: 318); *Gazetteer* (1914, II: 554).

the 'reserve militia' probably referred, not to the Shahsevan in particular, but rather to Qızılbash land-holders in general. Further, at the time of the appeal, the Shahsevan of Moghan and Ardabil were in the direct path of advancing Ottoman and Russian armies, in no position to send relief to the beleaguered Safavid ruler at Esfahan. Thirdly, if the name Shahsevan implied loyalty to the Safavid Shahs, as argued in Chapter Seven, it also represented two other linked values: fidelity to Shi'ism and opposition to the Sunni Ottomans. In fact, in the later 1720s, when Ardabil and much of Moghan were occupied by Ottomans, contemporary chronicles indicate that the local Shahsevan and other tribal groups rose repeatedly against them in the Safavid name, and, when finally defeated in 1728, rather than surrender to the arch-enemies of the Safavid Shahs, some at least of the Shahsevan took refuge across the Kor river in territory newly occupied by the Russians. When Nader Afshar recovered this a few years later for Tahmasp Safavi, the Shahsevan duly resumed allegiance. In other words, the known behaviour of the Shahsevan in the 1720s indicates extreme loyalty to the Safavids, in conformity with their name, but contrary to the influential image purveyed by Malcolm and Sykes.

The second occasion of 'betrayal' was during the Russo–Iranian Wars of the early nineteenth century. After Agha Mohammad Khan established the Qajar dynasty in the 1790s, Russian forces returned to Transcaucasia and the Shahsevan were again in the thick of a major international conflict. Between 1806 and 1828, as narrated in Chapter Eight, Shahsevan warriors fought valiantly on many occasions, both in defence of their own pasturelands and in the Qajar army elsewhere. Eventually, however, following two Russian expeditions into their territory in the winters of 1826–7 and 1827–8, the Meshkin chiefs surrendered, provided the invaders with supplies and even harried the Iranian army.

This defection, recorded in numerous accounts, established a stereotype of the Shahsevan as unreliable frontier guards and bandits. Although the tribesmen did much in the ensuing decades to confirm at least their reputation as bandits, it must be remembered that the Ardabil chiefs had remained loyal to the Qajars, that the Meshkin chiefs gave in only under duress, and that those who blame them for this and their subsequent lawlessness give no consideration to their motivations, of which we have no knowledge, but among which must have been economic factors such as loss of control of their winter quarters, and rapacious demands by Qajar officials.

We should remember, too, that, after the fall of the Safavid dynasty and the subsequent formation of the Shahsevan tribal confederacy in Moghan and Ardabil by Nader Afshar, the relevance of the three original

Shahsevan values (loyalty to the Safavids, fidelity to Shi'ism, and opposition to the Sunni Ottomans) would have rapidly decreased. At the time Russia annexed Moghan, none of those values could have provided unambiguous ideological guidance for the tribes' political behaviour. Nothing is known of Shahsevan motivations and religious inclinations in the eighteenth century, but the Safavid mystique persisted for some time: Nader Shah Afshar was possibly still acting in the Safavid name when he made Badr Khan chief of the Shahsevan; Karim Khan Zand claimed to be a deputy for the Safavids; among Safavid pretenders Esma'il Mirza (1728) and Sam Mirza (1743) attracted Shahsevan and Moghanlu adherents respectively, and Mohammad Hasan Qajar hoped for their support for his protégé Esma'il III in 1757, as did Fath 'Ali Khan of Qobbeh for 'Abbas Mirza in 1784. That this support was unreliable must indicate a growing disillusionment. The Shahsevan would have been no more devoted to the dynasty established by Agha Mohammad Qajar, at least in the early decades, than they had been to other eighteenth-century powers: the Afshar, Afghan and Zand chiefs and local lords such as the khans of Gilan, Qara-Bagh and Qobbeh, who had competed for Nader's throne and for the allegiance of the other khans and tribal groups of Azarbaijan. Moreover, the Shahsevan had not yet learned to hate the Russians, who had given them refuge from the Ottomans less than a century before.

The third occasion of supposed disloyalty was during the Constitutional Revolution in the early twentieth century, when judgments of Shahsevan actions are marked by a similar disregard of economic factors and possible complexities of motivation and ideology. Like other nomads, they had a bad press, among both historians and journalists of the time; commonly dismissed as inveterate brigands, their involvement in the siege of Tabriz and the sack of Ardabil was enough to label them as implacable anti-Constitutionalists.

Most writers on the Shahsevan in the late nineteenth and early twentieth centuries conspire to deny them any political or religious motivation, and ignore the economic factors in their situation, portraying them as 'much addicted to theft and pillage'.[4] Europeans, influenced by various often mutually contradictory traditions – Scottish clans, Indian hill-tribes, warlike Pathans in the case of the British; steppe nomads and Caucasian mountaineers in the case of the Russians – display a generally Hobbesian view of the Shahsevan as savages, sometimes balanced by a contrary, Rousseauian image of hospitable nomads. Most foreign agents

---

[4] Sir G. Buchanan, comments on *Rossiya* article in Reuter from St Petersburg, 27.7.1912, passed on to Grey in London, Dp 237 in *Further Correspondence*, Part XXXI.

and journalists, Iranian officials and local historians saw banditry as the problem, culminating in the sack of Ardabil. They did not allow that it might have economic causes or political motivations, but interpreted it as a primitive cultural phenomenon, not worth civilized respect.[5]

Among Iranian writers, Mostoufi, seeking to justify Reza Shah's disarmament and settlement of the tribes, noted that the Shahsevan won their name by fighting for the state under the Safavids and Nader Shah Afshar; during Qajar times, however, particularly the Constitutional period, they were of no economic or political benefit to the state and people of Iran but rather occupied themselves with raiding.[6] Recently published accounts of the experience of *äshrarlıq* in the towns of the region, often by local officials or scholars, not surprisingly take a perspective hostile to the Shahsevan, sometimes express a conventional admiration for their hospitality and their martial qualities, but castigate them as uneducated and irreligious, and show no appreciation of their economic circumstances or possible political values. Safari, for example, in his monumental history of Ardabil, while lauding Shahsevan virtues of courage, honour and hospitality, has no doubts about the predatory motivations of at least some of the tribesmen. Explicit in both his urban perspective on the barbarity and ignorance of the tribespeople and his eagerness to absolve his fellow-townspeople of any blame for the events of 1909, he records how some Ardabilis rejoiced when the tribesmen sacked the Ardabil bazaar, since this appeared to give the lie to claims that their motivation was political and religious.[7]

Tigranov's verdict on Shahsevan political potential in 1903 was very much the same, though based on a rather different diagnosis:

An offensive operation could attract the Shahsevan if they are promised at least material gain. Feelings of patriotism towards their common homeland are not found among them, nor is faith in the government and administration, whose policy of creating disputes among the tribes and destroying them, rather than fostering devotion to themselves, they understand very well, responding with open or concealed hatred. The possibility of arousing religious fanaticism among them is also very remote: they are hardly religious, they hate and despise the cowardly and self-interested clergy, who have begun to enlarge their estates at the expense not only of [Shahsevan] lands but also of [Shahsevan] peasants. Finally, the respect the Administration pays only to the clergy evokes among the Shahsevan [chiefs] hatred and powerless fury towards them. One can say with certainty that the

---

[5] Even Oberling, influenced perhaps by such sources, says that 'by the nineteenth century the Shahsevens had degenerated into a lawless rabble' (1964a: 44). Exceptions to this economically blind interpretation include a few long-term observers such as Consul Abbott, quoted in Chapter Ten.   [6] Mostoufi (1947, III/2: 306).

[7] Safari (1971: 280 and *passim*, esp. 160; 1974: esp. 2–7). For Meshkin see Sa'edi (1965: esp. 79f.). For Qara-Dagh see Baiburdi (1962). For Khalkhal see Rava'i (1984: esp. 146).

Shahsevan will serve anybody they please, if he can gain their trust and guarantee them some sort of respect and material gain.[8]

European newspapers, particularly (after the 1907 agreement) the British, were strongly influenced by the Russians to see the Shahsevan as bandits with 'predatory instincts', a 'frontier problem' comparable to that of the British on their North-West Frontier in India. For example, the *Times* correspondent in St Petersburg, persuaded by the Russians' interpretation of events in Ardabil in 1909 and their plan for a 'final solution', commented:

The interests of the [Russian] Empire demand a cessation of the anarchy on its borders. A punitive expedition against the Shahsevans would have been undertaken long ago had they indulged their marauding propensities on our Indian border.[9]

In summer 1912, the *Times* correspondent justified Fidarov's campaign against the Shahsevan as follows:

These lawless tribes are a veritable scourge to their peaceful countrymen, and, under the guise of patriotic resistance to alleged invaders, are trying to get rid of the uncomfortable interference of forces whose presence in Northern Persia has rendered that section enviably quieter than the British sphere in the South.[10]

These comments echoed the official Russian view, as purveyed in *Rossiya*:

The operations are devoid of any political significance. It is merely a question of an expedition demanded by local interests which were in need of active protection. The Shahsevens are not a political party, but are a wild marauding people who roam about the country on and in the vicinity of the Russian frontier.[11]

In 1920, when a Bolshevik column on its way from Astara to Ardabil 'fell among thieves' in the shape of Shahsevan warriors (probably Alarlu), the *Times* special correspondent in Tehran commented:

Thus the Shahsavends, after having looted their own countrymen and emissaries of the Government from time immemorial, have at last turned patriots by accident and wrung a wry chuckle from Tehran.[12]

Such comments were commonplace for many years. About the only dissenting voice is that of Arfa; writing of Shahsevan highway robberies in 1914, he explains that they were

nomad tribes very unruly and predatory but at the same time intensely patriotic and loyal to the throne as their name indicates . . . They had fought fiercely against the Russian occupation forces in 1911, and although they sustained heavy losses, had never been subdued by the considerable Russian forces sent against them.[13]

---

[8] Tigranov (1909: 146).   [9] *The Times*, 7.11.1909.   [10] *The Times*, 18.7.1912.
[11] See note 3 above.   [12] *The Times*, 1.6.1920.   [13] Arfa (1964: 54–5).

A closer examination of the Shahsevan role in these events, and a knowledge of the historical and sociological background of the tribes, compel a more complex interpretation of their political behaviour. Rather than motivated simply by blind reaction and lust for booty, Shahsevan actions in the Constitutional period must be evaluated in the light of three main factors: the reasons for the 'brigandization' of eastern Azarbaijan in the early twentieth century; the tribespeople's varying assessments, in terms of a presumed royalist and Islamic political ideology, of the appeal of various figures and forces that sought to gain their allegiance; and the complex patterns of internal rivalries within and between the tribes.

Banditry, as described in Chapter Eleven, was certainly a common activity and caused a great deal of harm and suffering in the region, although its extent was often grossly exaggerated, particularly by Russia. But it would be a mistake to see it as merely an addiction, a cultural imperative or a principle of social organization; rather it was a pastoral people's response to difficult economic and political circumstances.[14]

In the millennium of their presence in Southwest Asia, Turkic tribes have been notorious for their predatory activity. Noting that the Turkic 'tribe' is a political and not an ethnic or descent group, Oberling observed that:

Traditionally, the chief's job was to make war (i.e. to get booty), and protect his tribesmen from other tribes whose leaders were similarly inclined. As a rule, there was a direct correlation between the military prowess of a chief and the size of his following.[15]

However strong the sense of moral duty which successful dynasties such as the Safavids and Qajars managed to instil, they could not secure the allegiance of subordinate tribal chiefs without offering material rewards – spoils. The chiefs too relied on a supply of spoils with which to ensure the support of their own tribal followings, or at least to pay their armed henchmen.

In some ways, the tribal policy of the early Qajars resembled that of the early Safavids. They rewarded their most loyal followers with lucrative governorships, land grants and tax concessions; they controlled the tribes through the chiefs, giving them authority, legitimacy and responsibility; they were at first successful in their military campaigns, another source of spoils. The similarity soon ends, however, for while the Safavids enjoyed a heyday of a century and a half and were then, thanks largely to Shah 'Abbas I, allowed nearly another century of peaceful decline before suddenly succumbing to Afghan, Ottoman and Russian aggression, the

---

[14] Cf. Hobsbawm (1965).
[15] Oberling (1964b: 61). See also Nikitine's warnings, quoted in Chapter Four.

Qajar dynasty was less than two decades old when it confronted irresistible aggression, though even then it was not allowed to fall, for the Imperial powers, which could easily have destroyed the dynasty, co-operated in preserving it for another century. Nevertheless, as Oberling observed,

as Persia suffered defeat after defeat in the nineteenth century, the flow of spoils dwindled rapidly, with the result that the tribesmen lost their most lucrative (and only legal) source of loot. As a consequence, banditry became ever more prevalent [especially in the last three Qajar reigns] . . . The ambitious tribal leader now had to build his reputation solely on his exploits as a highwayman.[16]

Though an exaggeration for most of the country, this is fair comment on economic and political conditions towards the end of the Qajar era in Moghan and Ardabil, resembling those that prevailed there (though for different reasons) two centuries earlier, at the end of the Safavid era: overcrowded pastures, tribal disunity, the formation of competitive clusters and coalitions, and banditry. The difference is that in 1700 the Shahsevan confederacy had not yet been formed, while in 1900 it had already disintegrated.

If the brigandization of Moghan and Ardabil is explicable in terms of the economic and political history of the region during the nineteenth century, does lust for booty account for Shahsevan behaviour in the early years of the twentieth century? We should at least consider again the implications of the values and political ideology to which the Shahsevan are reputed to have subscribed.

The first value (support for the Safavid Shahs) was long outdated, but the Qajars, like the Safavids, cultivated a sacred public image of the Shah himself, and in due course those Shahsevan tribes that stayed in Iran after the Treaty of Torkman–Chai came to owe the established monarchy some of the loyalty which their ancestors had given to the Safavids. The two other values of the original Shahsevan complex were equally transformed. Fidelity to Shi'ism was generalized to Islam and could at times direct former hatred of Sunni Ottomans against their new and aggressive neighbours, the infidel Russians. Although the Shahsevan remained quite unmoved by respect for administrative officials or mullahs with whom they came into contact, they continued to profess duty to the ultimate secular power and religious authority: to the Shah and to Islam as represented by the chief mojtaheds. On a few occasions, the call of Shah and Islam, uttered by respected leaders, brought a powerful if short-lived unity to the tribes.

These related values could rarely guide the Shahsevan unambiguously

[16] Oberling (1964b: 62).

in their responses to the complex external forces which this period introduced. If they were to observe their duty to the Qajar dynasty and to
Islam, what attitude should they take towards the Russians, who were
Christians and aggressive neighbours and yet became not only the allies
but the protectors and paymasters of the dynasty? To the
Constitutionalists, who opposed and then deposed Mohammad 'Ali
Shah and yet swore allegiance to his successor? To Rahim Khan, known
supporter of Mohammad 'Ali, yet with suspect motives and a chequered
past as a local bandit leader on terms of deadly rivalry with important
Shahsevan tribes? To Sattar Khan, hero and leader of the Constitution,
whose personality and behaviour, when he came to Ardabil, accorded
with none of the Shahsevan values?

The reformist movements that led to the Constitutional Revolution of
1905–6 received considerable support from religious leaders (and hence
from the masses who followed them) who, like the merchants and
intellectuals, were opposed to the Shah's policy of 'selling the country' to
infidels and foreigners. The fact that the Shahsevan tribes did not react
decisively in the first year or two of the Revolution may reflect the contradiction they would have seen in the clerical leaders' support for the
Constitution and opposition to the Shah. After the Revolution, some
members of the religious classes awoke to the secular implications of the
Constitution and Nationalism, and defected to the Royalist party. With
the prominent part played in the Nationalist movement by non-Muslims,
the Shahsevan by 1909 could see that their duty, to both Shah and Islam,
lay in opposition to the Constitution, and they were able to unite for this
purpose even if it meant accepting the Russian support offered by Rahim
Khan Chalabianlu.

The Royalist cause was soon discredited, however, losing the support
of the clerics and also of the Russians, whose ulterior motives in
Azarbaijan were revealed by their military occupation. The Shahsevan,
accepting Mohammad 'Ali's deposition and Soltan Ahmad Shah's
succession, broke into open rebellion against the Russian troops, who,
though they could still use Shahsevan banditry as an excuse for their presence, now feared that the Nationalists might recruit the tribes' support,
and determined to crush them and destroy their military effectiveness.
This plan had only partially succeeded when the War and the Bolshevik
Revolution prevented its completion.

Thus, in most situations during the early twentieth century, it was not
possible for the Shahsevan to act in a fashion at once consistent with both
loyalty to Shah and fidelity to Islam; but where it was possible so to act,
then they did so. It is important to establish this consistency, not only
because it corrects the historical record, but also because Shahsevan

chiefs at the time claimed to be primarily motivated by these values (Shah and Islam).[17]

A few writers on the period have acknowledged the importance of values. Cottam, reiterating the conventional view that the Shahsevan 'had consistently opposed the Constitutionalists and had been a major source of support for Muhammad Ali Shah', explains their resistance to the Russians as motivated by xenophobia and religious hatred, quoting the message sent to Samad Khan in 1912.[18] Arfa's assessment of the Shahsevan as patriotic royalists (see above) is consistent with the perspective expressed to me, in discussions in the 1960s, by old Shahsevan men of different classes who remembered those times and found nothing shameful in the actions of their fathers and grandfathers half a century earlier. I recorded legends of complaints made by the Russian Tsar to the Shahs Naser ad-Din and Mozaffar ad-Din, on their visits to St Petersburg, about banditry by such notorious Shahsevan chiefs as Nurollah Bey Qoja-Beyli, his son Bahram Khan, and Mohammad-qoli Alarlu; the Shah, instead of punishing his 'errant' subjects, pardons or even honours and rewards them for keeping the Russians on his frontier sensible of his power.[19]

Nevertheless, if the Shahsevan did not betray their professed ideals, their political attitudes and behaviour throughout the period were consistent with two other imperatives, namely material gain and the prosecution of internal rivalries. If duty to Shah and duty to Islam were in contradiction, these imperatives would sway them, and would sway different chiefs in different directions. Possibly the main factor influencing Shahsevan political attitudes at this period was relations between and within the tribes themselves, as described in Chapter Twelve. The chiefs were never all united; indeed, many were willing to support the Constitution, and some did throughout.

In the years following the Russian withdrawal, the Shahsevan devoted themselves politically to these inter-tribal rivalries and alliances, though they remained alert to threats and opportunities presented by external political forces. Of the Turks, the British, the Nationalists, the Democrats and the Bolsheviks, none offered the combined values of Shah and Islam, so none received unequivocal support from the Shahsevan. When Reza Khan seized power, however, and set about gaining control of the country, he made sure at first to court the religious leaders and to rebuff

---

[17] See the telegrams and the Treaty of 1909, Chapter Twelve.

[18] Cottam (1964: 56–7), referring to Mirza Firooz Khan; see Chapter Twelve.

[19] See Appendix Three. No Shahsevan has yet published a chronicle of those times which might take the perspective of at least one sector of tribal society and represent a tribal view of their history and identity. See Chapter One.

charges of secular intentions, and when he sent his army to pacify the Shahsevan it was not so much by superior force or by an appeal for national security that he persuaded most of them to submit without a fight, but rather by advertising his support for both Islam and the reigning Shah, Soltan Ahmad Qajar. If the Shahsevan disapproved when he abandoned these values by creating a new dynasty and a secular state, they could no longer resist, since they had been disarmed and subjected to the control of the new National Army. Twenty years later, however, during the Soviet occupation of Azarbaijan in the Second World War, and under the subsequent Democrat regime of 1946, the Shahsevan chiefs, with few exceptions, refused co-operation and maintained their allegiance to both Shah and country; but, perhaps because it runs counter to European images of the latter-day Shahsevan, this loyalty is not mentioned in many English sources.[20]

From tribalism to feudalism

By and large the commentators discussed so far, principally Western and non-Marxist, focus their attention on the significance of the name Shahsevan. Whether through paucity of reliable data for the relevant periods, or through lack of interest, they avoid consideration of the circumstances, perspectives and motivations of the population bearing the name.

Another group of authors, mainly Russian and Soviet, show awareness of the importance of the economic base in the socio-political history of the Shahsevan, though they largely ignore the role of ideology and religious values, and are besides somewhat uncritical and selective in their use of historical sources. They speculate on the development of the Shahsevan confederacy from its supposed origins until it first became an object of study in the mid-nineteenth century. With few exceptions, they support their theories with little documentation other than Malcolm's account of the formation of the 'tribe', nineteenth-century legends of Yunsur Pasha's acquisition of pasture-lands in Moghan, and records of Shahsevan surrender to the Russians there in 1728, letting their imaginations or their ideological inclinations tell them what must have happened.

The contributions of two authors are of particular relevance here: the Russian officer Colonel L. F. Tigranov, and the Soviet writer F. B. Rostopchin. Articles by two more recent Soviet historians, B. P. Balayan and H. A. Dälili, are of less interest and should be discussed first.

Balayan, an Armenian who visited the Shahsevan during the Second

---

[20] An exception, again, is Arfa (1964: 340, 342).

World War, was concerned with the possible common origins in Moghan of the Shahsevan and the Qashqa'i. On the Shahsevan, he considers three sets of evidence: (a) early Safavid sources showing the presence in Moghan of the Tekelu Qızılbash, and the immigration from Ottoman to Iranian domains of groups of Sil-Süpür and Jalali which 'became Shahsevan'; (b) Shahsevan traditions of immigration from Anatolia; and (c) the official story of the origin of the Shahsevan as a tribe formed by Shah 'Abbas I, which he accepts and supports with lengthy references to Safavid histories. Unfortunately these references are unconvincing as proof for Malcolm's story, and Balayan also fails to note the inconsistencies between his three sets of evidence, so that the rest of his study, speculating about the organization of the Shahsevan 'tribe' in Moghan in Shah 'Abbas' time, has no base in reality.[21]

The Azarbaijani Dälili uses almost exclusively Russian and Persian sources in reconstructing the early history of the Shahsevan, but misses writings by Tigranov, Rostopchin, Balayan and even Minorsky. He elaborates the official story of Shahsevan origins as the trusted private guards of Shah 'Abbas, and suggests a gradual alienation from the Shah and an eventual eighteenth-century bid for independence at Ardabil. He attacks a number of earlier writers, both Soviet and 'bourgeois', for their errors: the Shahsevan were not of heterogeneous origins, nor from Anatolia, he says, but they were from the start a unified 'tribe' (taifa) of Afshars from Urmiyeh. They had welcomed Russian citizenship in 1728 because it was preferable to the oppression inflicted by the Ottomans and because Moghan was then in a state of poverty and famine; and they did not divide into two branches until the nineteenth century. Now much of this may be true, and Dälili refers to a number of otherwise inaccessible Russian archive sources, but his use of the better-known sources is so uncritical, casual and often naive that his version of the eighteenth-century Shahsevan must remain suspect.[22]

The ideas of Tigranov and Rostopchin are of more interest, even if little better supported. The former, whose often perceptive observations on the Shahsevan in 1903 I have quoted at several points, betrays ignorance of the sources in his version of their history. He accepts and elaborates (but does not acknowledge) Malcolm's account of Shah 'Abbas' creation of a new tribe to counter the rebellious Qızılbash and to defend his western frontiers. The privileges of the new tribe attracted recruits from the Qızılbash tribes themselves. Under 'Abbas' successors, Tigranov continues, the clergy grew powerful and the nomad tribes began to break

---

[21] Balayan (1960). See my comments in Chapter Four and Tapper (1974: 343f.).
[22] Dälili (1974 and 1979). See also my comments in Chapters Five, Six and Seven.

down; by 1722 they were unable to offer resistance to the Afghan invaders; few of the tribes retained the name Shahsevan. Some of the Qızılbash-Shahsevan managed to recover their power in the eighteenth century, but the groups in the Ardabil region were among the first to decay, with a brief interlude of unity under Nader Shah. By the nineteenth century, when the Russians became familiar with them, the Shahsevan tribes of Moghan and Ardabil were, Tigranov considered, already in the last stages of disintegration. The desperate social and economic condition of the tribes around 1900, which he describes in great detail, he attributes partly to the historical process and partly to the evils and incompetences of the Iranian administration of the Ardabil province.[23]

Rostopchin, who visited the Shahsevan in the 1920s, was familiar with sources relating to the nineteenth century; although his ideas on earlier Shahsevan history are obscured by Marxist–Leninist jargon and preconceptions, some of them, with adjustments of dating, are plausible. He reproduces both Malcolm's story and Minorsky's doubts as to its validity, but he continues to accept that Shah 'Abbas did create a tribal militia called Shahsevan, for he pursues Tigranov's arguments concerning the military nature and purposes of the tribe. Using a historical materialist framework, and referring to studies of other tribal groups for comparison, he attempts a reconstruction of the developmental stages of Shahsevan tribal organization. The original politico-military amalgamation of distinct Turkic tribal groups enjoyed certain economic privileges, in return for which they were expected to mobilize when called; after a number of such calls, 'the Shahsevan union took on the character of a closed military corporation'. From the beginning, the confederacy would have consisted of both a propertyless mass seeking economic security, and powerful tribal leaders who seized or were granted control of the pastures, the main productive resource. In the eastern Transcaucasus, the struggle for the choice pasture lands, intensified by the rapid increase in livestock and consequent overcrowding of those pastures, transformed the original military cohesion of the corporation into a 'caste' structure, cross-cut by tribal factions and alliances. Shah 'Abbas cleverly manipulated this struggle, says Rostopchin, to prevent the emergence of excessively powerful chiefs, and crystallized the basis of the Shahsevan political confederacy.

Rostopchin locates these processes, without a shred of evidence, in the early seventeenth century. The eighteenth century, he considers, saw the breakdown of the Shahsevan confederacy and the transition from the

---

[23] Tigranov (1909: 104–9).

tribal (primitive-communal) to the feudal stage (or socio-economic formation). When the military purpose of the original confederacy was no longer relevant, and the Shi'i religious classes gained control of Iran under the late Safavids, he argues, the artificial cohesion of the Shahsevan broke down and they split into their constituent units, one of which was the Ardabil–Moghan group. Over the following centuries further decay of Shahsevan organization was intensified by extortionate taxation and predatory expeditions by government authorities, until by the end of the nineteenth century the condition of the tribes could be summarized as sedentarization, feudalism, and brigandage.[24]

The major flaw in these theories of Shahsevan tribal development is that no credible evidence has yet been produced for the formation of a Shahsevan tribe before the end of the seventeenth century. The evidence in this book indicates that the confederacy as such did not exist in the early eighteenth century, when the Russians first contacted the Shahsevan; it was formed shortly after, but when the Russians returned at the end of the century it was hardly yet in the state of final disintegration that Tigranov and Rostopchin suggest. The processes of formation and development that Rostopchin discusses probably did occur, but a century or more later than he thinks, and in rather different circumstances. Neither Russian nor Soviet authors consider the extent to which, at the time the Russians were most familiar with the Shahsevan, the breakdown of the confederacy was precipitated by Russian imperial pressures. When the confederacy did disintegrate, with the fall from power of the paramount chiefs, this was due ultimately as much to the Russian advent, and the tribal response to it, as to any internal evolutionary – or devolutionary – process.

From patriotism to pastoralism

The commentators discussed so far represent the history of the Shahsevan from perspectives reflecting two versions of their origins. Most writers adopt Malcolm's version, focusing on the Shah's act of creation, which is the perspective of the central state, with its concern for order and loyalty to the ruler. The perspective of the *elbeys* is evident in Russian and Soviet analyses of the development and breakdown of their central control of the tribes, which start from legends of Yunsur Pasha's advent and acquisition of present Shahsevan territory, legitimating a tribal hierarchy based on his descendants' control of the main pastoral resource.

None of these commentators considers the perspectives of ordinary

---

[24] Rostopchin (1933: 88–97).

Shahsevan nomads, partly through lack of interest, but partly because they were not accessible until recently. Several Russian writers, from Ogranovich to Tigranov, describe social and economic conditions, religious beliefs and practices in some detail, but with a generality and an evident lack of sympathy that make it difficult to infer how ordinary tribe-people of the past saw themselves and what motivated their practices. The few Shahsevan comments or statements of belief that are recorded would seem to have come from the chiefly elite.

In the 1960s, Shahsevan constructions of their recent history and identity were varied. To a great extent, these variations reflected class and descent status. I came across a few scions of the older noble class, who did preserve traditions of Anatolian or Kurdish origins, and stories of Yunsur Pasha and the old *elbey* dynasty and their relatives, in which former Shahs rewarded their loyalty by granting authority over the tribes and rights over much of the land of the region. For them, the loss of these rights and authority meant the disintegration of the Shahsevan tribal confederacy: they would probably have agreed with the analysis of writers such as Tigranov and Rostopchin.

The most powerful chiefs during the Pahlavi period had no connexion with the house of Yunsur Pasha, and rarely referred to former paramount chiefs and nobles. They and their families – the new nobles – had often, as the most formally educated class among the tribespeople, learnt the 'official' story of Shahsevan origins from standard histories and school texts. As they (and a number of local townspeople) told it to me, it made no reference to the right of any particular group or class to lands or authority, but nicely accorded with current official images of Shahsevan loyalty to the Pahlavi Shah and a history of warlike patriotism. They depicted themselves as patriotic defenders of Iran and Islam, who had fought glorious battles against the Russians and earned their authority over their followers – and rights to both pastures and farmlands – in a time when the government was weak. They accepted the character of the Shahsevan as a powerful and vigorous tribal minority which, posing an age-old threat to the stability of government, was disarmed and (tem-porarily) settled under the Pahlavi regime. Their representation of Shahsevan tribalism – martial qualities, independence of authority, and predatory activities – coincided with (and has to some extent both formed and been formed by) that found in twentieth-century local histories.

Popular memory did not generally go back further than the time of *äshrarlıq*. By the time of the disarmament (1923), the old hierarchy of *elbey*s and *beyzadä* was a thing of the past, and the division between Meshkin and Ardabil tribes was of little relevance. Many nomads in the 1960s knew that the Qoja-Beyli and 'Isalu tribes were related as former nobles, and some were able to include Sarı-Khan-Beyli and Bala-Beyli; stories were told of Farzi Khan and 'Ata Khan, but none except their descendants knew of Yunsur Pasha or Shah-qoli Bey, or that they had been paramount chiefs. Most now believed that there had always been thirty-two independent Shahsevan tribes; that it was only through political necessity that weaker tribes, now or in the past, subordinated themselves to dominant chiefs of other tribes. For some time, indeed, Shahsevan have quoted their lack of an indigenous paramount chief among the criteria that distinguish them from tribal groups elsewhere.

If sources before 1919 are silent on the popular dogma of 'thirty-two tribes', this perhaps confirms that earlier informants were from the chiefly class. Just as likely, it reflects radical changes in Shahsevan tribal structure and relations with central government. Certainly, the dogma during the Pahlavi era accorded with egalitarian notions among the ordinary nomads.

In the 1960s 'Shahsevan', as a category of the population of eastern Azarbaijan, signified 'tribally organized pastoral nomads', as opposed to the category 'Tat', which denoted settled peasants. The basis for this opposition must be sought in economic and political history.

Before 1923, when the region was dominated by tribal chiefs, the main criterion defining the Shahsevan was membership of a recognized *taifa*. Though most tribespeople were pastoral nomads, living in tent-camps and raising sheep, many were based on tribal villages and practised agriculture. All tribespeople gave their allegiance to one of the chiefs, a partial sacrifice of independence that nevertheless gave a degree of economic security. *Tat*, by contrast, signified peasants, eking out a living as cropsharing tenants or labourers on the land of some absentee landowner and continually vulnerable to tribal raids and exactions. Shahsevan who were forced to abandon their tribal camps or villages quickly became regarded as Tat. A Tat could become Shahsevan by joining a chief's retinue of servants, but more permanent membership of a *taifa* as a pastoralist or agriculturalist was impossible without access to tribal lands, which were already the object of severe competition among the tribespeople themselves. Thus the Tats, without property or protection, formed a residual category, while Shahsevan could, through their place in the tribal organization, claim association with the dominant forces in the region. Symbolic elements in tribal unity and chiefship were stressed: Shahsevan identity was associated more clearly with particular names, dress and behaviour than with pastures, flocks and tents.

After 1923, however, these latter elements became prominent. The chiefs were suppressed, and the tribes lost their political dominance of the region. Government authority prevailed, officially favouring sedentary agricultural pursuits and village forms of organization. Among the pastoral nomads, economic security now came less from allegiance to tribal groups and deposed chiefs than from ownership or occupation of pastures. Migrations and the *alachɪq* tent became symbols of central importance to Shahsevan identity, though paradoxically Tat carpenters made the tent-frames.[25] The opposition between Shahsevan and Tat continued to form the theme of much local folk literature, but it depended now more on economic than on political criteria. The Shahsevan were still *'ashayer*, tribesmen, as opposed to *rayät*, Tat peasants, but these terms increasingly signified nomad versus settled; more often they were *obalɪ*, camp-dwellers, or *köçärä*, nomads as opposed to *kätlɪ*, villagers, or *oturaq*, settled; besides, in the nomad context, *'ashayer* signified independent pastoralist, opposed to *choban*, hired herdsman.

In most contexts, *taifa* affiliation was still an essential criterion for Shahsevan identity; but no two individuals would agree on a list of the recognized *taifa*. There was uncertainty, both locally and in twentieth-century sources on the Shahsevan, about whether to include neighbouring tribes (settled or nomadic), such as those of Talesh, Khalkhal, Sarab, Qara-Dagh and districts to the south, many of whom had had close relations with the Shahsevan, and some of whom at least shared important cultural items such as the *alachɪq*. Within the Moghan–Meshkin region, moreover, villagers with no traceable Shahsevan history were taking their flocks and pitching *alachɪq*s in pastures they had bought or rented in tribal areas; some openly disclaimed Shahsevan identity, but many claimed membership in one or other Shahsevan *taifa*; and others (Khioulu, Larili) had even created a new *taifa* by adding the suffix *-lu/li* to their village name. Although long-established nomads were slow to recognize such claims, mere adoption of their way of life was now sometimes enough for acceptance among the Shahsevan.[26]

Ordinary Shahsevan in the 1960s saw themselves as peaceful, tent-dwelling pastoralists, with a heroic past as patriotic defenders of their frontier territory against the Russians. They stressed their membership of specific tribes, but claimed to be no longer subject to the chiefs; they would declare that they no longer obeyed anyone but God and the Shah, that *khan*, *tärkhan*, *häshtärkhan* (khans, privileges, turkeys) were finished. This was then a 'false consciousness' since several chiefs, though officially deposed, and with their resources threatened by Land Reform, nevertheless retained considerable economic power and political influence over

---

[25] There are other, social structural reasons for the increasing symbolic importance of nomadism, see Tapper (1979a: *passim*).   [26] Cf. Haaland (1969).

the tribespeople, as we saw in Chapter Thirteen.[27] Loyalty to the monarchy was strong, while complaints about administrative officials were constant and justified. An old man from Pir-Evatlu *taifa* told me in 1963, 'A Shah should hire a shepherd for his people, to graze his sheep, care for them, fatten them and receive his wages; but this Shah has hired wolves to look after his people.'

The Shahsevan tribes: cultural identity and historical continuity

In the 1960s, Shahsevan nomads considered that they belonged to an *el* (tribal confederacy, also 'people') which comprised thirty-two *taifa*; each *taifa* had a chief (*bey*) and a number of sections (*tira*), each of which had an elder (*aq-saqal*); these divided again into camps (*oba*) of changing composition. The only overall chief (*elbey*) most people recalled was the army officer appointed in Pahlavi times. Definitions of *el*, *taifa* and *tira* varied. Each had significances beyond that of a level in a hierarchy. *Taifa* implied political allegiance to a chief but more importantly (as we shall see) cultural unity, though not common descent – some component *tira* were known to have come from elsewhere. *El* was a political confederation of *taifa*; it was also a term for a mass of nomads. A *tira* was a section of a larger political group, led by an elder, but was often also a lineage (*göbäk*, agnatic descent group), and bore the name of the apical ancestor, though some *tira* included more than one lineage and some groups of *tira* within a tribe claimed common descent to form a large lineage or clan. Usually, but not always, *tira* (and lineage) coincided with *jamahat*, basic nomadic community. *Taifa* and *tira* bore recognized names, while the name of a lineage or a *jamahat* (where they did not coincide with a *tira*) were known only to members and their immediate neighbours.[28]

The group to which outsiders and officials most often referred in their representations of the Shahsevan was the *taifa*. This complex group needs to be examined more closely. Central governments had recognized the *taifa* by approving if not appointing the chiefs, subordinate to an *elbey*; the Qajars usually chose this official from the original noble dynasty; under the Pahlavis he was an army officer, an outsider. After World War Two, each *taifa* was issued with a banner, to be used on ceremonial occasions.[29] Recognition was also inscribed in official and unofficial lists of *taifa*, as

---

[27] Cf. Black (1972).

[28] Sections, lineages and communities are discussed in detail in R. Tapper (1979a: esp. 120f.).

[29] For example the Shah's visit to Ardabil in 1947 (Safari 1992: 127); I did not see any of these banners, and do not know how many were issued.

well as by constant reproduction of the *el–taifa–tira–oba* model of Shahsevan group structure, which (as suggested in Chapter One) homogenized and fixed a complex and changing reality, and sometimes preserve the names of *taifa* long after they had settled or broken up. After 1960, although removal of the chiefs implied abolition of the *taifa* too as political groups, they continued to be listed as the main components of the Shahsevan.

Official recognition of *taifa* in effect stressed the political dimension of what, for the nomads, was essentially a cultural group. Few *taifa* were ever independent political units within the confederation, and so vast was the gap in size (100:1) – and power – between the smallest *taifa* and the confederation as a whole that *taifa* have always formed alliances or clusters, weaker chiefs subordinating themselves and their *taifa* to more powerful ones.[30] In earlier Qajar times, government dealt with *taifa* indirectly, through the hierarchy of *elbey* and noble chiefs. By 1900, the nobles had lost power, government control had weakened, and inter-*taifa* relations were characterized by raiding, warfare and alliance; the main political actors were a few dominant, successful chiefs who headed not only their own *taifa* but a number of weaker ones, each cluster totalling 1,000 to 3,000 households. After disarmament, government removed the power of the dominant chiefs and recognized each chief of a *taifa*, aiming to integrate each *taifa* into the national administrative structure. None the less, to deal with thirty to forty individual *taifa* of varying size, it proved convenient to use the more influential chiefs, each of whom had a following of lesser chiefs and their *taifa* who were themselves anxious to have this political insulation from government.

Tribal clusters were probably the most significant Shahsevan political entities: a balance between the forces of the administration and the influence of the chiefs concerned.[31] Within the larger *taifa*, similarly, there were often one or two further levels of political organization between that of the section and that of the *taifa*: a powerful elder might gather an unnamed cluster of subordinate sections; in some cases several sections

[30] Cf. Johnson's argument (1982) concerning scalar stress, to the effect that the maximum number of units before hierarchization or division is fourteen, and the optimum number seven. Shahsevan social groups conform to this with uncanny precision: households averaged seven members; herding units comprised three to four households; section/communities averaged twenty-five households, i.e. seven average-sized herding units, with a maximum of fifty households, i.e. fourteen herding units; *taifa* averaged 175 households, i.e. seven average sections, with a maximum of ?350 before splits; in fact in larger *taifa*, there is hierarchization into major and minor sections. There were six or seven tribal clusters, each of roughly seven *taifa* (7 × 175 = 1,225 families) totalling 7,000–10,000 households.

[31] These clusters were roughly the same size as the Basseri tribe and other major component 'tribes' of the Khamseh, Qashqa'i, Qara-Daghi and other confederacies.

formed a named subtribe, whose leader was not recognized as a chief and which never claimed independence as a *taifa*.

There was no special term for any of these extra political levels: a tribal cluster might be called an *el*, a named subtribe variously a *taifa* or *tira*; lesser *taifa* in a tribal cluster might be called *tira* of the dominant *taifa*. Formal (indigenous or official) models of tribal political structure recognized neither section clusters (which could be termed *göbäk*, if common descent were a factor, but without political connotations) nor tribal clusters.

Few Shahsevan considered discussion of such matters interesting or important, but as a result of the complexity and variation, informants rarely agreed on a list of the *taifa*, and it was most unlikely that any list would amount to exactly thirty-two. More knowledgeable informants, if pressed, would say that there might once have been thirty-two tribes, but many had settled or broken up, while new ones had formed by processes of segmentation or otherwise, so that there were probably about forty groups with the status of *taifa*.

Taifa lists deserve detailed study. They vary widely in length and content, and reflect the interests of the compilers – tax collectors, army officers, foreign agents, the livestock department, individual chiefs or section leaders, ordinary tribesmen – but they all sanction the idea of all *taifa* as equivalent, independent components of the Shahsevan. The first known list, dating from 1843, unfortunately gives no numbers, but a range of lists between 1870 and 1986 permits some tentative comparisons.[32]

Taifa average 150 to 200 households in size, but have always ranged widely, from under 50 to nearly 1,000 households, from one to over twenty sections. Over the period covered, many have remained near the average size (Mast-'Ali-Beyli, 'Ali-Babalu, 'Isalu, Hosein-Hajjili, Seyetler, Beydili, Takleh), others have remained comparatively large, 200 or more tents (Qoja-Beyli, Geyikli, Hajji-Khojalu with Gabali, Ajirli, Moghanlu, Talesh-Mikeilli of Meshkin), others have always had fewer than 100 (Kalash, Homunlu, Khalfali, Yekali). A few have grown (Qutlar, Kor-'Abbaslu), several have shrunk considerably (Sarı-Khan-Beyli, Jeloudarlu, Udulu, Pir-Evatlu, Damirchili, Jahan-Khanomlu), and many have settled (most of the Ardabil division).

Almost all *taifa* whose names *disappear* from the lists are recorded as settling in villages: I have no record of a small *taifa*, once listed as such, being absorbed by another, except possibly the two former noble *taifa*

---

[32] My own composite version is in Appendix Two. See also R. Tapper (1972: 697f. and Appendix III).

Qara-Qasemli and Nouruz-'Ali-Beyli, which became parts of Sarı-Khan-Beyli and Qoja-Beyli, though the first at least has a village in Moghan bearing its name; and Janyarlu, which took over Talesh-Mikeilli leadership.

Among the former noble *taifa*, several have formed by fission: Asefli and Khamesli from Polatlu; 'Isalu from Qoja-Beyli, and probably Qutlar/Kalesar from Damirchili. No other *taifa* have formed this way; most names which first appear in the list only after 1870 are known to have originated otherwise:

- Kor-'Abbaslu, Kalash, Hosein-Hajjili, Shah-'Ali-Beyli, Seyetler, Gabali, Terit, Ja'farli all wintered in western and southern parts of Iranian Moghan in 1870, hence escaped Ogranovich's attention that year.
- The Ojarud *taifa* Alarlu and Delaqarda did not count as Shahsevan until the twentieth century, when they were cut off from their Talesh neighbours.
- Some new *taifa* appear to have originated, at least in recent times, from a particular village with which they were exclusively associated: Terit (from Aslanduz), Seyetler-Zarenji (Aq-Tepe), Qaralar/Khioulu (Jabdaraq and Khiou), Larili (Larud/Lari).
- Aq-Qasemli and Rezalu, who seem to have enjoyed a brief existence around the turn of the century, were presumably once villagers, and later returned to that condition.
- Hoseinakli, which is counted in some of the latest lists, is a major Qara-Dagh *taifa*, though it has pastures in the Meshkin/Arshaq district.
- There are several groups of *taifa* which are related in ways that are not clear to me and that may have changed. One group are Beydili, Ajirli, Homunlu and Aivatlu, members of the former Yeddi-Oimaq complex. Another group is that of Milli, Seyetler, Khalfali.
- Seyetler are said to have come from Khalkhal; Khosroulu and Ja'farli from Qara-Bagh. The origins of Janyarlu, Ja'far-qoli-Khanlu and Ilkhchi ('horse-herders') are unknown to me, but there is no indication that they are related to any other taifa.[33]
- Several former subtribes of Qoja-Beyli were occasionally mentioned to me in the 1960s as taifa in their own right: Hampa,

---

[33] On Ilkhchi, cf. Sa'edi's study (1964) of an Ahl-e Haqq village of that name near Maragheh.

Petili, Sarı-Nasirli, Qara-Musalu, Hajji-Khanlu. So was Hajjili, a subtribe of Hajji-Khojalu, and Khırda-Pai, a subtribe of Moghanlu.

Thus among the commoner *taifa* there are few changes in the lists that cannot be accounted for in terms of emigration from or immigration to pastoral nomad society. While former 'noble' *taifa* have experienced the fission and fusion processes characteristic of lineage structures elsewhere, most of the commoners, through a century of political upheaval, have displayed no signs of these processes but rather a remarkable continuity as named and unified groups, despite wide differences and changes in size.

Why and how? What is involved in maintenance of *taifa* identity by the commoners? First, as we have seen, central government contributed by recognizing *taifa* through appointing their chiefs. But it would be hard to argue that the unity and identity of commoner *taifa* depended only on official recognition and the political effectiveness of their chiefs. I know of no commoner *taifa* which lost its identity except by a combination of settlement and dispersal. One commoner *taifa* (Ajirli) temporarily broke up as a result of weak leadership, the parts subordinating themselves politically to chiefs of different tribes, but the *taifa* did not lose its identity, and a more effective chief was able to reunite it in later years. If a chief at any period extended his influence over other *taifa*, these would become part of his personal political following, not members of his *taifa*. In Pahlavi times, the wealthier and more powerful chiefs became part of a regional, non-tribal elite, largely independent of any backing by tribal followers, while the *taifa* persisted into the 1990s without their chiefs.

Few if any commoner *taifa* (certainly none of the larger ones) claimed common descent for all their sections,[34] which is perhaps not surprising, as membership of a *taifa* as such brought no political or economic advantage, such as access to joint grazing lands. In many pastoral societies grazing rights are held jointly by substantial descent groups, and access depends on being able to claim membership of such a group. Among the Shahsevan, however, at least since the mid-nineteenth century, groups no larger than the tribal sections held rights in individual pastures.

If a *taifa* had no descent ideology and no joint estate, it was almost always territorially defined. Government officials when giving lists would think of the chiefs with whom they had to deal, or note groups as they passed an official checkpoint; nomad informants usually enumerated *taifa* by thinking where they were likely to be found by a traveller passing

[34] The only exception I knew of was Khalfali, a small *taifa* some of whose members told me they were all one *göbäk*, though they produced no pedigree leading to a common ancestor. However, they did not consider this criterion of descent or origins to be so important as that of political history: see Appendix Two.

through the pastures, whether in Moghan or in the mountains. It was easier perhaps for smaller *taifa* to remain territorially compact. Some maintained their identity by being associated exclusively with one particular settlement. The rest were usually associated with contiguous pastures, though all members of a *taifa* had no regular occasion to congregate in one place. In the mountains, sections and camps of a *taifa* often became widely separated by buying or renting pasture among neighbouring camps and even *taifa*, but tribal identity did not suffer so long as all stayed together in winter quarters; here, a few larger *taifa* (Geyikli, Kor-'Abbaslu, Ajirli) did have grazing lands in two separate areas, but even then political and cultural unity survived such separation and separated sections usually resisted absorption by neighboring *taifa*. With no ideology of common descent, however, many *taifa* were known to include sections which once belonged to others. A change of allegiance might result from moving into another *taifa*'s territory:[35] in its new territory, among the first acts of such a section was to marry into the new tribe.

Marriage, indeed, was a key to *taifa* identity. Field data from the 1960s indicate a strong tendency for *taifa* endogamy, varying according to the size and influence of the *taifa* and as between chiefly families and commoners. The men of three commoner sections from two large *taifa* (Geyikli, Talesh-Mikeilli) contracted a total of eighty-nine marriages, 90 per cent of which were with woman from the same *taifa*. Between 35 and 40 per cent of men's marriages were to women of the same section, leaving over half the marriages linking different sections of the same tribe in a complex web of alliances.[36]

Though unity did not depend on political leadership, the chief could often promote cohesion in his *taifa*. In many cases, the chief traditionally controlled the marriages of commoners, who had at least to seek his approval for a match. He could thus not only prevent the formation of commoner factions based on marriage alliances, he could also – like the Qajars and other ruling dynasties – conciliate powerful elders by arranging marriage alliances with them himself. Though I have no systematic data on them, such manoeuvres certainly took place, for example in Geyikli.

Another way in which a chief could promote *taifa* cohesion was in feasts, particularly for weddings and circumcisions of members of his own family. In the 1960s, when former chiefs held major feasts largely in order

---

[35] For an example from Geyikli, see R. Tapper (1979a: 197f.). Op't Land (1961: 28, 33) mentions a section of Ja'farli which quarrelled with the chief and went to become a section of Qoja-Beyli in about 1940.

[36] R. Tapper (1979a: 142, 292). These conclusions were supported by more fragmentary data on other marriages in these *taifa*, and in the smaller tribes 'Arabli and Khalfali.

to impress fellow-members of the regional elite, they also helped to keep alive the identity and honour of the *taifa* by reproducing (and sometimes reconstructing) traditional *taifa* customs on a scale which commoners might emulate but could not match in their own feasts.

The immediate relatives of a powerful chief rarely married with commoners of their *taifa*, but spread their marriages between lineage endogamy and links with other chiefly families or powerful outsiders. Less powerful chiefly families married more like commoner lineages, mainly within the *taifa*. Thus in 'Arabli, a small *taifa* of some fifty families, men of the small chiefly lineage had made twenty-five marriages, seventeen of them (68 per cent) within the *taifa*, of which ten (40 per cent) were within the lineage and seven (28 per cent) with commoner women; eight wives (32 per cent) came from outside the *taifa*. In the larger chiefly lineage of Ajirli, a *taifa* of four hundred families, men had made sixty-four marriages, thirty-seven of them (58 per cent) within the *taifa*, of which twenty-one (33 per cent) were within the lineage and sixteen (25 per cent) with commoner women; twenty-seven wives (42 per cent) were outsiders. More recent marriages show no particular change of pattern.[37]

There are no systematic marriage data available for former noble *taifa*, whether during or since the time of their dominance, but there seems to have been little intermarriage between the chiefly dynasty and the commoners, the former intermarrying extensively with their distant cousins from other noble *taifa*, and also with closer lineage cousins. The chiefly lineages of commoner *taifa* which emerged later as dominant (such as Geyikli) attempted to establish control of their following by adopting some of the practices peculiar to former noble – and Royal – dynasties, for example, avoidance of marriage with commoners. The partial information I collected on marriages of the chiefly lineage of Geyikli (a tribe of some 700 families) indicated many links with both close agnates and other Shahsevan and Qara-Daghi chiefly families, and few – but significant ones – with commoners. At the same time, once established, a new dynasty became liable to the divisive rivalries which had been peculiar to the noble dynasties in the past. Such rivalries developed in the chiefly dynasties of Geyikli, Hajji-Khojalu, Alarlu, as described in Chapter Eleven, and in more recent times within Ajirli and Moghanlu. In each case they threatened to divide the *taifa* permanently; that each *taifa* resisted fission was not simply due to political and administrative controls by government, but also perhaps to the insecurity felt by

---

[37] In both cases, data on daughters of the lineage were incomplete. It should be noted that the above data on marriage choices must be treated with great caution, not so much for their incompleteness but because they give no indication of the meanings of the categories and the choices for the participants; cf. N. Tapper (1991).

commoner chiefly dynasties as opposed to former nobles. The cohesive elements of commoner *taifa* may have also played a part; in particular, the strong tendency to endogamy and the maintenance of a complex web of marriage links between sections not only prevented politically effective factions from forming, but erected and maintained a cultural boundary around the *taifa* as a social group.

Different section-communities within a *taifa* were closely linked, not so much by political commitment as by ties of affinity and friendship, shared values and customs. As a culturally homogeneous group, the *taifa* was an arena for competition on ceremonial and ritual occasions: members of a *taifa* played the same game with the same rules. Although neighbouring sections might be known for differences of custom, such as greater or weaker preference for marriage with cousins, such differences were felt to be much slighter than those distinguishing *taifa* from each other.

People would talk of other *taifa* in terms implying differences in kind (*taifa* means species, even class: insects as opposed to animals), relating these to differences of origins or history in a way they would never talk of fellow-tribesmen from different sections. Members of each *taifa* asserted its uniqueness and superiority in some respect, sometimes pointing to tangible differences, for example, in herding and husbandry practices, ceremonial customs, dialect and vocabulary.[38] Although there was no arena for social competition between *taifa*, nor any objective ranking according to either nobility or size,[39] size and wealth were important factors in the political situation, if only because they usually affected the degree of independence a *taifa* was able to maintain. Yet there was no straight correlation of size, wealth and influence, particularly in the 1960s, when former chiefs of relatively small *taifa* were sometimes of more consequence than those of some of the larger *taifa*. *Taifa* were known not only for comparative wealth and size, but for moral qualities: this *taifa* was more honest, that contained more thieves, that one was more religious. Outsiders (including myself) who had dealings with Shahsevan often had pronounced preferences for some *taifa* over others, influenced rarely by any objective criteria, but more by the degree of hospitality and co-operation they had experienced.[40]

On the whole most commoners remained economically and socially isolated from members of other *taifa*. When migrating groups from two

---

[38] Groups of *taifa*, located together, shared the tricks of speech and verbal inflections which distinguish for example Qara-Baghi, Ardabili, Khalkhali, Moghan/Meshkini dialects of Azari; none, to my knowledge, spoke like people from Sarab or Tabriz.

[39] Some chiefly informants distinguished 'primary' from 'secondary' tribes, on rather imprecise grounds of relative 'importance'.

[40] Cf. Chapter Nine for comments by nineteenth-century Russian officials.

different *taifa* passed, they would openly ignore each other as strangers, exchanging little or no information; often they did not know, or care to know, the identity of the others. *Taifa* were socially almost self-contained, and section-communities were economically independent in relations with settled people, the market and the administration. But there were a few marriage links (more with smaller *taifa*) and other kinds of relationships outside the *taifa*; these were more frequent between elders of adjoining sections of two *taifa*, and effectively maintained both the boundary between the *taifa* and a channel of communication across it.

Contact between members of neighbouring *taifa* of the same tribal cluster was rarely more intensive than between neighbours belonging to different clusters. Only when clusters were on terms of active hostility were actual political barriers strong enough to disrupt intermittent social relations across them. Normally, the only special factors to unite *taifa* of the same cluster were their neighbourhood and their allegiance (and contributions of armed horsemen) to the same powerful chief. Between chiefs, on the other hand, there was a regular system of communication, involving not only marriage but general social interaction on a scale and level which differentiated chiefs as a class from most commoners.

The identity, cohesion and continuity of commoner *taifa* thus depended partly on administrative recognition and on territoriality, and most of all on a high degree of endogamy and shared culture.[41] In 1966, in most of the nomadic *taifa*, those at least with which I was familiar, the sense of unity and identity was very much alive. The *taifa* remained territorially distinct, and so far as I was aware there was no weakening in the tendency to endogamy, nor in the maintenance of cultural distinctiveness. The political identity of the *taifa*, as I have suggested, was never of prime importance; it was even less so after the chiefs were formally deposed, even if many continued to play a role in the affairs of their former followers, and even if censuses and other government action relating to the Shahsevan continued to deal with *taifa*. In the 1990s, government policies towards pastoral nomads (*'ashayer*) specifically addressed a population organized in tribes and clans based on sentiments of solidarity and not subject to any chiefs (see Chapter One). With all overt political attributes of the *taifa* gone, Shahsevan living widely dispersed in the region and elsewhere still referred to each other by *taifa* names and, indeed, Shahsevan friends I encountered in Tehran still expressed a preference for marriage with people of the same *taifa* origins.

---

[41] Features of the second type of nomadic community identified in Chapter One (cf. Tapper 1979b).

Concluding remarks: tribes and states

From the foregoing, it is clear that an account of the history of a people such as the Shahsevan must comprehend the varied interests, perspectives – and indeed histories – of three very different kinds of actor: the rulers of the state and their administrative entourages; the elite of chiefs with their retinues, a warrior class who controlled access to land; and the commoners in their nomadic communities who did the herding and pastoral production and were themselves divided into flock owners and shepherds.

The complex interactions between these actors constituted the field commonly referred to as tribe–state relations, much debated in recent decades by students of tribal societies in Iran and elsewhere, as summarized in Chapter One. Daniel Bradburd, in a trenchant critique of these debates, has suggested that the so-called 'tribe–state' issue had little to do with 'tribes', a term best reserved for relatively small pastoral groups, but rather concerned the state-like tribal confederacies; that the issue was indeed a matter of state formation and the problems faced by rulers, would-be rulers and chiefs; that confederacies were the creations of ambitious chiefs, rather than central governments; and finally, that if chiefs (or central governments) represented confederacies as 'tribes', this was an ideology which falsely identified ruler with ruled in order to legitimate the former and disguise their exploitation of the latter. In this light, relations between 'tribes' and 'states' in Iran are strictly comparable, he suggests, with state formation processes in Europe and elsewhere.[42]

This book provides some support for Bradburd's argument. First, he has in effect reformulated Barth's two-level analysis of the Basseri (as outlined in Chapter One), which I have found useful and valid for the Shahsevan: the basic pastoral nomad communities (the Basseri 'camp', the Shahsevan *jamahat/tira* section) arise in economic and ecological circumstances quite different from the wider political context of chiefs, tribes, confederacies and states. I have identified larger communities (the Shahsevan *taifa* or the Basseri *tireh*) which also exhibited a degree of cultural cohesion and continuity even where incorporated into an administrative structure by either chiefs or agents of the state; in the Shahsevan case, I have called them 'tribes'. However, whether we locate 'tribes' with the pastoralists, as Bradburd does, or with the chiefs, as Barth does, is largely a matter of definition.

Secondly, state formation processes are clearly evident in Shahsevan

---

[42] Bradburd (1987), reviewing van Bruinessen (1978), Garthwaite (1983), Tapper (1983a), Beck (1986) and other works; see also Bradburd (1990).

history. At least three can be identified: the process by which rulers, would-be rulers and chiefs seek legitimate power; the expansion of Shahsevan identity; and the devolution of tribal power. These processes have unfolded in the context of rivalries between tribal leaders, interactions involving government officials, shifting frontiers, invading armies, and other forces; an environment of both states and would-be states competing for manpower, arms, spoils, taxes.

On the other hand, there is no evidence that the 'creation' of the Shahsevan confederacy, whenever it occurred, was the act of an ambitious chief. We have seen Shahsevan chiefs forming tribal clusters, but always in a context of struggle with rival chiefs and with agents of central government, and I would maintain that the latter, in the Shahsevan case, was ever the creator of both chiefs and confederacies. Bradburd's main focus is on nineteenth-century Iran, and in particular on the formation then of the major centralized confederacies (Bakhtiari, Qashqa'i and Khamseh) of the Zagros; by that time, however, both the Kurdish confederacies and the Shahsevan (to which he also refers) were disintegrating, having formed over a century earlier in very different circumstances to those of the Zagros groups, notably in frontier locations – a factor which Bradburd correctly identifies as crucially determinant.

Finally, the notion of 'tribe' as an ideology of control touches on an issue which Bradburd does not address, namely the role of descent and genealogy. Much of the debate on this issue[43] fails to distinguish between, on the one hand, descent as an integrating ideology associated with pastoral nomadic tribes, and on the other, the dynastic pedigrees used by chiefs and rulers both to legitimate their authority and to separate them from those they rule.

Let me elaborate some of these points.

Until the development of the territorial nation-state, rulers or would-be rulers in Iran sought to conquer and control people, not territory. Until territory (such as the Moghan pastures) became commercialized, sovereignty over it was useless without people to exploit and defend it, people who could be taxed and provide military support. In order to persuade people of their continued right to levy taxes and recruits, rulers sought legitimacy. In our context, the most potent legitimating ideology for a ruler was usually some form of popular Islam: personal holiness/sanctity or holy descent from the Prophet or a Sufi saint. Chiefs could not normally claim such personal religious authority, but they too established dynasties claiming descent from original immigrant leaders, granted territory by a legitimate ruler. Both rulers and chiefs had to back

---

[43] Which has continued in the pages of *JRAI* (Salzman 1995).

their claims with military force and success in battle, bringing material rewards in the form of booty. Rulers were expected to make grants of land to their supporters, but took a risk in doing so, since, if ever either the ideology were discredited or the supply of spoils dried up, grant-holders had a base from which to pursue their own ambitions for autonomy, defection (if on a frontier) and challenge to the ruler.

This constant tension between rulers and supporters was at the base of 'tribe–state' relations. A classic example was the early Safavids' problems with the Qızılbash (Chapter Two); and a classic, ideal resolution was Shah 'Abbas' (mythical) creation of the Shahsevan as his personal 'tribe', variously depicted as 'countering the power of the Qızılbash', or as 'recruited from all the Qızılbash tribes'. As we saw in Part I, although there is no evidence that 'Abbas 'created the Shahsevan tribe' in this way, he did reform his army so as to remove the tribal threat to his state, and he did break up and resettle the tribes. Later rulers with their own 'tribal problems' (notably Nader Shah and some of the Qajars) took similar measures when they could. They created (and destroyed) tribal confederacies and dynasties directly; they recognized (or deposed) local chiefs, gave them land grants and authority over tribal populations, and influenced the formation and operation of local political groups (the tribal clusters).

But the 'creation' of confederacies involved more than collecting tribal groups and putting them under central control; rulers also indirectly 'created' the whole tribal system by controlling its terms of existence through print and propaganda. As we have seen, in this chapter and in Chapter One, administrators have defined tribes, both by naming them and by labelling them (for example, as loyalists or traitors); historians and other academics have played a role too, by constructing tribes (*ilat*, *'ashayer*) politically and terminologically as pastoral nomads with chiefs and genealogies.

In the early eighteenth century, when Safavid control was weak, the Shahsevan was only one among several disunited groups in a region which soon became a contested frontier. Nader Shah united many of these groups as Shahsevan under Badr Khan, and they probably reached their greatest unity under his son Nazar 'Ali Khan. Their vulnerable location, and strong local competition from the khanates of the southern Caucasus, inhibited the Shahsevan khans from developing greater ambitions, and indeed not only did the khan dynasty split, but they may not have controlled several local groups (Moghanlu, Beydili, Alarlu and others) who were still mentioned separately. The Shahsevan absorbed these groups under the Qajars, paradoxically after the centralization of the confederacy broke down. In the present century, the administration tended to include many neighbouring tribes too (those of Qara-Dagh, Khalkhal, Sarab, Talesh) as Shahsevan, which became almost synonymous with 'nomadic tribes of Eastern Azarbaijan'. This expanded body reached its greatest power (or was perceived to do so) when briefly united, paradoxically again, under a non-Shahsevan leader, Rahim Khan Chalabianlu; but once more the frontier situation, local rivalries and Russian Cossacks put paid to any ambitions to move beyond the local context.

In other words, in the case of the Shahsevan, if not of other tribal groups in Iran, social and political developments have followed two apparently contradictory, but in fact complementary processes. On the one hand, since the early eighteenth century, the overall identity label 'Shahsevan' appears to have expanded to include increasing numbers of groups of divergent origins; on the other, from a peak of centralization and unity in the late eighteenth century, the locus of power in the confederacy and the 'interface' with the state has gradually 'devolved', from the *elbey* dynasty to the cluster chiefs, to the *taifa* chiefs, and to the elders of the communities.

A chief of a state-like confederacy had similar problems, on a smaller scale, to the ruler of a state. He too sought armed followers, resources (pastures and booty) with which to pay them, a population to tax, and legitimation of his control.[44] A chiefly dynasty would sometimes 'naturalize' their difference from the tribal commoners as 'ethnic', reserving a special descent name for themselves (the Shahilu chiefs of the Qashqa'i, the Sarı-Khan-Beyli of the Shahsevan) while attaching a more generalized ethno-linguistic name (Turk, Lor, Baluch . . .) to the commoners. By their marriage practices (endogamy, and alliances with regional elites) they would further reproduce the difference, leading to their settlement, detribalization and alienation from the commoners.

The original legitimating ideology of the Shahsevan chiefs was (we presume) mystical devotion to the Safavid Shahs as Sufi leaders. With the demise of the Safavids in the eighteenth century and the appointment of the first paramount chief by a non-Safavid, non-Sufi Shah, this royalist and religious ideology lost power, and the authority of Badr Khan and his successors must have been based largely on dynastic ties and land grants. By the mid-nineteenth century, after two catastrophic wars had located a new frontier in their territory, the *elbey*s too lost power and authority (control of pastures and ability to tax), became settled and were replaced by a range of new leaders who seized control of the pastures and of the

---

[44] Earlier (Tapper 1983b) I analysed the problem of tribal leadership by proposing two 'ideal types': the brigand and the chief.

right to tax, while pursuing a lucrative line in banditry. Yet *in extremis* the old call of Shah and Islam could still unite and legitimate, and it continued to be invoked, formally, in the twentieth century. If, in the nineteenth or twentieth centuries, the Shahsevan failed to follow direct religious leadership, let alone a millennial movement such as energized some other tribal peoples at the time, this is not surprising. Millennial movements typically emerged when outsiders were seen to possess extreme cultural and technological superiority. The Shahsevan saw no superiority in the Russians; they felt themselves equal or superior to any opponents.

Speculations about ideology, political allegiance, and hostilities, apply only to the ruling chiefly elite, those who until recently were the ones who had to deal with state authorities and neighbouring groups, including settled society. Are the actions and ideas of the pastoral commoners in their nomadic communities relevant to these discussions of state formation and the tribes and confederacies? There has been unresolved debate about the relation between elite and commoners: how far it was exploitative or protective, and how it was perceived by the commoners in the past. For the Shahsevan at least, the problem, as mentioned above, is that we can know very little about the ordinary tribespeople, their standard of living, motivations, religious beliefs, identity, before the present. Until the detailed, if coloured, reports of late-nineteenth century Russian officials such as Ogranovich, we are dependent on even more impressionistic observations by passing travellers, from Olearius to Morier, and their hints at the abject poverty and ignorance of the nomads. We are reduced to extrapolating from twentieth-century ethnographic studies – as I have done here, in suggesting, for example, that at least since the eighteenth century Shahsevan nomads have been organized, as they were recently, in two kinds of nomadic communities, whose reproduction over time depended more on shared culture and marriage practices than on 'creation' by chiefs or rulers.

Lois Beck has pointed to another apparent paradox of tribalism in twentieth-century Iran: is it politically 'left' or 'right'?[45] Some observers, as we have seen, identify the tribes with reaction and opposition to (usually urban-based) progressive forces; others point to them as representatives of a classic democratic, egalitarian tradition with, in many areas, a revolutionary history of resistance to tyranny. Perhaps the paradox is resolved by pointing to the tribal chiefs, with their landed and other interests, as the reactionaries, and the commoners as the democrats.

In the Shahsevan case, I suggest that the commoners in their nomadic

---

[45] Beck (1980).

communities were not only more or less equal socially and economically, but they maintained a classic, grass-roots nomad-tribal egalitarian ideology. Some writers on nomadic societies hold that such an ideology, often in the form of a segmentary lineage structure, is a false consciousness, fostered by tyrannical chiefs to disguise their exploitation.[46] With the Shahsevan, there were good historical and social reasons which would have produced and maintained such an ideology, whether or not chiefs (or rulers) constructed their identity as descent-based 'tribes'. First, the nomads would have been influenced by Shi'a ideals of equality before God and the illegitimacy of worldly power; secondly, times of disorder (*äshrarlıq*) allowed equality of opportunity to work, and validated ideas of equality of worth; finally, socio-economic equality was reproduced through marriage practices (even where the basic communities were not descent groups, they intermarried and formed groups of kin).[47]

The state's 'creation' and recreation of the tribal system continues with renewed vigour under the Islamic Republic, as we saw in Chapters One and Thirteen. Khomeini reversed the repressions of the Pahlavis by identifying the tribes as 'Treasures of the Revolution'. Where Shah 'Abbas (mythically) created the 'Shahsevan', the Islamic Republic has attempted to recreate them as 'Elsevan'. Tribal organization in the old sense no longer exists. The state has finally abolished the centralized chiefdoms and confederacies, condemned as socially unjust and politically unnecessary and incompatible with a modern state structure, and, through the Organization for Nomadic Affairs, has taken over the political and economic functions of the former tribal chiefs. It has redefined *'ashayer*, *il* and *taifeh* to include no reference to tribal political organization or chiefship, but specifically to imply both pastoral nomadism and the moral ties of kinship, or shared economic interest. It has in effect recognized the socio-cultural and economic significance of the basic nomadic communities.

---

[46] E.g. Black (1972), Bradburd (1987).
[47] In the twentieth century, nomad commoners would have encountered further democratic-egalitarian ideals in the propaganda of the Musavatists (1920s) and the Democrats (1940s), besides the Bolsheviks and the Soviets.

The Shahsevan of Kharaqan and Khamseh: origins and traditions

In the nineteenth and twentieth centuries there have been two distinct sets of tribes called Shahsevan, though there is evidence that the ancestors of most of the tribes in each set co-existed in the Ardabil region in the early eighteenth century. No detailed ethnographic study has been conducted among the Shahsevan tribes of Kharaqan and Khamseh, and I have no personal knowledge of them, but it seems appropriate here to summarize what is known of their origins and traditions.

In Chapters Five and Seven I discussed evidence that Nader Afshar removed Shaqaqi, Inallu Shahsevan and Afshar tribal groups from the Moghan–Ardabil region in 1730. The Shaqaqi returned by the 1750s, though they settled around Sarab to the south of their former home. There is no record that the Inallu or Afshar groups ever came all the way back from Khorasan; rather, evidence indicates that they returned to the Khamseh and Kharaqan regions, where they settled and have remained, and constitute the second of the two major groups of tribes bearing the name Shahsevan.

In these regions, centred approximately on Zanjan, Qazvin and Saveh, there were by the middle of the nineteenth century five tribal groups known as Shahsevan: Inallu, Baghdadi, Qurt-Beyli, Doveiran and Afshar-Doveiran.[1] At least three of these groups appear to have been in the Ardabil–Moghan region early in the previous century, along with the ancestors of the Shahsevan tribes there now.

---

[1] From the mid-nineteenth century on, sources on these groups are relatively prolific, though I have come across no study of their traditions so comprehensive as those published for the Moghan and Ardabil Shahsevan. Some information is to be found in Napier (1902), Fortescue (1922), Minorsky (1934a; 1951–2), Ardalan (1972), Housego (1978), Bellingeri (1978), Tanavoli (1985), Afshar-Sistani (1987), Hasani (1990), Shahsevand-Baghdadi (1991). Varjavand's account of the tribes in the Qazvin area (1970) has nothing new to add to those by Fortescue and Minorsky from which his own derives.

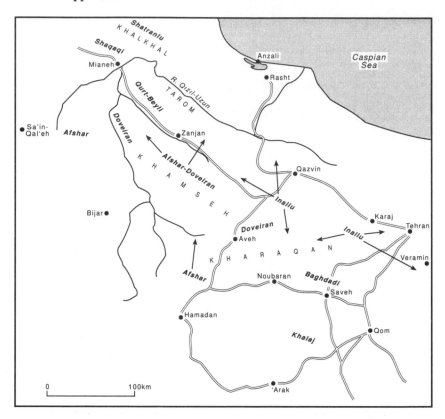

Map 9. Khamseh and Kharaqan, to show places mentioned in Appendix One

The Inallu/Inanlu of Kharaqan and Saveh

Inallu was one of the Oghuz Turkish nomad groups from Central Asia that began moving into Azarbaijan in the eleventh century; since then, groups bearing the name have been recorded in different parts of Anatolia and Iran. A major group of Inallu formed part of Shamlu Qızılbash, and more recently two groups have been prominent in Iran: the Inallu Shahsevan of Kharaqan and Saveh; and the Inallu of Fars, one of the five tribes of the Khamseh confederacy.[2] Smaller groups of Inallu, both nomad and settled, are to be found in Azarbaijan.[3]

The Inallu tribe wintering between Tehran, Saveh and Qazvin and

---

[2] Not to be confused with the Khamseh region of the northwest, or any other of the districts named Khamseh (= five).

[3] In Ardabil and Moghan (see Appendix Two); in Qara-Dagh; and among the Hajji-'Alili of Maragheh (Oberling 1964b: 82).

summering in Kharaqan, according to Fortescue, 'are said to have been moved from the Mughan plain by Agha Muhammad Khan Kajar', while Minorsky says they 'used to live in Mughan, whence they were transported by Nadir Shah (?) to Khamsa to form a bulwark against the incursions of the Bilbas Kurds'.[4] The Inanlu of Fars, according to Hasan Fasa'i, came there in the Mongol era, and the Abolverdi dynasty have headed the tribe since Safavid times. The Fars and Shahsevan Inallu appear to be of different origins, but one of the two main sections of the latter, named Gökpar, may have originated with the former, one of whose twenty-five sections is also called Gökpar. Fasa'i was told by a leading member of the Gökpar Inallu Shahsevan that in Shah 'Abbas' time, when some of the tribes became Shahsevan, his ancestors separated from the Fars Gökpar tribe and became Shahsevan; but it is not stated whether they then went to Moghan or elsewhere.[5]

In the traditions of the Moghan Shahsevan (Markov's and Radde's versions), a group of Inallu is said to have come from Anatolia to Moghan at the same time as Yunsur Pasha. In the early eighteenth century, the Inallu Shahsevan were indeed a major force in the Moghan area (Chapter Five), but references to a substantial Inallu tribe there cease after 1730. By the late nineteenth century, when groups said to have originated as Inallu 'clans' (Pir-Evatlu, Kalash, Kor-'Abbaslu, Geyikli, Yortchi, Dursun-Khojalu) were separate tribes among the Moghan Shahsevan, Markov and Radde record only ninety families of Inallu. We can conclude that the Inallu must have been among those removed from Moghan by Nader Afshar.[6]

Inallu are mentioned not far from their present habitat of Kharaqan and Saveh in 1779, soon after the death of Karim Khan Zand: Agha Mohammad Qajar, returning from Fars to Mazandaran to raise his tribesmen in a bid for supremacy, came across some Inanlu Kurds (*sic*) who had been sent by Karim Khan to reside near Veramin, Sa'uj-Bolagh and Saveh; he took them with him to Mazandaran.[7] From the mid-nineteenth century, the Inallu were a major tribal group in Kharaqan and Saveh, and provided cavalry for the Iranian army.

The Baghdadi Shahsevan of Saveh and Qom

This group has a somewhat different history, though they were closely allied with the Inallu by the mid-nineteenth century. According to Fortescue,

---

[4] Fortescue (1922: 326); Minorsky (1934a: 268).
[5] Fasa'i (1896, II: 309); cf. Karimzadeh (1974).
[6] Perhaps it is they whose return from Khorasan is mentioned by al-Hoseini (1974: fol. 20b), see Chapter Five.   [7] Nami (1938: 246).

The Baghdadi are narrated to have migrated from Persia during the Safavi period and settled near Baghdad, whence they returned to Shiraz during the reign of Nadir Shah. During the reign of Karim Khan Zand they had no fixed abode. They joined Agha Muhammad Khan Kajar, who settled them in their present habitat.[8]

A more recent researcher tells a slightly different story, based on interviews with the chiefs and documents owned by them: at Nader Shah's orders, 12,000 families of Moghan Shahsevan, led by the brothers Qasem 'Ali Khan and Qara Bey, were sent to watch the western marches of Iran (Baghdad?). Later, Karim Khan sent them to Shiraz, where they resided in Zand times; after his death they wished to return to Moghan, their original home, but Agha Mohammad Qajar prevented them and settled them between Hamadan, Qazvin and Saveh; under Naser ad-Din Shah they acquired private rights to their pastures. In the same writer's investigations, however, Inanlu are counted as one of the three branches of the Baghdadi (the others are Lak and Arekhlu), and it may be only this branch that has traditions of Moghan origins.[9]

Yet more recently, 'Ataollah Hasani has argued that sections of the Baghdadi came from the Bayat Turks; he has found traces of the Baghdadi in the Kerkuk region of Iraq, in Syria and southern Turkey, as well as in Khorasan, where legends among present Baghdadi chiefs state that Nader Afshar removed their ancestors after his expedition to Baghdad. After his death, they moved to Shiraz; then, under Agha Mohammad Qajar, to Saveh. Their leader, 'Ali Khan, was one of Karim Khan Zand's experienced military commanders, who campaigned in the Gulf in the 1750s, then in 1759 was detailed to kill off the settled Afghans in Mazandaran in Karim Khan's Nouruz massacre. Later, with difficulty he routed the Qajars. In 1762 he was commander of Karim Khan's western flank at the battle of Urmiyeh, and a year later he accompanied Nazar 'Ali Khan Zand to capture the rebel Zaki Khan. His end came in 1765 when, having been sent to reduce Taqi Khan Dorrani at Kerman, he was shot by a sniper.[10] Though he is only named 'Ali Khan Shahsevan in the sources, Hasani argues that he was from the Qasemlu branch of the group that later became known as Baghdadi.[11] I know of no reference to the Baghdadi by name before the mid-nineteenth century, when they are

---

[8] Fortescue (1922: 326). According to Minorsky (1934a: 268), however, the Baghdadi are said to have come from Shiraz in the time of Shah 'Abbas I.
[9] Ardalan (1972: 133).   [10] See Perry (1979).
[11] Hasani (1990, I: 12–16). Napier, Fortescue, Minorsky, Ardalan and (in most detail) Hasani all give lists of the Baghdadi subsections: a few names echo those of ancient Oghuz or Qızılbash groups, but on the whole they give little indication of the origins of the Baghdadi before the move to Baghdad. Despite her name, Shahsevand-Baghdadi includes virtually no information on the Baghdadi Shahsevan in her book (1991), which focuses on the Moghan Shahsevan.

mentioned among the Persian forces fighting in Afghanistan; later they became the chief recruiting ground for the Iranian Cossacks.

The Qurt-Beyli Shahsevan of Mianeh and Khamseh

The Qurt-Beyli are recorded as a substantial group in the Khamseh and around Mianeh in the nineteenth century, but I can find no mention of their traditions, and by the twentieth century this name no longer appears.

They may be of Afshar origins: in his study of the Oghuz and their descendants, Sümer mentions Kutbeyli, an Afshar clan in southeast Anatolia in the fifteenth century; nothing is known of their later fate, but perhaps they came to Iran with the Imanlu Afshars and the Inallu, with both of whom they are associated.[12] Maybe they are the Q.t.beglu tribe near Zanjan mentioned by Chelebizadeh as submitting to the Ottomans in 1727.[13]

They may also be connected with the Qurt Bey who, according to the traditions published by Markov and Radde, brought his people to Moghan from Anatolia with Yunsur Pasha. This is indicated by a minor discrepancy between Markov's and Radde's accounts. Markov states that certain groups separated from Qurt Bey's tribe and went to live on the 'Araks' (sc. Aras) river, while Radde gives their destination as 'Arak', that is 'Eraq-e 'Ajam, the large area of western Iran sometimes taken to include the Khamseh region. Movement to the Aras would not have meant much of a separation from Qurt Bey's group, if the latter was with Yunsur Pasha in Moghan (which is after all bounded by the Aras), and would thus hardly warrant special mention. For this reason, Radde's 'Arak' is to be preferred, except for the fact that the tribes listed in both sources as having left Qurt Bey (Qozatlu, Polatlu, Damirchili, Talesh-Mikeilli, Khalifali, Moghanlu, Udulu, Moratlu, Zargar) are all now found among the Shahsevan of Moghan, that is, they at any rate did not move to Iraq.[14] The puzzle remains.

The Doveiran and Afshar-Doveiran of Khamseh and Tarom

These groups, according to Fortescue,

are all Turki and are of mixed origin but appear to have been brought from Ardabil and other parts of Azarbaijan and mingled with the Kizil Bash tribes, already in Khamseh, into the Shahsavan confederation [of the Baghdadi and

[12] Sümer (1967: 263, 268).   [13] Chelebizadeh (1740: f. 120b).   [14] See Chapter Three.

Inallu tribes] . . . Duvairan were a strong Shahsavan tribe brought from Mughan and Ardabil by Fath Ali Shah, and settled in the fertile Kizil Uzun valley for their 'Qishlaq' with 'Yailaq' in the highlands West of the valley bordering on the Afshar district of Azarbaijan . . . owing to oppression and bad times they have melted away to Ardabil and other parts of Azarbaijan, and only a remnant are left.[15]

The Afshar-Doveiran (also known as Shahsevan-Afshar) are so called to distinguish them from two other neighbouring groups of Afshar, those of Sa'in-Qal'eh and those between Khamseh and Saveh, although all these groups are said to have come from Moghan at the same time, together with the Doveiran. The Afshar-Doveiran used to go to summer quarters in Tarom, but settled in the nineteenth century in Khamseh. Housego, who visited these groups in the 1970s, says that they did not recognize the name 'Duvayran'; Tanavoli says that the name should be 'Davayoran' (Dävä-yörän), meaning 'camel-drivers'.[16]

Either the Doveiran or the Afshar-Doveiran, or both of them, may be identified with the Erili/Eyerli Afshar who settled in Tarom and Khalkhal in the eighteenth century. Musa Bey Erili Afshar of Khalkhal, leader of a group of Shahsevan, was one of Nader Shah's assassins.[17] Musa Bey's brother, Amir Guneh Khan Erili Afshar of Tarom, was a military veteran fighting under Karim Khan Zand and later under 'Ali Morad Khan against the Qajars. Another close relative, presumably, was Zo'lfeqar Khan Erili Afshar, appointed by Karim Khan to govern Zanjan and Khamseh in 1763; in 1772 he rebelled with Shaqaqi allies, was defeated and taken to Shiraz, but was later reinstated, with his family kept as hostages. He was independent again briefly in 1779, when he captured Hedayat Khan of Gilan and replaced him with his own agents, but soon after he was killed by 'Ali Morad Khan Zand. Neither Zo'lfeqar Khan nor Amir Guneh Khan was referred to as Shahsevan, but in 1918 Zo'lfeqar Khan, chief of the Shahsevan Doveiran, claimed his namesake as his ancestor.[18]

A rival for control of Zanjan was an 'Ali Khan Shahsevan of Khamseh, first mentioned in 1779 as an ally of Hedayat Khan of Gilan and 'Ali Morad Zand. A few years later he turned against them, defecting to Agha Mohammad Qajar. In 1783 he seized Rasht and freed his brother-in-law Ebrahim from Enzeli, where Hedayat Khan had imprisoned him; in 1786 he helped Agha Mohammad Khan in the capture of Tehran, but later in the year the Qajar had him killed.[19] He is given no tribal name other than Shahsevan, but being from Zanjan it is likely that he too was from the Doveiran or Afshar-Doveiran, and later sources call him 'Ali Khan Afshar

[15] Fortescue (1922: 322–3).   [16] Housego (1978: 11), Tanavoli (1985: 30).
[17] Mohammad Kazem (1960, III: fol. 249b); Golestaneh (1965: 12). See Chapter Five.
[18] Fortescue (1922: 323, 396).   [19] Butkov (1869, II: 304).

Khamseh.[20] He is not to be confused with the earlier 'Ali Khan Shahsevan, Karim Khan's general.

Other named Shahsevan chiefs in the Zand forces are of so far unidentified affiliations: Sarmast Khan, who was in charge of Sistani cavalry in the west soon after Nader's death, and Reza-qoli Khan at Shiraz under Lotf 'Ali Khan in the 1780s.[21] Some of the sources confuse both the 'Ali Khans mentioned with a third, who was contemporary with both of them but was chief of the Shaqaqi from 1747–86 and father of Sadeq Khan. Butkov, for example, states that Sadeq Khan was son of 'Ali Khan (Shahsevan) of Zanjan, which is most unlikely. The confusion was compounded by a further possible 'Ali Khan, one of Sadeq Khan's brothers, appointed by him to govern Zanjan.[22]

Other 'Shahsevan' groups

Among tribal groups related to the Shahsevan are their neighbours in Qara-Dagh (Arasbaran), such as the Chalabianlu and Hajji-'Alili, and in Khalkhal, such as the Shatranlu and Dalikanlu. All these groups figure prominently in the narrative of this book, especially in Part IV, and indeed since the early twentieth century official documents and reports have increasingly classified them in association with, if not under the name of, the Shahsevan of Moghan and Ardabil, although there is no evidence, nor has it been claimed, that they share common origins with the majority of Shahsevan.[23] There are those, however, who claim a common origin in Moghan for the Shahsevan and the Qashqa'i of Fars, though there are no recorded contacts between these groups in recent history.[24]

---

[20] E.g. Hedayat (1994: 294f.).   [21] Golestaneh (1965: 133); Nami (1938: 353).

[22] Dälili (1979: 28).

[23] On the tribes of Qara-Dagh, see Baiburdi (1962), Oberling (1964b), Bazin (1982). On the tribes of Khalkhal, see Fortescue (1922), Oberling (1964a), Rava'i (1984).

[24] See Oberling (1974), and my discussion in Tapper (1972: 809–13).

Appendix two

Lists and histories of Shahsevan tribes

The value of tribal lists as documents is qualified by their nature and inherent interest as social constructions (see Chapter Fourteen), which leads, among other variations, to considerable differences in length. For example, among official lists I collected in the 1960s, one given by a senior official responsible for the Ministry of Agriculture's relations with the Shahsevan amounted to forty-eight tribes; another, by the Moghan Office of Tribes, numbers forty; while the Meshkin gendarmerie's 1963 list numbered twenty-one. Only a few discrepancies in length and content were due to differences of jurisdiction.

In the sources, tribes are sometimes ordered according to size and importance, sometimes according to territorial propinquity or common origins. There is no obviously preferable order, so in the list, and the accompanying table (Figure 12), I have listed the tribes alphabetically (as did the recent Census, though according to the Persian alphabet), within four categories:

    1. The tribes of Meshkin
    2. The tribes of Ardabil
    3. Tribes that have settled/disappeared since about 1900
    4. Tribes that have emerged since about 1900.

With transliteration of tribal names, I have attempted a compromise between the usually Persianized literary versions and a phonetic version of how they are pronounced by Shahsevan themselves.

Sources for the table and lists:

1843 = Abbott (1844). 'I was not able to obtain any account of the number of each separate division.'

1870 = Ogranovich (1870); also gives numbers of *qıshlaqs*, their location, some details of *yailaqs*.

1878 = Markov (1890) (Krebel's list); also gives locations of *yailaqs*, some names of chiefs.

1884 = Radde (1886) ('checked by Ogranovich, May 1884'); similar to 1878.

1886 (a) = Mizban (1992); Amin Nezam's 1884 list of tribes and Moghan pastures, from Amir Leshkar's 1922 document. Some names (marked ++) appear more than once, attached to different chiefs. This list includes several major groups which do not appear in 1886 (b), including Hajji-Khojalu, Geyikli, 'Isalu, and the Qara-Daghi tribe Hajji-'Alili.

1886 (b) = Mizban (1992); rearrangement of pastures by Mostafa-qoli Khan Amir Toman in 1886 (see Chapter Eleven).

1903 = Tigranov (1909); also gives locations, names of chiefs, some detailed tribal histories.

1919 = Anon. (1919): good on chiefs and locations of main tribes; numbers are inflated.

1956 = Iranian Army HQ in Meshkin-Shahr, recorded by Oberling (1964a); most numbers are highly inflated.

1959 = Taj-Gardun (1959); apparently based on a census of families.

1960 = figures from Iranian Army Files at Tabriz, of undetermined date, recorded by Oberling during 1960 field research (1964a); more accurate than 1956, with a few exceptions such as Ajirli; gives locations, names of sections.

1961 = Sadeq (1961); like 1959, apparently based on a quite accurate census; though differing on figures for individual tribes, their totals agree on about 5,000 nomad families, 30,000–40,000 individuals. I read them after completing Tapper (1966), and was at first inclined to dismiss their figures as too low, but later came to accept them as good guides.

1966 = My own summary records of 1963–6, based on several of the above, plus half a dozen official lists, a score or more lists given by private individuals (some of which are given in detail in Tapper 1972: Appendix 3), and my own observations and experience.

1986 = Census of Nomads (1987), distilled by Kamali (1989); locations and names of tribal sections given, some of them being names of former tribes. The census appears to be accurate: the total Shahsevan nomad population is given as 47,248, in 5,897 households. Some tribes included did not figure earlier, e.g. Zakhurashlu, and the Qara-Daghi tribe Hoseinakli.

Name of tayfa	List 1843	1870 ff	1878 ff	1884 ff	1886 (a)	1886 (b)	1903 ff	191` ff
1. Tribes of Meshkin								
Aivatlu	-	-	-	-	+	+	30	-
Ajirli	-	700	185	200	+	+	150	-
'Ali-Babalu	-	200	120	200	+	+	150	-
'Arabli	-	100	90	120	+	+	100	-
Bala-Beyli	+	100	50	100	-	+	75	-
Bey-Baghlu	-	50	50	70	+	+	20	-
Beydili	+	600	150	50	-	-	150	-
Damirchili	+	800	150	200	++	++	300	-
Gabali	-	-	50,70	50	+	-	-	-
Gamushchi	-	50	100	100	-	-	-	-
Geyikli	(+)	400	+	70	+	-	200	100
Hajji-Khojalu	-	600	100	300	+	-	500	100
Homunlu	-	50	20	30	+	+	200	-
Hosein-Hajjili	-	-	110	80	+	+	100	-
Inallı	-	400	90	90	-	-	-	-
'Isalu/'Isa-Beyli	-	200	210	200	+	-	150	7-80
(Sarı)Ja'farli	-	-	100	100	-	+	100	-
Janyarlu	-	-	70	80	(+)	(+)	35	-
Jeloudarlu	-	300	120	350	-	+	100	-
Kalash	-	250?	70	70	+	+	70	-
Khalafli	-	50	-	-	-	-	25	-
Khalifali/Khalfali	+	400	100	80	++	+	100	+
Kor-'Abbaslu	-	-	50	50	-	+	25	-
Larili/Lahrud	-	-	30	100	+	-	-	-
Mast-'Ali-Beyli	-	800	8	150	++	++	50	-
Milli	+	250	15	40	-	-	(25)	-
Moghanlu	+	300	450	700	+	++	800	100
Moratlu	+	200	50,30	100	+	++	40	-
Nouruz-'Ali-Beyli	+	400	110	150	+	+	110	+
Pir-Evatlu	-	500	150	150	+	+	30	400
Qara-Qasemli	-	-	58	150	+	+	100	-
Qoja-Beyli	+	200	100	250	+	+	500	150
Qurtlar/Qutlar	+	-	-	50	-	-	-	-
Sarı-Khan-Beyli	+	400	250	400	+	+	250	-
Sarvanlar	-	100	50	50	-	-	-	-
Seyetler	-	-	100	100	-	+	-	-
Seyetler-Zarenji	-	-	+	-	+	?	100	-
Shah-'Ali-Beyli	-	-	150	150	+	+	100	-
Talesh-Mikeilli of Meshkin	+	400	250	300	+	+	200	-
Terit/Trit	-	-	-	-	-	+	-	-
Udullu	+	100	140	120	+	+	200	-
Zargar	+	100	50	100	+	+	50	4-50

1956 ff	1959 ff	1960 ff	1961 ff	1966 ff	1986 ff	1986 oba	Name of tayfa
60	+	-	-	(S)	23	6	Aivatlu
600	374	3200	482	400	476	139	Ajirli
200	39	60	159	+	34	21	'Ali-Babalu
100	44	230	48	50-60	38	17	'Arabli
150	19	50	74	+	48	20	Bala-Begli
40	30	25	53	+	17	6	Bey-Baghlu
200	136	-	156	100-150	167	33	Beydili
100	121	59	99	+	137	35	Damirchili
-	259	-	398	+	313	56	Gabali
-	-	-	-	(S)	-	-	Gamushchi
>600	539	620	307	700	507	116	Geyikli
1500	248	480	331	+	361	56	Hajji-Khojalu
150	45	19	64	+	28	11	Homunlu
300	202	100	139	150-200	134	18	Hosein-Hajjili
300	-	-	-	-	-	-	İnallı
1000	146	150	279	(S)	100	24	'Isalu/'Isa-Beyli
150	10	50	46	50	15	4	(Sarı)Ja'farli
+	-	+	118	+	(+)	(+)	Janyarlu
50	46	95	82	50	142	53	Jeloudarlu
150	45	37	75	70	30	11	Kalash
-	+	-	26	+	-	(+)	Khalafli
60	37	35	60	50	78	16	Khalifali/Khalfali
100	211	-	172	150	126	32	Kor-'Abbaslu
-	+	-	27	60	98	28	Larili/Lahrud
250	98	80	119	(S)	105	25	Mast-'Ali-Beyli
100	123	46	?43	+	(37)		Milli
2000	703	1170	764	1000	842	291	Moghanlu
-	56	30	49	+	43	11	Moratlu
-	-	-	+	-	-	-	Nouruz-'Ali-Beylii
150	+	10	92	5(S)	-	-	Pir-Evatlu
50	+	-	45	-	-	-	Qara-Qasemli
3000	400	960	593	500	277	93	Qoja-Beyli
250	43	260	55	+	353	73	Qurtlar/Qutlar
300	46	15	131	+	74	30	Sarı-Khan-Beyli
40	27	-	60	50	46	25	Sarvanlar
350	123	140	122	50-60	142	45	Seyetler
300	-	50	5	(S)	-	-	Seyetler-Zarenji
-	-	-	33	+	26	4	Shah-'Ali-Beyli
260	200	-	228	4-500	139	58	Talesh-Mikeilli of Meshkin
80	43	15	29	+	(+)		Terit/Trit
50	34	22	74	+	21	10	Udullu
50	+	-	15	+	-	-	Zargar

List Name of tayfa	1843	1870 ff	1878 ff	1884 ff	1886 (a)	1886 (b)	1903 ff	1919 ff
2. Tribes of Ardabil								
Alarlu/Arallu	-	-	-	-	-	-	-	300
Asefli-Khamesli	-	-	-	-	-	-	-	120-15
Delaqarda	-	-	-	-	-	-	-	500
Dursun-Khojalu	+	350	250(S)	300(S)	-	-	+	6-700
Jahan-Khanomlu	+	300	150	150	-	+	150	300
Khamesli	-	-	110	-	-	-	200	4-500
Polatlu	+	600	100	250,150	+	+	(S)	1200
Qozatlu	+	400	50	70	-	-	50	4-500
Reza-Beyli	+	50	25	100	-	-	(S)	400
Takleh	+	600	100	150	-	+	100	400
Talesh-Mikeillu of Ardabil	+	200	+	250	+	+	150	800
Yekali	-	50	15	40	-	-	30	-
Yortchi	+	400	500	950	-	-	(S)	2000
3. Tribes that have settled/disappeared since about 1900								
Abi-Beyli	+	100	50(S)	70 (S)	-	-	-	-
Aq-Qasemli +	-	-	-	-	+	-	25	-
Rezalu					+		15	
Baibagli	+	100	+	-	+	+	(S)	-
Band-'Ali-Beyli	+	+	-	-	-	-	-	-
Farajollah-Khanlu	+	50(S)	50(S)	-	-	-	-	-
Fathollah-Khanlu	+	50(S)	50(S)	-	-	-	50(S)	-
Ilkhichi	-	-	20	25	-	-	-	-
Qahraman-Beyli	-	50	20(S)	30(S)	-	-	-	-
Sheikhli	+	250	S	100(S)	-	-	(S)	-
Yeddi-Oimaq	-	-	110	80	+	+	+	-
4. Tribes that have emerged since about 1900								
Ja'far-qulu-Khanlu	-	-	-	-	-	-	-	-
Kalesar	-	-	-	-	-	-	-	-
Qaralar/Khioulu	-	-	-	-	-	-	-	-
Qaralar-Jabdaraq	-	-	-	-	-	-	-	-
Madadli	-	-	-	-	-	-	-	-
Sarı-Nasirli	-	-	-	-	-	-	-	-
Zakhurashlu	-	-	-	-	-	-	-	-
Sarı-Khanlu	-	-	-	-	-	-	-	-
Hoseinakli	-	-	-	-	-	-	-	-

Figure 12. Lists of Shahsevan tribes, 1843–1986.

956 ff	1959 ff	1960 ff	1961 ff	1966 ff	1986 ff	1986 oba	Name of tayfa
950	-	100	-	+	4	1	Alarlu/Arallu
200	-	-	-	+	-	-	Asefli-Khamesli
300	-	20	-	+	-	-	Delaqarda
-	-	(S)	-	(S)	-	-	Dursun-Khojalu
50	66	-	87	+	106	11	Jahan-Khanomlu
500	-	10	+		11	6	Khamesli
650	-	-	+	(S)	-	-	Polatlu
30	-	-	-	-	-	-	Qozatlu
500	14	-	21	(S)	13	2	Reza-Beyli
-	58	58	120	+	187	24	Takleh
50	-	-	-	-	-	-	Talesh-Mikeilli of Ardabil
50	-	45	-	+	31	3	Yekali
-	-	(S)	+	(S)	-	-	Yortchi
-	-	-	-	-	-	-	Abi-Beyli
-	-	-	-	-	-	-	Aq-Qasemli + Rezalu
-	-	-	-	-	-	-	Baibagli
-	-	-	-	-	-	-	Band-'Ali-Beyli
-	-	-	-	-	-	-	Farajollah-Khanlu
-	-	90	-	-	-	-	Fathollah-Khanlu
-	-	-	-	-	-	-	Ilkhichi
-	-	-	-	-	-	-	Qahraman-Beyli
-	-	-	-	-	-	-	Sheikhli
-	-	+	-	+	+	-	Yeddi-Oimaq
-	-	100+	-	+	17	10	Ja'far-qulu-Khanlu
-	-	150	-	+	-	-	Kalesar
-	-	-	18	+	39	13	Qaralar/Khioulu
-	-	-	-	-	56	19	Qaralar-Jabdaraq
-	-	300	-	-	-	-	Madadli
-	-	-	-	+	34	14	Sarı-Nasirli
-	-	-	-	-	151	9	Zakhurashlu
-	-	-	-	-	2	2	Sarı-Khanlu
-	-	-	-	+	312	46	Hoseinakli

1. The Meshkin division

AIVATLU: Two groups, one a *tirä* of TAKLEH; see also BEYDILI.

AJIRLI: See BEYDILI. 'Ibadollah Bey (c. 1900) was unable to hold the AJIRLI tribe together, as was his son Ne'mat, and most of them went to ALARLU in Ojarud, leaving the rest under Nouruz QOJA-BEYLI. Nosrat Bey reunited the AJIRLI in northern Moghan in c. 1940; he later served the Democrats as chief of Shahsevan in 1946, then was killed soon after. His third son Qotaz was chief until the 1960s and continued active until the Revolution. Meanwhile many AJIRLI *qıshlaqs* were taken over by the canals and 200–300 families settled in Moghan.

'ARABLI: Both Olearius (in 1639) and Gärber (in 1730) mention Arab nomads in Moghan; but there is no recorded link between these and the 'ARABLI *taifa* of the nineteenth and twentieth centuries. See also BEYDILI.

BALA-BEYLI: Had pastures near their parent tribe, SARI-KHAN-BEYLI. Before the closure, they had no farming settlements; afterwards many went to Russia, the rest being allotted *qıshlaqs* in southeast Moghan, near TALESH-MIKEILLI, to whom they later became attached; a few founded a village on the banks of the Aras which survives today. *Tiräs* include KHALAFLI.

BEY-BAGHLI: Not to be confused with BAI-BAGLI tribe of Ardabil. See BAND-'ALI-BEYLI below.

BEYDILI: (See Chapter Three); part of the Shamlu Qızılbash, associated with AJIRLI and INALLU, all three names being found in Moghan in the early eighteenth century. A century later, both BEYDILI and AJIRLI were still mentioned separately from the Shahsevan; both were populous but comparatively poor. Neither they nor their neighbours and associates (YEDDI-OIMAQ, HOMUNLU, AIVATLU, 'ARABLI and others) had any farming settlements before the closure. Some, however, had pastures in Iranian Moghan, particularly in the northern part, along the Aras towards the Russian frontier and the Hasan-Khanlu settlements, which they retained after the closure. None of these tribes took a leading part in the subsequent inter-tribal disputes: they attached themselves to either QOJA-BEYLI or ALARLU, and only Jahangir Bey of BEYDILI was a chief of any influence. Cf. documents of Savad Jahangirzadeh. BEYDILI used to be with ALARLU in Ojarud, then in the 1930s many settled, partly in Arshaq, partly in Northern Moghan where their *qıshlaqs* were under irrigation.

DAMIRCHILI: Despite the 1849 report (Chapter Ten) of a feud with HAJJI-KHOJALU, DAMIRCHILI were reputedly a peaceful, populous and wealthy tribe, though exceeded in all three respects by their associates MOGHANLU. They had no farms before the closure; their *qıshlaqs* in the northern part of Russian Moghan were replaced by rather poor hilly pastures in Khoruslu, but their pastures on the southern slopes of Savalan were good. They comprised two or three major sections, one of which later became a separate tribe known variously as QURTLAR and QARAJALU/KALESAR. Dependants may have included MILLI and SEYETLER.

GABALI: See HAJJI-KHOJALU.

GEYIKLI: Neighbours of HAJJI-KHOJALU in both Moghan and the mountains, GEYIKLI was a comparatively small tribe of heterogeneous origins in the mid-nineteenth century. At that time, 'Ali-Reza and his son Mohammad 'Ali, who had arrived from Qara-Bagh at the time of the Russian wars, took over the chiefship from the former ruling lineage, whose scions scattered throughout GEYIKLI and other tribes and settlements in the region. Around the same time, GEYIKLI were joined by a section of the YORTCHI of Ardabil. Towards the end of the century, the tribe multiplied and the new ruling lineage grew large and powerful, assuming the trappings of nobility by marrying with other chiefly lineages rather than with commoners of GEYIKLI. This was somewhat premature, for around 1900, weakened by dynastic disputes, the lineage nearly lost control to the head of a commoner section. This rival died young, however, and the ruling lineage reunited itself and retained control for the last decades of *khankhanlıq*. Towards the end of that period, another dispute developed, a blood-feud between Hajji Faraj and his nephew 'Aleshan Khan (who killed the former's eldest son Bala Khan). The whole tribe split on a territorial basis into two divisions, known (and apparently recognized administratively) as the first and second *qesmat*, but not losing the common GEYIKLI name. For many years in alliance with HAJJI-KHOJALU, GEYIKLI were similarly traditional enemies of the QOJA-BEYLI. Under Hajji Faraj, the tribe grew so powerful that it managed eventually to become independent of HAJJI-KHOJALU and then to wrest control of two large village bases – Khiou and Zeiveh – from QOJA-BEYLI. From this time, the chief of GEYIKLI had the allegiance of a number of smaller commoner tribes: HÜSÜN-

HAJJILI, KALASH, KOR-'ABBASLU, SHAH-'ALI-BEYLI, and later
SEYETLER and MILLI. When 'Aleshan Khan died, his following (it is
said) turned to his powerful commoner henchman Esma'il Khan, but
the dynastic quarrel was patched up through the mediation of Javat
Khan HAJJI-KHOJALU, and in 1941 Hatam Khan, Faraj's second son,
won over Esma'il Khan, reunited the tribe and remained in firm
control as chief until the 1960s.

HAJJI-KHOJALU: Possibly descended from the Aq-Qoyunlu group Khoja-
Hajjilu; and/or from the Hajji-Kazili mentioned by Olearius. Recorded
in the traditions as associated with BEYDILI, AJIRLI and YEDDI-OIMAQ,
and thus possibly of Shamlu origins. In the nineteenth century, HAJJI-
KHOJALU were the most powerful of the 'commoner' tribes of Meshkin,
who had traditional *qıshlaqs* near Aslanduz (where they were associated
with the INALLU), and *yailaqs* on Qosha-Dagh at the western end of the
Savalan range. They have always been the westernmost of the
Shahsevan tribes, having certain of the Qara-Dagh tribes as neighbours
in both summer and winter quarters. In 1849 they are recorded as
fighting the DAMIRCHILI tribe, though the cause is unclear since their
pastures did not adjoin. In the early 1870s, harsh winters and punishment for banditry reduced their population from several hundred to
only seventy households, the remainder being scattered among the
other tribes,[1] but in subsequent years their numbers soon swelled, and
after the closure they were again capable of defending their *qıshlaqs*, the
choicest in Iranian Moghan, from the rapacious CHALABIANLU tribe of
Qara-Dagh. When Artamonov visited them in 1889, the chiefs had
settled numbers of poor farmers in small hamlets in their pastures
along the Dara-Yort valley, providing them with 'protection' in return
for over half the harvest of wheat and rice. Under their powerful chief
Hazrat-qoli and later his cousin Javat Khan, they successfully opposed
the QOJA-BEYLI. After 1900, by virtue of their distance from Russian
Moghan and the comparative inaccessibility of their territory, they
became even more successful at banditry than their rivals. Javat Khan
fought General Fidarov in 1912; later he married the widow of Rahim
Khan CHALABIANLU, and united the two tribes to fight Amir Arshad
HAJJI-'ALILI. They clashed over the town of Ahar. After his brother
Hajji-Aqa was killed, Javat drove Amir Arshad out of Ahar. He survived
until World War II (see Appendix Three). The tribes GABALI and
HAJJILI have always had the status of sub-tribes of HAJJI-KHOJALU. So
also, perhaps, had TERIT.

---

[1] Ogranovich (1876: 203).

HOMUNLU: See BEYDILI.

HOSEIN-HAJJILI/HÜSÜN-AJILI: See GEYIKLI.

INALLU: Originating with the Shamlu Qızılbash, a major group of INALLU were active in Moghan in the 1720s, but most were removed to Khorasan by Nader Afshar shortly afterwards; they later returned as far as the Kharaqan and Saveh districts (see Appendix One); there are also INALLU nomads near Marand, west of Qara-Dagh. However, a number of small groups named INALLU remained settled in the Ardabil region, one of them near Aslanduz.

'ISALU/'ISA-BEYLI: See QOJA-BEYLI.

JA'FARLI/SARI-JA'FARLI: Possibly two different tribes. JA'FARLI said to have come from Qara-Bagh in the 1820s.

JANYARLU: A diminished tribe (1903), mostly settled in Russia; migrate and mix with TALESH-MIKEILLI (q.v.), to whom chiefs sold *yailaqs*.

JELOUDARLU: See SARVANLAR. One *tirä* is QAHRAMANLU.

KALASH: See GEYIKLI. Not to be confused with Talesh tribe of GALESH.

KHALAFLI: Not to be confused with KHALFALI. See BALA-BEYLI.

KHALIFALI/KHALFALI: See MOGHANLU, MILLI (and there is a separate tribe called KHALIFALU-YE OJARUD; cf. 1919, 1960). Savat Bey and a group of elders told me in 1964 that KHALFALI was all one lineage, though they produced no pedigree leading to a common ancestor. They considered that they used to be a section of MOGHANLU (see Chapter Thirteen), though the lists show that KHALIFALI was a separate tribe in 1843, then was attached to QOJA-BEYLI before 1900.

KOR-'ABBASLU/KÜRAVAZLI: See GEYIKLI. One *tirä* is TRIT.

LARILI/LARUD: From the Meshkin village of Larud.

MAST-'ALI-BEYLI: See BAND-'ALI-BEYLI (below).

MILLI: Associated with SEYETLER, KHALFALI.

MOGHANLU: See Chapter Three. MOGHANI nomads, not surprisingly, have been recorded in Moghan since the seventeenth century, and were possibly of indigenous Kurdish, rather than Turkish origins.[2] It is likely that they became Turkicized in the eighteenth century, changing their name to MOGHANLU; they were not fully assimilated to the Shahsevan confederacy until the nineteenth century. Always among the more populous of the nomad tribes, their numbers increased throughout the nineteenth century until at the time of the closure they were the largest of all, with some 700 families. They have always been known as law-abiding and wealthy, raisers not raiders of stock. As reported by Markov, they suffered considerably in the incidents of December 1885, but they were usually powerful enough to hold their own against other tribes, though there is no record of their being involved in feuds themselves. It may have been these characteristics that led the authorities, after the closure, to appoint MOGHANLU chief Morad 'Ali Bey as 'overseer' of the Shahsevan. This chief was moreover married to a daughter of the assistant of the Ardabil governor responsible for the administration of the Shahsevan. I was told by an old man of another tribe that Morad 'Ali Bey and his associates 'were so powerful that even the wolves were afraid of their sheep, and not a thief was to be seen', but the QOJA-BEYLI chiefs at least did not acknowledge Morad 'Ali's authority (see Appendix Three). MOGHANLU had no farming settlements. Their winter pastures lay along the Aras in the northern part of Russian Moghan, but probably some of them already had to use part of Iranian Moghan before the closure. Afterwards they secured extensive if inadequate *qıshlaqs* in the Quru-Chai region of Iranian Moghan, southeast of HAJJI-KHOJALU and GEYIKLI. Their fine summer quarters stretch across the Savalan range just west of the peaks. The small tribe of KHALFALI, whose winter and summer pastures adjoined those of MOGHANLU, eventually became dependent on them, although originally attached to QOJA-BEYLI. *Tiräs* include REZA-BEYLI, QARALAR.

MORATLU: Linked with UDULU and ZARGAR.

NOURUZ-'ALI-BEYLI: Once populous, began to decline after the closure of the frontier; they had no villages and seem to have broken up and joined other tribes such as QOJA-BEYLI.

PIR-EVATLU: Neighbours of GEYIKLI, whose size and fortunes fell as theirs rose. In *äshrarlıq*, joined QOJA-BEYLI against GEYIKLI, with little success. Settled in Moghan irrigation project.

---

[2] Moghanlu are also recorded in Armenia (Bournoutian 1992).

QARA-QASEMLI: See SARI-KHAN-BEYLI, BAND-'ALI-BEYLI.

QOJA-BEYLI: Notorious for banditry under their chief Nurollah Bey, they were banned from Moghan at Russian request in 1867. They then occupied the Barzand village and district, which was not only favoured with fertile soil and abundant water, but lay across the road from Ardabil to Belasuvar, down which passed both considerable caravan traffic and the other tribes on their seasonal migrations. QOJA-BEYLI now levied tolls on the caravans, and their chiefs extorted both cash and animals from the migrating tribes, suppressing any resistance by force. Meanwhile they raided neighbouring districts of Russia.[3] In 1871 the Governor of Ardabil led a punitive expedition against them, burned Barzand village and confiscated property to recompense victims of their raids. Nurollah Bey escaped to Tehran with a large sum of money, but returned soon after with orders from the Court to the effect that QOJA-BEYLI lands and property should be restored to them. The tribe reoccupied Barzand district and continued to rob and oppress the surrounding population, until in 1876 the heir apparent was persuaded by the Governor of Baku to remove QOJA-BEYLI from the frontier to the Urmiyeh region. They bribed their way back to the vicinity of Sarab, and eventually to their former lands at Barzand.[4] By this time QOJA-BEYLI comprised two divisions, at feud with each other: the larger, headed by Nurollah Bey, continued to be known as QOJA-BEYLI or to be distinguished as 'Ali-Hasanli after Nurollah Bey's father; the smaller division, headed by his cousin Aqa Bey, was named after the latter's father 'ISA-BEYLI or 'ISALU, and continued to be permitted to migrate to Russian Moghan, where they had pastures near Belasovar. The 'ISALU chiefs had only a small retinue, while their rivals not only had a vast retinue of fugitives and impoverished nomads in the service of Nurollah Bey and his relatives, but also counted a number of distinct subtribes among their commoners. At the end of 1880, cavalry from QOJA-BEYLI were used by Hasan 'Ali Khan Garusi (later the Amir Nezam) in subduing the rebellions of the Kurdish chiefs Sheikh 'Obeidollah and Hamzeh Aqa near Sauj-Bolagh. The following autumn the Russians again complained of QOJA-BEYLI banditry on the frontier, and demanded that the tribe be removed to Mianduab or some other distant locality. The Iranians thought such a move would be difficult at that time of year, and General Schindler wrote to Consul

---

[3] Rostopchin (1933: 104), quoting articles in the newspaper *Kavkaz* from 1872. See also Nassery Bilasawar (1993).

[4] Markov (1890: 29–30). See Appendix Three for Nurollah Bey.

Abbott that it would bring QOJA-BEYLI into renewed contact with the
Kurds, with whom they were now at feud, recalling that previously they
had easily found their way back from exile and would presumably do so
again.[5] A strong detachment was sent to subdue them, but it is unclear
whether either section of QOJA-BEYLI was actually removed to
Kurdistan. According to Radde, the section complained of was 'ISALU,
and they at least were banned from Moghan, though allowed back sur-
reptitiously in 1883.[6] A recent source relates that the Governor of
Ardabil and Meshkin at this time, General Hasan 'Ali Khan Afshar,[7]
forced the whole tribe of QOJA-BEYLI to emigrate to Mianduab, where
they stayed for ten years, while he rebuilt Barzand village and fortified it
and Khiou against the marauding tribes; however in 1889 Artamonov
observed that the QOJA-BEYLI villages in Barzand, having been
destroyed ten years before by the Governor of Azarbaijan (Hasan 'Ali
Khan, Amir Nezam Garusi), were deserted.[8] The main section of
QOJA-BEYLI was now further divided into two subsections, one headed
by Sardar Bey and named JURUGHLU, the other headed by Nurollah
Bey and later his son Bahram Khan and known as NUROLLAH-BEYLI.
Artamonov spoke to Sardar Bey in 1889, and his section at least must
have continued to nomadize in northeast Azarbaijan, where they soon
took over the whole stretch of land between Sarı-Qamish and the Dara-
Yort valley, and from the 1890s onwards they expanded their raiding
activities over both Russian and Iranian territory. Among the measures
which the Amir Nezam is said to have taken at this time were the reduction of the hegemony of the QOJA-BEYLI and the creation of a balance
of power among the Shahsevan: at his instigation the HAJJI-KHOJALU
tribe under Hazrat-qoli successfully opposed JURUGHLU and refused to
pay taxes to them. At the same time, the ALARLU tribe from Ojarud
provided a powerful balance in the east. At some stage Nurollah Bey's
son Bahram Khan became active in the west, where he took over the
district between Zeiveh and the Dara-Yort valley and pursued the
conflict with HAJJI-KHOJALU. A report that in 1907 Shahsevan nomads
were finally driven by the Kurds from winter pastures near Mianduab[9]
may refer to NUROLLAH-BEYLI, but their chief Bahram Khan himself at
least was back in northeast Azarbaijan long before then. In 1903
Tigranov reported that of the 500 households of QOJA-BEYLI (headed
by Sardar Bey), 100 were of the chiefly suite, 200 were other 'genuine

[5] FO 450/8, Abbott to Thomson, no. 97 of 29.12.1880; same to same, no. 55 of 6.12.1881;
     Eqbal (1946: 23).   [6] Radde (1886: 441).
[7] First appointed in 1879 (FO 450/8, Abbott to Thomson, no. 17 of 20.6.1879).
[8] Sa'edi (1965: 82–3); Artamonov (1890: 411).
[9] Belyaev (1910: 8), quoted by Rostopchin (1933: 108).

Shahsevan' (i.e. commoners), and the remaining 200 were the retinue of refugee peasants from both sides of the frontier who performed economic services for the chiefs. 'ISALU contained 150 households, only 20 to 30 of which were the chiefly family's retinue; in opposition to QOJA-BEYLI, they regularly offered their services to the Administration for the suppression of bandits and rebels, but were becoming disillusioned by lack of appreciation and reward.[10] QOJA-BEYLI continued to have the allegiance of most of the Meshkin Shahsevan nomad tribes throughout the period of rebellion: see Chapter Twelve and Figure 11.

QURTLAR/QUTLAR: Difficult to identify; perhaps because there were few in Moghan and Savalan until recently; possibly two different groups: one a section of DAMIRCHILI, the other an Ardabil tribe, possibly same as KALESAR/QARAJALU.

SARI-KHAN-BEYLI: I cannot trace any immediate connexion between this tribe and the *elbey* dynasty which bore the same name, but whose members seem either to have settled or to have joined the SARVANLAR or JELOUDARLU *taifa* by the twentieth century. In the mid-nineteenth century SARI-KHAN-BEYLI was a *taifa* of several hundred families. Before the closure they owned a few villages in Arshaq and one or two also in Barzand, but they were mainly nomadic, having *qıshlaq* near Salyan and *yailaq* on the northeast flanks of Savalan. In 1885 many of the tribe fled and hid in Russian settlements, where they managed to remain – there is a Sarı-Khan-Beyli village in their former pastures. Those who stayed in Iran were allotted *qıshlaqs* near Barzand and became subsidiaries of QOJA-BEYLI. Their villages lay on the Ardabil Governor's route to Moghan, and suffered in consequence, being very poor. One *tirä* is QARA-QASEMLI.

SARVANLAR: SARVANLU were recorded as a branch of the Afshar in 1716. By the nineteenth century, they and JELOUDARLU were associated with the Meshkin *elbeys*. In due course they absorbed the remnants of the dynasty, after the wealthier scions had left the region, while JELOUDARLU largely comprised the former retinue. Neither tribe had settlements before the closure, nor pastures in Russian Moghan, though JELOUDARLU, the larger, would hire *qıshlaqs* there from other tribes. After the closure they were both to be found in east-central Moghan, and they were attached to QOJA-BEYLI.

---

[10] Tigranov (1909: 113–17).

SEYETLER: One *tirä* is named MILLI. Separate from SEYETLER/SADAT-ZARENJI.

TALESH-MIKEILLI OF MESHKIN: In 1843, 'The Tâlish Michaielli have . . . just been removed by order of the Government to Arâk to which they formerely belonged.'[11] (This may refer to the Ardabil group, see below.) They had pastures on the frontier near Belasovar, where they founded a large settlement in about 1870, while 200–300 households continued to migrate to summer pastures on the northern flanks of Savalan, near Qotur-Sui. By 1903 they had other settlements near Belasovar and in Arshaq, and were reckoned a strong tribe. Mingled with them were the remnants of the tribe of JANYARLU, most of whom had settled in Russia. Chiefs from JANYARLU seized power from Babash Bey c. 1920: 'Abdollah Bey, succeeded by son Pasha Bey, latter by his son Fazlollah Bey (d. 1965), then his nephew Farhad.

TERIT/TRIT: See GEYIKLI, KOR-'ABBASLU, HAJJI-KHOJALU.

UDULU: With MORATLU, ZARGAR.

ZARGAR: With MORATLU, UDULU.

2. The Ardabil division

ALARLU (ARALLU): Not recognized as Shahsevan until the twentieth century. Based on villages in Ojarud, near Garmi and Langan, they had some *yailaqs* on Baghrou and later acquired some on Savalan too. Situated along the Russian frontier, under their chief Mohammad-qoli Khan after 1900 they became as notorious as the QOJA-BEYLI for their raids, and indeed they were powerful rivals of the latter tribe. From among the Shahsevan, the BEYDILI, 'ALI-BABALU, JAHAN-KHANOMLU and other tribes became their followers. So also, later, AJIRLI.

DELAQARDA/DELAQADAR: Presumably descended from the Dulqadir Qızılbash, DELAQARDA were mentioned among the Ardabil tribes resisting the Ottomans in 1726. By the nineteenth century they were based in Ojarud and associated with ALARLU, like whom they only recently became counted among the Shahsevan. See JAHAN-KHANOMLU.

---

[11] Abbott (1844: 27); no other source confirms this.

DURSUN-KHOJALU: Attached to neighbouring YORTCHI, their lands lay on the southeast slopes of Savalan. Settled early, though a small section migrated to Moghan until the closure. In 1903 they numbered 1,720 households in 39 villages, but they had no effective leadership. The villages, owned by various townsmen, all comprised the *tiyul* of a wealthy Tabriz official, and were completely in the hands of his agent at Ardabil.

JAHAN-KHANOMLU: The only Ardabil tribe, apart from KHAMESLI, to remain nomadic in 1903, without any village base. Had *qıshlaq* near Salyan, and *yailaq* on the eastern slopes of Savalan. According to Seidlitz the JAHAN-KHAN tribe (which he traced to Jahan Khan Qara-Qoyunlu) was integrated with the DELAGARDA.[12] After the closure they associated with KHAMESLI, migrating with them to new winter pastures in southeast Khoruslu and Ojarud.

KHAMESLI/ASEFLI-KHAMESLI: See POLATLU.

POLATLU/FULADLU: In the Ardabil division, the only tribe claiming noble descent. The chiefs owned villages in a large stretch of country southeast of Ardabil, where much of the tribe settled long before the closure. The tribe divided into two sections, usually at feud, of which the larger, mainly settled and occupied in agriculture, retained the name POLATLU (although it had a further subdivision JURUGHLU, not to be confused with the QOJA-BEYLI section), while the smaller, wholly nomadic, became known as KHAMESLI or ASEFLI-KHAMESLI. Their *qıshlaqs* in Russian Moghan were along the river Kor, by the main trade route passing through Moghan, and they became notorious for banditry there. Their *yailaqs* were on Baghrou above their villages. Artamonov called them the best armed of the Shahsevan: they were renowned for skill in assembling cartridges, and 'when this tribe migrates, then no less than ten full-grown healthy camels accompany them in a special convoy loaded with supplies of ammunition'.[13] After the closure, POLATLU themselves completely settled; in 1903 their 32 villages (1,500 families) were almost all owned by the chiefs, but a few had recently been bought by powerful landowners from Ardabil. KHAMESLI continued as pastoral nomads and bandits along the frontier, having been allotted new winter pastures in Barzand and Ojarud. See Chapter Eleven.

QOZATLU: Once as large as POLATLU, YORTCHI and DURSUN-KHOJALU, QOZATLU was based on villages south of Ardabil, bordering the territo-

---

[12] Seidlitz (1879: 497).   [13] Artamonov (1890: 455).

ries of YORTCHI, POLATLU, and the SHATRANLU of Khalkhal. The villagers suffered heavily from oppression and extortion, and in 1877 abandoned their lands to join their nomadic section in southern Russian Moghan; having no animals, they took to raiding across the Akosha river and the Lankaran–Salyan caravan route. Later they were persuaded to return to their ten villages, where they remained in 1903, diminished in population (450 households), very poor and oppressed by landowners. The chiefly class had disappeared or taken refuge with the YORTCHI chiefs. After the closure, fifty nomad families migrated with thirty families of YEKALI between *qıshlaq* in Ojarud and *yailaq* on eastern Savalan.

REZA-BEYLI: See MOGHANLU.

TAKLEH/TAKILEH: Presumed descendants of the Tekelu Qızılbash; Takleh are recorded in Moghan from the sixteenth century, and may have remained separate from the Shahsevan until the nineteenth. In 1843, they were recorded as part of the Meshkin division. Once numerous, by the end of the nineteenth century TAKLEH were weak: their villages were owned and administered by the same officials as those of their neighbours the DURSUN-KHOJALU. Several hundred families lived in villages between DURSUN-KHOJALU territory and Ardabil, but a section of one hundred or more families migrated between Russian Moghan (where they rented *qıshlaqs* in various places) and *yailaqs* above their villages on eastern Savalan. This section continued to migrate after the closure, being allotted *qıshlaqs* along the frontier north of Belasovar, where they remained in the 1960s, though many were lost to the canals. One *tırä* is named QARALAR: Olearius reported nomads called QARA'I and TAKLEH in Moghan in 1639; though QARA'I/QARALAR is a common name, these were probably ancestors of some of the twentieth-century QARALAR of Meshkin, of whom the most likely is the present section of the TAKLEH. Cf. AIVATLU and QARALAR.

TALESH-MIKEILLI OF ARDABIL: Neighbours of JAHAN-KHANOMLU in Moghan and Savalan and companions on the migration. Were once also completely nomadic, but by the closure of the frontier had a village of one hundred houses near their summer quarters; their connexion with the larger tribe of the same name in the Meshkin division is not clear.

YEKALI: See on QOZATLU; a small tribe, once completely nomadic but now with a village north of Ardabil.

YORTCHI: Possibly descended from the Aq-Qoyunlu group of this name, YORTCHI are said to have had a special role choosing Nader Shah's camp-site (*yort*). Apart from a small group who joined GEYIKLI,[14] they were almost fully sedentarized by mid-nineteenth century in a large area southwest of Ardabil, but maintained summer quarters on Bozgush near by. In 1903 the chiefs were reckoned the wealthiest in the district, but oppressed their numerous villages, which were consequently very poor. Traditional enemies of POLATLU, the YORTCHI chiefs were loyal to the Qajars even after Mohammad 'Ali Mirza had put Khosrou Khan *elbey* Yortchi to death in 1902.[15]

3. Tribes settled/disappeared since about 1900

ABU-BEYLI, AQA-BAQERLI, AQ-QASEMLI (WITH REZALU), FATHOLLAH-KHANLU, FARAJOLLAH-KHANLU, HAMZA-KHANLU, MIRZA-RAHIMLI, PASHA-KHANLU: Settled in villages near Ardabil.

BAI-BAGLI: Not to be confused with BEY-BAGHLU of Meshkin. Almost fully sedentarized in Arshaq before the closure, which did not affect them directly.

BAND-'ALI-BEYLI, a large tribe divided in the second half of the nineteenth century into MAST-'ALI-BEYLI, 'ALI-BABALU, and QARA-QASEMLI. They had *qishlaqs* along the Kor and in the central part of Russian Moghan. None had farms before the closure, after which some MAST-'ALI-BEYLI went to Russia, while the rest of these tribes joined QOJA-BEYLI or ALARLU. Not much inclined to banditry, and consequently poor, they remained substantial groups, with good pastures in southeast Moghan and southern Savalan. QARA-QASEMLI was joined by the small tribe of BEY-BAGHLU, which had one village in Meshkin.

ILKHICHI: Name of a village in Angut.[16]

QAHRAMAN-BEYLI: Possibly descended from the Qaramanlu tribe. Settled in Meshkin before 1900. See HAJJI-KHOJALU, GEYIKLI, JELOUDARLU, DELAQARDA.

SHEIKHLI: Despite the common name, plausibly the nineteenth-century SHEIKHLI of Ardabil descend from those mentioned in Moghan in 1704 (Chapter Four).

---

[14] Tapper (1979a: 197).   [15] See Chapter Twelve.
[16] Cf. Ahl-e Haqq village of this name south of Mt Sahand (Sa'edi 1964).

YEDDI-OIMAQ: Possibly identical with either HOMUNLU or BEYDILI; certainly subsumed by them.

4. Tribes that have emerged since 1900

JA'FAR-QOLI-KHANLU, MADADLI, SARI-NASIRLI, ZAKHURASHLU.

KALESAR: See DELAQARDA, QURTLAR, DAMIRCHILI.

QARALAR/KHIOULU (QARALAR-E JABDARAQ; QARALAR-E KHIOU): See HÜSÜN-AJILI, MOGHANLU, TAKLEH.

HOSEINAKLI: A major Qara-Dagh tribe, but by the 1980s counted as part of the Shahsevan; so also HAJJI-'ALILI.

Appendix three

Some Shahsevan voices

The following is a selection of stories I recorded during fieldwork among the Shahsevan. Habib Sabri, from the Moghan village of Ultan where I stayed for a few weeks in summer 1963, was an old man who, like most of his tribe Pir-Evatlu, had given up pastoral nomadism and settled many years earlier, but had vivid memories of his youth as a nomad warrior, forty to fifty years earlier. 'Emran Imani, elder of the Hajji-Imanlu section of Geyikli tribe, was my host for many months in 1966, then in his late forties: I have written about him (as 'Akbar') and his family in my *Pasture and Politics*, where I noted that he was a good story-teller. When I re-established contact with his family in 1992, I learned that he had died in 1989 (his grandson Mehdi Mizban has also written an MA thesis (1992) about the family). Hasan Panahi, from another section of Geyikli, was the same age as 'Emran and a close friend. Both 'Emran and Hasan were regular companions of Hatam Bey, the most distinguished of the former Shahsevan chiefs, who was then in his seventies, and died a few years later. I recorded the stories from 'Emran, Hasan and Hatam Bey during the winter of 1966 in Moghan.

'Emran Imani of Geyikli on Nurollah Bey Qoja-Beyli

In the time of Naser ad-Din Shah, the Shah summons Nurollah Bey Qoja-Beyli to Tehran to account for his misdeeds. In those days there were no government representatives in Azarbaijan, though there were in Araq. People say to Nurollah Bey, 'The Shah may have summoned you to Tehran, but don't go, he'll kill you; he wants you to account for your misdeeds.' 'Even if the Shah has summoned Nurollah Bey Qoja-Beyli to Tehran to die', he tells them, 'Nurollah Bey will not pay any attention to your warnings; I'm going.'

So he takes one servant and sets off from Moghan for Tehran. In those days there were no cars nor even proper roads, so they go by horse; and it takes them twenty days or a month to get there. He arrives in Tehran and rests for a little, then after a couple of days he has a letter written to the Shah, as follows: 'God save Your Majesty! Nurollah Bey Qoja-Beyli, whom you sent for, is here, come to your feet, ready, at your service.'

Taking the letter, he approaches the inner court and says to the sentry, 'May I have permission to deliver a letter to the Shah?' The sentry tells him, 'I'm afraid I can't give you permission, but if you'll hand me the letter I'll take it and deliver it to His Majesty myself.' But it seems that the Shah has heard this conversation, since he immediately orders the sentry to let Nurollah Bey come in.

He passes through the courtyard door and enters the inner court. The Shah comes out onto the balcony, and Nurollah Bey finds himself in the royal presence. He takes out the letter and presents it to the Shah, who reads it and sees that this is indeed the Nurollah Bey whom he had summoned on such-and-such a date and at such-and-such a time.

'Nurollah Bey', he says, 'Weren't you frightened of coming here to see me?'

'No', replies he, 'God save Your Majesty, I wasn't frightened.'

The Shah is most surprised at this boldness, and goes on: 'Nurollah Bey, I'm going to ask you three questions; if your answers are satisfactory, I shan't harm you; but if not, I shall have one of your wrists cut off and one of your eyes put out.'

Well, if a man gets such an order from the Shah, he must be very bold indeed to remain unafraid! Nurollah Bey says, 'God save Your Majesty, go ahead.'

'Nurollah Bey', says the Shah, 'Where is strength?'

'Sire', replies Nurollah Bey, 'Strength is in gun-powder!'

'Bravo, Nurollah Bey!' cries the Shah. 'Nurollah Bey', he goes on.

'Sire?' replies Nurollah Bey.

'Nurollah Bey, where is pleasure?'

'Sire', replies Nurollah Bey, 'Pleasure is in meat!'

'Bravo, Nurollah Bey!' cries the Shah. 'Splendid! Nurollah Bey', he continues, 'which are prettier, your women or ours?'

'Sire', replies Nurollah Bey, 'Our women are prettier!'

'Eh?!' cries the Shah.

'Yes', says Nurollah Bey.

'How's that?' asks the Shah.

'Because, Sire', explains Nurollah Bey, 'If it rained cats and dogs for twenty-four hours and we put all those women out in the rain, then the rain would wash the rouge and powder off your women, and the dirt off ours, and then you'd see which of them were prettier!'

'Bravo, bravo!' cries the Shah. 'Nurollah Bey, I shall grant you a boon, just ask me whatever you like.'

At first Nurollah Bey – who was very smart, a really cunning fellow – says, 'Sire, all I want is good health for Your Majesty.'

'No, Nurollah Bey, you must ask me for something.'

'Sire', says Nurollah Bey, 'Since you're so kind as to grant me this boon, give me all the land between Taulan and Lakiwan for my horses to graze.' (This was Taulan on the Dara-Yort, and as far as Arshaq.)

So the Shah writes him out a Royal Farman, and gives it to him, saying, 'Nurollah Bey, take your leave if you want to, it's up to you; if you like, you may stay here.'

Nurollah Bey takes another few days' rest, then comes back to see the Shah and ask permission to leave. He enters the Royal Presence once more and says, 'Sire, your servant requests permission to take his leave.'

The Shah replies, 'You're very welcome, Nurollah Bey, have a good journey and come again.'

At that time Nurollah Bey was paramount chief of all the Shahsevan, the Shahsevan delegate, as it were. The thirty villages he acquired are still in the hands of his descendants; the Shah had no idea where 'the land between Taulan and Lakiwan' was, he thought it must be one village, or something like that. Nurollah Bey was a very clever chap, and scored quite a triumph there, getting the Shah to write him a Farman for all that land.[1]

Hajji Hatam Bey of Geyikli, on Nurollah Bey and Bahram Khan Qoja-Beyli

When Naser ad-Din Shah went to Russia, the Emperor complained to him, 'Nurollah Bey Qoja-Beyli is pillaging on Russian territory.' On his return, Naser ad-Din Shah came through Astara, and the chiefs of all the Shahsevan tribes went there to greet him. When they arrived in Ardabil, he gave the order to the Governor: 'Take Nurollah Bey to Belasovar and have him shot from the cannon's mouth.' So they took Nurollah Bey to Belasovar, on the Iranian side, so as to tie him to the cannon.

Now one of Nurollah Bey's henchmen, one of the chiefs, went to see Amir Bahador-e Jang, who was Naser ad-Din Shah's Minister, and grandfather of the present Bahadors. He said, 'Sir, tell His Majesty that, even if the Emperor and his government complain that a servant and subject of His Majesty is pillaging in Russia, Nurollah Bey of the Shahsevan has not done wrong. Tell him, rather than putting Nurollah

---

[1] The land concerned is a huge area between the Dara-Yort valley and Qoja-Beyli territory around Barzand. In a later discussion, not recorded, there was argument over exactly which villages were involved. See Chapter Eleven, and Appendix Two.

Bey to death, he ought to do him honour. Nurollah Bey is not at fault, that the Imperial Government complains about him to His Majesty.'

So Amir Bahador pardoned him. They say a telegram was sent to the Governor, telling him to leave Nurollah Bey alone.

Once Mozaffar ad-Din Shah went to Russia, and the Imperial government, in Baku or Moscow, complained that Nurollah Bey's son Bahram Khan was pillaging in Russia. Mozaffar ad-Din Shah came here to Ardabil; all the chiefs were gathered there, and he ordered them to have Mahmad-qoli Khan and Bahram Khan tied to the cannon. So the Governor, Khan Hakim, sent officials to bring Mahmad-qoli Khan of Alarlu and Bahram Khan Bey to Belasovar to be tied to the cannon.

Then Morad 'Ali Moghanlu went to see Khan Hakim – Morad 'Ali at that time was the leader of all the Shahsevan chiefs, just as we were later. He went to see the Governor one evening and asked him, 'Sir, I have a request.'

'What is it?'

'Sir, don't tie Mahmad-qoli and Bahram Khan to the cannon; it's me that you should do it to.'

'Why?'

'I sent those two to Russia to carry out the pillaging which the Emperor has complained to the Shah about. I did this because Qara-Baghi horsemen were always coming to Iran and stripping our homes of property. Now a daughter of ours is in Russia, and she saw how they would come here to steal our bridal clothing. She sent us word, saying, "Are there no men among the Shahsevan? The Qara-Baghis go and steal our Shahsevan bridal clothing, so that the Qara-Baghi women can wear them at their weddings. Have you no men?" So it was on her orders that I despatched Bahram Khan and Mahmad-qoli. First you should tie me to the cannon, and then you may deal with the other two.' So saying, he offered his own back to the cannon.

His meaning was this: 'The Iranian government and the Shah really should do us honour. The Qara-Baghis came and took our women's bridal clothing, our daughter sent word to us, and so I sent Bahram Khan and the rest; and they went and seized animals from Russia.' But Morad 'Ali Bey didn't offer to give any of the animals back, and he didn't take animals from Bahram Bey and his family, you see. In fact, he went and raided the other Shahsevan, and took animals from them to give back [to the Russians].

Hasan Panahi of Geyikli on Javat Khan Hajji-Khojalu

In the time of Mahmad 'Ali Shah, the Russians passed through Astara into Iran. They fought through Gilan, Rasht and Pahlavi, and came to

Karaj, where they summoned Mahmad 'Ali Shah, who came to see them. They said, 'Sir, sign here, we have taken Iran in battle.' Mahmad 'Ali Shah replied, 'Sir, there's been no battle in Iran; I set up this *khankhanlıq* in Azarbaijan, putting the chiefs in authority, since some of the people were disobeying the laws' – Mahmad 'Ali Shah had indeed set up *khankhanlıq* over the tribesmen here. The Russians told him, 'No, we have taken Iran in battle.' He answered, 'No, I've not fought a battle, but I'm tired of this monarchy; for seven generations we have reigned in Iran, but I no longer want the monarchy.' So he resigned there and then.

His son, who was then twelve years old, succeeded to the throne and became Ahmad Shah. The Russians came back to Azarbaijan. Their forces were in two sections: one went to deal with Alarlu, the other came here to deal with Geyikli, Qoja-Beyli and Hajji-Khojalu. Javat Amir Tuman gathered the tribesmen together – in those days our chief was Hajji Faraj [father of Hatam Bey] – he gathered the Geyikli, Qoja-Beyli and Hajji-Khojalu tribes, and they fought in Shah-Dagh. The other section of the Russian forces went and fought Najaf-qoli [Alarlu] in Deman. Najaf-qoli slaughtered them and captured several guns and a large quantity of rifles; he routed them, past Deman and back into Russia.

Javat Amir Tuman meanwhile fought at Shah-Dagh, during the migration; Shah Dagh is part of the Savalan mountain pastures. At one place on Shah-Dagh, which we call Qashqa-Mesha, Javat killed 1,900 Russians. The few that were left, he chased past Dash-Burun here and back to Baku.

[Reza Khan] wrote to Tehran, 'I have pacified Azarbaijan, send an agent to collect all the arms from Azarbaijan and take them away; send an agent, and let him establish authority here.' So they appointed 'Abdollah Khan Amir Lashkar, to come to Azarbaijan and collect the arms. He came and wrote a note to Javat Amir Tuman, 'Come and meet me.' Javat would not go, so he wrote a second time; Javat still would not go to meet him. 'Abdollah Khan came himself to his home, which was in Shah-Dagh; he said, 'Amir, don't you respect the Iranian state, that you don't come to meet me?' Javat smiled and answered, 'Abdollah, I do respect the Iranian state, but they aren't important. I myself have served the country here, and have grown old here. I have had the strength to fight a state like that of Russia – I can show you the skulls of 1,900 of them that I killed in Qashqa-Mesha – I didn't respect the Russian state. As for the Iranian state, well, I was myself serving Iran. I have grown old: it should be you coming to meet me!'

'Abdollah Khan came and took Javat Amir Tuman's hand and kissed it, saying, 'Amir, you're right, it was my duty to come to meet you.' Then Javat Amir Tuman and Najaf-qoli collected the weapons from Azarbaijan, and delivered them to 'Abdollah Khan, who took them away. After that, Reza Shah came and ruled in Iran.

Habib Sabri of Pir-Evatlu, on the Battle of Sarı Khan (1921)

In the days of Nikolai there were no Soviets. Nikolai believed in himself on earth and God in Heaven, but had no respect for anyone else. He wanted to come and take our lands and kill us. We took up our rifles and cartridge-belts, mounted our horses, and rode off to stop the Russians, the forces of Nikolai. Five of us – five horsemen, five cousins – defended this place and beat the Russians off. Three times they sounded the trumpet, ordered the troops to march over here, but we killed them. Praise the Unity of God, we put up such a fight here, our Shah himself couldn't have done so well. We put them to flight, with our own weapons.

Four times I have seen battles with the Soviets. We Shahsevan had come and camped at our qishlaq near 'Ali-Reza-Abad; over where the dam is now, the Soviets had set up their artillery. Above those saplings, look, there is a hill, they call it Dash-Burun. From there, they had brought an army against us. They were firing their cannon in the air, while we were packing our women and children onto the animals with one hand, and fighting with the other. Shells were bursting in the air and bullets falling on our women and children . . . the artillery shells were so long, look; you haven't seen them? they were so long and so wide, and there was explosive in the nose, so that wherever it landed it would burst. But another sort of shell burst in the air; inside were sixty bullets; the shell was made from the powder, the bullets and the casing . . . those were the bullets that rained down on top of us.

Well, we beat them off, and managed to escape that camp and come here. Sarı Khan was with us too. This Sarı Khan was a refugee from the Soviets; he was a grandson of Mostafa Khan Shirvan-Shah from Shirvan – haven't you heard of Shirvan, didn't the reapers tell you they'd been there?[2] Sarı Khan was exiled from Shirvan and came here, a refugee from the Soviets. He stayed one year with Hömü here . . . They were six horsemen, Sarı Khan and his two brothers and three servants, and also their sister. First they stayed with Ayaz Bey [Qoja-Beyli] then, seeing that Pir-Evatlu were powerful and could fight well, they came to Pir-Evatlu, to Hömü's house, and then moved to Aqa-Kishi Bey's home.

We had just moved, and were pitching our tents over there, just about

---

[2] On Mostafa Khan of Shirvan, see Chapter Eight. The reapers were presumably Iranian subjects who used to cross the frontier to work in the harvest on the Soviet side.

where Pir-Evatlu village is now. It was very dark and misty, being still late winter. Ah, in those days we were young and brave, and we knew how to ride our horses, and I was always ahead of the others, showing off . . .

We camped there, and some days passed. We built some shelters from cane, for the sheep. A young man, about your age, came to our camp; he had been sent to find out where the camps were; he was a spy, and he came and discovered our movements. He stayed a couple of days with Aqa-Kishi Bey, a relative of his. Then he went back and told them where he had been; the Russians meanwhile had collected a force of some 2,000 infantry and some artillery, cannon and machine-guns, in Qara-Donlu. The spy informed them that Aqa-Kishi Bey, our chief – chief of Pir-Evatlu – was camped here, Yadollah of 'Arabli a little further down (this side of Böyük-Khanlu), by the Ajirli Beys' *qıshlaq*, and Nouruz-Beyli were camped in the *qıshlaq* of Qara-Nurollah, near Yel-Aqarshı, along with the small group of Petili. Nouruz Bey himself was a little up from Petili, near the entrance to Lula-Dara. Sarı Khan had a fine *alachıq* beside that of Aqa-Kishi Bey.

So they collected their army at Qara-Donlu and marched against us at dusk, coming past Bahram-Tapa. At dawn we heard sounds in the distance; we got up and saw that there was gunfire coming from Yel-Aqarshı, from over those hillocks there, towards the south. It turned out later that the spy had told them where all the camps were and how to find them, and they had decided to come along the Taza-Kand road, but somehow they had gone too far. That's why we heard the shooting from the Yel-Aqarshı direction. But we asked each other what it was, we couldn't think what the shooting might mean. We ran up to the top of that hillock above Pir-Evatlu village, and told each other it must be a band of Petili returning from a sheep-raid, or something.

Then Sarı Khan came up with one of his brothers, bringing a pair of field-glasses; he put them to his eyes and then suddenly shouted to Aqa-Kishi Bey to come at once. Just as now we hang on to our spades, so in those days we never put down our guns and cartridge-belts. Aqa-Kishi Bey ran up and asked what the matter was. 'Russians', said Sarı Khan. 'What do you mean, Russians?' asked Aqa-Kishi Bey, 'How can it be Russian shit-eaters here?' 'I don't know', replied Sarı Khan, 'but Russians they are', and he passed the field-glasses to Aqa-Kishi Bey. He looked for himself, and confirmed that it was indeed the Russians. We leaped onto our horses and hurredly organized the breaking of camp, to get the animals and stuff away from the river.

I was with Amir-qoli – he was a brave man! – we hurried to get our animals out of reach of the Russians, but as we were busy at this, we saw another Russian troop in Qara-Daghlu village, advancing towards us along the river. We each took up our rifles and opened fire on them, and they turned back. Meanwhile, firing was still coming from the other direction, so we came back to camp to see what was happening. Then the five of us mounted our horses and spurred them and rode to meet the troops: Sarı Khan, Böyük Aqa son of As'ad, Aqa-Kishi Bey, Amir-qoli, and myself – by Hazrat 'Abbas, you never saw such horsemen, such fine shots!

We charged the enemy, while Petili charged them from the other side, though Petili weren't really much use. The soldiers turned tail, they couldn't face us, and we chased them without hesitation, from here to Kazem-Otaran, that hill in Ajirli *qıshlaq*. On this side of Kazem-Otaran, Sarı Khan and Aqa Reza dismounted and beat about 100 of their cavalry down to the river banks, over there by Böyük-Khanlu, and they crossed back to Russia. Their cavalry and infantry were falling, just like a flock of sheep when a wolf attacks. They were more or less wiped out, let me tell you, and their bodies lay all over the place, so much did God favour us.

One of the gunners was hit . . . they had cannon; you should know about those cannon we handed over to Reza Shah. We were attacking one machine-gun post . . . They weren't like the machine-guns now, they had 250 rounds on a belt like this, which had to be fed into it as it fired; each bullet could hit that tree over there; then you had to keep the muzzle clear . . . you see, we learned how to use it ourselves; we captured one of the gunners and got him to show us. You'd fire it like this, press the trigger so, with one or two fingers, and those 250 bullets would keep coming out until the belt was empty.

We captured a cannon too. One was abandoned, the other side of Kazem-Otaran hill, together with its shells and four horses to haul the carriage. Not like the machine-guns they have now. The machine-gun too had wheels, and two horses to pull it, one black, the other chestnut.

We took them along, and brought them cautiously up to Bahram-Tapa; we were just above Taza-Kand when poor Sarı Khan said we should ride on after them and kill them, like wolves among the sheep. He told Aqa-Kishi Bey – he knew us all by name – that he would chase the Russian bastards up to Qara-Donlu, even up to Qara-Qaya. Off we went, but then the soldiers made a stand. Ayaz Bey's horse was shot, and one of our men from Pir-Evatlu, Ahmad Khan, was asked to give his grey to Ayaz Bey; so he gave it up and was left behind, but as he went back he was shot himself.

After Ahmad Khan was shot, we turned to try to dislodge the Russians from their trenches above Mahmad-Rezalu. There we were fighting, when Sarı Khan, who was lying propped up on his elbow like this, was hit by a machine-gun bullet, which entered his heart and passed out through his back; and he fell back. Then Böyük Aqa saw a grey horse passing, and he leaped onto his own chestnut to go and catch it, but as he cantered off he was hit. Amir-qoli saw this, and cried out that his uncle was shot; he rode after him, but he too was hit and fell beside his uncle.

Now we had lost Sarı Khan, Amir-qoli and Ahmad Khan, so we could no longer go after the soldiers. Of course, we were warriors, but if four out of six of us had fallen, the other two must turn back and see to them. We were headed for Taza-Kand, and would have crossed into Russia, but this happened. We had to look after our own dead, our leaders. We no longer cared about any troops attacking us.

A man from Khosroulu was among the fallen, Aqa Hasan Bey's eldest son, brother of Kichik Khan. We turned back to look to our own casualties: Böyük Aqa, Amir-qoli, Ahmad Khan, Sarı Khan, four of them. As for the wounded Russians, we killed them of course . . .

So back we went, taking with us that brown Russian cannon, and the 250-shot machine-gun, the very ones which are probably now in some government office. I myself was the one who handed them over, and now when I go into a government office they ignore me. If only there were shooting battles like in those days, now in these last days of my life, then you'd see what sort of a man I am.

What does our Shah know of us here, what does he care now about our condition? He has delivered us into the hands of a bunch of tyrants, and humiliated me in the world; and he's dishonoured his own throne. That's it, there's nothing left to be said. A Shah should hire a shepherd for his people, to graze his sheep, care for them, fatten them, and take his wages; but this Shah has hired wolves and inflicted them on the people; believe me, many go hungry, and flee to Russia.[3]

'Emran Imani on the time of the Democrats (1940s)

After the Shahrivar coup, when the Russians came to Iran; in the time of the Democrats [1945–6]; the Russian authorities were suspicious of Hatam Khan [Geyikli] and Amir Aslan ['Isalu], so they ordered the Democrat authorities to take some troops, lay hold of Hatam and Amir Aslan and send them to the Russian Consul in Tabriz.

They chased Hatam Khan and Amir Aslan for some time, but eventually captured them. Six soldiers took them and brought them before the Consul in Tabriz. One of the six was from Qara-Bagh and acted as interpreter. When they arrived in the Consul's presence, he said to the Consul, 'Sir, you ordered us to capture Hatam Khan and Amir Aslan and bring them to you; here they are, at your orders.'

---

[3] This is one of many accounts of the 'Battle of Sarı Khan' recorded in 1963 from Pir-Evatlu, 'Arabli and Ja'farli participants. I published a synthetic account in Tapper (1966).

He asked, 'Which one is Amir Aslan, and which Hatam?' The interpreter pointed them out. As he did so, the Consul shook Amir Aslan warmly by the hand. Having shaken the Consul's hand, Amir Aslan put his own hand in his trouser pocket.

The Consul told the interpreter, 'Ask this Amir Aslan: when I am so friendly as to shake you by the hand, why do you then put your hand in your pocket? Aren't you afraid of me?'

Amir Aslan tells the interpreter, 'Tell the Consul' (not 'submit', in polite language, just 'tell', you see) 'Tell the Consul that Amir says he's afraid of no one but God; he's only afraid of God.'

The Consul is astonished. He smiles, grasps Amir Aslan once more by the hand, shows him great friendliness, and takes them both to his own house. There he sits them down and entertains them, serves them tea and sweets, and orders the soldiers, 'Take them, prepare a nice house, have them kept in custody there, and feed them three times a day.'

They stayed about three months in custody there, then they were set free and went back home. That's how it happened.

After the Shahrivar coup, the Democrats outlawed some of us, and they were after us, trying to take us prisoner. Well, autumn came and we were on the migration, approaching Moghan.[4] We arrived in the district of Angut, near Zeiveh. There everybody gathered in Hatam Khan's home and discussed what was best to do. 'What shall we do?' people said. 'We can't go to Moghan; Moghan is the frontier and the Soviets are there; we'd better spend the winter in these Khoruslu hills, and if the Democrats come after us, we'll hold the hills against them.'

Well, Hatam Khan collected fifteen armed horsemen (I was one of them). We mounted and rode off to take a look at the frontier (round here) and see what was going on, intending then to come back and work out what to do. We came and rode along the frontier here, looked about and couldn't see a thing going on, so we went back homewards.

As we came past Borran – you know, the place where all those cafés are now – well, Hatam Khan was riding ahead (we were eighteen horsemen) and I was riding just behind him. In those days there was no motor-road, and there were no cars on those tracks; but suddenly I heard the sound of a car. Hatam Khan was way in front, so I cantered up beside him (we were riding up the Dara-Yort valley), and called out to him. He stopped and asked what I wanted. 'Bey', I said, 'Excuse me, I can hear a car coming.' The Bey reined in his horse, and we both stopped. All of a sudden, we saw

---

[4] It is not entirely clear, but this must have been the autumn of 1946, as the Democrat regime was about to fall. See Chapter Thirteen.

a jeep come up. As it did so, we recognized it: it was Mohammadov and Mohammad Jalili [Sarı-Khan-Beyli], two of the most important Soviet officials, top brass of the Democrat regime. It turned out they had been to Hatam Khan's home, and having got hold of his poor son Bala Khan [killed in a car accident in 1964] they were now coming after Hatam Khan himself, to take him prisoner too. It seems they were doing a bunk and they wanted to take Hatam Khan and his son with them to Soviet territory.

They stopped their car. Mohammad Jalili got out and they made Bala Khan get out too. They waved to Hatam Khan, shouting, 'Bey, it's us, Mohammad Jalili and Bala Khan, come on, ride over here and join us.'

Hatam Khan answered, 'I've no business over there.' At the same time, he ordered us, 'Everyone dismount and load and aim your rifles at them; be ready to open fire when I give the order.' (We were all armed, of course.) So we all dismounted and lay down with our rifle-sights to our eyes, while the Bey stayed on horseback.

They called to Hatam Khan again, and he replied, 'I have no business with you, and you have none with me. You have no right to come after me.' He refused to join them. Then Hajji Mahmud Khan [younger brother of Hatam] went to join Mohammadov and Mohammad Jalili, and again they called to Hatam Khan to come over too; this time he did. As he came over, Mohammadov said to him, 'Hatam Khan, the reason you're annoyed, if you'll excuse my saying so, is that the Democrat government made Karbala'i Nosrat [Ajirli] Chief of the Tribes. If you say so, we'll have him dismissed, and we'll replace him with anyone you want.'

Hatam replied, 'I'm not the one to make or break any Chief of the Tribes. I've nothing to do with you, nor you with me.'

Hatam Khan and the rest of us wanted to take these men prisoner, kill them, smash up their jeep and throw it into the river, but Hajji Mahmud Khan wouldn't let us. 'It's none of your business', he said, 'Let them go.' So, having rescued Bala Khan and sent them away, we went home ourselves.

When we got home, we held a meeting to discuss what to do. These Democrats had two garrisons, with 150 men each, one in Taza-Kand near Garmi,[5] the other in Qala-Barzand. Hatam Khan said, 'In the morning I'll collect a hundred armed horsemen, and we'll go and capture them and seize their weapons.'

So a hundred of us rode off, first to attack Qala-Barzand. We got there about half an hour before sunset and laid siege to the buildings where the garrison was quartered. By nightfall we had them surrounded, and we

---

[5] Not the Taza-Kand in Moghan, mentioned in an earlier story.

were able to make sure that none of them could get away. There was some shooting for about an hour during the night, then it stopped. Meanwhile, we kept them surrounded until dawn. Day broke; it was winter, and thick snow lay everywhere; early in the morning Hatam Khan sent Baghish Bey Qoja-Beyli, saying, 'Go and tell the Feda'i [Democrats], 'Don't get your-selves killed; surrender your weapons and you'll go free; if you don't, we'll kill you."

Baghish Bey went along, with some of us as escort. He called out to the Democrat leader, a man called Aziz, 'Give up your arms, and we'll let you all go free; if you don't, we'll kill you.' They answered, 'We won't give up our arms; we've sent for some of those black Russian planes, they're coming in an hour.' When they said this, we opened fire, and we killed two of them.

Baghish Bey called to them again, 'Don't get yourselves killed, give up your arms and we'll let you go free.' They answered, 'You're from Qoja-Beyli, you're a liar and we won't give our arms to you, since if we do you'll still kill us. Fetch Hatam Khan, bring him out and have him stand on that roof there for us to see; when we've seen him, we'll give up our arms.'

Hatam Khan was in his tent. A messenger was sent to fetch him, and he came and climbed onto the roof of a nearby house so that they could see him. When they saw him, they laid down their arms and came out into the yard.

Now on that day they [the garrison] had been paid, a matter of some 50,000–60,000 tomans in cash. The Qoja-Beyli wanted to go and seize this money. Hatam Khan said, 'If anyone lays a finger on that money, I'll have him machine-gunned down.'

Well, Hatam Khan had them all taken and assembled in the mosque. There he entertained them royally, gave them dinner, took over their arms and set them free. He allowed every one of them to go home, saying that since they were Iranians, subjects of the Iranian state, he wouldn't have them killed. Hatam Khan captured 150 rifles, heavy and light machine-guns there, together with 50,000 rounds of ammunition. We loaded these onto mules and pack-horses and took them away to attack the Feda'is in Tazeh-Kand.

Well, then we rode off to attack Tazeh-Kand, where they had their other garrison. They had heard how we had let the Barzand garrison go free after they had given up their arms. We came and laid siege to this garrison in Tazeh-Kand, and Hatam Khan sent a man to tell them, 'Don't get yourselves killed; give up your arms and go free.' So there they handed over their arms, very peacefully and with the minimum of fuss, and Hatam Khan let them all go home. That's the story of how we captured their weapons.

Hatam Khan let all the Feda'is go except two: 'Aziz and Emam-Verdi. When Khiou fell [December 1945], the Chief of Police escaped in women's clothes. Now previously he was acquainted with 'Aziz from Qara-Qaya,[6] so when he escaped he came to Qara-Qaya by night, to his friend 'Aziz, who ran a café there, to ask to be taken to Amir Aslan's house where he could take refuge. On his arrival at 'Aziz's café, wearing these women's clothes, he said to 'Aziz (who recognized him), "'Aziz, I've got 6,000 toman which I'll give you if you find me a man who'll take me by night to Amir Aslan's house.' 'Aziz – the cowardly bastard – fetched a man, took the 6,000 toman, and then informed the Feda'i. The Feda'i captured the Chief and sent him back to Meshkin-Shahr; there they handed him over to the Feda'i authorities, who tied him to a tree and shot him.

As for Emam-Verdi, he was from Alcha-Dara. When Meshkin-Shahr fell, the Feda'i captured the officers of the army and the police, but the regiment commander Colonel Adib-Amini got into his car and made his escape towards Ardabil. Now Emam-Verdi got wind of this, and with a few Feda'i he cut Adib-Amini off in the Gen-Dara gorge. They opened fire; the car tyres were shot up, the car came to a halt, and they captured Adib-Amini and killed him on the spot. On one of his fingers there was a gold ring set with precious stones; Emam-Verdi cut off the finger and took off the ring.

We captured this same Emam-Verdi at Barzand, along with 'Aziz of Qara-Qaya at Taza-Kand. Hatam Khan had them loaded onto mules, and we took them to Meshkin-Shahr, where we handed them over to the authorities saying, 'This is the same Emam-Verdi who killed Adib-Amini, cut off his finger and took his gold ring; and this is 'Aziz the café-keeper from Qara-Qaya who, when the Chief of Police came and offered him 6,000 toman to take him to Amir Aslan, took the money, but handed him over to the Feda'i, who took him back to Meshkin-Shahr, tied him to a tree and shot him.'

So we captured Emam-Verdi of Alcha-Dara, and 'Aziz of Qara-Qaya, and handed them over to the Iranian authorities in Meshkin-Shahr; they were tied to the same willow-tree on which the Police Chief was shot, and executed in their turn. That's how it happened.

Habib Sabri on pastoral life among the Shahsevan

In the old days I was a Shahsevan, and my home was an *alachïq*. When we moved camp to another site, 10–15 km away, we'd load the *alachïq* onto a

---

[6] Not the Qara-Qaya in Moghan, mentioned in an earlier story.

camel, and on another we'd load the storage bags, and the wife would ride on top, or she'd ride a mare. Myself, I'd saddle my stallion and ride that. I'd hire a shepherd to graze my flock, a hundred, five hunded, maybe a thousand sheep; and a drover for the cattle, and a servant for the camels. We'd migrate for maybe 10–15 km, then we'd choose a site, and pitch the tents for the night. Then in the morning off we'd go again. That's how the Shahsevan lived.

When we got to *yailaq*, everyone had his own pasture, inherited from his ancestors, as recorded by Amir Nizam. We'd camp in the greenest parts; we'd spend a month in this site, and a month in that, as each is grazed, till the end of summer, and then we'd come back again. The ewes' milk is finished, the lamb-herd grazes his lambs and takes the milk, the shepherd takes his dues and his contract is renewed, and we come back to Moghan. Then we went to the villages to get provisions, e.g. wheat-flour and fodder, as much as we could afford. Thus we returned here to Moghan. Here too, in this very spot, was our ancestral pasturage, where Pir-Evatlu alone could settle. If the year was dry, the animals went hungry and we had to feed them barley and straw, but in a green year things went much better; then when spring came we'd be off again on migration.

Once a year the government would tax us, each tribe according to size. Some were registered for 1,000 toman, some for 500, some for 200. They'd collect this tax once a year, and then leave us alone, not like today. If someone had committed an offence, theft or murder for example, then the government would take him away, and maybe they'd put him to death, or perhaps imprison him. There he'd have to stay with chains on his legs for two or three years, until his sentence was up. That was the way the law worked among the Shahsevan.

Then came the time of *äshrarlıq*, when we'd go off plundering in Russia; we'd go plundering everywhere, and everyone had his own rifle and his own horse. In those days the weak and poor were defenceless and sought the protection of the rich and powerful, for example Qoja-Beyli and Nouruz Bey, or Hajji-Khojalu and Javat Khan. Javat Khan fought many battles against the Russians. Once General [Fidarov] came and swept Iran clean; everyone ran away, except Javat and his men. Then once again the Iranian regime was restored, and the Russians returned to their own country, leaving us to our own government.

The Shahsevan meanwhile kept their traditional nomadic life. A man with many sheep was rich, one with few was poor; and the poor man went and became the rich man's shepherd, or his lamb-herd, or his camel-herd. That's the way we lived.

Bibliography

ABBREVIATIONS

AA – American Anthropologist
ANASSR – Academy of Sciences of the Azarbaijan Soviet Socialist Republic (II – Institute of History)
ANSSSRIV – Academy of Sciences of the USSR, Oriental Institute
BM – British Museum/British Library
BSOAS – Bulletin of the School of Oriental and African Studies
EI – Encyclopedia of Islam
EIr – Encyclopedia Iranica
FO – Foreign Office Files (Public Record Office), London (see also IOL)
IJMES – International Journal of Middle East Studies
IOL – India Office Library and Records
IS – Iranian Studies
ISSR – Institute of Social Studies and Research (Tehran University)
JRAI – Journal of the Royal Anthropological Institute
JRAS – Journal of the Royal Asiatic Society
JRCAS – Journal of the Royal Central Asian Society
JRGS – Journal of the Royal Geographical Society
MEJ – Middle East Journal
MOOI – Moyen Orient et Océan Indien
RAS – Royal Asiatic Society
SI – Studia Iranica
ZDMG – Zeitschrift der Deutschen Morgenländischen Gesellschaft

Abbott, Keith Edward 1844. *Narrative of a Journey from Tabreez along the shores of the Caspian Sea, to Tehrān.* PRO, FO 251/40.
    1864. *Notes on Azerbaijan.* PRO, FO 60/286, 19.4.1864. Published in Amanat (1983).
Abdullaev, Gasi Bekhbudovich 1958. *Iz Istorii Severo-Vostochnogo Azerbaydzhana v 60–80–kh. gg. XVIII v.* Baku, ANASSRII.
    1965. *Azerbaydzhan v XVIII veke i Vzaimootnosheniya ego s Rossiey.* Baku, ANASSRII.
Abdurakhmanov, Asim Akhmadoghlu 1964. *Azerbaydzhan vo Vzaimootnosheniyakh Rossii, Turtsii i Irana v Pervoy Polovine XVIII v.* Baku, ANASSRII.
Abou-Zeid, Ahmed 1965. 'Honour and shame among the Bedouins of Egypt'. In J. G. Peristiany (ed.) *Honour and Shame; the Values of Mediterranean Society,* London, Weidenfeld and Nicolson.

389

Abraham de Crète, Catholicos 1876. 'Mon histoire et celle de Nadir Chah, Chah de Perse'. In *Collection d'Histoires Arméniens*, transl. M. Brosset, vol. II. St Petersburg.

Abrahamian, Ervand 1982. *Iran Between Two Revolutions*. Princeton University Press.

Adle, Chahryar 1984. Review of Anon. (1982). *Abstracta Iranica* 7, p. 80.

Afshar, Iraj (ed.) 1995. *Khaterat va Asnad-e Mostashar ad-Douleh: Majmu'eh-ye Panjom, Gusheha'i az Siasat-e Dakheli-ye Iran, 1330–1335*. Tehran, Talayeh, 1374.

Afshar-Naderi, Nader 1968. *Monografi-ye Il-e Bahme'i*. Tehran, ISSR, 1347.

Afshar-Sistani, Iraj 1987. *Moqaddameh'i bar Shenakht-e Il-ha, Chador-Neshinan va Tavayef-e 'Ashayeri-ye Iran*, 2 vols. Tehran, private, 1366.

Afushteh'i Natanzi, Mahmud b. Hedayatollah 1971. *Naqavat al-Athar fi Dhikr al Akhyar*, ed. Ehsan Eshraqi. Tehran, Bongah-e Tarjomeh va Nashr-e Ketab, 1350.

Ahmad Mirza ('Azod ad-Douleh Soltan Ahmad Mirza) 1976. *Tarikh-e 'Azodi*, ed. 'Abd al-Hosein Nava'i. Tehran, Babak, 2535 (orig. 1304/1886–7).

Äliyev, F. M. n. d. 'XVIII Äsrin 1 Yarısında Azärbayjanda Khälq Azadlıq Häräkäti'. Diss., Azerb. S. S. R. Tarikh Inst., Archiv.

Allouche, Adel 1983. *The Origins and Development of the Ottoman–Safavid Conflict (906–962/1500–1555)* (Islamkundliche Untersuchungen Band 91). Berlin, Klaus Schwarz.

Altstadt, Audrey L. 1992. *The Azerbaijani Turks. Power and Identity under Russian Rule*. Stanford, California, Hoover Press.

Amanat, Abbas 1983. *Cities and Trade. Consul Abbott on the Economy and Society of Iran 1847–1866*. London, Ithaca.

Amanollahi-Baharvand, Sekandar 1992. *Kuch-Neshini dar Iran: Pazhuheshi dar-bareh-ye 'Ashayer va Ilat*. Tehran, Agah, 1370.

Amir-Khizi, Esma'il 1960. *Qiyam-e Azarbaijan va Sattar Khan*. Tabriz, Tehran, 1339.

Anderson, Benedict 1983. *Imagined Communities. Reflections on the Origins and Spread of Nationalism*. London, Verso.

Andreski, S. 1954. *Military Organization and Society*. London, Routledge and Kegan Paul.

Andrews, Peter A. 1987. 'Alachïkh and küme: the felt tents of Azarbaijan'. In Rainer Graefe and Peter Andrews, *Geschichte des Konstruierens* III (Konzepte SFB 230, Heft 28), Stuttgart, Kurz, pp. 49–135 (expanded version of article with same title, published in *Mardom-Shenasi va Farhang-e 'Ammeh-ye Iran* 3, 1977–8, pp. 19–45).

Anon. 1919. 'The Tribes of Azerbaijan.' FO 248/1225, no. 191, 17.1.1919.

Anon. 1982. *Tarikh-e Qızılbashan*, comp. Mir Hashem Mohaddes (after a MS of 1007–1013). Tehran, Behnam, 1361.

Anon. 1992 (comp.). *Farman-ha va Raqam-ha-ye Doureh-ye Qajar, I: 1211–60*. Tehran, Mo'assaseh-ye Pazhuhesh va Motale'at-e Farhangi, 1371.

Arakel of Tabriz (Arakel de Tauriz, Vartabed) 1874. 'Livre d'histoires'. In *Collection d'Historiens Arméniens*, transl. M. Brosset, vol. I. St Petersburg.

Ardalan, Zafardokht 1972. 'Nezam-e khanavadagi dar il-e Shahsevan'. In Hamid Zarrinkub (ed.), *Proceedings of Second Congress of Iranian Studies* 2, Mashhad, 1351, pp. 128–63.

Arfa, Hasan 1964. *Under Five Shahs.* London, John Murray.

Arjomand, Said Amir 1984. *The Shadow of God and the Hidden Imam. Religion, Political Order and Societal Change in Shi'ite Iran from the Beginning to 1890.* Chicago and London, University of Chicago Press.

Artamonov, L. N. 1890. *Severniy Azerbaydzhan. Voyenno-geogr. Ocherk.* Tiflis.

Asad, Talal 1973. 'The Bedouin as a military force: notes on some aspects of power relations between nomads and sedentaries in historical perspective'. In Cynthia Nelson (ed.) *The Desert and the Sown.* Berkeley, University of California Institute of International Studies, pp. 61–73.

    1986. 'The concept of cultural translation in British social anthropology.' In James Clifford and George Marcus (eds.) *Writing Culture,* Berkeley, University of California Press. (Repr. in Asad 1993.)

    1993. *Genealogies of Religion: Discipline and Reasons of Power in Christianity and Islam.* Baltimore, Johns Hopkins University Press.

Asef, Mohammad Hashem, Rostam al-Hokama 1969. *Rostam al-Tavarikh.* Ed. Mohammad Moshiri. Tehran, 1348. See also Hoffman (1985).

Astarabadi, Mirza Mohammad Mahdi Koukabi 1962. *Jahangosha-ye Naderi (Tarikh-e Naderi),* ed. Abdollah Anvar. Tehran, Anjoman-e Asar-e Melli (Publ. no. 45), 1341.

Atkin, Muriel 1979. 'The strange death of Ibrahim Khalil Khan of Qarabagh'. *IS* 12 (1–2), pp. 79–107.

    1980. *Russia and Iran, 1780–1828.* Minneapolis, University of Minnesota Press.

Aubin, Eugène 1908. *La Perse d'Aujourd'hui.* Paris, Colin.

Aubin, Jean 1959. 'Shah Ismail et les notables de l'Iraq persan (Etudes Safavides I)'. *Journal of the Economic and Social History of the Orient* 2/1, pp. 37–81.

    1984. 'Revolution chiite et conservatisme. Les soufis de Lahejan, 1500–1514 (Etudes safavides II)'. *MOOI* 1, pp.1–40.

    1988. 'L'avènement des Safavides réconsidéré (Etudes safavides III)'. *MOOI* 5, pp. 1–130.

Avdeyev, Mikhail 1927. *Mugan i Salyanskaya Step. Naselenie-zemlepolzovanie – Vodnoe Khozyaistvo. (Obsloedovanie 1925g.).* Baku, Soviet Truda i Oborony.

Avery, Peter 1965. *Modern Iran.* London, Benn.

Avery, Peter, Gavin Hambly and Charles Melville (eds.) 1991. *From Nadir Shah to the Islamic Republic,* The Cambridge History of Iran Vol. VII. Cambridge, Cambridge University Press.

Averyanov; see Shkinskiy and Averyanov.

Azadi, Siawosch and Peter A. Andrews 1985. *Mafrash.* Berlin, Reimer, and Munich, Weltkunst.

Babaev, K. 1973. 'Voennaya reforma Shakha Abbasa I (1587–1629)'. *Vestnik Moskovskogo Universiteta, Vostokovedenie 1,* pp. 21–9.

Bacqué-Grammont, Jean-Louis 1976. 'Une liste d'émirs Ostâğlû révoltés en 1526'. *SI* 5, pp. 91–114.

    1987. *Les Ottomans, les Safavides et Leurs Voisins. Contribution à l'histoire des relations internationales dans l'Orient islamique de 1514 à 1524.* Leiden, Netherlands Historical and Archaeological Institute in Istanbul.

Baddeley, John F. 1908. *The Russian Conquest of the Caucasus.* London.

Bahmanbegi, Mohammad 1945. *'Orf va 'Adat dar 'Ashayer-e Fars.* Tehran, Azar, 1324.

    1989. *Bokhara-ye Man, Il-e Man.* Tehran, Agah, 1368.

Bahrami, 'Abdollah 1965. *Khaterat az Akher-e Saltanat-e Naser ad-Din Shah ta avval-e Kudeta*. Tehran, no publ., 1344.

Baiburdi, Sarhang Hosein 1962. *Tarikh-e Arasbaran*. Tehran, Ebn Sina, 1341.

1969. 'Panj farman-e tarikhi'. *Barrasi-ha-ye Tarikhi* 4 (2–3), 1348, pp. 67–75.

Bakhash, Shaul 1978. *Iran: Monarchy, Bureaucracy and Reform under the Qajars 1858–1896*. London, Ithaca.

Bakikhanov, Abas Kuli Aga Kudsi 1926. *Gyulistan-iram (Golestan-e Eram)*. Baku, Travaux de la Société Scientifique d' Azerbaidjan.

Balayan, B. P. 1960. 'K voprusu ob obshchnosti etnogeneza Shakhseven i Kashkaytsev'. *Vostokovedcheskiy Sbornik* (Yerevan) 1, pp. 331–77.

Bamdad, Mehdi 1968. *Sharh-e Hal-e Rejal-e Iran dar Qarn-e 12 va 13 va 14 Hejri*, 6 vols., Tehran, Zavvar, 1347.

Barbaro, Josafa and Ambrogio Contarini 1873. *Travels to Tana and Persia* (Hakluyt Society, First series 49), transl. by William Thomas and S. A. Roy, ed. by Lord Stanley of Alderley. London.

Barfield, Thomas J. 1991. 'Tribe and state relations: the Inner Asian perspective', in Khoury and Kostiner (1991).

Barker, Paul 1981. 'Tent schools of the Qashqa'i: a paradox of local initiative and state control'. In Michael E. Bonine and Nikki R. Keddie (eds.), *Modern Iran: the Dialectics of Continuity and Change*. Albany, State University of New York Press.

Barth, Fredrik 1961. *Nomads of South Persia: the Basseri Tribe of the Khamseh Confederacy*. London, Allen and Unwin. (Persian translation by Kazem Vadi'i, Tehran, ISSR, 1964.)

1992. 'Method in our critique of anthropology'. *Man (N.S.)* 27, pp. 175–7.

Barthold, V. V. 1914. *K Istorii Orosheniya Turkestana*. St Petersburg. (Repr. in *Sochineniya* III, Moscow, 97–233.

Bates, Daniel 1973. *Nomads and Farmers*. Ann Arbor, Museum of Anthropology.

Bausani, Alessandro 1962. *I Persiani*. Florence, G. C. Sansoni.

Bavar, Mahmud 1945. *Kuhgilu va Ilat-e An*. Gachsaran, private, 1324.

Bayani, Khanbaba. 1974. *Tarikh-e Nezami-ye Iran: Jang-ha-ye doureh-ye Safaviyeh*. Tehran, Setad-e Bozorg-e Arteshtaran, 1353.

Bayat, Kaveh 1991. *Fa'aliyat-ha-ye Komunisti dar doureh-ye Reza Shah (1300–1310)*. Tehran, Entesharat-e Sazman-e Asnad-e Melli-ye Iran, 1370.

Bazin, Louis 1988. 'Les turcophones d'Iran: aperçus ethno-linguistiques'. In Digard (1988), pp. 43–54.

Bazin, Marcel 1982. 'Le Qara Dâg d'après Asghar Nazariân'. *Revue Géographique de l'Est* (1–2), pp. 19–59.

Beck, Lois 1980. 'Revolutionary Iran and its tribal peoples'. *MERIP Reports* 87, pp. 14–20.

1982. 'Nomads and urbanites: involuntary hosts and uninvited guests'. *Middle Eastern Studies* 18 (4), pp. 426–44.

1986. *The Qashqa'i of Iran*. New Haven, Yale University Press.

1991a. 'Tribes and the state in nineteenth- and twentieth-century Iran'. In Khoury and Kostiner (1991).

1991b. *Nomad: A Year in the Life of a Qashqa'i Tribesman in Iran*. Berkeley, University of California Press.

1992. 'Qashqa'i nomads and the Islamic Republic'. *Middle East Report* 177, vol. 22 (4), July–August, pp. 36–41.

Bedlesi, Sharaf ad-Din (Chèref-ou'ddîne) 1868–75. *Chèref-Nâmeh ou Fastes de la Nation Kourde*, trans. and ed. François Charmoy, 2 vols., St Petersburg.

Begdili, Gholam Hosein 1988. *Tarikh-e Begdili. Madarek va Asnad*. Tehran, Bu 'Ali, 1367.

Begdili, Mohammad Reza 1993. *Ilsevanha (Shahsevanha)-ye Iran*. Tehran, Pasargad, 1372.

Belyaev, D. 1910. 'Ocherk severo-vostochnoy chasti Persidskogo Kurdistana'. *Izv. Shtaba Kavk. Voyennogo Okr.*, no. 29 (quoted by Rostopchin).

Bell of Antermony, John 1764. 'A journey from St Petersburg in Russia to Ispahan in Persia . . .' In *Travels from St Petersburg in Russia to diverse Parts of Asia*, vol. I, London.

Bellan, L. L. 1932. *Chah 'Abbas I*. Paris, Geuthner.

Bellingeri, Giampiero 1978. 'Una recente ricognizione tra gli Shāhseven della Khamsè'. *Oriente Moderno* 58 (11), pp. 555–61.

Benjamin, S. G. W. 1887. *Persia and the Persians*. London, John Murray.

Bessaignet, Pierre 1961. *The Shahsavan, an Example of Settlement accompanied by Cultural Transplantation* (Problems around the Sedentarisation of Pastoral Tribes, Paper No. 1). Tehran, ISSR.

Black, Jacob 1972. 'Tyranny as a strategy for survival: Luri facts versus an anthropological mystique'. *Man (N.S.)* 7, pp. 614–34.

1976. 'The Economics of Oppression: Ecology and Stratification in an Iranian Tribal Society'. Unpubl. thesis, London University.

(Black-Michaud) 1986. *Sheep and Land. The Economics of Power in a Tribal Society*. Cambridge, Cambridge University Press/Paris, Maison des Sciences de l'Homme.

Bosworth, C. E. 1967 (2nd edn 1980). *The Islamic Dynasties. A Chronological and Genealogical Handbook*. Edinburgh University Press.

Bournoutian, George A. 1992. *The Khanate of Erevan under Qajar Rule*. Costa Mesa, California, Mazda Publishers.

Bradburd, Daniel 1987. 'Tribe, state and history in Southwest Asia: a review'. *Nomadic Peoples* 23, pp. 57–71.

1990. *Ambiguous Relations: Kin, Class and Conflict among Komachi Pastoralists*. Washington and London, Smithsonian.

Brooks, David 1983. 'The enemy within: limitations on leadership in the Bakhtiari'. In Tapper (1983a).

Browne, E. G. 1910. *The Persian Revolution of 1905–1909*. Cambridge, Cambridge University Press.

1928. *A Literary History of Persia*. Vol. IV, *Modern Times (1500–1924)*. Cambridge, Cambridge University Press.

Brydges, Sir Harford Jones 1833. *The Dynasty of the Kajars*. (Transl. from Donboli's *Ma'aser-e Soltaniyeh*). London.

Busse, Heribert 1974. *History of Persia under Qajar Rule*. (Transl. from Fasa'i's *Farsnameh-ye Naseri*). New York, Columbia University Press.

Butkov, P. G. 1869. *Materiali dlya Novoy Istorii Kavkaza s 1722 po 1803 god*, 3 vols. St Petersburg.

Calmard, J. 1989. 'Azīz Khan Mokrī.' *EIr* 3, pp. 261–3.

(ed.) 1993. *Etudes Safavides* (Bibliothèque Iranienne 39). Paris/Tehran, Institut Français de Recherche en Iran.

Campbell, J. 1931. 'The Russo-Persian frontier, 1810'. *JRCAS* 18, pp. 223–32.

Casimir, Michael J. and Aparna Rao (eds.) 1992. *Mobility and Territoriality. Social and Spatial Boundaries among Foragers, Fishers, Pastoralists and Peripatetics.* Oxford, Berg.

Census 1987. *Socio-Economic Census of Nomadic Tribes* (multiple volumes). Statistical Centre of Iran (Plan and Budget Organization) and Iran's Tribal Affairs Organization (Ministry of Jehad-e-Sazandegi).

Chardin, Jean (later Sir John) 1811. *Voyages du Chevalier Chardin en Perse, et autres Lieux de l'Orient*, ed. L. Langlès, 10 vols., Paris.

Chehabi, Houchang E. 1993. 'Staging the emperor's new clothes: dress codes and nation-building under Reza Shah'. *IS* 26 (3–4), pp. 209–33.

Chelebizadeh. Küçükçelebizâde Isma'il Asim 1740. *Tarih-e Çelebizâde.* Constantinople, 1153.

Cohn, Bernard S. 1987. *An Anthropologist among the Historians and Other Essays.* Oxford, Oxford University Press.

Contarini 1873. See Barbaro.

Cook, John 1770. *Voyages and Travels through the Russian Empire, Tartary, and part of the Kingdom of Persia.* Edinburgh.

Cottam, Richard W. 1964. *Nationalism in Iran.* Pittsburgh University Press.

Cribb, Roger 1991. *Nomads in Archaeology.* Cambridge University Press.

Crone, Patricia 1986. 'The tribe and the state'. In J. A. Hall (ed.) *States in History*, Oxford, Blackwell.

1993. 'Tribes and states in the Middle East'. *JRAS* 3 (3), pp. 353–76.

Curzon, Hon. George Nathaniel 1894. *Persia and the Persian Question*, 2 vols. London.

Cyren, Otto 1913. 'Fran Schahsewenzernas Land'. *Ord och Bild*, pp. 297–307.

Dahl, Gudrun and Anders Hjort 1976. *Having Herds. Pastoral Herd Growth and Household Economy.* Department of Social Anthropology, University of Stockholm.

Dälili, Hüseyin Älioghlu 1971. 'Qarabagh khanlığının banisi Pänahäli Khan haqqında yeni mä'lumat'. *Tarikh, Fälsäfä, Huquq* 1, pp. 42–7.

1974. 'Shahsevän tayfası vä onun Azärbayjanın siyasi häyatındaki möuqeyi haqqında'. *Tarikh, Fälsäfä, Huquq* 4 (3), pp. 23–30.

1979. *Azärbayjanın jänub khanlıqları XVIII äsrin ikinji yarısında.* Baku, ANASSRII.

Danesh-Pazhuh, Mohammad Taqi 1968–9. 'Dastur al-Moluk-e Mirza Rafi'a va Tazkerat al-Moluk-e Mirza Sami'a'. *Majalleh-ye Daneshkadeh-ye Adabiyat-e Tehran*, pt I: 15, 1347, pp. 504–75; pt II: 16, 1347–8, pp. 62–93; pt III: 16, 1347–8, pp. 198–322; pt IV: 16, 1347–8, pp. 416–40; pt V: 16, 1347–8, 540–64.

1974. ''Amar-e mali va nezami-ye Iran dar 1128, ya tafsil-e 'asaker-e firuzi-ye ma'sir-e Soltan Hosein-e Safavi, az Mirza Mohammad Hosein Mostoufi'. *Farhang-e Iran Zamin* 20, 1353, 1–4, pp. 396–421. (See also Kunke.)

d'Arcy Todd, E. 1938. 'Itinerary from Tabríz to Ṭehrán *via* Ahar, Mishkín, Ardabíl, Ṭálish, Gílán and Kazvín, in 1837'. *JRGS* 8, pp. 29–39.

de Bruin, Cornelis 1759. *Travels into Muscovy, Persia and divers Parts of the East-Indies.* London.

de Clairac, Louis André de la Mamye 1750. *Histoire de Perse depuis le Commencement de ce Siecle.* Paris.

de la Maze, Père 1723. 'Journal du voyage . . . de Chamakie a Ispahan'. In *Nouveaux Mémoires des Missions de la Compagnie de Jesus dans le Levant* III. Paris.

della Valle, Petro 1972. *I Viaggi di Pietro della Valle. Lettere dalla Persia* (Il Nuovo Ramusio 6), ed. F. Gaeta and L. Lockhart. Rome, Instituto Poligrafico dello Stato.

de Morgan, Jacques 1912. 'Le féodalité en Perse, son origine, son développement, son état actuel'. *Revue d'Ethnographie et de Sociologie* 1912 mai–août (5–8), pp. 169–90.

de Planhol, Xavier 1968. *Les Fondements Géographiques de l'Histoire de l'Islam.* Paris, Flammarion.

1993. *Les Nations du Prophète. Manuel Géographique du Politique Musulmane.* Paris, Fayard.

Dickson, Martin 1958. 'Sháh Táhmasp and the Úzbeks (The Duel for Khurásán with 'Ubayd Khán 930–946/1524–1540)'. Unpubl. Dissertation, Princeton University.

1962. 'The fall of the Safavi dynasty'. *J. American Oriental Society* 82, pp. 503–17.

Digard, Jean-Pierre 1973. 'Histoire et anthropologie des sociétés nomades: le cas d'une tribu d'Iran'. *Annales: Economies, Sociétés, Civilisations* 28 (6), pp. 1423–35.

1979. 'Les nomades et l'état central en Iran: quelques enseignements d'un long passé d'hostilité réglementée'. *Peuples Méditerranéens* 7, pp. 37–53.

1987. 'Jeux de structures: segmentarité et pouvoir chez les nomades Baxtyari d'Iran'. *l'Homme* 27 (2), pp. 12–53.

(ed.) 1988. *Le Fait Ethnique en Iran et en Afghanistan.* Paris, Editions du Centre National de Recherche Scientifique.

Donboli, 'Abd al-Razzaq Beg Maftun 1972. *Ma'aser-e Soltaniyeh*, ed. Gholam Hosein Sadri-Afshar. Tehran, Ebn Sina, 1351 (original edn 1241/1827).

Dorn, B. 1967. *Geschichte Shirwans. Beiträge zur Geschichte der Kaukasischen Länder und Völker,* Pt II. Leipzig. (Orig. St Petersburg 1840).

Douglas, William O. 1952. *Strange Lands and Friendly People.* London, Gollancz.

Dunsterville, L. C. 1920. *The Adventures of Dunsterforce.* London, Edward Arnold.

Dupré, Adrien 1819. *Voyage en Perse.* Paris.

Eagleton, W. 1963. *The Kurdish Republic of 1946.* OUP.

Echraqi, Ehsan 1975. 'Le Kholâsat al-Tawârikh de Qâzi Ahmad connu sous le nom de Mir Monshi'. *SI* 4, pp. 73–89.

Efendiev, Oktay 1975. 'Le rôle des tribus de langue turque dans la création de l'état safavide'. *Turcica* 6, pp. 24–33.

1981. *Azerbaydzhanskoe Gosudarstvo Sefevidov v XVI veke.* Baku, ANASSRII.

Eichwald, E. 1834. *Reise auf dem Caspischen Meere und in den Caucasus.* Stuttgart and Tübingen.

Eickelman, Dale F. 1989. *The Middle East, An Anthropological Approach.* Englewood Cliffs, Prentice Hall. (2nd edn. Original edn 1981.)

Emerson, John 1990. 'Some general accounts of the Safavid and Afsharid period, primarily in English'. In Melville (1990).

1993 'Adam Olearius and the literature of the Schleswig-Holstein missions to Russia and Iran, 1633–1639'. In Calmard (1993).

Eqbal, 'Abbas 1941. *Tarikh-e Mofassal-e Iran.* Tehran, 1320.

1946. 'Hasan 'Ali Khan Amir Nezam Garusi'. *Yadgar* 3 (2), pp. 8–33.

1947. 'Sharh-e hal-e 'Aziz Khan Sardar-e Koll Mokri'. *Yadgar* 4 (1–2), pp. 37–62.

Equipe 1979, Equipe écologie et anthropologie des sociétés pastorales (eds.) *Pastoral Production and Society.* Cambridge, Cambridge University Press/Paris, Maison des Sciences de l'Homme.

Evans-Pritchard, E. E. 1937. *Witchcraft, Oracles and Magic among the Azande.* Oxford, Oxford University Press.

1940. *The Nuer.* Oxford, Oxford University Press.

Evliya Chelebi (Evliya Efendi) 1850. *Narrative of Travels in Europe, Asia, and Africa in the Seventeenth Century,* transl. Ritter Joseph von Hammer. London.

Falsafi, Nasrollah 1985. *Zendagani-ye Shah 'Abbas-e avval,* 3 vols. Tehran, 'Elm 1364 (first edn 1953–60/1332–9).

Farzad, Hosein 1945. *Enqelab va Tahavvol-e Azarbaijan.* Tabriz, Danesh, 1324.

Fasa'i, Hajji Mirza Hasan 1895–6. *Farsnameh-ye Naseri.* Tehran, lithogr., 1313.

Fawcett, Louise L'Estrange 1992. *Iran and the Cold War: the Azerbaijan Crisis of 1946.* Cambridge, Cambridge University Press.

Floor, Willem 1993. 'Fact or fiction: the most perilous journeys of Jan Jansz. Struys'. In Calmard (1993).

FO Prints, Affairs of Persia. Further Correspondence respecting the Affairs of Persia. Parts I–XXXV (Jan. 1905–Sept. 1913). IOL, L/P&S/20.

FO Prints, Persia and Arabia. Further Correspondence respecting the Affairs of Persia and Arabia. Parts I–XXI (July 1899–Dec. 1904). IOL, L/P&S/20.

Foran, John 1993. *Fragile Resistance: Social Transformation in Iran from 1500 to the Revolution.* Boulder, Westview Press.

Fortescue, Capt. L. S. (comp.) 1922. *Military Report on Tehran and adjacent Provinces of North-West Persia.* Calcutta. IOL, L/P&S/20, C.200.

1924. 'The western Alburz and Persian Azerbaijan'. *Geographical Journal* 63 (April), pp. 301–17.

Fragner, Bert 1975a. 'Ardabīl zwischen Sultan und Schah. Zehn Urkunden Schah Ṭahmāsps II'. *Turcica* 6, pp. 177–225.

1975b. 'Das Ardabīler Heiligtum in den Urkunden'. *Wiener Zeitschrift zur Kunst Morgenländes* 67, pp. 169–215.

1980. *Repertorium persicher Herrscherurkunden: Publizierte Originalurkundern (bis 1848).* Freiburg, Schwarz.

1986. 'Social and economic affairs'. In Jackson and Lockhart (1986), pp. 491–567.

Franz, Erhard 1981. *Minderheiten in Iran. Dokumentation zur Ethnographie und Politik* (Aktueller Informationsdienst Moderner Orient. Sondernr. 8). Hamburg, Deutsches Orient-Institut.

Fraser, J. B. 1838. *A Winter's Journey (Tâtar) from Constantinople to Tehran,* 2 vols. London.

Frye, Richard 1960. 'Ardabil'. *EI* (2nd edn) 1, pp. 625–6.

Fryer, John 1909–15. *A New Account of East India and Persia, being Nine Years' Travels, 1672–1681,* 3 vols. London, Hakluyt Society.

Ganzer, Burkhard 1994. 'Constructing tribal identity in Iran'. *Man (N.S.)* 29, pp. 182–3.

Gärber, Major Johann Gustav 1760. 'Nachrichten, von denen an der westliche

Seite der Caspischen See . . . in dem Jahre 1728'. In G. F. Müller's *Sammlung Russischer Geschichte* 4, St Petersburg, pp. 1–147.

Garrod, Oliver 1946. 'The Qashqai tribe of Fars'. *JRCAS* 33, pp. 293–306.

Garthwaite, Gene R. 1983. *Khans and Shahs: a Documentary Analysis of the Bakhtiyari in Iran.* Cambridge, Cambridge University Press.

Garusi, Hasan 'Ali Khan, Amir Nezam 1910. *Monsha'at-e Amir-Nezam*, ed. Mohammad Mahdi. Tabriz, 1328.

Gazetteer 1914. Gazetteer of Persia, Vol. II *(North-West Persia)*. Simla, General Staff India.

Gellner, Ernest 1983. 'Tribal society and its enemies'. In Tapper (1983a).

Ghaffari Kashani, Mirza Mohammad Abo'l Hasan 1887. *Golshan-e Morad.* Tehran, 1300 (BM Or. 3592; orig. 1210/1796).

Gholsorkhi, Shohreh 1995. 'Pari Khan Khanum: a masterful Safavid Princess'. *IS* 28, pp. 143–156.

Gilbar, Gad G. 1976 'Demographic developments in late Qajar Persia, 1870–1906'. *Asian and African Studies* 11 (2) (1976–7), pp. 125–56.

    1978. 'Persian agriculture in the late Qajar period, 1860–1906: some economic and social aspects'. *Asian and African Studies* 12 (3), pp. 312–65.

    1983. 'Trends in the development of prices in late Qajar Iran, 1879–1906'. *IS* 16 (3–4), pp. 177–98.

Gingrich, Andre 1992. 'Concepts and confusions: understanding Middle Eastern Societies'. *Current Anthropology* 33 (1), pp. 129–31.

Glassen, Erika 1968. 'Die frühen Safaviden nach Qāzī Ahmad Qumī'. Dissertation, Freiburg-im-Breisgau.

Glatzer, Bernt 1983. 'Pashtun nomads and the state', in Tapper (1983a).

Gmélin, Samuel Gottlieb (*et al.*) 1779. *Histoire des Découvertes faites par Divers Savans Voyageurs dans Plusieurs Contrées de la Russe, & de la Perse* . . ., 3 vols., Berne, La Haye.

Golestaneh, Abo'l Hasan b. Mohammad Amin 1965. *Mojmal al-Tavarikh*, with Zein al-'Abedin Amir Kuhmarreh'i's *Zeil va Hashiyeh*, ed. Modarres Rezavi. Tehran 1344.

Good, Mary-Jo 1977. 'Social hierarchy in provincial Iran: the case of Qajar Maragheh'. *IS* 10 (3), pp. 129–63.

Griswold, William J. 1983. *The Great Anatolian Rebellion 1000–1020/1591–1611* (Islamkundliche Untersuchungen, Band 83), Berlin, Klaus Schwarz.

Grönke, Monika 1993. *Derwische im Vorhof der Macht. Sozial- und Wirtschaftsgeschichte Nordwestirans im 13. und 14. Jahrhundert* (Freiburger Islamstudien 15). Stuttgart, Franz Steiner.

Gurney, John D. 1983. 'A Qajar household and its estates'. *IS* 16 (3–4), pp. 137–76.

    1990. 'Rewriting the social history of late Qajar Iran'. In Melville (1990).

Haaland, Gunnar 1969. 'Economic determinants in ethnic processes'. In Fredrik Barth (ed.), *Ethnic Groups and Boundaries*, London, Allen and Unwin.

Hambly, Gavin R. G. 1963. 'Aqa Muhammad Khan and the establishment of the Qajar dynasty'. *JRCAS* 50 (2), pp. 161–74.

    1991a. 'Āghā Muhammad Khān and the establishment of the Qājār dynasty' and 'Iran duing the reigns of Fath 'Alī Shāh and Muhammad Shāh'. In Avery *et al.* (1991), chapters 3 and 4.

1991b. 'The Pahlavī Autocracy: Riza Shāh, 1921–1941' and 'The Pahlavī Autocracy: Muhammad Riza Shāh, 1941–1979'. In Avery *et al.* (1991), chapters 6 and 7.

Hammer (Hammer-Purgstall), Joseph Ritter von 1965. *Geschichte des Osmanischen Reiches*. Graz, Akad. Druck und Verlagsanstalt.

Haneda, Masashi, 1981. Review of Savory (1978). *SI* 10, pp. 335–8.

1984. 'L'evolution de la garde royale des Safavides'. *MOOI* 1, pp. 40–64. (Transl. as 'The Evolution of the Safavid Royal Guard', *IS* 22 (2–3), 1989, pp. 57–86.)

1987. *Le Châh et les Qizilbāš. Le Systeme Militaire Safavide* (Islamkundliche Untersuchungen 119). Berlin, Klaus Schwarz.

Hanway, Jonas 1753. *An Historical Account of the British Trade over the Caspian Sea ... The Revolutions of Persia*. London.

Hart, David M. 1989. 'Rejoinder to Henry Munson, Jr., "On the irrelevance of the segmentary lineage model in the Moroccan Rif"'. *AA* 91, pp. 765–9.

Hasani, 'Ataollah 1990. 'Tarikhcheh-ye Il-e Shahsevan-e Baghdadi'. Unpubl. thesis, 5 vols., Islamic Free University, Tehran, 1369.

Hawaiian Agronomics 1971. *The Study of Animal Husbandry and Agricultural Complex of Moghan Region: Reconnaissance Survey and Preliminary Investigation.* Honolulu, Hawaiian Agronomics Company (International), and Tehran, Animal Husbandry Organization, Ministry of Agriculture.

Hedayat, Mahdi-qoli, Mokhber as-Saltaneh 1965. *Khaterat va Khatarat*. Tehran (2nd edn), 1344.

Helfgott, Leonard M. 1977. 'Tribalism as a socio-economic formation in Iranian history'. *IS* 10 (1–2), pp. 36–61.

1980. 'The structural foundations of the national minority problem in revolutionary Iran'. *IS* 13, pp. 195–214.

1983. 'Tribe and uymaq in Iran: a reply'. *IS* 16 (1–2), pp. 73–8.

Heyadat, Reza-qoli Khan 1994. *Fehres al-Tavarikh*, ed. 'Abd al-Hosein Nava'i and Mir Hashem Mohaddes. Tehran, Research Centre for Social Sciences and Cultural Studies, 1373.

Hinz, Walter 1936. *Irans Aufstieg zum Nationalstaat im fünfzehnten Jahrhundert.* Berlin and Leipzig.

Hobsbawm, Eric 1965. *Primitive Rebels. Studies in Archaic Forms of Social Movement in the 19th and 20th Centuries.* New York, Norton.

Hoffman, Birgitt 1985. *Persische Geschichte 1694–1835, erlebt, erinnert und erfinden. Das Rustam al tawārīh in deutscher Bearbeitung* (Islamwissenschaftliche Quellen und Texte aus deutschen Bibliotheken, Vol. 4), 2 parts. Bamberg, AKU.

Holmes, William Richard 1845. *Sketches on the Shores of the Caspian, Descriptive and Pictorial*. London.

al-Hoseini, Mahmud 1974. *Tarikh-e Ahmadshahi*, 2 vols., ed. Dustmorad Seyed Moradov. Moscow, Nauka.

Housego, Jenny 1978. *Tribal Rugs. An Introduction to the Weaving of the Tribes of Iran.* London, Scorpion.

Houtum-Schindler, General A. 1898. *Eastern Persian Irak.* London, John Murray.

Huart, C. 1927. 'Kara Bāgh'. *EI* (1st edn) 2 (2), p. 727.

İnalcık, Halil 1994. 'Part I The Ottoman State: Economy and Society, 1300–1600.' In Halil İnalcık and Donald Quataert (eds.), *An Economic and*

Social History of the Ottoman Empire 1300–1914, Cambridge, Cambridge University Press.

Ingold, Tim (ed.) 1994. *The Past is a Foreign Country*. Manchester, Group for Debates in Anthropological Theory.

'Iranskiy', 1924. 'Cherez voyennuyu diktaturu k nats. gosudarstvu'. *Novy Vostok* 5, pp. 100–13.

Irons, William G. 1974. 'Nomadism as a political adaptation: the case of the Yomut Turkmen'. *American Ethnologist* 1 (4), pp. 635–58.

1975. *The Yomut Turkmen: a Study of Social Organization among a Central Asian Turkic-speaking Population*. Ann Arbor, University of Michigan, Museum of Anthropology.

Ismail-zade, D. I. 1960. 'Iz istorii kochevogo khozyaystva Azerbaydzhana pervoy polovini XIX v'. *Istoricheskiy Zapiski*, pp. 96–136.

Issawi, Charles (ed.) 1971. *The Economic History of Iran, 1800–1914*. University of Chicago Press.

ISSR (comp.) 1987. *Manabe' va Ma'akhez-e 'Ashayer-e Iran be Farsi*. Tehran, 'Ashayer Publications (High Council of the Tribes).

Jackson, Peter and Laurence Lockhart (eds.) 1986. *The Timurid and Safavid Periods*, The Cambridge History of Iran Vol. 6. Cambridge, Cambridge University Press.

Jahanbani, Sepahbod Amanullah 1957. *Marz-ha-ye Iran va Shuravi*. Tehran, Ibn Sina.

Jahangir Mirza, 1948. *Tarikh-e Nou*, ed. 'Abbas Eqbal. Tehran, 'Elmi, 1327.

Janebolahi, Mohammad Hosein 1991–2. 'Gozaresh az safar be yeilaqat-e ['ashayer-e] Ilsevan va Arasbaran'. *Zakhayer-e Enqelab* 15 (summer 1370), pp. 89–106 and 18 (spring 1371), pp. 43–55.

Jaubert, P. Amédée 1821. *Voyage en Arménie et en Perse, fait dans les années 1805 et 1806*. Paris.

Jävanshir, Ähmädbäy 1961. *Qarabagh Khanlıqının Tarikhi (1747–ji ildän 1805–ji ilä qädär)*. Baku, ANASSRII.

Jenkinson, Anthony 1885–6. *Early Voyages and Travels to Russia and Persia* (Hakluyt Society, First series 72–3). London.

Johnson, Gregory A. 1982. 'Organizational structure and scalar stress'. In Colin Renfrew, Michael Rowlands and Barbara Abbott Segraves (eds.), *Theory and Explanation in Archaeology*, New York, Academic Press.

Jonabadi, Mirza Beg bin Hasan Hasani n. d. *Rouzat as-Safaviyeh* (BM Or 3388).

Kamal Khan b. Jalal Monajjem 1677. *Zobdat at-Tawarikh*. (RAS MS P.56; original 1088).

Kamali, 'Abbas 'Ali 'Abdali, 1989. *Negareshi bar Ouza'-e Eqtesadi-ye Ejtema'i va Farhangi-ye Jame'-e 'Ashayeri-ye Azarbayjan-e Sharqi*. Tabriz, Plan and Budget Org., East Azarbaijan (1368).

Kara Chemsi (Réchid Safvet Kara Chemseddine Oglu) 1916. 'Les Turcs en Perse'. *Revue de Hongrie* (Budapest) 17 (1 April), pp. 14–25, (15 June), pp. 12–23; and 18 (1 July–15 August), pp. 26–39, (15 Sept.), pp. 17–30.

Karimzadeh, Mohammad 1974. 'Shahsevan-ha-ye Fars (pishineh-ye tarikhi va shenakht-e Shahsevan-ha'. *Honar va Mardom* 12 (136–7), Bahman/Esfand 1352, pp. 75–9.

Karimzadeh-Tabrizi, Mohammad 'Ali 1971. 'Chand farman-e tarikhi'. *Barrasi-ha-ye Tarikhi* 5 (5), pp. 177–86.

Kasravi Tabrizi, Ahmad 1938. *Tarikh-e Hijdah Saleh-ye Azarbaijan, ya Dastan-e Mashrutiyat dar Iran*. Tehran, 1316.

Kazemzadeh, Firuz 1968. *Russia and Britain in Persia, 1864–1914. A Study in Imperialism*. New Haven and London, Yale University Press.

Keddie, Nikki and Mehrdad Amanat 1991. 'Iran under the later Qājārs, 1848–1922'. In Avery *et al.* (1991), chapter 5.

Keihan, Mas'ud 1933. *Jughrafiya-ye mofassal-e Iran*. Tehran, 1311.

Khakhanov, A. 1908. 'Shakhseveni (k sobitiyam na Kavkazsk. granitse)'. *Moskovski Yezhenedelnik* 22, pp. 26–8.

Khazanov, A. 1984. *Nomads and the Outer World*. Cambridge, Cambridge University Press.

Khoury, Philip S. and Joseph Kostiner (eds.) 1991. *Tribes and State Formation in the Middle East*. Berkeley, California University Press / London, I. B. Tauris.

Khuzani Esfahani, Fazli ben Zein al-'Abedin n.d. *Afzal at-Tawarikh*, 2 vols. Vol. I, Eton College MS 172; Vol. II, BM Or. 4878.

Khwandmir, Ghiyas ad-Din b. Homam 1954. *Habib as-Siyar*, ed. Hayyam. Tehran 1333.

Kiavand (Rakhshkhorshid), 'Aziz 1989. *Hokumat, Siyasat va 'Ashayer az Qajariyeh ta Konun*. Tehran, 'Ashayer Publications, 1368.

Kinneir, J. Macdonald 1813. *A Geographical Memoir of the Persian Empire*. London.

Kobychev, V. P. 1962. 'Krestyanskoe zhilishche narodov Azerbaydzhana v XIX v'. *Kavkasky Etnograficheski Sbornik* 3, pp. 3–68.

Koetz, Walter N. 1983. *Persian Diary 1939–41*. Ann Arbor, University of Michigan.

Kotov, K. F. 1958. *Khozheniye Kuptsa Fedota Kotova v Persiyu*, ed. A. A. Kuznetsov. Moscow, ANSSSRIV.

Krech III, Shepard 1991. 'The state of ethnohistory'. *Annu. Rev. Anthropol.* 20, pp. 345–75.

Krusinski, Pere Tadeusz Juda, S. J. 1728a. *Histoire de la Derniere Revolution de Perse*, ed. J. A. du Cerceau, transl. Bechon. Paris.

1728b. *The History of the Revolution of Persia: taken from the Memoirs of Father Krusinski*, transl. anon. London.

Kuhmarreh'i. See Golestaneh.

Kunke, Marina 1991. *Nomadenstämme in Persien im 18. und 19. Jahrhundert* (Islamkundliche Untersuchungen Band 151). Berlin, Klaus Schwarz.

Lambton, A. K. S. 1953. *Landlord and Peasant in Persia*. Oxford, Oxford University Press.

1961. 'Persian society under the Qājārs'. *JRCAS* 48 (2), pp. 123–39.

1969. *The Persian Land Reform 1962–1966*. Oxford, Oxford University Press.

1971. 'Īlāt.' *EI* (2nd edn) 3, pp. 1095–110.

1977. 'The tribal resurgence and the decline of the bureaucracy in the eighteenth century'. In Thomas Naff and Roger Owen (eds.), *Studies in Eighteenth-Century Islamic History*. Carbondale, S. Illinois University Press.

1987. *Qajar Persia: Eleven Studies*. London, I. B. Tauris.

1991. 'Land tenure and revenue administration in the nineteenth century'. In Avery *et al.* (1991).

Lapidus, Ira M. 1988. *A History of Islamic Societies*. Cambridge, Cambridge University Press.

1991. 'Tribes and state formation in Islamic history'. In Khoury and Kostiner (1991).

Larijani, Hojjatollah Hasan (comp.) 1990. *Ketab-Nameh-ye 'Ashayer-e Iran.* Tehran, 'Ashayer Publications (ONA, High Council of the Tribes), 1369.

Leach, E. R. 1954. *Political Systems of Highland Burma.* London, Athlone.

Lerch, Johann Jacob 1769. 'Auszug aus dem Tagebuch von einer Reise . . .' *Büsching's Magazin* 3, pp. 1–44.

1776. 'Nachricht von der Zweiter Reise nach Persien von 1745 bis 1747'. *Büsching's Magazin* 10, pp. 365–476.

Le Roy Ladurie, Emmanuel 1975. *Montaillou.* Paris, Gallimard.

Leviatov, V. N. 1948. *Ocherki iz Istorii Azerbaydzhana v XVIII veke.* Baku, Izd. ANASSRII.

Lewis, I. M. (ed.) 1968. *History and Social Anthropology* (ASA Monographs no. 7). London, Tavistock.

Lindner, Rudi Paul 1982. 'What was a nomadic tribe?' *Comparative Studies in Society and History* 24, pp. 689–711.

1983. *Nomads and Ottomans in Medieval Anatolia.* Bloomington, Indiana University Press.

Lockhart, Laurence 1938. *Nadir Shah.* London, Luzac.

1958. *The Fall of the Safavi Dynasty and the Afghan Occupation of Persia.* Cambridge, Cambridge University Press.

1959. 'The Persian army in the Safavid period'. *Der Islam* 34, pp. 89–98.

Loeffler, Reinhold 1973. 'The national integration of Boir Ahmad'. *IS* 6, pp. 127–35.

1978. 'Tribal order and the state: the political organization of Boir Ahmad'. *IS* 11, pp. 145–71.

MacGregor, C. M. 1879. *Narrative of a Journey through the Province of Khorassan and on the N. W. Frontier of Afghanistan in 1875.* London.

Madatov, Prince 1837. *Zhizn General-Leytenanta Knyazya Madatova.* St Petersburg.

Magee, Lieut. G. F. 1948. *The Tribes of Fars.* Simla (compiled Nov. 1945); IOL, V. 2068, A. 1179–ME/46, Secret.

Malcolm, Sir John 1815. *The History of Persia,* 2 vols. London. (2nd edn 1829).

Manz, Beatrice Forbes 1989. *The Rise and Rule of Tamerlane.* Cambridge, Cambridge University Press..

Maraghe'i, Mohammad Hasan Khan, Sani' ad-Douleh, E'temad as-Saltaneh 1877–80. *Mer'at al-Boldan-e Naseri,* 4 vols. Tehran, 1294–7.

1889. *Ketab al-Ma'asir wa'l-Asar.* Tehran.

Markov, Vladimir 1890. 'Shakhseveni na Mugani. Istoriko-etnograficheskiy ocherk'. *Zap. Kavk. Otd. Russk. Geogr. Obshch.* 19 (1), pp. 1–62.

Martin, B. G. 1965. 'Seven Safawid documents from Azarbayjan'. In S. M. Stern (ed.) *Documents from Islamic Chanceries, First Series.* Oxford, Oxford University Press.

Marx, Emanuel 1977. 'The tribe as a unit of subsistence: nomadic pastoralism in the Middle East'. *AA* 79, pp. 343–63.

Maslovskiy 1914. 'Materiali sobrannye iri Shtabe Ardebilskogo Otryada. Zamyetka o Shahsevenakh'. *Izv. Shtaba Kavk. Voyennogo Okr.* 37, pp. 1–23, 47.

Masson, Chas. 1842. *Narrative of Various Journeys in Balochistan, Afghanistan, and the Panjab; including a Residence in those countries from 1826 to 1830*, 3 vols. London.

Mazzaoui, Michel 1972. *The Origins of the Ṣafawids: Šīʿism, Ṣūfism and the Ġulāt.* Wiesbaden, Franz Steiner.

McChesney, R. D. 1981. 'Comments on "The Qajar Uymaq in the Safavid period, 1500–1722"'. *IS* 14 (1–2), pp. 87–105.

Mélikoff, Irène 1975. 'Le problème Qizilbash'. *Turcica* 6, pp. 49–67.

Melville, Charles (ed.) 1990. *Pembroke Papers I, Persian and Islamic Studies in Honour of P. W. Avery.* Cambridge University, Centre of Middle East Studies.

  1993 'From Qars to Qandahar: the itineraries of Shah 'Abbas I (995–1038/1587–1629)'. In Calmard (1993).

Melzig, Herbert 1938. *Resa Schah: der Aufstieg Irans und die Grossmächte.* Stuttgart, Berlin, Leipzig, Union deutsche Verlagsgesellschaft.

Membré, Michele 1993. *Mission to the Lord Sophy of Persia (1539–1542)*, transl. with introduction and notes, A. H. Morton. London, SOAS.

Minorsky, Vladimir 1934a. 'Shāh-sewan'. *EI* (1st edn) 4 (1), pp. 267–8. (First published in French edn, 1926.)

  1934b. 'Shaḳāḳī'. *EI* (1st edn) 4 (1), p. 290.

  1936. 'Muḳān'. *EI* (1st edn) 3, pp. 710–711.

  1938. 'Muḳān'. *EI* (1st edn) Supplement, pp. 152–3.

  (tr. and explained) 1943. *The Tadhkirat al Mulūk. A Manual of Safavid Administration* (Gibb Memorial Series, NS 16). London, Luzac.

  1951–2. 'Aynallu/Inallu'. *Rocznik Orientalistycny* 17, pp. 1–11.

  1964. 'Persia: religion and history'. *Iranica* (Tehran), pp. 242–259.

Mirjafari, Hossein 1979a. 'The Ḥaydarī-Niʿmatī conflicts in Iran', transl. and adapted, J. R. Perry. *IS* 12, pp. 135–62.

  1979b. 'Shahsevan tribes in Iran'. *The Turkish Studies Association Bulletin* 3 (1), pp. 1–3.

Mirza Firooz Khan 1912. 'Shahsevans v. Cossacks'. *The Near East*, 2 August, p. 383.

Mizban, Mehdi 1992. 'Il-e Shahsevan (Moured-e Motaleʿeh Taifeh-ye Geyiklu, Tireh-ye Hajji-Imanlu)'. Unpubl. thesis, Islamic Free University, Tehran, 1371.

Moerman, Michael 1965. 'Ethnic classification in a complex civilization: who are the Lue?' *AA* 67, pp. 1215–30.

  1968. 'Who the Lue are'. in June Helm (ed.) *Essays on the Problem of Tribe.* Seattle, University of Washington Press.

Mohammad Kazem, Vazir of Marv 1960. *Nameh-ye Alam-ara-ye Naderi.* Moscow, ANSSSRIV.

  1990. *Alam-ara-ye Naderi*, 3 vols., ed. with introduction, notes and indices, Mohammad Amin Riahi, 2nd edn. Tehran, 'Elm, 1369.

Mohammad Maʿsum 1978. *Ḫulāsat as-Siyar. Der Iran unter Schah Ṣafī (1629–1642) nach der Chronik des Muhammad Maʿṣūm b. Ḫuāǧagī Iṣfahānī*, selections transl., with introduction, Gerhard Rettelbach. Munich, Rudolph Trofenik.

Mojtahedi, Mehdi 1948. *Rejal-e Azarbayjan dar Asr-e Mashrutiyat.* Tehran, Naqsh-e Jahan, 1327.

Momen, Moojan 1985. *An Introduction to Shiʿi Islam. The History and Doctrines of Twelver Shiʿism.* New Haven and London, Yale University Press.

Monaco, Adriano 1928. 'L'Azerbeigian Persiano'. *Bolletino della Reale Società Geografica Italiana* Series 6, vol. 5, pp. 25–70, 143–70, 262–94.

Monteith, W. 1833. 'Journal of a tour through Azarbdbijan [sic] and the shores of the Caspian'. *JRGS* 3, pp. 1–59.

1856. *Kars and Erzeroum*. London.

Moore, Arthur 1914. *The Orient Express*. London, Constable.

Moosa, Matti 1988. *Extremist Shiites: the Ghulat Sects*. Syracuse University Press.

Morgan, David 1986. Review of Reid (1983). *BSOAS* 49 (2), p. 434.

1988. *Medieval Persia 1040–1797*. London, Longman.

Morier, James 1812. *A Journey through Persia, Armenia, and Asia Minor, to Constantinople in the Years 1808 and 1809*. London.

1818. *A Second Journey through Persia, Armenia, and Asia Minor, to Constantinople, between the Years 1810 and 1816*. London.

1837. 'Some account of the Íliyáts, or wandering tribes of Persia . . .' *JRGS* 7, pp. 230–42.

Morton, Alexander H. 1974. 'The Ardabil shrine in the reign of Shāh Tahmāsp I, Part I'. *Iran* 12, pp. 31–64.

1975. 'The Ardabil shrine in the reign of Shāh Tahmāsp I, Part II'. *Iran* 13, pp. 39–58.

1986. Review of Reid (1983). *JRAS*, pp. 281–2.

1993a. See Membré (1993).

1993b. 'The *chūb-i ṭarīq* and *Qizilbāsh* ritual'. In Calmard (1993).

Mostoufi, 'Abdollah 1945–7. *Sharh-e Zendagani-ye Man ya Tarikh-e Ejtema'i va Edari-ye Doureh-ye Qajar*, 3 vols. Tehran, Zavvar, 1324–6.

Müller, Hans (ed. and transl.) 1964. *Die Chronik Ḫulāṣat at-Tawārīḫ des Qāzī Ahmad Qumī: Der Abschnitt über Schah 'Abbās I*. Wiesbaden, Steiner.

Munson Jr, Henry 1989. 'On the irrelevance of the segmentary lineage model in the Moroccan Rif'. *AA* 91, pp. 386–400.

Musävi, T. M. 1977. *Orta Äsr Azärbayjan Tarikhinä dair Farsdilli Sänädlär (XVI–XVIII äsrlär)*. Baku, ANASSRII.

Naba'i, Abu'l Fazl 1987. 'Shahsevan(Elsevan)-ha-ye Azarbaijan'. *Faslnameh-ye Tahqiqat-e Joghrafia'i* 2(1), 1366, pp. 181–98.

Nader Mirza ben Badi' al-Zaman Mirza 1905. *Tarikh va Jughrafiya-ye Dar al-Saltaneh-ye Tabriz*, ed. 'Abbas-qoli Lesan al-Molk Sepehr. Tehran, 1325.

Nafisi, Sa'id 1956 and 1965. *Tarikh-e Ejtema'i va Siyasi-ye Iran dar Doureh-ye Mo'aser*, 2 vols. Tehran, Sharq, 1355 and 1344.

Na'ini, Mohammad Ja'far ben Mohammad Hosein 1974. *Jame'-e Ja'fari*, ed. Iraj Afshar. Tehran, Anjoman-e Asar-e Melli, 1353.

Nami Esfahani, Mirza Mohammad Sadeq al-Musavi 1938. *Tarikh-e Giti-Gosha'i*, with two supplements by 'Abd al-Karim b. 'Ali Reza ash-Sharif and Mohammad Reza Shirazi, ed. Sa'id Nafisi. Tehran, Eqbal, 1317.

Napier, Major H. D. 1902. 'Report on a Journey Isfahan-Hamadan-Saveh-Tehran'. *FO Prints Persia and Arabia* Part X (82), *IOL*, I./P&S/20.

Nassery Bilesawar, Ahad 1993. *Dasht-e Moghan dar Gozargah-e Tarikh*. Private, 1372.

Nikitine, Basil 1922. 'Notice sur la province persane de Talech'. *Revue du Monde Musulman* 1992 (1), pp. 121–38.

1929. 'Les Afšārs d'Urumiyeh'. *Journal Asiatique* 214 (Jan.–Mar.), pp. 122–3.

Oberling, Pierre 1960. 'The Turkic Peoples of South Iran'. Ph.D. thesis, Columbia University, University Microfilms.
1964a. *The Turkic Peoples of Iranian Azerbaijan*. American Council of Learned Societies, Research and Studies in Uralic and Altaic Languages, Project no. 51.
1964b. 'The tribes of Qarāca Dāg.' *Oriens* 17, pp. 60–95.
1974. *The Qashqā'i Nomads of Fārs*. The Hague, Mouton.
1985. 'Afšār'. *EIr* 1, pp. 582–6.
ODDM 1966. 'Report of Dashte Moghan Development Centre'. Unpublished report, Azarbaijan Water and Power Authority, October.
Ogranovich, I. A. 1870. 'Svedeniya o Shakhsevenakh'. *Kavkazskiy Kalendar na 1871* 2, pp. 68–84.
1872. 'Muganskaya step . . .' *Kavkaz* (Tiflis), 1872 nos. 1, 11, 37, 45, 82, 85, 102, 130, 144.
1876. 'Provintsii Persii Ardebilskaya i Serabskaya'. *Zap. Kavk. Otd. Imp. Russk. Geogr. Oshch.* 10 (1), pp. 141–235.
Okazaki, Shoko 1986. 'The great Persian famine of 1870–71'. *BSOAS* 49, pp. 183–92.
Olearius, Adam 1669. *The Voyages and Travells of the Ambassadors*, transl. John Davies, 2nd edn. London.
ONA 1990. Study and Research Unit of the Organization for Nomadic Affairs, 'Bar-rasi-ye ta'arif va mafahim-e vazheh-ha-ye 'ashayer'. *Zakhayer-e Enqelab* 11, summer 1369, pp. 77–81.
1992. 'Ta'arif va mafahim-e be-kar-rafteh dar sarshomari-ye ejtema'i-eqtesadi-ye 'ashayer-e kuchandeh-ye Tir-mah 1366'. *Zakhayer-e Enqelab* 19, summer 1371, pp. 17–24.
Opie, James 1992. *Tribal Rugs: Nomadic and Village Weavings from the Near East and Central Asia*. N.p., Lawrence King.
Op't Land, C. 1961. *The Shah-Savan of Azarbaijan: A Preliminary Report* (Problems around the Sedentarisation of Pastoral Tribes, Paper No. 4). Tehran, ISSR.
1962. *The Permanent Settlement of the Dachte–Moghan Development Project Area* (Problems around the Sedentarisation of Pastoral Tribes, Paper No. 5). Tehran, ISSR.
Pakdaman, Nasser (ed.) 1983. *Studies on the Economic and Social History of Iran in the Nineteenth Century*, special issue of *IS* 16 (3–4).
Papers Relative to the War. Papers Relative to the War between Persia and Russia in 1826, 1827 and 1828. IOL, L/P&S/20, A.7, Vol. I.
Pehrson, Robert 1966. *The Social Organization of the Marri Baluch*, ed. from his notes, Fredrik Barth. New York, Viking.
Peirce, Leslie P. 1993. *The Imperial Harem. Women and Sovereignty in the Ottoman Empire*. Oxford, Oxford University Press.
Perry, John R. 1971. 'The last Safavids, 1722–1773'. *Iran* 9, pp. 59–69.
1975. 'Forced migration in Iran during the 17th and 18th centuries'. *IS* 8 (4), pp. 199–215.
1979. *Karim Khan Zand: a History of Iran 1747–1779*. University of Chicago Press.
Pesyan, Najaf-qoli 1949. *Marg Bud, Baz-Gasht ham Bud (Tarikhcheh-ye Ferqeh-ye*

Demkrat-e Azarbaijan va Hezb-e Kumleh-ye Kordestan, az Soqut-e Padganha-ye Azarbaijan ta Esteqrar-e Niru). N.p., Emruz, 1328.

Petrushevskiy, Ilya Pavlovich 1947. 'Vakfnie imeniya Ardabilskogo mazara v XVII v.', *Trudi Instituta Imeni A. Bakikhanova ANASSR* 1, pp. 24–41.

1949. *Ocherki po Istorii Feodalnikh Otnosheniy v Azerbaydzhane i Armenii v XVI–nachale XIX vv.* Leningrad, Vostochniy Nauchno-issledovatelskiy Institut.

1977. Contributions to M. S. Ivanov (ed.) *Istoriya Irana*. Moscow, Izd. Mosk. Univ.

1985. *Islam in Iran*, transl. Hubert Evans. London, Athlone.

Philips Price, M. P. 1946. 'Soviet Azerbaijan'. *JRCAS* 33 (2), pp. 188–200.

Porter, Sir Robert Ker 1821-2. *Travels in Georgia, Persia, Armenia, Ancient Babylonia, etc., etc., during the Years 1817, 1818, 1819, and 1820,* 2 vols. London.

Puturidze, Vladimir 1961. *Persidskie Istoricheskie Dokumenti v Knigokhranilishchakh Gruzii*. Tiflis, Izd. AN Gruz. SSR.

Qara-Baghi, Mirza Jamal Javanshir 1959. *Tarikh-e Qara-Bagh*. Baku, ANASSRII.

Qomi, Qazi Ahmad, 1980. *Kholasat al-Tawarikh*, ed. E. Eshraqi. Tehran University Press, 1359. See also Müller (1964), Glassen (1968), Echraqi (1975).

Rabino di Borgomale, H.-L. 1917. *Les Provinces Caspiennes de la Perse: le Guilân (Revue du Monde Musulman* 32). Paris.

Radde, Gustav 1886. *Reisen an der Persisch-Russischen Grenze. Talysch und Seine Bewöhner*. Leipzig, Brockhaus.

Rakhshkhorshid, 'Aziz 1962. *Ouza'-e Zendegi-ye Deh-Neshinan-e Dasht-e Moghan* (Problems around the Sedentarisation of Pastoral Tribes, Paper No. 3). Tehran, ISSR.

Rava'i, Naser-e Daftar 1984. *Khaterat va Asnad-e Naser-e Daftar Rava'i*. Ed. Iraj Afshar and Behzad Razzaqi. Tehran, Ferdousi, 1363.

Rawlinson, Major H. C. 1841. 'Notes on a journey from Tabriz . . . in October and November 1838'. *JRGS* 10, pp. 1–64..

Refik, Ahmet 1930. *Anadolu'da Türk Aşiretleri (966–1200)*. Istanbul, Devlet.

Reid, James J. 1978. 'The Qajar uymaq in the Safavid period'. *IS* 11, pp. 117–43.

1979. 'Comments on "Tribalism as a socio-economic formation"'. *IS* 12 (3–4), pp. 275–81.

1980. 'The Qarāmānlū: the growth and development of a lesser tribal elite in sixteenth- and seventeenth-century Persia'. *SI* 9, 195–209.

1983. *Tribalism and Society in Islamic Iran 1500–1629*. Malibu, Undena.

1984. 'Studying clans in Iranian history: a response'. *IS* 17 (1), pp. 85–92.

Ricks, Thomas M. 1973. 'Towards a social and economic history of eighteenth-century Iran'. *IS* 6, pp. 110–128.

Roemer, Hans Robert 1985. 'Die turkmenischen Qïzïlbaš. Gründer und Opfer der safawidischen Theokratie'. *ZDMG* 135 (2), 1985, pp. 227–240.

1986. 'The Safavid period'. In Jackson and Lockhart (1986).

1989a. *Persien auf dem Weg in die Neuzeit. Iranische Geschichte von 1350–1750* (Beiruter Texte und Studien, Vol. 40). Beirut/Stuttgart, Franz Steiner Verlag (revised version of Roemer 1986).

1989b. 'Loyalitätsappelle bei Türken Irans und Ägyptens im Mittelalter'. In

Maria Macuch, Christa Müller-Kessler and Bert G. Fragner (eds.) *Studia Semitica necnon Iranica (Festschrift to Rudolph Macuch)*, Wiesbaden, Harrassowitz.

1990. 'The Qizilbash Turcomans: founders and victims of the Safavid theocracy'. In Michel M. Mazzaoui and Vera B. Moreen (eds.) *Intellectual Studies on Islam*, Salt Lake City, University of Utah Press. (Translation of Roemer 1985).

Röhrborn, Klaus-Michael 1966. *Provinzen und Zentralgewalt Persiens im 16. und 17. Jahrhunderten*. Berlin, De Gruyter.

1979. 'Regierung und Verwaltung Irans unter den Safawiden'. In H. R. Idris and K. Röhrborn, *Regierung und Verwaltung des Vorderen Orients in Islamischer Zeit* (Handbuch der Orientalistik, Abt. 1, Vol. 6, Abschn. 5, Teil 1). Leiden, Brill.

Rosaldo, Renato 1986. 'From the door of his tent: the fieldworker and the inquisitor'. In James Clifford and George E. Marcus (eds.) *Writing Culture. The Poetics and Politics of Ethnography*. Berkeley, University of California Press.

Rosenfeld, Henry 1965. 'The social composition of the military in the process of state formation in the Arabian desert'. *JRAI* 95, pp. 75–86, 174–94.

Ross, E. Denison 1896. 'The early years of Shāh Ismāʿīl, founder of the Ṣafavī dynasty'. *JRAS* 2, pp. 249–340.

Rossow, Robert, Jr. 1956. 'The battle of Azerbaijan'. *MEJ* 10 (1), pp. 17–32.

Rostopchin, F. B. 1933. 'Zametki o Shahsevenakh'. *Sovetskaya Etnografiya* 1933 (3–4), pp. 88–118.

Routes in Persia, Vol. II (North-Western Persia). Simla, General Staff, India, 1922. IOL, L/P&S/20, C101.

Rubruck 1900. *The Journey of William of Rubruck to the Eastern Parts of the World, 1253–55*, trans. and ed. by William Woodville Rockhill. London, Hakluyt Society.

Rumlu, Hasan Beg 1931, 1934. *A Chronicle of the Early Ṣafawīs, being the Ahsanu't-tawārīkh of Ḥasan-i-Rūmlū*, 2 vols., ed. and transl. C. N. Seddon. Baroda, Oriental Institute.

1979. *Ahsan al-Tawarikh*, Vol. XII, ed. ʿAbd al-Hosein Nava'i. Tehran, Babak, 1357.

Sabahi, Houshang 1990. *British Policy in Persia 1918–1925*. London, Frank Cass.

Sadeq, ʿAli-Goshad 1961. 'Motalaʿeh-ye Eqtesadi-ye Damdari-ye Ilat-e Shahsevan'. Unpubl. thesis, Faculty of Agriculture, Tabriz University, 1340.

Saʿedi, Gholam Hosein 1964. *Ilkhchi* (Monograph 5). Tehran, ISSR, 1342.

1965. *Khiou ya Meshkinshahr: Kaʿbeh-ye yailaqat-e Shahsevan* (Monograph 7), Tehran, ISSR, 1344.

1968. *Tup. Dastan.* Tehran, Ashrafi, 1347.

Safaʾi, Ibrahim 1974. *Yeksad Sanad-e Tarikhi*. Tehran, Sharq, n.d. (1353).

Safari, Baba 1971, 1974, 1992. *Ardabil dar gozargah-e tarikh*, 3 vols. Vols. 1 and 2, Tehran, private, 1350 and 1353; vol. 3, Ardabil, Islamic Free University, 1371.

Safizadeh, Fereydoun 1984. 'Shahsevan in the grip of development'. *Cultural Survival Quarterly* 8(1), pp. 14–18.

Sahlins, Marshall 1968. *Tribesmen*. Englewood Cliffs, Prentice Hall.

Salzman, Philip Carl 1978a. 'Does complementary opposition exist?' *AA* 80, pp. 53–70.

1978b. 'Ideology and change in Middle Eastern tribal society.' *Man (N.S.)* 13, pp. 618–37.

1995. 'Understanding tribes in Iran and beyond.' *JRAI (N.S.)* 1, pp. 399–403.

Sarwar, Ghulam 1939. *History of Shāh Ismāʿīl Ṣafawī.* Aligarh, Muslim University (private).

Savory, R. M. 1978. See Torkman (1978).

1980a. *Iran under the Safavids.* Cambridge, Cambridge University Press.

1980b. 'Ḳizil-bāsh'. *EI* (2nd edn) 6, pp. 243–5.

1986. 'The Safavid administration system'. In Jackson and Lockhart (1986).

1987. *Studies on the History of Ṣafavid Iran.* London, Variorum Reprints.

Schimkoreit, Renate 1982. *Regesten Publizierter Safawidischer Herrscherurkunden. Erlasse und Staatsschreiben der Frühen Neuzeit* (Islamkundliche Untersuchungen 68). Berlin, Klaus Schwarz.

Schneider, Jane, and Rayna Rapp 1995. *Articulating Hidden Histories: Exploring the Influence of Eric R. Wolf.* Berkeley, University of California Press.

Schweizer, Günther 1970. 'Nordost-Azerbaidschan und Shah Sevan-Nomaden: Strukturwandel einer nordwestiranischen Landschaft und ihrer Bevölkerung'. In Eckart Ehlers, Fred Scholz and Günther Schweizer, *Strukturwandlungen im Nomadisch-Bäuerlichen Lebensraum des Orients* (Beihefte, *Geographische Zeitschrift*), Wiesbaden, Steiner.

1973. 'Lebens- und wirtschaftsformen Iranischer Bergnomaden im Strukturwandel: das Beispiel der Shah Sevan'. In Carl Rathjens, Carl Troll and Harald Uhlig (eds.) *Vergleichende Kulturgeographie der Hochgebirge des südlichen Asien* (Erdwissenschaftliche Forschung, vol. V), Wiesbaden, Steiner.

1974. 'The Aras–Moghan development project in Northwest Iran and the problems of nomad settlement'. *Applied Sciences and Development* 4, pp. 134–48.

S.D.D. Sbornik Diplomaticheskikh Dokumentov, Kasayushchikhsya Sobitiy v Persii s Kontsa 1906 g. po Iyul 1909 g., 7 vols. St Petersburg, Ministerstvo Inostrannikh Del, 1911–13. (Translated into Persian by Parvin Manzavi as *Ketab-e Naranji: Asnad-e Siyasi-ye Vezarat-e Kharejeh [Russiyeh-ye Tezari] dar bareh-ye Ruydad-ha-ye [Enqelab-e Mashruteh-ye] Iran.* Tehran, Parvaz, 1366–68.)

Seddon, C. N. See Rumlu (1934).

Seidlitz, N. von 1879. 'Historisch-ethnographische Skizze des Gouvernements Baku . . .' *Russische Revue* 15, pp. 193–236, 445–67, 492–513. Revised and augmented translation of 'Etnograficheskiy ocherk Bakinskoy gubernii', *Kavkazskiy Kalendar na 1871 god* 2, Tiflis 1870, pp. 1–67.

Sepehr Kashani, Mohammad Taqi Lesan al-Molk 1958. *Nasekh al-Tavarikh,* ed. Jahangir Qaʾem-Maqami. Tehran, Amir Kabir, 1337.

Sh-f M-z-f 1908. 'Shakhseveni'. *Kavkaz* 100. (Quoted by Rostopchin; see von Hahn.)

Shahbazi, ʿAbdollah 1990. *Moqaddameh'i bar Shenakht-e Ilat va ʿAshayer.* Tehran, Ney, 1369.

Shahsevand-Baghdadi, Parichehreh 1991. *Barrasi-ye Masa'el-e Ejtema'i, Eqtesadi va Siyasi-ye Il-e Shahsevan.* Tehran, 'Ashayer Publications, 1370.

Shahshahani, Soheila 1986. 'History of anthropology in Iran'. *IS* 19, pp. 65–86.

Sheean, Vincent 1927. *The New Persia.* New York, Century.

Shirazi, 'Abdi Beg ('Ali Zein al-'Abedin?) 1990. *Takmilat al-Akhbar (Tarikh-e Safaviyeh az Aghaz ta 978 HQ)*, edited, with introduction and critical notes, by Dr 'Abd al-Hosein Nava'i. Tehran, Nashr-e Ney, 1369.

1570. *Sarih al-Melk.* See Morton (1974 and 1975).

Shirvani, Zein al-'Abedin 1898. *Bostan al-Siyahat.* Tehran, Sana'i (lithog.), 1315 (orig. 1246/1831).

Shkinskiy, Y. F. and P. I. Averyanov 1900. *Otchet o Poyezdke po Severnomu Azerbaydzhanu v kontse 1899 g.* Tiflis.

Singer, André 1982. 'Ethnic origins and tribal history of the Timuri of Khurasan'. *Afghan Studies* 3 and 4, pp. 65–76.

Smith, John Masson, Jr. 1978. 'Turanian nomadism and Iranian politics'. *IS* 11, pp. 57–81.

Sohrweide, Hanna, 1965. 'Der Sieg der Ṣafaviden in Persien und seine Rückwirkungen auf die Schiiten Anatoliens im 16. Jahrhundert'. *Der Islam* 41, pp. 95–223.

Southall, Aidan 1976. 'Nuer and Dinka are people: ecology, ethnicity and logical possibility.' *Man (N.S.)* 11, pp. 463–95.

Spooner, Brian 1987. 'Anthropology'. *EIr* 2, pp. 107–16.

Spuler, Bertold 1960. *The Muslim World, II: The Mongol Period*, transl. F. R. C. Bagley. Leiden, Brill.

Stauffer, Thomas 1965. 'The economics of nomadism in Iran'. *Middle East Journal* 19, pp. 284–302.

Stöber, Georg 1978. *Die Afshar: Nomadismus im Raum Kerman (Zentraliran).* Marburg/Lahn, Geographisches Institut der Universität Marburg.

Street, Brian 1990. 'Orientalist discourse in the anthropology of Iran, Afghanistan and Pakistan'. In Richard Fardon (ed.) *Localizing Strategies: Regional Traditions of Ethnographic Writing*, Edinburgh, Scottish Academic Press.

1992. 'Method in our critique of anthropology'. *Man (N.S.)* 27, pp. 177–9.

Struys, Jean 1681. *Les Voyages.* Amsterdam.

Sumbatzade, A. S., S. A. Taqieva, and O. S. Malikov (eds.), 1985. *Jänubi Azärbayjan Tarikhinin Ocherki (1828–1917).* Baku, Elm.

Sümer, Faruk 1967. *Oğuzlar (Türkmenler).* Ankara University Press.

1976. *Safevî Devletinin Kuruluşu ve Gelişmesinde Anadolu Türklerin Rolü (Şah İsmail ile Halefleti ve Anadolu Türkleri).* Ankara, Güven.

Sweet, Louise E. 1965. 'Camel raiding of North Arabian Bedouin: a mechanism of ecological adaptation'. *AA* 67, pp. 1132–50.

Swietochowski, Tadeusz 1985. *Russian Azerbaijan, 1905–1920: the Shaping of National Identity in a Muslim Community.* Cambridge, Cambridge University Press.

Sykes, Sir Percy 1930. *A History of Persia* (3rd edn). London, Macmillan.

Szuppe, Maria 1994, 1995. 'La participation des femmes de la famille royale à l'exercice du pouvoir en Iran safavide au XVIe siècle'. *SI* 23, pp. 211–58, 24, pp. 61–122.

Tagieva, Sh. A. 1956. *Natsionalno-osvoboditelnoe Dvizhenie v Iranskom Azerbaydzhane v 1917–1920 gg.* Baku, ANASSR.

1964. *XIX Äsrin sonu vä XX Äsrin Ävvällärindä İranda Torpaq Mülkiyyäti Formaları vä Torpaqdan İstifadä Qaydaları.* Baku, ANASSR.

1969. *XIX Äsrin sonu vä XX Äsrin Ävvällärindä İran Kändlilärinin Väziyyäti.* Baku, Elm.

Taheri, Amir 1970. 'A week in the Shah-savan country. Where Nader was crowned'. *Kayhan International,* 28.11.1970.

Taherzadeh-Behzad, Karim 1955. *Qiyam-e Azarbaijan dar Enqelab-e Mashrutiyat-e Iran.* Tehran, 'Eqbal.

Taimaz, S. 1979. *Seh Maqaleh dar Bareh-ye Torkman-Sahra, Dasht-e Moghan, va Rustaha-ye Digar.* Tehran, 'Elm, 1358.

Tairov, M. Mehti and P. A. Pavlenko 1922. *Shakhseveniya,* ed. F. M. Isayeva. Baku.

Taj-Gardun, Toraj 1959. 'Motala'eh ru-ye Nezhad-e Gusfand-e Moghani va Tarz-e Galleh-dari-ye Il-e Shahsevan'. Unpubl. thesis, Faculty of Agriculture, Tabriz University, 1338.

Tanavoli, Parviz 1985. *Shahsavan: Iranian Rugs and Textiles.* New York, Rizzoli.

Tapper, Nancy and Richard Tapper 1982. 'Marriage preferences and ethnic relations among Durrani of northern Afghanistan'. *Folk* 24, pp. 157–77.

Tapper, Nancy 1978. 'The women's subsociety among the Shahsevan nomads of Iran'. In Lois Beck and Nikki Keddie (eds.) *Women in the Muslim World,* Cambridge, Mass., Harvard University Press.

1991. *Bartered Brides: Politics, Gender and Marriage in an Afghan Tribal Society.* Cambridge, Cambridge University Press.

Tapper, Richard 1966. 'Black sheep, white sheep and red-heads: a historical sketch of the Shahsavan of Azarbaijan'. *Iran* 4, pp. 61–84.

1972. 'The Shahsavan of Azarbaijan: A Study of Political and Economic Change in a Middle Eastern Tribal Society'. Unpubl thesis, University of London.

1974. 'Shahsevan in Safavid Persia'. *BSOAS* 37 (2), pp. 321–54.

1979a. *Pasture and Politics: Economics, Conflict and Ritual among Shahsevan Nomads of Northwestern Iran.* London, Academic Press.

1979b. 'The organization of nomadic communities in pastoral societies of the Middle East'. In Equipe (1979), pp. 43–65.

1979c. 'Individuated grazing rights and social organization among the Shahsevan nomads of Azarbaijan'. in Equipe (1979), pp. 95–114.

(ed.) 1983a. *The Conflict of Tribe and State in Iran and Afghanistan.* London, Croom Helm.

1983b. 'Introduction'. In Tapper (1983a), pp. 1–82.

1983c. 'Nomads and commissars in the Mughan steppe: the Shahsevan tribes in the Great Game'. In Tapper (1983a), pp. 401–35.

1985. 'One hump or two? Hybrid camels and pastoral cultures'. *Production Pastorale et Société* 16, pp. 55–69.

1986. 'Raiding, reaction and rivalry: Shāhsevan tribes in the constitutional period'. *BSOAS* 49 (3), pp. 508–31.

1988a. 'Ethnicity, order and meaning in the anthropology of Iran and Afghanistan'. In Digard (1988).

1988b. 'History and identity among the Shahsevan'. *IS* 21 (3–4), pp. 84–108.

1991a. 'Anthropologists, historians and tribespeople on tribe and state formation in the Middle East'. In Khoury and Kostiner (1991).

1991b. 'The tribes in eighteenth and nineteenth century Iran'. In Avery *et al.* (1991).

1994. 'Change, cognition and control: the reconstruction of nomadism in Iran'. In C. M. Hann (ed.) *When History Accelerates*, London, Athlone.

n.d. 'Peaked caps and wooden doors: Reza Shah and the tribes of Iran'. MS.

Tavahodi, Kalimollah 1987–8. *Harakat-e Tarikhi-ye Kord be Khorasan dar Defa' az Esteqlal-e Iran*, 3 vols. Mashhad, Kushesh, 1359, 1364, 1367.

Tavernier, Jean-Baptiste 1678. *The Six Voyages of John Baptista Tavernier through Turky into Persia and the East-Indies*, 2 vols., transl. J. Philips. London.

Tenreiro, António 1923. *Itinerário*. In António Baião (ed.) *Itinerários da Índia a Portugal por terra*, Coïmbra, Imprensa da Universidade, pp. 1–127.

Tigranov, L. F. 1909. *Iz Obshchestvenno-ekonomicheskikh Otnosheniy v Persii*. St Petersburg.

Toğan, Zeki Velidi 1943. 'Azerbaycan.' *İslam Ansiklopedisi* 2, pp. 91–118.

Torkman, Eskandar Beg Monshi 1971. *Tarikh-e 'Alam-ara-ye 'Abbasi*, 2 vols., ed. Iraj Afshar. Tehran, Amir Kabir, 1350.

1978. *History of Shah 'Abbas the Great (Tarikh-e 'Alamara-ye 'Abbasi) by Eskandar Beg Monshi* (Persian Heritage Series No. 28), 2 vols., transl. R. M. Savory. Boulder, Colorado, Westview.

and Mohammad Yusof 1938. *Zeil-e Tarikh-e 'Alam-ara-ye 'Abbasi*, ed. Soheil Khwansari. Tehran, 1317.

Torkman, Mohammad (ed.) 1991. *Asnadi dar bareh-ye Hojum-e Englis va Rus be Iran (1287–1291 AHS)*. Tehran, IPIS.

Towfiq, F. 1987. "Ashayer'. *EIr* 2, pp. 707–24.

Ulug Beg 1926. *Don Juan of Persia, A Shiah Catholic 1560–1604*, ed. and transl. G. Le Strange. London, Routledge.

Vahid Qazvini, Mohammad Taher 1951. *'Abbas-Nameh ya Sharh-e Zendagani-ye 22–Saleh-ye Shah 'Abbas-e Sani (1052–1073)*, ed. Ebrahim Dehqan. Arak, Davudi, 1329.

van Bruinessen, Martin 1978. *Agha, Shaikh and State*. Utrecht, private (2nd edn, London, Zed, 1992).

1983. 'Kurdish tribes and the state of Iran: the case of Simko's revolt', in Tapper (1983a).

Varjavand, Parviz 1965. *Ravesh-e Bar-rasi va Shenakht-e Koll-e Ilat va 'Ashayer*. Tehran, ISSR, 1344.

1970. *Sarzamin-e Qazvin*. Tehran, Anjoman-e Asar-e Melli, 1349.

Volynskiy, Artemii; see Zevakin.

von Hahn, C. 1910. 'Die Schahsewenen und die russische Straf-expedition auf persisches Gebiet'. *Asien* (Deutsch-Asiatischen Gesellschaft) 9 (5 February), pp. 66–7.

von Thielmann, Baron Max 1875. *Journey in the Caucasus*, 2 vols., transl. Chas. Heneage. London.

Watson, R. G. 1866. *A History of Persia*. London.

Wehrmacht (transl.) 1941. *Iran: Darstellung Irans, Verfaszt vom Generalstab der Sowjetrussischen Armee, Moskau 1941*. Oberkommando der Wehrmacht, A

Ausl/Abw. Ag Ausland Nr. O2440/42 Ausl I (D 4). Bundesärchiv (Militärarchiv) RW5/v.487.

Wilber, Donald 1948. *Iran, Past and Present.* Princeton University Press (6th edn 1981).

Woods, John 1976. *The Aqqoyunlu: Clan, Confederation and Empire: a Study of 15th/9th Century Turko–Iranian Politics.* Minneapolis and Chicago, Bibliotheca Islamica.

  1986. Review of Reid (1983). *IJMES* 18 (4), pp. 529–32.

Wratislaw, Albert Charles 1924. *A Consul in the East.* Edinburgh, Blackwood.

Wright, Susan 1992. 'Method in our critique of anthropology: a further comment'. *Man (N.S.)* 27, pp. 642–4.

  1994. 'Constructing tribal identity in Iran'. *Man (N.S.)* 29, pp. 183–6.

Yapp, M. E. 1980. *Strategies of British India. Britain, Iran and Afghanistan 1798–1850.* Oxford, Oxford University Press.

  1983. 'Tribes and states in the Khyber 1838–1842'. In Tapper (1983a).

Yazdi, Molla Jalal ad-Din Monajjem n.d. *Tarikh-e 'Abbasi.* BM Or. 6263 and Add. 27241.

  1987. *Tarikh-e 'Abbasi ya Ruznameh-ye Molla Jalal,* ed. Seifollah Vahid-Niya. Tehran, Vahid, 1366 (based on MSS in National and Malik Libraries, Tehran).

Yekrangian, Mir Hosein 1957. *Golgun-e Kafnan.* Tehran, 'Elmi, 1336.

Zahedi, Sheikh Hosein b. 'Abdal 1924. *Selselat al-nasab-e Ṣafaviyeh.* Berlin, Iranschähr.

Zapiska 1828. 'Zapiska o narodakh i sposobakh provintsii Ardebilskoy, sostavlena 1828 g'. *Azerbaydzhan Central Government Military Historical Archives,* file 446. No. 172. pp. 1–4. (quoted by Dalili)

Zeinaloghlu, Jahangir 1924. *Mukhtäsär Azärbaijan Tarikhi.* Istanbul, Shams, 1342.

Zevakin, E. 1929. 'Azerbaydzhan v nachale XVIII veka'. *Izv. Obshchestva Obsledovaniya i Izucheniya Azerbaydzhana* 8 (quoted by Abdurakhmanov).

Index of topics

agriculture, cultivation 171–2, 226–7,
232–4, 287–8, 293
see also settlement
alachıq (Shahsevan tent) 25, 68, 76, 291–3,
333, 381, 387
see also tents
alliances 15, 113–15, 120, 145, 242, 286,
335
see also chequer-board patterns,
marriage, tribal clusters, tribal
coalitions, Tribal Union.
Anglo-Russian Convention of 1907 248,
271
anjoman (local organizations) 244, 251,
254–5
änjini (raiding parties) 244
aq-saqal
see elders
'ashayer 86, 333, 342, 345, 348
see il, nomadism, tribe
äshrarlıq, khankhan(lıq) 221–47, 284,
286–7, 321, 331, 348, 363, 366,
379, 388

banditry, raiding 95, 162, 170, 179, 222,
233, 240, 242–7, 250–2, 273–4,
319–26
by Qoja-Beyli tribe 202, 367–9
ending of 284–5, 308
in Moghan 102–3, 117, 157, 190, 192,
202, 207–9, 212, 233
raiding parties 244–6, 252, 271, 276
beys 26, 32–3, 67, 135, 170, 180, 185–9,
208, 224, 229, 236–46, 273–8,
284–9, 295–8, 302–11, 313–14,
331–6, 338–40, 342
see also chiefship, *elbeys*
beyzadä ('nobles') 58, 64, 186–7, 238–9,
331
bölgi-yılı 268–9

camels 177, 200, 231, 245, 310, 313, 371,
388

canals
see irrigation
Census of Nomads (1987) 11, 26, 357
chequer-board patterns 17, 139, 144, 275–6
see also alliances, tribal clusters
chiefship, leadership 7–8, 10–20, 22–3, 75,
130–1, 283–4, 305, 314, 323,
326–7, 343–8
Qızılbash amirs 44–8, 76
see also beys, elbeys
cholera 83, 86, 161, 172, 206, 222
class, hierarchy 1, 15–16, 58, 186, 189, 238,
316, 329–32, 343, 347
tabaqeh 50, 53, 75, 81, 86
see also beyzadä, chiefship, egalitarianism
hampa, nökär
clothing 288, 292, 332
community, nomadic 14, 16–19, 22–4, 135,
174, 229, 291, 314, 317, 341–3,
346–8
jamahat among Shahsevan 14, 26–7, 135,
239–40, 334, 343
jama'at, cemaat 22, 50–1, 53–4, 65, 75,
106
see also tribes
confederacy, tribal 7, 13, 15–18, 24, 45–7,
74
among Shahsevan 25, 109, 129–46, 219,
324, 327–31, 334, 343–8
conscription 288, 305
Constitution, Constitutional Revolution
218, 237, 248–82, 320, 325–6
crime
see law
Crown Lands
see land
cultivation
see agriculture

Democrat Party/Government 296–8,
326–7, 348, 362, 383–6
descent
as ideology 7, 15–16, 22–3, 44–5, 47, 67,

412

Index of places, peoples, persons, dynasties, parties, companies

Index of authors quoted or discussed

Index of tribal names